Linear Control System
Melsa, Schultz 1969
McGraw
Chapter 6, Page 245.

Decision Systems for Inventory Management and Production Planning

A Volume in the Wiley Management and Administration Series

Elwood S. Buffa, Advisory Editor University of California, Los Angeles

PRINCIPLES OF MANAGEMENT: A Modern Approach Fourth Edition Henry H. Albers
OPERATIONS MANAGEMENT: Problems and Models Third Edition Elwood S. Buffa
PROBABILITY FOR MANAGEMENT DECISIONS William R. King
MODERN PRODUCTION MANAGEMENT: Managing the Operations Function Fifth Edition Elwood S. Buffa
CASES IN OPERATIONS MANAGEMENT: A Systems Approach James L. McKenny and Richard S. Rosenbloom
ORGANIZATIONS: Structure and Behavior, Volume 1 Second Edition Joseph A. Litterer
ORGANIZATIONS: Systems, Control and Adaptation, Volume II Joseph A. Litterer
MANAGEMENT AND ORGANIZATIONAL BEHAVIOR: A Multidimensional Approach Billy J. Hodge and Herbert J. Johnson
MATHEMATICAL PROGRAMMING Claude McMillan
DECISION MAKING THROUGH OPERATIONS RESEARCH, Second Edition Robert J. Thierauf and Robert C. Klekamp
QUALITY CONTROL FOR MANAGERS & ENGINEERS Elwood G. Kilpatrick
PRODUCTION SYSTEMS: Planning, Analysis and Control Second Edition James L. Riggs
SIMULATION MODELING: A Guide to Using Simscript Forrest P. Wyman
BASIC STATISTICS FOR BUSINESS AND ECONOMICS, Second Edition Paul G. Hoel and Raymond J. Jessen
COMPUTER SIMULATION OF HUMAN BEHAVIOR John M. Dutton and William H. Starbuck
INTRODUCTION TO GAMING: Management Decision Simulations John G. H. Carlson and Michael J. Misshauk
PRINCIPLES OF MANAGEMENT AND ORGANIZATIONAL BEHAVIOR Burt. K. Scanlan
COMMUNICATION IN MODERN ORGANIZATIONS George T. and Patricia B. Vardaman
THE ANALYSIS OF ORGANIZATIONS, Second Edition Joseph A. Litterer
COMPLEX MANAGERIAL DECISIONS INVOLVING MULTIPLE OBJECTIVES Allan Easton
MANAGEMENT SYSTEMS, Second Edition Peter P. Schoderbek
ADMINISTRATIVE POLICY: Text and Cases in the Policy Sciences Richard M. Hodgetts and Max S. Wortman, Jr.
THE ECONOMICS OF INTERNATIONAL BUSINESS R. Hal Mason, Robert R. Miller and Dale R. Weigel
BASIC PRODUCTION MANAGEMENT, Second Edition Elwood S. Buffa
FUNDAMENTALS OF MANAGEMENT COORDINATION: Supervisor, Middlemanagers and Executives Thomas A. Petit
QUANTITATIVE BUSINESS ANALYSIS David E. Smith
OPERATIONS MANAGEMENT: The Management of Productive Systems Elwood S. Buffa
PERSONNEL ADMINISTRATION AND HUMAN RESOURCES MANAGEMENT Andrew F. Sikula
MANAGEMENT SCIENCE/OPERATIONS RESEARCH: Model Formulation and Solution Methods Elwood S. Buffa and James S. Dyer
MANAGEMENT PRINCIPLES AND PRACTICES Robert J. Thierauf, Robert Klekamp and Daniel Geeding
ESSENTIALS OF MANAGEMENT SCIENCE/OPERATIONS RESEARCH Elwood S. Buffa and James S. Dyer
AN INTRODUCTION TO MANAGEMENT Joseph A. Litterer
FORECASTING: METHODS AND APPLICATIONS Spyros Makridakis and Steven Wheelwright
POLICY FORMULATION AND STRATEGY MANAGEMENT Robert Schellenberger and Glenn Boseman
DECISION SYSTEMS FOR INVENTORY MANAGEMENT AND PRODUCTION PLANNING Rein Peterson and Edward A. Silver

Decision Systems for Inventory Management and Production Planning

Rein Peterson
York University

Edward A. Silver
University of Waterloo

JOHN WILEY & SONS

New York • Chichester • Brisbane • Toronto • Singapore

Library of Congress Cataloging in Publication Data

Peterson, Rein, 1937–
Decision systems for inventory management and production planning.

(The Wiley series in management and administration)
Bibliography: p.
Includes index.
1. Inventory control—Decision-making.
2. Production planning—Decision-making.
I. Silver, Edward Allan, 1937– joint author.
II. Title.
HD55. P44 658.7'87 78-4980
ISBN 0-471-68327-2

Printed in the United States of America
10 9 8 7 6

About The Authors

Rein Peterson

Rein Peterson is a professor on the Faculty of Administrative Studies, York University, Toronto, Canada, where he is the Coordinator of the Management Science Area. Formerly he served the Faculty of Administrative Studies as Associate Dean, as Director of Research and as Chairman of the Faculty Council.

Born in Europe, he considers himself part Quebecois having spent thirteen formative years in Montreal, before moving in turn to London, Ontario; Ithaca, New York: New York City; and then to Toronto. Prior to his academic career he worked as a prospector, and as a professional engineer/project manager helping to locate and build iron mines, new towns and railways in Northern Quebec and Ontario.

He was awarded his Ph.D. at Cornell University, having received his M.B.A. from the University of Western Ontario and B.Eng. from McGill University. Before coming to York, Professor Peterson served on the Faculties of Columbia University, Harpur College and the University of Western Ontario.

Professor Peterson has served as an elected member of The Council of The Institute of Management Sciences (T.I.M.S.), as the editor in charge of a special issue of *Management Science* devoted to Canadian authors and as Programme Director of the XXII International T.I.M.S. Conference in Kyoto, Japan.

He is an active consultant to business and government, and serves on several Governmental advisory committees. His most recent book dealt with Canadian economic and business policy: *Small Business: Building A Balanced Economy*, Press Porcepic, Toronto, 1977.

Edward A. Silver

Edward A. Silver is a professor of management sciences at the University of Waterloo. He has previously taught at Boston University and, as a visiting professor, at the Swiss Federal Polytechnique Institute in Lausanne, Switzerland. During his career, the undergraduate and graduate courses in which he has instructed have included production planning and inventory control, operations management, production engineering, decision analysis, operations research, applied probability and statistics, Markov processes, and dynamic programming.

Dr. Silver has presented seminars and talks at national and international meetings of a number of professional societies as well as at educational institutions throughout North America and Europe. An important activity has been his participation in several executive development programs related to the production/inventory field. He has published over 30 articles in a number of professional journals.

A native of Montreal, Professor Silver completed a Bachelor of Civil Engineering at McGill University and a Science Doctorate in Operations Research at the Massachusetts Institute of Technology. He is a licensed professional engineer and is a member of a number of professional societies including the American Production and Inventory Control Society, the Canadian Operational Research Society, the Institute of Management Sciences, the Operational Research Society (UK), the Operations Rescarch Society of America, and Sigma Chi.

Dr. Silver spent four years as a member of the Operations Research Group of the International consulting firm, Arthur D. Little Inc. In addition, subsequent consulting experience has included a number of studies in the inventory/production field for a variety of industrial and government clients in North America.

To Mari and Michael Daniel

To Maxine, Michelle, Norman, and Heidi

Preface

Inventories represent one of the major investments made by a firm. Expenses associated with inventory management and production planning are often a substantial portion of the total expenditures incurred by an organization. In the aggregate, inventories affect the economy through business cycles. Individually they determine the degree to which purchasing, manufacturing, and distribution can be rationalized to ultimately provide competitive customer service.

Inventory management and production planning have been studied in considerable depth by management theorists. Yet, those of us who, through consulting work, come into intimate contact with managerial decision procedures in this area, are repeatedly surprised to find how limited, and ad hoc, many of the existing decision systems actually are. The rate at which theory has been developed has far outstripped the rate at which decision practices of firms have been successfully upgraded. A major gap exists between the theoretical solutions on the one hand and the real world problems on the other.

Our primary objective in this book is, therefore, to bridge this gap through the development of *operational* inventory management and production planning decision systems, which allow management to capitalize on readily implementable improvements to their current practices. We shall also try to demonstrate how theories of inventory control and production planning must be recast, made more comprehensive, and much more responsive to management policies.

In contrast with most published books in this field, we do not attempt to collect and evaluate a large number of theoretical models for different types of problems, nor do we simply recount our own personal consulting experiences and methods. Rather we believe we have achieved a reasonable balance between a survey of the most important theoretical problems and techniques in this area, and *practical solution approaches which are theoretically sound* as well as comprehensible and usable by practitioners. In other words, we blend some theory (to show the rationale behind decision rules) with practical advice (when existing theory fails) and philosophy (to provide perspective). In particular, we present a comprehensive treatment of the following topics:

1. the importance of inventories to top management decision making and policy makers in the economy as a whole.

2. the interaction between *aggregate* production/inventory policies and decisions on an *individual* item basis.

3. the seasonality of forecasted demand for individual items.

4. the uncertainty of future demand for individual items, including many options for incorporating top management's risk-taking attitudes in setting safety stocks.

5. hierarchical decision systems which incorporate overall corporate policies and individual managerial styles into the planning for production rates, work force sizes and inventory levels.

6. implementation considerations involved in designing decision systems, including computer programmes and other implementation aids that can be used in practice.

Part 1 presents a discussion of the inventory management and production planning decisions as components of total business strategy. Included are relevant material on business policy, aggregate economics, cost measurement, an introduction to the important concept of exchange curves, and a chapter devoted to the determination of forecasting strategy and the selection of forecasting methods.

Part 2 presents heuristic approaches to *individual item control, based on the popular and widely used economic order quantity.* No practical compromises are made on the very real problems of seasonal demand, probabilistic demand, and the many different attitudes of management towards costing the risk of insufficient capacity in the short run. The recently developed Silver–Meal heuristic is presented for the first time in its completely operational form.

Part 3 deals with special classes of items including the most important (Class A) and the large group of low activity items (Class C). Also discussed are procedures for dealing with so-called style goods.

Part 4 presents a comprehensive discussion of the problems of coordination of items. Related to multi-stage manufacturing processes we treat the important topic of Material Requirements Planning. Also coordination of items at a single stage is considered for purposes of achieving group discounts or simply reducing overall replenishment costs. A special chapter is devoted to a discussion of reasonable solutions to some of the more perplexingly complex problems of inventory management.

Part 5 presents a discussion of the aggregate production planning problems. Many unused, theoretical models exist in this area, while current practice is grossly underdeveloped and ad hoc in nature. In this section we present strategies and methods for increasing the level of implementation, including a discussion of hierarchical decision systems.

Part 6 discusses the important practical problems of planning, implementation and control of large decision systems. We pool, in this section, our consulting experience with psychological-sociological research findings on bringing about change. The concluding chapter includes a brief listing of *suggested topics for further research which we believe have substantial potential payoff.*

Extensive problem sets have been provided at the end of each chapter. In addition, a number of supplementary problems are available in the Solutions Manual. Finally, six case studies, entitled MIDAS Canada, are interwoven with the material in the text to provide a context for technical topics and a means of reference to existing managerial practice.

We have developed computerized versions of most of the decision rules presented throughout the text. Our original intention was to include these, together with test examples, in an appendix

i. To demonstrate in explicit detail the feasibility of using the proposed decision rules (in fact, many of the rules have also been programmed for use on a *hand* calculator)

ii. To allow practitioners to make direct use of some of the proposed decision rules, for example, by inserting them directly as subroutines in existing decision systems

iii. To permit faculty to assign homework involving lengthy calculations (such as the aggregate effects of decision rules) that would be prohibitive to complete by hand

The length of the text precluded the inclusion of the programmes. Those readers interested in procuring a copy should contact Professor Edward A. Silver.

Lengthy mathematical proofs have been placed in appendices of the individual chapters. In addition, a few sections, requiring a level of mathematical understanding higher than the rest of the book, *have been marked with asterisks.* In all cases, these sections can be omitted without a loss of continuity. This style of presentation has been deliberately chosen so that sufficient material of interest is made available to the analytically inclined reader, while at the same time providing a meaningful text for the less analytically oriented manager without the latter becoming bogged down in mathematical details.

We believe that the book will be of interest to faculty and students in programmes of business administration, industrial engineering, and management sciences/operations research. At the same time the book should also be appealing to practicing analysts and managers at both ends of the currently existing gap between theory and practice.

Possible paths through the book for different types of users include:

1. Undergraduate business and community college programmes—Chapters 1, 2, 3, 4, 5, 6, 8, 10, 11.

2. Industrial engineering, management sciences/operations research programmes—

a. 1 term course on inventory management—Chapters 3, 4 (short range forecasting), 5, 6, 7, 8, 9, 10, 11, 19, 20.
b. 1 term course primarily on aggregate production planning—Chapters 1, 2, 3, 4 (medium range forecasting), 12, 13, 14, 15, 16, 17, 18, 19, 20, Case Studies (E–F).

3. Graduate business (MBA) programmes (as a part of the production management offerings or as a illustration of a functional area application of the management sciences approach to problem solving)—

a. 1 term course on inventory management—Chapters 1, 2, 3, 4 (short term forecasting), 5, 6, 8, 19, 20, Case Studies (A–D).

b. 1 term course primarily on production planning—Chapters 1, 2, 3, 4 (medium range forecasting), 12, 13, 15, 16, 17, 18, 19, 20, Case Studies (E–F).

4. Managers exclusively interested in policy issues (perhaps on an executive development programme basis)—Chapters 1, 2, 3, 4, 16, 19, 20, Case Studies (A–F).

5. Practicing inventory/production managers and consultants (the latter both internal and external)—

a. As related to purchasing managers, industrial distributors, and retailers—Chapters 1, 2, 3, 4, 5, 6, 8, 11, part of 13, 19, 20, Case Studies (A–D).
b. As related to manufacturing managers and production planners—all of the above as well as Chapters 12, 15, 16, 18, Case Studies (E–F).

6. Researchers including faculty members, masters and doctoral students, and non-academic researchers (to be used both as a source of research topics and a statement of the state of the art)—Chapters 6, 7, 8, 9, 10, 12, 13, 14, 15, 17, 18, 20.

The pioneers of production management, such as Henry Ford, managed to remove a great deal of the variability and, consequently, the risk and uncertainty from the area of manual labor. Apparently what is needed now are similar breakthroughs in managing the increasing diversity of information and daily decisions that continually impinge on top and middle management. Hopefully, this book is an important step in the right direction. *Il faut "reculer pour mieux sauter."*

Acknowledgments

In an undertaking of this magnitude there are always a number of individuals, besides the authors, who have an important impact on the final contents of the manuscript. Special mention must be made of two authorities in the field who, early in our careers, encouraged us to work in the general area of inventory management/production planning, namely Robert G. Brown, as a colleague of EAS at Arthur D. Little Inc., and Martin K. Starr, as a colleague of RP at Columbia University.

The manuscript, as is often the case, had its origin in the teaching notes used by the authors for several years in courses they taught at Boston University, Columbia University, the University of Waterloo, the University of Western Ontario, and York University. A large number of students (including many part-time students holding employment in industry) have provided excellent critiques. We would like to particularly thank Maged Abo El-Ela, Blyth Archibald, Ronald Craig, Alan Daley, and Robert Thompstone. A special note of appreciation is in order to Frank Steinmoeller for his effective development and testing of the computer routines and to Blyth Archibald, T. Marley, A. Russell McGillivray, and Pardeep Roy for their excellent work on the Solutions Manual.

A significant portion of the book has developed out of research supported by Grant Number A7417 from the National Research Council of Canada, Grant Number 9740-16 of the Defence Research Board of Canada, Grant Number 16-585 from the Canada Council, and Grant Number 69-151 from the Ford Foundation. The authors gratefully acknowledge this support.

A number of our professional colleagues have provided helpful comments concerning the earlier research papers and the drafts of the manuscript. In addition, other colleagues have provided us with drafts of papers in the more advanced topic areas. We appreciate these important inputs from individuals such as Kenneth Baker, William Berry, Elwood Buffa, John Buzacott, Morris Cohen, Guy Curry, Donald Daly, Chandrasekhar Das, W. Steven Demmy, Adolf Diegel, Richard Ehrhardt, Donald Gross, Warren Hausman, Arnoldo Hax, David Herron, Edward Ignall, Alan Kaplan, Jack Kleijnen, Howard Kunreuther, Alastair MacCormick, Eliezer Naddor, Steven Nahmias, E. F. Peter Newsom, L. S. Rosen, David Schrady, Lee Schwarz, Harvey Wagner, D. Clay Whybark, and Gene Woolsey.

A number of senior managers also have had an influence on the development of this book, for example, J. Alexander, formerly President, A. L. & W. Sports; E. Brewer, Controller, CIBA-GEIGY; D. B. McCaskill, former President of Connaught Labs Ltd.; and R. Walker, Formerly Vice President—Manufacturing, Fuller Brush Co.

Finally, on such a monumental task a special work of thanks is necessary for those individuals who have edited, typed, and proofread the many drafts of the manuscript. These appreciated people include Diane Hammar, Lobin Ling, Patricia Robinson and, particularly, Joan Bennewies and Mari Peterson. *Sic vos non vobis.*

Contents

Decision Systems for Inventory Management and Production Planning

PART 1

Inventory Management and Production Planning Decisions as Components of Total Business Strategy

A lack of agreement as to the relative importance and role of inventories in overall business strategy has impeded the introduction of modern methods of decision making. Too many in top management have tended to view inventory as the result of a year end accounting of "all the dumb things we undertook last year". Analysts, for their part, have too readily adopted formulations of the inventory management and production planning decisions that are largely mathematical in content and which too often have not captured adequately the realities of the managerial context.

In Chapter 1 we review some of the analytical approaches that have been taken and the attitudes assumed by managers and analysts. Analytical formulations of the inventory management and production planning decisions need to have more direct inputs from top management to be effective in practice. Many of the benefits gained and costs incurred in carrying inventory are difficult to assess quantitatively and can seldom be determined directly from accounting records. Subjective value judgments must be accepted by analysts as valid substitutes for hard data when the latter is lacking. Top management is best qualified to make such judgments.

The individual item inventory problem is primarily one of coping with a large amount of data, variables, and physical entities. In Chapter 2, we describe the diverse nature of inventory as well as its statistical properties. The sheer magnitude of the problem and the effects of managerial expectations and decisions on the fluctuation of aggregate inventory investment are related to the business cycle.

Given the voluminous information, the competing internal and external motives for stocking inventory and all the other demands made upon management, the question as to how much inventory is really enough is impossible to answer unless all the controllable aspects of inventories are precisely identified. In Chapter 3, we define the major decision variables and discuss the planning problem at the level of the firm. A methodology making possible the direct introduction of value judgments into analytical formulations is outlined along with conceptual and physical aids for coping with the sheer magnitude of the task involved.

Since managerial expectations about the future have such a tremendous impact on the inventory management and production planning decisions, forecasting the demand variable is given special treatment in a separate chapter. In Chapter 4, we present the many techniques and the strategies that could be adopted to cope with the unknown future.

CHAPTER ONE

The Context of Inventory Management and Production Planning Decisions

Inventory management and aggregate production planning have been studied in considerable depth and are probably the most technologically advanced segments of the administrative sciences. Yet, those of us who, through consulting work, come into intimate contact with managerial decision procedures in this area, are repeatedly surprised to find how limited, ad hoc and crude many of the existing decisions systems actually are. The rate at which theory has been developed, has far outstripped the rate at which decision practices have been successfully upgraded. Moreover, while some existing theory is well developed, important segments of the total problem area have been overlooked by analysts in the past. We have tried with this book to fill some of the gaps in theory and in practice.

In this chapter we explore some of the reasons why theory has outstripped practice and propose a more realistic context for dealing with inventory and production planning decisions in the future. Undoubtedly a great potential remains for improvement in current managerial practices, as well as for meaningful research into heretofore underdeveloped theoretical questions.

1.1 *Introduction*

In the aggregate, inventories affect the economy through business cycles. Individually they provide the means by which we can efficiently organize operations such as purchasing, manufacturing and/or distribution so that ultimately the end user receives any desired level of service.

At the level of the firm, inventory is among the largest investments made and therefore logically deserves to be treated as a major policy variable, highly responsive to the plans and style of top management. Yet, to date, in most firms, both analysts and managers have been relatively unsuccessful in convincing top management to give this area the due consideration that it logically deserves.

The same is not the case at the level of the economy as a whole. Aggregate inventory fluctuations receive very close scrutiny from senior governmental analysts and policy makers, industrial lobbyists, labor unions, and politicians. This strange paradox is an important part of the basic challenge that our book tries to examine and help resolve. It is our hope that through the development of a comprehensive, yet practically useable, set of decision rules and decision systems we can demonstrate to senior management that it is now feasible to manage inventories more effectively than has been the case ever before.

1.1.1 *The Problem Defined*

Inventories play an essential and pervasive role in any enterprise because they make it possible:

To order larger quantities of goods, materials or components from suppliers at advantageous prices

To provide reasonable customer service through supplying most requirements from stock without delay

To maintain more stable operating and/or workforce levels

To take advantage of shipping economies

To plan overall operating strategy through decoupling of successive stages in the chain of: acquiring goods, preparing products, shipping to branch warehouses, and finally serving customers

In general, the larger the inventory, the easier it is to plan operations and work force levels; the easier it is to reduce costs of purchasing, manufacturing, and shipping; the easier it is to provide prompt customer service. At the same time, though, a larger inventory also requires a larger investment of money and has associated with it higher costs such as storage, handling, risk of obsolescence, and data-processing. These latter costs must be balanced off against any advantages achieved from stocking larger amounts in inventory. This then, simply stated, is the basic problem to be resolved—the balancing of the many cost advantages and disadvantages to attain an *appropriate* level of inventory investment for a particular organizational setting.

While it is simple to state the problem in words, it turns out to be not-so-easy to determine appropriate inventory policy in practice. *Most of the benefits gained and costs incurred in carrying inventory are difficult to assess and can seldom be determined directly from accounting records.* This is because questions, such as those listed below, do not always have straightforward, *quantifiable* answers:

What is the value of good customer service?

How stable a workforce or operating level should be maintained?

What is the value of decoupling successive operating stages?

What degree of centralization or decentralization in operations should prevail?

What is the cost of wrong decisions that result from forecast errors?

How quickly and in which way should aggregate inventory investment be adjusted in response to inflationary pressures?

How sophisticated a decision-control system is warranted given the available managerial talent and the competitive environment?

Part of the reason why such questions have proven to be difficult to answer in the past is that they involve overall company policy and cannot be answered from the limited point of view of inventory management or cost accounting, *alone.* Ultimately, the size of an appropriate, balanced inventory investment must be justified in terms of the extent to which it contributes to the effectiveness of overall organizational policies and profitability. Such justifications usually contain significant subjective judgments. These subjective judgments really should not be left to clerks or analysts, as is the case in many organizations. To make top management involvement feasible, we must develop decision systems which can accept as input top management opinion on qualitative questions, and which then yield consistent decisions for operating personnel to implement.

1.1.2 *The Role of Top Management*

The key organizational role of top managers is aggregate business planning, strategy, and control. Senior management has the responsibility for defining in broad outline what needs to be done, and how and when it should be done. Top management also must act as the final arbiter of all conflicts between the operating divisions and has the ultimate responsibility for seeing that the general competitive environment is monitored and adapted to effectively. Throughout the book we shall assume and argue for the role of top management shown schematically in Figure 1.1.

In Figure 1.1 a myriad of external variables, many of which are beyond direct managerial control, are shown to impinge on top management who sift through and evaluate the voluminous information (some of it incorrect, some of it misleading). In fact, top management is presented as a filter which reduces the large amount of data on external forces to relatively well-defined goals, guidelines and constraints for use by lower levels of administration or as input to well defined decision systems.

Figure 1.1 The Desired Role of Top Management in the Inventory Management and Production Planning Process.

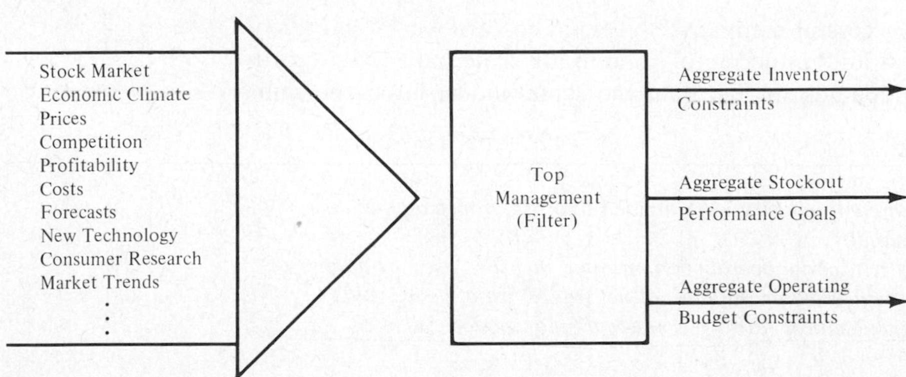

While advocating the top management role illustrated in Figure 1.1, we do not intend to imply that the filtering process is always decisive, clear cut and feasible in practice as the schematic shows it. Given the many uncertainties among the input variables, top management may not always be able to clearly differentiate between goals and constraints, let alone provide guidelines.

However, it is clear that, regardless of the organization and regardless of the timing, at some point top management's feelings about financial constraints, performance levels and operating budgets will *always* have a bearing on the inventory management and production planning decisions made. In Figure 1.1, we propose that top management concerns be brought to bear explicitly right from the beginning, rather than after the fact when aggregate inventory is suddenly discovered to be out of kilter. In the next section we will present some data on what happens in companies where such a role is accepted by senior management.

1.1.3 *Productivity and Performance of Existing Inventory Decision Systems*

Many existing companies are relatively successful in managing the productivity of their investment in inventories, but a surprising number of organizations leave decisions in this crucial area to rules of thumb, guesswork or chance. A large majority of organizations consider inventory control a middle or lower management responsibility—a technical subject consisting of mathematical formulae, cost accounting, measurement and the drudgery of keeping track of thousands of individual items of stock.

Burr W. Hupp,[10] using data that were originally compiled by Dun's Review on the inventory management policies of merchants (retailers and wholesalers) from 17 industries, concluded that:

> *If the typical unsuccessful company did as well (as a successful one) it could double its sales with no increase in quantity of goods on hand. Or, with no change in sales, it could reduce stock by* 50 *percent.*

That is, a typical "successful company"* seemed to turnover** its inventories twice as often as an "unsuccessful" one in the same industry. According to Hupp, the companies studied sold the same goods, hired the same

---

* *Companies in each industry were divided into two groups on the basis of recent profitability.*

** *Turnover is a favorite overall performance measure used by many managers and is defined as the ratio of net sales (cost of goods sold) to average dollar inventory during some calendar period such as* 12 *months.*

type of operating personnel, and had access to the same tools and techniques of successful inventory management. The one major factor that was not the same in all companies studied was the attitude of top management. In the more successful companies top management tended to become more directly involved with *aggregate* inventory and production planning policy determination. In Table 1.1 we summarize the inventory performance of the sample of companies reported on by Hupp.

Considerable variability exists in the turnover ratios listed in Table 1.1. Turnover ratios differ not only between successful and unsuccessful companies but also between types of merchants. This latter fact is attributable largely to the differences that exist between industries in their cost structures, in the volatility of their seasonal sales patterns, in the industry norms of competition, in the degree of profitability that has been achieved in the past *and in the managerial styles of doing business.* That is, top management style and the type of industry involved does have a marked influence on the inventory performance achieved by any particular company.

In similar research carried out by Hill,[9] companies in the retail and wholesale trades were found typically to have greater top management involvement in the management of inventories. In most other industries top

Table 1.1 Typical Inventory Turnover Ratios

		Ratio of Net Sales to Inventory (Net Sales per $1.00 of Inventory)	
Types of Merchants	Number of Companies	Successful Company Ratio	Unsuccessful Company Ratio
Retailing:			
Building Materials	96	15.1	5.2
Department Stores	202	7.3	3.9
Discount Stores	180	7.5	4.4
Gasoline Service Stations	84	21.2	5.4
Groceries and Meats	156	23.0	12.7
Tires, Batteries, and Access.	69	8.4	3.9
Variety Stores	63	6.0	3.5
Women's Specialty Shops	208	9.4	4.9
Wholesaling:			
Chemicals and Allied Products	55	16.2	7.3
Drugs and Sundries	110	10.2	5.6
Electrical Parts, Supplies	156	10.2	5.6
Electronics Equipment	56	5.6	3.3
Household Appliances	111	10.6	4.8
Machinery and Equipment	211	10.9	5.0
Metals and Minerals	68	11.4	4.1
Paper	157	9.7	5.5
Petroleum Products	75	41.1	13.0

management tended to become concerned only from time to time if inventory got "out-of-line," which often meant higher than the same time last year. More concern was also likely to be expressed when money supply from conventional sources became so tight that a reduction in the investment in inventory was perceived as being the most ready source of cash in the short-run.

About half of the organizations studied by Hill had no predetermined budgets nor limits on inventory. Most of the representatives of the organizations interviewed said they had some *aggregate* inventory budgets or limits which were usually arbitrarily set in terms of number of days supply, flat dollar limits, or as a percentage of total sales. Many organizations interviewed attempted to shift inventory management to a greater degree on their suppliers. A major inventory control programme which always received top management recognition was the standardization of products, parts and raw materials—always carried out with the view to *reducing* the total number of stock keeping units (s.k.u.) carried and thereby total inventory investment. The latter finding reflects some of the top management attitudes toward inventories which we shall explore in Chapter 2.

1.1.4 *Progress in Inventory Management and Production Planning Practices*

Progress towards greater top management involvement in rational processes of inventory management has been slow in coming. About twenty years ago Melnitsky, an early writer in this area, concluded rather acerbically that:

> *The aborigine knew nothing of inventory control, and, quite possibly, his 20th century corporate counterpart is equally unenlightened. The changeover from inventory to inventory control bears no date. Some concerns plunged into the healthful waters of scientific management of inventories well before the first World War; others are still on the shore contemplating on the advisability of wetting their toes.*[14]

Such a harsh evaluation of top management involvement may still hold true in many organizations today, *but unlike Melnitsky we believe the fault has not and does not lie today with reticent managers alone.*

The general acceptance of a radically new technology has always taken two or three decades in the past. Witness the discovery of something as obviously superior as the diesel engine and the subsequent slow changeover from steam. It seems that new conceptions always need a period of maturation during which details can be improved upon, made more practicable, and when original claims about increased productivity and performance can be mellowed through the test of time.

By comparison, to the historical acceptance of innovations, rational inventory management and production planning theory are relatively new, and on schedule towards becoming eventually generally accepted. After all, most of the theory in this area was developed during the last 25 years. At the same time the majority of existing top managers and policy makers did not receive their formal managerial training, nor did they garner their experiences in the context of the relatively novel decision systems developed in the last two decades. Therefore, those of us who are advocating improvement in managerial technology must temper our impatience by pursuing a strategy of implementation that allows for a smooth transition in systems as well as managerial values.

We do not wish to leave the reader with an impression that there are no successful implementations of inventory management and/or production planning decision systems in existence, which operate with full support and involvement of top management. One of the most impressive inventory decision systems that the authors have seen, in this context, was implemented by the Canadian Tire Corporation Ltd. C.T.C. is a chain of franchised dealers, in many ways similar to Western Auto Stores in the U.S.A., who sell, at retail, auto parts and accessories, home hardware and house improvement items, as well as some housewares and sporting goods. According to Dean Muncaster, the president:

> *In the development of in-store inventory procedures . . . the principal accolades must go to some dealers who joined us in the last few years . . . they in effect had developed an in-store, computer based system . . . These fellows have developed models that they believe will handle every seasonal sales pattern of merchandise that we sell in our stores. It's a . . . sophisticated system, but it's simple in the sense that it doesn't cause people to have to change their in-store habits a whole lot. It's done in mini-computers so that the costs are reasonable and having been dealer-inspired and dealer-oriented we don't have any of the ivory tower syndrome to contend with.**

We believe that many writers like Melnitsky have reacted overly impatiently. If senior management in some of our companies have not adopted our new decision systems as fast as we would like, then at least some of the fault must be ours. Perhaps we, who develop and design decision models for inventory management and production planning, have not done a good enough job of convincing managers of the validity or usefulness of our

---

* *For a complete description of the C.T.C. experience, see the interview conducted by Leonard S. Simon and reported in* Interfaces, *Vol.* 4, *No.* 3, *May,* 1974, *pp.* 12–22.

models. Perhaps our models have not always been as suitable for management purposes as we have led ourselves to think.

1.2 *The Reluctant Advocates*

Many analysts assume that the scientific method is the only alternative to "straight thinking" on managerial problems, often also implying that it is something that can be done only by "scientists." Such a point of view is, perhaps unintentionally, too imperialistic and certainly has impeded the upgrading of management decision making procedures.

The scientific method, as a type of thinking and decision making process dates back essentially to seventeenth century England, most notably to the writing of Sir Francis Bacon. In essence, it is predicated on basically asking:" If I do *A*, how likely is it that *B* will be the result?" Managers, by necessity, have to spend considerable time trying to predict the course of future events in attempting to adapt to changing conditions. Risk is an inherent part of such a process. The scientific method can help to refine the risk taking process by focussing attention on the realities of the situation and generating additional information through a well-reasoned evaluation of the relevant facts, assumptions, and courses of action, appropriately weighted by their respective probabilities of success.

However, too many management science practitioners view the scientific decision making aids which they develop as being *obviously* superior replacements for existing methods. As a result, they feel it hardly necessary to promote the use of their methods. That is, they are *reluctant advocates* of the use of the scientific method in management decision making. This has, in turn, led to a circular kind of reasoning in management practice. As reluctant advocates, management scientists have had limited success in convincing senior management that management science methodology is operational. As a result, many of the existing planning procedures used by management, especially in the area of corporate planning, turn out to be relatively ineffective. Consequently, managers become progressively more pessimistic about their own ability to plan rationally and become even more resistant to using unfamiliar scientific methods developed by scientists who "have never had to meet a payroll."

It is unfortunate that in response to managerial resistance to new decision technology so many management scientists and operational researchers have opted for a style of involvement which is predicated on acting merely as staff technicians who provide logical (mathematical) solutions to only some well defined types of management problems. Management science in practice, more often than not, consists of the *application* of the scientific method in ways which, in concept, are not as mysterious nor as complex as they are sometimes (unnecessarily) made to appear. By aspiring to remove themselves from the mainstream of decision making (in line positions of management) many operational researchers are (inadvertently) retarding the upgrading of managerial decision making and are relegating themselves to an unnecessarily low status in the decision making hierarchy.

1.3 Heuristic Decision Systems

All managers plan on the basis of what they perceive will happen in the future. Since all predictions about the future turn out to be erroneous to some unknown degree, managers must constantly adapt their original plans on the basis of information that continuously comes to their attention. In fact, one should expect that decisions made in such a context will be revoked or, at best, supplemented by subsequent decisions. That is, management is a process of constant adaptation to change. Such a process of decision making is analogous to the adaptive feedback control or cybernetic control system illustrated by the decision system in Figure 1.2, where we have included automatic decision rules as part of the heuristic decision process controlled by a human decision maker.

The word "heuristic" comes from the Greek *heuriskein*, helping to discover or learn, and is often used today to describe methods of problem solution and/or investigation which encourage the decision maker to learn and to decide on his own, using the best available resources at his command. In the context of this book, by heuristics, we shall mean decision rules which are designed to yield satisfactory, that is reasonable, yet mathematically *suboptimal*, answers to complex real problems.

Figure 1.2 A Heuristic Decision System.

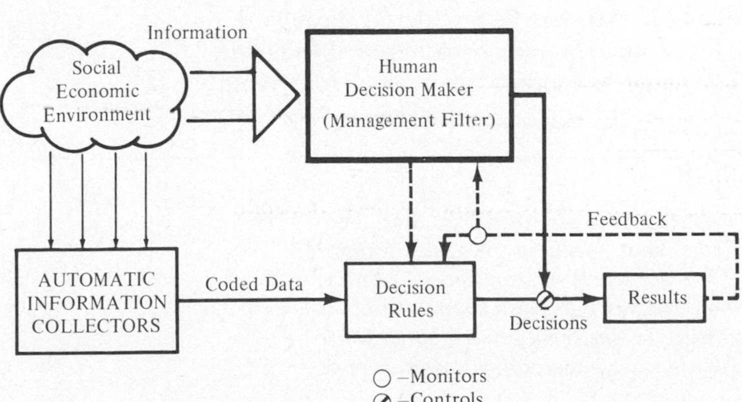

In Figure 1.2, heuristics are shown as being used under the direct control of the manager who allows some routine decisions to be made automatically, but always retains the option of intervening through either directly modifying the decisions generated or through specifying extraordinary inputs to prespecified decision rules. Presumably the manager would intervene only when he learns or discovers information that would improve the solution to the problem under review. The process illustrated in Figure 1.2 is the manner in which we recommend that the decision systems for inventory management and production planning designed in this book be implemented in practice. Note that decisions, under normal circumstances, are routinely generated by coded information collected from the environment (for example, unit sales) and management by exception is exercised only when deemed necessary. Such a decision system strikes an effective division of labor between computer-based decision models, the rapid, rigorously-programmed processors of coded information, and the creative and adaptive decision maker who intervenes when the decision model is insufficient. Such a marriage deals most effectively with real problems, often yielding near-optimal results.*

1.4 *The Focus of the Book*

The existing gap between decision theory and practice seems to have developed primarily for two reasons: First, top management in the recent past has been preoccupied with rapid economic growth at the expense of operating efficiency. Secondly, many management scientists and economists, being left to their own devices, have been overly preoccupied with developing mathematically elegant decision models that have had limited practical value for decision making at the level of the firm.

Elaboration on the first of these two points is in order. The economies of most Western countries have experienced an uprecedented expansionary era of post-war development since 1944. Growth was first achieved through the rapid exploitation of the large stored up demand, backlogged during the war. Subsequently, new-found consumer prosperity maintained the rapid

* *For an excellent discussion of Heuristics see Martin K. Starr,* Production Management; Systems and Synthesis. *Second Edition. Prentice-Hall, 1972, p. 136. We are using the concept "heuristics" in the most general sense. Some readers may wish to quibble about the fact that most of our heuristics in this book have a single objective function and many of them do not have explicit lower or upper bounds on other criteria.*

growth. Growth was also achieved through the opening up of new domestic markets and markets in developing countries. In such an economic environment, it made sense for top management to marshal all efforts towards meeting rapidly rising sales, often at almost any cost. Inventory management and production planning were of secondary priority during this period. In order to meet the profit goals set for their companies in the early 1950s, when labor costs began to rise, top management responded by implementing policies which decreased the use of manual labor and which increased the use of mechanized manufacturing equipment.

A departure from this traditional response to rising costs began to emerge in the 1960s when top management were introduced to a new form of technological change. Large-scale computers became available for controlling a firm's operations. Given this new means of monitoring and control, top management started automating many clerical jobs and in turn became more demanding in requesting information about the cost of daily operations. Such operating data, more readily available to all, made inventory management and production planning decisions more visible and brought them, at least potentially, under closer scrutiny by all members of the top management team.

The remainder of the 1970s and 1980s promise to have an even more important impact on management thinking. The early part of the 1970s brought reduced growth and extensive changes in the market place. The consumer has begun to demand maximum productive variety (or maximum choice) at the same price, as has been pointed out by Moran.[15] The number of different products needed to satisfy existing markets is becoming larger. Product life cycles, correspondingly, are becoming shorter. This need for increased diversity, unless properly planned for, threatens to greatly increase the costs of operation. For one thing, all products and markets today must be monitored and planned for much more closely than in former years. The efficient allocation of internal resources is by necessity, once again, receiving considerable attention from top management.

The pioneers of production management, such as Henry Ford, managed to remove a great deal of the variability, and, consequently, the risk and uncertainty, from the area of manual labor. Apparently what is needed in the context of future reality are similar breakthroughs in managing the increasing diversity of information and daily decisions that continually impinge on top and middle management. It is towards this end that the decision systems described in this book are directed.

Problems for Chapter 1

Problem 1.1

Refer to Figure 1.1. Give examples from current newspapers that illustrate the effect of prevailing general economic conditions on inventory investment. How should your examples from the newspaper affect top management's guidelines regarding aggregate inventory constraints, performance goals, and budget contraints?

Problem 1.2

Have an interview with a senior executive of a large company and see how much importance he attaches to the control of inventories in his company. Try to determine whether different top executives in the same company view inventories differently. Based on your interview, do you think it is possible to have top management directly involved in inventory management and production planning "right from the beginning" as proposed in Chapter 1? Discuss.

Problem 1.3

Analyse the financial statements for the last five years of two companies from different industries. (For example a grocery chain and an electronic goods manufacturer.) Calculate their turnover ratios. Try to explain why their turnover ratios are different. Are there any trends apparent that can be explained?

Problem 1.4

Talk to a person who is responsible for inventory control at a *medium sized* company in your community. Why does this firm carry the current amount of inventories? What kind of decision rules are being used? Evaluate their current inventory management policies.

Problem 1.5

Investigate the inventory control procedures at a *small* (owner-managed) company. When does a company become too small to have its inventories managed scientifically?

REFERENCES FOR CHAPTER 1

1. Broffman, Morton H. "What Management Expects of Production and Inventory Control." *APICS Quarterly Bulletin*, Vol. 2, No. 1, January, 1961.

2. Chinal, Jean P. "The Systems Approach: A French Experience." *Interfaces*, Vol. 5, No. 2, February, 1975, pp. 47–56.

3. Daly, D. J. and Peterson, Rein. "On Bridging the Gaps." *Management Science*, Vol. 20, No. 4, Part I, December, 1974, pp. 550–569.

4. Dickie, H. F. *Key Consideration in Inventory Management.* American Management Association Manufacturing Series, No. 207, 1953.

5. Dickie, H. F. "Six Steps to Better Inventory Management." *Factory Management and Maintenance*, July, 1956.

6. Dyer, Dickie "Why Inventory Doesn't Get Managed." *Modern Distribution Management*, Vol. 6, No. 23, November 22, 1972, pp. 3–6.

7. Grayson, C. Jackson. "Management Science and Business Practice." *Harvard Business Review*, July-August, 1974, pp. 41–48.

8. Hadley, B. and Whitin T. "A Review of Alternative Approaches to Inventory Theory." Rand RM-4185-PR, September, 1964, 165 pp.

9. Hill, Richard E. "Does Top Management Manage Inventory?" *Production and Inventory Management*, First Quarter, 1974, pp. 32–36.

10. Hupp, Burr W. "Inventory Policy is a Top Management Responsibility." in *Readings in Physical Distribution Management*, edited by D. J. Bowersox, Bernhard J. Lalonde, and Edward W. Smykay. McMillan, 1969, pp. 179–184.

11. Lampkin, W. "A Review of Inventory Control Theory." *The Production Engineer*, Vol. 46, No. 2, 1967, pp. 57–66.

12. Meador, Charles Lawrence and Ness, David N. "Decision Support Systems: An Application to Corporate Planning." *Sloan Management Review*, Winter, 1974, pp. 51–68.

13. Meal, Harlan C. "Policy Conficts and Inventory Control." *Financial Executive*, December, 1963, pp. 13–17.

14. Melnitsky, Benjamin. *Management of Industrial Inventory.* Conover-Mast Publications, New York and Chicago, 1951, pp. 3–4.

15. Moran, William T. "The Marketing-Production Interaction." Chapter 15, in Starr, Martin K. *Production Management: Systems and Synthesis.* Second Edition, Prentice Hall, 1972, pp. 463–507, and pp. 194–196.

16. Sandhusen, Richard L. "Managing Inventory for Profit." *Industrial Distribution*, February, March, May, and July, 1972.

17. Tilles, S. "The Manager's Job: a Systems Approach." *Harvard Business Review*, January, February, 1973, pp. 153–161.

18. Wagner, H. M. "A Manager's Survey of Inventory and Production Control Systems." *Interfaces*, Vol. 2, No. 4, August, 1972, pp. 31–39.

CHAPTER TWO

The Nature of Inventories

Some two hundred years ago the management of inventories was, relatively, a simpler matter. Inventories were considered by merchants, producers, and policy makers as primarily a measure of wealth. A businessman's or a country's wealth and power were assessed in terms of how many bushels of wheat, heads of cattle, pounds of gold, etc. were stored in warehouses. In 1677, Pappilon,[28] writing about inventories, pointed out that:

> *The stock or riches of the kingdom doth not only consist of our money, but also in our commodities and ships for trade and magazines furnished with all necessary materials.*[28]

More recently, especially since the 1920s, decision makers have started to put increased emphasis on the liquidity of assets such as inventories, until fast turnover has become a goal to be pursued for its own sake in many organizations. According to Whitin:[30]

> *Inventories are (now) often referred to as the "graveyard" of American business, as surplus stocks have been a principal cause of business failures. Inventories are also considered a destabilizing influence in business with cycles . . . As a result, businessmen have developed an almost pathological fear of increasing inventories.*[30]

Most of the pathological fears to which Whitin refers, date from the period 1920–21 when the first "Inventory Depression"* was recognized, and caused in turn, a phenomenon commonly known as "hand-to-mouth buying"[24,25,26] throughout the American economy. As the name suggests, during this Depression, too much emphasis was placed on the necessity of achieving rapid rates of inventory turnover. Many managers overreacted by trying to achieve near zero inventories. Top management had completely reversed their attitudes regarding the desirability of inventories from 200 years before.

Inventories are today viewed by most senior management as a large potential risk and seldom as a measure of wealth. A constant nagging fear seems to persist in the minds of most policy makers that merchandise stocked in excess of actual demand may require drastic price cuts, so as to be salable before it becomes worthless because of obsolescence through style or technological changes. Obsolescence through style changes is, in fact, of relatively recent origin, but promises to be of increasing importance in the future as product life cycles become shorter and shorter.

Most managers today recognize the importance of *balancing* the advantages and disadvantages of carrying any level of inventories. Nevertheless, some of the old fears and values still linger on. As one company president expressed it to us:

> *"I agree that inventories play a crucial role in my operations. But I cannot lose sight of the other side of the coin. While inventories are something I need to survive, they also represent stuff I can get stuck with."*

---

* *We shall discuss inventory depressions in some detail later in this chapter. For now let us define an inventory depression as a period marked by a slackening of business activity, much unemployment, falling prices and wages, etc. It is generally believed that such periods can be brought about by surplus inventories held widely by merchants and producers in the economy.*

When we consider past attitudes regarding inventories in a historical perspective, it is really not so surprising that changes in management decision behavior in this area have been slow in coming. The change in top management thinking from viewing inventories, first as a measure of wealth and power, then as a cause of fearful business failures, and now as something that must be tamed and managed rationally through the use of modern techniques, is equally as radical an innovation in concept as the changeover from steam to diesel power.

2.1 *Why Inventory Investment Fluctuates*

That total dollar inventory investment in any economy fluctuates in response to a complex set of factors is an empirical fact. Inventory investment is one of the most volatile components of our economy. During business cycles, changes in the rate of inventory investment have been larger in magnitude than those on any one of the other volatile components of the economy, such as expenditures on plant and equipment, housing, or durable consumption. This relative volatility of inventory investment is remarkable when you consider that approximately 34 percent of current assets and about 90 percent of the working capital of a typical company in the United States is invested in inventories. In absolute terms the 1976 book value of the stock of manufacturing and trade inventories was $276 billion or 16.5 percent of the GNP of the United States.*

Note that in Table 2.1 the lowest rate of increase in business inventories occurred in 1970 (actually during the first quarter of 1970). During the 1969/1970 recession no actual disinvestment of business inventories took place, only a slowdown in the rate of investment. This was an indication of the fact that the 1969/1970 recession would be a relatively mild period of readjustment (actually the mildest in the post war years). In contrast, for example, in the first quarter of 1975, inventories *decreased* 1.3 percent, indicating that a much more severe recession was taking place (see also Figure 2.1). Historically, a slowdown in the rate of inventory investment has always been followed first by a reduction in corporate profits and then, in

---

* *GNP is the market value of the newly produced goods and services that are not resold (to avoid double counting) in any form during a calendar year. It is a measure of the new wealth resulting from the productive activity of an economy and is approximately comparable to the annual sales of a business firm. Readers unfamiliar with economic terms can refer to Thomas F. Dernburg and Duncan M. McDougall.* Macro Economics. *McGraw-Hill, Second Edition,* 1963, *pp.* 1–48.

Table 2.1 Some Economic Indicators of the U.S. Economy

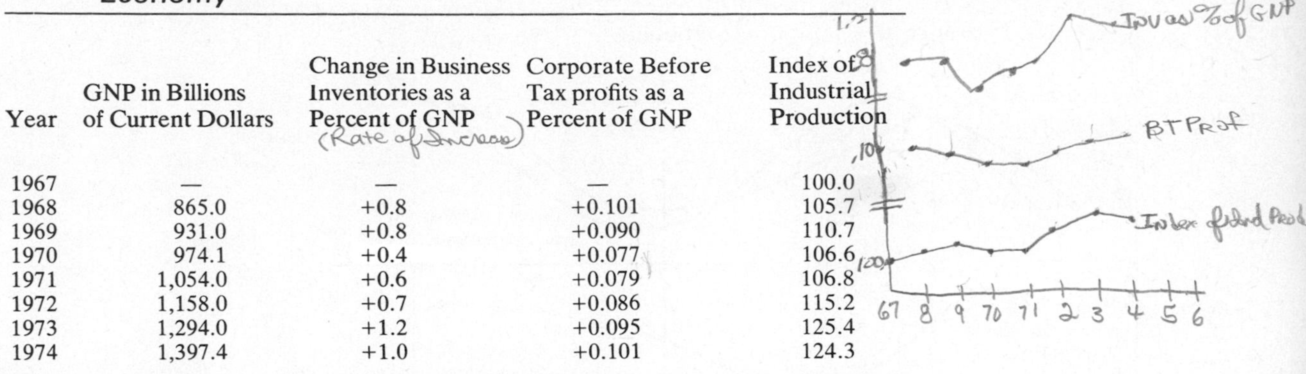

Year	GNP in Billions of Current Dollars	Change in Business Inventories as a Percent of GNP	Corporate Before Tax profits as a Percent of GNP	Index of Industrial Production
1967	—	—	—	100.0
1968	865.0	+0.8	+0.101	105.7
1969	931.0	+0.8	+0.090	110.7
1970	974.1	+0.4	+0.077	106.6
1971	1,054.0	+0.6	+0.079	106.8
1972	1,158.0	+0.7	+0.086	115.2
1973	1,294.0	+1.2	+0.095	125.4
1974	1,397.4	+1.0	+0.101	124.3

Source: Business Conditions Digest, U.S. Department of Commerce, selected issues.

turn, by a slowdown in the rate of industrial production, resulting eventually in a lower level of employment and less money in consumers' pockets for spending on the necessities of life. Five of the major business downturns in the period from the end of World War II to 1969 have been attributed to "excess" inventory. The most recent recession, in the middle 1970s, is also considered to be the result of a major readjustment in the economy of the size and nature of inventory stocks.

2.1.1 *The Business Cycle*

Many economists have tried to compile comprehensive models of the business cycle to explain all patterns of fluctuations that have occurred historically.[10] No one has succeeded, to date, in building an all-purpose model. The major point which seems to emerge from all this research is that each cycle has in the past been somewhat different, especially with regard to its exact timing and relative magnitude. Some underlying common variables, which can be gleaned from past cycles, about the recurrent timing of the cyclical process are illustrated in Figure 2.1.

We shall start describing the cycle in Figure 2.1 at the point "A" where, due to overoptimistic expectations, too many products are manufactured by the economy and cannot be sold. These surplus goods increase aggregate inventories to the extent that producers start to reduce the scale of their operations until the rate of sale exceeds the rate of production of goods. The resulting disinvestment in inventories creates a recession during which prices, production, and profits fall and unemployment is prevalent. Eventually an economic recovery is generated by a slowing in the rate of inventory liquidation. Some top managers, expecting that prices will recover, start to slowly expand their operations while costs are low. Thus the stage is set for the expansionary, recovery phase. On May 9, 1975, an article appeared in the

Figure 2.1 The Business Cycle.

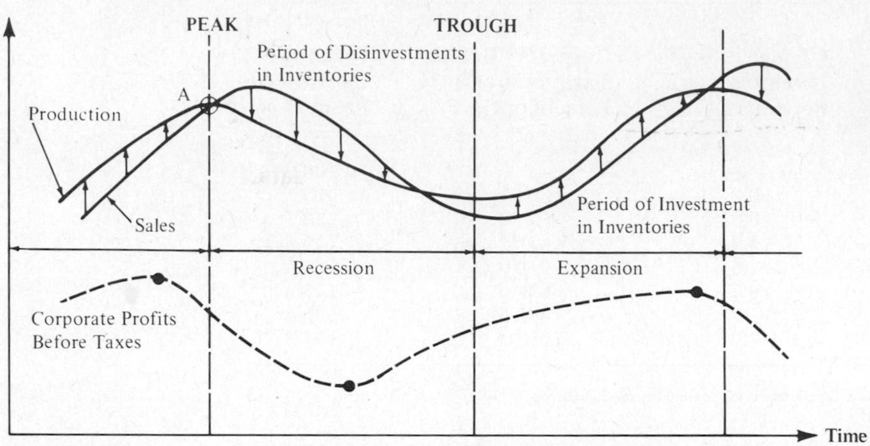

business section of the *Toronto Globe and Mail*, proclaiming:

Figure 2.2

Record inventory drop buoys New York prices

The New York market buoyed by news of a record drop in inventory levels in March, registered a broad advance in much busier trading.

Advances outnumbered declines by more than two to one, with 1,084 issues up and 429 down.

The Dow Jones industrial average finished up 0.63 points at 850.13.

At the opening, prices received a lift when the Government reported that business inventories declined a record $1.92-billion in March, the largest monthly plunge on record.

The March decline was nearly double the drop reported in February. Economists say the decline is an important indication that the economy is beginning to recover.

More and more firms slowly start to hire additional labor, purchase more raw materials, and thereby infuse more money into circulation in the economy. Consumers, with money to spend once again, start to bid up prices of available goods. Once prices of goods start to rise, more and more businessmen get on the bandwagon by expanding their operations and thereby accentuate the expansionary phase of the cycle.

The boom that results eventually is brought to an end when costs of materials are bid up once again by competing firms, when labor unions begin demanding higher wages, and when the scarcity of money for further expansion causes the banks to raise their interest rates. The crisis phase which follows is a period of uncertainty and hesitation on the part of consumers and businessmen. The latter find that their warehouses are restocked with excess inventory which, once again, cannot be sold. The business cycle then is ready to repeat itself as explained above.

This explanation is, of course, highly simplified, but it does illustrate the main forces, especially the role of inventories, at work during each cycle. Note that the expectations of businessmen and consumers and the ability of decision makers to react quickly and correctly to change is an important determinant of the length and severity of a cycle.

In Figure 2.1 the following key relationships are illustrated by the data. The peaks and troughs in corporate profits before taxes precede the peaks and troughs in production. Inventory investment lags slightly and thereby contributes to higher cyclical amplitudes in production than is necessary, given the relative amplitude in the fluctuating demand for goods by end users.

2.1.2 *Empirical Studies of Inventory Fluctuations*

Much has been written as a result of empirical studies of aggregate inventory behavior in the economy.[20,22] But it is difficult to find a sufficient amount of consensus in the opinions offered by economists to provide many directly useful operating rules for management. It is generally agreed that expectations about the future held collectively by decision makers in the economy are the major determinants of whether and to what degree inventory investment will fluctuate. The severity of inventory fluctuations depends on the degree to which expectations are in error and *on the speed with which decision makers are capable of reacting to errors in their expectations in a rational manner.* Expectations about the future have been shown to depend on the following variables: the trend of recent sales and new orders, the volume of unfilled orders, price pressures, the level of inventories in the recent past, the ratio of sales to inventories (turnover ratio), interest rates on business loans, the current level of employment, *and the types of decision making systems used by management.*

Hirsch and Lovell[17] present the following useful conclusions:

1. Both large and small firms are much more flexible at adjusting production schedules to unexpected changes in market conditions than is customarily assumed in discussions about classical economics models of the business cycle (such as presented in section 2.1.1)*

---

* *Most classical economic theory assumes that a company will always ship exactly that which is ordered; this of course is not always possible, nor desirable. See Rein Peterson. "An Optimal Control Model for Smoothing Distributor Orders: An Extension of the H.M.M.S. Aggregate Production-Work Force Scheduling Theory." unpublished Ph.D. thesis, Cornell University,* 1969.

2. A comparison of the behavior of large and small firms did not reveal a noticeable difference in the degree of forecasting precision achieved, but empirical evidence suggests that an advantage of being small is that it permits a more rapid realignment of production schedules when unexpected market developments cause errors in forecasting sales,

3. Three types of error seem to be involved in a typical firm's short-run response to its changing environment:

a. Firms do not fully exploit the information provided from past experience in formulating their expectations about the future.

b. Firms do not adequately consider production smoothing considerations (such as presented in Chapters 15 to 18 of this book) in formulating their production schedules.

c. Firms consistently underestimate the magnitude of future inventory stocks; as a result of this unwarranted optimism, the average firm generally finds itself with more capital than planned tied up in inventory.

In studying expectations, D. J. Daly[8] attributes the unwarranted optimism which management often exhibits to the difficulties that top management experience in acquiring timely information about what is currently happening in their companies. Delays in responding to relevant changes in the economic environment result. Action by top management is sometimes further hampered because of a failure to adjust available data for seasonality.* In such cases top management is in danger of confounding cyclical effects with those of seasonal movement and could respond in a inappropriate manner:

> *The need for seasonal adjustments is almost taken for granted by most economists and statisicians . . . . However as one moves away from the national aggregates and toward a finer level of industrial and regional detail . . . seasonally adjusted data are less readily available . . . many large and most small companies rely on (seasonally) unadjusted data. Insofar as this is the case, it contributes to an accentuation of inventory fluctuations as the companies respond to their reading of the surrounding economic climate.*[9]

In sum, research evidence seems to corroborate the assumption that much

---

* *We shall discuss the adjustment of time series for seasonality, cyclical, trend, and random effects in Chapter 4.*

of aggregate inventory behavior depends upon the prevailing attitudes of the people who direct industry, trade, and finance. When businessmen as a whole are optimistic as to future possibilities of economic gain, they expand their operations and investment in inventories is increased. Nevertheless inventory fluctuations and business cycles are not the result of rising and falling expectations alone. An important factor is the quality of the decisions made and the management technology used. In the next section we shall see that managerial decision systems and the structure of a physical production-distribution system in a particular industry can play an important role.

2.1.3 *Studies of Structurally Induced Inventory Fluctuations*

Over 20 years ago, economists attempted to establish to what extent decision makers in the economy maintained their inventory levels in a fixed ratio to sales.[1]

$$I_t^* = kD_t \tag{2.1}$$

Economists refer to Eq. 2.1 as the *fixed accelerator.* It is also more commonly called by accountants: the *turnover ratio.* Economists who examined the empirical data concluded that this, the most simple form of the accelerator, is not consistent with observed management behavior. Actual inventory investment is not usually maintained in direct proportion to sales either because management doesn't want to or is not able to do so in most industries. As we shall see there are logical reasons for not doing so.

Using greater variety and detail of data for the post-war period, some economists have more recently researched a modified version of the accelerator called the *flexible accelerator.*[21] These new studies assumed that business firms attempt only a partial adjustment of stocks to their desired levels during each production period. The flexible accelerator studies revealed that in the past only about 50 percent of the difference between desired and actual inventories is made up over any twelve month period. Some evidence also emerges which indicates that adjustments are being made progressively faster, with perhaps now up to 60 percent of the discrepancy being corrected during a 12 month period in recent years. This latter change is attributed largely to improved computer-based inventory control systems and more astute ordering decision rules.

It has been known by economists for some time that the more nearly the apparent inventory decision behavior of an industry or a company's distribution system approaches the fixed accelerator, the more severely will the inventory level fluctuate in that system. Why this happens can be readily demonstrated with a simplified example.

Suppose that a merchant, for example, a distributor, wants to maintain his desired inventory investment in a constant ratio to his sales, $I_t^* = kD_t$. For illustrative purposes, suppose that he uses two times current sales as his desired level of inventory, $I_t^* = 2D_t$. Then the pattern of distributor orders and inventory levels in Table 2.2 will result in response to the retail sales pattern assumed. Note that an order placed at the *end* of period $t-1$ is delivered at the beginning of period t, that is, with zero lag.

In Table 2.2 sales are constant at 100 units for three periods. As a result, desired inventory is set at 200 and the merchant orders 100 units each period and inventory on hand remains at 200. Now suppose that in period 3, sales increased 10 percent to 110. Required order size (column 5) must now rise by 10 units to replace the inventory sold, plus an additional 20 units because the desired level of stock has now risen to 220. (We are assuming here that the decision maker tries to adjust his inventories towards desired levels abruptly. As was already mentioned, in practice such adjustments tend to be more gradual.) That is, total orders in period 3 must increase by 30 percent. If the increase in sales continues at the rate of 10 units per period for another period, then the total orders placed in period 4 will also grow at a 10 units per period rate.

If the increased sales level turned out to be of short duration (as we have shown it) and returned in period 5 back to its original level of 100, total orders would have to fall drastically by 80 units, or 57 percent, in reponse to a 17 percent reduction in sales. That is, the ordering rule used by the merchant greatly amplifies the rate of change of ordering in comparison with the rate of change in sales. *Note that a fixed accelerator or turnover decision rule will cause desired inventory levels to fluctuate in response to any, even a random, fluctuation in sales.*

More complicated models of the acceleration effect have been studied by Forrester[11] at M.I.T., where he has directed a large research programme exploring the behavior of complex systems. For a model of a *four*-level

Table 2.2 The Acceleration Effect—Distributor Level

Period, t	Period Starting Inventory, $I_{s,t} = (I_{e,t-1}) + (O_{t-1})$ (1)	Retail Sales, D_t (2)	Desired Inventory, I_t^* (3)	Period Ending Inventory $I_{e,t} = I_{s,t} - D_t$ (4)	Required Order Size, $O_t = I_t^* - I_{e,t}$ (5)
0		100			
1	200	100	200	100	100
2	200	100	200	100	100
3	200	110	220	90	130
4	220	120	240	100	140
5	240	100	200	140	60
6	200	100	200	100	100
7	200	100	200	100	100

distribution system consisting of mailing, order processing, and shipment delays, as well as production lead times, Forrester reports behavior similar to our simple example above. In response to a 10 percent increase in retail sales, production at the factory level increased to a peak of 40 percent, that is, four times as much as the actual increase at the retail level. The ordering decision rules used in the model were more complex than those we assumed in Table 2.2. The ordering behavior was described by a series of 40 equations designed to realistically represent purchasing rates, delivery rates, and adjustments for orders in process and in the pipeline. All adjustments were made gradually over a period of time.

2.1.4 *The Management of Aggregate Inventory Fluctuations*

Some authorities, in the past, have contended (and a few still do) that fluctuations in economic activity were not only inevitable (beyond our control), but that they also conformed to a regular pattern known as the *business cycle.* Many people currently reject the inevitability of the cycle. But most everyone agrees that economic activity has not and will not proceed at an even pace. A period of rapid expansion in economic activity will probably always be followed by a significant contraction in the scale of operations during the succeeding period. This does not mean that we cannot take steps to significantly dampen the severity of inventory fluctuations or shorten the length of the periods of economic readjustment.

Klein and Popkin[19] concluded on the basis of their studies that, if 75 percent of the fluctuations in inventory investment could have been controlled, the U.S. economy would not have experienced any postwar recessions. As a result of findings like this, a general outcry has been heard in many quarters, demanding that excessive inventory fluctuations be dampened, to reduce the violence done by business cycles to the quality of everyday life. To this end, some politicians and lawmakers have suggested that an inventory fluctuation tax should be imposed on companies who fluctuate their inventories "excessively." To date, most of these proposals to tax inventory fluctuations have come to naught, simply because it is difficult to determine conclusively how much fluctuation in inventories is warranted and how much is not for any particular firm.*

Furthermore, research results suggest that governmental intervention through manipulation of interest rates would not significantly affect the inventory investment of a firm. This latter fact is really not that surprising. In Chapter 3, we shall consider the relative magnitudes of the costs involved

---

* *As an example, consider the reserve currency proposals originally advocated by Benjamin Graham.* Storage and Stability. *Princeton Press,* 1937.

in an inventory decision. As we shall see, in most companies, during relatively stable economic periods, the cost of carrying inventories is around 25 cents per dollar of inventory investment carried per year. Unless government policy is designed to encourage hyperinflation, top management will always find it more economical to delay purchases of inventories in the face of rising prices *below* 25 percent per year.

Many serious questions remain unanswered about the actual desirability of "social control." Most objectives of social control tend to be in direct conflict with those of manager–entrepreneurs. For example, a government policy of varying inventories counter-cyclically as part and parcel of some economic stabilization scheme, could cause serious operating difficulties at the level of the firm.

The raising of the general level of management competence in inventory management and production planning is, we believe, the only course open to those who advocate better social control of inventories. Traditionally, government policy makers and top management have formulated policies using inventory records that are highly aggregated. Before the days of computer-based data processing, we really had no other reasonable, inexpensive alternative. Today we are no longer constrained in this manner, since it is now possible to design relatively inexpensive information systems that quickly yield real-time inventory data at any required level of detail. Managerial and governmental decision making behavior and the thinking of analysts who design inventory decision systems has not kept pace with these changes. There is a lingering tendency to continue using overly aggregated averages for policy making.

Overall averages, of course, give a very limited picture of whether the inventories in various departments, or in the mix of particular products or of entire lines are in proper balance. Inventory exists physically in discrete units and therefore at least some of the decisions must be based on detailed information. The management problem, in any case, is primarily one of managing the diversity among thousands of different items whose nature and quantity is continually changing over time.

2.2 *Some Statistical Properties of Aggregate Inventories*

In previous sections we examined statistical data and economic rationales on the fluctuation of aggregate inventories. In this section we shall present some of the static statistical properties that characterize typical inventory systems. These relationships shall prove to be invaluable conceptual aids in helping management direct its efforts more effectively when managing the large numbers and the diversity of factors in a typical inventory system.

We shall see that the importance and magnitude of inventory investment varies from one industry to another, as well as with the location of the firm within a distribution system of an industry. Secondly, in most companies a small percent of the products account for a large percent of the total annual dollar sales volume. Finally, we shall see that the variability of demand for a product over any time period can be empirically related to its dollar volume over the same period.

2.2.1 *The Distribution of Inventories within Industries*

The form and physical location of inventory investment, and, therefore, the nature and relative importance of inventory decisions are not the same in all industries. In some industries, from the point of view of top management, the problem is primarily one of controlling raw materials, in others it is one of controlling finished goods, whereas, for example, in the capital goods industry, most organizational effort must be concentrated on the control of work-in-process inventories.

In the case of the manufacturers of railroad rolling stock and the garment industry, manufacturing is carried out primarily to specific customer order. One simply does not stock many diesel engines because of the tremendous cost of carring inventory, as is evident from Table 2.3. One stocks a minimum of finished goods in the garment industry because of the vagaries of taste and style. However, note from Table 2.4 that in the latter case a lot of inventory investment is tied up in work-in-process presumably in readiness for quick response to cues from the market place.

In direct contrast is the case of consumer goods, for example rubber tires, where success depends largely on the immediate availability of finished goods on demand. Minimum investment in inventories is held in raw materials and work–in-process. Production is seldom to-order; brand preferences and repeat sales of the same product to the same customer are common.

Capital goods and the steel mills operate to a large degree as prescription centers where raw materials are assembled or mixed to-order. Moderate finished goods inventories exist partly to help smooth out production rates.

Table 2.3 The Relative Concentration of Inventory Investment Across Three Canadian Industries[a] (In Percent of Total Inventory Investment)

	Raw Materials	Work-In-Process	Finished Goods
Iron and Steel Mills	50	29	21
Railroad Rolling Stock Manufacturers	40	52	8
Rubber Tires Manufacturers	15	10	75

[a] Based on figures reported in "Inventories, Shipments and Orders in Manufacturing Industries", *Statistic Canada*, 1969.

Table 2.4 Inventory Distribution in Three U.S. Industries (Percent of Total Inventory Investment)[a]

	Raw Material	Work-In-Process	Manufacturer's Finished Goods	In the Distribution System
Capital Goods	60	16	24	0
Garment Industry	28	60	4	8
Consumer Goods	4	12	28	56

[a] Adapted from Donald D. Hall. "Hard Nosed Inventory Management" in Robert E. Finley and Henry R. Pioboro (Eds.) *The Manufacturing Man and His Job.* The American Management Association, Inc., 1966.

2.2.2 The Distribution by Annual Dollar Usage Value (DBV) within a Firm

Managerial decisions regarding inventories must ultimately be made at the level of an individual item or product. The specific unit of stock to be controlled will be called a *stock keeping unit (or s.k.u.), where an s.k.u. will be defined as an item of stock that is completely specified as to function, style, size, and color.* That is, two physical objects are exactly the same only if they are fully interchangeable. The same-style shoes in two different sizes would constitute two different s.k.u. Each combination of size and grade of steel rod in raw stock constitutes a separate item. An oil company must regard each segregation of crude as a separate s.k.u. A soap company must view supplies of the same brand, and size, of soap flakes as two distinct s.k.u., especially *if they differ in color.* Note that such a classification system can result in the demand for two s.k.u. being highly correlated in practice, because certain portions of customers will always be willing to substitute, for example, a blue widget for one that is red.*

The close examination of a large number of actual multi–s.k.u. inventory systems has revealed a useful statistical regularity in the demand rates of items in inventory. Typically, somewhere in the order of 20 percent of the s.k.u. account for 80 percent of annual dollar demand. This suggests, as we shall discuss later in this chapter, that all s.k.u. in a firm's inventory should

* *A word of caution may be appropriate here. What we have given here is the typical "text book" definition of an s.k.u. In practice, of course, one can define an s.k.u. in any way one pleases depending on the decision being made and depending on the level of detail at which one wants to control inventories.*

not be controlled to the same extent. Figure 2.3 illustrates graphically the typical Distribution by Value (DBV) observed empirically in practice.

A DBV curve can be calculated as follows: The value, v, in dollars per unit, and the annual demand, D, in units, of each s.k.u. in inventory are identified. Then the product Dv is calculated for each s.k.u. and the Dv values for all s.k.u. are ranked in decending order starting with the largest value as in Table 2.5. Thereupon the corresponding values of the cumulative percentages of total dollar demand and the cumulative percent of the total number of units in inventory are plotted on a graph such as Figure 2.3. Experience has revealed that inventories of consumer goods will typically show a lesser concentration in the higher value s.k.u. than will an inventory of industrial s.k.u.[23]

The derivation of a table, such as Table 2.5 is one of the most valuable tools for handling the diversity of disaggregate inventories because it helps to identify the s.k.u. in inventory which are the most important. These s.k.u. will be assigned a higher priority in the allocation of management time and financial resources in any decision system we design. Note that the ranking is on the basis of Dv. Both the demand and the cost of an item are continually

Figure 2.3 Distribution by Value of s.k.u.'s.

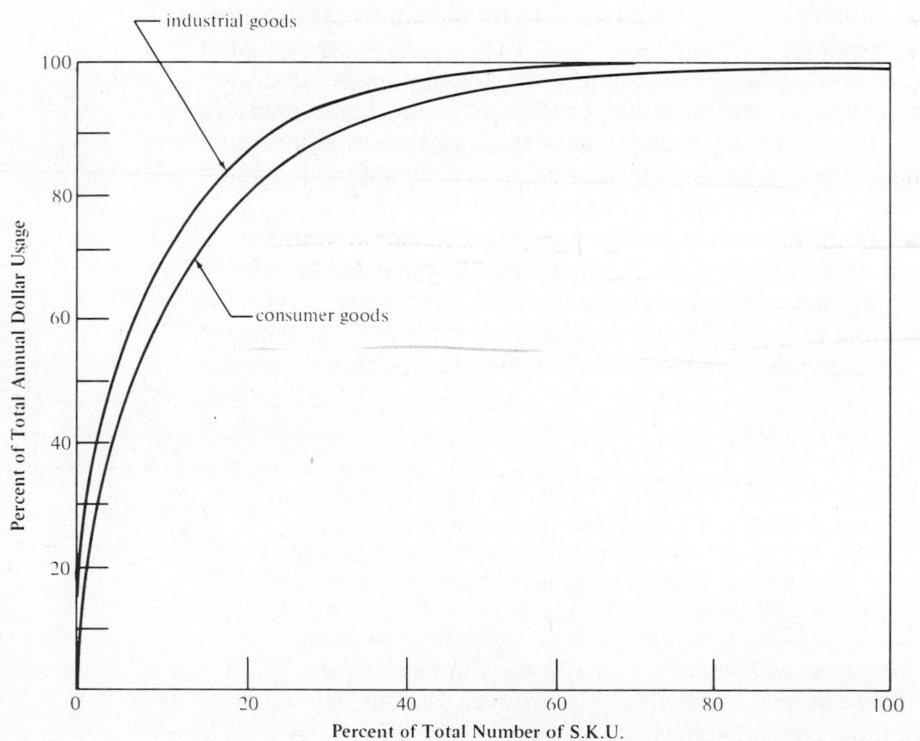

Table 2.5 Example Listing of s.k.u. by Descending Dollar Usage

Sequential Number	S.k.u. I.D.	Cumulative Percent of s.k.u.	Annual Usage Value (Dv)	Cumulative Usage	Cumulative Percent of Total Usage
1	—	0.5	$3,000	$3,000	13.3
2	—	1.0	2,600	5,600	24.9
3	—	1.5	2,300	7,900	35.1
—	—	—	—	—	—
—	—	—	—	—	—
—	—	—	—	—	—
—	—	—	—	22,498	—
199	—	99.5	2	22,500	100.0
200	—	100.0	0	22,500	100.0

subject to change. As a result the relative priority assigned to any product is also always changing. That is, the DBV is a dynamic, not a static, concept.

2.2.3 The DBV and the Lognormal Distribution*

The empirically observed relationship between the cumulative percent of items and the cumulative percent of total demand (i.e., the DBV in Figure 2.1) can in many situations be represented quite accurately by the Lognormal probability distribution. The assumption of such a closed-form mathematical relationship can be very useful when managing diversity, as we shall see in later chapters. The statistical properties of the Lognormal are discussed in Appendix B. We shall only highlight its properties at this time. We do not intend to imply that *all* DBV can be accurately approximated by a lognormal.

The Lognormal Distribution is completely specified by two parameters, m and b. Parameter $m = \sum Dv/n$, is the mean of the distribution. Herron[16] describes a graphical method for calculating the other parameter, b, which is a measure of the spread of the distribution, although it is not the standard deviation.** If we plot the cumulative fraction of s.k.u. versus its corres-

---

* *Some readers may wish to skip this section on a first reading of the chapter because it presents details on the mathematical properties of the DBV which will be utilized in later chapters. The basic conceptual basis of the DBV has already been covered fully in the previous section.*

** *The parameter b is actually the standard deviation of the Normal distribution which can be derived by taking the logarithm of each value of the Lognormal distribution. (See Appendix B). The standard deviation of the Lognormal is equal to* $m\sqrt{\exp(b^2)-1}$.

ponding cumulative fraction of total annual dollar usage on a graph, where both axes are marked off according to Normal probability scales, then for a lognormal distribution the resulting points would lie on a straight line with a slope of 1 as in Figure 2.4. This straight line will intersect an ordinate erected at the 50 percent mark of the horizontal scale of Figure 2.4 and allow the reading off of the value of parameter b.

The straight line labelled "A" in Figure 2.4, is for the 4886 s.k.u. in the Warmdot Company inventory, a manufacturer of heating and air conditioning equipment described and analysed in great detail in Brown.[3] For line "A" the value of m is \$2,923, (not on graph) and that of b can be read from the graph as 2.40. Line "B" describes the 849 s.k.u. in the inventory of the Professional Products Division of MIDAS (Canada) Corporation for which m equals \$2,048 and b is equal to 1.56. (The MIDAS (A) case is described following Chapter 2. Further details regarding the composition of the Professional Products Division's inventory will be given in Chapter 3.) Note that the bottom 50 percent of s.k.u. account for less than 1 percent of total annual dollar usage for Warmdot and about 6 percent of total annual dollar usage for MIDAS. According to Herron, typically the inventories of merchants (wholesalers, retailers, etc.) have b's in the range of 0.8 to 2.0; industrial producers are in the range 2 to 3; and highly sophisticated hardware suppliers (who are subject to rapid technological innovations) have b's in the 3 or 4 range.

These relationships, based on the Lognormal distribution, shall prove to be useful in subsequent chapters when relatively rough estimates are required about the aggregate characteristics of a particular firm's inventory system. This is possible partly because the b parameter tends to be relatively constant for different stocking locations of a single firm as well as for different firms within the same industry. The other parameter, m (the average annual dollar usage per s.k.u.), obviously must vary, but it is relatively easy to compute for a given population of items of interest.

2.2.4 *Some Statistical Properties of the Variability of Demand**

For many finished goods and especially service parts, demand can be reasonably constant throughout the year. For such s.k.u. one can write that:

$$d_t = \bar{d} + e \tag{2.2}$$

where

$$E(d_t) = \bar{d}$$

---

* *Some non-technical readers may wish to skip this section on the first reading of this material.*

In Eq. 2.2 the demand over period t, d_t, is shown as the sum of a constant known level demand rate, $\bar{d}$, and a stochastic error term e. The mean error, $E(e)$, is usually assumed to be zero so that the expected or average value of demand d_t, $E(d_t)$, is the constant demand rate $\bar{d}$. Therefore the variance of

Figure 2.4 Distribution Curves for Two Different Multi-item Inventories.

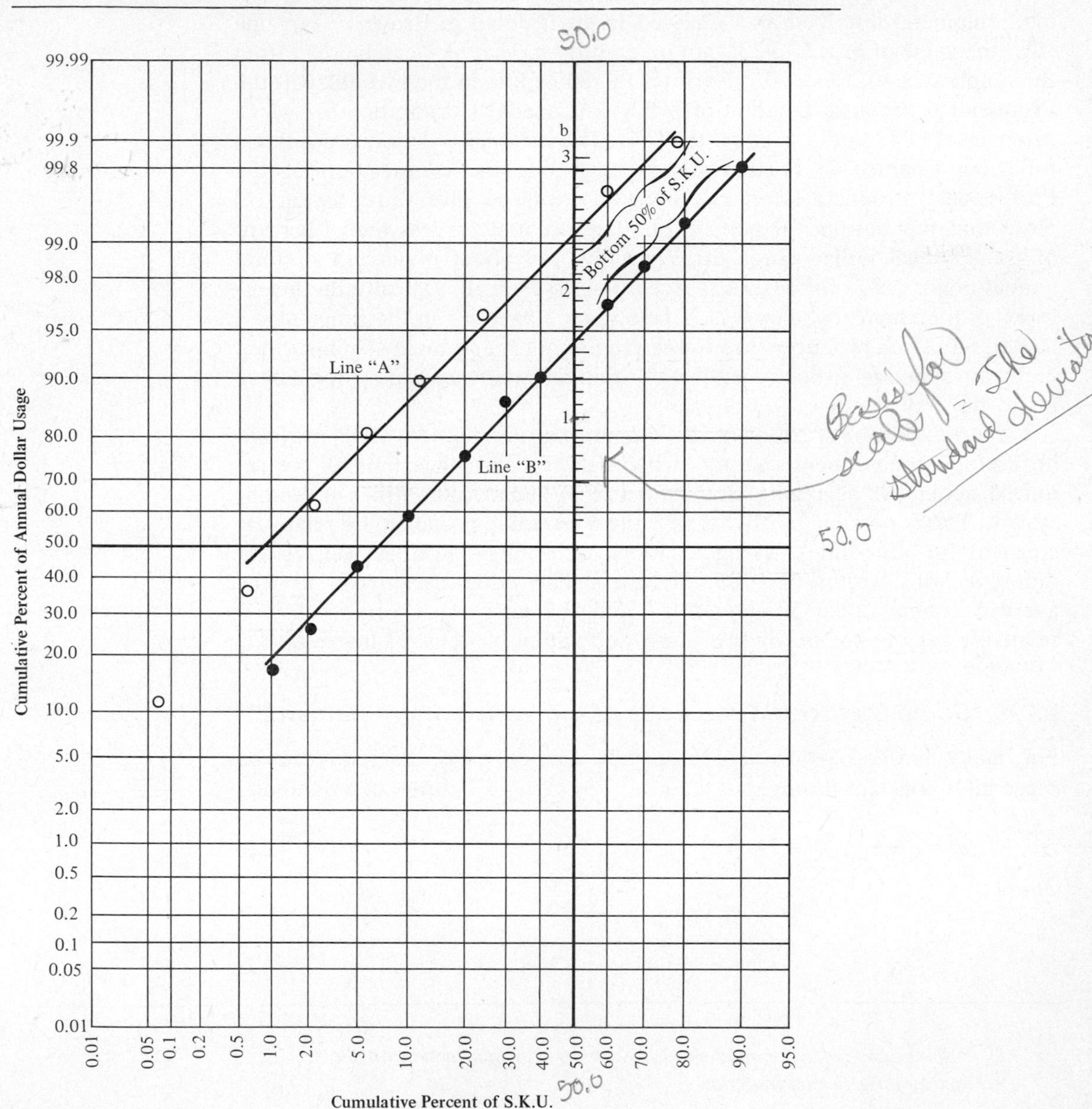

demand or equivalently of the errors, is given by:

$$\text{Var}(d_t) = E[(d_t - \bar{d})^2] = E(e^2) = \sigma_t^2 \tag{2.3}$$

The square root of the variance, denoted by σ, is called the standard deviation of demand. It has been found, in a number of empirical studies of existing inventory populations, that the average demand rate $\bar{d}$ (in units) is highly correlated with the standard deviation, σ (in units). Brown has suggested that the correlation between the mean demand rate and its variability can be reasonably estimated by the following equation:*

$$\sigma_t = a_1(\bar{d}_t)^{b_1} \tag{2.4}$$

or equivalently

$$\log \sigma_t = \log a_1 + b_1 \log \bar{d}_t$$

where:

a_1, b_1 are regression coefficients determined empirically.

$\bar{d}_t$ is the average demand in units over some period, t.

σ_t is the standard deviation of demand over the same period, t.

Eq. 2.4 will prove useful in later chapters when we wish to approximate demand variability over lead time. For the 849 s.k.u. from the MIDAS (Canada) Corporation Professional Products Division we fitted the following equation by regression:

$$\sigma_1 = 1.3(D/12)^{0.65} \tag{2.5}$$

where:

σ_1 is the standard deviation of demand over a one month period.
D is the demand rate in units/year.

Many other empirical models have been suggested by researchers such as

---

*Sometimes Eq. 2.4 is estimated in the form $\sigma_t v = a_2(\bar{d}_t v)^{b_2}$

Burgin and Wild,[7] Harrison and Green,[14] Stevens,[29] and Hausman and Kirby.[15]

The Hausman–Kirby results suggest that additional information concerning order frequency, unit cost, etc., is of value for estimating σ_1 of low unit-volume items. This was found to be the case in another study reported by Oppenheimer.[27] In the latter study, performed at the Operations Research Center at M.I.T., a relationship was also found between the unit price, the average demand rate, and the variance of demand.

The most complete study in this vein, done to date, is reported by Kaplan[18] who considered many explanatory variables in addition to unit price and annual demand. The study was carried out on 13,000 low volume s.k.u. of the U.S. Army. Kaplan used a stratification procedure rather than using a single regression relation and found that the most important single predictor of variance was, D, the rate of customer demand. But for very low frequencies it was useful to further stratify the s.k.u. by annual dollar usage (Dv).

Three cautionary comments regarding these studies need to be made. All the above studies assumed that a constant non-seasonal demand rate held for the sample s.k.u. But a significant portion of s.k.u. in any random sample can exhibit pronounced seasonal patterns (a topic which we shall examine thoroughly in Chapter 4). Secondly, the variance about the average demand rate, $\bar{d}$, that is Var (e), is not the same thing as forecast error variance, as is often incorrectly assumed. It is simply the variance of the raw demand data about its mean. Finally, the demand for s.k.u. does not occur one unit at a time. Demand, especially for low volume items, can be "lumpy" with 5 or 6 s.k.u. being demanded per order followed by a period of zero demand.

It is important not to forget that *the true justification for all these models is purely empirical*. Such models turn out to be convenient and helpful in the management of low dollar usage s.k.u., which as we saw in the previous section, account for more than 50 percent of all s.k.u. Some researchers have tried to force rationalizations on an interesting empirical *phenomenon*, thereby confusing the practitioner who is less interested in such intellectual exercises.

2.3 Concluding Comments

In this chapter we have examined the nature of inventories in detail and found them to be diverse physically, statistically, and from the point of view of the values held by policy makers who manage inventory fluctuations at the level of the economy and the firm. While we have made much of controlling inventory fluctuations, decision makers should not expect to be able to eliminate all inventory fluctuations. Certain systematic inventory fluctuations are an unavoidable part of doing business and must remain:

1. Most industries face a seasonal demand for their product and services. As a result, desired inventory levels must also be seasonal, to some degree.

2. All corporate planning is based on forecasts which, after the fact, will always turn out to be in error to some degree. As a result, inventory levels must always be adjusted, post hoc, to match reality.

3. The amount of managerial effort and expense needed to eliminate or control all erratic behavior usually proves to be uneconomical. As a result, some residual erratic behavior must always be allowed to remain.

4. No matter how much we reduce the information lags, the delivery times, and how well we design the decision rules used in distribution systems, some acceleration will always occur.

Starting with Chapter 3 we begin our rational examination of the inventory and production planning decision with the goal of trying to better understand which causes of inventory fluctuations can be more effectively brought under control than is the case in current practice.

Problems for Chapter 2

Problem 2.1
Read the article, TRIMMING STOCKS, *The Wall Street Journal*, May 6, 1975, front page. Summarize the three main issues regarding inventories discussed, and comment.

Problem 2.2
Why do inflation and supply shortages tend to increase real inventories? What is the effect of a reduction in the rate of inflation on inventory investment?

Problem 2.3
Update Figure 2.1 and explain what has happened to inventory investment since 1976 in the U.S. economy as reflected by the economic indicators involved. What has happened to the book value of the stock of manufacturing and trade inventories as a percent of GNP since 1976?

Problem 2.4
Design a decision system for a distributor that won't accelerate random sales fluctuations at the retail level. Fluctuations in the manufacturer's order rate are not allowed to exceed 50 percent of the average order rate which has been 40 units-per-month for the past several years. Make any other assumptions you wish. Test your decision system using the following data and comment on your approach.

Month	Retail Sales	Month	Retail Sales
1	40	7	25
2	50	8	35
3	45	9	40
4	30	10	45
5	55	11	35
6	40	12	55

Problem 2.5
A company uses 20 different raw materials for producing exercise books. Using the values-per-unit and the annual usages shown, draw the distribution-by-value curve on ordinary graph paper and on the lognormal paper as illustrated in Figures 2.3 and 2.4 respectively.

a. How well do they compare with theory?

b. How many items account for 80 percent of dollar usage?

c. What is the value of the parameter m of the lognormal curve?

d. From the lognormal graph estimate the parameter b.

Item #	Cost-per-Unit (v)	Annual Usage (D)
1	217.00	1,000
2	200.00	26,000
3	140.00	5,000
4	61.00	3,000
5	30.00	11,400
6	25.00	19,000
7	14.70	40,000
8	7.50	9,600
9	7.50	5,000
10	5.00	4,900
11	3.50	40,000
12	2.50	38,000
13	2.25	24,000
14	2.00	4,450
15	1.90	5,000
16	0.80	20,000
17	0.50	36,000
18	0.41	20,000
19	0.26	50,000
20	0.15	56,000

Problem 2.6

For the MIDAS (Canada) Corporation data (Eq. 2.5) estimate the standard deviation of demand over a one month period for an s.k.u. that has been selling at the rate of 127 units per month over the past 8 months. What assumptions need to be made to achieve such an estimate? How is this estimate of the standard deviation of demand related to the standard deviation of forecast errors?

Problem 2.7

Use two methods to estimate the standard deviation of demand over a two-month period for the following MIDAS data:

Month #	Demand
1	10
2	8
3	19
4	11
5	14
6	13
7	7
8	12
9	13
10	10
11	16
12	17

REFERENCES FOR CHAPTER 2

1. Abramovitz, Moses. *Inventories and Business Cycles.* New York: The National Bureau of Economic Research, 1950.

2. Aitchison, J. and Brown, J. A. C. *The Lognormal Distribution.* Cambridge University Press, 1957.

3. Brown, R. G. *Decision Rules for Inventory Management.* Holt, Rinehart and Winston, 1967.

4. Brown, R. G. *Statistical Forecasting for Inventory Control.* New York: McGraw-Hill, 1959.

5. Buchan, J. and Koenigsberg, E. *Scientific Inventory Management.* Prentice-Hall, 1976.

6. Buffa, E. S. and Taubert, W. H. *Production: Inventory Systems, Planning and Control.* Irwin, Revised Edition, 1972.

7. Burgin, T. A. and Wild, A. R. "Stock Control: Experience and Useable Theory." *Operational Research Quarterly,* Vol. 18 (1967) pp. 35–52.

8. Daly, D. J. "Seasonal Variations and Business Expectations." *Journal of Business,* July, 1959, pp. 259–261.

9. Daly, D. J. "Forecasting With Statistical Indicators." Bert G. Hickman (Ed.), *Econometric Models of Cyclical Behavior,* Vol. 2, National Bureau of Economic Research, Columbia University Press, 1972.

10. Evans, Michael K. *Macroeconomic Activity: Theory, Forecasting and Control.* Harper and Row, 1969, pp. 321–345.

11. Forrester, Jay W. "Industrial Dynamics." *Harvard Business Review,* July–August, 1958.

12. Hadley, G. and Whitin, T. *Analysis of Inventory Systems.* Prentice-Hall, 1963.

13. Hanssmann, F. *Operations Research in Production and Inventory Control.* Wiley, 1962.

14. Harrison, P. T. and Green, M. "On Aggregate Forecasting." *Warwick University Statistic Report No. 2,* England, 1972.

15. Hausman, Warren H. and Kirby, Robert M. "Estimating Standard Deviations for Inventory Control." *AIIE Transactions,* Vol. 11, No. 1, 1970.

16. Herron, D. P. "Profit Oriented Techniques for Managing Independent Demand Inventories." *Production and Inventory Management,* Vol. 15, No. 3 (1974) pp. 57–74.

17. Hirsch, Albert C. and Lovell, Michael C. *Sales Anticipations and Inventory Behaviour.* John Wiley and Sons, 1969.

18. Kaplan, Alan J. "Estimation of Demand Variability Parameters." *IRO Report No. 183,* USAMC Inventory Research Office, Frankford Arsenal, Philadelphia, PA., 1974.

19. Klein, L. R. and Popkin, J. "An Econometric Analysis of the Postwar Relationship Between Inventory Fluctuations and Change in Aggregate Economic Activity." *Inventory Fluctuations and Economic Stabilization Part III.* Washington D. C.: Joint Economic Committee, 1961, pp. 71–86.

20. Lovell, Michael C. "Determinants of Inventory Investment", in *Models of Income Distribution* (edited by Irwin Friend), Princeton University Press, 1964.

21. Lovell, Michael C. "Manufactures' Inventories, Sales Expectations, and the Acceleratior Principle." *Econometrica*, Vol. 29, No. 3, (July, 1961) pp. 293–314.

22. Mack, Ruth P. *Information, Expectations and Inventory Fluctuation.* Columbia University Press, 1967.

23. Magee, John F. and David U. Boodman. *Production Planning and Inventory Control.* Second Edition. McGraw Hill, 1967, pp. 165–159.

24. McGill, H. N. "Hand to Mouth Buying and its Effect on Business." *Industrial Management*, Vol. 73, No. 6 (1927) pp. 344–347.

25. McNair, Malcolm P. "Significance of Stock-turn in Retail and Wholesale Merchandising." *Harvard Business Review*, Vol. 1, 1922–1923.

26. Nash, C. W. "How We Get 12 Turns a Year." *Factory*, Vol. 33, (1924) pp. 329–331.

27. Oppenheimer, Gottfried. "Ordnance Logistics Studies—IV: Discussion Notes for Operating Supply Personnel on Mathematical Methods of Supply Control." *Interim Report No.* 19, O.R. Center, M.I.T., May, 1963.

28. Pappilon, A. "A Treatise Concerning the East India Trade (1677)," 1696 reprint, p. 4. Quoted in Viner, J. *Studies in the Theory of International Trade.* New York: 1937, p. 20.

29. Stevens, C. F. "On the Variability of Demand for Families of Items." *Operational Research Quarterly*, Vol. 25, No. 3 (1974) pp. 411–419.

30. Whitin, Thomson M. *The Theory of Inventory Management.* Princeton University Press, 1957, p. 219.

Midas Canada Corporation (A)*

NOTE: *Throughout the book we shall refer to examples which are related to the decision systems explained in the MIDAS case series. We have tried to write the chapters so that they can be read without a detailed knowledge of the cases. Nevertheless the reader is encouraged to read the cases for a fuller appreciation of the points of view we are trying to express.*

The MIDAS CANADA CORPORATION is a wholly owned Canadian subsidiary of a large international conglomerate with head offices located in England. The company's Canadian facilities, namely an assembly plant and warehouse, were located in Toronto, Ontario. It distributed, in Canada and the United States, "Superchrome" branded high technical quality sensitized films, papers and processing chemicals from a modern, highly efficient plant in Germany where an active ongoing product research and development program was maintained. From Japan, MIDAS imported "Takashi" branded X-Ray Systems which it installed and maintained through service contracts in hospitals and private clinics. The

Figure 1 Product Flow Chart.

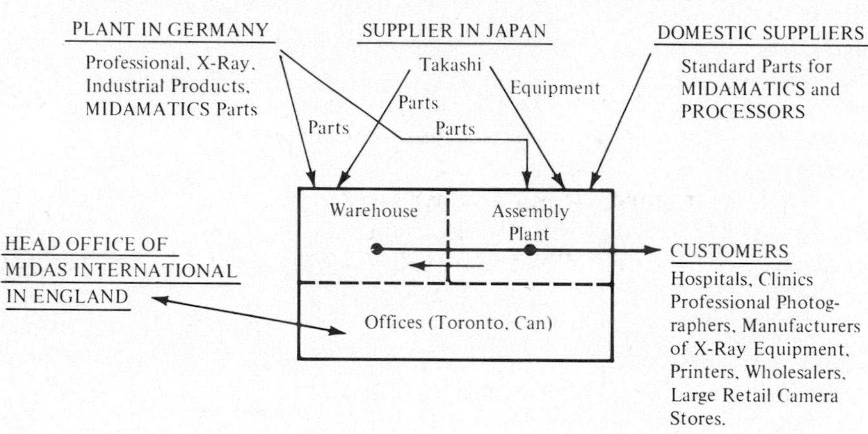

* *The MIDAS cases describe actual decisions systems which are based on consulting experiences of the authors. They do not describe the situation at any single company, but are in fact a compendium of actual situations which have been compressed into the environment of a single firm and industry for discussion and illustrative purposes. The cases are not intended as presentations of either effective or ineffective ways of handling administrative problems.*

Canadian company also assembled, under license from MIDAS INTERNATIONAL, two lines of film processing equipment: the manually operated MIDAS STABILIZATION PROCESSOR used for rapid development of black and white paper and the MIDAMATIC, a much more expensive automatic rapid processor of X-Ray film.

A total of $1.1 million was invested in inventories in Toronto on May 31, 1976 distributed among 2103 stock keeping units (s.k.u.) as shown in Table 1. On May 31, 1976, a total of 14 s.k.u. were out of stock, a situation which the Inventory Control Manager labelled as being "normal and typical for this time of year."

The industry in Canada was dominated by one large company and was served by seven other companies, one of which was MIDAS. Keen competition was prevalent both as to price and technical quality. Most customers displayed fierce brand-loyalty and were quite proficient in their ability to judge the technical quality of a film, a processing chemical or a paper offered for sale.

The Canadian company usually employed more than 60 persons and had an annual sales of over $8 million. It was organized into four sales divisions: The X-Ray Film Division, the Professional Products Division, the Industrial Products Division, and the Equipment Division. The organization chart is given in Figure 2.

The Equipment Division

The Equipment Division was by far the largest Division in the company, accounting for about 60 percent of total sales. Whereas the other three Divisions acted merely as sales agents for products manufactured in Germany, the Equipment Division sold products which it either assembled, or installed itself. The Division was divided into two functions: the sales office and the Assembly Plant. The Assembly Plant consisted of 17 employees reporting to a manager. Four salesmen and a manager operated the sales office.

STABILIZATION PROCESSORS were assembled from standard parts available in Canada. In the case of MIDAMATICS, sixty percent of the components were imported from Germany, with the remainder being available from suppliers in Canada. Spare parts for repair and maintenance of existing PROCESSORS and MIDAMATICS were kept in inventory and were listed as "finished goods" in Table 1, columns 5 and 6. During May, 1976, 14 MIDAMATICS and 311 PROCESSORS were assembled. Parts for these machines were stored separately even though they were identical to the spare parts that were used for repairs and maintenance of existing machines. Parts for assembly were listed as "Raw Materials" in Table 1, column 8. Company policy did not allow any assembled

Table 1 Composition of Midas-Canada Corporation Inventory Investment

Division	No. of. s.k.u. (1)	Turnover Ratio[a] (2)	Annual Sales 1976 Forecast (3)	Total Inventory (31/5/76) (4)	Finished Goods Cycle Stock (5)	Finished Goods Safety Stock (6)	Work in Process (7)	Raw Materials (8)	Seasonal Inventory (9)
Equipment	644	6.84	5.168,000[b]	453,100	50,800[c]	123,300[c]	153,000[d]	123,000[e]	3,000[f]
X-Ray	207	3.93	690,000	105,300	32,700	71,400	—	—	1,200
Industrial	403	3.89	1,070,000	165,100	46,900	116,350	—	—	1,850[g]
Professional	849	4.20	1,740,000	248,700	72,400	173,200	—	—	3,100[g]
(Obsolete)	—	0.00	0	128,000[h]	—	—	—	—	—
OVERALL	2103	4.73	$8,668,000	$1,100,200	$202,800	$484,250	$153,000	$123,000	$9,150

[a] Cost of goods sold assumed to be 60 percent of sales.
[b] Sales of spare parts amounted to $968,00.
[c] Spare parts of MIDAMATICS, Processors, and Takashi system only.
[d] Mostly semifinished MIDAMATICS being assembled.
[e] $91,000 of MIDAMATIC parts and $32,000 of Processor parts awaiting assembly.
[f] Processors only. See Table 9 of MIDAS (F) Case.
[g] Repackaged bulk chemicals only. See Table 9 of MIDAS (F) Case.
[h] Estimated value of dead stock, currently not listed in sales catalogue.

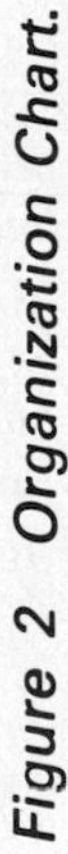

Figure 2 Organization Chart.

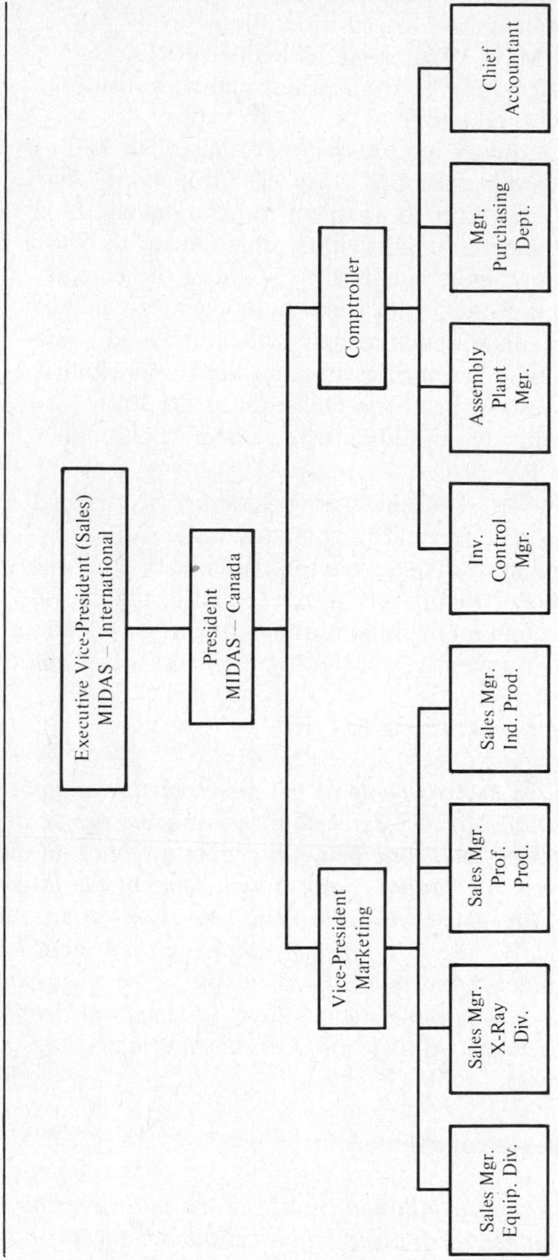

MIDAMATICS or PROCESSORS to be kept in finished goods inventory. However, due to production smoothing considerations (to be discussed in detail in Case F) during May, 1976, some assembled PROCESSORS were in inventory in anticipation of future sales and were listed as "Seasonal Inventory" on Table 1, column 9.

All chemicals arrived from Germany in 200-gallon drums or in 200-pound barrels and were repackaged and labelled by the Equipment Division in 1 gallon plastic bottles (sold four to a carton) or into envelopes and boxes weighing up to 4 pounds, and sold either singly or up to 6 to a carton. The use of large bulk containers significantly reduced the cost of shipment from Germany. During May, 1976, some bulk chemicals had been repackaged ahead of immediate needs to help with work load smoothing in the Assembly Plant. These inventories became the responsibility of the X-Ray Division, the Industrial Products Division, or the Professional Products Division, respectively, and were listed under "Seasonal Inventory" in Table 1, column 9.

The Assembly Plant also installed Takashi X-Ray Systems. No original Takashi equipment was kept in inventory. The company ordered the X-Ray equipment directly from the Japanese manufacturer only after successfully bidding on a contract. Such contracts stipulated an installed price plus a fee for maintaining the equipment in continuous repair. A selection of replacement parts was kept in inventory, see columns 5 and 6 in Table 1.

The vice-president in charge of marketing felt that

> *in the future we will have to keep some of the more popular original units in stock. These installations are not as customized as some people around here like to think. The long lead time between getting the bid and delivery from Japan is hurting us. We cannot compete with some of the larger companies on delivery, and therefore must try to beat them on price or on post-installation service. We are in danger of not being even invited to bid on jobs which require quick turnaround. For example, a lot of hospitals are currently in the process of upgrading their X-Ray systems and demand fast delivery once they have made up their mind to allocate some funds from the budget for this purpose.*

The Inventory Control Manager commented:

> *We offer the best repair and installation service in the industry. Our products and prices are competitive and profitable. Although success has generated its own problems, it is getting increasingly more difficult to promise fast delivery on our MIDAMATICS because of the steadily increasing work load on our assembly facilities in Toronto. The Assembly Plant is always complaining that our orders arrive in bunches instead of being spaced out over the year and that we are always rushing them to get faster delivery.*

I believe that a good design engineer could look at our Takashi, Midamatic and Stabilizer lines and reduce, through product standardization, the number of different screws, nuts, bolts and brackets that we now keep in inventory. I think that in this way the work load on the Assembly Plant could probably be made more manageable.

The X-ray Film Division

Two types of X-ray film, (rapid process and manual process) in many sizes, were sold through 9 dealers who also manufactured X-ray equipment and usually carried a complete line of sundry technical supplies for hospitals, clinics and veterinary hospitals. Some film was sold directly to the federal and provincial governments and to larger hospital group purchasing departments through competitive tenders which quoted prices that were close to those charged to MIDAS dealers. All X-ray film was manufactured in Germany, where it was dated upon manufacture. Each quantity of film sold subsequently received a further code number which recorded the date of sale to a MIDAS dealer. According to the Inventory Control Manager:

> *. . . like fresh food, photographic sensitized materials deteriorate with age. As with some foods it is possible to halt the process of deterioration by, for example, freezing. But with most photographic papers and films it is commercially uneconomical to do so.*

The Division also sold chemicals that were used to develop X-ray film. These included liquid developers, fixers and starters, and various powdered substances. Chemicals were packaged by the Equipment Division from bulk shipments made from Germany.

In addition to the above fast moving items, the X-Ray Division also sold a variety of supplementary products. These consisted of Tungsten screens, used by technicians to get better contrast, and cassettes which made it easier to handle film.

The Industrial Products Division

In addition to X-ray film MIDAS-CANADA distributed specialized films and stabilization papers, along with dry and liquid developing chemicals, to industrial printers, craft jobbers, and large in-house captive printing shops. Four company salesmen called on the larger offset printing, letterpress, and rotogravure plants in Canada and in the northern portion of the U.S.A. In addition, about one-third of the Division's sales were handled through wholesalers who sold a variety of other kinds of printers' supplies.

Professional Products Division

This Division sold 90 percent of its products to wholesalers who in turn supplied retail camera stores. Products included general purpose photographic films and papers, stabilization papers, general purpose flat films, black and white roll films, and a variety of dry and wet developing chemicals. A total of 849 s.k.u. were kept in inventory, including 10 s.k.u. of "Superchrome" film which were kept in a specially-designed climate-controlled room kept at 35 degrees Fahrenheit, under lock and key. These items were display transparency color films available in flat or in roll form and used by professional photographers. Only a select, small number of professional photographers bought these films directly from MIDAS. These very expensive films had a life of less than 12 months and were considered by professional photographers to be at the forefront of current technological development. The Inventory Control Manager commented that

> *I don't let anyone else handle these films but myself. I worry at night about that darn air-conditioning unit failing on me. With good reason, we jokingly refer to the climate-controlled room as Fort Knox.*

Product Identification

All stock keeping units were identified by a 3-letter, 3-number code. The first letter identified the selling division: X for X-ray, I for Industrial Products, P for Professional Products and E for the Equipment Division. The second letter recorded whether the product was produced for stock by the plant in Germany (Code: S) or was manufactured to order (Code: M). If the item was available domestically in Canada the second letter was coded D.

The third letter was either F, C, P, or M identifying the s.k.u. as being either film, chemical, paper or some other miscellaneous item respectively. This was true for all divisions except for products in the Equipment Division where the third letter (either M, S, T, or C) identified the s.k.u. as being a part of either the MIDAMATIC, STABILIZER, TAKASHI, or common to more than one product line, respectively. For example, s.k.u. XMF-014 identified a film (product number 14) manufactured to order in Germany and sold by the X-Ray Division.

Company Policy Regarding Inventories

No written, formal set of guidelines existed regarding the control of inventories. The final responsibility for inventory management rested with the company's Comptroller. The Comptroller believed that

> *because there is no certainty of how customers will store our films . . . our own stocks must be kept as low as possible, consistent of course with maintaining reasonable customer delivery. Therefore at any point in time, we try to maintain several orders outstanding on the plant in Germany for the same stock keeping unit. The basic idea is to keep a steady flow of material moving from Germany to our warehouse. In this way the stock sits only a short period of time on our shelves before being sold—about 3 months on average. Besides, by doing this, we keep our book inventories low. The head office in England does not invoice us until 30 days after the date of shipment from Germany. As a result, the more stock we keep in the pipeline the better we look on the Balance Sheet.*

---

*Midas Canada Corporation (B)**

In this case we describe how inventory transactions were recorded and how the level of inventory for each of the 2103 s.k.u. was monitored. Also described is the warehouse receiving, preparation and control system.

** The MIDAS cases describe actual decision systems which are based on consulting experiences of the authors. They do not describe the situation at any single company, but are in fact a compendium of actual situations which have been compressed into the environment of a single firm and industry for illustrative purposes. The cases are not intended as presentations of either effective or ineffective ways of handling administrative problems.*

The Inventory Recording and Control System

The Inventory recording and control system at MIDAS was manual and was based on a commercially available "Vertical Visi-Record" card system. For each s.k.u. three cards were kept in sequence in a bin on wheels (also called a tub file) which was located in the Stock Keeping Clerk's office. These three cards were called the Record Card (Figure 1), the Travel Card (Figure 2), and the Backorder Card (Figure 3).

The Record Card (Figure 1) recorded the dates of all transactions in column 1, the Sales Order or Purchase Order numbers in column 2, the quantities received in column 3, and the Balances on Order in column 4. In column 5 was recorded the number issued on a particular Sales Order. In column 6 the cumulative number of units issued during the current month to date was calculated.

Balance on Hand was recorded in column 7. Column 8 was reserved for recording any quantities which were held in abeyance for an important expected order or demand but for which a Sales Order had not as yet been issued. The last column recorded the Balance Available which was calculated from:

$$\text{Bal. on Order} + \text{Bal. on Hand} - \text{Quant. Alloc.} = \text{Bal. Avail.}$$

For example, on Figure 1, on May 28 three units of IMM-177 were issued via Sales Order number 73149 resulting in total issued to date of 129, a Balance on Hand of 273, and a Balance Available of 673. A total of 400 units remained on order from the plant in Germany. Similarly, on June 4 an order for 120 units was placed on Purchase Order number 35373. On June 5 a shipment of 200 units arrived as a result of Purchase Order number 34999, placed several weeks earlier.

On the top right hand corner of the Record Card was recorded the Minimum Balance Available allowed. If the Balance Available dropped to or below the specified figure then this was a signal for placing an order for more units. The Minimum Available Balance for IMM-177 for June was given as 606. The order placed on June 4 was placed at an Available Balance level of 630 units. Apparently the Inventory Control Manager decided to place the order at that point in time rather than wait a couple of more days until the Balance Available dropped closer to 606.

Also on top of the Record Card were listed the retail list price, the cost of IMM-177 to MIDAS-CANADA and the prices charged to dealers as a function of their annual dollar purchase volume from MIDAS. On the top left hand corner of the card was recorded the number of Record Cards that had been filled for a particular s.k.u. The Record Card illustrated in Figure 1 was the 30th card to date that had been used to record transactions regarding IMM-177.

Figure 1 MIDAS CANADA CORPORATION—The Record Card.

3 2 1

IMM-177

LIST $12.00

COST 4.59

DEALER UNDER $400 8.40

DEALER OVER $400 7.20

#30

MIN 606

DATE		REFER	REC'D	BAL ON ORDER	ISSUED	TOTAL ISSUED	BALANCE ON HAND	QUANT ALLOCATED	BALANCE AVAILABLE
May	27	Brought Forw.		400		126	2 76		6 76
	28	73149			3	129	2 73		6 73
	28	73188			5	134	2 68		6 68
	28	73220			1	135	2 67		6 67
	28	73204			4	139	2 63		6 63
	28	73309			6	145	2 57		6 57
	28	73299			5	150	2 52		6 52
	29	73332			3	153	2 49		6 49
	29	73318			3	156	2 46		6 46
	29	73360			2	158	2 44		6 44
	30	73416			1	159	2 43		6 43
	30	73430			2	161	2 41		6 41
	31	73412			3	164	2 38		6 38
	31	73483			2	166	2 36		6 36
	31	73485			6	172	2 30		6 30
June	4	35373		520			2 30		7 50
	4	73546			4	4	2 26		7 46
	4	73603			4	8	2 22		7 42
	4	73616			3	11	2 19		7 41
	5	34999	200	320			4 19		7 41
	5	73663			4	15	4 15		7 37

CARD GRAPHIC SYSTEMS LIMITED Toronto
FORM 778

BAL ON ORDER + BAL ON HAND − QUANT ALLOCATED = BAL AVAILABLE

6.5 X 10 X 1.

INVENTORY CONTROL

When the Balance Available (column 9, Figure 1) dropped below the minimum Balance Available allowed, listed on top of the Record Card (i.e. ·606 for IMM-177), the Inventory Clerk pulled the Travel Card (Figure 2) from the vertical tub file. The clerk recorded in column 1 the current Balance Available (from column 9 of the Record Card), the date in column 2, and suggested an order quantity in column 3. Then he sent the Travel Card to the Inventory Control Manager who determined the actual quantity to be ordered. The Inventory Control manager in turn recorded the date on which he processed the order in column 4 and placed his initials in column 5. His decision as to the quantity to be ordered appeared in column 8. In the past the Inventory Control Manager had usually ordered the difference between the Maximum Balance Available which was listed on the top right hand corner of the Travel Card (e.g. for IMM-177, Maximum was 757) and the current Balance Available as given in column 1.* However, he was free to round off the actual quantity ordered or to ignore the rule if in his opinion impending future events made an alternative quantity more attractive. This was especially true for special items such as Superchrome and the more expensive, slow moving Professional and Industrial Products. For such items the Inventory Control Manager admitted that he went completely "by the seat of his pants." He relied heavily on his intimate knowledge of the industry, his customers and suppliers, some of whom he had dealt with over 23 years.

Note that column 1 of Figure 2 is actually labelled "Balance On Hand." In the past the Inventory Control Manager had based his ordering decisions on the Balance on Hand figures, as suggested by the Vertical Visi-Record card system. After a while he found it very difficult to keep track of outstanding orders and started to base his decisions on the Balance Available figures. As a result, column 1 of Figure 2 was in fact mislabelled on all the Travel Cards. The Inventory Control Manager was somewhat unsure whether he had done the right thing:

> *I've always wondered how other people who use Visi-cards manage to make decisions using The Travel Card as it was originally intended?*

After determining the order quantity the Inventory Control Manager sent the Travel Card to the purchasing department. There a clerk typed up a purchase order, entered the purchase order number in column 9 of

---

* *The determination of Maximum and Minimum levels of Balance Available will be discussed in MIDAS CANADA CORPORATION (D) case.*

Figure 2 MIDAS CANADA CORPORATION—The Travel Card.

IMM-177

MAX. 757

PRICE	QTY.	PRICE	QTY.	PRICE	QTY.	PRICE	QTY.

MIN. 606

	VENDOR	TX	D'Y	VIA	LD.D. COST	PER	LEAD	F.O.B.	TERMS
1	Germany				4 59		12-16	4.33	
2									
3									

YEAR	JAN	FEB	MAR	APRIL	MAY	JUNE	JULY	AUG	SEPT	OCT	NOV	DEC	TOTAL
1973	172	109	127	172	159	103	48	87	132	171	201	54	1535
1974	159	127	130	169	172								

BAL ON HAND	DATE	QUANT REQ'D	DATE REQ'D	APP BY	V	P.O. NUMBER	QUANT ORD'D	PRICE PER	DEL'Y PROM'D	DATE	QUANT REC'D	BAL ON ORDER
Brought forward												300
487	1/24 76	200	1/26 76	Rc.		34999	200					500
528	2/1 76	200	2/1 76	Rc.		35007	200					700
						34531				2/7 76	100	600
570	3/1 76	200	3/5 76	Rc.		35102	200					800
						34543				3/15 76	200	600
						34581				3/15 76	100	500
						34630				4/23 76	200	300
502	5/1 76	300	4/30 76	Rc.		35212	300					600
						34801				5/7 76	200	400
630	6/4 76	100	6/4 76	Rc.		35373	120					520
						34999				6/5 76	200	320

CARD GRAPHIC SYSTEMS LIMITED toronto FORM 640

PERMANENT REQUISITION

5 X 9.9 X 1

Figure 2, and returned the Travel Card to the Inventory Control Clerk, who then updated the balance on order columns on both the Record and Travel Cards.

For example, on January 24, 1976, the Inventory Control Clerk noticed that the Balance Available had fallen to 487 which was below the Minimum allowed for January.* She pulled the Travel Card and sent it to the Inventory Control Manager who processed the order on January 26, deciding to place an order for 200 units. The Travel Card was then sent to purchasing where a purchase order number of 34999 was assigned and a purchase order was typed up. Then the Travel Card was returned to the Inventory Control Clerk who updated the Balance on Order from 300 to 500.

Also recorded on the Travel Card was the arrival of orders. When an order had been received and checked by the warehouse, a copy of the accompanying packing slip was forwarded to the Inventory Control Clerk. Note that on the bottom line of Figure 2 a quantity of 200 units on purchase order 34999 arrived on June 5 reducing the Balance on Order to 320.

On the top of the Travel Card were recorded the Maximum and Minimum allowable Available Balances, as well as the Vendor's name, his prices, and the estimated lead time needed to get delivery. IMM-177 was supplied exclusively by the MIDAS-INTERNATIONAL plant in Germany. When more than one vendor was available, such as for some domestically available parts for the assembly of MIDAMATICS and PROCESSORS, the Inventory Control Manager was responsible for deciding which vendor would get an order. In such cases he would record the vendor number under the column headed "V" along with the price per unit and promised delivery dates in the appropriate columns.

During the second week of March, 1976, IMM-177 was out of stock. In such cases the Inventory Control Clerk filled out the Backorder Card (Figure 3) and notified the Inventory Control Manager. Customer sales orders that were on backorder were listed in the order they were received. Note that once the delayed order arrived on March 15 (see Figure 2) the backorders were filled in the same order that they had been received. In this particular case the Inventory Control Manager dispatched a panel truck to pick up the order from the railway station, rather than wait for regular delivery. The extra cost of expediting the order in this manner was charged to the Industrial Products Division, whose product was involved.

---

* *Each month has a different set of Maxima and Minima to be discussed in Case* D.

Figure 3 MIDAS CANADA CORPORATION—The Back-order Card.

DESCRIPTION: IMM-177

DATE		CUSTOMER	REF NO	QUANTITY ORDERED	QUANTITY SHIPPED	QUANTITY BACK ORDERED	TOTAL BACK ORDERED
3/7	76	Goldare	2387	12	5	7	7
3/7	76	Black	2372	4		4	11
3/7	76	Jones	2378	5		5	16
3/8	76	B&W	2427	2		2	18
3/8	76	Kenny's	2404	3		3	21
3/12	76	Weinberg	2409	3		3	24
3/13	76	United	2381	6		6	30
3/15	76		2387			7	23
3/15	76		2372			4	19
3/15	76		2378			5	14
3/15	76		2427			2	12
3/15	76		2404			3	9
3/15	76		2409			3	6
3/15	76		2381			6	0

CARD GRAPHIC SYSTEMS LIMITED toronto FORM 805 — CARD GRAPHIC BACK ORDER CONTROL — 5.5X7.7X1

The Warehouse Receiving, Preparation, and Control System

Orders normally arrived at the warehouse by railroad car or by truck in cardboard cases along with a packing slip. An invoice had usually preceded the shipment by mail. The packing slip, the invoice and the original

Figure 4 MIDAS CANADA CORPORATION—The Case Card.

Case No. 7664

17	XMF-014
100	IMM-177
75	XMF-038
4	PMP-747
30	PMF-198
50	PMF-231

purchase order were compared. Only if discrepancies were noted, was the box opened to determine its exact contents. Otherwise the boxes were stored without being opened. A copy of the packing slip was sent to the Inventory Control Clerk to notify her of the arrival of orders.

For each arriving box a Case Card see Figure 4) was prepared by cutting the description of its contents from the packing slip and pasting it on a 4×6 inch file card. (Cut and paste was used to minimize clerical errors.) Each carton also received an identification number. Under such a system, inventory of the same s.k.u. could be located in several different cartons. For this reason a Case Control Card (see Figure 5) was also prepared listing the date of arrival, the quantity, and the carton numbers where stock pertaining to a particular s.k.u. was located. Inventory was stored in cartons because in this form it took up less space and provided a simple First-In, First-Out system of stock use.

About one month's sales of inventory was kept loose on metal shelves from which stock pickers daily compiled orders to be sent to customers. No record was kept of how much of a particular s.k.u. was left at any point in time on the shelf. It was the responsibility of the warehouseman to visually keep the shelves stocked from the packing cartons described above. To guide the warehouseman, on the edge of each shelf, directly under the product's location, was recorded the amount that represented approximately one month's sales. When a shelf location became depleted the warehouseman consulted the Case Control Card for that particular s.k.u. He recorded the date on the card and the quantity of stock he was removing from the carton in question. For example, according to Figure 5, on February 7, he removed 100 units of IMM-177, leaving a zero balance in case 7664 which had arrived in the warehouse on January 11, 1976. Upon removing the 100 units from case 7664 he also recorded this fact on the Case Card (See Figure 4).

The President, on several occasions, commented on the existing control systems as follows:

> *The present system seems to involve a tremendous amount of paper handling, recording and checking. Even with all this activity we seem to lose*

Figure 5 MIDAS CANADA CORPORATION—The Case Control Card.

IMM-177

DATE	CASE	IN	RMDR.	RMDR.	RMDR.	DATE	CASE	IN	RMDR.	RMDR.	RMDR.
1/11/76	7664	100		100/0	2/7						
2/7/76	8355	100		100/0	2/14						
3/15/76	8498	200		200/0	3/15						
3/15/76	8499	100		100/0	3/26						
4/23/76	8548	200		200/0	5/2						
5/7/76	8586	200		200/0	5/20						
6/5/76	9090	200									

considerable amount of stock, through pilferage I presume. After all, everyone is interested in photography to some extent. Although I must admit that some stock just gets lost in the boxes and is found much later either damaged, too old to be sold, or is no longer in our sales catalogues. Surely the present system could be improved upon!

CHAPTER THREE

The Inventory Planning Decision

Some military organizations stock over 600,000 items in inventory. Large retailers, such as department stores, stock some 100,000 goods for sale. A typical medium-sized manufacturing concern keeps in inventory approximately 10,000 types of raw materials, parts and finished goods.

Items held in inventory can differ in many ways. They may differ in cost, weight, volume, color, or physical shape. Units may be stored in crates, in barrels, on pallets, in cardboard boxes, or loose on shelves. They may be packaged by the thousands or singly. They may be perishable because of deterioration over time, perishable through theft and pilferage, or subject to obsolescence because of style or technology. Some items are stored in dust-proof temperature-controlled rooms while others can lie in the mud, exposed to the elements.

Demand for goods in inventory also can occur in many ways. Items may be withdrawn from inventory by the thousands, by the dozen, or unit by unit. Items may be substitutes for each other, so that, if one item is out of stock, the user is usually willing to accept another. Items can also be complements, that is, customers will not accept one item unless another is also available. Units could be picked up by a customer, or they may have to be delivered by company-owned vehicles or shipped by rail, boat, airplane, or transport truck. Some customers are willing to wait for certain types of products, others expect immediate service on demand. Many customers will order more than one type of product on each purchase order submitted.

Goods arrive into inventory also by a variety of modes and in quantities that can differ from how they will eventually be demanded. Some goods arrive damaged; others differ in number or kind from that which was ordered. Some items are unavailable because of strikes or other difficulties at a supplier's plant. Delivery of an order may take hours, weeks, or even several months.

The management of inventories is therefore basically *a problem of coping with large numbers and with a diversity of factors external and internal to the organization.* Some decision systems for inventory management and production planning fail in practice simply because of this basic diverse nature of inventories. For example, Thomson M. Whitin,[20] who examined in 1957 the collapse of inventory decision systems at several United States military establishments concluded that:

> *The failure of the National Military Establishment to establish effective inventory control has been to a large extent due to the sheer magnitude of the task.*

We have seen tremendous progress in the technology of inventory control since 1957, including the successful installation of a very modern inventory control system by the aforementioned National Military Establishment. But one basic fact remains: inventory control is still a problem of managing diversity and coping with large magnitudes.

In specific terms, the problem of managing diversity is made difficult by the fact that the control of total dollar inventory investment, at the level of the economy, can only be achieved by policies at the level of the firm, where detailed decisions must be implemented one stock keeping unit at a time, day in and day out. Conceptually the jump from aggregate, economy-level considerations, to the control of nuts and bolts in, say, a warehouse in Delaware, is enormous.

3.1 *The Bounded Rationality of Man*

An inescapable fact alluded to in the first two chapters was the need to view the inventory and production planning problem from a systems standpoint. Before we plunge into a detailed discussion of the possible solutions to the problem as we have posed it, let us consider explicitly and realistically our expectations regarding the nature of the results we seek.

Herbert Simon[17] has pointed out that all decision makers approach complex problems with a framework or model that simplifies the real situation encountered. A human being's brain is simply incapable of absorbing and rationalizing *all* the many relevant factors in a complex decision situation. A decision maker cannot effectively conceive of the totality of a large system *without assistance from extra-cerebral systems.* All decision makers are forced to ignore some relevant aspects of a complex problem and base their decision on a smaller number of carefully selected factors. These selected factors always reflect a decision maker's personal biases, abilities, and perception of the reality he thinks he faces, as well as the decision technology that is available to him at any point in time.

The inventory planning decision is a complex systems problem. It extends beyond the intuitive powers of most decision makers because of the many interconnected systems, both physical and conceptual, that have to be coordinated, rationalized, adapted to, or controlled. The inventory decision ideally must be viewed *simultaneously* from the point of view of: the individual s.k.u. in its relation to other similar s.k.u., the total aggregate inventory investment, the Master Plans of the organization, the production-distribution systems of suppliers and customers, and the economy as a whole.

The challenge is therefore two-fold. Since a decision maker's ability to cope with diversity is limited, decision systems and rules must be designed to help expand the bounds put upon his ability to rationalize. However, since most decision makers probably have already developed personalized approaches to the inventory decision, decision systems have to be designed and their use advocated in the context of existing resources, managerial capabilities, and even sheer mythologies.

Inventory management and production planning as practiced today, like the practice of accounting, because of the predominance of numerical data and a relatively long history, is a mixture of economically sound theory, accepted industrial practices, tested personalized approaches and outright fallacies. Our goal in this book (which also should be that of any decision maker in the inventory area) is to influence the amount of sound theory that actually gets used, while trying to clarify existing fallacies. However, one must accept the fact that existing theory is, and will be, for some time to come, insufficient to do the whole job. There will always be room for personalized, tested-in-practice, approaches to fill the gaps in theory.

Therefore within this book, we shall in effect weave our own brand of personalized approaches with theory and thereby also contribute to the existing mythology. This is why, from an intellectual point of view, we find the inventory planning decision both challenging and exciting.

3.2 *Strategies for Managing Diverse Individual Item Inventories*

As Plossl[15] has pointed out, the standard cost accounting definitions for reporting individual item inventory investment are of limited help in resolving the inventory planning decision.* Accountants are interested in reporting total value in such classes as raw material, purchased and manufactured components, work-in-process, finished product, supplies, etc. Why do they use these classifications? The answer is simple; these categories are convenient for scorekeeping and *convenient for accountants* who must track the flow of costs from one stage to the next.

What comes in from outside sources is raw material or purchased parts. When work begins, these are transferred to work-in-process and labor overheads are added. The result is finished goods ready to ship to customers. The chain is completed by accounts payable and accounts receivable. Outside of this chain there are also "supplies" and "miscellaneous" classes which are used as handy catchalls for cost items that cannot be identified with individual products. Unfortunately these readily available accounting categories are not convenient, especially to top management, when answering the question: how much inventory investment is enough?

A number of somewhat obvious alternative strategies have been developed to help cope with this incongruity. The managerial decision aids are basically of two kinds, conceptual and physical:

A. Conceptual Aids

1. The large number of physical units of inventory are classified into a smaller number of relatively homogeneous organizational (as opposed to accounting) categories. Managers then manage inventories in the context of these smaller number of decision classifications (e.g. Anticipation Inventory).

---

* *Parts of this section and the next are adapted from: Plossl, George W. "How Much Inventory is Enough?"* Production and Inventory Management, *June,* 1971, *pp.* 1–22.

2. The complexity of the inventory planning decision is also reduced by identifying through analysis and empirical research (rather than through personal preference) only the most important variables for explicit consideration. This is an especially important essence of the operational theory which we expound in this book (e.g. ordering costs, carrying costs).

B. Physical Aids

1. Decision makers often resort to mechanized-automatic information collection and digestion procedures which summarize environmental data and which suggest analytical or heuristic solutions derived through management science methods. On the basis of such pre-digested, more compact information the decision maker can deal more quickly and effectively with a larger number of decisions. For example, the forecasting decision systems of Chapter 4 fall in this category.

2. A decision maker's physical span of control is also expanded by harnessing the *principle of management by exception* through the use of computer-based and/or manual clerical systems that free the manager from the mass of unimportant routine situations. Agreed upon decision rules or systems are used within computer systems or by clerks on a routine basis. When the system or clerk encounters factors that cannot be handled routinely, only then is the situation brought to the attention of higher level decision makers (e.g. A-B-C Classification).

The identity of the most important conceptual variables of the inventory planning decision will be examined first in sections 3.2.1 and 3.2.2, and expanded upon throughout the remaining parts of this chapter and the book. The physical aids of classification for better control are discussed subsequently in section 3.3.

3.2.1 *Functional Classifications for Aggregate Inventory Control*

In answering the question: how much inventory is enough? the most common mistake made in practice is that the turnover ratio is used uniformly across many s.k.u. to control inventories with little regard to their differing functions or the degree of compatibility between individual items. As Plossl reports, the inventory planning decision often gets delegated to a controller who in sheer frustration imposes controls on categories of inventories which he had previously defined for accounting purposes only. For example, percent of sales limits on sales divisions, finished goods warehouses, or raw materials stockpiles are often set in this manner. *While the turnover ratio and percent of sales measures are useful tools for reporting results after the fact, we shall discover that they should not be applied uniformly for control purposes.*

We recommend four broad decision categories for controlling aggregate inventories: cycle stock, safety stock, anticipation inventories, and pipeline inventories. In our opinion, senior management can and must express an opinion on how much aggregate inventory is required in each of these broad categories. While we cannot expect that such opinions will always have clear cut, simple answers, they do focus attention on viewing inventories as being controllable and not as the "residue of the sum total of all the mistakes we made over the past year."

Cycle inventories result from an attempt to order in batches instead of one unit at a time. The amount of inventory on hand, at any point in time, *that results from such batches,* is called *total cycle stock* (TCS).

For most finished goods and service parts inventories, demand is reasonably smooth and sufficiently frequent that it is necessary to carry stock on hand at all times. In Figure 3.1 cycle stock varies from zero to a maximum of Q, the number of units ordered at any one time. Implicit in the above graph is the assumption that stock is withdrawn continuously one unit at a time and a quantity Q arrives every T periods of time. The case when demand is lumpy and intermittent, is illustrated in Figure 3.2. The determination of the Q in Figure 3.1 will be discussed in Chapters 5, 11, and 13 and the lumpy demand case will be discussed in Chapters 8, 12 and 14.

Figure 3.2 depicts a demand pattern where little or no demand occurs on most days, but sudden demand peaks occur at infrequent intervals. In Figures 3.1 and 3.2 cycle stock is shown as being superimposed upon safety stock, a point that will be discussed at length later.

Often the theoretical total cycle stock (TCS) for an inventory of n items is defined as

$$\text{TCS} = \sum_{i=1}^{n} Q_i v_i / 2 \tag{3.1}$$

where v_i is the dollar value of each individual s.k.u. That is, on the average only one half of the order quantity, Q, is assumed to be on hand for every s.k.u. In practice actual cycle stock will differ from Eq. 3.1 to the degree that demand is lumpy and if the order quantity is not always Q (for example Q_1, Q_2, or Q_3 in Figure 3.2).

In either case, the amount of cycle stock on hand at any time depends directly on how frequently orders are placed. As we shall see, this will be determined in part by senior management who will specify the desired tradeoff between the cost of ordering and the cost of having cycle stock on

Figure 3.1 Inventory Pattern—Smooth Demand.

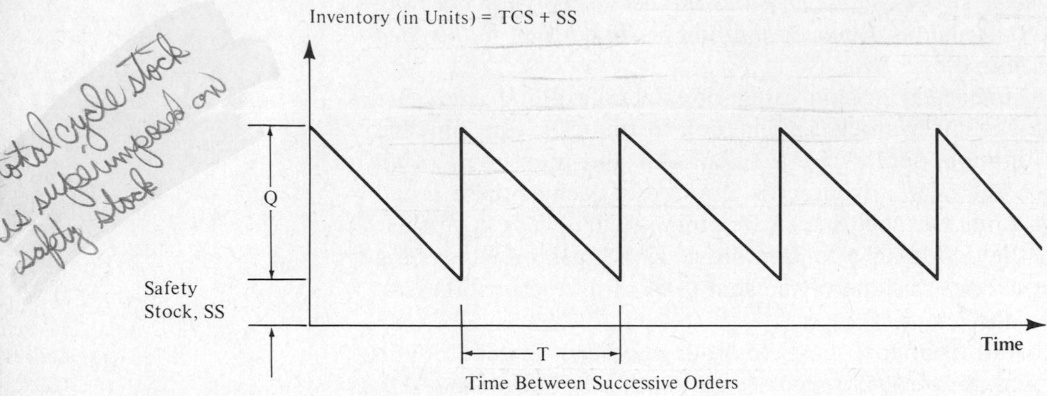

hand. Note that the less often one orders, the more cycle stock will be on hand, on the average.

Other considerations also enter the order frequency decision. Longer production runs tend to lower manufacturing costs and make it easier for production management to organize their affairs. We shall see that producers and merchants also vary the size of their order quantities because of other considerations such as the economies of bulk shipping and quantity discounts.

Figure 3.2 Inventory Pattern—Lumpy Demand.

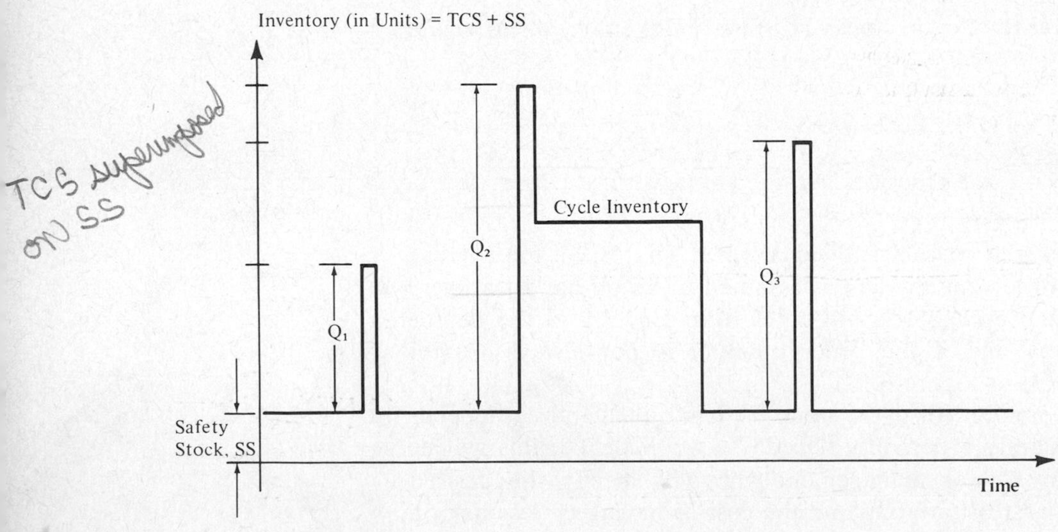

Safety stock is the amount of inventory kept on hand, on the average, to allow for the uncertainty of demand and the uncertainty of delivery schedules over the replenishment lead time. Safety stocks are not needed when the future rate of demand and the length of time it takes to get delivery of an order are known with certainty. The level of safety stock is controllable in the sense that this investment is directly related to the level of desired customer service (that is, how often customer demand is met from stock). In Figures 3.1 and 3.2 safety stock is shown as the amount on hand when delivery of an order takes place. Actually both figures depict the idealized average (or expected) situation over a large number of periods of time. During some periods of time, demand will be greater than the shown expected levels and the replenishment order will not arrive exactly on time. At such times one must dip into safety stock to meet the surge in demand. If demand uses up the entire safety stock before a replenishment arrives, then a stockout will occur. Aggregate safety stock can be simply calculated from Eq. 3.2 by adding up the safety stock for all n items:

$$\text{Aggregate Safety Stock} = \sum_{i=1}^{n} SS_i v_i \tag{3.2}$$

The determination of safety stock levels in response to prespecified managerial measures of customer service will be discussed in Chapters 6, 7, 8, 9, 10, 11, and 13.

Anticipation inventory consists of stock accumulated in advance of an expected peak in sales. Anticipation stocks can also consist of inventories built up to meet labor strikes, war crises, or any other event which is expected to result in a period of time during which the possible rate of acquisition of s.k.u. into inventory is likely to be lower than the rate of demand.

When demand is regularly lower than average during some parts of the year, excess inventory (above cycle and safety stock) can be built up so that during the period of high anticipated requirements, extra demand can be serviced from stock rather than from, for example, working overtime in the plant. Anticipation stocks can also occur because of seasonality on the supply side. For example, tomatoes which ripen during a rather short period are sold throughout the year as ketchup.

Management's expectations about the nature and length of future economic events play an important role in the fluctuation of inventories. In Part V of the book, in Chapters 15–18, we shall consider the rational determination of anticipation inventories as a part of the production planning decision.

Pipeline (work-in-process) inventories include goods in transit, on trucks or in railway cars, between levels of a multi-echelon distribution system or between adjacent work stations in an assembly line. For example, products en route to a branch warehouse, products being held in distributor warehouses, products en route from warehouses to retailers and the products on the shelves of retailers together comprise the *pipeline inventory from a producer's point of view.* Distributors, in turn, would view only the goods en route to retailers, and the retailers' current stocks, as pipeline inventory which is of relevance to their decision making.

Note that our four functional categories were defined so as to concentrate attention on the organizational purposes of the inventories, especially with regard to control and manageability, rather than accounting scorekeeping (for example: raw materials, supplies, finished components, etc.). Most managers are intuitively aware of the functions that inventories in each of the four conceptual categories must play. Some of the benefits (and costs) may even be measured by existing cost accounting systems.

Most accounting systems will not keep track of opportunity costs, such as, customer disservice through lost sales or the costs of extra paper work generated by an order that must be expedited to meet an unexpected emergency.

Table 3.1 Functional Classification and Cost-Benefit Relationships Summarized [15]

Category	Function	Benefits
Cycle Stock	Uncoupling manufacturing operations and user from supplier.	Quantity discounts; reduced costs of setups, freight, material handling, paperwork, and inspection, etc.
Safety Stock	Vendor lead-time variations; unexpected demand variations.	Increased sales; reduced cost of freight, substitution of higher value product, customer disservice, clerical handling, telephone, telegraph, and packaging; reduced downtime and overtime.
Anticipation Stock	Smoothing of production to meet seasonal sales or marketing promotions. Provide hedge against raw material price increases. Insurance against interrupted supply.	Reduced total costs of overtime, hiring, layoff, unemployment insurance, training, scrap, rework, and subcontracting. Lower material costs.
Pipeline Stock (Work-in-process)	Fill distribution pipeline with inventories in transit, at branch warehouses, as consigned materials.	Reduced costs of freight, material handling, and packaging; Reduced operating costs.

While it will not be always possible to precisely measure the costs and benefits of each subgroup of organizational inventories, many experienced managers have garnered over the years a sense of perspective regarding the effect of reducing or increasing the amount of inventory investment allocated into each of these four different organizational purposes. One of our goals in this book is the development of procedures to harness this experimental perspective along with measurable costs and benefits and analytical techniques to yield better decisions from an overall systems viewpoint.

It is quite possible that an individual manager may not have had sufficient experience to have developed an intuitive feel for the four organizational categories that we have defined above. This could be the case especially in respect to the many phases of a large organization's operations. In such cases, instead of classifying a company's total aggregate inventory investment, it may be more meaningful to a manager to deal with a smaller inventory investment, such as in a divisional grouping. In the MIDAS (A) case, the four sales managers of the X-Ray, Industrial, Professional, and Equipment Divisions, felt qualified to provide an opinion as to how much inventory was enough for only their own divisions. The Inventory Control Manager, on the other hand, categorized *total* company inventory investment into imported, purchased domestically, or manufactured items for purposes of cost-benefit tradeoffs.

Meaningful functional groupings do vary from organization to organization. But, from a theoretical and practical viewpoint, at some point in time, the four organizational categories: cycle stock, safety stock, anticipation stock, and pipeline inventories, need to be analyzed from a cost-benefit standpoint so as to provide an aggregate perspective for the control of individual s.k.u.

3.2.2 *Cost and Conceptual Classifications for Individual Item Inventory Control*

The cost of carrying an item in inventory will depend naturally enough on its value. The *unit value of a s.k.u.*, in dollars per unit, for which we shall give the symbol "v," is for the case of a merchant simply the price that he pays for an item to his supplier. As we shall see in Chapter 5, the price of an item can depend on the size of the quantity ordered. For producers, the value of an item is usually somewhat more difficult to determine. However, one thing is certain; it is seldom the conventional accounting or "book value" assigned to it in most organizations. The value of an item ideally should measure the actual amount of money that has been spent on the s.k.u. to make it available for fulfilling demand, including such costs as transporting units from a supplier to the merchant's warehouse. Producers must determine the actual variable costs of making a s.k.u. ready for sale, using cost concepts which result in a value, v, that is in concept equivalent to the price charged by outside suppliers of merchants *plus* other related variable costs. This is not always a trivial task, as we shall see.

The *cost of carrying items in inventory*, for which we shall assign the symbol "r," includes the opportunity cost of the money invested, the expenses incurred in running a warehouse, the costs of special storage requirements including deterioration of stock, overtime, obsolescence, insurance, and taxes. We shall express r as the cost to carry one dollar of inventory for one year ($/$/year). By far the largest portion of the carrying cost is made up of the opportunity costs of the capital tied up that otherwise could be used elsewhere in an organization and the opportunity costs of warehouse space claimed by inventories. Neither of these costs are measured by traditional accounting systems.

The opportunity cost of capital, in the context of the inventory planning decision can be defined easily enough. It is, theoretically speaking, the return on investment that could be earned on the next most attractive opportunity that cannot be taken advantage of because of a decision to invest the available funds in inventories. Such a marginal cost concept is difficult to implement in practice. For one thing, the next most attractive investment opportunity can change from day to day. Does this mean that the cost of the capital portion of carrying should also be changed from day to day? From a theoretical point of view, the answer is yes.

In practice such fluctuation is difficult to administer; instead the cost of capital is set at some level by decree and is changed only if major changes have taken place in a company's environment. For example, after due consideration by senior management, a policy is declared that "only investments which earn more than r percent can be implemented." The value of r, of course, has to depend on the degree of risk inherent in an investment. (For the same reason the banks charge a higher rate of interest on second mortgages than on the first.) As a result, in practice the opportunity cost of capital can range from the banks' prime lending rate, which has fluctuated in Canada and the United States between 6 and $10\frac{1}{2}$ percent in the recent past, to 50 percent and above for small companies that are suffering from severe capital rationing (shortages) because they lack the collateral to attract additional sources of working capital. Inventory investment, at least in total, is usually considered to be of relatively low risk because in most cases it can be converted to cash relatively quickly. However the degree of risk inherent in inventory investment varies from organization to organization. Some of the most important impediments to quick conversion to cash can be obsolescence, deterioration, pilferage, and the danger of a lack of immediate demand at normal price. Each of these factors increases the cost of capital over and above the prime rate because of a possible lack of opportunity of quick cash conversion.

Not only is r dependent on relative riskiness of s.k.u. it also depends on the costs of storage which are a function of: bulkiness, weight, special handling requirements, insurance, and possibly taxes. Such detailed attention is seldom given to all s.k.u. in inventory. To make the inventory decision more manageable both from a theoretical and practical point of view a single value of r is usually assumed to apply for most items. To make some allowance for the fact that items do differ as to their cost of carrying, the value of r is usually expressed as a percent of v. Notice that this assumes that more expensive items are apt to be riskier to carry and more expensive to handle or store. Such a convenient relationship doesn't always hold true for all s.k.u.*

The *cost of replenishment, A,* usually is expressed as a fixed number of dollars per order placed by a merchant or per production setup in the case of the producer. We must distinguish between the ordering cost for items purchased from an outside supplier (or possibly shipped from a company-owned central warehouse) and *setup costs* for items manufactured within the company. The ordering cost should include the cost of: order forms, postage, telephone calls, typing of orders, addressing, recording of transactions, following up on unexpected situations, receiving, and possibly inspection.

The setup cost, the equivalent of the ordering cost incurred by producers, includes all the cost elements that we enumerated above. But, in addition there are also other costs related to interrupted production. For example, the wages of a skilled mechanic who has to adjust the production facilities to allow production of the ordered s.k.u. can be considerable. Then, once a setup is completed, there usually follows a period of time during which the facility is unlikely to produce within rated effectiveness. During this period the production worker "learns" to get used to the new setup, procedures, and materials. Scrap costs are likely to be higher than normal while the worker adjusts his rhythm to the new procedures, gradually reaching full efficiency. The latter two factors are normally called the "learning effect" and these costs are taken as a part of the setup cost because they are the result of a decision to place an order (see, for example, Conway and Schultz[6] or Hirschmann[10]). Finally, notice that during the period of the setup and learning period, opportunity costs are in effect incurred because production time on the machines is being lost during which some other item

---

* *The units of r are dollars per dollar invested in inventory per year. For example, if v equals* \$10.00 *and r is set at* 25 *percent, we would say it costs* \$2.50 *per year to carry one unit of this item. Alternatively, if such a procedure is deemed inappropriate, one could directly specify, for example, that it costs* \$3 *per year to carry an item, thereby circumventing the common percentage value of r. However, note that this would in effect imply a value of r equal to* 30 *percent rather than* 25.

could be manufactured. Note that the latter opportunity cost is only incurred if the production facility in question is being operated at capacity.

Another important variable of the inventory planning decision that is hard to measure is *the cost of insufficient capacity or the cost of being out of stock.* In the case of a producer these costs amount to the expenses that result from the tearing down of existing production setups to run emergency orders and the attendant costs of expediting and rescheduling, split lots, etc. In addition, common to both merchant and producer, are the costs that can result from not servicing customer demand. The disruption costs that result in rescheduling the plant can be estimated relatively easily. But the costs of customer disservice are much more nebulous. Will the customer be willing to wait until he can have the item backordered or is the sale lost for good? How much goodwill is lost as a result of inability to be of immediate service—will he ever return? Will he tell his colleagues of our disservice? what alternative sources does he have? Such questions can in principle be determined empirically through an actual study for only a limited number of s.k.u. For most items the risks and costs inherent in disservice have to remain a matter of educated, considered opinion, not unlike the determination of the risks inherent in carrying inventories. In Chapters 6 and 7 we shall examine a number of different methods of modelling the costs of disservice.

A stockout can only occur during periods when the inventory on hand is "low." Our decisions as to when an order should be placed will always be predicated on how low the inventory stock should be allowed to be depleted, so that the expected number of s.k.u. demanded during a replenishment lead time will not result in a stockout more often than a specified number of times. We shall define the *replenishment lead time*, as the time that elapses from the moment at which it is decided to place an order, until it is physically on the shelf for satisfying customer demands. The symbol L will be used to denote the replenishment lead time. It is convenient to think of the lead time as being made up of five distinct components:

1. Administrative time at the stocking point (order preparation time): the time that elapses from the moment at which it is decided to place the order until it is actually transmitted out from the stocking point.

2. Transit time to the supplier: this may be negligible if the order is placed by telephone, but transit time can be several days if a mailing system is used.

3. Time at the supplier: this time constitutes the primary variable component. Its duration is materially influenced by the supplier's stock situation when the order arrives.

4. Transit time back to the stocking point.

5. Time from order receipt until it is available on the shelf: this time is often neglected when it should not be. Contributing factors include inspection and cataloging.

We shall see that the variability of demand over L can be due to several causes. If demand varies in a reasonably predictable manner *depending on time of the year,* we shall say it is *seasonal.* If it is essentially unpredictable we shall label the variability random. Demand over lead time also varies because the time between ordering and receipt of goods is seldom constant. Strikes, inclement weather or supplier production problems can delay delivery. During periods of low sales, lead times can turn out to be longer than expected because the supplier is accumulating orders to take advantage of the efficiency inherent in longer production runs. On the other hand, longer lead times can result because high demand is causing backlog in the supplier's plant. Since it is infeasible to try to deal with all the large number of possible reasons for variation in lead time demand, only one or two probability distributions are usually used in decision models to summarize all sources of variation.

3.3 The A-B-C Classification as a Basis for Designing Individual Item Decision Models

Many existing inventory management systems can be significantly improved upon by simply adopting decision rules that do not treat all s.k.u. and/or categories of aggregate inventory investment equivalently. Certainly, in the case of MIDAS (CANADA) CORPORATION, an expensive line of film such as *Superchrome* deserves more managerial attention than the less expensive miscellaneous hardware items, such as sheet metal screws, used to assemble Stabilization Processors. Similarly, in designing a decision system MIDAS must take into account the fact that it can have more control over the finished goods inventory produced by the Assembly Department than over the amount of inventory in the pipeline between the plant in Germany and the warehouse in Toronto. On what basis, then, should the amount of operating funds and managerial effort available be allocated to controlling each of the many s.k.u. in inventory?

In Chapter 2, we saw that somewhere in the order of 20 percent of the s.k.u. account for approximately 80 percent of the total annual dollar usage ($\sum Dv$). Assuming that s.k.u. with higher annual dollar volume deserve more managerial attention, because they can potentially yield higher profits, we recommend the assigning of a priority rating to each and every s.k.u. in inventory according to its Dv value. It is common to use three priority ratings: A (most important), B (intermediate in importance), and C (least important).

Recall that the Distribution By Value (often reasonably fit by a lognormal distribution) which we developed in Chapter 2 was derived by ranking in decreasing order the Dv values for all s.k.u. Note that, as a result, an expensive slow moving item (with a low demand, D, and high per unit cost, v) and a less expensive fast moving item (with a high D and low v) could receive an approximately similar priority ranking. While such a weighting might be appropriate from a managerial point of view, it can lead to some difficulties in the analysis of the demand during a replenishment lead time. For this reason we shall recommend later that the s.k.u. in each of the A, B, and C categories be further grouped according to whether they are *slow or faster moving items*, in terms of average usage during a lead time, and not only by annual dollar usage, Dv.

Other bases for an A-B-C type of classification are sometimes used. Some large volume consumer distribution centers plan the allocation of warehousing space on the basis of cubic feet per unit using an A-B-C curve. The s.k.u.'s with (high volume and large cubic feet) are stored closer to the retail sales counter. Similarly a distribution by (profit × volume) per s.k.u. is sometimes used to identify the best selling products. Items at the lower end of such an A-B-C curve become candidates for being discontinued. Finally, if top management wants to reclassify any items differently from the procedures described, because they believe (for example) that blue widgets are crucial to operation, so be it.

The number of categories appropriate for a particular company depends on its circumstances and the degree to which it wishes to differentiate the amount of effort allocated to various groupings of s.k.u. For example, one can always subdivide the Distribution by Value into further categories such as "moderately important," etc., as long as the resulting categories receive differentiated treatment in terms of how much expense and managerial time is allocated to controlling the s.k.u. within them. A minimum of 3 categories is almost always used and we shall use this number to present the basic concepts involved.

Class A items should receive the most personalized attention from management. The first 5 to 10 percent of the s.k.u., as ranked by the Distribution by Value Curve, are usually designated for this, the class of most important items. Usually these items also account for somewhere in the neighborhood of 50 percent or more of the total annual dollar movement ($\sum Dv$) of the population of items under consideration.

At MIDAS careful attention was given to A items, especially regarding the level of customer service being achieved. Some of the most expensive *Superchrome* items were not even stocked; instead salesmen placed orders in such a way as to ensure the arrival of the goods by air freight from Germany as soon as the relatively small number of individual customers actually needed a film of this type. For other A items, the Inventory Control

Manager was directly responsible for monitoring and expediting any orders that seemed to be in danger of not being filled within the normal lead time period. In Chapters 8, 9, 10, 13, and 14 we shall discuss decision systems that are suitable for use with class A items.

Class B items are of secondary importance in relation to class A. These items, because of their *Dv* values or other considerations, rate a moderate but significant amount of attention. By far the largest number of s.k.u. fall into this category. Usually more than 50 percent of total s.k.u., accounting for most of the remaining 50 percent of the annual dollar usage, are worthy of being labelled B items in any inventory. Some books on inventory control tend to recommend a somewhat lower portion of total s.k.u. for the B category. When a computer facility is available we suggest that as many s.k.u. as possible be monitored and controlled by a computer-based system, with management by exception intervention routines appended. Given the increasing costs of clerical labor and the attendant potential costs of human error, versus the constantly decreasing cost of data processing, we believe this propensity toward greater computerization will continue to look more attractive in the future. Having a larger proportion of s.k.u. on a computer system has also the advantage of making a larger data bank available for more effective and timely management reporting and sales analysis.

In Chapters 5, 6, 7, 8, 12, and 13 of the book we present a large number of decision systems that are suitable for use with class B items. Some of these models are also useful for controlling A items, although in the case of A items such models are *more* apt to be overruled by managerial intervention. As well, model parameters, such as costs and the estimates of demand will be reviewed more often for A items.

Class C items are the relatively numerous remaining s.k.u. that make up only a minor part of total dollar investment. For these s.k.u. decision systems must be kept as simple as possible. One objective of A-B-C classification is to identify this third large group of s.k.u. which can potentially consume a large amount of data processing and record keeping time. Typically for low value items most companies try to keep a relatively large number of units on hand to minimize the amount of inconvenience that could be caused by a stockout of such insignificant parts.

It is common to specify a large safety stock for C items (because of the low unit cost). This is done because many orders arrive requesting say, one A item, two B items, and six inexpensive C items. Unless the probability of stockout per individual s.k.u. is kept low, the chance that *at least one* of the six C items is out of stock could be quite large, thereby causing potentially serious problems such as partial shipments, customer disservice, etc. As a result, the usual goal in stocking C items is to minimize the number of total orders and administrative costs generated subject to constraints specifying a relatively high minimum customer service level and a limit on the maximum length of time a s.k.u. can remain in storage because of obsolescence, threat of pilferage, and deterioration.

For C items especially, and to a lesser degree for the others, as much grouping of s.k.u. into control groups based on similar annual usage rates, common suppliers, similar seasonal patterns, same end users, common lead times, etc., is desirable so as to reduce the total number of discrete decisions that must be processed.* Each control group can be designed to operate using a single order rule and monitoring system; for example, if one s.k.u. in the group requires an order because of low inventories, most of the other items will also be ordered at the same time to save on the cost of decision making. Two bin systems, because they require a minimum of paperwork, are especially popular for controlling class C items. They will be discussed in Chapters 6 and 11 of this book.

The classification into A-B-C categories at MIDAS had the objective of trying to put as many s.k.u. on a class B, computer-based decision system as possible.** Items that required special individualized attention were classified as "A." All remaining items were put into category C as shown in Table 3.2.

Table 3.2 MIDAS Professional Products Division A-B-C Classification

Classification	Number of s.k.u.	percent s.k.u.	ΣDv (dollars)	ΣDv Percent of Total Dv
A. s.k.u. with $Dv \geq \$6{,}000$	66	7.8	\$961,404.60	53.6
B. s.k.u. with $240 \leq Dv \leq \$6{,}000$	561	66.1	\$808,943.05	45.1
C. s.k.u. with $Dv \leq \$240$	222	26.1	\$23,317.65	1.3
TOTALS	849	100.0	\$1,793,665.30	100.0

---

* *At MIDAS, because most of the films were supplied from Germany, common lead times for large classes of products were not unusual. Within these classes a large number of s.k.u. (especially the same films cut to different sizes) exhibited similar demand and seasonal patterns.*

** *For smaller inventory systems that are not computerized, the same logic makes sense. Instead of computers one would try to routinize automatic decision making by use of manual-based clerical systems. Under such circumstances the fraction of s.k.u. classified as B items should probably be reduced somewhat and the fraction of C items should increase to take advantage of the lower cost of less paperwork and clerical handling.*

Figure 3.3 MIDAS Professional Products Division ABC Classification.

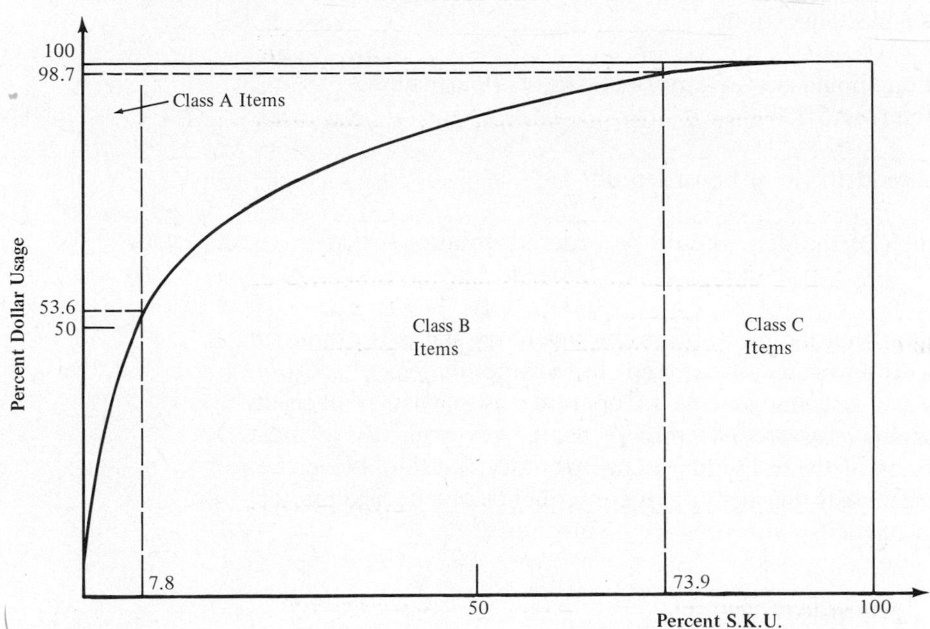

Note the relatively small number of s.k.u. in Class A and the low total dollar volume in Class C. While Figure 3.3 is typical, the precise number of members in each of the above categories depends, of course, on how spread out the Distribution by Value curve actually is. For example, the greater the spread of the distribution, the more s.k.u. fall into Class C.

An A-B-C classification need not be done on the basis of the Distribution By Value Curve *alone.* Recall that management should feel free to move s.k.u. between categories on the basis of other criteria. For example, some inexpensive s.k.u. may be classified as "A" simply because they are crucial to the operation of the firm. The Distribution by (dollar) Value Curve provides only a quick, but rough, first cut at the categorization eventually used.

3.4 *Modelling Uncertainty in Individual Item Decision Models*

In previous sections of this chapter we examined the individual item inventory planning decision in the context of the many cost and functional *categories that need to be controlled.* In the remaining sections we shall focus on other aspects of the decision problem and describe the variables and tradeoffs involved more precisely.

In simple terms, the *individual item* inventory decision consists of providing answers to three basic questions:

1. How often should the inventory status of a particular s.k.u. be determined?

2. When should the item be ordered?

3. How much of the item should be ordered on any particular order?

It should be evident that the more often the inventory status is examined (because of the uncertain nature of demand) for a large number of s.k.u. in inventory, the more it is going to cost to operate any particular decision system. These *systemic costs* are not usually dealt with explicitly in most analytical formulations of the individual item inventory decision. Nevertheless these are very real costs that result as a consequence of a decision model chosen to control a particular subcategory of inventory.

3.4.1 *General Considerations*

Obviously all inventory decision models require the estimation of future demand. The degree to which one can predict the future varies with the kind of item being considered. From an analytical and practical point of view we can choose to capture (in a model) the reality of how well we can predict the future in four ways. We can postulate that the demand for a s.k.u. is either:

1. Approximately constant/level and is:
   a. known with certainty or is
   b. known probabilistically

2. Varies with calendar time according to a pattern that is:
   a. known with certainty or that is
   b. known probabilistically

With models that assume approximately constant demand, known with certainty (case 1a above), we can capture the sales pattern over a month by dividing annual demand D by 12, weekly demand by approximately $D/52$ and daily demand by approximately $D/250$ (assuming 250 working days per year), and so on, for any period of time. A good example of such a s.k.u. would be a fixed contract held by a company to deliver each week the same specified quantity of goods to a government agency.

Alternatively, for some s.k.u. only *on the average* are sales-per-month, per-week, or day approximately constant (case 1b). That is, the actual sales for any particular month, week or day varies randomly (probabilistically) around an approximately constant mean. For such cases our decision models will have to take into account the probabilities that various sized deviations away from a constant mean can occur. For example, the weekly demand for some food staples is relatively constant. But the vagaries of weather, the timing of children's colds and other household happenings can change the day of the week on which a housewife makes her regular shopping trip. In particular, on some weeks she may not be able to make her regular shopping trip at all, thus increasing the amount of goods bought the following week.

For case 1b we shall be interested in modelling the variability of demand over the lead time so as to be able to calculate the safety stock needed to provide prespecified levels of customer service. We shall recommend either the Normal, Poisson, or Laplace probability distributions for modelling the variability of lead time demand. Our choice of the appropriate mathematical probability distribution shall depend on the relative importance of the s.k.u. (class A, B, or C) and on whether demand over lead time is relatively large (continuous) or low (intermittent).

We now turn to the two cases (2a and 2b) of time-varying demand. Case 2a, that where the pattern is approximately deterministic, is illustrated by the requirements through time of a component once the production schedules through time of its parent items have been specified.

Case 2b is typical of any seasonal item where considerable uncertainty in demand exists. An example would be the sales of a particular make of camera. The peak demand occurs each year around Christmas but the magnitude of sales is not known with certainty.

Decision models which have been designed to handle seasonal demand, known with certainty (case 2a), are generally much more complex than models which assume that demand is approximately constant. It is only recently that operationally feasible decision rules, such as the Silver–Meal Heuristic (to be discussed in Chapter 8) have become available. The last category of models, case 2b: seasonal demand known probabilistically, are by far the most complex models. From a practical point of view relatively few usable decision rules are available at present.

3.4.2 *Modelling the Variability of Lead Time Demand—A Two-Tiered A-B-C Classification*

It is common to model the variability of lead time demand of high volume s.k.u. by assuming that the sales rate follows approximately the *continuous* Normal Probability distribution. For a discussion of why such an assumption is usually reasonable see R. G. Brown.[4] For slow moving items which sell only, say, 5 or 6 units a year, a similar assumption of continuity can lead to unreasonable decisions and significant errors. It is therefore better sometimes to assume instead that the sales of slow moving items follow some other probability distribution.[1]

All decision systems and rules developed in this book are related to the two-tiered A-B-C classification in Table 3.3 which is an extension of the concepts we discussed in Section 3.3. In this section we present *only a summary of all the assumptions* that will be made concerning the modelling of lead time demand in the many decision models to be developed later on. Some of the ideas presented may well be unclear or unfamiliar to some readers at this time and these readers may have to return to the summary presented in Table 3.3 later on.

In modelling the variability in lead time demand of *fast moving A items*, we shall recommend using the Normal probability distribution. The required two parameters, $\bar{x}_L$ and σ_L, should be estimated from the most recently available data on historical experience regarding forecasts of lead time demand and the accuracy of such forecasts. The mechanized forecasting systems which we shall describe in Chapter 4 are well suited for this purpose, because they are designed to keep an updated record of both forecasted mean lead time demand, $\bar{x}_L$ and its variability σ_L. Such data manipulation and storage, even by fast computers, can, for a large number of s.k.u., become an appreciable expense which is warranted only for the A and B items in inventory.

Slow moving A items will be modelled according to the Poisson or Laplace distributions. Where demand for an expensive replacement part, for example, occurs without warning it may be worthwhile from a managerial standpoint to model explicitly the probabilities of random breakdowns (rare events). On the other hand, management may be indifferent about achieving such fine precision, especially when there is no easy logical explanation for why demand for a s.k.u. should be Poisson distributed. For the latter cases we recommend the use of the Laplace distribution. However one should not lose sight of the fact that the number of slow moving A items

Table 3.3 A Two-Tiered A-B-C Classification

Dv Category	Fast Moving s.k.u., $\bar{x}_L \geq 10$	Slow Moving s.k.u., $\bar{x}_L < 10$	Estimate of σ_L
A items	Normal	Poisson or Laplace	Based on actual measurements
B items	Normal	Laplace	Based on actual measurements
C items	Normal	Laplace	Based on aggregate regression relationship or $\sigma_L \doteq \sqrt{\bar{x}_L}$

will be usually relatively small. Therefore, for this category of s.k.u., management may well choose to ignore all these mathematical niceties and revert to "good old gut feel." Additional comments on this point will be made in Chapter 9.

Fast moving B items will be handled analytically exactly in the same manner as was explained above for the fast moving A items. The only difference will occur in actual practice—decisions generated by management science models for s.k.u. in this category are less likely to be overruled by managerial intervention than is the case for A items.

Slow moving B items will be handled somewhat differently from their class A counterparts. The Poisson distribution can become computationally cumbersome for a large number of s.k.u. For slow-moving B items we shall recommend the exclusive use of the Laplace distribution to model lead time demand. Note that for most B items we shall recommend that the variability of lead time demand be measured directly, as was the case for A items.

Fast moving C items shall also be modelled using the Normal distribution, except that the amount of data-processing necessary to estimate $\bar{x}_L$ and σ_L will be drastically reduced. The value of $\bar{x}_L$ must be estimated, although not usually by a mechanized, forecasting system. In addition, we do *not* recommend that the value of σ_L be measured directly through forecasting systems. Instead we recommend the use of the regression relationships between $\bar{x}_L$ and σ_L presented in section 2.2.4 of Chapter 2. In Chapter 4 we shall also treat the important issue of how to relate the estimated variability over one time period (the lead time) to that over another time period (the basic forecast update period) by means of a regression relationship.

Slow moving C items deserve the least amount of managerial and data-processing attention. For these items we shall recommend the exclusive use of the Laplace distribution to model lead time demand. Slow moving C items often exhibit some type of erratic (unexpected) demand spurts. Therefore the extra protection that results from assuming the Laplace distribution (a point we shall demonstrate in Chapter 11) is welcome for these items, especially since the extra carrying costs incurred are small. If regression estimates of the relationship between σ_L and $\bar{x}_L$ are available as discussed under fast-moving items, then the variability of lead time demand should be captured in this fashion. Alternatively (and this holds true also for fast-moving C items) one may want to *resort* to setting:

$$\sigma_L = \sqrt{\bar{x}_L} \tag{3.3}$$

and/or if a regression relationship between variability in one period to that of another is unavailable:

$$\sigma_L = \sqrt{b}\,\sigma_1 \tag{3.4}$$

where

σ_1 is the estimate of variability over some base period (usually one month).

b is the number of *base periods** equivalent to a lead time, L.

Eq. 3.3 makes a *convenient* assumption which actually holds true for the Poisson distribution and not, in general, for the Laplace. Eq. 3.4 depends on the somewhat questionable assumption that demands in successive base periods are independent.

It is possible that a decision maker may not wish to distinguish between slow- and fast-moving items to the extent described above, perhaps because it may be felt that the added precision may not be worth the added costs of data-processing and managerial workload. Two simpler options are possible.

The decision maker could choose not to categorize B and C items into slow- and fast-movers. Instead he would use the decision models described above for fast-moving B and C items for all items respectively in these categories. A items would continue to be treated by the separate procedures for slow- and fast-moving items given in Table 3.3.

The other option consists of treating both slow- and fast-moving items in the A, B, and C categories in the same way—according to the procedures outlined above for fast-moving items. That is, lead time demand could always be assumed to vary normally, although $\bar{x}_L$ and σ_L would be estimated by different procedures depending on the data-processing costs merited by the class in question.

3.5 *Explicit Measurement of Costs*

It often comes as a surprise to engineers and management scientists that cost accountants and managers cannot always determine exactly the costs of some of the variables they specify in their models. According to L. S. Rosen,

> *Many aspects of accounting have developed over time on the basis of conventions that have been widely adopted simply because some people feel that they have proven to be useful in practice. What is not often appreciated by non-accountants is the fact that we possess no magic formulae or methods for measuring relevant costs for a specific managerial decision.*

* *A base period is defined as the period over which forecast errors are collected and calculated.*

> *Different costs are relevant for different purposes; and unless the user's needs are known the wrong type of cost can be furnished by an accountant ... Many costs assembled for stockholder's financial reports, for example, are particularly useless or dangerous for other purposes because highly arbitrary methods are used to allocate costs to different functions of a business.**

That cost measurement is in practice a problem that has not been conclusively solved, is evident from the fact that a number of alternative cost accounting systems are in use. The basic problem arises because it is not possible and often is not economical to trace all costs (variable, semi-variable or fixed) to each and every individual s.k.u. in inventory. An allocation process which distributes, somewhat arbitrarily, fixed or overhead costs across all units is inevitable. Rosen categorizes some of the many possible cost systems in his book, as we have summarized in Table 3.4.[16]

Table 3.4 Costing and Control Alternatives

Basic Characteristic of System (1)	Which Valuation? Actual? Predetermined? Standard? (2)	Include vs. Exclude Fixed manufacturing overhead in inventory cost? (3)
A Process costing methods	A Actual direct material Actual direct labor Actual manufacturing overhead	A Full absorption costing (includes fixed portion of manufacturing over-head)
	B Actual direct material Actual direct labor Predetermined manufacturing overhead	
B Job order costing methods	C Actual direct material Predetermined direct labour overhead	B Direct variable costing (does not include fixed portion of manu-facturing overhead)
	D Standard direct material Standard direct labor Standard manufacturing overhead.	

---

* *Private correspondence (L. S. Rosen is Professor of Accounting at York University, Toronto)*

In Table 3.4, column 1, *Process Costing* is defined as an accounting method whereby all costs are collected by cost centers such as the paint shop, the warehouse, etc. After a predetermined collection period each s.k.u. that passed through the process will get allocated a share of the total costs incurred in the cost center. For example, all chairs painted in a particular month could be allocated exactly the same painting cost (which could be different the next month).

Alternatively, *Job Order Costing* could be used. Under this accounting method a particular order for chairs would be kept track of as it progressed through the shop and all costs incurred by this particular order would be recorded. Thereby the "cost" of producing the same chair under either of the two costing systems could be very different. The reason for having these two different systems in practice is simple. The job order costing system is more expensive in terms of the amount of bookkeeping required but provides information for more detailed cost control than process costing. (Note that the accountant has to select between decision systems for collecting and keeping track of costs just like we must design inventory decision systems that are appropriate in terms of the level of sophistication warranted.)

In addition to selecting between bookkeeping systems the accountant must decide on the basis of valuation. He has four choices according to column 2 of Table 3.4. Under *standard costing* materials, labor, and factory overhead are charged against each production unit in accordance with a standard (hourly) rate regardless of how much actual effort (time) it takes. Any deficit (negative variance) between total standard costs charged and actual costs incurred over a costing period (say a year) is charged as a separate expense item on the income statement and does not end up as part of the cost of an item, v_i. Alternatively, surpluses (positive variances), that is, where production takes less time than the standard, can artificially inflate v_i unless all items produced are revalued at the end of an accounting year. The possibility of a difference between standard and actual costs results from the fact that standards may have been set for different purposes or they may have been set at ideal, long run or perceived "normal" rates that turn out, after the fact, to be unattainable. Existing standards can also be out of date and not indicative of prevailing conditions.

Under *actual costing*, product cost, v_i, is determined on the basis of accumulated actual cost directly incurred during a given period of time. Materials, labor, and overhead costs are accumulated, which are then spread over all units produced during the period. Note that, as a result, the cost of a given item may vary from one time period to another.

The term *predetermined* in Table 3.4 refers to the allocation of costs to an s.k.u. based on short term budgets as opposed to engineered standards. Predetermined cost allocations are usually somewhat arbitrary and may not reflect the amount of expense (as could be determined from a careful engineering study) incurred by a s.k.u. Predetermined costing has the virtue of ensuring that, from an accounting point of view, all costs incurred over a costing period get allocated somewhere.

Cost accounting systems are further differentiated in column 3 of Table 3.4 by whether they utilize absorption costing or direct costing. Under *absorption costing* (also called full costing) little distinction is made between fixed and variable manufacturing costs. All overhead costs are charged according to some formula, such as percent of direct labor hours used, to the product being manufactured. The concept of *direct costing* involves the classification of costs into fixed and variable elements. Costs that are a function of time rather than volume are classified as fixed and are not charged to individual s.k.u.. For example, all fixed manufacturing expenses, executive and supervisory salaries, and general office expenses are usually considered to be fixed since they are not directly a function of volume. However, note that some costs are in fact semi-variable, they vary only with large fluctuations in volume. A doubling of the production rate, for example, could make it necessary to hire extra supervisory personnel.

Semi-variable costs (Figure 3.4) are often handled in practice by assuming that volume can be predicted with sufficient accuracy so that over a relevant

Figure 3.4 Semi-Variable Costs.

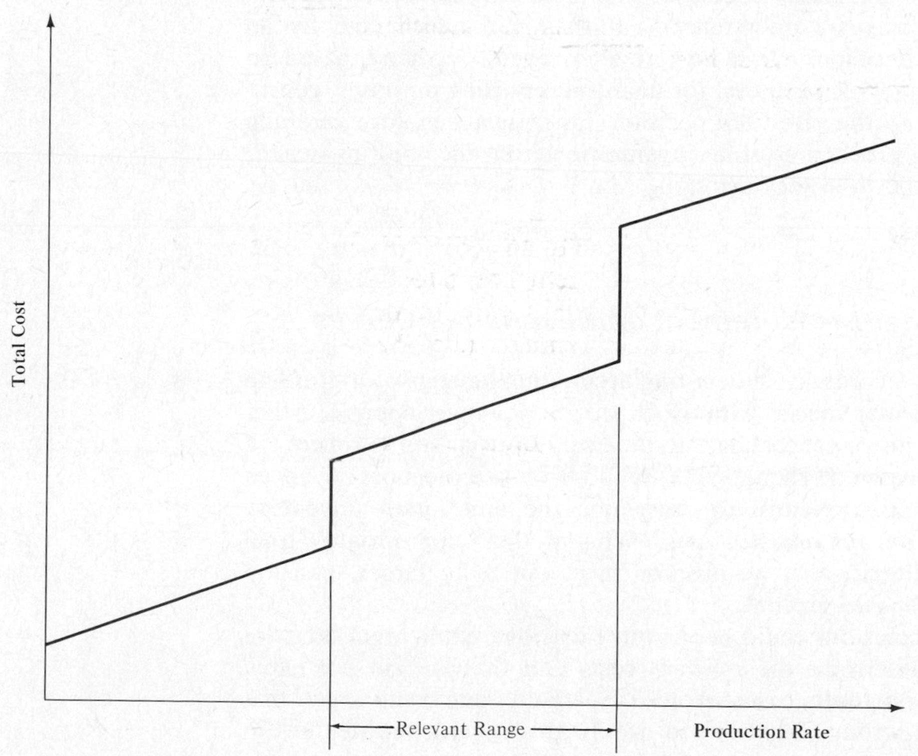

range, costs can be viewed as being only of two kinds: variable and fixed. This is not always a simple matter.

It should be clear that the first step in any attempt at explicit cost measurement has to be a determination of what assumptions are made by the existing cost accounting system within a firm. As Rosen points out, a small business needing information for external reporting and bookkeeping purposes may choose from Table 3.4 a system (one selection from each of the 3 columns) that is (A, A, A) because it may be the least costly from a bookkeeping standpoint. A similar company wishing to postpone tax payments may choose (A, A, B) and so forth.

Note that while the above description of costing systems provides many options, the most important costs of all, from an inventory planning standpoint do not appear at all. Inventory and production planning decisions require the estimation of *opportunity costs.* These costs do not appear in conventional accounting records. Accountants are primarily concerned with the recording of *historical costs,* whereas decision makers must anticipate *future costs* so that they can be avoided if possible. Existing cost data in standard accounting records therefore may not be relevant to decision making or at best have to be recast to be useful.

To a decision maker a *relevant cost* is a cost that will be incurred in the *future* if a particular action is chosen. Alternatively it could be a cost which can be avoided if a particular course of action is not chosen. Therefore, overall overhead costs are only relevant if they can be affected by an inventory planning decision. Allocated (predetermined) overhead, based on some ad hoc formula which is useful for financial reporting purposes, generally is not relevant to the inventory decision. One must therefore carefully examine the costing procedures of an organization from the point of view of their relevancy to the inventory decision.

3.6 *Implicit Cost Measurement and Exchange Curves*

Suppose we examine carefully the existing accounting systems of a firm and determine the particular species with which we are dealing. Suppose further that we modify the historical cost data to the best of our ability to reflect the opportunity costs involved. Then, finally, suppose we use the most advanced techniques of inventory control to determine the appropriate inventory investment, *based on our adjusted costs.* What if this "appropriate" total investment in inventories that we propose turns out to be larger than top management is willing to accept?

Two possible conclusions could be drawn. First, one could argue that we did not correctly determine the relevant costs and that we did not allow properly for the opportunity costs involved. Secondly, one could argue that top management is wrong. But what to do? In this regard, the key lies in realizing that *the inventory planning decision deals with the design of an entire system: consisting of an ordering function, a warehousing system, and the servicing of customer demand—all to top management specification.* One can not focus on an individual s.k.u. and ask: what is the *marginal cost* of stocking this or that individual item without considering its impact on other s.k.u. or on the system as a whole! Robert G. Brown[5] argues that there is no "correct" value for *r*, the cost of carrying inventories, in the accounting-explicit measurement sense. Instead the carrying charge, *r*, he says is a top management policy variable, that can be changed from time to time to meet the changing environment. The only "correct" value of *r*, according to Brown, is the one that results in a total system where aggregate investment, total number of orders per year and the overall customer service level are in agreement with what top management wants.* For example, the specification of a low *r* value would generate a system with relatively large inventory investment, good customer service, and low order replenishment expenses. Alternatively, higher values of *r* would encourage carrying of less inventories, poorer customer service and higher ordering costs.

There is of course, no reason, from a theoretical point of view, why all costs (including *A*, *v* and the cost of disservice) could not be considered as policy variables. In practice this is in effect what is often done, at least partially, by many inventory consultants. An attempt is first made to measure all costs explicitly so as to provide some baseline data ("ballpark" estimates). Thereupon the resulting inventory decision system is modified to conform to all aggregate specifications. Only cost estimates that serve the cause of attaining the aggregate specifications get ultimately used during implementation.

As we shall see in Chapter 5, such an approach is feasible in practice partly because most of the decision models for inventory management are relatively insensitive to errors in cost measurement. For example, we shall see that an economic order quantity that is 50 percent *larger* than one that would result from using "true" costs results in only a 17 percent increase over the theoretically possible minimum total operating cost. Errors on the low side are somewhat more costly. An economic order quantity that is 50 percent *less* than the mathematically optimal quantity, increases total operating costs by 25 percent.

In Chapters 5 to 7 we shall describe in detail a methodology called *Exchange Curves*, for dcsigning inventory decision systems using cost information *and/or* policy variables specified by top management.

---

* *For an earlier discussion of the imputation of costs see for example, Martin K. Starr and David W. Miller.* Inventory Control: Theory and Practice, *Englewood Cliffs, N. J., Prentice Hall,* 1962, *pp.* 93–104 *and pp.* 120–125.

In the remaining pages of this Chapter we shall introduce only the basic concepts involved with the aid of a simple numerical example. Suppose we had an inventory system consisting of the 5 s.k.u. given in Table 3.5.

Table 3.5 A Contrived Example

Item, i (1)	D_i (2)	A_i (3)	v_i (4)	Q_i (5)
1	2,400	$10	$5	?
2	6,000	10	4	?
3	1,200	10	2	?
4	4,800	10	3	?
5	3,600	10	1	?
				?

Note that someone has explicitly estimated for each item the D_i, the annual demand for item i, its cost of ordering A_i and its value v_i. The problem is to determine what quantities Q_i to order. In Chapter 5 we shall see that the optimal or economic order quantity is given by:

$$Q_i = \sqrt{\frac{2A_iD_i}{v_ir}} \tag{3.5}$$

Table 3.5 contains all the information necessary to calculate Eq. 3.5, except, as is most often the case, the carrying charge r.

Also, even if we had an estimate of r, there would always be some doubt whether the total cycle stock implied by this particular set of A, v, r, and D values is acceptable to top management. Recall that the theoretical total cycle stock in dollars is given by:

$$\text{TCS} = \sum_{i=1}^{5} Q_iv_i/2 \tag{3.6}$$

If we decided to order Q_i of item i which sold at a rate of D_i per year then the total number of orders generated for the 5 items (N) would be:

$$N = \sum_{i=1}^{5} D_i/Q_i \tag{3.7}$$

In Chapter 5 we shall derive, using economic order quantity concepts (and based on all items having the same A value), the following 2 key relationships based on which the Exchange Curve for trading off cycle stock investment versus total number of orders per year, shown in Figure 3.5, is drawn:*

$$(TCS)N = \tfrac{1}{2}\left(\sum_{i=1}^{5} \sqrt{D_i v_i}\right)^2 \tag{3.8}$$

$$\frac{TCS}{N} = \frac{A}{r} \tag{3.9}$$

Figure 3.5 Cycle Stock vs. N Exchange Curve.

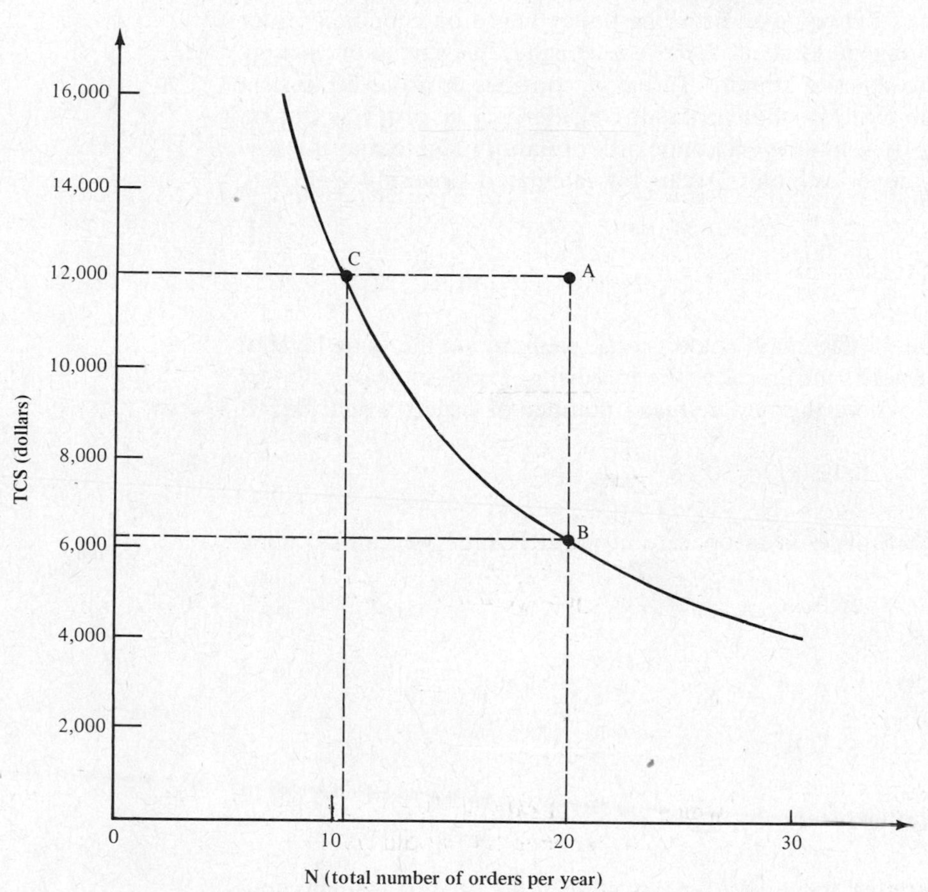

* *The next two equations also appear as Eqs. 5.14 and 5.15 in Chapter 5. We have omitted the proofs here. The interested reader should refer ahead to Chapter 5.*

Using data from Table 3.5 we can calculate Eq. 3.8 to be

$$(\mathrm{TCS})N = \$121{,}748.25 \tag{3.10}$$

Note that Eq. 3.10 is a hyperbola which can be drawn graphically as in Figure 3.5.

Also shown on Figure 3.5 is point A which represents the fact that currently for these 5 items top management stocks \$12,000 of cycle stock on the average and places 20 orders per year. Since point A lies off the Exchange Curve (as is usually the case in practice) it is clear that management of this particular firm is not following an ordering policy based on economic order quantities. Top management could achieve a considerable saving in carrying costs by choosing to operate at point B, that is, continue to order 20 times a year but reduce the cycle stock investment considerably by ordering less on each order (that is, by using the economic order quantity). Note that the new reduced inventory level at point B can be calculated precisely from Eq. 3.10:

$$\mathrm{TCS} = 121{,}748.25/20 = \$6{,}087.41$$

Alternatively, top management could choose to maintain the same level of cycle stock investment and reduce the ordering expense drastically by moving to point C where the new reduced number of orders would be:

$$N = 121{,}748.25/12{,}000 = 10.15$$

If top management decided to operate at point B then we can calculate from Eq. 3.9

$$\mathrm{TCS}/N = A/r$$

$$6{,}087.41/20 = 10/r$$

or

$$r = \$0.03/\text{dollar/year}$$

Note that the imputed value of r, above, appears to be unreasonably low given the fact that it is even lower than the prime bank rate in recent history. What is wrong? Well perhaps the original estimate of the order cost, A, was in error. (From our experience we have never met a cost accountant who was willing to bet his job on guaranteeing any value of A he derived as being unquestionable.) Suppose everyone in the firm felt that their intuitions were much better served by a value of r of \$0.25/dollar/year (a favourite rule of thumb of consultants for many years) then we could calculate that:

$$TCS/N = A/r$$

$$6{,}087.33/20 = A/0.25$$

or

$$A = \$76.09$$

Is this all a lot of nonsense? Are we just playing with numbers, which we then pretend to be relevant costs? Undoubtedly some dyed-in-wool comptrollers, of the old school of explicit cost measurement, most likely would conclude that we had lost our senses. But note that these figures do serve to produce *an inventory system which has the overall desired characteristics specified by top management.*

In case it wasn't already clear from the example above, any A and r values chosen by top management through a tradeoff, trial and error procedure using Figure 3.5 can be substituted into Eq. 3.5 to calculate the missing Q_i's in Table 3.5 which will sum up to the desired total cycle stock provided we use the relationships in Eqs. 3.8 and 3.9.

As we shall see in Chapters 6 and 7, similar Exchange Curves can be developed for determining safety stocks and the level of customer service on a total system basis. We shall not discuss them here. The basic concepts are the same as for the cycle stock case considered above.

One last topic does remain to be discussed at this juncture. Are top managers really able to make tradeoffs such as we discussed above? Not *all* managers can make such tradeoffs, nor are the theoretical relationships of Exchange Curves always easy to derive.

In research carried out by the authors, the following main four lessons about Exchange Curves emerged:[14]

1. Some managers will have difficulty in trading off TCS versus N because they are unable to separate out cycle stock from total company inventory which consists of anticipation stock, safety stock, pipeline inventories, etc.

2. Managers have as much difficulty as anyone in thinking in terms of opportunity costs. What are the true meanings of A and r? Is the number of orders really going to affect the size of the purchasing/order department?

3. In industries where seasonal demand is prevalent for most s.k.u. managers find the separation of cycle stock and safety stock considerations very difficult.

4. The Exchange Curve concepts are easier to implement in a merchant rather than in a producer context; in the latter one may have to allow for a multitude of other multiechelon effects.

Does this mean that we are doomed to muddling through forever as far as measuring inventory related costs are concerned, as Rosen implied in the previous section? Probably so, for there are no magical, inviolable answers to cost measurement just as we shall see in Chapter 4 that there are no real ways of foretelling the future. It just *seems* more reasonable to some people that one *should* be able to *always* measure costs. As Vatter[19] points out:

> *I am certain that the two human traits . . . the search for the simple answer and the reverence for mathematics can cause a lot of trouble for cost accountants. Cost figures may actually be misleading if they are computed to fit one purpose and used for another purpose. The validity and results of a business decision may be traced to the way in which costs were marshalled in tackling the problem.*

It is ironic to reflect on the historical fact that classical economics assumed in their theories for many years that "engineers" could always marshal any available resources to organize production facilities so as to yield an optimum output for any combination of factors (labor, capital, and land). Engineers and (presumably management scientists) being burdened so unjustly, in turn assumed that "accountants" could measure the relevant costs needed by their models. Perhaps we, in turn, have "passed the puck," to coin a Canadian metaphor, to top managers who may not be any better equipped to provide us with the needed answers.

Problems for Chapter 3

Problem 3.1

In the MIDAS (A) case a number of problems that require top management input are raised:

i. Should Takashi subassemblies be stocked?
ii. Should MIDAMATICS be assembled only to order?
iii. Should a major programme be undertaken to reduce the number of s.k.u. through product standardization?
iv. Should MIDAS continue to stock *Superchrome* given its high costs of storage and low volume?
v. Should MIDAS continue to keep its book inventories low and the pipeline from Germany full of many small orders?

a. How do you think top management would go about resolving the above issues?
b. Do you agree that top management can and should resolve the above issues?
c. Which of the above issues do you think operating management would be capable of handling *alone?*

Problem 3.2

Draw a flow chart which traces the flow of paperwork, information, and the decision points within the procedures described in the MIDAS (B) case. Are there any deficiencies that could lead to clerical or managerial error? Are they in a position to upgrade the decision making rules within their system? Recommend changes by pointing out how your procedures would be superior. Illustrate your modifications on your flowchart.

Problem 3.3

The Inventory Control Manager at MIDAS was trying to decide on how to model the replenishment lead time of shipments he received from West Germany. Typically 20 to 30 s.k.u. were ordered at a time from the MIDAS INTERNATIONAL plant and arrived in Toronto in a single container. For the last 8 containers received from West Germany the following data was collected by a clerk and presented to the manager.

Container No.	Transit Time (Days)	Time Taken At Plant in Germany (Days)
357	93	10
358	79	4
359	86	7
360	102	14
361	106	28
362	129	8
363	110	11
364	107	5

Transit time in the above table included the number of days it took the container to travel from the time it left the plant in West Germany to the time it arrived at the warehouse in Toronto.

a. How long would you estimate the replenishment lead time to be *on the average?* Would you include any data? Would you request any additional data?
b. Would you recommend the use of the Poisson or Normal or Laplace Probability distribution to model the variability exhibited? Should a mathematical distribution be used at all? Discuss.
c. If the replenishment lead time were set at 120 days, estimate the probability that a longer lead time could actually result, assuming that lead time length varied according to the:

i. Poisson distribution
ii. Normal distribution
iii. Laplace distribution

d. How do the estimates in (c) compare to historical data?

Problem 3.4

Discuss the fundamental differences in approach required to analyse the following two types of inventory control problems:

a. A one-opportunity type of purchase that promises large savings

b. A situation where the options remain the same from one buying opportunity to the next

Problem 3.5

Assuming that you have no data on total annual dollar movement ($\sum Dv$), which of the following s.k.u. (and under what circumstances) should be classified as A, B, or C items?:

a. Spare parts for a discontinued piece of manufacturing equipment

b. Bolts and washers

c. Subassemblies

d. Imported s.k.u.'s for resale

e. Motor oil

f. Perishable food stuffs

g. A Right Handed PS-37R-01

h. Widget invented by the company owner's nephew

i. Platinum bushings

j. Describe and classify one example of A, B, and C from your experience

If, in addition, you were supplied with figures on the total annual dollar movement ($\sum Dv$) for each s.k.u. how could such figures affect your classification above? What other information would you like to have?

Problem 3.6

Given no other information, what would you estimate the standard deviation over a 3-month lead time to be, if the standard deviation of forecast error over a two month period has been 58 units?

Problem 3.7

The May-Bee Company distributes fire fighting equipment. Approximately 50 percent of the company's s.k.u. are imported and the rest are acquired from domestic suppliers. May-Bee sales have been increasing at a steady rate and future trends appear very optimistic. The company is wholly-owned by a Mr. Brown who relies heavily on his bank for working capital. His current credit limit is set at $150,000 and he is experiencing some resistance from his banker in getting more cash to increase his investment in inventories to meet an anticipated increase in sales.

In the past Brown has used only simple decision rules for ordering from his suppliers. He orders a 3-week supply of s.k.u. which cost more than $10 per unit and a 6-week supply of items which cost less than $10 per unit.

Last year May-Bee's average inventory was around $1,000,000. He paid $19,500 interest on his bank loan, $80,000 rent for his warehouse, and $15,000 to insurance companies. Brown believes it would be profitable to increase his bank loan because he feels he could probably earn 14–15% on the borrowed money.

The following six items represent 30 percent of May-Bee's annual dollar sales volume and according to Brown are his bread and butter.

S.k.u. Number	Value/Unit v ($)	Annual Demand D (units)
1	15.78	6,400
2[a]	40.50	2,200
3[a]	18.30	4,500
4	8.40	3,500
5	9.70	6,000
6[a]	25.00	4,800

[a] Items imported from the same supplier.

Brown gets directly involved with the ordering of imported items because for these items he has to go to the bank to get a letter of credit and on the average spends about 60 minutes per order doing so. An order for imported items had in the past included from 1 to 10 s.k.u.

The table below gives a summary of the costs involved in placing an order. These estimates were supplied by the persons involved, who guessed at the amount of time involved in each activity.

Person Involved	Hourly Rate ($)	Time Per Order (minutes) Domestic[a]	Imported
Typist	$3.00	20	24
Inventory clerk	3.20	20	20
Receiver	4.50	30	30
Bookkeeper	4.20	20	20
Mr. Brown	20.00	20	60

Domestic Orders usually included 1 to 5 s.k.u.

Apart from the above there was a charge of $10 per order which represented the bank charge for the letter of credit for imported items whereas the bank charges were only 25¢ per order for items acquired from domestic suppliers.

a. The above cost description was compiled by the bookkeeper. In your opinion are there any costs that have been left out? Comment.

b. Compute May-Bee's carrying cost (r).

c. Compute the cost of placing an order for a single domestic and for a single imported s.k.u.

d. Compute the E.O.Q. for all six items.

e. Compute the theoretical total cycle stock (T.C.S.) under present ordering rules (6-items).

f. Compute the T.C.S. for the six items using E.O.Q.'s.

g. Compute the difference in T.C.S. under e) and f). Estimate the change in T.C.S. for all the 100 items.

h. Compute the total number of replenishments for the sample of six items under the present system and under the E.O.Q. policy.

i. Using Eq. 3.8 (from the text) draw an exchange curve for the imported items. From the graph calculate the increase or decrease in T.C.S. if the combined total number of orders for the three imported items is changed to 36 per year.

j. Compute the total relevant costs (ordering costs plus holding costs) under the present system and under the E.O.Q. policy. What are the estimated savings (percent) for the six items, if the E.O.Q. policy is applied throughout the whole population?

Problem 3.8

An inventory mostly made up of machined parts, consisted of 6,000 s.k.u. valued (at full cost) by the accounting department at $420,000. The company had recently built a new warehouse at a cost of $185,000 which was financed through a 12% mortgage. The building was to be depreciated on a 25-year basis. The company's credit rating was sound and a bank loan of $50,000 was under negotiation with the bank. The main operating costs per year in the new warehouses were estimated to be as follows:

Municipal and Other Taxes	$5,732.67
Insurance on building and contents	3,200.00
Heating/Air conditioning	12,500.00
Electricity and Water	3,200.00
Labor (Supervisor, 3 clerks and a half-time janitor)[a]	69,000.00
Pilferage	5,000.00
Obsolescence	5,000.00
Total	$103,632.67

[a] Includes 60 percent manufacturing overhead.

It was estimated that on the average each s.k.u. involved one dollar of labor cost per dollar of material cost.

a. Recommend a value for the carrying cost, r in $/$/year.

b. Suppose that your recommended value for r is accepted by management and the accounting department. You proceed to calculate the E.O.Q. quantities for all 6,000 items and discover that the new warehouse is too small to physically accommodate all the inventory that is indicated by your calculations. What action would you take now?

c. Alternatively suppose that your recommended value for r is accepted by management and the accounting department, but that the total dollar investment (based on E.O.Q.'s) that you estimate will be needed is approximately $800,000. Top management is unwilling to have a total investment greater than $500,000. What action would you take under such a circumstance?

REFERENCES FOR CHAPTER 3

1. Archibald, B., Silver, E. A. and Peterson, R. "Selecting the Probability Distribution of Demand in a Replenishment Lead Time." Working Paper No. 89, Department of Management Sciences, University of Waterloo, Waterloo, Ontario, Canada, August, 1974.

2. Bacigalupo, Paul F. "Can Inventories be Managed?" *Production and Inventory Management,* 1st Quarter, 1975, pp. 17–24.

3. Beranek, W. "Financial Implications of Lot-Size Inventory Models." *Management Science,* Vol. 13, No. 8, April, 1967, pp. 401–408.

4. Brown, R. G. *Smoothing, Forecasting and Prediction of Discrete Time Series.* Prentice Hall, Englewood Cliffs, N.J., 1963, pp. 275–281.

5. Brown, Robert G. *Decision Rules for Inventory Management.* New York, Holt, Rinehart and Winston, 1967, pp. 29–31.

6. Conway, R. W. and Schultz Jr., A. "The Manufacturing Progress Function." *Journal of Industrial Engineering,* Vol. X, No. 1, January-February, 1969, pp. 39–54.

7. Dickie, H. F. "ABC Inventory Analysis Shoots for Dollars, Not Pennies." *Factory Management and Maintenance,* July, 1951.

8. Dyer, Dickie. "Don't Get Casual with the Cost to Stock." *Modern Distribution Management,* October 9, 1973, pp. 3–7.

9. Girling, A. J. and Morgan, P. W. "Exchange Curves for Fixing Batch Quantities." *OMEGA*, Vol. 1, No. 2, 1973.

10. Hirschmann, J. "Profit from the Learning Curve." *Harvard Business Review*, Vol. 42. No. 1, January-February, 1964, pp. 125–139.

11. Mayer, R. R. "Selection of Rules of Thumb in Inventory Control." *Journal of Purchasing,* May, 1972.

12. McFadden, F. R. "On Lead Time Demand Distributions." *Decision Sciences,* Vol. 3, pp. 106–126, April, 1972.

13. Parr. J. O. "Formula Approximations to Brown's Service Function." *Production and Inventory Management,* Vol. 13, pp. 84–86, First Quarter, 1972.

14. Peterson, R. and Silver E. A. "Exchange Curves: Implicit Parameter Determination Through Aggregate Considerations In Multi-Item Production-Inventory Models." presented at Joint TIMS/ORSA Meetings, Boston, April 22–24, 1974.

15. Plossl, George W. "How Much Inventory is Enough?" *Production and Inventory Management,* June, 1971, p. 4.

16. Rosen, L. S. *Topics in Managerial Accounting.* Second Edition, McGraw-Hill, Ryerson, 1974.

17. Simon, Herbert A. *Models of Man, Social and Rational.* New York, John Wiley and Sons, Inc., 1957, pp. 196–206.

18. Slater, W. "Determining Cost

Factors in Order Quantity Formulae." *APICS Quarterly Bulletin*, July, 1965, pp. 8–21.

19. Vatter, William J. "Tailor-Making Data for Specific Uses." Chapter 16 in Rosen, L. S. *Topics in Managerial Accounting.* 2nd Edition, McGraw-Hill, Ryerson, 1975, p. 195.

20. Whitin, Thomson M. *The Theory of Inventory Management.* Princeton University Press, 1957, p. 219.

Midas Canada Corporation (C)*

Four Times a year each of the managers of the four sales Divisions prepared Sales Target Reports which estimated the dollar sales by quarter for each major product category for the 12 month period ahead. (See Table 1.) The Inventory Control Manager, in turn, prepared from the Sales Target Reports a number of reports which became the bases for planning. One set of summaries, called *Purchase Budgets,* he submitted to production planners in Germany. Purchase Budgets stated how many square meters in total of each type of photographic paper, for example, MIDAS-CANADA was going to buy in each of the next four quarters. The sales of individual s.k.u. were not forecasted on Purchase Budgets only major product groupings such as major grades of paper and bulk chemicals were projected. The quantities stated in the Purchase Budget for the most imminent quarter were considered to be firm commitments; subsequent quarterly estimates could be modified later on if the need arose.

He also used the Sales Target Reports to prepare *Sales Forecasts* (in units) for the Assembly Plant, from which the Master Plan for the Equipment Division was compiled twice a year. The Master Plan stated the number of units of each product line that was to be assembled or repackaged each month, how many workers were required to carry out planned production and how much inventory would be carried from one

Table 1 Timing of Sales Target Reports

Time of Preparation	
October	January to December
January	April to March
April	July to June
July	October to September

* *The MIDAS cases describe actual decision systems which are based on consulting experiences of the authors. They do not describe the situation at any single company, but are in fact a compendium of actual situations which have been compressed into the environment of a single firm and industry for illustrative purposes. The cases are not intended as presentations of either effective or ineffective ways of handling administrative problems.*

month to the next. In converting dollar sales estimates to units the Inventory Control Manager used a number of rules of thumb. He figured that on the average a PROCESSOR would sell for $500, a MIDAMATIC for $25,000 and that bulk chemicals would yield approximately $2 per pound or gallon.

According to the Inventory Control Manager:

> *A lot of discussion goes on between the Sales Managers and myself before the Purchase Budgets are prepared. I don't accept the Sales Targets at face value. As everyone knows, salesmen are eternal optimists. I have been in this business 23 years and have a pretty good feel for what is reasonable and what is not. Unfortunately, because of the large number of products, I don't have the time nor the manpower to actually go back and check in detail the sales history on each product every time. Now and then they slip one past me.*

Sales Forecasts of Individual Items

For most of the 2103 s.k.u. in inventory no forecast of future sales was made. Once a month the Inventory Control Manager and the Comptroller along with 3 assistants reviewed the sales of all items by summing the sales over the most recent 5 month period using the data recorded on Travel Cards (see Figure 2, case B). These 5 month totals became the bases for determining Order points and order quantities that will be discussed in case D.

These monthly sessions lasted usually two twelve hour days and were referred to as "marathons." It was generally agreed that the manual updating system was becoming overly burdensome. During the year the head office Computer Center in England started to summarize past sales of individual s.k.u. and product groups in an effort to help out. Unfortunately these computer printouts arrived in Toronto sometimes several months out of date and utilized methods that were not completely understood by the Toronto office. As a result, MIDAS-CANADA was considering, during the latter part of 1976, the installation of a small computer of their own to handle all the record keeping, sales forecasting and order generation currently being done manually.

Stock keeping units needed for the assembly of PROCESSORS, MIDAMATICS and Takashi Systems were "forecasted" differently and were not a part of the marathon sessions. Four times a year the Inventory Control Manager calculated the number of assembled products (PROCESSORS, for example) that would be sold in a particular month from the Sales Target Reports. Then, in turn, he broke down each PROCESSOR into subcomponents and parts that had to be ordered. For example, each PROCESSOR consisted of 4 EDM-001 parts, 1 EDM-002 part, 6 EDM-003 parts, etc. By multiplying the number of each s.k.u. needed per PROCESSOR by the number of PROCESSORS forecasted for any month he was able to determine the total number of each s.k.u. needed each month to meet the assembly schedule. Such a procedure, commonly referred to as explosion into components, was one of the key factors in the Assembly Plant planning system. The Inventory Control Manager kept no safety stocks in assembly parts, and ordered only enough parts to meet the demand per month forecasted through explosion of predicted demand for PROCESSORS, MIDAMATICS, and Takashi Systems, because he felt that the explosion method of forecasting yielded quantities that were almost certain to accrue.

For some of the most expensive s.k.u. (A items) neither of the above two procedures were used. For speciality items, such as *Superchrome*, which were kept locked in a climate controlled vault, the Inventory Control Manager prepared sales estimates every month by telephoning some of his key large customers and asking them to estimate their needs for a one month period, two months ahead. (It took 2 to 4 weeks to receive delivery from Germany for specialty items such as *Superchrome.*) These estimates were considered as commitments by the Inventory Control Manager, who guaranteed delivery of orders up to the level estimated by the key customers telephoned by him. If a key customer habitually overestimated his actual sales of specialty items, then the Inventory Control Manager either dropped him from his list of customers whom he telephoned or asked the customer to sign a sales order which committed him to a fixed order quantity. The Inventory Control Manager usually ordered ten to twenty percent more of each specialty item than was estimated by the customers whom he telephoned. Customers not on his telephone list had to take their chances of getting their orders serviced from the ten to twenty percent increment which he added to the committed orders. Committed orders were recorded separately as "Quantities Allocated" on the Record Card (see column 8, Figure 1, in case B).

For the remaining specialty items the Inventory Control Manager assumed that the demand this year would be approximately the same as last year. In such cases he defined last year's demand as being the sum of actual sales plus the number of backorders (see Figure 3, case B) that were not filled. Only under unusual circumstances did he depart from this procedure, by multiplying last years's demand by an additional factor, in response to information that came to his attention.

In reviewing the existing forecasting procedures the Inventory Control Manager admitted that he found them very time-consuming. He also worried about what would happen when he retired from the Company:

> *The computer forecasts are of no use to me. All they do is report back to me the data that I mailed to them in the first place. We would be better off*

if they took my figures and carried out the sums and multiplications we have to go through during our marathon sessions. But the computer forecasts arrive too late from England to be of any use and appear to be less accurate than my own—especially for seasonal items. Apparently they use some sort of a mathematical model called Triple Exponential Smoothing. I can't see how they can make up for all the intuitive judgments I have to make, on the spot, in coming up with my own estimates of future sales. I sometimes worry about what will happen when a man with less experience than I takes over my job when I retire. There are not too many of us old timers around any more.

CHAPTER FOUR

Forecasting: Strategy and Tactics

Let's face it, there is really no way of judging the future except by the past. Yet, most of us would agree, that it would be foolish to rely solely on the past in planning for the future. This is the *forecaster's dilemma* that confronts every person who is about to make a conjecture about the unknown future.

Most successful decision makers resolve the *forecaster's dilemma* through a judicious combination of historical fact and interpretation, with judgments based on hunches about the future. Because it is so tempting to speculate about the future one must always be on guard in such a process against wishful thinking and unfounded emotion. While making judgments about the future, it is important to make every effort in ensuring that predictions are based on informed opinions, sufficiently believable for the taking of the risks involved.

In this chapter we shall concentrate mainly on the *tactics* (*or techniques*) *of forecasting*. We shall have relatively little to say about how one forms valid and believable *judgments* about the future. In the final analysis, such matters, while very important, belong in our opinion to the realm of metaphysics. We shall make some suggestions regarding the selection of overall forecasting strategy.

Robert G. Brown[7] distinguishes between forecasting and prediction. He uses "prediction" when referring to subjective opinions about future events and reserves "forecasting" for the casting forward of historical patterns through objective computations made on past data. We shall follow the same convention.

4.1 *What to Expect From a Good Forecasting System*

Forecasts are unavoidable in decision making. Every decision in inventory management and production planning requires an estimation of future demand. We need forecasts: to set up performance standards for customer service, to plan the allocation of total inventory investment, to place replenishment orders, to identify needs for additional production capacity, and to choose between alternative operating strategies. Only one thing is certain after such decisions are made—*the forecasts will be in error*. What remains to be determined, is the exact size of the resulting errors and whether any past decisions need to be altered in response. Forecasts are at best imprecise, at worst misleading!

A primary concern in designing a forecasting system for inventory control is the development of mechanical, routine, computerized if possible, ways of calculating demand estimates for as many s.k.u. as possible in a typical inventory. M. J. Netzorg,(28) a management consultant with almost 30 years experience, described the typical environment in which the demand for individual s.k.u. is forecasted:

> *. . . we seldom have the time to make genuinely new forecasts . . . For most items we get no market research support . . . The only new information we get routinely is a month's net sales figures, by item, by region, to compare to the forecasts made earlier for that month . . . therefore one mustn't promise or even aim at accurate forecasts from month to month, but only forecasts that wouldn't crucify production and customer service.*

Furthermore, according to Netzorg, in most inventory systems only the demand for high volume s.k.u. is clearly seasonal, whereas the seasonality of low value (C items) tends to get lost in erratic sales patterns. As a result, he ignores seasonality in forecasting C items. He recommends a simple twelve-month moving average to forecast the lowest volume items and he reduces the length of the moving average gradually to six months for the highest volume items among the slow movers. Consistent with this viewpoint we advocate that the more sophisticated forecasting models, described in this chapter, apply only to the more important (A and B) items.

From the point of view of inventory management and production planning an *ideal forecast* should therefore:

1. Estimate expected demand in physical units.

2. Estimate probable range of actual demand around the expected value point (i.e., forecast error).

3. Be timely—available sufficiently in advance of any decision that must be made.

4. Be updated periodically so that revisions to decisions taken can be made promptly.

5. Balance the cost of forecast errors made versus the cost of generating forecasts.

6. Allow human judgment to override mechanical forecasts (whose primary advantage is the handling of massive amounts of historical data).

We have previously defined the challenge of inventory management as one of coping with large numbers of diverse s.k.u. Part of this challenge is the problem of keeping track of the historical sales patterns for each of the many individual items and their projection into the future. Because of the sheer massiveness of such a data-processing task, short term forecasts for inventory management must be made quickly, inexpensively, and easily. The number of pieces of information required to make a forecast must be kept at a minimum. The logic of the forecasting technique must be clear and relatively simple to understand to be usable by a variety of users, who are in return expected to supply *value judgments which transform forecasts into predictions.*

Since prediction of future sales is so closely linked with the judgment of forecasters, *an ideal forecaster* should:

1. Be familiar with the economic, industry and product-specific contexts of his projections.

2. Know the true value of his forecasting techniques.

3. Be able to state clearly his objectives and assumptions.

4. Be able to gather pertinent data and be able to validly expunge it of extraordinary observations.

5. Be humble in his opinions.

Finally *an appropriate forecasting strategy* for any organization depends on:

1. The number and the competence of existing forecasters. (In most companies no one man can do it all.)

2. The amount of budget made available for generating forecasts.

3. The availability of computer-based data processing facilities.

4. The timing and accuracy of forecasts required.

5. The availability and extent of historical and current data.

6. The ability of decision makers (managers) to cope with sophisticated statistical and/or other rational approaches.

A large number of techniques and systems for casting forward past patterns exist. We shall present only a small selection of these which we have found useful in our own consulting experience. These techniques, at best, can form only a part of any total forecasting system which must be imbedded within the particular style of management being practiced.

4.2 *Aggregate Longer-Term Forecasts*

We shall begin with a short overview of techniques that are usually applied to longer term forecasts such as are required by the aggregate production planning models discussed in Chapters 15–18. There is, of course, no hard and fast rule that prevents their use in forecasting individual item demand.

The techniques in this section require that the time series being forecast be relatively stable, especially with regard to annual seasonal swings and long-term trends. An aggregated time series, consisting of several products, usually is more stable than the sales pattern of an individual s.k.u. It is for this reason that we group the techniques in this section under the heading aggregate longer-term forecasts. When a time series is not stable and when we are dealing with individual s.k.u. we recommend the use of techniques to be discussed in Section 4.3. We start with a description of the general concepts involved.

4.2.1 *The Components of Time Series Analysis*

Any time series can be thought of as being composed of five components: level, trend (G), seasonal variations (F), cyclical movements (C), and irregular random fluctuations (e). Level captures the scale of a time series. Trend identifies the rate of growth or decline of a series over time. Seasonal variations can be of two kinds: (a) those resulting from natural forces and (b) those arising from man-made conventions. For example, in the northern United States and in Canada, the intensity of many types of economic activity depends on prevailing weather conditions. On the other hand, department store sales increase before Easter and Christmas, a circumstance related to man-made events. Cyclical variations or alternations between expansion and contraction of economic activity are the result of business cycles. Irregular fluctuations in time series analysis are the residue that remain after the effects of the other four components are identified and removed from the time series. Such fluctuations may be the result of *unusual* weather conditions, *unexpected* labor strife and all other forms of *unpredictable* events. In any case, they represent our ignorance as to what else may be affecting the time series we are studying.

Using these concepts one can formulate a *multiplicative model* of a time series:

$$\begin{aligned}\text{Sales} &= (\text{Trend}) * (\text{Seasonal}) * (\text{Cycle}) * (\text{Irregular}) \\ &= G * F * C * e \qquad (4.1)\end{aligned}$$

There are statistical procedures for isolating each of the four components from any time series (see, for example, Chapters 19–21, Spurr and Bonini[36]). Having identified the G, F, and C for a desired future period, one can compute a forecast from Eq. 4.1.

The choice of a multiplicative model is of course arbitrary. In the initialization procedure for the Winters Model, discussed later in section 4.3.6 of this chapter, a mixed additive-multiplicative model is used. The reader may wish to quickly scan those pages at this time.

4.2.2 *Least Squares Regression Analysis**

An alternative technique for forecasting the aggregate sales is given below for the data in Table 4.1:

Table 4.1 Historical Sales Data—MIDAS PSF Film

Year	t	d_t	Q_2	Q_3	Q_4
1974	1	412	0	0	0
	2	680	1	0	0
	3	477	0	1	0
	4	826	0	0	1
1975	5	471	0	0	0
	6	733	1	0	0
	7	529	0	1	0
	8	888	0	0	1

By using a computerized least squares regression package the following equation was fitted to the data:

$$\hat{d}_t = 399.13 + 14.125t + 250.88Q_2 + 33.25Q_3 + 373.13Q_4 \tag{4.2}$$

Note that Eq. 4.2 consists of a linear trend ($14.125t$) and seasonal "dummy variables" Q_2, Q_3, Q_4 which take on the value of 1 for the appropriate quarter and zero otherwise. Q_1 is always set to zero, that is, all seasonals are measured relative to the first quarter. Eq. 4.2 is a *linear* regression forecasting equation which allows for *seasonality.*

In general, of course, the trend in sales is not always linear. Alternatively a *curvilinear trend* could be fitted to the data, for example as in Eq. 4.3:

$$\hat{d}_t = w_1 + w_2 t + w_3 t^2 \tag{4.3}$$

Actually any order of polynomial could be fitted by regression. The reader is referred to a standard statistical text for examples of how polynomial trend lines can be fitted by regression.[17] In concept and in terms of the computerized regression packages there is very little difference between linear and curvilinear regression. The real difficulty that a forecaster faces in such

---

* *We shall assume that the reader is somewhat familiar with regression analysis. This section is intended to serve only as a reminder as to the models available. The reader who is unfamiliar with regression should refer to a statistics text such as Wesolowsky.*[40]

cases is in deciding whether for a particular time series it is more appropriate to assume a curvilinear rather than a linear trend. Furthermore, as was mentioned earlier, regression models assume that the underlying statistical process is stable. That is in the judgment of the forecaster, the cyclical pattern and gradient of the time series have been "similar" from year to year and probably will continue into the future in a "similar" fashion.

Before considering the case of less stable demand patterns, one last topic related to regression forecasts remains to be mentioned. In section 4.1 we listed, as one of the requirements of a good forecast, an estimate of the probable range of actual demand around the expected (forecasted) value. That is, a forecasting system always should include an estimate of the possible forecast error. An estimate of the standard deviation of forecast error can be obtained from regression theory.[36] In practice, this estimate of forecast error is too often neglected, reducing the value of the forecast given.

4.3 *Individual Item Short Term Forecasts*

When dealing with forecasts of demand for individual s.k.u., it is less likely that the demand patterns from year to year remain relatively constant ("similar"). For these circumstances we shall recommend in this section several models which attempt to allow for changes in demand patterns over time.

4.3.1 *The Moving Average*

The moving average method assumes that the following data generating process underlies a time series:

$$d_t = \bar{d} + e \tag{4.4}$$

where:

d_t is actual sales over period t (a random variable).

$\bar{d}$ is the expected (or average) sales for period t.

e is a random variable with a mean of zero and constant variance σ_e, over time.

The model in Eq. 4.4 describes a situation where the basic underlying demand generating process is constant from one period to the next, but random unforeseen events can alter the actual demand from the constant rate ($\bar{d}$) for any particular period. We need to forecast (monitor) demand in such situations because in practice we usually do not know the exact value of $\bar{d}$. Furthermore, the value of $\bar{d}$ is always subject to a sudden change to a new level in response to say the arrival of a new competitor in the market which reduces the share of the total market available to the product being forecasted.

A moving forecast of level demand can be calculated from:

$$\bar{d}_{t,N} = (d_t + d_{t-1} + \ldots + d_{t-N+1})(1/N) \tag{4.5}$$

$$= \bar{d}_{t-1,N} + \frac{d_t - d_{t-N}}{N}$$

where:

$\bar{d}_{t,N}$ is the N period moving average calculated at time t (the end of period t).

N is the number of past periods selected for calculating the moving average.

Note that the moving average is simply the mean of the N most recent observations. By taking an N period average the forecaster hopes to smooth out the random fluctuations, e, to obtain a good estimate of the basic underlying average demand rate, $\bar{d}$. Provided that the model in Eq. 4.4 holds, we know from statistical theory that $\bar{d}_{t,N}$ is a best estimator (forecastor) of $\bar{d}$ and that the standard error of the estimate (the forecast error) is given by:

$$\hat{\sigma}_{\bar{d}} = \frac{\sigma_e}{\sqrt{N}} \tag{4.6}$$

Note that the larger the value of N the more precise will be the estimate of $\bar{d}$, provided Eq. 4.4 holds stable for long periods of time. But the size of N also determines how responsive $\bar{d}_{t,N}$ is to the most recent fluctuation, e_t. Only a few time series of demand actually follow the model given in Eq. 4.4 *exactly*, especially for long periods of time. The value of $\bar{d}$, while constant over significant intervals of time, usually shifts up or down moderately in practice in response to sudden changes in market conditions. Under unstable circumstances a smaller value of N is preferable. In the moving average $\bar{d}_{t,N}$ each historical sales observation is weighted by $1/N$. The smaller the value of N the greater the weight put on the most recent data. We shall discuss the selection of an appropriate size for N in conjunction with the selection of smoothing constants later in this chapter. Recall that at MIDAS all inventory decision rules were based, in effect, on a five month moving average forecast of demand.

4.3.2 *Simple Exponential Smoothing*

An alternative approach to forecasting the level demand process in Eq. 4.4 is called simple exponential smoothing:

$$\begin{aligned}\bar{d}_t &= ad_t + (1-a)\bar{d}_{t-1} \\ &= \bar{d}_{t-1} + a(d_t - \bar{d}_{t-1}) \qquad (4.7)\end{aligned}$$

where:

$\bar{d}_t$ is the exponentially smoothed average calculated at time t.

a is a smoothing constant, $0 \leq a \leq 1$.

Note that $\bar{d}_t$ is calculated by taking a fraction (a) of current demand plus a fraction (1-a) of the most recent smoothed average, $\bar{d}_{t-1}$. (See also Figure 4.1 for an interpretation of the second line of Eq. 4.7.) The difference $(d_t - \bar{d}_{t-1})$ is an estimate of e_t, the random fluctuation in Eq. 4.4. Practically speaking, one doesn't ever really know whether any particular difference $(d_t - \bar{d}_{t-1})$ results from a random fluctuation or whether a significant shift in $\bar{d}$ has occurred. As a result, the simple exponential smoothing model always hedges by assuming that only a fraction of the forecast error should be used to revise $\bar{d}_t$ (the second line of Eq. 4.7).

Figure 4.1 The Components of an Exponentially Smoothed Average.

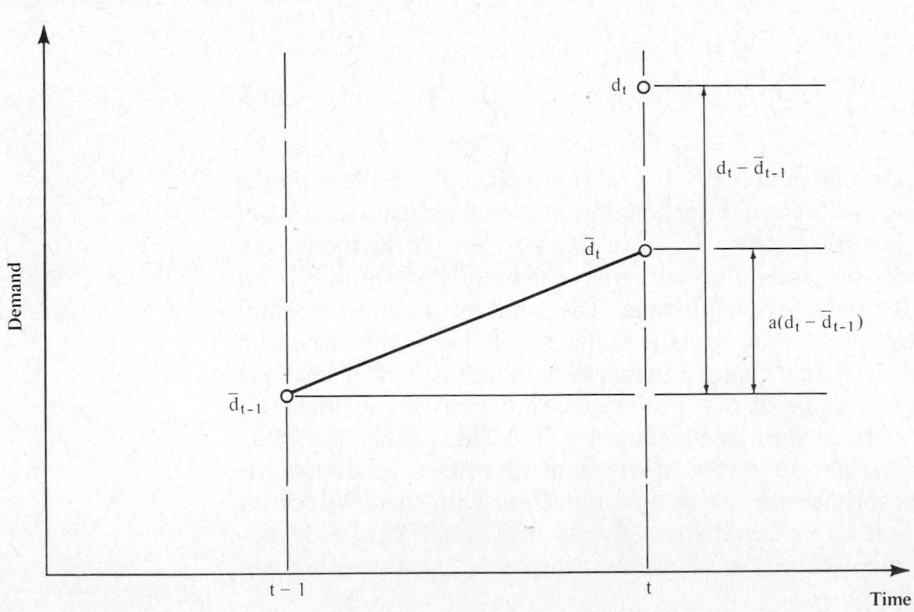

In practice the value of a ranges from 0.01 to 0.30. The longer the forecast update period, the larger should be the smoothing constant, a. Over a longer period conditions are more likely to have changed.

If we substitute in Eq. 4.7 the corresponding equation for the smoothed value $\bar{d}_{t-1}$, and then recursively substitute the corresponding equation for the smoothed value $\bar{d}_{t-2}$, and so on, we get:

$$\begin{aligned}\bar{d}_t &= ad_t + (1-a)\bar{d}_{t-1} \\ &= ad_t + (1-a)[ad_{t-1} + (1-a)\bar{d}_{t-2}] \\ &= ad_t + a(1-a)d_{t-1} + (1-a)^2\bar{d}_{t-2} \\ &= ad_t + a(1-a)d_{t-1} + a(1-a)^2 d_{t-2} \\ &\quad + \ldots + a(1-a)^k d_{t-k} + \ldots + (1-a)^t \bar{d}_0 \\ &= a\sum_{k=0}^{t-1}(1-a)^k d_{t-k} + (1-a)^t\bar{d}_0 \qquad (4.8)\end{aligned}$$

In Eq. 4.8 $\bar{d}_0$ represents the initial value assigned to the smoothed average. In practice, $\bar{d}_0$ is usually taken as equal to the average of the most recent observations, if available. If such data is not available, then the forecaster must guess at an initial value and let the smoothing process in Eq. 4.7 modify his guess through subsequent iterations until a reasonably stable value of $\bar{d}_t$ is achieved. Often a high value of a is used over the run-in-period until a stable value is attained.

The name, *exponential smoothing*, derives from Eq. 4.8 where the historical sales data of period t—k are respectively weighted by $a(1-a)^k$. The greater the age of a sales figure, the larger the value of k. Therefore, each past sales figure contributes *exponentially* less and less to the prevailing smoothed average, $\bar{d}_t$. This is in direct contrast to the moving average method, $\bar{d}_{t,N}$, where all historical data used received the same weighting, $1/N$.

Simple exponential smoothing models also require less computation and less storage of data than is the case with moving averages. This is especially important if the forecasting procedures for thousands of s.k.u. have to be computerized. A simple exponential smoothing model requires only the storage of 2 pieces of data (the smoothing constant, a, and the last smoothed average, $\bar{d}_{t-1}$) as opposed to the N pieces of data required to calculate $\bar{d}_{t,N}$.

Every simple exponential smoothing model implies, *in theory*, a moving average of an equivalent number of months. Brown[6] calculates a theoretically equivalent value of a, (equivalent only in terms of the average age of data used):

$$a = 2/(N+1) \qquad (4.9)$$

A moving average of $N=12$ months is often used to average out (eliminate) seasonal cycles in a time series. A common mistake made in practice, because of Eq. 4.9, is that in simple exponential smoothing of monthly data, a smoothing constant of $a=2/(12+1)=0.154$ is used with the intent of eliminating seasonal cycles. *But an a of* 0.154 *will not eliminate seasonal variation, because Eq.* 4.9 *only equates the average age of the data being used.*

Illustration

For MIDAS product PSF-008, a film ordered from Germany, we would proceed as follows. A five month moving average would be equivalent on the average to an $a = 2/(5+1) = 1/3$. That is, a value of 1/3 would result in an average age of data used by the exponentially smoothed average of $(N-1)/2$ or two months.

Table 4.2 Moving Average and Simple Exponential Smoothing Forecasts For PSF-008, using N=5 and a=1/3 (all data in×10² square meters)

Year (1)	Month t (2)	Sales d_t (3)	5-Mo. Moving Avg. $\bar{d}_{t,5}$ (4)	Exponen. Smoothed Avg. $\bar{d}_t$ (5)	Forecasts $\hat{d}_{t+1}=\bar{d}_{t,5}$ (6)	Forecasts $\hat{d}_{t+1}=\bar{d}_t$ (7)
1977	1	52				
	2	48				
	3	36		(50.0)		
	4	49		(49.7)		
	5	65	50.0	(54.8)	50.0	54.8[a]
	6	54	50.4	54.5	50.4	54.5[a]
	7	60	52.8	56.3	52.8[a]	56.3
	8	48	55.2	53.6	55.2	53.6[a]
	9	51	55.6	52.7	55.6	52.7[a]
	10	62	55.0	55.8	55.0	55.8[a]
	11	66	57.4	59.2	57.4	59.2[a]
	12	62	57.8	60.1	57.8	60.1
1978	1					

[a] Closer to actual sales.

In Table 4.2, the average of the first 5 month's sales (50.0) is taken as the initial value for the exponentially smoothed average and plotted opposite $t=3$ the mid-point of the 5-month range of the average. Then the exponentially smoothed average in column 5 for month 4 is calculated by taking:

$$\bar{d}_4 = \tfrac{1}{3}\, d_4 + \tfrac{2}{3}\, \bar{d}_3$$

$$= \tfrac{1}{3}\,(49) + \tfrac{2}{3}\,(50)$$

$$= 49.7$$

The same procedure was repeated for all subsequent months. For months 4 and 5 no exponentially smoothed forecasts were issued to allow the effect of setting initial conditions at $\bar{d}_3 = 50.0$ to be smoothed out. This is commonly referred to as the "run-in-period."

In column 4 the five month moving averages are calculated using Eq. 4.5. Two forecasts are then issued by setting:

$$\hat{d}_{t+1} = \bar{d}_{t,N} \quad \text{(in column 6)}$$

and

$$\hat{d}_{t+1} = \bar{d}_t \quad \text{(in column 7)}$$

Note that the exponential smoothing forecast outperforms the five month moving average forecast for 6 of the 7 months of 1977, illustrated in Table 4.2. This appears to be a result of the fact that using an $a = 1/3$ makes the simple exponential smoothing forecast more responsive to recent sales data variation than the five month moving average. Since the time series, d_t appears to be undergoing changes, this degree of responsiveness appears to be warranted for the particular example shown.

In general, one has to determine the appropriate value of a or N experimentally for as many cases as possible by trial and error simulation using past sales data in a manner similar to Table 4.2. However, the analyst should guard against spending too much time in super fine-tuning.

4.3.3 *Double Exponential Smoothing*

Double exponential smoothing is used when the forecasted time series exhibits a linear trend. The following data-generating model is assumed to underlie the process:

$$d_t = \bar{d} + Gt + e \tag{4.10}$$

where:

G is the rate of change in demand per period t (the gradient).

The model in Eq. 4.10 describes a situation where the basic demand is constantly increasing (or decreasing) at a rate G (see Figure 4.2). Actual demand at any time t varies randomly about the trend line.

We have previously defined a simple exponential smoothing average as:

$$\bar{d}_t = ad_t + (1-a)\bar{d}_{t-1}$$

Figure 4.2 The Components of a Doubly Smoothed Exponential Average.

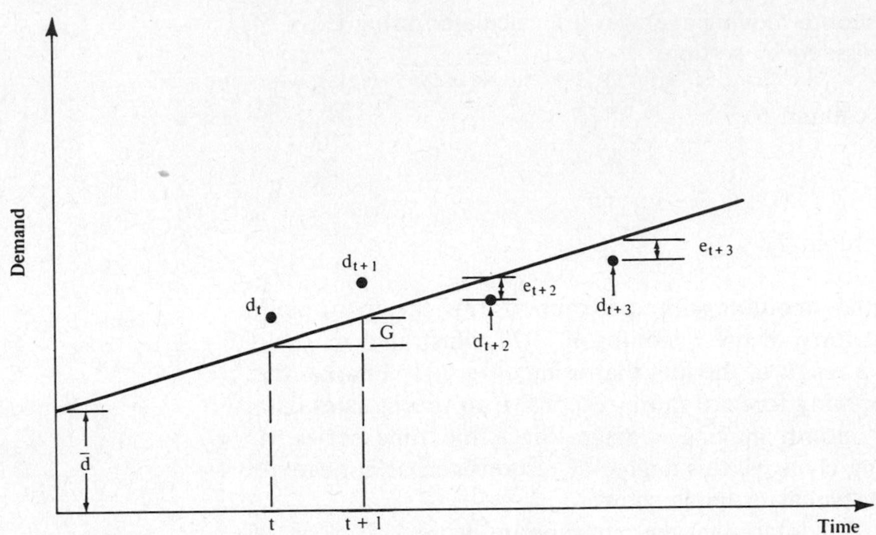

Similarly a doubly smoothed exponential smoothing average can be defined by the following equation:

$$\bar{d}_t^{(2)} = a\bar{d}_t + (1-a)\bar{d}_{t-1}^{(2)} \tag{4.11}$$

The superscript (2) in Eq. 4.11 denotes the fact that we are dealing with a doubly smoothed average. Brown has shown that the intercept and slope of the trend line can be estimated by setting:*

$$\begin{aligned} \bar{d} &= 2\bar{d}_t - \bar{d}_t^{(2)} \\ G &= \frac{a}{1-a}(\bar{d}_t - \bar{d}_t^{(2)}) \end{aligned} \tag{4.12}$$

* *For* detailed derivations, see R. G. Brown[6], pp. 128–144. *The derivations are based on minimizing the sum of discounted least squares, similar to deriving the normal equations in linear regression. The discount factor is intimately related to the smoothing constant, a.*

and the forecast equation becomes:

$$\hat{d}_{t+j} = \bar{d} + Gj = [2\bar{d}_t - \bar{d}_t^{(2)}] + \left[\frac{a}{1-a}(\bar{d}_t - \bar{d}_t^{(2)})\right]j \tag{4.13}$$

where:
j is the number of periods into the future that the forecast is projected

Note that if there is no linear trend, then $G = 0$ and from Eq. 4.12, $\bar{d}_t = \bar{d}_t^{(2)}$. Substituting into Eq. 4.13 we would simply get:

$$\hat{d}_{t+j} = \bar{d}_t$$

That is, the double exponential smoothing model simplifies to the simple exponential case, discussed in the previous section. A numerical illustration of double exponential smoothing, using the data for PSF-008 from Table 4.2, is shown in Table 4.3, column 5. Double exponential smoothing forecasts for PSF-008 are given in column 8. Note that the sum of columns 6 and 7 in any period t, add to the forecast shown for the subsequent period $(t+1)$, actually made at the beginning of that period (or equivalently, at the end of period t).

4.3.4 *Triple Exponential Smoothing*

A triple exponential smoothing model is used in forecasting when the underlying time series is believed to consist of a linear trend whose slope is continually increasing or decreasing over time. That is, suppose the following underlying time series model holds true:

$$d_t = \bar{d} + G_1 t + \tfrac{1}{2} G t^2 + e \tag{4.14}$$

Note that the derivative of d_t with respect to t is:

$$G_1 + G_2 t$$

That is, the slope of the curve defined in Eq. 4.21 changes with time at the rate of G_2. A common error made by some forecasters is to assume that triple exponential smoothing models allow explicitly for the seasonality of demand. This, of course is not the case, as is evident from Eq. 4.14. The computation procedure for triple smoothing becomes quite involved and is discussed in detail by Brown.*

---

* R. G. Brown,[6], pp. 132–142. *Once again the derivation involves minimizing the sum of least squares as in ordinary linear regression. Brown also has treated mathematically the more general case of higher order smoothing.*

Table 4.3 Double Exponentially Smoothed Averages (For PSF-008, Using $a = 1/3$)

Year (1)	Month t (2)	Sales d_t (3)	Single Smooth. Avg. $\bar{d}_t$ (4)	Double Smooth Avg. $\bar{d}_t^{(2)}$ (5)	$\bar{d} = 2\bar{d}_t - \bar{d}_t^{(2)}$ (6)	$G = [a/(1-a)](\bar{d}_t - \bar{d}_t^{(2)})$ (7)	Forecast (8)
1977	1	52					
	2	48					
	3	36	(50.0) ⟶	(50.0)			
	4	49	(49.7)	(49.9)			
	5	65	(54.8)	(51.5)			
	6	54	54.5	52.5	56.5	1.0	
	7	60	56.3	53.8	58.9	1.3	57.5
	8	48	53.6	53.7	53.4	−0.1	60.2
	9	51	52.7	53.4	52.0	−0.3	53.3
	10	62	55.8	54.2	57.4	0.8	51.7
	11	66	59.2	55.9	62.5	1.7	58.2
	12	62	60.1	57.3	63.0	1.4	64.2
1978	1						64.4

4.3.5 *Autoregressive Models*

Forecasting methods accounting for correlations in the sequence of observations in a time series are called autoregressive models. For example, if d_t and d_{t+1} are two successive values in a time series, then a *first order* (linear) autoregressive model would assume that:

$$d_{t+1} = w_4 + w_5 d_t + e \tag{4.15}$$

where the coefficients w_4 and w_5 in Eq. 4.15 must be estimated from past sales data by least squares regression methods. Actually, in general, one does not have to limit oneself to first order or linear models such as in Eq. 4.15. The number of independent variables on the right hand side of the equation is limited only by a modeller's ability to rationally explain any correlations that are found empirically to exist between the dependent and independent variables. For example, a second order model including a quadratic term in period t could be specified as:

$$d_{t+1} = w_6 + w_7 d_t + w_8 d_t^2 + w_9 d_{t-1} + e$$

As an example of first order autocorrelation we chose another product XMC-081, a chemical manufactured to order by MIDAS International in Germany. Historical sales data and the resulting autoregressive forecasts are given in Table 4.4.

Table 4.4 First-Order Autoregression Forecasts for XMC-081

Year (1)	Month t (2)	Sales d_t (3)	Sales d_{t-1} (4)	Forecast (5)	Forecast Error (6)
1977	1	52	50		
	2	86	52		
	3	102	86		
	4	118	102		
	5	135	118		
	6	130	135		
	7	150	130		
	8	156	150		
	9	159	156		
	10	161	159		
	11	167	161	164.6	−2.4
	12	150	167	169.7	19.7

By using the first 10 months of data from column 3 as the dependent variable and the first 10 months of data from column 4 as the independent variable we estimated the following forecast equation by linear regression:

$$\hat{d}_{t+1} = 27.7 + 0.85 d_t \tag{4.16}$$

The slope coefficient for Eq. 4.16, is highly significantly different from zero (the associated $t = 9.50$). Therefore, a strong first order autocorrelation seems to be present in the data. Using Eq. 4.16, we issued in columns 5 and 6 of Table 4.4, two forecasts for months $t = 11$ and 12. For sake of brevity we will not discuss here the logical reasons of why there was autocorrelation in the time series for XMC-081. Before Eq. 4.16 is accepted as a forecast equation such rationalizations should be clearly verbalized. Unfortunately, with thousands of s.k.u. to be forecasted, this is not always feasible in practice. As a result, exponential smoothing models are more commonly used in individual item inventory control because the modelling strategy used emphasizes *feedback*. That is, forecast errors are monitored and cause the basic forecast model to change in response. This does not happen routinely with the autoregression such as Eq. 4.16, unless the linear regression equation is reestimated periodically.

4.3.6 *The Winters Exponential Smoothing Model with Seasonal Factors*

A number of exponential smoothing models, that incorporate seasonal and trend factors directly, have been proposed. Most of these models differ only on specifics, while implementing the same basic smoothing concept. For example, some models incorporate trend and seasonal indices through additive factors, others propose the use of multiplicative terms. McClain and Thomas[26] explored the relationships among several of the more common exponential smoothing models and concluded that they were equivalent in the sense that one could achieve identical forecasts if the smoothing constants were selected carefully. We shall therefore present only one exponential smoothing forecasting model that was originally proposed by Peter Winters[42].

In the Winters model:

$$\bar{d}_t = a[d_t / F_{t-N}] + (1-a)[\bar{d}_{t-1} + G_{t-1}] \tag{4.17}$$

where:

$\bar{d}_t$ is the simple exponentially smoothed level* (deseasonalized) calculated at the end of period t.

---

* *We previously defined $\bar{d}_t$ as a smoothed average. We shall follow the terminology used in the original Winters article in this section. Conceptually the definition of $\bar{d}_t$ has not changed.*

$\bar{d}_{t-1}$ is the simple exponentially smoothed level (deseasonalized) calculated at the end of period $t-1$.

d_t is the actual sales during period t.

a is a smoothing constant, $0 \leq a \leq 1$.

N is the number of periods in the season.

F_{t-N} is the multiplicative seasonal factor obtained one season earlier, namely at the end of period $(t-N)$.

G_{t-1} is the trend for period $(t-1)$.

Seasonality factors are updated once every season according to:

$$F_t = b[d_t/\bar{d}_t] + (1-b)F_{t-N} \tag{4.18}$$

b is the seasonal smoothing constant, $0 \leq b \leq 1$.

Trend is accounted for linearly and the trend factor is updated each period using:

$$G_t = c[\bar{d}_t - \bar{d}_{t-1}] + (1-c)G_{t-1} \tag{4.19}$$

where:

c is the trend smoothing constant, $0 \leq c \leq 1$.

G_t is the per period additive trend factor.

Eqs. 4.17, 4.18, 4.19 give exponentially smoothed values updated according to patterns evident in historical data. The forecast, based on these values, is given by:

$$\hat{d}_{t+j} = [\bar{d}_t + jG_t]F_{t+j-N} \tag{4.20}$$

where:

$\hat{d}_{t+j}$ is the forecast for j periods hence from time t. The hat on d_{t+j}, as earlier, designates an estimate.

Initial Conditions—The series of equations leading up to Eq. 4.20 must at some point in time receive initial values for the 3 basic types of parameters: $\bar{d}_0$, G_0, and (F_i; $i=-N+1, -N+2, \ldots, -1, 0$). The effect of initial conditions on the stability and reliability of subsequent forecasts depends on the size of smoothing constants used and the length of the time series preceding $t=0$ (the present period) over which initial conditions are determined. Most exponential smoothing models have to be initialized in a somewhat arbitrary, though hopefully logical fashion. As a result, it is advisable to use a sufficiently long run-in period during which initial parameters can be stabilized over a sample of past time series data, by use of the revision (updating) process specified by Eqs. 4.17, 4.18, 4.19. The effect of initial values $\bar{d}_0$ and G_0 will usually be attenuated sooner than those for (F_i; $i=-N+1, -N+2, \ldots, -1, 0$) because $\bar{d}_t$ and G_t are revised every period, whereas the seasonal factors F_t are revised only once every N periods (that is, once every season).*

Winters proposed the following procedure for obtaining initial values. The steps below should be followed by referring to Figure 4.3:

a. Calculate the average sales per period over the last two N period seasons, (usually a year in length). (The present period is subscripted as $j=0$, therefore the two initialization years have negative subscripts.)

$$V_1 = \frac{1}{N} \sum_{j=(-2N+1)}^{-N} d_j$$

$$V_2 = \frac{1}{N} \sum_{j=-(N-1)}^{0} d_j \tag{4.21}$$

b. Then the initial value G_o, the trend per period, is given by:

$$G_0 = \frac{V_2 - V_1}{N} \tag{4.22}$$

---

* *The initialization procedure that we describe assumes the existence of 2 years of historical data. This amount of data will not always be available, for example, for new products. In such cases we must resort to asking knowledgeable persons to provide us with guesstimates for the values of level, trend, and seasonal factors. Alternatively we could use the historical time series of another product that is considered to behave in a like manner. In either case the effect of these initial estimates must subsequently be carefully monitored during a run-in period of at least one season in length. During this period the use of large values for all smoothing constants is advisable and month by month the consequences of the initial guesstimates should be fed back to knowledgeable persons.*

Figure 4.3 Graphical Representation of Initialization ($N=4$).

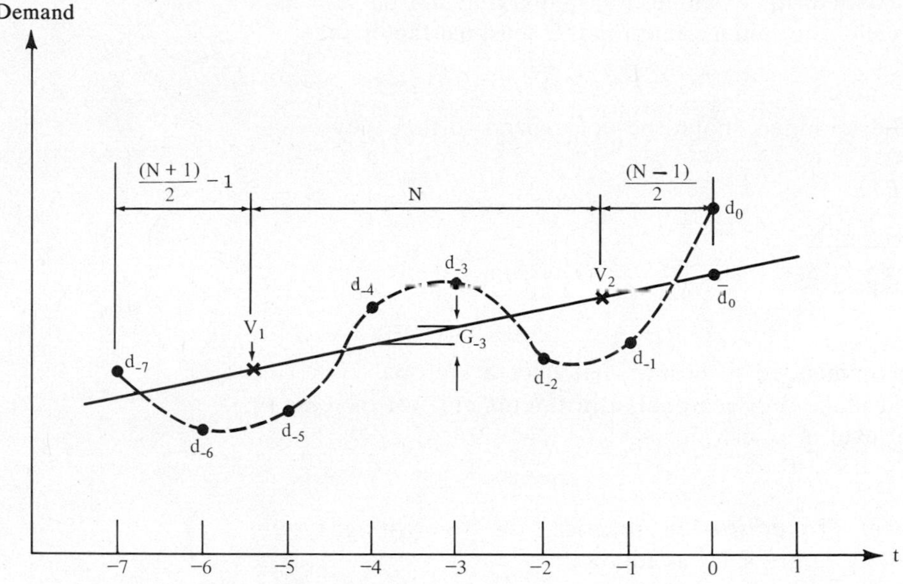

c. And the initial value $\bar{d}_0$ can be calculated from the level at the midpoint of the most recent season, V_2:

$$\bar{d}_0 = V_2 + G_0\left(\frac{N-1}{2}\right) \tag{4.23}$$

where $\bar{d}_0$ is the smoothed level at the end of the most recent season.

d. The initial seasonal factors can then be derived from:

$$F_t = \frac{d_t}{V_i - \left(\frac{N+1}{2} - j\right)G_0} \tag{4.24}$$

where:

V_i is the level at the midpoint of the appropriate season (year) and j is the position of the period t within the season, e.g., for January, $j=1$; for February, $j=2$, etc.

e. The seasonal factors for each of the initial years (if more than one year's data is available) should be averaged. That is, all F's calculated, for example, for January should be averaged to yield one initial value for the seasonal factor for January, etc.

f. Finally, the seasonals should be normalized so that they add to N.

$$F_j = \frac{(\text{Average } F_j)\, N}{\sum_{i=1}^{N} \text{Average } F_i}$$

The last step was recommended to ensure that over a seasonal cycle, the seasonal factors would make only seasonal adjustments and not increase or decrease the average level of sales.

Computational Procedure—In practice, the forecasting system would be used to predict future sales as follows:

a. The initial values of $\bar{d}_0$, G_0 and (F_i; $i = -N+1, -N+2, \ldots, -1, 0$) are calculated.

b. At the end of the period $t = 1$ actual sales, d_t, are recorded.

c. Equation 4.17 is applied to revise $\bar{d}_t$.

d. Equation 4.18 is applied to revise F_t.

e. Equation 4.19 is applied to revise G_t.

f. Equation 4.20 is applied to forecast sales d_{t+j} for ($j = 1, 2, \ldots$) periods into the future.

g. At the end of period $t+1$ actual sales are recorded and steps c, d, e, f are repeated, etc.

Illustration

The quarterly sales for product EDM-617, a bracket used by the assembly department at MIDAS, during the past two years are given in Table 4.5.

Table 4.5 Quarterly Sales EDM-617

Year, i	Quarter	Period, t	Demand, d_t
1974 (1)	1	−7	43
	2	−6	57
	3	−5	71
	4	−4	46
1975 (2)	1	−3	50
	2	−2	61
	3	−1	85
	4	0	47

The following computations are required to forecast sales for quarter 1, 1976:

Initialization

a. The average sales for years 1 and 2 are:

$$V_1 = \frac{43+57+71+46}{4} = 54.3$$

$$V_2 = \frac{50+61+85+47}{4} = 60.8$$

b. The initial value of trend is given by:

$$G_0 = \frac{V_2 - V_1}{N} = \frac{60.8-54.3}{4} = 1.6 \text{ units/period}$$

c. The initial value for level is given by:

$$\begin{aligned}\bar{d}_0 &= V_2 + G_0\left(\frac{N-1}{2}\right)\\ &= 60.8 + 1.6\left(\frac{4-1}{2}\right)\\ &= 60.8 + 2.4\\ &= 63.2 \text{ units.}\end{aligned}$$

d. The initial values of the seasonal factors are given by

$$F_t = \frac{d_t}{V_i - \left(\dfrac{N+1}{2} - j\right)G_0}$$

where j (equal to 1,2,3,4) is the position of period t in a season.

For example, for quarter 1, 1974 ($t=-7$):

$$F_{-7}=\frac{d_{-7}}{V_1-\left(\frac{4+1}{2}-1\right)G_0}$$

$$=\frac{43}{54.3-1.5(1.6)}$$

$$=0.83$$

Similarly the initial seasonal factors for other periods can be calculated, as shown in Table 4.6.

Table 4.6 Initial Seasonal Factors

Year	Quarter, j	Period, t	Seasonal Factor, F_t
1	1	−7	0.83
	2	−6	1.07
	3	−5	1.29
	4	−4	0.81
2	1	−3	0.86
	2	−2	1.02
	3	−1	1.38
	4	0	0.74

The average values of the seasonality factors from Table 4.6 must be stored for the second year:

$$F'_{-3}=\frac{F_{-7}+F_{-3}}{2}=\frac{0.83+0.86}{2}=0.85$$

Similarily:

$$F'_{-2}=1.05$$

$$F'_{-1}=1.34$$

$$F'_0=0.78$$

Next, the seasonality factors must be normalized so as to add to unity.

The sum of Seasonality factors,

$$
\begin{aligned}
S &= F'_{-3} + F'_{-2} + F'_{-1} + F'_0 \\
&= 0.85 + 1.05 + 1.34 + 0.78 \\
&= 4.02
\end{aligned}
$$

$$
\begin{aligned}
F_{-3} &= F'_{-3}\, N/S \\
&= 0.85 \times 4/4.02 \\
&= 0.85
\end{aligned}
$$

As a result, the normalized initial seasonal factors become those given in Table 4.7.

Table 4.7 Normalized Initial Seasonal Factors

Period, t	Seasonality Factors, F_t
−3	0.85
−2	1.04
−1	1.33
0	0.78
	4.00

The Forecasts—The Forecast of sales for 1976, quarter 1 ($j = 1$) can now be calculated from Eq. 4.20:

$$
\begin{aligned}
\hat{d}_{t+j} &= [\bar{d}_t + jG_t]F_{t+j-N} \\
\hat{d}_1 &= [\bar{d}_0 + 1G_0]F_{-3} \\
&= [63.2 + 1.6]0.85 \\
&= 55.1 \text{ units}
\end{aligned}
$$

Similarily:

$$
\begin{aligned}
\hat{d}_2 &= [\bar{d}_0 + 2G_0]F_{-2} \\
&= [63.2 + 3.2]1.04 \\
&= 69.1 \text{ units}
\end{aligned}
$$

$$
\begin{aligned}
\hat{d}_3 &= [\bar{d}_0 + 3G_0]F_{-1} \\
&= [63.2 + 4.8]1.33 \\
&= 90.4 \text{ units}
\end{aligned}
$$

$$
\begin{aligned}
\hat{d}_4 &= [\bar{d}_0 + 4G_0]F_0 \\
&= [63.2 + 6.4]0.78 \\
&= 54.3 \text{ units}
\end{aligned}
$$

We could forecast as many periods, j, into the future as we desired by *reusing* the appropriate seasonal factors. Of course, for larger j values we would expect the accuracy of our forecasts to diminish.

Up-dating Trend, Smoothed Level, and Seasonality Factor— Suppose the actual sales for quarter 1 of 1976 were 69 units. The apparent Level, Seasonality Factor, and Trend can now be updated (revised). Assume that the smoothing constants, a, b, and c have values 0.2, 0.2, and 0.1 respectively:

a. The revised value of Level is given by (see Eq. 4.17):

$$\begin{aligned}\bar{d}_1 &= a[d_1/F_{-3}) + (1-a)[\bar{d}_0 + G_0] \\ &= 0.2[69/0.85] + 0.8[63.2 + 1.6] \\ &= 68.1\end{aligned}$$

b. The revised Seasonality Factor is given by (see Eq. 4.18):

$$\begin{aligned}F_1 &= b[d_1/\bar{d}_1] + (1-b)F_{-3} \\ &= 0.2[69/68.1] + 0.8(0.85) \\ &= 0.88\end{aligned}$$

c. The revised estimate of trend is given by (see Eq. 4.19):

$$\begin{aligned}G_1 &= c[\bar{d}_1 - \bar{d}_0] + (1-c)G_0 \\ &= 0.1[68.1 - 63.2] + 0.9(1.6) \\ &= 1.93\end{aligned}$$

Note that sales for period 1 were forecasted as 55.1 units. Actual sales turned out to be 69 units, that is, a forecast error of −13.9 units resulted. Because of the forecast error the Level was adjusted upward from 64.8 to 68.1 units, the seasonality factor was adjusted upward from 0.85 to 0.88 and the apparent trend estimate was increased from 1.60 to 1.93 units. These new estimates can now be substituted into the forecast Eq. 4.20 and a set of revised forecasts calculated. For 1976, quarter 2 ($t = 1, j = 1$):

$$\begin{aligned}\hat{d}_{t+j} &= [\bar{d}_t + jG_t]F_{t+j-N} \\ \hat{d}_2 &= [\bar{d}_1 + 1G_1]F_{-2} \\ &= [68.1 + 1.93]1.04 \\ &= 72.8 \text{ units}\end{aligned}$$

Similarily all subsequent forecasts can now be revised (see Table 4.8).

Table 4.8 Effect of Forecast Error In Period 1 on Forecasts of Demand for Later Periods

Period, t	Forecast Calculated at $t=0$	Forecast Calculated at $t=1$
1	55.1	69 (Actual)
2	69.1	72.8
3	90.4	95.7
4	54.3	57.6

Note that in Table 4.8 all forecasts for future periods had to be revised as a result of the forecast error of −13.9 units in quarter 1, 1976.

Once the figure for actual sales in quarter 2, 1976 becomes available, the above procedures must be repeated—the three parameters (level, seasonal factor, and trend) revised and a new set of revised forecasts issued.

4.3.7 *Fourier Series Methods for Forecasting a Seasonal Time Series*

In choosing to model a time series using Fourier methods a forecaster assumes that the process being forecast is periodic, at least in terms of seasonal factors. A periodic function is one whose values repeat after a while. The length of time before any series of values is repeated is called a period. Any periodic time series can be reproduced mathematically by adding a sufficient number of sine and cosine functions in a Fourier Series (see, for example, Selby[35]). R. G. Brown[5] describes a transcendental forecasting model of this type. While such models are becoming more common in practice, we prefer the Winters model in modelling seasonality, because we have found it easier for most managers to understand.

4.3.8 *The Box–Jenkins Technique*

We have examined two basic strategies of designing forecasting models. In the first strategy, used by the techniques of time series decomposition, linear regression, and autoregression, a forecast of the next value in a time series was derived from *previous values* of the same time series. The second strategy, implemented by the techniques of exponential smoothing, the transcendental model, and the moving average method, put emphasis on tracking *forecast errors* to determine an appropriate forecast. These two statistical design strategies in general do not lead to the same set of forecast values.

Box and Jenkins[4] have recently developed a systematic approach to modelling and forecasting discrete time series where *both* types of strategy are combined. Their generalized model, called the Autoregressive Integrated Moving Average Model (ARIMA), consists of several possible separate model combinations which can be chosen by an analyst. The analyst is provided with statistical aids with which to rationally eliminate available inappropriate model combinations until he is left with the one he considers most suitable. Judgement and the industrial experience of a forecaster play a very important part in the modelling process. The ARIMA methodology consists of three distinct steps:

1. An *identification procedure* for selecting potential models from the generalized ARIMA

2. The *estimation* of model parameters

3. An approach to *diagnostically check* the models to see if improvements can be made

The Box–Jenkins technique does not analyse the actual values in a time series directly, but instead models the *difference* between successive variable values and the mean value of the forecasted variable.

Theoretically speaking, the Box–Jenkins technique is probably the most general and complete. While the technique can be a highly successful short term forecasting technique, it has not been widely applied in practice in the area of individual item inventory control. Applications to date include forecasts of telephone installations, electric power generation and sales, common stock price movements, and in the control of chemical processes. Applications to date of the technique have been held back because of the level of mathematical notation used by most explanations and presentations of the technique.

In our experience we have found the Box–Jenkins model highly sensitive to historical values, which must be carefully selected so as not to mislead the estimation procedures. Outliers, especially, must be carefully handled. We do not recommend the use of ARIMA for forecasting the demand for individual s.k.u. primarily because it is relatively more expensive than exponential smoothing. The Box–Jenkins model is theoretically sound and future developments in this area will undoubtedly make it practically more usable by non-specialists. The method at present is useful where only a few time series need to be forecasted and where the attendant extra expense is warranted.

4.4 *Selection of the Exponential Smoothing Constants*

In this chapter we have discussed exponential smoothing techniques at some length. These techniques were presented as being particularly suitable for forecasting individual items in inventory control because they do not require the retention of a lot of historical data for each s.k.u. from one forecast period to the next and because they are relatively easy to understand. However, an exponential smoothing model's ability to track (especially sudden) changes in the sales pattern of an individual s.k.u. is critically dependent upon values of the smoothing constants (a, b, c) selected. Smoothing constants also determine the stability of any forecasting system subject to random fluctuations.

In general, the smoothing constant, a, is chosen by practitioners to be somewhere between 0.01 and 0.30. A large smoothing constant places substantial emphasis on current sales information, causing an exponential smoothing forecast to react quickly to changes in the expected pattern of the time series. A small smoothing constant results in emphasis being placed on previous sales data, thereby resulting in a stable forecast model that is less responsive to fluctuations in current sales.

Two basic strategies to selecting smoothing constants have been suggested. One approach requires a *judgment*, by the forecaster for each s.k.u., regarding the extent to which a particular time series is subject to random variations and/or major shifts in level. Guided by experience and some theoretical findings, as well as simulation techniques on occasion, the forecaster selects smoothing constants he deems appropriate. The second approach, called *adaptive smoothing*, is more dynamic in that initially selected smoothing constants are changed in response to forecast performance criteria built into the forecasting systems. Such decision models are usually computerized using equations which automatically adapt smoothing constants up or down in response to the size of recent forecast errors.

4.4.1 *Static Smoothing Constants*

By describing (or assuming that one knows) the critical characteristics of a time series *beforehand*, it is possible to determine mathematically optimal static smoothing constants in certain situations.[7,10] But, it is usually debatable whether the rigid assumptions required by such mathematical derivations, can be made before the fact. As a result, some intuitive or heuristic approach must usually be resorted to in practice.

Based on mathematical analysis, McClain[25] warns about possible instability of exponential models such as proposed by Winters. Of particular interest to us is his finding that if one increases the trend smoothing constant, c, when a change in trend is anticipated or apparent, the forecast may overshoot and oscillate about the new trend line. Therefore, we recommend that in the Winters model (see Eq. 4.18), the smoothing constant for trend, c, be kept small (say, no greater than 0.05). We also recommend that c should always be smaller than a, the smoothing constant for level. McClain and Thomas[26] have shown that the largest value of c which does not lead to oscillatory behavior under certain conditions is found by solving:

$$a = 4c/(1+c)^2 \tag{4.25}$$

Strictly speaking, Eq. 4.25 was derived only for the case when there are no seasonal terms in the forecast model and when an unexpected impulse occurred in the time series.

An empirical methodology for selecting smoothing constants is presented by Berry and Bliemel[3] and Winters.[42] They use a computer simulation approach applied to historical sales data to select smoothing constants for individual s.k.u.. The combination of a, b, and c which minimizes the standard deviation of forecast errors over a *historical* forecast period is selected for use in forecasting future sales. Two procedures called *grid search* and *pattern search* are compared with respect to forecast error and computing time.

The use of computer simulation to determine the smoothing constants for the thousands of s.k.u. in most inventories is cost-wise prohibitive. In practice, when static smoothing constants are used, a common set of a, b, and c is used for groups of s.k.u. that are deemed to be similar. Sometimes such a common set of smoothing constants is chosen through simulation. More often the set of smoothing constants is selected somewhat arbitrarily through experience in other similar situations. For example, we have found $a = 0.2$, $b = 0.1$, $c = 0.05$ reasonable in many situations.

4.4.2 *Adaptive Smoothing*

Adaptive smoothing techniques have been developed to deal with the problem of choosing the smoothing constant a, (for level) so that a forecasting system responds only to real shifts in a time series and ignores random variations, e_t. All adaptive smoothing approaches raise the value of the smoothing constant a in response to an apparent *drastic* change in level. Subsequently the value of a is lowered once the forecasting model has reached a new steady state, through an updating procedure, for example, as described by Eqs. 4.17 to 4.19.

Roberts and Whybark have compared four commonly used adaptive forecasting techniques which they categorize as shown in Table 4.9.[33]

Table 4.9 Classification of Adaptive Techniques

Method of Selecting, a	Periodic Evaluation	Continuous Evaluation
Unconstrained or Computed Value of Smoothing Constant	Eilon and Elmaleh	Trigg and Leach
Constrained or Pre-specified Choice of Smoothing Constant	Roberts and Reed	Whybark

The Eilon and Elmaleh approach to adaptive smoothing consists of setting the smoothing constant a to a fixed value, whereupon forecasts are made for a specified number of periods (called the evaluation interval). At the end of the evaluation interval, forecast errors are computed (post hoc) using the sales time series that actually occurred. Forecast errors are also computed for a range of permitted values ($a = 0.1$ to 0.9) to see what size forecast errors *would have* resulted if one of these values of a had been used over the evaluation interval.[16] The permitted value of the constant that would have minimized the forecast error variance over the historical evaluation interval is then used until the next evaluation interval. This procedure is repeated periodically over and over again.

Roberts and Reed have defined a technique for setting the smoothing constant for level (a) called evolutionary operation, which computes the sample error variance resulting over the evaluation interval from any prevailing smoothing constant and the error variance which would have resulted if the smoothing constant a had been 0.05 greater or less.[9,27,32] If it can be shown by a statistical test that the larger or smaller smoothing constant would have produced a smaller forecast error variance, then the value of a is set to the higher or lower value.

In 1967 Trigg and Leach[39] suggested a continuous evaluation approach which consists of the calculation of a tracking signal after each forecast period:

$$E_t = \bar{e}_t / |\bar{e}_t| \tag{4.26}$$

where:

E_t is the tracking signal.

$\bar{e}_t$ is the smoothed forecast error.

$|\bar{e}_t|$ is the smoothed *absolute* forecast error.

The forecast error and the absolute forecast error are both exponentially smoothed as follows:

$$\begin{aligned} e_t &= d_t - \hat{d}_t \\ \bar{e}_t &= he_t + (1-h)\bar{e}_{t-1} \\ |\bar{e}_t| &= h|e_t| + (1-h)|\bar{e}_{t-1}| \end{aligned} \tag{4.27}$$

where h is the tracking signal smoothing constant, $0 \le h \le 1$.

For an unbiased forecasting procedure the smoothed forecast error $\bar{e}_t$ should fluctuate about zero. Consider two consecutive forecast errors, one of which is positive, the other negative. It is seen from Eq. 4.27 that in the computation of $\bar{e}_t$ the effects of these two errors will tend to cancel one another. In contrast, in the computation of $|\bar{e}_t|$, where the absolute value of e_t is taken, no cancelling occurs. Continuing this line of reasoning we can write that:

$$-|\bar{e}_t| \le \bar{e}_t \le |\bar{e}_t|$$

The limiting equalities are achieved if all errors are positive or all errors are negative. From Eq. 4.26 the equivalent limits on the tracking signal E_t are:

$$-1 \le E_t \le 1$$

Moreover, E_t will be close to one of the limits if most of the errors are of the same sign, an indication that the forecasting system is biased (most of the forecasts are too high or most of the forecasts are too low). When such is the case we wish to adapt more rapidly to the new data, that is, we wish to increase the smoothing constant.

The Trigg–Leach approach to adaptive smoothing does precisely this by setting the smoothing constant for level (only) equal to the *absolute* value of the tracking signal at the end of each forecast period:

$$a_t = |E_t| \tag{4.28}$$

A similar approach has been proposed by D'Amico.[12]

An alternative approach to continuous monitoring of forecast errors was suggested by Whybark.[41] A change in the smoothing constant is triggered when a *single* forecast error is found to lie outside a range of ±4 standard deviations around zero, or when *two consecutive* forecast errors, in the same direction, lie outside ±1.2 standard deviations. The smoothing constant is immediately set to a high value for the next forecast period after the detection of a shift and then is reduced somewhat for the following periods. The smoothing constant is eventually returned to a base value until another shift is detected.

Whybark in his comparison of the four techniques (of Table 4.9) concluded that adaptive models require additional computation and this cost must be balanced in each and every application against the substantially improved forecasts. Continuous review approaches, as would be expected, performed better in his experiments, which involved time series characterized by random step shifts in level. For the selection of an appropriate adaptive smoothing technique we suggest the use of simulation models which have been calibrated to the cost and time series environment in which they must subsequently perform. (A brief discussion of simulation will be presented in Chapter 9.)

4.5 *Measuring the Variability of Forecast Errors*

In subsequent chapters we shall consider procedures for calculating safety stocks. Each of these procedures will require an estimate of forecast error variability over lead time (or lead time plus review interval). The most common measure used in practice is developed from the standard deviation of historical forecast errors.

4.5.1 *Estimating the Standard Deviation of Forecast Errors Over the Forecast Update Period*

The straightforward statistical estimate is

$$\sigma_1 = \sqrt{\sum_{j=1}^{n} (e_j - \bar{e})^2/(n-1)} = \sqrt{\frac{\sum_{j=1}^{n} e_j^2 - n(\bar{e})^2}{n-1}} \tag{4.29}$$

where

σ_1 is the estimated forecast error standard deviation over a one month forecast period (as indicated by the subscript).*

e_j is the forecast error $(d_j - \hat{d}_j)$ in period j.

* *In practice we could have a forecast period of any length, that is σ_1 or $\sigma_2, \ldots,$ or σ_n. The length of the forecast period is often referred to as the base period. We shall assume a base period of one month, its most common value in practice, for ease of presentation.*

$\bar{e}$ is the average forecast error over the last n periods. If the past forecasts have been unbiased then, $\bar{e} \doteq 0$.

Eq. 4.29 is easy enough to calculate for a single s.k.u. But for an inventory consisting of thousands of s.k.u. this relatively simple equation is not as practical computationally to use as the mean absolute deviation (MAD_1), which is defined as:

$$\text{MAD}_1 = \sum_{j=1}^{n} |e_j|/n \tag{4.30}$$

where $|e_j|$ is the absolute value of the forecast error for forecast period j.

In practice the MAD estimate is usually calculated recursively using the following smoothing equation:

$$\text{MAD}_{1,t} = h|d_t - \hat{d}_t| + (1-h)\text{MAD}_{1,t-1} \tag{4.31}$$

where h is a smoothing constant, $0 \leq h \leq 1$.

Note from Eqns. 4.27 and 4.31 that the MAD is the smoothed absolute forecast error. One important advantage of calculating MAD rather than σ_1 results from the fact that Eq. 4.31 requires the storage from one forecast period to the next of only one piece of data (i.e. $\text{MAD}_{1,t-1}$) per s.k.u., assuming that a common smoothing constant h is used for all items. In contrast Eq. 4.29 may require the storage of up to 3 pieces of data ($\sum e_j^2$, $\sum e_j$, and n) per s.k.u.; if a significant number of s.k.u. have a common number of periods of historical data, n, then the average data requirements per s.k.u. could be reduced to somewhere between two and three.

An equally important advantage of MAD is the fact that it is more up-to-date, since the smoothing Eq. 4.31 assigns progressively less weight to forecast errors the older they are. In contrast Eq. 4.29 weights all historical forecast errors equally. As pointed out in Appendix C for normally distributed forecast errors:

$$\sigma_1 = \sqrt{\pi/2}\,\text{MAD}_1 \doteq 1.25\,\text{MAD}_1$$

or equivalently,

$$\text{MAD}_1 = 0.80\sigma_1 \tag{4.32}$$

We have used the subscript on MAD_1, as with σ_1, to denote that the measure is for forecasts over the unit time period (usually, as is the case here, one month in length).

Another measure of variability that is commonly used, especially when σ_1 is developed manually by clerks, is the range of historical forecast errors.

The range of past forecast errors, R_e, is defined as the difference between the largest and the smallest observed errors. It is known that the expected value of the range of a sample from a normal distribution is proportional to the standard deviation. That is,

$$E(R_e) = k_2 \sigma_1 \tag{4.33}$$

where k_2 is a constant depending on sample size.* From Eq. 4.33 we can obtain an unbiased estimate of σ_1 from the ratio R_e/k_2. The values of k_2 for a range of sample sizes are given in Table 4.10.

Table 4.10 k_2 Factors for Calculating σ_1 from R_e

Sample Size, n	k_2	Sample Size, n	k_2	Sample Size, n	k_2
2	1.13	11	3.16	20	3.74
3	1.69	12	3.26	21	3.76
4	2.06	13	3.34	22	3.82
5	2.33	14	3.41	23	3.86
6	2.53	15	3.47	24	3.90
7	2.70	16	3.53	25	3.93
8	2.85	17	3.58		
9	2.97	18	3.64		
10	3.07	19	3.69		

The values in Table 4.10 were derived by simulating a large number of random draws from a unit normal distribution and calculating the ratio of the sample range to the sample standard deviation for each sample size n. Each simulation was terminated when the sample standard deviation was approximately equal to 1 (the population standard deviation of a unit normal).

We have presented in this section a number of *direct* methods of calculating σ_1. Recall that these direct methods are applicable for A and B items as we discussed in Chapter 3 (see Table 3.3). For C items a different approach for estimating the variability of forecast errors is to make use of an empirical regression relationship (Eq. 2.4) discussed in Chapter 2:

$$\sigma_t = a_1(\bar{d}_t)^{b_1} \tag{4.34}$$

* *This concept is widely used in the development of statistical control charts in quality control. Most quality control books use the notation of d_2 for the constant. To avoid confusion with demand d_t we have opted for k_2. The subscript 2 has no significance in our context.*

where:

a_1 and b_1 are regression coefficients determined empirically (these are *not* smoothing constants).

$\bar{d}_t$ is the mean demand over some period t.

σ_t is the standard deviation of *demand* (not forecast errors) over the same period t.

Normally $t = 1$, the unit forecast period (here taken as one month) in Eq. 4.34. Recall that Eq. 4.34 was derived from a regression of the *standard deviation of demand* against the mean demand over the same period and not from a comparison of the viability of forecast errors and mean demand.

Eq. 4.34 is also useful in computing initial values for $\text{MAD}_{1,t-1}$ in Eq. 4.31. Sometimes Eq. 4.34 is resorted to in practice for A and B items, when direct calculation of forecast error variance is deemed overly expensive by top management. We do not recommend this latter practice for A and B items, except as a last resort.

4.5.2 *Estimating the Standard Deviation of Forecast Errors Over a Lead Time (or a Review Interval plus a Lead Time)**

Once we have calculated the standard deviation of forecast errors over some base period, usually one month, we may still face the problem of having to estimate the forecast error, σ_L, over any length of lead time, L. Since the length of lead time, L, is not always equal to one month, we need some way of converting σ_1 for a base period of one month to any lead time, L. We have found that for most inventory systems the following model satisfactorily captures empirically the required relationship:

$$\sigma_L = L^{c_1}\sigma_1 \tag{4.35}$$

where:

σ_L is the standard deviation of forecast errors over a lead time period of L months.

* *Our discussion here is restricted to the case of continuous review systems where the key time interval in establishing safety stocks is the lead time L. We shall discuss the case of periodic review in Chapter 6.*

L is the length of the lead time in months (L need *not* be an integer).

σ_1 is the standard deviation of forecast errors over a one month period.

c_1 is a coefficient that must be estimated empirically.

To estimate Eq. 4.35 for the MIDAS Professional Products inventory we proceeded as follows. We selected 10 representative s.k.u., 6 from the A category and 4 from the B category for which 5 years of historical monthly sales data was available. (For C items we recommend the use of Eq. 4.34.) Using the first two years of data we initialized the Winters exponential smoothing model by the procedures described in section 4.3.6. That is, for each of the 10 representative s.k.u., we obtained the data needed to initialize the Winters forecast equation (i.e., Eq. 4.20):

$$\hat{d}_{t+j} = [\bar{d}_t + jG_t]F_{t+j-N}$$

Then for the third, fourth and fifth years of sales data, Eq. 4.20 along with the Winters updating procedures described in Eqs. 4.17, 4.18, and 4.19 were used to issue the forecasts listed in Table 4.11. In all the cases the model parameters were updated monthly. For each forecast in Table 4.11, the forecast figure was compared to the actual sales that resulted over the period L and the forecast errors were recorded for each forecast period t:

$$\text{Forecast Error} = e_{tL} = \sum_{j=1}^{L} \hat{d}_{t+j} - \sum_{j=1}^{L} d_{t+j}$$

$$L = 1, 2, \ldots, 6; \text{ and for } j, t \text{ described in Table 4.11} \qquad (4.36)$$

Table 4.11 Forecasts Simulated to Estimate c_1

Length of L	Forecasts	
1	$\hat{d}_{t+1} = [\bar{d}_t + G_t]F_{t+1-12}$;	$t = 0, 1, \ldots, 35$
2	$\sum_{j=1}^{2} \hat{d}_{t+j} = \sum_{j=1}^{2} [\bar{d}_t + jG_t]F_{t+j-12}$;	$t = 0, 2, 4, \ldots, 34$
3	$\sum_{j=1}^{3} \hat{d}_{t+j} = \sum_{j=1}^{3} [\bar{d}_t + jG_t]F_{t+j-12}$;	$t = 0, 3, 6, \ldots, 33$
⋮		
6	$\sum_{j=1}^{6} \hat{d}_{t+j} = \sum_{j=1}^{6} [\bar{d}_t + jG_t]F_{t+j-12}$;	$t = 0, 6, 12, \ldots, 30$

For each lead time L forecast errors were then summarized by computing the standard deviation of forecast errors over each lead time:

$$\sigma_L = \left(\frac{1}{n-1}\sum_t (e_{tL} - \bar{e}_L)^2\right)^{1/2} \tag{4.37}$$

where

$\bar{e}_L = \sum_t (e_{tL}/n)$, the average error for the L under consideration.
n = the number of lead times of length L used.

As a result of all the above calculations the set of forecast errors described in Table 4.12 were available for plotting the graph in Figure 4.4. Using σ_L calculated from the forecast errors in Table 4.12, log (σ_L/σ_1) was plotted against log L for each L, for each of the 10 representative s.k.u. as shown in Figure 4.4. Eq. 4.35 can be written as:

$$\sigma_L/\sigma_1 = L^{c_1}$$

$$\log(\sigma_L/\sigma_1) = c_1 \log L \tag{4.38}$$

Therefore the slope of the line through the origin and the 50 ratios of σ_L/σ_1 (one for each combination of s.k.u. and lead time L) in Table 4.12 is an estimate of c_1 in Eq. 4.38. The line $c_1 = 0.50$ was fitted by eye to the data. The $c_1 = 0.50$ line fits the data only approximately. For MIDAS we chose to use this approximation which gives:

$$\log(\sigma_L/\sigma_1) = 0.50 \log L$$

$$\sigma_L = L^{0.50}\sigma_1 \tag{4.39}$$

$$= \sqrt{L}\sigma_1$$

Table 4.12 Amount of Sample Data for each of the 10 Representative S.K.U.

Lead time, L (1)	Number of Forecast Errors Generated, n (2)
1	36
2	18
3	12
4	9
5	7
6	6

Figure 4.4 Relative Standard Deviations of Forecast Errors versus Lead Time.*

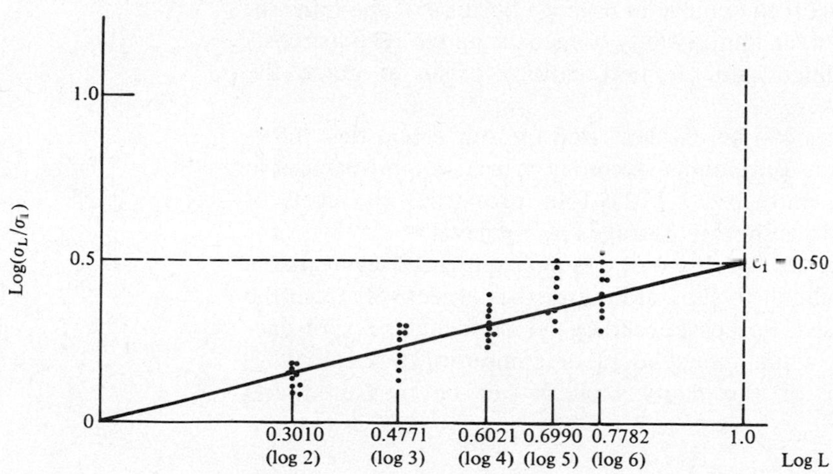

This result also follows theoretically from an assumption of forecast errors in non-overlapping periods being independent. From Eq. 4.39 for an $L = 3$ months we would get $\sigma_3 = \sqrt{3}\sigma_1$. That is, the forecast error standard deviation for 3 months is the square root of three, times the forecast error standard deviation for one month, the base period. Equation 4.39 may *not* be a reasonable approximation in all cases. We recommend that an analysis such as in Figure 4.4 be carried out for every inventory system, from which an appropriate c_1 value should be chosen.

4.6 *Selecting an Appropriate Forecasting Strategy*

We have presented in this chapter only a selection from the myriad of available techniques for forecasting demand. Each of these techniques costs a different amount to operate, provides a different amount of information for general planning purposes, aside from a numerical forecast, and results in different forecast error distributions. Ultimately the merit of any one of these forecasting procedures depends on how well it performs in the context

* *The linear graph paper used here requires the computation of logarithms before plotting. This can be avoided by the use of special log-log paper.*

in which it is used. In every case a compromise has to be struck between the cost of forecast errors that result from currently used procedures and the temptation of spending more on new methods that promise to do better. Such compromises are difficult to achieve in practice because of the inherent uncertainties involved, the near impossibility of measuring the relevant costs and because no well defined general methodology exists to guide the intuition of a decision maker.

All forecasting procedures can be characterized by four properties: information and computational requirements, accuracy in use, responsiveness to sudden shifts in demand, and cost. Of the four properties the costs of computing time, information gathering, storage and retrieval are inextricably dependent on the particular configuration of computing technology available to the organization. It is difficult to separate these costs objectively from the type of equipment being used. Forecast accuracy (which includes responsiveness), on the other hand, while independent of computing technology, is difficult to judge because of the many ways it can be measured and evaluated.

4.6.1 *Evaluating Forecast Accuracy*

Most analysts and managers end up selecting forecasting procedures intuitively using commonly accepted statistics (such as the variance, the mean, the mean absolute deviation, the range, etc.) all of which are based on historical forecast errors. We use the word "intuitively" to describe such comparisons for two reasons. One cannot, in general, make valid claims statistically about the significance of the relative size of these statistics. For example, if procedure one results in a historical error variance of σ_a^2, and procedure two has an error variance of σ_b^2 the significance of the statistical difference between the two variances cannot be tested by currently known techniques because the two series of forecast errors are correlated to an unknown extent.[30] Secondly, statistics such as the variance imply definite assumptions about the relative cost of forecasting errors (i.e., the cost of a forecast error increases as the square of its magnitude). The expected cost of forecasting errors can seldom be stated as explicitly and simply in a specific application.

Some analysts resort to the use of an intuitive criterion and reason as follows:

> *If one forecast method is best as judged by each of several different statistics that were derived from different (cost) assumptions, then we can feel fairly confident about its superiority under general circumstances.*[34]

That is, if one particular forecasting method always has the lowest variance of forecast errors, lowest mean absolute deviation of forecast errors, etc.

then it can be judged to be the best. *But only in exceptional cases will a single forecasting method be judged best by all possible statistics that could be reasonably used to measure forecasting effectiveness.* If one single procedure does not clearly dominate all others in this manner, it usually becomes difficult to achieve consensus via an intuitive criterion.

Furthermore, in adopting such an approach to evaluation, the decision maker assumes erroneously that the best forecasting strategy always consists of selecting a *single* procedure from a set of alternatives. We have shown elsewhere that:[31]

> *In general, the optimal forecasting strategy does not consist of selecting a single forecasting procedure from a set of alternatives. The optimal procedure is in general some combination of available forecasting procedures.*

A combination forecast that is a linear combination of two others can be constructed as follows:

$$\hat{d}_c = kX + (1-k)Y \tag{4.40}$$

where:

k is a constant between zero and one.

X is a random variable, the forecast issued by procedure one.

Y is a random variable, the forecast issued by procedure two.

$\hat{d}_c$ is the combination forecast which is a linear combination of X and Y and is issued after X and Y have been established.

If we chose as our objective the minimization of the variance of the combination forecast's errors, the optimal value, k^*, for the coefficient, k, can be determined from setting:

$$\frac{d\sigma^2(\hat{d}_{ec})}{dk} = 0$$

It can be shown that

$$k^* = \frac{\sigma^2(Y_e) - r_{XY}\sigma(X_e)\sigma(Y_e)}{\sigma^2(X_e) + \sigma^2(Y_e) - 2r_{XY}\sigma(X_e)\sigma(Y_e)} \tag{4.41}$$

where:

$\sigma^2 (d_{ec})$	is the variance of the errors resulting from the combined forecast in Eq. 4.40.
$\sigma^2 (Y_e)$, $\sigma^2 (X_e)$	are the variances of the forecast errors of Y and X respectively.
r_{xy}	is the correlation coefficient between X and Y.

The value of k^* is not easy to determine in practice because the estimates for the σ^2 and r_{xy} terms tend to be unstable.[2,4,15,30]

4.6.2 *Evaluating Forecasting Procedures*

To establish any forecasting procedure as the best, one must demonstrate that the use of a particular procedure will result in the *lowest expected total cost* up to some future decision horizon. Comparing forecast error statistics as in the previous section is really insufficient. Total cost should include both the cost of obtaining a forecast and *cost in use* of the forecasting errors made:

$$\begin{aligned} &E(\text{Total Cost of selecting a procedure}) \\ &\qquad = E(\text{Cost of Forecast Errors in Use}) \\ &\qquad + E(\text{Cost of Operating a Procedure}) \end{aligned} \tag{4.42}$$

In practice, however, the application of this apparently simple expected total cost criterion is usually impossible because:

1. It is very difficult to measure the relative cost of forecast errors in use.

2. The general form of the joint probability distribution of future forecast errors is generally not known and difficult to determine empirically.

But this does not mean that one should not even try to make the tradeoffs shown graphically in Figure 4.5.

In an excellent article on choosing between forecasting techniques, Chambers, Mullick and Smith[8] provide some data on the relative cost of operating various forecasting procedures, *in the computing environment* that existed at Corning Glass Works in 1970. More importantly they spell out in great detail, with examples, the tradeoffs that need to be made in Figure 4.5. They point out that most managers assume that when they ask a forecaster to prepare a projection, this request in itself provides sufficient information for the forecaster to go to work and do his job. This is almost never true. Successful forecasting begins with a collaboration between manager and

Figure 4.5 Cost of Forecasting Versus Cost of Inaccuracy.

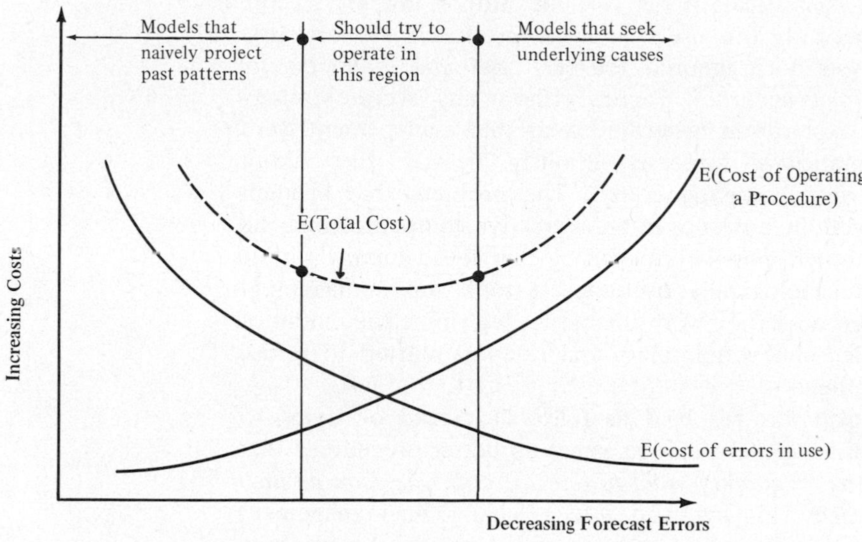

forecaster in which they work out answers to the following questions:

> What is the purpose of the forecasts—how will they be used?
>
> What are the dynamics and components of the *system* about which the forecast will be made?
>
> How important is the past in estimating the future?

The tradeoff in Figure 4.5 is always between selecting models that pretend to understand the underlying causes of time series fluctuations and those which do not.

4.6.3 *In Conclusion: Strategy Over Tactics*

One of the authors was once asked to mediate between competing forecasting groups at a large international corporation. Each group was obviously very sophisticated in mathematical time series analysis and very clever in coaxing the most obscure of patterns out of historical data through spectral analysis. None of the nine highly trained mathematician-forecasters involved had ever really examined closely a retail outlet or wholesaler through which the products that they forecasted were being sold. To most of them, products (in their naiveté) were characterized by amplitudes and phase angles.

Top management for their part were somewhat intimidated with all the apparent computerized sophistication (as was the author initially). Little collaboration existed between the users and the producers of forecasts. Management and analysts both ignored the fact that *you really cannot foretell the future with great accuracy*. Tactics without any overall strategy prevailed. Upon closer exploration it became clear that management were not taking the mathematicians' forecasts seriously, because they didn't understand how they were being generated. The problem that brought matters to a head involved the entrance of an aggressive competitor into the market who claimed through massive advertising that the company's basic product concept was technologically obsolete. It took top management several weeks to react because they were unable to determine the extent of the impact on their sales until wholesalers and retailers started to refuse previously planned shipments.

Eventually the situation was resolved as follows. Instead of trying to foretell the future, top management agreed to set up better procedures that would allow the company to *quickly react to forecast errors as soon as their magnitude was determined*. This involved a basic change in management philosophy. No longer were forecast errors a surprise event. They were fully anticipated and everyone in the decision hierarchy prepared contingency plans in response. All agreed that it was at least equally as important to develop techniques for responding to errors, as it was to try and measure and predict them—the major emphasis of this chapter. In the process, six of the high-powered time series analysts were laid off, resulting in a substantial reduction of overall costs associated with forecasting as well as in a better *forecasting strategy*.

Problems for Chapter 4

Problem 4.1

For the MIDAS (C) case draw a flow chart which summarizes all the different methods used by the company to develop forecasts for s.k.u.

a. Which s.k.u. are explicitly forecasted and which are not? Do you agree with their approach? (You may also wish to read Case (D).)

b. Would you allow the Inventory Control Manager to continue to override explicit decision rules at his own discretion?

c. How do you react to the Inventory Control Manager's quote at the end of Case C? What action do you recommend?

d. Comment on the attempted computerization of forecasting procedures at MIDAS. Is the company ready for sophisticated methods?

Problem 4.2

Evaluate the forecasting procedures described in the MIDAS (C) case in terms of the factors described in Section 4.1. Do they have a good forecasting system?

Problem 4.3

National Optical Distributors (N.O.D.) imports expensive optical instruments from an overseas manufacturer. A particular item CT2-9 costs $2,700 per unit and has a 30–40% margin. Orders have to be placed 1 year in advance and an order size cannot be reduced although a few extra units may be added by the supplier if so desired by N.O.D.

N.O.D. has already placed an order for 135 items for 1976 and has 45 units in stock. How many items should be ordered for 1977? Past demand is as follows:

In Year	Demand
1970	58
1971	48
1972	42[a]
1973	83
1974	106
1975	73 (First 9 months)

[a] There was a shortage in 1972.

Problem 4.4

Suppose that the following are sales of beer in the Kitchener-Waterloo area by month for the 3 years shown:

	Jan	Feb	Mar	Apr	May	June
1968	73	69	68	64	65	98
1969	80	81	83	69	91	140
1970	95	66	81	100	93	116

	Jul	Aug	Sept	Oct	Nov	Dec
1968	114	122	74	56	72	153
1969	152	170	97	122	78	177
1970	195	194	101	197	80	189

a. Plot the data roughly to scale.
b. Is there a trend present?
c. Is there any seasonality? Discuss.
d. Are there any anomalies? Discuss.
e. What is your forecast of demand for Jan. 1971? For June 1971?

Problem 4.5

a. Use a four-quarter moving average to deseasonalize the historical quarterly sales (in units) of STABILIZATION

PROCESSORS by MIDAS in the City of Buffalo:

Year	Quarter	Sales	Year	Quarter	Sales
1970	4	156	1974	1	163
1971	1	132		2	151
	2	100		3	175
	3	149		4	168
	4	148	1975	1	155
1972	1	129		2	147
	2	112		3	169
	3	163		4	168
	4	165	1976	1	154
1973	1	148		2	137
	2	143		3	181
	3	171		4	197
	4	171			

Note: To deasonalize sales, divide sales by the approximate 4 quarters moving average for each quarter.

b. Issue a forecast for processor sales in the Buffalo area for 4 quarters in 1977.

Problem 4.6

a. Use a multiple regression analysis computer programme to fit a regression line to the data given in Problem 4.5.

b. Issue a forecast for processor sales in the Buffalo area for 4 quarters in 1977.

c. How do the forecasts issued in Problems 4.5 and 4.6 compare?

Problem 4.7

The table below shows the sales (units) of a product for the last 12 years. Forecast the sales for the 13th year using simple exponential smoothing and a three-year moving average. Which method is better? (Use a smoothing constant, $a = 0.20$).

Year	Sales
1	519
2	405
3	683
4	597
5	709
6	511
7	389
8	650
9	721
10	785
11	631
12	712

Problem 4.8

A common way of testing forecasting procedures consists of monitoring how a particular procedure responds to a step function in sales or a one period transient change in sales level. (Needless to say, the step and transient functions are only two of the many functions that can be used).

Time	Step Function	Transient Change
1	100	100
2	100	100
3	150	150
4	150	100
5	150	100
6	150	100
7	150	100
8	150	100
9	150	100
10	150	100

a. Use both a simple and a double exponential smoothing model (with appropriate smoothing constants) to track both of the above sales patterns. For initial conditions, assume at the start of time 1 (end of period 0) that $\bar{d} = 100$, $G = 0$.

b. Plot the corresponding *forecast errors* under each procedure.

c. Which forecasting procedure performed better? Discuss.

Problem 4.9

Southern Consolidated manufactures gas turbines. Some of the parts are bought from outside while the important ones are made in the Company's plant. CZ-43 is an important part which wears out in approximately two years and has to be replaced. This means CZ-43 has to be manufactured not only to meet demand at the assembly line but also to satisfy its demand as a spare part. The gas turbine was first sold in 1961 and the demand for CZ-43 for 1961–1974 is given below.

Forecast the total demand for CZ-43 for 1975.

Year	Demand as Spare Part	Demand for Assembly	Total Demand
1961	3	87	90
1962	6	48	54
1963	14	43	57
1964	30	31	61
1965	41	49	90
1966	46	31	77
1967	42	37	79
1968	60	42	102
1969	58	47	105
1970	67	32	99
1971	70	25	95
1972	58	29	87
1973	57	30	87
1974	85	23	108

Problem 4.10

The following table shows the number of housing starts during each month for the period January 1972–December 1974 in Canada. Choose a model from the chapter and forecast the number of housing starts for each of the 4 quarters of 1975. Discuss the appropriateness of the model you have chosen.

Month	1972	1973	1974
Jan.	9,423	11,187	13,506
Feb.	10,735	8,880	9,029
March	13,565	13,300	13,291
April	15,493	18,456	15,782
May	20,746	19,453	19,880
June	21,862	20,946	19,528
July	19,564	22,417	16,095
Aug.	19,082	19,622	14,857
Sept.	20,905	19,879	13,628
Oct.	22,592	22,069	12,994
Nov.	18,976	18,079	11,489
Dec.	14,011	17,255	9,358

Problem 4.11

Union Gas reports the following (normalized) figures for gas consumption by households in a metropolitan area of Ontario:

	Jan.	Feb.	Mar.	Apr.	May	June
1972	196	196	173	105	75	39
1973	227	217	197	110	88	51
1974	216	218	193	120	99	59
1975	228					

	July	Aug.	Sept.	Oct.	Nov.	Dec.
1972	13	20	37	73	108	191
1973	27	23	41	90	107	172
1974	33	37	59	95	128	201

a. Using a simple (single) exponential smoothing model (with $a = 0.10$), determine the forecast for consumption in i) Feb. 1975; ii) June 1976.

b. Do the same using the Winters seasonal smoothing model with $a = 0.20$, $b = 0.05$, $c = 0.10$ using the initialization procedures outlined in the chapter.

c. Plot the demand data and the two sets of forecasts roughly to scale. Does there appear to be a point of abrupt change in the demand pattern? Discuss your results briefly.

Problem 4.12

A major manufacturer of slide rules reports the following quarterly pattern of sales (in hundreds of units) of slide rules. You have been asked to develop inventory planning decision rules to be used for the next two years.

	1970				1971			
Quarter	1	2	3	4	1	2	3	4
Sales	68	53	219	75	56	47	236	82

	1972				1973				1974
Quarter	1	2	3	4	1	2	3	4	1
Sales	72	46	214	67	44	51	158	66	24

a. Using the Winters seasonal smoothing model, determine the forecast of sales for each of the second and third quarters of 1974. Use $a=0.20$, $b=0.10$, $c=0.05$ and initial values as follows: $\bar{d}_0=100$, $G_0=0$ and

Quarter	1st	2nd	3rd	4th	Total
i	1	2	3	4	
F_i	0.6	0.4	2.2	0.8	4.0

b. Plot the sales data and the forecasts for the Winters model.

c. From the plot of sales data alone, discuss any noticeable change in the time series. Using an eyeball procedure, now estimate the two sales forecasts asked for in a). Discuss how you might refine these estimates.

Problem 4.13

a. What are the two types of errors that one attempts to balance in selecting the value(s) of the smoothing constant(s) in exponential smoothing?

b. A newly developed adaptive smoothing package allows for an adjustment in the smoothing constant in the following fashion: One keeps track of the exponentially smoothed error (same as $\bar{e}_t$ in Eq. 4.27). The smoothing constant (the weight given to the most recent data) is varied with the magnitude of the smoothed error, increasing as the magnitude of the smoothed error increases. Does this method make sense? Discuss briefly.

Problem 4.14

Consider a s.k.u. for which it has been decided to use the following underlying model:

$$d_t = \bar{d} + e$$

Smoothing procedures involve the following:

$$\text{MAD}_{1,t} = h\,|d_t - \hat{d}_t| + (1-h)\text{MAD}_{1,t-1}$$

$$\text{Smoothed Error} = \bar{e}_t$$
$$= h(d_t - \hat{d}_t) + (1-h)\bar{e}_{t-1}$$

$$\text{Forecast} = \hat{d}_{t+1} = \hat{d}_t + a\,(d_t - \hat{d}_t)$$

Assume that for regular smoothing we use $h=0.03$ and $a=0.06$, and for fast smoothing we use $a=0.20$ (for our example we won't need h for fast smoothing). Assume that we start at the beginning of month 1 with regular smoothing and initial values:

$$\hat{d}_1 = 100, \quad \text{MAD}_{1,0} = 4, \quad \bar{e}_0 = 0$$

Using the data below, update $\text{MAD}_{1,t}$, $\bar{e}_t$ and $\hat{d}_t$ for each period shown. When $|\bar{e}_t|/\text{MAD}_{1,t}$ exceeds 0.1, switch to fast smoothing for the next 6 months, then return to regular smoothing. For simplicity do not bother calculating $\bar{e}_t$ and $\text{MAD}_{1,t}$ after the switch to fast smoothing is made. Plot the forecasts thus derived against actual sales.

Month, t	1	2	3	4	5	6	7	8	9	10	11	12
Demand, d_t	101	93	106	101	79	74	80	68	79	84	65	70

Problem 4.15

Compare the ability of the Trigg–Leach and Whybark adaptive smoothing models to track the following time series of sales.

Month, t	1	2	3	4	5	6
Demand, d_t	231	226	239	287	290	265

Month, t	7	8	9	10	11	12
Demand, d_t	281	290	287	296	280	275

Assume the following: i) in the Whybark model the 3 levels of the smoothing constant, a, are 0.3, 0.2 and 0.1, ii) initial estimates of $|e| = 10$ and $\bar{e} = 0$, iii) $h = 0.1$, iv) $\sigma_1, = 1.25 \text{ MAD}_1$. Use the simple (single) exponential smoothing model to generate forecasts, assuming an initial value of $\bar{d}_0 = 100$. Plot the two sets of forecasts, as well as actual sales, and discuss your results briefly.

Problem 4.16

For purposes of calculating the safety stock of a particular item, we are interested in having an estimate of the MAD of forecast errors. No historical forecasts are available but historical monthly demand data for three years are available. An analyst on your staff has proposed the following procedure for estimating the MAD:

Step 1: Plot the three years of data.
Step 2: Fit the best straight line to it (either by eye or through a statistical fit).
Step 3: For each month find the absolute deviation

$$x_t = |d_t - \hat{d}_t|$$

where: d_t is the actual demand in month t and $\hat{d}_t$ is the value read off the straight line (found in Step 2) at month t.
Step 4: MAD = average value of x_t over the 36 months.

a. Discuss why the MAD found by the above procedure might be *lower* than that actually achievable by statistical forecasting.

b. Discuss why the MAD found by the above procedure might be substantially *higher* than that actually achievable by a forecasting procedure.

Hint: The use of diagrams may be helpful.

Problem 4.17

In Chapter 4 we suggested two methods, Eqs. 4.33 and 4.34, for estimating σ_1, the standard deviation of forecast errors over a base period (assumed to be 1 month for this example).

a. Discuss the relative advantages and shortcomings of these two methods. When would each method be most appropriate? Illustrate your answer numerically.

b. Ideally what is the most desirable way to estimate σ_1?

Problem 4.18

In Figure 4.4 we summarized a methodology for estimating σ_L from σ_1. If for a MIDAS item σ_1 is estimated to be equal to 137 what would be a good estimate of σ_5?

REFERENCES FOR CHAPTER 4

1. Adam Jr., Everett E., Berry, William L. and Whybark, D. Clay "Forecasting demand for Medical Supply Items Using Exponential and Adaptive Smoothing Models." Paper No. 381, Institute for Research in the Behavioral, Economic and Management Sciences, Purdue University, November, 1972.

2. Bates, J. M. and Granger, C. W. "The Combination of Forecasts." *Operational Research Quarterly*, Vol. 20, No. 4, 1969.

3. Berry, William L. and Bliemel, Griedelm W. "Selecting Exponential Smoothing Constants: An Application of Pattern Search." Technical Paper No. 341, Institute for Research, Graduate School of Industrial Administration, Purdue University, Lafayette, Indiana, April 1972.

4. Box, G. E. P. and Jenkins, G. *Time Series Analysis; Forecasting and Control.* Holden-Day. San Franciso, California, 1970.

5. Brown, R. G. *Decision Rules for Inventory Management.* Holt, Rinehart and Winston, New York, 1967.

6. Brown, R. G. *Smoothing, Forecasting and Prediction.* Prentice-Hall, Englewood Cliffs, N.J., 1963.

7. Brown, R. G. *Statistical Forecasting for Inventory Control.* McGraw-Hill, New York, 1959.

8. Chambers, John C., Mullick, Satinder K. and Smith, Donald D. "How to Choose the Right Forecasting Technique." *Harvard Business Review*, July–August, 1971, pp. 45–74.

9. Chow, Wen M. "Adaptive Control of the Exponential Smoothing Constant." *Journal of Industrial Engineering*, Vol. 16, 1965.

10. Cox, D. R. "Prediction by Exponentially Weighted Moving Averages and Related Methods." *Journal of the Royal Statistical Society*, Vol. 23, 1961, pp. 414–422.

11. Dalkey, Norman and Helmer, Olaf. "An Experimental Application of the DELPHI Method to the Use of Experts." *Management Science*, Vol. 9, No. 3. April, 1963.

12. D'Amico, Peter. "Forecasting System Uses Modified Smoothing." *Journal of Industrial Engineering*, Vol. 3, 1971, pp. 15–20.

13. De La Valle, D. and Poussin, N. Sarofim. "Leading Indicators: A Tool for Corporate Forecasting." *Sloan Management Review*, Spring, 1973.

14. Dickinson, J. P. "Some Stastistical Results in the Combination of Forecasts." *Operational Research Quarterly*, Vol. 24, No. 2, 1973, pp. 253–260.

15. Dickinson, J. P. "Some Comments on the Combination of Forecasts." *Operational Research Quarterly*, Vol. 26, No. 1, 1975, pp. 205–210.

16. Eilon, S. and Elmaleh, J. "Adaptive Limits in Inventory Control." *Management Science*, Vol. 16, 1970, pp. B533-B-548.

17. Ezekiel, Mordecai and Fox,

Karl A. *Methods of Correlation and Regression Analysis.* Fourth Edition, New York, John Wiley, 1970.

18. Goodman, M. L. "A Look at Higher-Order Exponential Smoothing for Forecasting." Operations Research, Vol. 22, No. 4, July–August, 1974, pp. 880–888.

19. Haber, S. and Sitgreaves, R. "A Methodology for Estimating Expected usage of Repair Part with Application to Parts with No Usage History." *Naval Research Logistics Quarterly*, Volume. 17, No. 4, December, 1970, pp. 535–546.

20. Harrison, P. J. "Exponential Smoothing and Short-Term Sales Forecasting." *Management Science*, Vol. 13, No. 11, July, 1967, pp. 821–842.

21. Harrison, P. J. and O. Davies. "The Use of Cumulative Sum (CUSUM) Techniques for the Control of Product Demand." *Operations Research* Vol. 12, No. 2, March–April, 1964, pp. 325–333.

22. Kirby, R. M. "A Comparison of Short and Medium Range Statistical Forecasting Methods." *Management Science*, Vol. 13, No. 4, December 1966, pp. 202–210.

23. Mabert, Vincent A. and Radcliffe, Robert C. "Forecasting—A Systematic Modeling Methodology." Paper No. 489, Institute for Research in the Behavioral, Economic and Management Sciences, Purdue University, 1974.

24. Mackenzie, E. "An Analysis of General Exponential Smoothing." *Operations Research*, Vol. 24, No. 1, January–February, 1976, pp. 131–140.

25. McClain, J. O. "Dynamics of Exponential Smoothing with Trend Seasonal Terms." *Management Science*, Vol. 20, No. 9, May, 1974, pp. 1300–1304.

26. McClain, J. O. and Thomas, L. J. "Response Variance Tradeoffs in Adaptive Forecasting." *Operations Research*, Vol. 21, March–April, 1973, pp. 554–568.

27. Montgomery, Douglas C. "Adaptive Control of Exponential Smoothing Parameters by Evolutionary Operation." *AIIE Transactions*, Vol. 2, 1974, pp. 268–269.

28. Netzorg, M. J. "Background of Experimental Roughing." Canadian Association of Production and Inventory Control Seminar, Toronto, Canada, May 9, 1974.

29. Parker, G. C. and Segura, Edilberto L. "How to Get a Better Forecast." *Harvard Business Review*, March–April, 1971, pp. 99–109.

30. Peterson, Rein. "A Note on the Determination of Optimal Forecasting Strategy." *Management Science*, Vol. 16, No. 4, December, 1969, pp. B165–B169.

31. Peterson, Rein and Lamont, J. G. D. "On the Consolidation of Competing Forecasts." *International Technical Conference Proceedings, A.P.I.C.S.*, Toronto, March 1972, pp. 1–11.

32. Roberts, S. D. and Reed R. "The Development of a Self-Adaptive Forecasting Technique. "*AIIE Transactions*, Vol. 1, 1969, pp. 314–322.

33. Roberts, Stephen D. and Whybark D. Clay. "Adaptive Forecasting Techniques." *International Journal of Production Research*, Vol.

12, No. 6, 1974, pp. 635–645.

34. Schussel, George. "Sales Forecasting With a Human Behavior Simulator." *Management Science*, Vol. 13, June, 1967, pp. B593–B611.

35. Selby, Samuel M. *Standard Mathematical Tables*. The Chemical Rubber Company, Cleveland, Ohio, 1965, pp. 410–414.

36. Spurr, William A. and Bonini, Charles P. *Statistical Analysis for Business Decisions*. Revised Edition, Irwin, 1974.

37. Stevens, C. F. "On the Variability of Demand for Families of Items." *Operations Research Quarterly*, Vol. 25, No. 3, September, 1974. pp. 411–419.

38. Trigg, D. W. "Monitoring a Forecast System." *Operational Research Quarterly*, Vol. 15, 1964, pp. 271–274.

39. Trigg, D. W. and Leach, A. G. "Exponential Smoothing With an Adaptive Response Rate." *Operational Research Quarterly*, Vol. 18, 1967, p. 53.

40. Wesolowsky, G. *Multiple Regression and Analysis of Variance*. John Wiley, 1976.

41. Whybark, D. Clay. "A Comparison of Adaptive Forecasting Techniques." *Logistic Transportation Review*, Vol. 8, 1973.

42. Winters, P. R. "Forecasting Sales by Exponentially Weighted Moving Averages." *Management Science*, Vol. 6, 1960, pp. 324–342.

PART 2

Economic Order Quantity Decision Systems for Managing Individual Item Inventories

In the preceding section we have laid the groundwork in terms of specifying the environment, goals, constraints, relevant costs, and forecast inputs of inventory decision models. Now we turn our attention to the detailed logic required for short range planning and scheduling. In contrast with the macro (aggregate) approaches which will be taken in Part V in dealing with medium range planning and scheduling, here we shall be concerned primarily with decision making on an individual item or stock keeping unit (s.k.u.) basis. However, as discussed in Chapter 3, aggregate considerations will often still play a crucial role in the following manner: in most of the decision rules there is a parameter whose value can be implicitly specified through selecting an operating point on an exchange curve which shows the aggregate consequences (across a population of inventoried items) of using different values of this policy parameter. Management can select the aggregate operating point, thus implying a value of the parameter which is to be used in the item by item decision rules.

Within this part of the book we shall deal with the so-called B items which, as we have seen earlier, comprise the majority of items in a typical inventory situation. Unlike for C items, which will be handled in Part III, there are usually significant savings to be derived from the use of a reasonably sophisticated control system. On the other hand, the potential savings per inventoried item are not of the same order of magnitude as those realizable for individual A items. The combination of these two factors dictates that a hybrid system be used that combines the relative advantages of man and machine. The management by exception control system, often automated (possibly manual rather than computerized, depending upon the total sales volume of the items involved), that we shall describe is reasonably sophisticated, requiring human intervention on a relatively infrequent basis. Such automated control systems, when applied in practice, have resulted in significant improvements in the control of B items.

In Chapter 5 we shall first answer the question of how much to replenish in the context of an *approximately level demand pattern*. Then, in Chapters 6 and 7, the discussion will be concerned with the situation where the *average* demand rate stays approximately level with time but there is a random component present, that is, the mean or forecast demand stays constant or changes slowly with time but there definitely are forecast errors present (in contrast with Chapter 5). When demand is known only in a probabilistic sense, two additional questions must be answered: "how often should we review the stock status?" and "when should we place a replenishment order?" Chapter 6 will cover, in an introductory fashion, the key issues of control under probabilistic demand. In Chapter 7 considerably more detail will be presented, including some of the more complex mathematical logic. In Chapter 8 we shall consider the more general situation of a demand pattern where the mean or forecast demand changes appreciably with time, an obvious example being that of a seasonal demand pattern. The relaxation to this more general case considerably complicates the analysis. Therefore, the decision system, to be suggested, is based upon a reasonable heuristic decision rule. All of the material in Chapters 5 through 8 ignores possible benefits of coordinating the replenishments of two or more items. We shall return to this important topic in Chapters 12 and 13 of Part IV.

Midas Canada Corporation (D)*

The company's stated inventory control policy was "to have zero stockouts." Since customers could obtain almost equivalent products in most cases from a competitor it was the opinion of the President of MIDAS-CANADA that every effort should be made to avoid back orders or stockouts. Air freight at a cost of approximately $0.50 per pound was sometimes used to meet the demand from an important large customer. However, if a large customer placed an unusually large order without prior warning that depleted the available stocks, then it was the company's policy to bill him for part of the costs of air freight involved. On occasion MIDAS filled an important customer's order by supplying a competitor's film at below retail price, thereby absorbing a loss on the sale.

On slow moving items company salesmen were instructed to make no delivery promises until they had checked with the Inventory Control Manager. Some customers were asked to sign a non-cancellable purchase order and, if their credit rating was poor, a deposit was required before an order was accepted. The Inventory Control Manager tried to order all slow moving items directly from Germany and thereby keep a minimum of inventory on hand of slow moving s.k.u.

Lead Times

The length of the lead time for receiving delivery depended on whether the plant in Germany produced the particular item for stock or to order. Because films tended to deteriorate over time, only the more popular items were manufactured for stock. Parts for MIDAMATICS and items sold by the Industrial and Professional Products Divisions which were stocked by the plant in Germany arrived at the warehouse 8 to 12 weeks

* *The MIDAS cases describe actual decision systems which are based on consulting experiences of the authors. They do not describe the situation at any single company, but are in fact a compendium of actual situations which have been compressed into the environment of a single firm and industry of illustrative purposes. The cases are not intended as presentations of either effective or ineffective ways of handling administrative problems.*

after an order was placed. Made to order items took longer, with the lead time varying from 12 to 16 weeks. The plant in Germany grouped orders whenever possible and shipped them via specially designed containers that could be unloaded directly from a cargo ship onto a railroad flatcar in Halifax, Nova Scotia, and then delivered directly to the MIDAS warehouse in Toronto, Ontario.

Superchrome was shipped from Germany by Air Cargo and arrived at the plant 2 to 4 weeks after an order was placed, depending on the work load at the manufacturing plant. *Superchrome* products were made to order.

All X-Ray films were produced to order and received special handling throughout the production-shipping process. As a result, the lead time for these s.k.u. was shorter, varying from 8 to 10 weeks. The remaining products sold by the X-Ray Division had lead times similar to the Professional and Industrial Products described above. For chemicals, an additional one to two weeks during some months of the year had to be allowed in addition to the 8 to 12 weeks lead time for delivery from Germany so that bulk shipments could be repackaged appropriately.

Takashi products arrived through the port of Vancouver on the west coast of Canada. Most items ordered by MIDAS were stocked by the Japanese manufacturer and arrived from 10 to 12 weeks after an order was placed. Because delicate optical instruments were involved, extra care was taken throughout shipment to minimize breakage. Nevertheless some breakage inevitably occurred and one could never be sure of the exact quantity of goods that arrived safely.

The remaining miscellaneous items and parts mostly used by the Assembly Plant and which were obtained domestically in Canada, had lead times that varied from zero to two weeks. Many items were available on the same day from suppliers located in the Toronto area, provided MIDAS sent a truck to pick up the goods.

Lead times for assembled MIDAMATICS and STABILIZATION PROCESSORS had been always less than 2 weeks during 1976. Because of the increasing demand for both types of equipment the company was starting to build some PROCESSORS for finished goods inventory during slack periods.

The Determination of Order Quantities and Order Points

Once a month, the Inventory Control Manager and the Comptroller, along with 3 assistants, calculated by hand, during "a two day marathon session," for all but the most expensive s.k.u. and the parts used to assemble PROCESSORS and MIDAMATICS, the total sales over the most recent 5 month period. The total sales figure over the last 5 month period became the order up to quantity (called the "Maximum" by the Company). Whenever an order was placed the quantity ordered was taken as the difference between the "Maximum" and the current Balance Available (see Figures 1 and 2, case B). Eighty percent of the "Maximum" quantity was then taken as the Order Point (called the "Minimum" by the Company). Such systems are commonly referred to by practitioners as MIN/MAX Inventory Control Systems. (see Table 1).

The newly computed MIN/MAX quantities were compared to the ordering rules computed during the previous month and adjustments were made, when deemed appropriate, to Travel Cards of individual s.k.u. (see the top right hand corner of Figure 2, case B). The Inventory Control Manager did not blindly follow the 5 month rule described above. He sometimes modified the order up to quantities and order points because of some future events that he knew would take place.

Parts for the assembly of MIDAMATICS and PROCESSORS were not ordered in the above manner. The Inventory Control Manager tried to order the exact number of parts required each month to meet the planned assembly schedule. The parts for assembly and for repairs were kept physically separate. The Inventory Control Manager explained that:

> *The repairmen used to be lax in keeping track of spare parts they needed. They felt that they could always dip into the stock of parts which had been ordered for assembly if they ran short. By doing this they upset our assembly schedules several times. By separating the two inventories, we put a stop to that practice. Although I must admit that now we sometimes borrow from the stock of spare parts to meet unexpected demand for our assembled end-products. On occasion, because of this practice, we have been a little short of spare parts. I've often wondered whether there was any way of combining the inventory for both types of parts so that there would be enough safety stock to meet emergencies from either of the two sources.*

Table 1 Inventory Control Work Sheet

s.k.u.	Month 1	Month 2	Sales Month 3	Month 4	Month 5	Maximum = 5 Month Total	Order Point = 0.8 × Maximum
EDM-008	52	48	36	39	65	240	192
PMF-298	8	12	14	18	23	75	60
PSF-107	402	368	374	396	376	1916	1533
IMM-177	159	127	130	169	172	757	606
.	.	.	.	.	.	.	.
.	.	.	.	.	.	.	.
.	.	.	.	.	.	.	.

For very expensive items, such as all X-Ray and *Superchrome* films, the Inventory Control Manager personally placed orders once a month. He tried to order only enough items to meet actual sales for the one month period, one lead time period ahead. In most cases these orders were in response to non-cancellable purchase orders placed by customers, or commitments made to him over the telephone by customers he deemed dependable. He usually ordered ten to twenty percent more than the number of units he was able to identify through purchase orders or commitments to meet unexpected demand.

Proposed Changes to Existing Ordering Procedures

By the Summer of 1976 MIDAS-CANADA had decided to explore the possibility of setting up computerized procedures for controlling inventories, for generating more timely sales reports, and to help reduce the amount of manual clerical accounting procedures currently in use. The Comptroller took this opportunity to review the current ordering rules which were based on the total sales during the 5 most recent months' sales, as explained above. The Comptroller had always felt that the total dollar investment in inventories was too high. He also agreed with the Vice-President of Sales that the Company had failed to meet its stated policy of "zero stockouts." Based on a number of investigations and calculations, he proposed the new system of calculating order quantities and Order Points described in Figure 1.

The Inventory Control Manager was asked to comment on the Comptroller's proposal:

> *As far as I am concerned, one set of rules is as good as another as long as I am allowed the freedom to modify the calculated order quantities when I need to. I think the proposed change will probably be an improvement over our previous methods because it takes account of lead times. But it does not solve a big problem I face each quarter which is making sure that all the individual orders placed add up to the total I committed the Company to in the Purchase Budgets* which I submitted to the production planners in Germany.*

---

* *For a description of Purchase Budgets see case C.*

Figure 1

MIDAS CANADA CORPORATION

Inter-Office Memo

To: Inventory Control Manager

From: The Comptroller's Office

I have made a study of our present method of calculating Order Points and it seems to me that it has the following weaknesses:

1. We use 5 months of historical sales as a basis for our planning. That means that what happened 4 or 5 months ago weighs as heavily on what we order, as what happened last month.

2. The varying lead times of different products are not taken into account.

However it does appear to me that in the majority of cases these two points do offset each other, except that we seem to have too many overstocks of slow movers and understocks of fast movers. I propose that until further notice the following method be adopted for calculating Maximums. We have agreed that our products should at all times carry a 6 weeks' buffer stock. In addition we allow for 4 weeks of off-take inventory* that gets used up during the reorders cycle, for a total of 10 weeks inventory. Therefore, for an item that has, on the average, a lead time of 8 weeks the factor becomes (assuming 3 months = 13 weeks):

$$\frac{10 + 8}{13} \times \text{(3 months sales)} = 138\% \times \text{(3 months sales)}$$

Similarly for 10 week and 12 week lead times the factors become respectively 154% and 169%.

Order Points (Minimums) should continue to be calculated as being 80% of Maximum. The Maximum for most of our products under this proposed system will be 20 weeks sales, of which the 4 week reorder cycle is 20%, leaving 80% of Maximum as our Order Point just as before.

---

*By off-take inventory the Comptroller presumably meant cycle stock.

CHAPTER FIVE

An Order Quantity Decision System for the Case of Approximately Level Demand

In this chapter we are concerned with the question of how large a replenishment quantity to use under rather stable conditions (any changes in parameters occur slowly over time). Furthermore, there is relatively little or no uncertainty concerning the level of demand. This simplified situation is a reasonable approximation of reality on certain occasions. However, more important, the results obtained turn out to be important components of the decision systems when parameters change with time and/or demand is probabilistic.

In Section 5.1 we discuss the rather severe assumptions needed in the derivation of the economic order quantity (EOQ). This is followed in

Section 5.2 by the actual derivation. This derivation includes two cost parameters: i) the carrying charge r, and, ii) the fixed cost per replenishment, A. As discussed in Chapter 3, one or both of their values may be explicitly evaluated or may be implicitly specified through looking at the aggregate consequences of using different values of r (or A/r) and then selecting a suitable aggregate operating point which implies an r (or A/r) value. Section 5.3 shows how to develop the exchange curves, a crucial step in this latter (implicit) approach. In Section 5.4 we show that the total relevant costs are not seriously affected by rather large deviations of the replenishment quantity away from the minimizing value. This robust property of the economic order quantity is important from an operational standpoint. Section 5.5 is concerned with aids, such as tables and graphs, where items are grouped into broad categories to make implementation easier, particularly in a non-computerized system. The important case of quantity discounts is handled in Section 5.6. Section 5.7 deals with several types of limitations on replenishment quantities ignored in the earlier development of the EOQ. This is followed by the incorporation of other potentially important factors in Section 5.8.

5.1 *Assumptions Leading to the Basic Economic Order Quantity (EOQ)*

Let us first lay out the assumptions. Some of these may appear to be far removed from reality but, as we shall see, the EOQ forms an important building block in the majority of decision systems which we shall advocate. The reader is asked to bear with us as considerable discussion will be directed to this point later in this and subsequent chapters.

a. The demand rate is constant and deterministic.

b. The order quantity need not be an integral number of units.

c. The unit variable cost does not depend on the replenishment quantity; in particular, there are no discounts in either the unit purchase cost or the unit transportation cost.

d. The item is treated entirely independently of other items, that is, benefits from joint review and/or replenishment do not exist or are simply ignored.

e. The replenishment lead time is of zero duration; as we shall see later, extension to a *known* non-zero duration creates no problem.

f. No shortages are allowed.

g. The *entire* order quantity is delivered at the same time.

All of these assumptions will be relaxed later in this chapter or elsewhere in the book. However, in the derivation of the fundamental version of the economic order quantity it is necessary that they all be satisfied.

5.2 *Derivation of the Economic Order Quantity*

As discussed in Chapter 3 there are five fundamental categories of costs:

i. basic production or purchase costs

ii. inventory carrying costs

iii. costs of insufficient capacity

iv. control system costs

v. costs of changing work force sizes and production rates.

The fifth category is not relevant for the item-by-item control which we are considering here. Also, given that we are restricting attention to a particular type of control system (an order quantity system) the control system costs are not influenced by the exact value of the order quantity. Hence, they need not be taken into account when selecting the value of the order quantity.

Because of the deterministic nature of the demand the only cost relevant to the third category would be that which is caused by the decision maker deliberately choosing to run short of inventory before making a replenishment. For now, we shall ignore the possibility of allowing planned shortages.

Therefore, we are left with only the first two types of costs being relevant to the economic selection of the replenishment quantity.

Before proceeding further, let us introduce some notation:

Q—the replenishment order quantity, in units.

A—the fixed cost component (independent of the magnitude of the replenishment quantity) incurred with each replenishment, in dollars. (This cost component has been discussed at length in Chapter 3.)

v—the unit variable cost of the item. This is not the selling price of the item, but rather its value (immediately *after* the replenishment operation now under consideration) in terms of raw materials and value added through processing and assembly operations. The dimensions are \$/unit.

r—the carrying charge, the cost of having one dollar of the item tied up in inventory for a unit time interval (normally one year) that is, the dimensions are \$/\$/unit time. (Again, this cost component was discussed at length in Chapter 3.)

D—the demand rate of the item, in units/unit time.

TRC(*Q*)—the total relevant costs per unit time, that is, the sum of those costs per unit time which can be influenced by the order quantity *Q*. The dimensions are \$/unit time.

Because the parameters involved are assumed to not change with time, it is reasonable (and, indeed, mathematically optimal) to think in terms of using the same order quantity, *Q*, each time that a replenishment is made. Furthermore, because i) demand is deterministic, ii) the replenishment lead time is zero, and iii) we have chosen to not allow planned shortages, it is clear that each replenishment will be made when the inventory level is exactly at zero. A graphical portrayal of the inventory level with time is shown in Figure 5.1.

Note that the time between replenishments is given by Q/D, the time to deplete *Q* units at a rate of *D* units per unit time. (*D* is the usage over a period of time; normally 12 months is used.) Therefore, the number of

Figure 5.1 Behavior of Inventory Level with Time.

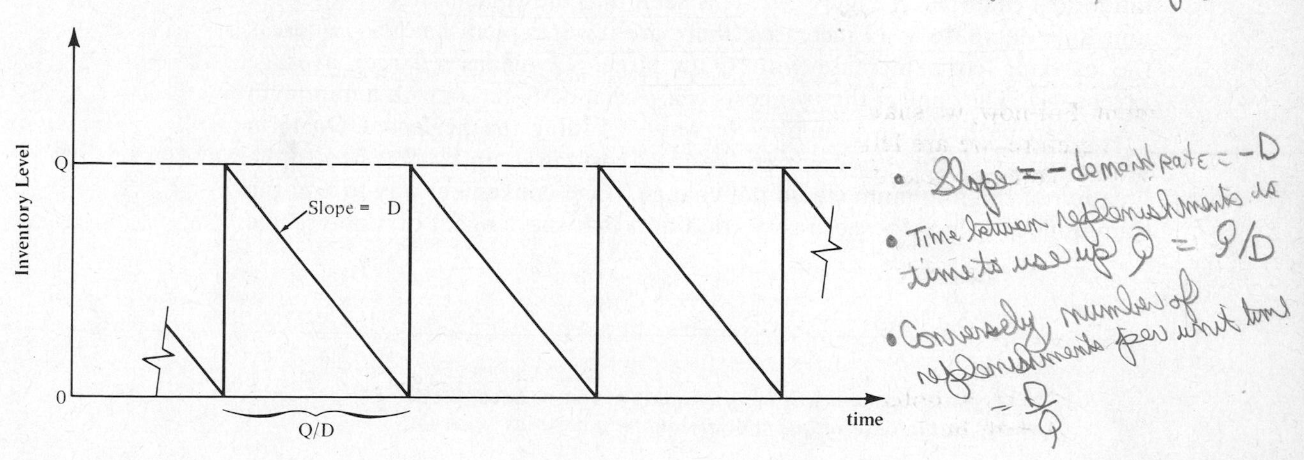

replenishments per unit time is D/Q. Associated with each of these is a replenishment cost given by $A+Qv$ where one of our assumptions insures that the unit variable cost v does not depend upon Q. Therefore, the replenishment costs per unit time (C_r) are given by

$$C_r = (A+Qv)D/Q$$

or

$$C_r = AD/Q + Dv \tag{5.1}$$

The second component in Eq. 5.1 is seen to be independent of Q and, hence, can have no effect on the determination of the best Q value. (It represents the constant acquisition cost of the item per unit time which cannot be affected by the magnitude of the order quantity.) Therefore, it will be neglected in further discussions.*

As discussed in Chapter 3, the common method of determining the costs of carrying inventory over a unit time period is through the relation

$$C_c = \bar{I}vr$$

where $\bar{I}$ is the average inventory level, in units. The average height of the sawtooth diagram of Figure 5.1 is $Q/2$. Therefore,

$$C_c = Qvr/2 \tag{5.2}$$

Combining Eqs. 5.1 and 5.2 and neglecting the Dv term, as discussed above, we have that the total relevant costs per unit time are given by

$$\text{TRC}(Q) = Qvr/2 + AD/Q \tag{5.3}$$

The two components of Eq. 5.3 and their total are plotted for an illustrative numerical example in Figure 5.2. It is seen that the replenishment costs per unit time decrease as Q increases (there are fewer replenishments), whereas the carrying costs increase with Q (a larger Q means a larger average inventory). The sum of the two costs is a u-shaped function with a minimum which can be found in a number of ways. (Adding the neglected Dv term would simply shift every point on the total cost curve up by Dv; hence, the location of the minimum would not change.) One convenient way to find the minimum is to use the necessary condition that the tangent or slope of the

---

**The Dv component will be of crucial interest in Section 5.6 where, in the case of quantity discounts, v depends upon Q.*

Figure 5.2 Costs as Functions of the Replenishment Quantity.

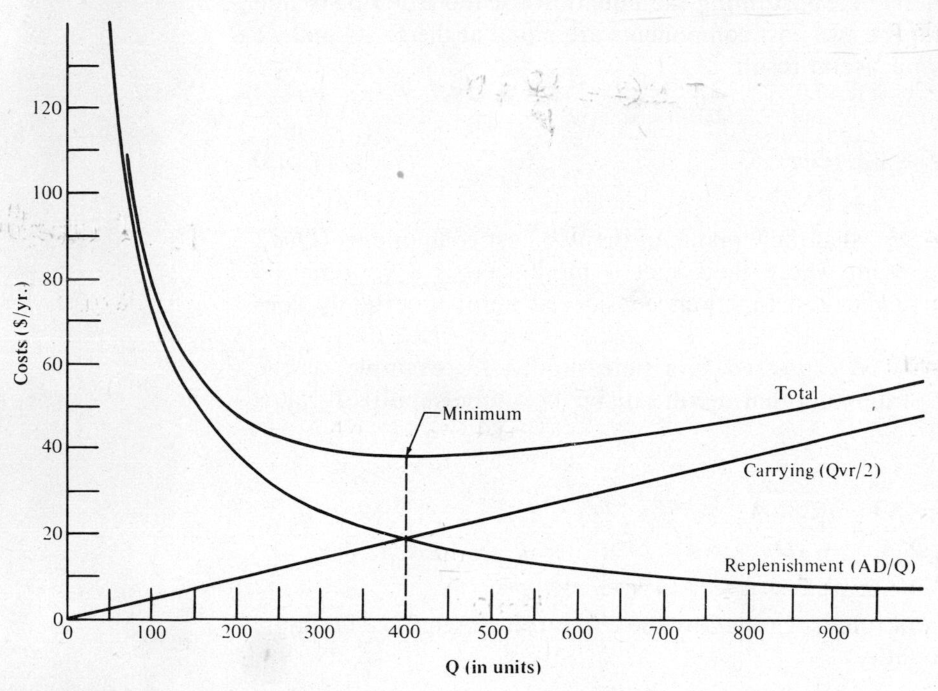

curve is zero at the minimum*:

$$\frac{d\,\mathrm{TRC}(Q)}{dQ}=0$$

that is,

$$\frac{vr}{2}-\frac{AD}{Q^2}=0$$

$$Q_{\mathrm{opt}} \quad \text{or} \quad \mathrm{EOQ}=\sqrt{\frac{2AD}{vr}} \tag{5.4}$$

---

* *A second condition for a minimum, namely that the second derivative is positive, is also satisfied, viz.*

$$\frac{d^2\mathrm{TRC}(Q)}{dQ^2}=2AD/Q^3>0 \text{ for any } Q>0.$$

This is the economic order quantity (also known as the Wilson lot size). This is one of the earliest and most well-known results of inventory theory (see, for example, Mennell[14]). Substituting the equation for the EOQ back into Eq. 5.3, we find that the two cost components are equal at the EOQ and we obtain the simple and useful result

$$\text{TRC(EOQ)} = \sqrt{2ADvr} \tag{5.5}$$

It should be emphasized that the equality of the two cost components ($Qvr/2$ and AD/Q) at the point where their sum is minimized is a very special property of the particular cost functions considered here; it certainly does not hold in general.

The EOQ can also be expressed as a time supply, for example, as the number of months of demand that it will satisfy. This time supply, T_{EOQ}, is given by

$$T_{\text{EOQ}} = \frac{12\text{EOQ}}{D} = \sqrt{\frac{288A}{rDv}} \tag{5.6}$$

MIDAS' new decision rules suggested by the comptroller (see Case D) imply a replenishment quantity

$$Q = (2 + 0.2L)D/52$$

where L is the replenishment lead time, in weeks. Expressed in months of supply this is

$$T_Q = \frac{12Q}{D} = \frac{3}{13}(2 + 0.2L)$$

Ignoring for now the dependence on the value of L, this says that MIDAS' decision rule would lead to items having the same time supply of replenishment even if they had different values of A, D and/or v. The EOQ result of Eq. 5.6 shows that the time supply should depend upon these factors (in fact, only items having the same value of the ratio A/Dv should have the same time supply), hence, there is room for improvement over MIDAS' rule, the latter not having been developed from explicit cost considerations. Note that Eq. 5.4 illustrates, among other points, that the preferred order quantity goes up as the square root of demand rather than being directly proportional to the D value.

We can also convert the EOQ to an implied turnover ratio (annual demand rate divided by the average inventory level)

$$TR = \frac{D}{\bar{I}} = \frac{D}{\text{EOQ}/2} = \sqrt{\frac{2Dvr}{A}} \tag{5.7}$$

a result which is again seen to depend upon the individual item factors D, v, and A. In particular, all other things remaining constant, we see that the turnover ratio increases in proportion to the square root of the demand rate, D.

Numerical Illustration (*Illustrated in Figure* 5.2) – Consider item EDM-073, a 3 ohm resistor used in the assembly of MIDAMATICS. The demand for this item has been relatively level over time at a rate of 2400 units/yr. The unit variable cost of the resistor is \$0.40/unit and the fixed cost per replenishment is estimated to be \$3.20. Suppose further that an r value of 0.24 \$/\$/yr. is appropriate to use. Then Eq. 5.4 gives

$$\text{EOQ} = \sqrt{\frac{2 \times \$3.20 \times 2400 \text{ units/yr.}}{\$0.40/\text{unit} \times 0.24\ \$/\$/\text{yr.}}}$$

$$= 400 \text{ units, that is, a 2 month supply } (D/6).$$

Note that the dimensions appropriately cancel. This would not be the case, for example, if D and r were not defined on the same unit time basis.

Equation 5.5 reveals that the total relevant costs per year for the resistor are

$$\text{TRC(EOQ)} = \sqrt{2 \times \$3.20 \times 2400 \text{ units/yr.} \times \$0.40/\text{unit} \times 0.24/\text{yr.}}$$

$$= \$38.40/\text{yr.}$$

A check on the computations is provided by noting that substitution of $Q = 400$ units in Eq. 5.3 gives a value of \$19.20/yr. to each of the two terms.

For this item, which has a lead time of 8 weeks, the MIDAS decision rule gives

$$Q = (2 + 0.2 \times 8)2400/52$$

$$\simeq 166 \text{ units (or 0.83 months of supply)}$$

a value considerably below the EOQ. Substitution of $Q = 166$ into Eq. 5.3 reveals that the total relevant costs for item EDM-073 using the MIDAS rule are \$54.23/yr. or some 41.2% higher than the costs incurred under use of the EOQ.

5.3 *Selection of the Carrying Charge (r), the Fixed Cost per Replenishment (A) or the Ratio A/r Based on Aggregate Considerations—the Exchange Curve*

Often it is difficult to explicitly determine an appropriate value of the carrying charge, r, or the fixed cost per replenishment, A, from basic cost considerations. An alternate method, which we discussed at length in Chapter 3, takes account of the aggregate viewpoint of management. In this and later sections we shall derive the relationships and graphs which we earlier asked you to accept on faith. For a population of inventoried items management may impose an aggregate constraint of one of the following forms:

i. The average total inventory cannot exceed a certain dollar value.

ii. The total fixed cost (or total number) of replenishments per unit time (for example, one year) must be less than a certain value.

iii. We should operate at a point where the tradeoff (exchange) between average inventory and cost (or number) of replenishments per unit time is at some reasonable prescribed value.

We consider two separate cases, the first where the fixed setup cost, A_i, for each item i, has been *explicitly* determined; the second where the A_i's cannot be determined explicitly but it is reasonable to assume that a common value of A holds (at least approximately) for all items in the portion of the inventory population under consideration. We designate the demand rate, unit variable cost, and order quantity of item i by D_i, v_i, and Q_i respectively. Also we let n be the number of items in the population.

Case 1—A_i's Known Explicitly

As shown in Part 1 of the appendix of this chapter, if we use an economic order quantity for each item, we obtain the total average stock (also called the total cycle stock) in dollars,

$$\text{TCS} = \frac{1}{\sqrt{r}} \frac{1}{\sqrt{2}} \sum_{i=1}^{n} \sqrt{A_i D_i v_i} \tag{5.8}$$

and the total cost* of replenishments per unit time,

$$TCR = \sqrt{r}\frac{1}{\sqrt{2}} \sum_{i=1}^{n} \sqrt{A_i D_i v_i} \tag{5.9}$$

Both TCS and TCR are seen to depend upon the value of the carrying charge *r*. Multiplication of Eqs. 5.8 and 5.9 produces the interesting result that

$$(TCS)(TCR) = \tfrac{1}{2}\left(\sum_{i=1}^{n} \sqrt{A_i D_i v_i}\right)^2 = \text{constant for a given population of items} \tag{5.10}$$

An equation of this latter type represents a hyperbolic relationship between TCS and TCR. Points on this hyperbola are obtained as follows. The quantity $\sum_{i=1}^{n} \sqrt{A_i D_i v_i}$ is evaluated once-and-for-all for the specific population of items. Then various pairs of TCS and TCR satisfying Eq. 5.10 are determined. To illustrate, suppose

$$\sum_{i=1}^{n} \sqrt{A_i D_i v_i} = 50{,}000$$

then Eq. 5.10 gives

$$(TCS)(TCR) = 1{,}250{,}000{,}000$$

Suppose, we wish to find the TCR value which goes with a TCS value of \$100,000. We have

$$TCR = \frac{1{,}250{,}000{,}000}{100{,}000} = \$12{,}500/\text{yr.}$$

These points are plotted on a curve (see Figure 5.3) with one axis being TCR and the other being TCS.

Division of Eq. 5.8 by Eq. 5.9 gives

$$\frac{TCS}{TCR} = \frac{1}{r} \tag{5.11}$$

---

* *By total cost we mean the sum of the A_iD_i/Q_i elements and not the D_iv_i components because changing the r value has no effect on the latter.*

Figure 5.3 An Exchange Curve for the Case Where the A_i's are Known Explicitly.

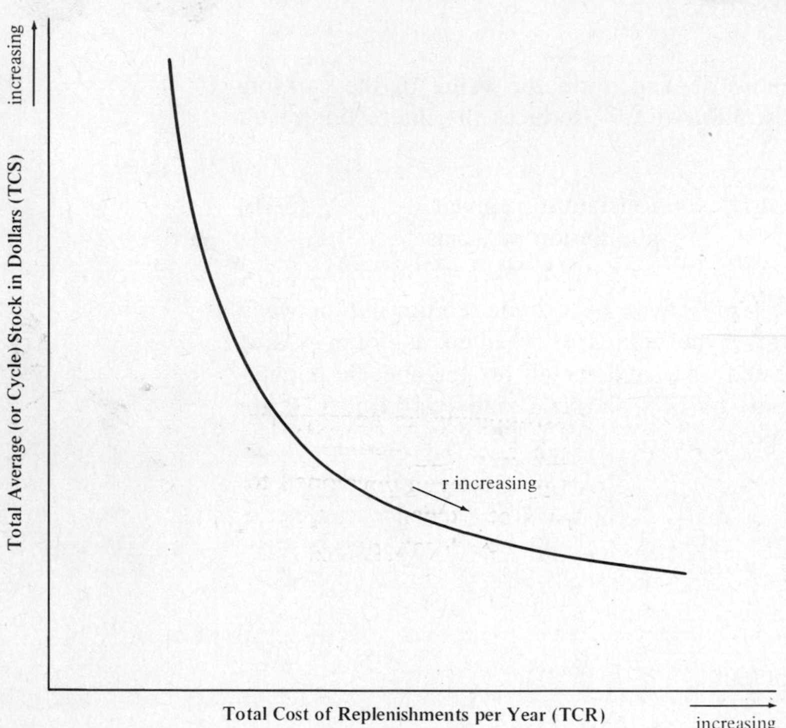

which shows that each point on the hyperbola has associated with it an implicit value of r. Moreover, Eqs. 5.8 and 5.9 show, for a given population of items, that the total average stock decreases as r increases while the total cost of replenishments per unit time increases with r.

Case 2—Common Unknown A

Again, as shown in Part 2 of the appendix of this chapter, if we use an economic order quantity for each item, we obtain the total average (or cycle) stock in dollars,

$$\text{TCS} = \sqrt{\frac{A}{r}} \frac{1}{\sqrt{2}} \sum_{i=1}^{n} \sqrt{D_i v_i} \tag{5.12}$$

and the total number of replenishments per unit time,

$$N = \sqrt{\frac{r}{A}} \frac{1}{\sqrt{2}} \sum_{i=1}^{n} \sqrt{D_i v_i} \tag{5.13}$$

Both TCS and N are seen to depend upon the value of the ratio A/r. Multiplication of Eqs. 5.12 and 5.13 gives

$$(\text{TCS})(N) = \frac{1}{2}\left(\sum_{i=1}^{n} \sqrt{D_i v_i}\right)^2 \tag{5.14}$$

which again is an hyperbola. Also, division of Eq. 5.12 by Eq. 5.13 gives

$$\frac{\text{TCS}}{N} = \frac{A}{r} \tag{5.15}$$

so that any point on the hyperbolic curve implies a value of A/r. Of course, if either A or r is known explicitly, the implicit value of A/r implies a value of the one remaining unknown parameter.

To summarize, in either of the above two cases, when an EOQ strategy* is used for each item, management can select a desired point on the tradeoff curve (with associated aggregate conditions), thus implying an appropriate value of r, A, or A/r (the latter parameters can now be thought of as management control variables). A computer routine has been developed to facilitate generation of either one of the two types of exchange curves. It should be noted that the use of r as a policy variable is closely related to a technique known as LIMIT (Lot-size Inventory Management Interpolation Technique) discussed by Eaton[5] or Harty et al.[9]

Exchange Curve for the MIDAS Professional Products Division

The Professional Products Division includes some 849 items, the majority of which are purchased from the same supplier in Germany. Therefore, it is realistic to think in terms of a fixed setup cost, A, which does not vary appreciably from item to item. Based on a detailed study of costs and policy factors management decided to set the value of A at \$3.20. The aforementioned computer routine was used to generate the exchange curve of

---

** When an aggregate constraint is to be satisfied it is not obvious that the best strategy for an individual item is to use an EOQ-type order quantity. In fact, the more mathematically oriented reader may wish to verify that, for example, minimization of the total number of replenishments per unit time subject to a specified total average stock (or minimization of total average stock subject to a specified total number of replenishments per unit time) does indeed lead to an EOQ-type formula. If a Lagrange multiplier approach is used, the multiplier turns out to be identical with r/A (or A/r).*

Figure 5.4 Aggregated Consequences of Different A/r Values–An Exchange Curve for the Professional Product Division of MIDAS.

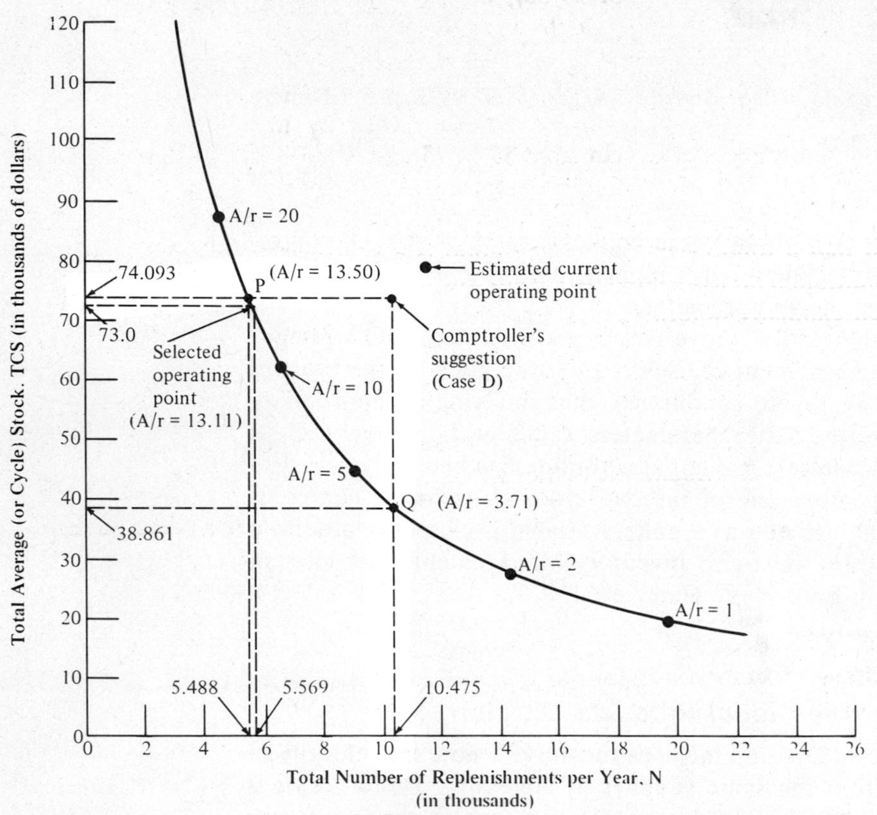

Figure 5.4. The $D_i v_i$ values needed in Eq. 5.14 were already available from the distribution-by-value analysis of Chapter 2. Two other points are also shown on Figure 5.4:

i. Current operating procedure (estimated by using the most recent replenishment quantity actually used for each of the items in the Division)

ii. The Q_i's implied by the decision rules suggested by the comptroller (Figure 1 of Case D)

It is seen that the comptroller's suggestion is preferable to current operating rules because it reduces both the total cycle stock and the total number of replenishments per year. However, further improvements are possible through the use of economic order quantities with a suitable value of A/r.

(This is because the comptroller's logic does not explicitly take economic factors into account—some inexpensive items are ordered too frequently while some fast-movers are not ordered often enough.) At one extreme, by operating at point P (with an implied A/r of 13.50), the same total cycle stock is achieved as by the comptroller's rule but the total number of replenishments per year is reduced from 10,475 to 5488 (a 47.6% reduction). Point Q (with an implied A/r of 3.71) represents the opposite extreme where the same total number of replenishments is achieved as by the comptroller's rule but the total cycle stock is cut from \$74,093 to \$38,861 (a 47.6% reduction). Decreases, compared with the comptroller's rule, are possible in both aggregate measures at any point between P and Q. Suppose management has agreed that a total cycle stock of \$73,000 is a reasonable aggregate operating condition. The associated A/r value (using Eq. 5.12) is 13.11. Since A has been explicitly determined, we have that

$$r = A \div A/r = 3.20 \div 13.11 = 0.244 \text{ \$/\$/yr.}$$

Rather than using a three decimal value for r, we choose to round to 0.24 \$/\$/yr. for convenience in subsequent calculations.

5.4 *Sensitivity Analysis**

In Chapter 3 we argued that the costs are insensitive to errors in selecting the exact size of a replenishment quantity. Let us now prove this statement for the case of the EOQ. Referring back to Figure 5.2, note that the total cost curve is quite shallow in the neighborhood of the EOQ. This indicates that reasonable sized deviations from the EOQ will have little impact on the total relevant costs incurred. Mathematically, suppose we use a quantity Q' which deviates from the EOQ according to the following relation:

$$Q' = (1 + p)\text{EOQ}$$

that is, $100p$ is the percentage deviation of Q' from the EOQ. The percentage cost penalty (PCP) for using Q' instead of the EOQ is given by

$$\text{PCP} = \frac{\text{TRC}(Q') - \text{TRC(EOQ)}}{\text{TRC(EOQ)}} \times 100$$

---

* *A detailed reference on this topic is Juckler.*[10]

Figure 5.5 Cost Penalty for Using a Q' Value Different From the EOQ.

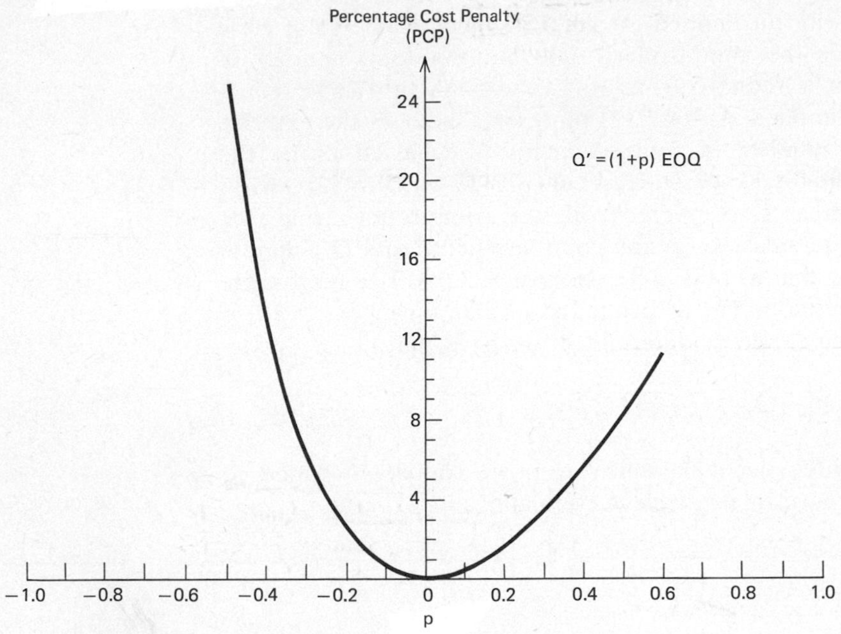

As shown in part 3 of the appendix of this chapter,

$$PCP = 50\left(\frac{p^2}{1+p}\right) \tag{5.16}$$

This expression is plotted in Figure 5.5. It is clear that even for values of p significantly different from zero the associated cost penalties are quite small.

To illustrate, consider the MIDAS item EDM-073 which was used as a numerical example in Section 5.2. The economic order quantity was found to be 400 units. Suppose that, instead, a value of 550 units was used. 550 is 1.375×400. Therefore, $p = 0.375$. Equation 5.16 or Figure 5.5 reveals that the percentage increase in total relevant costs is only 5.1%.

The insensitivity of total costs to the exact value of Q used has two important implications. First, use of an incorrect value of Q can result from inaccurate estimates of one or more of the parameters D, A, v, and r which are used to calculate the EOQ.* The conclusion is that it is not worth

---

* *It is worth noting that the cost penalty can actually be zero even if D, A, v, and r are inaccurately estimated, as long as the resulting ratio AD/vr is correct. For example, if both D and v are overestimated by the same percentage, the resulting EOQ will be the same as that resulting from use of the correct D and v values.*

making accurate estimates of these input parameters if considerable effort is involved; in most cases inexpensive, crude estimates should suffice. Secondly, certain order quantities may have additional appeal over the EOQ (for non-financial reasons or because of physical constraints which are not included in the basic EOQ model). The shallow nature of the total cost curve indicates that such values can be used provided that they are reasonably close to the EOQ. This seemingly trivial result is one of the important cornerstones of operational inventory control. Without this flexibility, implementable decision systems would be much more difficult to design.

5.5 *Implementation Aids*

Despite the simplicity of the EOQ formula of Eq. 5.4 it may often be unreasonable to expect a stock clerk to manually compute the square root relationship correctly on a consistent basis for many s.k.u. Consequently, several aids have been developed.

Special purpose slide rules and nomographs (see Davis[4]) are two types of aids. These are essentially mechanical devices. A promising development is that of special purpose preprogrammed desk top (or even portable) computers capable of computing not only EOQ's, but also some of the more elaborate formulae to be discussed in later sections of the book. In fact, almost all the programmes developed in conjunction with this book and designed for batch processing, have also been programmed on the Hewlett–Packard Model 65 electronic calculator. With such a device, the operator either inserts a card containing the values of A, D, v, and r or he keys in these numbers much as is done with a regular adding machine. Rather than elaborating further on such devices, we propose, in this section to show illustrations of two other common types of aids, namely graphical and table lookup procedures.

It should be emphasized that, even if a computer is available, it may be advantageous, at least initially, to use graphical or tabular aids. Such aids are more intuitively appealing to a practitioner than is the output from a computer. Moreover, they involve grouping of items into broad categories which also facilitates implementation.

5.5.1 *Graphical Procedures*

We shall illustrate only one of several possibilities. From Eq. 5.6 we have that the EOQ expressed as a time supply is given by

$$T_{\mathrm{EOQ}} = \sqrt{\frac{2A}{r}}\sqrt{\frac{1}{Dv}}$$

in years (if D is measured in units/yr).

or

$$T_{EOQ} = \sqrt{\frac{288A}{r}}\sqrt{\frac{1}{Dv}} \tag{5.17}$$

in months (if D is measured in units/yr). For a given value of A, Eq. 5.17 can be plotted as a function of Dv (assuming r is known). Repeating for several values of A results in a number of curves as indicated in Figure 5.6. (If more than one r value was possible, more than one set of curves would be necessary). The steps in using such a graph are as follows:

i. Evalute Dv for the item under consideration

ii. Look up this Dv value on the horizontal axis and move vertically to intersect the curve with the A value appropriate for the item.

iii. Move across horizontally from the intersection point to read the T_{EOQ} (in months) on the vertical scale.

iv. The EOQ is then given by

$$\text{EOQ} = \frac{D}{12} T_{EOQ}$$

Numerical Illustration—Consider product ISF-017, a box of 100 sheets of $8\frac{1}{2}$ in. × 11 in. stabilization paper sold by the Industrial Products Division. This product has been observed to have a relatively constant demand rate (D) of 200 boxes/yr. The unit variable cost (v) is \$16/box. Also assume that it is reasonable to use $A = \$3.20$ and $r = 0.24$ \$/\$/yr.
We have

$$Dv = \$3200/\text{yr}.$$

As shown in Figure 5.6, the intersection of a vertical line at \$3200/yr. and the curve corresponding to an A value of \$3.20 results in a T_{EOQ} of approximately 1.1 months. The replenishment quantity is thus

$$\begin{aligned} \text{EOQ} &\simeq (200/12 \text{ boxes/mo.}) \times 1.1 \text{ months} \\ &= 18 \text{ boxes} \end{aligned}$$

This method gives the true EOQ value, at least to the accuracy of reading the graph; hence, the cost error, if any, is negligible.

Figure 5.6 A Graphical Aid for Determining the EOQ.

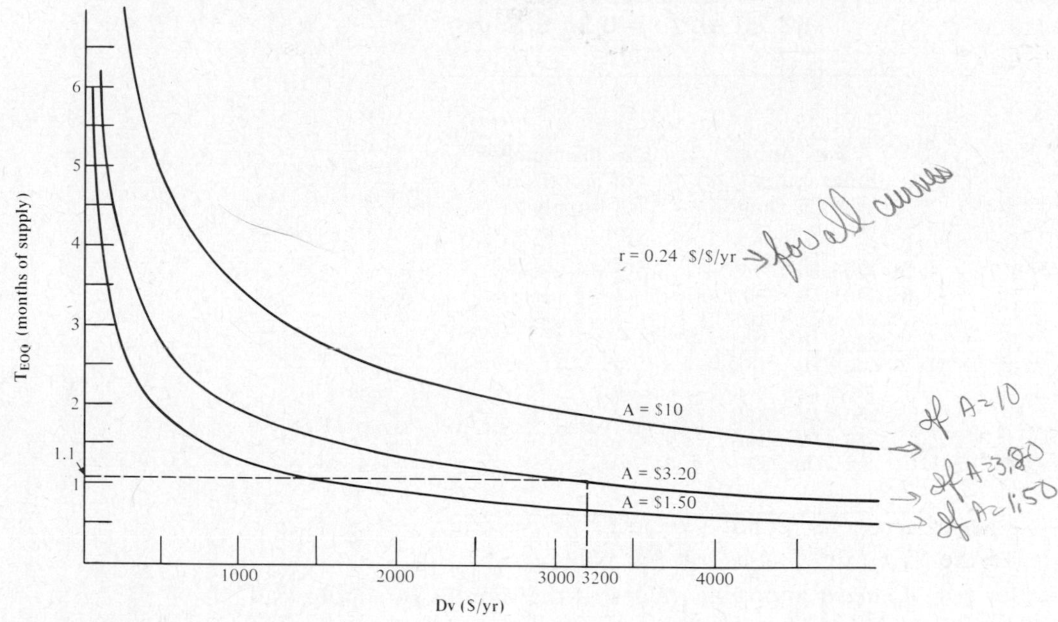

5.5.2 *Table Lookups*

An illustrative reference is the work of Welch.[21] The basic idea here is that one value of the order quantity (perhaps expressed as a time supply) is used over a range of one or more of the parameters. There is an economic tradeoff involved. The larger the number of ranges, the smaller are the percentage cost penalties resulting from not using the exact EOQ. However, the difficulty of compiling and using the tables increases with the number of ranges involved.

To illustrate let us consider a table usable for a set of MIDAS items having the same values of A and r. Suppose we deal with a group of items with $A = \$3.20$ and $r = 0.24$ \$/\$/yr. Furthermore, let us assume that management feels that the replenishment quantity of any item should be restricted to one of nine possible time supplies, namely $\frac{1}{4}$, $\frac{1}{2}$, $\frac{3}{4}$, 1, 2, 3, 4, 5, 6, and 12 months. Table 5.1 shows the months of supply to use as a function of the annual dollar usage (Dv) of the item under consideration. A numerical illustration of the use of the table will be given shortly. First, let us discuss how such a table is constructed.

Use of T months of supply is equivalent to use of a quantity $Q = DT/12$ provided D is measured in units/year which are the most common units. Use of Eq. 5.3 gives

$$\text{TRC (using } T \text{ months)} = \frac{DTvr}{24} + \frac{12A}{T}$$

Table 5.1 Tabular Aid for Use of EOQ (for $A=$ \$3.20 and $r=0.24$ \$/\$/yr.)

For annual dollar usage (Dv) in this range	Use this number of months of supply
$30{,}720 \leq Dv$	$\frac{1}{4}$ ($\simeq$ 1 week)
$10{,}240 \leq Dv < 30{,}720$	$\frac{1}{2}$ ($\simeq$ 2 weeks)
$5{,}120 \leq Dv < 10{,}240$	$\frac{3}{4}$ ($\simeq$ 3 weeks)
$1{,}920 \leq Dv < 5{,}120$	1
$640 \leq Dv < 1{,}920$	2
$320 \leq Dv < 640$	3
$160 \leq Dv < 320$	4
$53 \leq Dv < 160$	6
$Dv < 53$	12

Now consider two *adjacent* allowable values of the months of supply, call them T_1 and T_2. Equating the total relevant costs using T_1 months with that using T_2 months gives us the value of Dv at which we are indifferent to using T_1 and T_2, viz:

$$\frac{DT_1vr}{24}+\frac{12A}{T_1}=\frac{DT_2vr}{24}+\frac{12A}{T_2}$$

This reduces to

$$(Dv)_{\text{indifference}}=\frac{288A}{T_1T_2r}$$

To illustrate, for the given values of A and r in the MIDAS example, the indifference point for 1 month and 2 months is

$$(Dv)_{\text{indifference}}=\frac{288\times 3.20}{1\times 2\times 0.24}=\$1{,}920/\text{yr.}$$

In a similar fashion we can develop the rest of Table 5.1.

It should be emphasized that more than one value of A (and perhaps r) is likely to exist across a population of items. In such a case, a set of tables would be required, one for each of a number of possible A (and, perhaps, r) values.

Numerical Illustration—We use the same example as in the graphical case. Thus,

$$Dv = \$3200/\text{yr}.$$

The table indicates that a 1 month supply should be used. Therefore,

$$Q = \frac{D}{12} = 16.7,$$

say 17 boxes, that is, the film should be replenished in orders of 17 boxes. (The exact EOQ for this item is 18 boxes and the increase in costs for using 17 instead turns out to be only 0.3%.)

5.6 *Quantity Discounts*

A number of assumptions were made in Section 5.1 in order to derive the basic economic order quantity. One of the most severe of these was that the unit variable cost v did not depend upon the replenishment quantity. In many practical situations quantity discounts (on basic purchase price and/or transportation costs) exist. We must be able to modify the EOQ to cope with these conditions.

We shall restrict attention to the most common type of discount structure, namely that of an "all-units" discount. (The less common situation of an *incremental* discount structure has been treated in the literature by Hadley and Whitin.[8]) For the case of a single breakpoint, the unit variable cost behaves as follows:

$$v = \begin{cases} v_0 & 0 \le Q < Q_b \\ v_0(1-d) & Q_b \le Q \end{cases}$$

where v_0 is the basic unit cost without a discount and d is the discount expressed as a decimal fraction, given on *all* units when the replenishment quantity is equal to or greater than the breakpoint, Q_b. The *total* acquisition cost as a function of Q is shown in Figure 5.7. Note the discontinuity at the breakpoint.

Must now include Dv.

Now, it is essential to include the Dv component in a cost expression which is to be used for determining the best replenishment quantity. Proceeding exactly as in Section 5.2, but retaining the Dv component, we end up with two expressions for the total relevant costs, viz, for $0 \le Q < Q_b$,

$$\text{TRC}(Q) = Qv_0r/2 + AD/Q + Dv_0 \tag{5.18}$$

Figure 5.7 "All-Units" Quantity Discount.

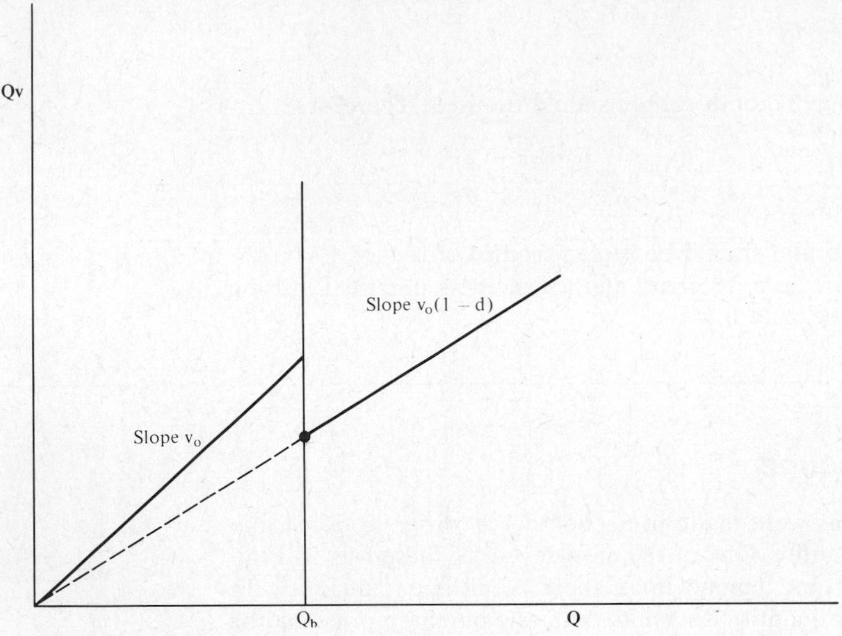

and for $Q_b \leq Q$

$$\text{TRC}\,(Q) = Qv_0(1-d)r/2 + AD/Q + Dv_0(1-d) \tag{5.19}$$

Although Eqs. 5.18 and 5.19 are valid for non-overlapping regions of Q, it is useful, in deriving an algorithm for finding the best Q, to compare the two cost expressions at the same value of Q. A term by term comparison of the right hand sides of the equations reveals that Eq. 5.19 gives a lower TRC (Q) than does Eq. 5.18 for the same Q. Therefore, if the lowest point on the Eq. 5.19 curve is a valid one (that is, at least as large as Q_b), it must be the optimum, since it is the lowest point on the lower curve.

It turns out that there are three possible types of solutions. These are illustrated in Figure 5.8. Taking advantage of the above property of Eq. 5.19 being the lower curve, the steps of an efficient algorithm for finding the best value of Q are:

Step 1 Compute the economic order quantity when the discount is applicable, that is,

$$\text{EOQ (discount)} = \sqrt{\frac{2AD}{v_0(1-d)r}}$$

Figure 5.8 Total Relevant Costs under "All-Units" Discount.

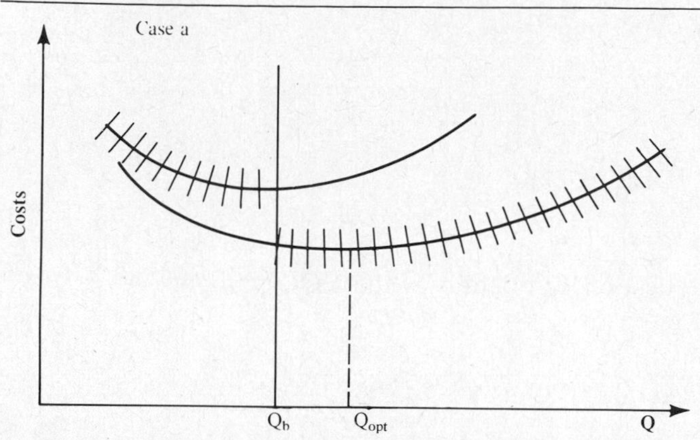

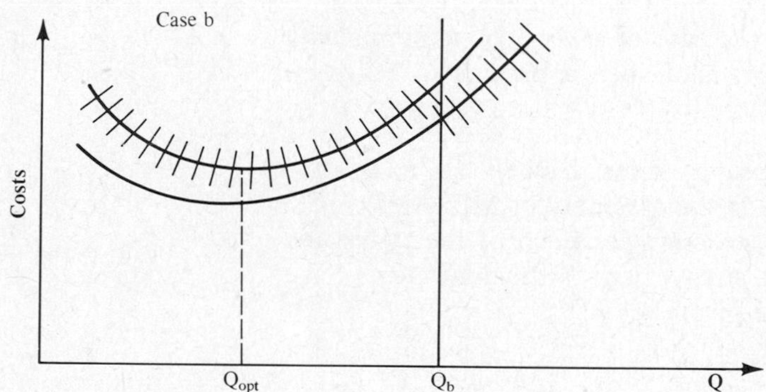

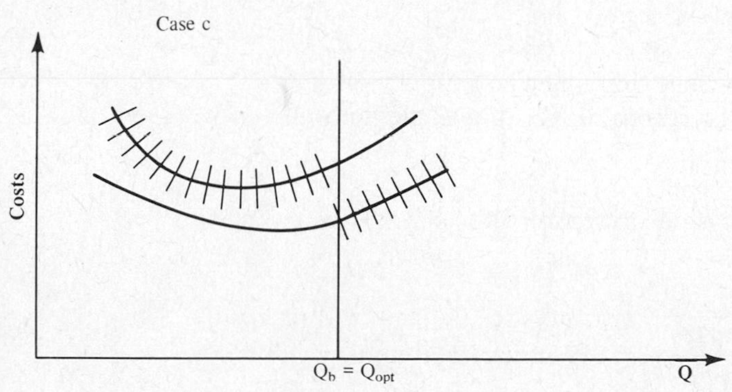

Step 2 Compare EOQ(d) with Q_b. If EOQ $(d) \geq Q_b$, then EOQ (d) is the best order quantity (case a of Figure 5.8)

If EOQ $(d) < Q_b$, go to step 3.

Step 3 Evaluate

$$\text{TRC (EOQ)} = \sqrt{2ADv_0r} + Dv_0$$

and TRC(Q_b), using Eq. 5.19.

If TRC (EOQ) < TRC (Q_b), the best order quantity is the EOQ without a discount (case b of Figure 5.8) given by

$$\text{EOQ (no discount)} = \sqrt{\frac{2AD}{v_0r}}$$

If TRC (EOQ) > TRC (Q_b), the best order quantity is Q_b (case c of Figure 5.8).

This logic can easily be extended to the case of several breakpoints with increasing discounts. A computer program of such a procedure has been developed.

Numerical Illustrations—Consider items EDM-010, EDM-012 and EDM-027, three components used in the assembly of MIDAMATICS. The supplier offers the same discount structure for each of the items and discounts are based on replenishment sizes of the *individual* items. The relevant characteristics of the items are given below.

Item	D units/yr.	v_0 \$/unit	A \$	r \$/\$/yr.
EDM-010	4160	2.40	1.50	0.24
EDM-012	104	3.10	1.50	0.24
EDM-027	416	14.20	1.50	0.24

Because of convenience in manufacturing and shipping, the supplier offers a 2% discount on any replenishment of 100 units or higher of a single item.

The computations are as follows:

EDM-010 (an illustration of case a of Figure 5.8)

Step 1

$$\text{EOQ (discount)} = \sqrt{\frac{2 \times 1.50 \times 4160}{2.40 \times 0.98 \times 0.24}} = 149 \text{ units} > 100 \text{ units}$$

Step 2 EOQ (discount) is greater than Q_b. Therefore, the Q to use is 149 units (perhaps rounded to 150 for convenience).

Case 2 *EDM-012* (an illustration of case b of Figure 5.8)

Step 1 EOQ (discount) = 21 units < 100 units.

Step 2 EOQ (discount) < Q_b, therefore go to step 3:

Step 3

$$\text{TRC (EOQ)} = \sqrt{2 \times 1.50 \times 104 \times 3.10 \times 0.24} + 104 \times 3.10$$
$$= \$337.64/\text{yr.}$$

$$\text{TRC}(Q_b) = \text{TRC (100)} = \frac{100 \times 3.10 \times 0.98 \times 0.24}{2} + \frac{1.50 \times 104}{100}$$
$$+ 104 \times 3.10 \times 0.98$$
$$= \$353.97/\text{yr.}$$

TRC (EOQ) < TRC (Q_b). Therefore, use the EOQ without a discount, that is,

$$\text{EOQ} = \sqrt{\frac{2 \times 1.50 \times 104}{3.10 \times 0.24}} \simeq 20 \text{ units.}$$

Case 3 *EDM-027* (an illustration of case c of Figure 5.8).
Step 1 EOQ (discount) = 19 units < 100 units.

Step 2 EOQ (discount) < Q_b, therefore go to step 3.

Step 3

$$\text{TRC (EOQ)} = \sqrt{2 \times 1.50 \times 416 \times 14.20 \times 0.24} + 416 \times 14.20$$
$$= \$5972.42/\text{yr.}$$

$$\text{TRC}(Q_b) = \text{TRC (100)} = \frac{100 \times 14.20 \times 0.98 \times 0.24}{2} + \frac{1.50 \times 4.6}{100}$$
$$+ 416 \times 14.20 \times 0.98$$
$$= \$5962.29/\text{yr.}$$

TRC (EOQ) > TRC(Q_b). Therefore, the best order quantity to use is Q_b, that is, 100 units.

Managers, buyers, purchasing agents, etc., rather than dealing with single items in isolation, often think in terms of a group of items purchased from a particular vendor. Thus, a potentially important discount situation has not been treated in this section, namely the case where a discount can be achieved by having a total order, involving two or more items, exceeding some breakpoint level. This topic will be addressed in Chapter 13 where we shall be concerned with coordinated replenishment strategies.

It should be mentioned that, in trying to achieve a quantity discount, one must be concerned about the implications of a large time supply, a topic to be discussed in the next section.

5.7 *Limits on Order Sizes*

The basic economic order quantity that we have derived considers only the costs of replenishing and carrying inventory. All the variables used reflect only financial considerations. There are a number of possible physical constraints, not explicitly included in the model, that might prevent use of the so-called best solution derived from the model. These include:

5.7.1 *Maximum Time Supply*

i. Shelf life (SL) of the commodity—Previously we derived the economic order quantity expressed as a time supply as

$$T_{\text{EOQ}} = \frac{\text{EOQ}}{D} = \sqrt{\frac{2A}{Dvr}}$$

As illustrated graphically in Figure 5.9, if this quantity exceeds the allowable shelf life SL, then the best feasible order quantity to use (that is, it produces the lowest feasible point on the cost curve) is the shelf life quantity itself,

$$Q_{\text{SL}} = D(\text{SL})$$

ii. Even without a shelf life limitation an EOQ that represents a very long time supply may be unrealistic for other reasons. A long time supply takes us well out into the future where demand becomes uncertain and obsolescence can become of significant concern. This is an important constraint on class C items as we shall see in a later chapter. A good example of obsolescence would be an impending engineering change.

Figure 5.9 Case of a Shelf-Life Constraint.

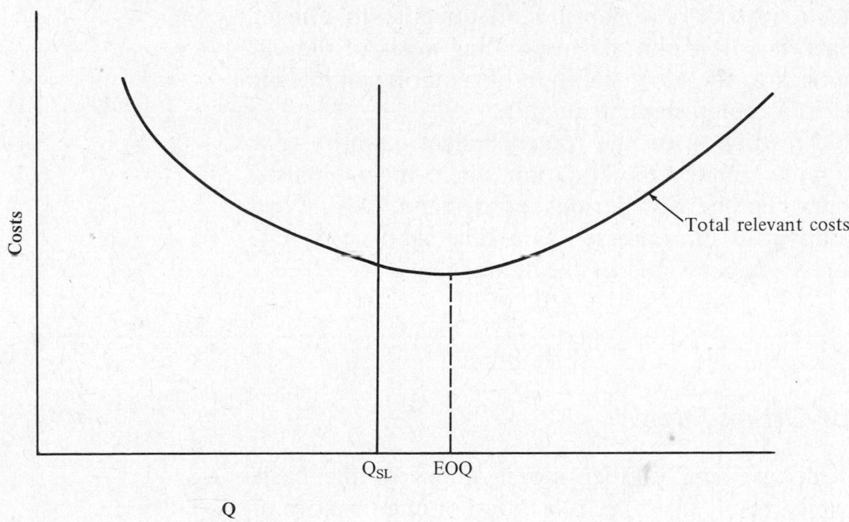

5.7.2 *Minimum Order Quantity*

The supplier may specify a minimum allowable order quantity. A similar situation exists in an in-house production operation where there is a lower limit on an order quantity which can be realistically considered. If the EOQ is less than this quantity, then the best allowable order quantity is the supplier or production minimum.

5.7.3 *Discrete Units*

The economic order quantity, as given by Eq. 5.4, will likely result in a non-integral number of units. However, it can be shown mathematically (and is obvious from the form of the total cost curve of Figure 5.2) that the best integer value of Q has to be one of the two integers surrounding the best (non-integer) solution given by Eq. 5.4. For simplicity we recommend simply rounding the result of Eq. 5.4, that is, the EOQ, to the nearest integer.*

---

* *Strictly speaking, one should evaluate the total costs, using Eq. 5.3, for each of the two surrounding integers and pick the integer having the lower costs. However, rounding produces trivial percentage cost penalties except possibly when the EOQ is in the range of only 1 or 2 units.*

Certain commodities are sold in pack sizes containing more than one unit; for example, MIDAS sells a certain type of film in a package of six units. Therefore, it makes sense to restrict a replenishment quantity to integer multiples of six units. In fact, if a new unit, corresponding to six of the old unit, is defined, then we're back to the basic situation of requiring an integer number of (the new) units in a replenishment quantity.

There is another possible restriction on the replenishment quantity very similar to that of discrete units, namely the situation where the replenishment must cover an integral number of periods of demand. Again, we simply find the optimal continuous Q expressed as a time supply (see Eq. 5.6) and round to the nearest integer value of the time supply.

5.8 *Incorporation of Other Factors*

In this section we briefly discuss four further modifications of the basic economic order quantity which result from the relaxation of one or more of the assumptions required in the earlier derivation. The treatment of one other important situation, namely where the quantity supplied does not necessarily exactly match the quantity ordered, can be found in Silver.[18]

5.8.1 *Non-Zero Constant Lead Time That is Known with Certainty*

As long as demand remains deterministic, the introduction of a known non-zero replenishment lead time (L) presents no difficulty. The inventory diagram of Figure 5.1 is unchanged. When the inventory level hits DL an order is placed and it arrives exactly L time units later just as the inventory hits zero. The costs are unaltered so that the best order quantity is still given by Eq. 5.4. As we shall see in Chapters 6 and 7, a non-zero lead time considerably complicates matters when demand is probabilistic.

5.8.2 *Finite Replenishment Rate*

m = production rate

One of the assumptions inherent in the derivation of the EOQ was that the whole replenishment quantity arrives at the same time. If instead, we assume that it becomes available at a rate of m per unit time (the production rate of the machinery used to produce the item), then the sawtoothed diagram of Figure 5.1 is modified to that of Figure 5.10. All that changes from the earlier derivation is the average inventory level which is now $Q/2\,(1-D/m)$. The total relevant costs are given by

$$\text{TRC}\,(Q) = \frac{Q(1-D/m)vr}{2} + \frac{AD}{Q}$$

Figure 5.10 Case of a Finite Replenishment Rate.

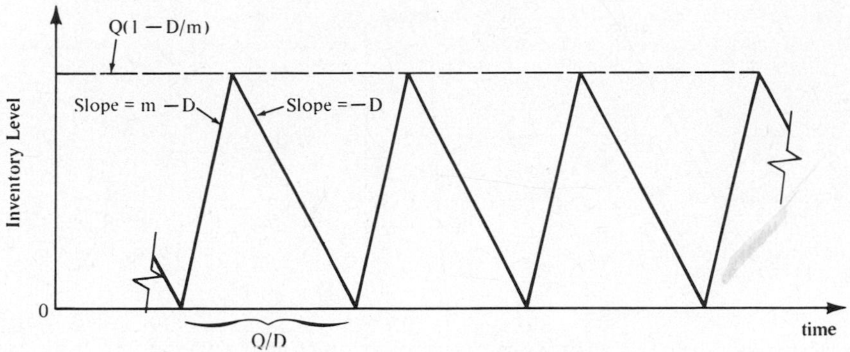

and the best Q value is now the finite replenishment economic order quantity,

$$\text{FREOQ} = \sqrt{\frac{2AD}{vr(1 - D/m)}}$$

$$= \text{EOQ} \cdot \frac{1}{\sqrt{(1 - D/m)}} \tag{5.20}$$

that is, the EOQ multiplied by a correction factor. The magnitude of this correction factor for various values of D/m is shown in Figure 5.11. Also shown are the cost penalties caused by ignoring the correction and simply using the basic EOQ. It is clear that D/m has to be fairly large before the cost penalty becomes significant, for example, even when D/m is 0.5 (that is, the demand rate is one half of the production rate) the cost penalty for neglecting the finite nature of the production rate is only 6.1%.

5.8.3 *Different Type of Carrying Charge*

In section 5.2 we assumed that the carrying charge was directly proportional to the average inventory level measured in dollars. Modifications are possible. Each can be handled with the resulting order quantity expression being somewhat more complex than Eq. 5.4. To illustrate:

Consider the situation where costs depend upon area or volume considerations as well as the value of the inventory. (It is intuitive that it should cost more per unit time to store a dollar of feathers than a dollar of coal.) Suppose that there is a charge of w dollars per unit time per cubic foot of space allocated to an item. Assume that this space must be sufficient to handle the maximum inventory level of the item. One situation where such a charge would be appropriate is where items are maintained in separate bins

Figure 5.11 Use of EOQ When There is a Finite Replenishment Rate.

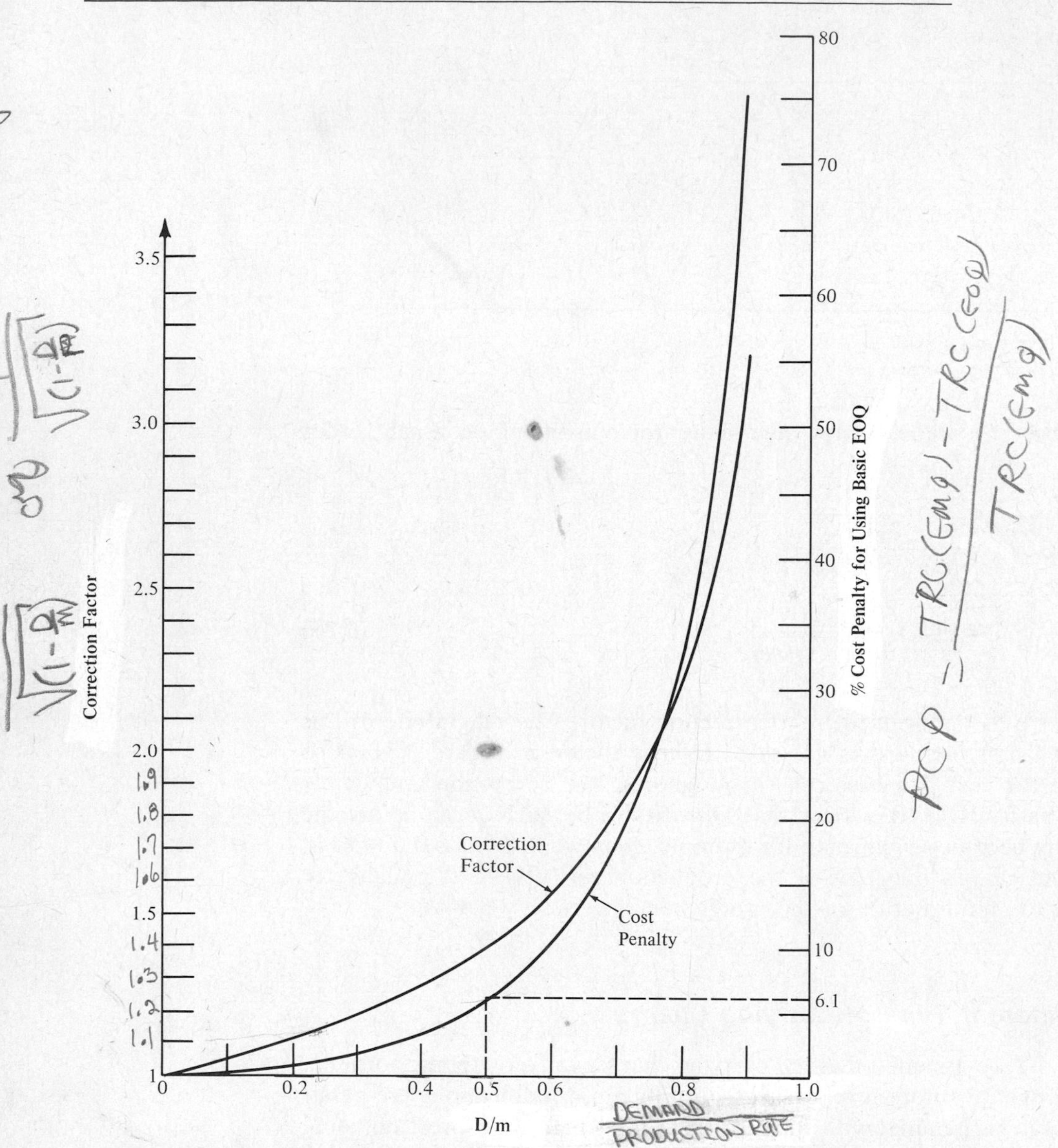

and a specific bin size (which must house the maximum inventory) is allocated to an item. The best replenishment quantity under these circumstances is

$$\sqrt{\frac{2AD}{2hw + vr}}$$

where h is the volume (in cubic feet) occupied per unit of the item.

5.8.4 A Special Opportunity to Procure

An important situation, often faced by both producers and merchants, is a one-time opportunity to procure an item at a reduced unit cost (a particular case being where this is the last opportunity to replenish before a price rise).

Because of the change in one of the parameters (the unit cost) the current order quantity certainly can differ from future order quantities (these future quantities will all be identical, namely the EOQ with the new unit cost). Thus the simple sawtooth pattern of Figure 5.1 no longer necessarily applies. Hence, we cannot base our analysis on the average inventory level and number of replenishments in a typical year (or other unit of time). Instead, in comparing two possible choices for the current value of the order quantity Q, strictly speaking, we should compare costs out to a point in time where the two alternatives leave us in an identical inventory state. To illustrate, suppose that the demand rate is 100 units/month and the new EOQ will be 200 units. Further, suppose that two alternatives under consideration for the current order quantity are 200 and 400 units. As shown in Figure 5.12, an appropriate horizon for cost comparison would be 4 months because, for both alternatives, the inventory level would be zero at that point in time. A comparison of costs out to 1.95 months, for example, would be biased in favor of the 200 unit alternative because the imminent (0.05 months later) setup cost under this alternative would not be included. An exact comparison for all alternatives is rather complex mathematically, particularly when there is a continuum of choices for the order quantity. For such an analysis, see Brown.[2]

We instead recommend an approximate approach, suggested by Naddor.[15] Let the decision variable, the current order quantity, be denoted by Q. Let the current unit cost be v_1 and the future unit cost be $v_2 (v_2 > v_1)$. The economic order quantity, after the price rise, is given by Eq. 5.4 as

$$\mathrm{EOQ}_2 = \sqrt{\frac{2AD}{v_2 r}} \tag{5.21}$$

Furthermore, from Eq. 5.5 the costs per unit time are then

$$\mathrm{TRC}\,(\mathrm{EOQ}_2) = \sqrt{2ADv_2 r} + Dv_2 \tag{5.22}$$

If the current order quantity is of size Q, then it will last for Q/D units of time. The average inventory during this period is $Q/2$. Hence, the total costs out to time Q/D are

$$\begin{aligned} TC(Q) &= A + Qv_1 + \frac{Q}{2} v_1 \frac{Q}{D} r \\ &= A + Qv_1 + \frac{Q^2 v_1 r}{2D} \end{aligned} \tag{5.23}$$

Figure 5.12 Comparison of Two Alternatives When the Order Quantity Changes with Time.

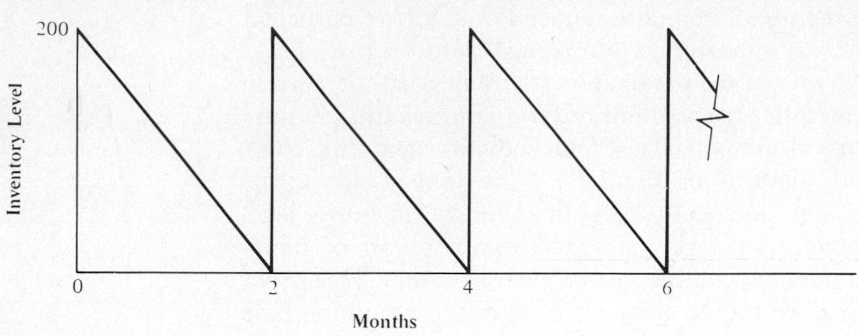

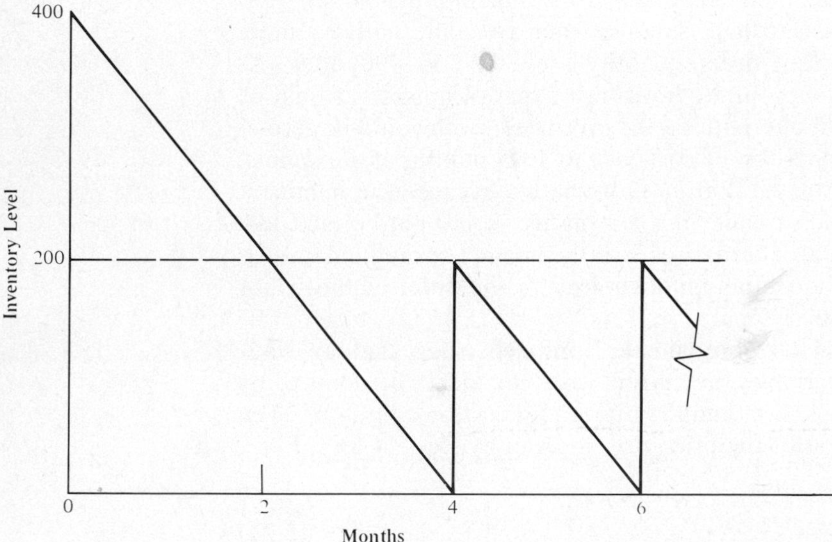

Consider the extreme case where Q was set equal to 0 so that the price increase would occur and we would immediately start ordering the new EOQ_2. Under this strategy total costs out to some time T would be, from Eq. 5.22,

$$T \cdot \sqrt{2ADv_2r} + DTv_2$$

It is reasonable to select the value of Q to maximize

$$F(Q) = Q/D\,\sqrt{2ADv_2r} + Qv_2 - TC(Q) \tag{5.24}$$

the improvement in total cost out to time Q/D achieved by ordering Q at the old price instead of not ordering anything at the old price. It can be shown that use of this criterion need not lead to the exact cost minimizing solution. What we are doing here, for the first time, is developing a heuristic rule; as discussed in Chapter 1, a heuristic is a plausible, relatively simple, procedure for selecting the value of the decision variable (in this case Q). A convenient approach to maximizing $F(Q)$ is to set $dF(Q)/dQ=0$. From Eqs. 5.23 and 5.24

$$F(Q)=\frac{Q}{D}\sqrt{2ADv_2r}+Qv_2-A-Qv_1-\frac{Q^2v_1r}{2D}$$

$$\frac{dF(Q)}{dQ}=\frac{1}{D}\sqrt{2ADv_2r}+v_2-v_1-\frac{Qv_1r}{D}=0 \tag{5.25}$$

or

$$Q_{\text{opt.}}=\frac{\sqrt{2ADv_2r}}{v_1r}+\frac{v_2-v_1}{v_1}\frac{D}{r}$$

that is,

$$Q_{\text{opt.}}=\frac{v_2}{v_1}\text{EOQ}_2+\frac{v_2-v_1}{v_1}\frac{D}{r} \tag{5.26}$$

Numerical Illustration—Consider a particular Toronto-based X-ray film dealer supplied by MIDAS. Suppose that MIDAS announces a price increase for product XMF-082 from \$28.00/box to \$30.00/box. The dealer uses approximately 80 boxes per year and estimates the fixed cost per order to be \$1.50 and the carrying charge as 0.20 \$/\$/yr.

From Eq. 5.21

$$\text{EOQ}_2=\sqrt{\frac{2\times1.50\times80}{30.00\times0.2}}\simeq6 \text{ boxes}$$

Then, Eq. 5.26 gives

$$Q_{\text{opt}}=\frac{30.00}{28.00}(6)+\frac{2.00}{28.00}\frac{80}{0.2}$$
$$=35.3, \text{ say } 35 \text{ boxes.}$$

The increase in unit price from \$28.00/box to \$30.00/box (a 7% increase) causes a one-time procurement quantity of 35 boxes instead of 6 boxes (an increase of almost 500%!), a much higher sensitivity than in the basic EOQ itself (see Section 5.4).

Substitution of each of $Q = 6$ and $Q = 35$ into Eq. 5.25 gives

$$F(6) = \$12.09$$

and

$$F(35) = \$42.23$$

so that the one-time cost savings of using the order quantity of 35 boxes are $(42.23 - 12.09)$ or \$30.14.

Two additional points are worth making:

i. The one-time purchase is likely to represent a large time supply. Obsolescence and other forms of uncertainty may dictate an upper limit on this time supply.

ii. The multi-item case, where a vendor offers a one-time price break on a range of products, is obviously of interest. In such a situation there is likely to be a constraint on the total amount that can be spent on the one-time purchase or on the total inventory (because of warehouse capacity). For illustrative purposes, let us consider the case of a constraint on the total amount that can be spent. For notation let

D_i be the usage rate of item i, in units/yr.

A_i be the fixed setup cost of item i, in dollars

v_{1i} be the unit cost of item i in the special opportunity to buy, in \$/unit

v_{2i} be the unit cost of item i in the future, in \$/unit

Q_i be the amount, in units, of item i to be purchased in the special buy

EOQ_{2i} be the economic order quantity of item i in units, under the future unit cost

n be the number of items in the group under consideration (we assume in the sequel that the items are numbered $1, 2, 3, \ldots, n$)

W be the maximum total amount in dollars, that can be spent on the special buy.

Then, the procedure for selecting the Q_i's is as follows:

Step 1: Determine the unconstrained best Q_i's by the analog of Eq. 5.26, namely

$$Q_i^* = \frac{v_{2i}}{v_{1i}} \text{EOQ}_{2i} + \frac{v_{2i} - v_{1i}}{v_{1i}} \frac{D_i}{r} \qquad i = 1, 2, \ldots, n \tag{5.27}$$

Step 2: Calculate the total dollar value of the unconstrained Q_i's and compare with the constraining value, viz:
From Eq. 5.27

$$\sum_{i=1}^{n} Q_i^* v_{1i} = \sum_{i=1}^{n} [v_{2i} \text{ EOQ}_{2i} + (v_{2i} - v_{1i}) D_i / r] \tag{5.28}$$

If $\sum_{i=1}^{n} Q_i^* v_{1i} \leq W$, we use the Q_i^*'s of step 1. If not, we go to Step 3.

Step 3: Compute the constrained best Q_i values. (The derivation is shown in part 4 of the appendix of this chapter):

$$Q_i^* = \frac{v_{2i}}{v_{1i}} \left\{ \text{EOQ}_{2i} + \frac{D_i}{r} \right\} - \frac{D_i}{\sum_{j=1}^{n} D_j v_{1j}} \times \left[\sum_{j=1}^{n} v_{2j} \left(\text{EOQ}_{2j} + \frac{D_j}{r} \right) - W \right] \qquad i = 1, 2, \ldots, n \tag{5.29}$$

A further interesting reference on this problem area is Gossett and Newlove.[17]

5.9 *Summary*

In this chapter we have specified a procedure for selecting the appropriate size of a replenishment quantity under demand conditions that are essentially static in nature, the assumption being that the demand rate is at a constant level which does not change with time. Under a rigorous set of assumptions the resulting order quantity is the well-known square root, economic order quantity.

We argued that one or both of the parameters r and A may be very difficult to obtain from explicit cost considerations. In such a case it was shown that a value of r, A, or A/r can be implicitly specified by selecting a desired operating point on an aggregate exchange curve of total average stock versus total number or costs of replenishments per year.

Sizable deviations of the order quantity away from the optimum value were seen to produce rather small cost errors. This robust feature of the

EOQ helps justify its widespread use in practice. Often, the limited savings achievable do not justify the effort required to develop overly sophisticated variations of the EOQ.

Several simple modifications of the basic EOQ were discussed; these modifications make the results more widely applicable. In the next two chapters we shall develop practical procedures for coping with an extremely important extension, namely where demand is no longer deterministic. Three other important extensions will be left to later chapters, namely

i. Situations where the average or forecast demand rate varies with time (Chapter 8).

ii. Situations (referred to as multi-echelon) where the replenishment quantities of serially related production or storage facilities should not be treated independently. (Chapter 12).

iii. Situations where savings in replenishment costs are possible through the coordination of two or more items at the same stocking point. (Chapter 13).

In each of these circumstances we shall see that the basic EOQ plays an important role.

Appendix to Chapter 5—Derivations.

1 Exchange Curve Equations when the A_i's are Known Explicitly

Suppose that we have n items in the population and we designate item i's characteristics by A_i, v_i, and D_i. Total average (or cycle) stock in dollars,

$$\text{TCS} = \sum_{i=1}^{n} \frac{Q_i v_i}{2}$$

and total cost of replenishments per unit time.

$$\text{TCR} = \sum_{i=1}^{n} A_i D_i / Q_i$$

If we use the EOQ for each item, we have, from Eq. 5.4,

$$Q_i = \sqrt{\frac{2A_i D_i}{v_i r}}$$

Therefore,

$$\text{TCS} = \sum_{i=1}^{n} \sqrt{\frac{A_i D_i v_i}{2r}} = \frac{1}{\sqrt{r}} \frac{1}{\sqrt{2}} \sum_{i=1}^{n} \sqrt{A_i D_i v_i}$$

which is Eq. 5.8.

Also,

$$\text{TCR} = \sum_{i=1}^{n} \sqrt{\frac{A_i D_i v_i r}{2}} = \sqrt{r} \frac{1}{\sqrt{2}} \sum_{i=1}^{n} \sqrt{A_i D_i v_i}$$

which is Eq. 5.9.

2 Exchange Curve Equations when A/r is Constant Across All Items

As above,

$$\text{TCS} = \sum_{i=1}^{n} \sqrt{\frac{A D_i v_i}{2r}} = \sqrt{\frac{A}{r}} \frac{1}{\sqrt{2}} \sum_{i=1}^{n} \sqrt{D_i v_i}$$

which is Eq. 5.12.

Now, the total number of replenishments per unit time is

$$N = \sum_{i=1}^{n} D_i/Q_i$$

$$= \sum_{i=1}^{n} \sqrt{\frac{D_i v_i r}{2A}} = \sqrt{\frac{r}{A}} \frac{1}{\sqrt{2}} \sum_{i=1}^{n} \sqrt{D_i v_i}$$

which is Eq. 5.13.

3. *Penalty for Using an Erroneous Value of the Replenishment Quantity*

The percentage cost penalty is

$$\text{PCP} = \frac{\text{TRC}(Q') - \text{TRC}(\text{EOQ})}{\text{TRC}(\text{EOQ})} \times 100 \tag{5.30}$$

where

$$Q' = (1+p)\text{EOQ} = (1+p)\sqrt{\frac{2AD}{vr}}$$

Substituting this Q' expression into the Eq. 5.3 representation of TRC, we obtain

$$\text{TRC}(Q') = (1+p)\sqrt{\frac{ADvr}{2}} + \frac{1}{1+p}\sqrt{\frac{ADvr}{2}}$$

$$= \sqrt{2ADvr}\,\tfrac{1}{2}\left(1+p+\frac{1}{1+p}\right) \tag{5.31}$$

Also from Eq. 5.5

$$\text{TRC}(\text{EOQ}) = \sqrt{2ADvr} \tag{5.32}$$

Substituting the results of Eqs. 5.31 and 5.32 into Eq. 5.30 gives

$$\text{PCP} = \left[\frac{1}{2}\left(1+p+\frac{1}{1+p}\right) - 1\right] \times 100$$

or

$$\text{PCP} = 50\left(\frac{1}{1+p} - 1 + p\right) = 50\left(\frac{p^2}{1+p}\right)$$

4. *Multi-item Special Opportunity to Procure*

As in Section 5.8.4. we would like to pick each Q_i so as to maximize

$$\frac{Q_i}{D_i}\sqrt{2A_iD_iv_{2i}r} + Q_iv_{2i} - A_i - Q_iv_{1i} - \frac{Q_i^2v_{1i}r}{2D_i}$$

However, there is the constraint (which we now know is binding because of the answer to Step 2 which caused us to go to Step 3)

$$\sum_{i=1}^{n} Q_iv_{1i} = W \tag{5.33}$$

We use a standard constrained optimization procedure, the Lagrange multiplier approach (See Appendix A). We maximize

$$L(Q_i\text{'s}, M) = \sum_{i=1}^{n}\left[\frac{Q_i}{D_i}\sqrt{2A_iD_iv_{2i}r} + Q_iv_{2i} - A_i - Q_iv_{1i} - \frac{Q_i^2v_{1i}r}{2D_i}\right] - M\left(\sum_{i=1}^{n} Q_iv_{1i} - W\right)$$

where M is a Lagrange multiplier.

Taking partial derivatives and setting them to zero,

$$\frac{\partial L}{\partial M} = 0$$

gives Eq. 5.33 and

$$\frac{\partial L}{\partial Q_j} = 0 \qquad (j = 1, 2, \ldots, n)$$

leads to

$$Q_j^* = \frac{v_{2j}}{v_{1j}}\text{EOQ}_{2j} + \frac{v_{2j} - (M+1)v_{1j}}{v_{1j}}\frac{D_j}{r} \qquad (j = 1, 2, \ldots, n) \tag{5.34}$$

where Q_j^* is the best constrained value of Q_j.

Therefore,

$$Q_j^* v_{1j} = v_{2j}\,\mathrm{EOQ}_{2j} + [v_{2j} - (M+1)v_{1j}]\frac{D_j}{r} \tag{5.35}$$

Summing Eq. 5.35 over j and using Eq. 5.33, there follows

$$\sum_{j=1}^{n} v_{2j}\,\mathrm{EOQ}_{2j} + \sum_{j=1}^{n} [v_{2j} - (M+1)v_{1j}]\frac{D_j}{r} = W$$

This is solved for $M+1$ and the result is substituted into Eq. 5.35, producing Eq. 5.29 of the main text.

Problems for Chapter 5

Problem 5.1

a. For MIDAS item EDM-073, used as an illustration in Section 5.2, suppose that A was changed to \$12.80. Now find

i. EOQ in units
ii. EOQ in dollars
iii. EOQ as a months of supply

Does the effect of the change in A make sense?

b. For the same item suppose that A was still \$3.20 but r was increased from 0.24/yr. to 0.30/yr. Find the same quantities requested in part a). Does the effect of the change in r make sense?

Problem 5.2

Suppose there are two identical machines that can be used to produce three items. Demand for item 1 will keep $1\frac{1}{4}$ machines busy while demand for each of items 2 and 3 will keep $\frac{1}{4}$ machine busy. How would you schedule production in such a situation? Why might the machines be loaded to capacity?

Problem 5.3

Consider an item where the unit variable cost v is not independent of the order quantity Q. More specifically, we have

$$v = a + \frac{b}{Q} \qquad (1)$$

a. Under these conditions, what is the order quantity that minimizes costs?

b. Check your result for the case of $b = 0$.

c. What physical reasons might there be for Eq. 1?

Problem 5.4

Suppose that all of the assumptions of the EOQ derivation hold except that we now allow backorders (that is, we deliberately let the stock level run negative before we order; backordered requests are completely filled out of the replenishment). Now there are two decision variables: Q and s (the level below zero at which we place an order).

a. Using a sketch and geometrical considerations find the average on-hand inventory level and the average level of backorders.

b. Suppose that there is a cost B_2v per unit backordered (independent of how long the unit is backordered) where B_2 is a dimensionless factor. Find the best settings of Q and s as a function of A, D, v, r, and B_2.

c. Repeat part b but now with a cost B_3v per unit backordered *per unit time*. The dimensions of B_3 are equivalent to those for r.

Problem 5.5

The famous Ernie of "Sesame Street" continually faces replenishment decisions concerning his cookie supply. The Cookie Monster devours the cookies at an average rate of 200 per day. The biscuits cost \$0.03 each. Ernie is getting fed up with having to go to the store once a week. His friend, Bert, has offered to do a study to help Ernie with his problem.

a. If Ernie is implicitly following an EOQ policy, what can Bert say about the implicit values of the two missing parameters?

b. Suppose that the store offered a special of 10,000 cookies for \$200. Should Ernie take advantage of the offer? Discuss. (*Hint:* Consult your local T.V. listing for the timing of and channel selection for "Sesame Street.")

Problem 5.6

A discount store sells plastic garbage bags in two package sizes as follows:

No. of Bags in Package	Cost for Package
10	\$0.49 (this is the normal package)
30	\$0.89 (this is a one-time special size)

A housewife is in a dilemma as to how many to purchase on this single shopping trip. She shops frequently for many different items so that the A factor can be neglected for this specific item. She estimates (with very little uncertainty) that her family uses 2 bags per week.

a. Express the optimal order quantity (up to a maximum of 90 bags) as a function of the carrying charge, r.

b. Also, give the optimal order quantity for $r = 0.07$/year.

Note: A package cannot be broken open in the store.

Problem 5.7

U. R. Sick Labs manufactures penicillin. Briefly discuss special considerations required in establishing the run quantity of such an item.

Problem 5.8

In a certain far east country the government is trying to prevent hoarding of a particular commodity. They do this by applying a reverse quantity discount, that is,

$$v = v_1 \quad \text{for} \quad Q < Q_{bp}$$

and

$$v = v_2 > v_1 \quad \text{for} \quad Q \geq Q_{bp}.$$

Suppose that a consumer feels that all of the other assumptions underlying the basic EOQ hold.

a. Develop a decision rule for finding the cost-minimizing value of Q as a function of D, A, v_1, v_2, Q_{bp} and r.

b. Illustrate for

$$D = 9000 \text{ units/yr.}$$

$$A = \$25$$

$$v_1 = \$0.25\text{/unit}; \; v_2 = \$0.36\text{/unit}$$

$$r = 0.2 \text{ \$/\$/yr.}$$

$$Q_{bp} = 2000 \text{ units.}$$

Problem 5.9

Consider an inventory with but four items with the following characteristics:

Item, i	D_i (units/yr.)	v_i (\$/unit)
1	7200	2.00
2	4000	0.90
3	500	5.00
4	100	0.81

The inventory manager vehemently argues that there is no way that he can evaluate A and r, however, he is prepared to admit that A/r is reasonably constant across the items. He has been following an ordering policy of using a 4-month time supply of each item. He has been under pressure from the comptroller to reduce the average inventory level by 25 percent. Therefore, he is about to adopt a 3-month time supply.

a. Develop an aggregate exchange curve assuming EOQ ordering rules.

b. Use the curve to suggest option(s) open to the manager which is (are) preferable to his proposed action.

Problem 5.10

The Acme company sells a particular product to a large number of customers. Demand is essentially constant at 100 units per month. Acme has been using a policy of running 1 month's supply every month. The production time of any reasonable sized lot is of negligible length. An analyst has estimated the following characteristics of the item:

unit variable cost – \$24.00 per dozen units.
selling price – \$30.00 per dozen units.
fixed cost per setup – \$8.00.
carrying charge – 0.24 \$/\$/yr.

a. What is the economic order quantity of the item?

b. What is the annual cost penalty of using the current policy?

c. What is the turnover ratio under the current policy? Under the EOQ strategy?

d. How can the turnover ratio be *lower* under the EOQ strategy which is supposed to be optimal?

Problem 5.11

A manufacturing firm located in Stratford produces an item in a 3-month time supply. An analyst, attempting to introduce a more logical approach to selecting run quantities, has obtained the following estimates of characteristics of the item:

$D = 4000$ units/yr.

$A = \$5.00$

$v = \$4$ per 100 units

$r = 0.25$ \$/\$/yr.

Note: Assume that the production rate is much larger than D.

a. What is the economic order quantity of the item?

b. What is the time between consecutive replenishments of the item when the EOQ is used?

c. The production manager insists that the $A = \$5.00$ figure has been pulled out of the air, that is, it is only a guess. Therefore, he insists on using his simple 3-month supply rule. Indicate how you would find the range of A values for which the EOQ (based on $A = \$5.00$) would be preferable (in terms of a lower total of replenishment and carrying costs) to the 3-month supply.

Problem 5.12

MIDAS can load and package their own brand of 35 mm slide film, or buy prepacked rolls of "Discount" brand film. If they load their own film, there is a production setup cost of \$20. The finished product is valued at \$1.23 a roll, and the production rate is 500 rolls/day. "Discount" film costs MIDAS \$1.26 per roll and the fixed ordering charge is \$3.00/order. In either case, an inventory carrying charge of 0.24 \$/\$/yr. would be used by the company. Demand for this item is 10,000 rolls per year. From the standpoint of replenishment and carrying costs, what should the company do? What other considerations might affect the decision?

Problem 5.13

In Figure 1 of MIDAS Case D it was pointed out that the comptroller was advocating a (min, max) system with specific rules for computing the minimum and maximum levels of each item. Suppose that for each item the values of of A, v, D, L, and r could be reasonably accurately ascertained.

a. Indicate how you would estimate the approximate cost savings of selecting the order quantity of an item through EOQ considerations rather than by the Comptroller's method. (*Hint:* Assume that the order quantity is approximately equal to the difference between the maximum and minimum levels.)

b. Illustrate for the following item: $A = \$3.20$; $v = \$10.00$; $D = 900$ units/yr.; $L = 10$ weeks; $r = 0.24$ \$/\$/yr.

REFERENCES FOR CHAPTER 5

1. Brown, R. G. "Use of the Carrying Charge to Control Cycle Stocks." *APICS Quarterly Bulletin,* Vol. 2, No. 3, July. 1961. pp. 29–46.

2. Brown, R. G. *Decision Rules for Inventory Management.* Holt, Rinehart and Winston, New York, 1967, pp. 201–3.

3. Buzacott, J. A. "Economic Order Quantities with Inflation." *Operational Research Quarterly,* Vol. 26, No. 3, September, 1975, pp. 553–558.

4. Davis, G. B. "The Preparation and Use of Nomographs." Ch. 15 in *Scientific Inventory Management.* J. Buchan & E. Koenigsberg. Prentice-Hall, Englewood Cliffs, N.J., 1963.

5. Eaton, J. A. "New-The LIMIT Technique." *Modern Materials Handling,* Vol. 19, No. 2, February, 1964, pp. 38–43.

6. Girling, A. and R. Morgan. "Exchange Curves for Fixing Batch Quantities." *OMEGA,* Vol. 1, No. 2, 1973, pp. 241–245.

7. Gossett, T. E. and G. H. Newlove. "Inventory Gains and Losses." *Management Services,* Vol. 2, No. 4, July–August, 1965, pp. 52–56.

8. Hadley, G. and T. Whitin. *Analysis of Inventory Systems.* Prentice-Hall, Englewood Cliffs, N.J., 1963, pp. 66–68.

9. Harty, J. D., G. W. Plossl and O. W. Wight. *Management of Lot-Size Inventories.* A special Education and Research Report of the American Production and Inventory Control Society, Chicago, Illinois, 1963.

10. Juckler, F. *Modèles de Gestion des Stocks et Coûts Marginaux.* Vandeur, Louvain, 1970.

11. Keachie, E. C. and R. J. Fontana. "Effects of Learning on Optimal Lot Size." *Management Science,* Vol. 13, No. 2, October, 1966, pp. 102–108.

12. Lindbäck, K. "The Economic Consequences of Deviations from Economic Lot Sizes." *International Journal of Production Research,* Vol. 6, No. 2, 1967, pp. 97–107.

13. Lippman, S. "Economic Order Quantities and Multiple Set-Up Costs." *Management Science,* Vol. 16, No. 1, September, 1969, pp. 118–138.

14. Mennell, R. F. "Early History of the Economical Lot Size." *APICS Quarterly Bulletin,* Vol. 2, No. 2, April, 1961, pp. 14–22.

15. Naddor, E. *Inventory Systems.* John Wiley and Sons, New York, N.Y., 1966, pp. 96–102.

16. Rutenberg, Y. "Calculation of Economical Order Quantities Using Ranges of Setup Costs." *Journal of Industrial Engineering,* Vol. XV, No. 1, January–February, 1964, pp. 44–46.

17. Schrady, D. "A Deterministic Inventory Model for Reparable Items." *Naval Research Logistics Quarterly,* Vol. 14, 1967, pp. 391–398.

18. Silver, E. A. "Establishing the Order Quantity When the Amount Received is Uncertain."

INFOR, Vol. 14, No. 1, February, 1976, pp. 32–39.

19. Snyder, R. D. "The Classical Economic Order Quantity Formula." *Operational Research Quarterly*, Vol. 24, No. 1, March, 1973, pp. 125–127.

20. Trippi, R. and D. Lewin "A Present Value Formulation of the Classical EOQ Problem." *Decision Sciences*, Vol. 5, 1974, pp. 30–35.

21. Welch, W. E. "How to Prepare Practical EOQ Tables." *Production and Inventory Management*, Vol. 10, No. 4, 1969, pp. 1–6.

22. Wilkinson, J. and A. Green. "A Graphical Approach to Price Break Analysis-2." *Operational Research Quarterly*, Vol. 23, No. 3, September, 1972, pp. 385–394.

CHAPTER SIX

Elements of Control for the Case of Probabilistic Demand

In the preceding chapter, which dealt with the determination of replenishment quantities, the decision rules resulted from an analysis which assumed a deterministic demand pattern. In several places we showed that the relevant costs associated with the selection of an order quantity were relatively insensitive to inaccuracies in the estimates of the various factors involved. However, the costs of insufficient capacity in the short run, that is, the costs associated with shortages or with averting them, were not included in the analyses. When demand is no longer assumed deterministic these costs assume a much greater importance. Clearly, the assumption of deterministic demand is inappropriate in many production and/or distribution situations. Therefore, the next two chapters are devoted to the theme of how to extend the system of the previous chapter so as to cope with the more realistic case of probabilistic demand where *average* demand is still approximately constant with time.

The introduction of uncertainty in the demand pattern significantly complicates the inventory situation from a conceptual standpoint. This, together with the plethora of possible shortage costing methods or customer service measures, has made the understanding and acceptance of decision rules for coping with probabilistic demand far less frequent than is merited by the importance of the problem. It is safe to say (as will be illustrated in Section 6.7.2 of this Chapter) that in most organizations an appropriate reallocation of buffer (or safety) stocks (which are kept to meet unexpected fluctuations in demand) can lead to a significant improvement in the service provided to customers.

It should be emphasized that in this and the next chapter we are still dealing with a single-stage problem. When one is concerned with a multi-echelon situation, a control system different from those proposed here is usually in order. One such control system is referred to as a material requirements planning system. We shall have more to say on this topic in Chapter 12.

We begin in Section 6.1 with a careful discussion of some important issues and terminology relevant to the case of probabilistic demand. Section 6.2 is concerned with the many different measures of service which may be relevant to any particular stocking situation. In Section 6.3 the important dichotomy of continuous versus periodic review is discussed. This is followed in Section 6.4 by an explanation of the four most common types of control systems. Section 6.5 deals with the selection of the reorder point for one type of continuous review system and one commonly used measure of service. As introduced in Chapter 3, we recommend the use of a two-tier type of control system; that is, the decision rule for items with relatively high average usage in a replenishment lead time is different from that for items with relatively low usage. To illustrate the dependence of the decision rules upon the service measure used, Section 6.6 is devoted to the case of another commonly utilized measure.

Section 6.7 deals with aggregate considerations, in particular, exchange curves displaying total buffer stock plotted against two aggregate measures of service as a function of a policy variable, the latter being the numerical value of the service level provided under the assumed measure of service. Section 6.8 provides a brief discussion of how the control variables are assigned values in the most common periodic review system. Finally, Section 6.9 addresses the issue of variability in the replenishment lead time itself.

The current chapter is meant to provide the reader with the essential elementary concepts of control in the face of probabilistic demand. Chapter 7, in contrast, will present in greater depth the logic for a variety of possible measures of service.

6.1 *Some Important Issues and Terminology*

6.1.1 *Different Definitions of Stock Level*

When demand is probabilistic it is useful to conceptually categorize inventories as follows:

i. On-hand stock—This is stock that is physically on the shelf; it can never be negative. This quantity is relevant in determining whether a particular customer demand is satisfied directly from the shelf.

ii. Net stock = (On-hand) − (Backorders) (6.1)

This quantity can become negative (namely, if there are backorders). It is used in some mathematical derivations and is also seen to be a component of the following important definition.

iii. Inventory Position (sometimes also called the available stock*)—The inventory position is defined by the relation

$$\text{Inventory position} = (\text{On-hand}) + (\text{On-order}) - (\text{Backorders}) - (\text{Committed}) \quad (6.2)$$

The on-order stock is that stock which has been requisitioned but not yet received by the stocking point under consideration. The inclusion of the "committed" quantity in Eq. 6.2 is based upon not being able to borrow from such stock for other purposes in the short run. If a commitment is made farther than a replenishment lead time in advance of use, such borrowing may be possible. As we shall see, the inventory position is a key quantity in deciding on when to replenish.

* *We have chosen to not use the words "available stock" because of the incorrect connotation that such stock is immediately available for satisfying customer demands.*

iv. Safety Stock—The safety (or buffer) stock is defined as the average level of the net stock just before a replenishment arrives. If we planned to just run out, on the average, at the moment when the replenishment arrived, the safety stock would be zero. A positive safety stock provides a cushion or buffer against larger-than-average demand during the effective replenishment lead time. The numerical value of the safety stock depends, as we shall see, upon what happens to demands when there is a stockout.

6.1.2 *Backorders versus Lost Sales*

Obviously of importance in inventory control is what happens to a customer's order when an item is temporarily out of stock. There are two extreme cases:

i. Complete backordering—Any demand, when out of stock, is backordered and filled as soon as an adequate sized replenishment arrives. This situation corresponds to a captive market, common in government organizations (particularly the military) and at the wholesale–retail link of some distribution systems (for example, exclusive dealerships).

ii. Complete lost sales—Any demand when out of stock is lost; the customer goes elsewhere to satisfy his need. This situation is most common at the retail-consumer link. For example, a housewife is unlikely to backorder a demand for a loaf of bread.

In most practical situations one finds a combination of these two extremes, whereas most inventory models have been developed for one or the other of the extremes. Nevertheless, most of these models serve as reasonable approximations because the decisions which they yield tend to be relatively insensitive to the degree of backordering possible in a particular situation. This is primarily a consequence of the common use in practice of high customer service levels; high service levels imply infrequent stockout occasions.

We shall now show that the numerical value of the safety stock depends upon the degree to which backorders or lost sales occur. Consider a particular replenishment lead time in which a stockout occurs. Under complete backordering, if demand occurs during the stockout, the net stock will be negative just before the next replenishment arrives. On the other hand, if all demands which occur when one is out of stock are lost, then the net stock will remain at the zero level throughout the stockout period. In other words, in a cycle when a stockout occurs, the value of the net stock just before the replenishment arrives depends upon whether or not backorders can occur. Because safety stock is defined to be the *average net stock* just before a replenishment arrives, its numerical value is thus influenced by whether or not backordering is possible under the actual circumstances.

6.1.3 The Three Key Questions to be Answered by a Control System under Probabilistic Demand

The fundamental purpose of a replenishment control system is to provide answers to the following three questions:

1. How often should the inventory status be determined?
2. When should a replenishment order be placed?
3. How large should the replenishment order be?

Under conditions of *deterministic* demand (discussed in the previous chapter) the first question is trivial because knowing the inventory status at any one point in time allows us to calculate it at all points in time (at least out to a reasonable horizon). Furthermore, under deterministic demand the second question is answered by placing an order such that it arrives precisely when the inventory level hits some prescribed value (usually set at zero). Again, under deterministic demand, the economic order quantity or a variation of it is the answer to the third question.

Under probabilistic demand the answers are more difficult to obtain. Regarding the first question, it takes resources (manpower, computer time, etc.) to determine the inventory status. On the other hand, the less frequently the status is determined the longer is the period over which the system must protect against unforeseen variations in demand in order to provide desired customer service. The answer to the second question rests upon a tradeoff between the costs of ordering somewhat early (hence, carrying extra stock) and the costs (implicit or explicit) of providing inadequate customer service. The factors relevant in answering the third question are similar to those discussed in the derivation of the basic economic order quantity, except that under some service criteria, specified by management, there is an interaction in that the answer to the second question, "when to replenish?" may be affected by the replenishment quantity used.

6.2 Alternative Measures of Service (or Risk)

When demand (and/or delivery capability) is probabilistic there is a definite chance of not being able to satisfy some of the demand on a routine basis directly out of stock. If demand is unusually large, emergency actions are required to avoid a stockout situation. On the other hand, if demand is lower than anticipated, the replenishment arrives earlier than needed, hence excess inventory is carried. Managers possess differing attitudes concerning the balancing of these two types of risks. There are three possible methods of modelling these attitudes so as to arrive at appropriate decision rules. The first of these, discussed in detail in Chapter 3, involves specifying (explicitly or implicitly) a way of costing a shortage once one knows certain characteristics of the shortage (for example, the total number of transactions backordered). An illustration is provided by the MIDAS context where "air freight at a cost of approximately $0.50 per pound was sometimes used to meet the demand from an important large customer."

The second approach, recognizing the extreme difficulties associated with costing shortages, skirts the problem by instead introducing a control parameter known as the service level. This becomes a constraint in establishing the decision rules; for example, one might minimize the sum of all other costs (replenishment, carrying, and control) subject to satisfying, routinely from stock, 95 percent of all demands. The following are among the more common measures of service:

i. Chance of no stockout in a replenishment cycle—equivalently, this is the fraction of cycles in which a stockout does not occur. A stockout is defined as an occasion when the on-hand stock *drops* to the zero level.

ii. Ready rate—the fraction of time during which the net stock is positive, that is, there is some stock on the shelf. If demand transactions are unit sized, this measure is equivalent with the following one.

iii. Fraction of demand satisfied routinely from shelf (that is, not being lost or backordered).

iv. Average time between stockout occasions.

As will become evident later in this chapter, we shall sometimes wish to aggregate measures of service across many items in an inventory population. This is difficult to do with the above four measures, but easier with the following three (which are really measures of inadequate service):

v. Expected number of stockout occasions per unit time—this is simply the reciprocal of measure iv), and is closely related to measure i), in that the expected number of stockout occasions per unit time is the product of the number of replenishment cycles per unit time and the probability of a stockout per cycle.

vi. Expected amount short per unit time—the expected number of units (or dollars) of demand per unit time not satisfied routinely from shelf stock. Although it is not immediately evident, this measure and measure iii) are closely related.

vii. Expected time-weighted shortages per unit time—with this measure, not only the number of units short, but the duration of backorder of each is important. If the time-weighting is linear, then one unit backordered for four weeks is equivalent to two units each being backordered for two weeks.

Each of these last three measures can be weighted by a factor known as the essentiality of the item. For example, if a particular item was deemed twice as important as another in terms of being in supply, then its essentiality would be double that of the other item.

The third approach to modelling the effects of shortages is to explicitly make future demand a function of the service now provided. Eilon[9] and Schwartz[21] have advocated this tack. We shall return to this viewpoint in Chapter 10 in a somewhat different problem context.

Unfortunately, there are no hard and fast rules for selecting the appropriate approach and/or measure of service. Which to use depends upon the environment of the particular company under consideration as well as management's attitude towards balancing the aforementioned two types of risks. However, relevant factors include:

i. The nature of the competition for the product being demanded.

ii. The nature of the customers (both in-house and out of house) involved, for example, parts for assemblies versus parts for spare usage.

iii. The amount of substitutability of products.

iv. Are the products purchased or manufactured?

v. How the company actually reacts to an impending shortage; for example, does it expedite?

6.3 *Continuous Versus Periodic Review*

The answer to the question "how often should the inventory status be determined?" specifies the review interval (R) which is the time that elapses between two consecutive moments at which we know the stock level. An extreme case is where there is continuous review, that is, the stock status is always known. In reality, continuous surveillance is usually not required; rather each transaction (shipment, receipt, demand, etc.) triggers an immediate updating of the status. Consequently, this type of control is often called "transactions reporting." Transactions reporting need not be computerized as evidenced by the hundreds of manual stock card systems (for example, "Kardex" or "VISI-Record") which have been used successfully over the years. With periodic review, as the name implies, the stock status is determined only every R time units; between the moments of review there may be considerable uncertainty as to the value of the stock level.

We now comment on the advantages and disadvantages of continuous and periodic review. Items may be produced on the same piece of equipment, purchased from the same supplier or shipped in the same transportation mode. In any of these situations coordination of replenishments may be attractive. In such a case periodic review is particularly appealing in that all items in a coordinated group can be given the same review interval (for example, all items purchased from a particular supplier might be scheduled for review every Thursday). Periodic review also allows a reasonable prediction of the level of the workload on the staff involved in issuing replenishment orders. In contrast, under continuous review a replenishment decision can be made at practically any moment in time, hence the load is less predictable. A rhythmic, rather than random, pattern is usually appealing to the staff.

Another disadvantage of continuous review is that it is generally more expensive in terms of reviewing costs and reviewing errors. This is particularly true for fast-moving items where there are many transactions per unit of time. However, for extremely slow-moving items very little costs are incurred by continuous review because updates are only made when a transaction occurs. On the other hand, we have the anomalous condition that periodic review may be more effective than continuous review in detecting spoilage (or pilferage) of such slow-moving items in that periodic review forces an occasional review of the situation, whereas, in transactions recording no automatic review will take place without a transaction occuring.

The major advantage of continuous review is that, to provide the same level of customer service, it requires less safety stock (hence, lower carrying costs) than does periodic review. This is because the period over which safety protection is required is longer under periodic review (the stock level has the opportunity to drop appreciably between review instants without any reordering action being possible in the interim).

6.4 Four Types of Control Systems

Recall that, in designing an inventory control system, we are really providing answers to the three questions:

1. How often should the inventory status be determined?
2. When should a replenishment order be placed?
3. How large should the replenishment order be?

There are a number of possible control systems. The physical operation of the four most common ones will be described in the next subsection. This will be followed by a brief discussion of the advantages and disadvantages of each of the systems.

6.4.1 Physical Operation

a. *Order Point, Order Quantity** *(s, Q) Systems*—This system involves continuous review (that is, $R = 0$). A fixed quantity Q is ordered whenever the inventory position drops to the reorder point s or lower. Note that the inventory position, and not the net stock, is used to trigger an order. The inventory position, because it includes the on-order stock, takes proper account of the material requested but not yet received from the supplier. In contrast, if net stock was used for ordering purposes, we might unnecessarily place another order today even though a large shipment was due in tomorrow. This system is often called a two-bin system because one physical form of implementation is to have two bins for storage of an item. As long as units remain in the first bin, demand is satisfied from it. The amount in the second bin corresponds to the order point. Hence, when this second bin is opened, a replenishment is triggered. When the replenishment arrives, the second bin is refilled and the remain-

* *The notation to be used is: s–order point; Q–order quantity: S–order-up-to-level.*

der is put into the first bin. It should be noted that the physical two-bin system will operate properly only when no more than one replenishment order is outstanding at any point in time.

b. Order Point, Order-Up-to-Level (s, S) System—This system again involves continuous review and a replenishment is made whenever the inventory position drops to the order point s or lower. However, in contrast to the (s, Q) system, here a variable replenishment quantity is used, enough being ordered to raise the inventory position to the order-up-to-level S. If all demand transactions are unit-sized, the two systems are identical because the replenishment requisition will always be made when the inventory position is exactly at s, that is, in this case, $S = s + Q$. As soon as the transactions can be larger than unit size the replenishment quantity in the (s, S) system becomes variable. Figures 6.1(a) and 6.1(b) illustrate the difference in the behavior of the two systems. The (s, S) system is frequently referred to as a min-max system because the inventory position, except for a possible momentary drop below the reorder point, is always between a minimum value of s and a maximum value of S. An illustration of a min-max system is provided in MIDAS Case D.

c. Periodic Review, Order-Up-to-Level (R, S) System—This system, also known as a replenishment cycle system, is in common use, particularly in companies not utilizing computer control. The control procedure is that every R units of time (that is, at each review instant) enough is ordered to raise the inventory position to the level S. A typical behavior of this type of system is shown in Figure 6.2.

d. (R, s, S) System—This is a combination of (b) and (c). The idea is that every R units of time we check the inventory position. If it is at or below the reorder point s, we order enough to raise it to S. If the position is above s, nothing is done until at least the next review instant. The (s, S) system is the special case where $R = 0$ and the (R, S) is the special case where $s = S - 1$. Alternatively one can think of the (R, s, S) system as a periodic version of the (s, S) system. Also, the (R, S) situation can be viewed as a periodic implementation of (s, S) with $s = S - 1$.

6.4.2 *Advantages and Disadvantages*

Our discussion will be rather general in that the advantages and disadvantages are dependent upon the specific environment in which the systems are to be implemented.

a. (s, Q) System—This is a simple system, particularly in the two-bin form, for the stock clerk to understand. Also a fixed order quantity has advantages in terms of less likelihood of error and also predictability of production requirements on the part of the supplier. One disadvantage of an (s, Q) system is that in its unmodified form it may not be able to

Figure 6.1 Two Types of Continuous Review Systems.

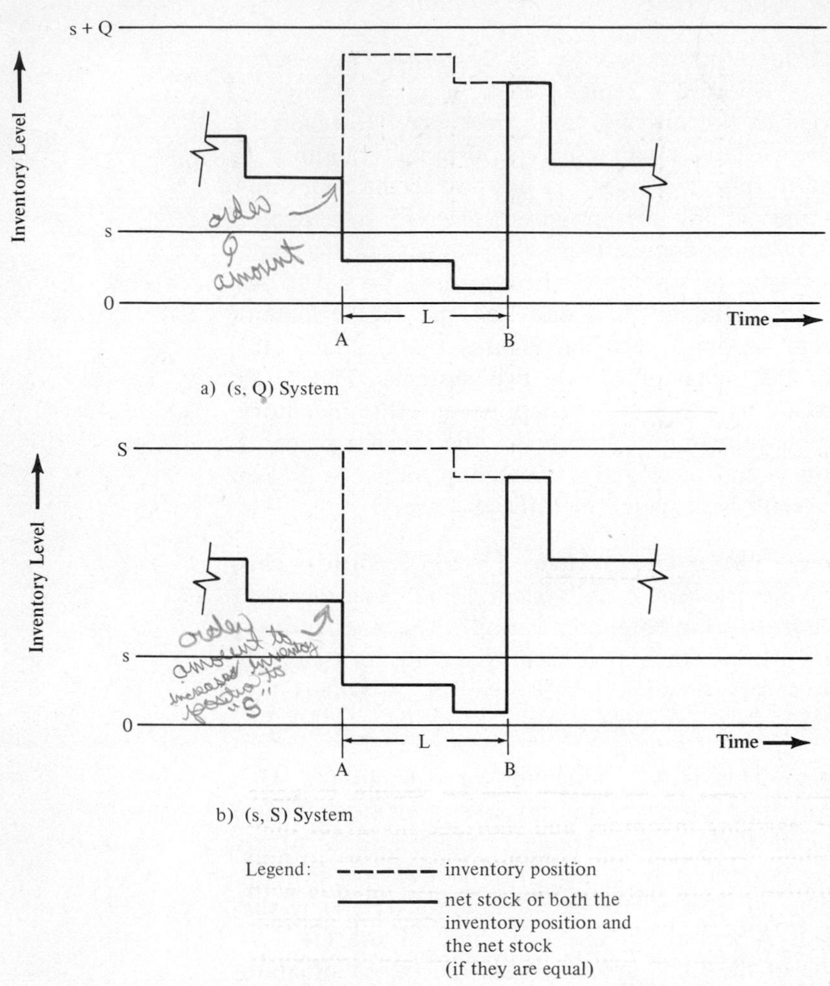

NOTE: Order placed at time A, arrives at time B.

effectively cope with the situation where individual transactions are of appreciable magnitude; in particular, if the transaction that triggers the replenishment in an (s, Q) system is large enough, then a replenishment of size Q won't even raise the inventory position above the reorder point (a numerical illustration would involve a Q value of 10 together with a demand transaction of size 15 occurring when the position is just 1 unit above s). Of course, in such a situation one could instead order an integer multiple of Q where the integer was large enough to raise the inventory position above s.

Figure 6.2 The (R, S) System.

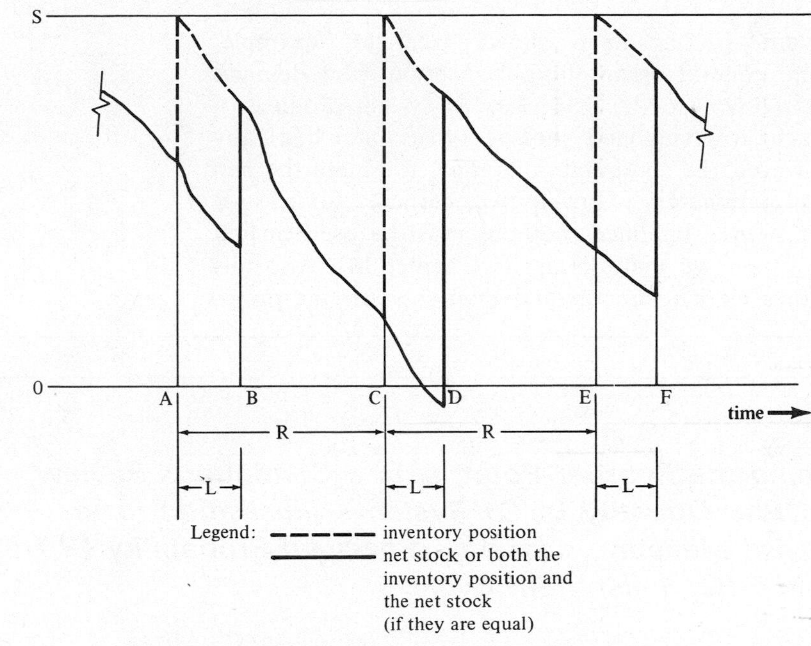

b. (s, S) System—The best (s, S) system can be shown to have total costs of replenishment, carrying inventory and shortage no larger than those of the best (s, Q). system. However, the computational effort to find the *best* (s, S) pair is prohibitive except perhaps where we are dealing with an item where the potential savings in the aforementioned costs are appreciable (that is, an A item). It is interesting that (s, S) systems are frequently encountered in practice. However, the values of the control parameters are usually set in a rather arbitrary fashion. (See, for example, MIDAS Case D). For B items (and even most A items) mathematical optimality does not make sense, rather we need a fairly simple way of obtaining ***reasonable*** values of s and S. This will be discussed further in Chapter 14. Another possible disadvantage of the (s, S) system is the danger of errors in requisitioning, etc. caused by the variable order quantity.

c. (R, S) System—Because of the periodic review property this system is much preferred to order point systems in terms of coordinating the replenishments of related items. In addition, the (R, S) system offers a regular opportunity (every R units of time) to adjust the order-up-to-level S, a desirable property if the demand pattern is changing with time. The main disadvantage of the (R, S) system is that the carrying costs are higher here than in continuous review systems.

d. (R, s, S) System—It has been shown (see, for example, Scarf[20]) that, under quite general assumptions concerning the demand pattern and the cost factors involved the best (R, s, S) system produces a lower total of replenishment, carrying and shortage costs than does any other form of system. However, the computational effort to obtain the *best* values of the three control parameters is prohibitive, certainly for class B items. Therefore, for such items, simplified methods must be used to find *reasonable* values (again, a topic we shall discuss in Chapter 14). Also this system is more difficult for a clerk to understand than some of the previously mentioned systems.

6.5 *Establishing the Reorder Point, s, in a Continuous Review, Order Point, Order Quantity (s, Q) System—Illustration for a Particular Service Measure, namely a Specified Probability (P_1) of No Stockout in a Replenishment Cycle*

The service measure which we shall use in this section is the probability of no stockout in a replenishment cycle; it will be denoted by the symbol P_1. It should be emphasized that we are not necessarily advocating use of this service measure, rather it is being used for illustrative purposes to convey some basic concepts in this introductory chapter. To show the effects of the particular service measure employed, decision rules based on a second measure of service will be presented in Section 6.6. Moreover, control systems under a variety of different measures of service will be discussed in Chapter 7.

6.5.1 *Protection Over the Replenishment Lead Time*

In a continuous review system a replenishment action can be taken immediately after any demand transaction. Once we place an order a replenishment lead time (L) elapses before the order is available for satisfying customer demands. Therefore, we want to place an order when the inventory is still adequate to protect us over a replenishment lead time. If the order is placed when the inventory position is at *exactly* the reorder point, s, then a stockout will not occur by the end of the lead time if and only if the total demand during the lead time is less than the reorder point. This is illustrated in Figure 6.3, where, for simplicity in presentation, we have assumed that at most one replenishment order is outstanding at any point

Figure 6.3 The Occurrence of a Stockout in an (s, Q) System.

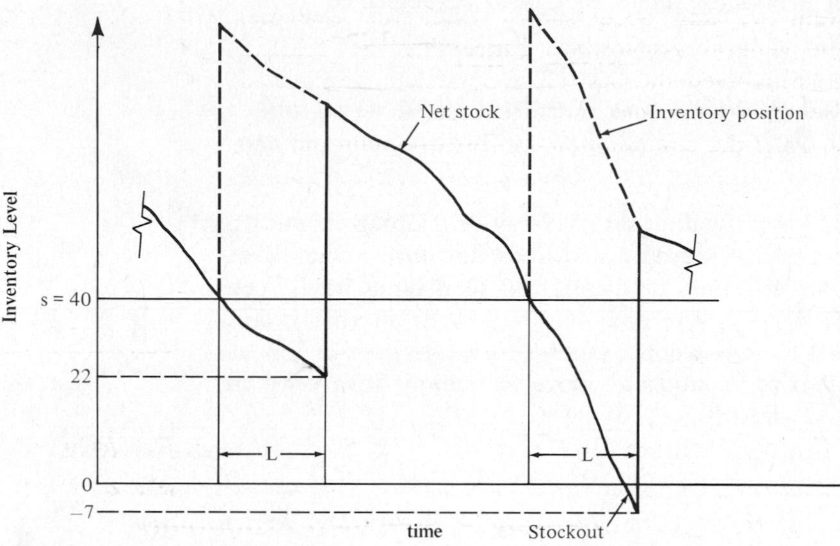

in time.* In the figure the reorder point is 40 units. In the first lead time shown the total demand is 18 so that the net stock just before the replenishment arrives is (40 − 18) or 22; that is, no stockout occurs. In contrast, in the second lead time the total demand is 47 resulting in a total backorder of (47 − 40) or 7 units when the replenishment arrives.

Note that above we assumed that the replenishment action is taken when the stock level is exactly at the reorder point *s*. Even for the situation of continuous review this may not necessarily be the case. To illustrate, suppose at a certain point in time the stock level for the item in Figure 6.3 was 42 units and a demand transaction of 5 units occurred. This would immediately drive the inventory level to 37 units which is an undershoot of the reorder point by 3 units. It is evident that, strictly speaking, no

---

* *The situation when two or more orders are simultaneously outstanding is somewhat more difficult to explain. Each order is initiated when the inventory position drops to the level s or lower. The level of the on-hand (or net) stock does not influence the placing of a new order. Certainly, however a low on-hand level may initiate an expediting action on an outstanding order to avoid an impending stockout.*

stockout occurs if and only if the sum of the undershoot and the total demand in the replenishment lead time is less than the reorder point. Except where explicitly noted otherwise, we shall make the simplifying assumption that the undershoots are small enough to be neglected.

6.5.2 *Empirical Analysis Using Actual Historical Lead Time Demand Data*

MIDAS' product XSC-023 is a 4 gallon set of X-ray developing chemicals. The demand for this item is not seasonal and does not have a significant trend. The actual demands observed in the last 10 lead times have been 64, 51, 48, 32, 93, 21, 47, 57, 41, and 46 units (sets) in that order. Suppose that management has specified that inventories be kept as low as possible subject to not having a stockout more frequently than once in every ten cycles, (that is, $P_1 = 0.90$).

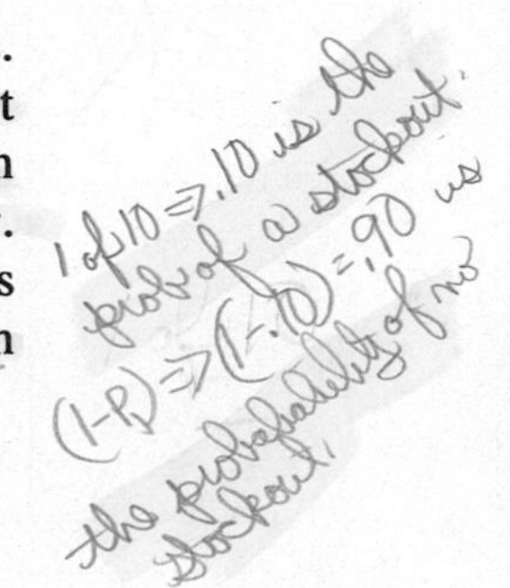

Table 6.1 Observed Historical Leadtime Demands for the Developing Chemicals Item

Lead Time Demand	Number of occurrences at or above this Value	Fraction of Occurrences at or above this Value
93	1	1/10 = 0.1
64	2	0.2
57	3	0.3
51	4	0.4
48	5	0.5
47	6	0.6
46	7	0.7
41	8	0.8
32	9	0.9
21	10	1.0

Certainly one method of establishing the reorder point would be as follows: The historical demand data, arranged slightly differently, are shown in Table 6.1. Based on these data, if any reorder point of 65 units or higher was used, only 1 stockout would have occurred in the ten lead times. Therefore, ***assuming the historical pattern is representative of future conditions***, a reorder point of 65 units would be used.

There are three potential weaknesses of this simple procedure:

i. Normally one is interested in high service levels, that is, a small chance of a stockout during a single replenishment cycle, subject, of course, to a reasonable cost of carrying the necessary safety stock. Therefore, we would usually prefer to have information about the demand in a considerable number of historical lead times to avoid guessing about the infrequent *outliers* against which we are trying to provide adequate protection.

ii. The method cannot easily cope with the situation where the basic demand rate is changing appreciably with time. For example, if the demands in the lead times in the numerical example had instead been seen in the following chronological order: 21, 32, 41, 47, 46, 48, 51, 64, 57, 93, that is, more or less increasing with time, then, unlike earlier, we would certainly not be willing to say that these values are equi-likely to occur in the next lead time. Rather, we would expect a lead time demand in the higher portion of the range.

iii. If for some reason the replenishment lead time was altered (for example, by negotiation with the supplier), the histogram of total demand during the old lead time (for example, 3 months) would be of limited value in estimating the probabilities of various total demands in the new lead time (for example, 2 months). In some cases it might be reasonable to assume that the *variability* would be unaltered, that is, only the average value of the total demand would change.

6.5.3 *A Decision Rule for Faster-Moving Items ($\bar{x}_L \geq 10$ units)*—Normally Distributed Forecast Errors*

As first discussed in Chapter 3, a two-tier type of control system is advocated. The classification of items is based on the average usage ($\bar{x}_L$) of the item during a replenishment lead time. Extensive tests by Archibald et

---

* *$\bar{x}_L$ is the average value (that is, the forecast) of the total demand in a replenishment lead time.*

al.[1] have revealed that for $\bar{x}_L \geq 10$ units it is reasonable to assume that a statistical forecasting system will produce forecasts whose deviations away from the actual demands (that is, the errors) tend to be normally distributed. The basic properties of this distribution are reviewed in Appendix C. A typical normal probability distribution of demand around the forecast value is shown in Figure 6.4. The curve is constructed such that the area under the curve, to the right of a vertical line through any point A, represents the probability that the total lead time demand will take on a value larger than A. (In fact, this statement holds for any probability distribution, not just the normal.)

Suppose that the forecast system outputs a forecast of demand ($\bar{x}_L$) in the next lead time of interest. Also, as discussed in Chapter 4, suppose it provides us with a measure (σ_L)* of forecast errors over a lead time. In the

Figure 6.4 Normally Distributed Forecast Errors.

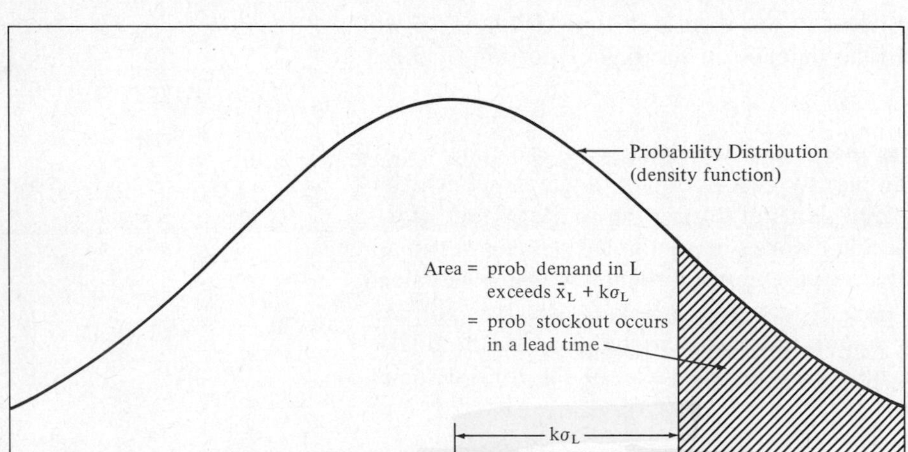

$\bar{x}_L$ – forecast demand over replenishment lead time
σ_L – standard deviation of errors of a forecast over a lead time

* *σ_L, the standard deviation of forecast errors over a lead time, measures the spread of the probability distribution of demand around the mean or forecast value. The basic output of the forecast system is MAD_1, the mean absolute deviation of forecast errors over a unit time interval (the forecast update period). As discussed in Chapter 4, MAD_1 is transformed to σ_1 which, in turn, is converted to σ_L.*

previous subsection we set about directly determining the required reorder point s. Here it turns out to be more appropriate to work indirectly using the following relationships

$$\text{Reorder point, } s = \bar{x}_L + (\text{safety stock}) \tag{6.3}$$

and

$$\text{safety stock} = k\sigma_L \tag{6.4}$$

where k is known as the safety factor.

Determination of a k value leads directly to a value of s through use of these two relations.

Suppose management has specified that the probability of no stockout in a cycle should be no lower than P_1 (conversely, the probability of a stockout should be no higher than $1\text{-}P_1$). Then, if forecast errors are normally distributed, we have the following simple decision rule (whose derivation will be discussed later in this section):

Decision Rule

Step 1 Select the safety factor k to satisfy

$$p_{u\geq}(k) = 1 - P_1 \tag{6.5}$$

where

$p_{u\geq}(k) =$ prob {unit normal variable (mean 0, standard deviation 1) takes on a value of k or larger}, a widely tabulated function (see Table C.1 in Appendix C).

Step 2 Safety stock, $SS = k\sigma_L$.

Step 3 Reorder point, $s = \bar{x}_L + SS$, increased to the next higher integer (if not already *exactly* an integer).

Numerical Illustration—For the developing chemicals item used in the preceding section suppose that MIDAS' forecast system had output the following values

$\bar{x}_L = 58.3$ units

$\sigma_L = 13.1$ units

Also, management desires a service level of $P_1 = 0.90$.

Equation 6.5 says that k should satisfy

$$p_{u\geq}(k)=0.10$$

From Table C.1 in Appendix C

$$k \simeq 1.28$$

$$SS = k\sigma_L = 1.28 \times 13.1 \text{ units}$$

$$= 16.8 \text{ units}$$

Reorder point, $s=58.3+16.8=75.1$, say 76 units.

Discussion of the Decision Rule—From Eq. 6.5 it is seen that the safety factor k depends only upon the value of P_1; in particular it is independent of any individual item characteristics such as the order quantity, Q. Therefore, all items for which we desire the same service level, P_1, will have identical values of the safety factor k.

From Eq. 6.5 $p_{u\geq}(k)$ must decrease as the desired service level (P_1) goes up. But, from Table C.1 in Appendix C it is seen that k increases as $p_{u\geq}(k)$ decreases. Therefore, we have the desirable behavior of the safety factor k increasing with increasing required service level.

The fact that the safety factor doesn't depend upon any individual item characteristics may cause one to reexamine the meaning of service here. Recall that service under the measure used in this section is prob{no stockout *per replenishment cycle*}. Consider two items, the first being replenished twenty times a year, the other once a year. If they both are given the same safety factor so as to both have a probability of 0.10 of stockout per replenishment cycle, then we'd expect $20 \times (0.10)$ or 2 stockouts per year for the first item and only 1 stockout every ten years (0.1 per year) for the second item. Therefore, depending upon management's definition of service, we, in fact, would probably not be giving the same service on these two items. As a result, somewhat more elaborate decision rules using other service measures are needed, a topic to be covered in depth in Chapter 7.

Derivation of the Rule—Suppose the reorder point is expressed as the sum of the forecast demand plus safety stock as shown in Eq. 6.3. Furthermore, suppose, as in Eq. 6.4, that the safety stock is expressed as the product of two factors

i. The safety factor k—the control parameter

ii. σ_L, the standard deviation of forecast errors over a lead time

Now, we know from the preceding section that

$$\text{prob}\,\{\text{stockout in a lead time}\} = \text{prob}\,\{\text{demand in } L \text{ exceeds } s\}$$
$$= \text{prob}\,\{\text{demand in } L \text{ exceeds } \bar{x}_L + k\sigma_L\} \quad (6.6)$$

As shown in Section C.4 of Appendix C, for normally distributed forecast errors,

$$\text{prob}\,\{\text{demand in } L \text{ exceeds } \bar{x}_L + k\sigma_L\} = p_{u\geq}(k) \quad (6.7)$$

From Eqs. 6.6 and 6.7 we have

$$\text{prob}\,\{\text{stockout in a lead time}\} = p_{u\geq}(k) \quad (6.8)$$

If the desired service level is P_1, then we must have

$$\text{prob}\,\{\text{stockout in a lead time}\} = 1 - P_1 \quad (6.9)$$

It follows from Eqs. 6.8 and 6.9 that we must select k to satisfy

$$p_{u\geq}(k) = 1 - P_1$$

which is Eq. 6.5.

Had we not chosen the indirect route of using Eqs. 6.3 and 6.4 we would have ended up with a more cumbersome result than Eq. 6.5, namely

$$p_{u\geq}[(s - \bar{x}_L)/\sigma_L] = 1 - P_1$$

Finally, because of the discrete nature of the reorder point we are not likely to be able to provide the exact level of service desired as this usually would require a non-integer value of s. Therefore, a non-integer value of s found in Eq. 6.5 is rounded up to the next higher integer with the predicted service level then being slightly higher than required.

6.5.4 A Decision Rule for Slower Moving Items ($\bar{x}_L < 10$ units)—Lead Time Demand Having a Laplace Distribution*

As mentioned earlier, the two-tier classification is based on the average usage of the item during a replenishment lead time. For slower moving items ($\bar{x}_L < 10$ units) Archibald et al.[1] found that the Laplace distribution is a better fit to the distribution of the total lead time demand than is the

* *The Laplace distribution is discussed in Appendix* B.

normal. Moreover, the Laplace is somewhat easier to use from a computational standpoint. If in certain situations it is desired for simplicity to reduce the number of options, then we recommend a single tier with the normal distribution being used for all B items.

If lead time demand has a Laplace distribution, then we are led to the following simple decision rule:

Decision Rule

Step 1 Select the safety factor k to satisfy

$$k = \frac{1}{\sqrt{2}} \ln \left[\frac{1}{2(1-P_1)} \right] \tag{6.10}$$

where ln x is the natural logarithm of x, a function easily calculated through the use of tables of logarithms, a slide rule or a hand electronic calculator.

Step 2 Safety stock, $SS = k\sigma_L$

Step 3 Reorder point, $s = \bar{x}_L + SS$, increased to the next higher integer (if not already exactly an integer).

Numerical Illustration—Another developing chemicals item, XSC-021, stocked by MIDAS, has a forecasted lead time demand ($\bar{x}_L$) of 8.5 units with an estimated standard deviation of forecast errors (σ_L) equal to 2.4 units. Suppose that management again desires a service level of $P_1 = 0.90$.

Equation 6.10 indicates that

$$\begin{aligned} k &= \frac{1}{\sqrt{2}} \ln \left[\frac{1}{2(1-0.9)} \right] \\ &= \frac{1}{\sqrt{2}} \ln 5 \\ &= \frac{1}{\sqrt{2}} (1.61) \\ &= 1.14 \end{aligned}$$

Then

$$SS = k\sigma_L = 1.14 \times 2.4 \text{ units} = 2.7 \text{ units}$$

and

$$s = 8.5 + 2.7 = 11.2, \quad \text{say 12 units}$$

Figure 6.5 Recommended Approach for the P_1 Service Measure.

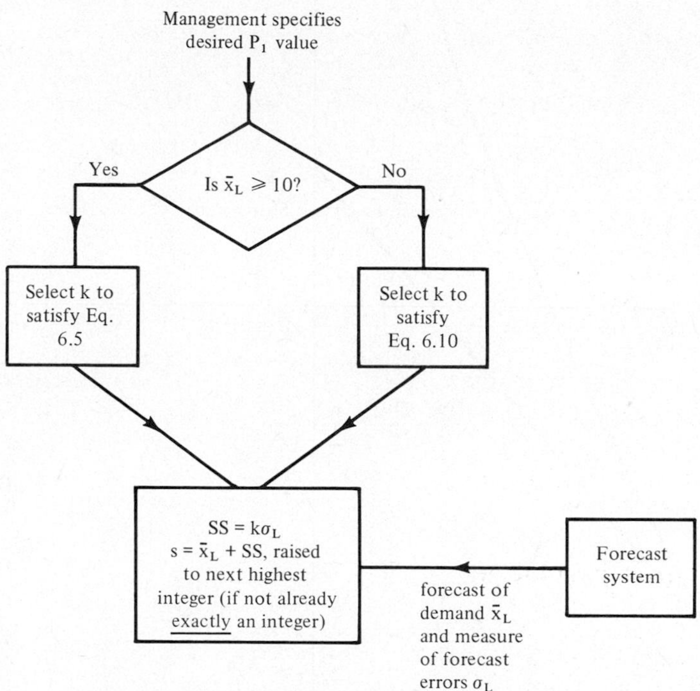

Derivation of the Rule—The approach is identical with that used in Section 6.5.3 for the normal distribution. The only difference is that, as can be shown from the results of Appendix B, for the Laplace distribution (and $k > 0$)

$$\text{prob}\,\{\text{demand in } L \text{ exceeds } \bar{x}_L + k\sigma_L\} = \tfrac{1}{2}\exp(-\sqrt{2}\,k)$$

Therefore,

$$1 - P_1 = \tfrac{1}{2}\exp(-\sqrt{2}\,k)$$

The solution, in terms of k, is Eq. 6.10.

6.5.5 *Summary of Recommended Approach for the P_1 Service Measure*

Figure 6.5 summarizes the logic to be followed in selecting the reorder point. A graphical aid which avoids the table lookup associated with Eq. 6.3 or the computation of Eq. 6.10, is shown in Figure 6.6.

Figure 6.6 Graphical Aid for P_1 Service Measure.

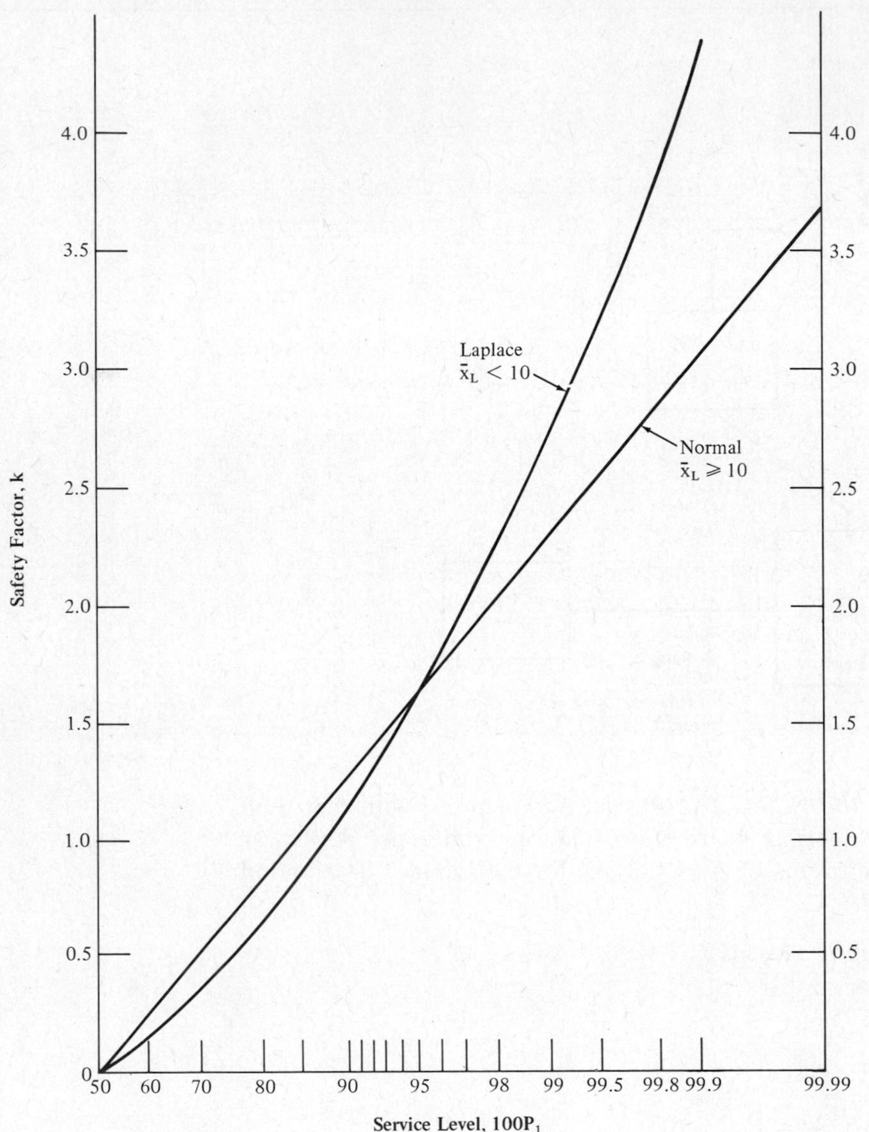

A fixed time supply of safety stock is a simple rule of thumb, often used in practice. The equation

$$\text{Safety stock,} \quad SS = k\sigma_L$$

clearly shows that, at least under the P_1 measure of service, a fixed time supply is inappropriate to use; the higher the measure of uncertainty (σ_L), the larger should be the safety stock. This makes intuitive sense—the size of the safety stock should be related to forecast errors in that it is carried to protect against such errors.

6.6 Use of an Alternative Measure of Service, Namely the Desired Average Time (TBS) Between Stockout Occasions, in Establishing the Reorder Point in an (s, Q) System

The P_1 service measure of the preceding section led to the same k value for all items having the same desired service level. For illustrative purposes we now introduce a second service measure, namely the desired average time (TBS) between stockout occasions.* As we shall see, now the safety factor k will differ from item to item. Again, we remind the reader that decision rules for a variety of other service measures (and shortage costing methods) will be presented in Chapter 7.

Once more we show a two-tier structure with a normal (Laplace) distribution being used for faster (slower) moving items with the boundary being an $\bar{x}_L$ value of 10 units. For a more compact presentation we blend the logic into a single (branching) decision rule. The single-tier alternative would be to use the normal distribution for all items.

Decision Rule

Step 1 Select the safety factor k to satisfy

$$p_{u\geq}(k) = \frac{Q}{D(\text{TBS})} \quad (\text{for } \bar{x}_L \geq 10 \text{ units}) \qquad (6.11)$$

or**

$$k = \frac{1}{\sqrt{2}} \ln\left[\frac{D(\text{TBS})}{2Q}\right] \quad (\text{for } \bar{x}_L < 10 \text{ units}) \qquad (6.12)$$

---

* *Equivalently, one could use the reciprocal of* (TBS) *which represents the desired average number of stockout occasions per year.*

** *Strictly speaking, Eq. 6.12 only holds for* $D(\text{TBS})/2Q \geq 1$. *However, any lower value would lead to a negative safety factor, normally not acceptable to management because it implies a greater than 50 percent chance of a stockout on each replenishment cycle.*

where, $p_{u\geq}(k)$, as earlier, is a tabulated function of the unit normal distribution,

Q is a *prespecified** replenishment quantity, in units.
D is the demand rate, in units/year.
TBS is the desired average time between stockout occasions, in years.

Step 2 Safety stock,

$$SS = k\sigma_L$$

where σ_L is the standard deviation of forecast errors over a lead time, in units.

Step 3 Reorder point,

$$s = \bar{x}_L + SS,$$

increased to the next highest integer (if not already exactly an integer) where $\bar{x}_L$ is the forecast demand over the lead time, in units.

Numerical Illustration—For the developing chemicals item, XSC-023, used in Section 6.5.3, suppose that

$$\bar{x}_L = 58.3 \text{ units}$$

$$\sigma_L = 13.1 \text{ units}$$

$$D = 200 \text{ units/yr.}$$

$$Q = 30 \text{ units}$$

and management specifies a desired TBS value of 2 years. Then, Eq. 6.11 gives

$$p_{u\geq}(k) = \frac{30}{200(2)} = 0.075$$

* *Likely developed by the economic order quantity methods of Chapter 5.*

From Table C.1 of Appendix C we have

$$k = 1.44$$

Then,

$$SS = 1.44 \times 13.1 = 18.9 \text{ units}$$

and,

$$s = 58.3 + 18.9 = 77.2, \quad \text{say 78 units}$$

Discussion of the Decision Rule—It is seen from Eqs. 6.11 and 6.12 that the safety factor k now depends upon characteristics of the individual item, namely D and Q. Note that all that is important is the ratio D/Q, the average number of replenishments per year, and not the individual components D and Q. For a given value of TBS Eq. 6.11 shows that $p_{u\geq}(k)$ decreases as D/Q gets larger. However, decreasing $p_{u\geq}(k)$ implies increasing k. Similarly, Eq. 6.12 shows directly that k increases with D/Q. In other words, we have the intuitively appealing result that as the number of replenishments per year increases, we must use a higher safety factor in order to achieve a given service level TBS. Similarly, for a given value of D/Q, k can be shown to increase with TBS, again intuitively correct.

The appearance of Q in the decision rule for finding the safety factor k indicates that a change in Q will affect the required value of the safety stock. Such effects of Q were ignored in the derivations of Chapter 5. For B items this turns out to be a reasonable approximation as we shall see in Chapter 9 where such interactions between Q and k will be more closely examined in the context of control of A items.

Derivation of the Rule—We illustrate the derivation of Eq. 6.11 (the case of the normal distribution). The only difference in the Laplace derivation is that $p_{u\geq}(k)$ is replaced by $\frac{1}{2}\exp(-\sqrt{2}\,k)$.

From Eq. 6.8 we have

$$\text{prob}\,\{\text{stockout in a particular replenishment lead time}\} = p_{u\geq}(k)$$

$$\text{The average number of replenishment lead times per year} = D/Q$$

Therefore, the expected number of stockout occasions per year is given by $(D/Q)p_{u\geq}(k)$. Now, the average time between stockout occasions is the reciprocal of the expected number of occasions per year (for example, if there are 10 stockout occasions expected per year, then the average time between occasions is 0.1 years). We want this average time to be equal to

TBS. Therefore, we require

$$\text{TBS} = \frac{1}{(D/Q)p_{u\geq}(k)} = \frac{Q}{Dp_{u\geq}(k)}$$

or

$$p_{u\geq}(k) = \frac{Q}{D(\text{TBS})}$$

Graphical Aids—The graphical aids of Figures 6.7 and 6.8 can be used to determine the safety factor k, thus avoiding the table lookup associated with Eq. 6.11 or the computation of Eq. 6.12. A further aid, of a tabular nature, will be discussed in connection with the control of C items in Chapter 11.

6.7 *Exchange Curves Involving Safety Stocks*

In Chapter 5 exchange curves were developed which showed the aggregate consequences, in terms of total cycle stock versus total number (or costs) of replenishments per year, when a particular policy (the EOQ) is used across a population of items. The curve was traced out by varying the value of a policy variable, either r or A/r. In a similar fashion exchange curves can be developed showing the aggregate consequences, in terms of total safety stock (in dollars) versus aggregate service, when a particular decision rule for establishing safety stocks (that is, reorder points) is used across a population of items. This is illustrated in Section 6.7.1 for the Professional Products Division of MIDAS. Again there is a policy variable for each type of decision rule, P_1 in one case, TBS in the other. Management's selection of an aggregate operating point implies a value of P_1 or TBS. Use of this implicit value in the individual item decision rules then leads to the desired aggregate consequences. An example, using the concept of an exchange curve, in Section 6.7.2 illustrates the type of improvement that is usually possible in moving away from the commonly used approach of basing safety stocks (or reorder points) on equal time supplies.

Management's ability to meaningfully utilize the safety stock versus service exchange curve hinges upon their capacity to think of inventories as being split into the two components of cycle stocks and safety stocks and to be able to make separate tradeoffs of cycle stocks versus replenishments and safety stocks versus aggregate service. Based on our experience, these conditions are not always met. Therefore, in Chapter 7 we shall discuss so-called composite exchange curves which show a three way exchange of total stock (cycle plus safety, in dollars) versus number of replenishments

Figure 6.7 Graphical Aid for TBS Service Measure and Fast Moving Items ($\bar{x}_L \geq 10$ units).

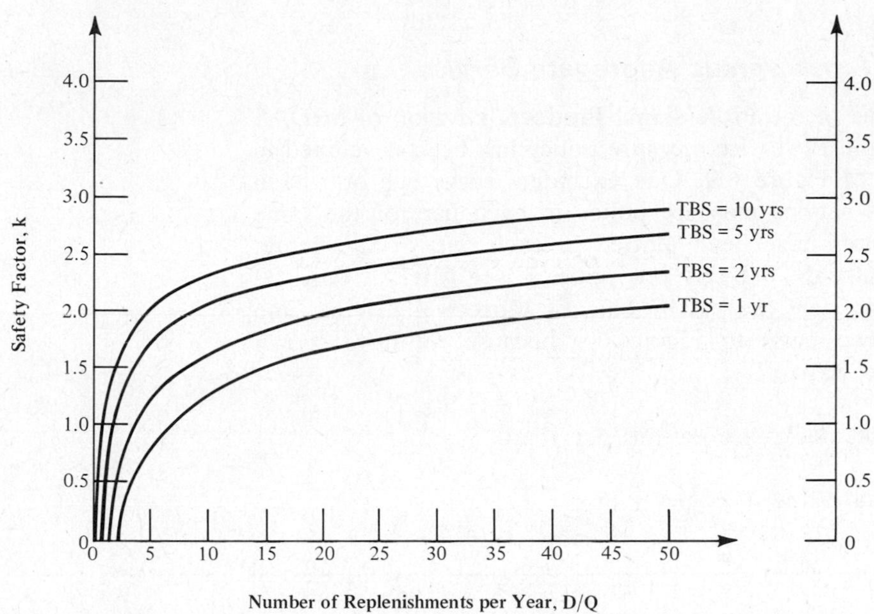

Figure 6.8 Graphical Aid for TBS Service Measure and Slow Moving Items ($\bar{x}_L < 10$ units).

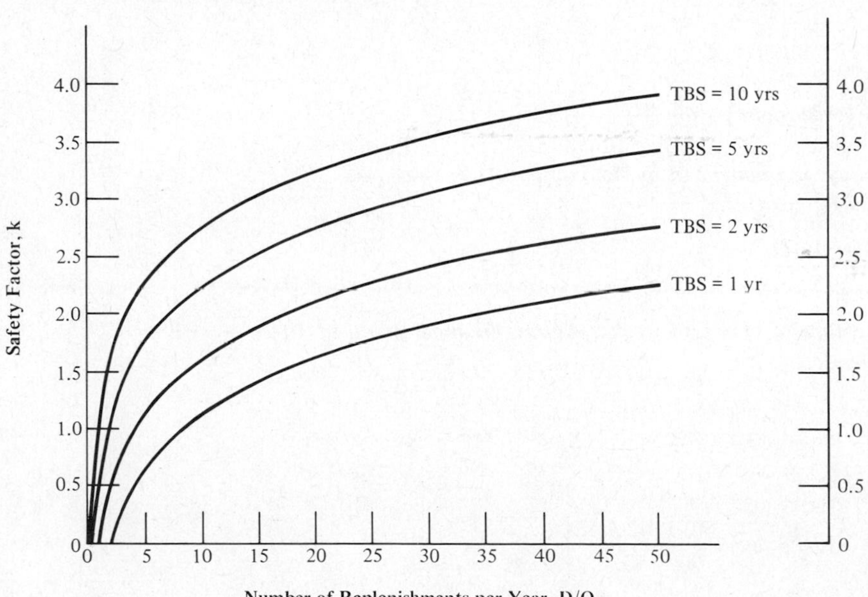

per year versus aggregate service. In addition, in Chapter 7 the safety stock versus service measure exchange curves will be extended to include a variety of policies of establishing safety stocks (hence, reorder points).

6.7.1 Total Safety Stock Versus Aggregate Service

For the 823 active items of the Professional Products Division of MIDAS an exchange curve for the P_1 service measure policy has been developed in each of the two parts of Figure 6.9. One exchange curve has also been developed for the TBS service measure policy in each part of the same figure. Finally, two points have been plotted in each part of the figure. These correspond to MIDAS' old and new policies (see MIDAS Case D) both of which are effectively the establishing of reorder points as time supplies.* There are two parts to Figure 6.9 because we have shown aggregate service in two ways:

i. Expected total stockout occasions per year

ii. Expected total value short per year

---

* *Translating from Case D, the old policy sets the maximum level* $(s_i + Q_i)$ *of item i as a 5 month supply. Then the order point,* s_i, *is 80% of this. Therefore*

$$s_i = 0.8\frac{5D_i}{12} = \frac{D_i}{3}$$

and

$$Q_i = (\textit{maximum}) - (\textit{order point}) = \frac{5D_i}{12} - \frac{D_i}{3} = \frac{D_i}{12}$$

Under the new policy, recommended by the comptroller's office, the maximum of item i is set at

$$\frac{10 + L_i}{13}\frac{D_i}{4} \quad \textit{or} \quad \frac{(10 + L_i)D_i}{52}$$

where L_i *is the lead time of item i, in weeks. Again, the order point,* s_i, *is 80% of this. Therefore*

$$s_i = \frac{(8 + 0.8\,L_i)D_i}{52}$$

and

$$Q_i = (\textit{maximum}) - (\textit{order point}) = \frac{(2 + 0.2\,L_i)D_i}{52}$$

Figure 6.9a Exchange Curves of Safety Stock Versus Expected Stockout Occasions for the Professional Products Division of MIDAS.

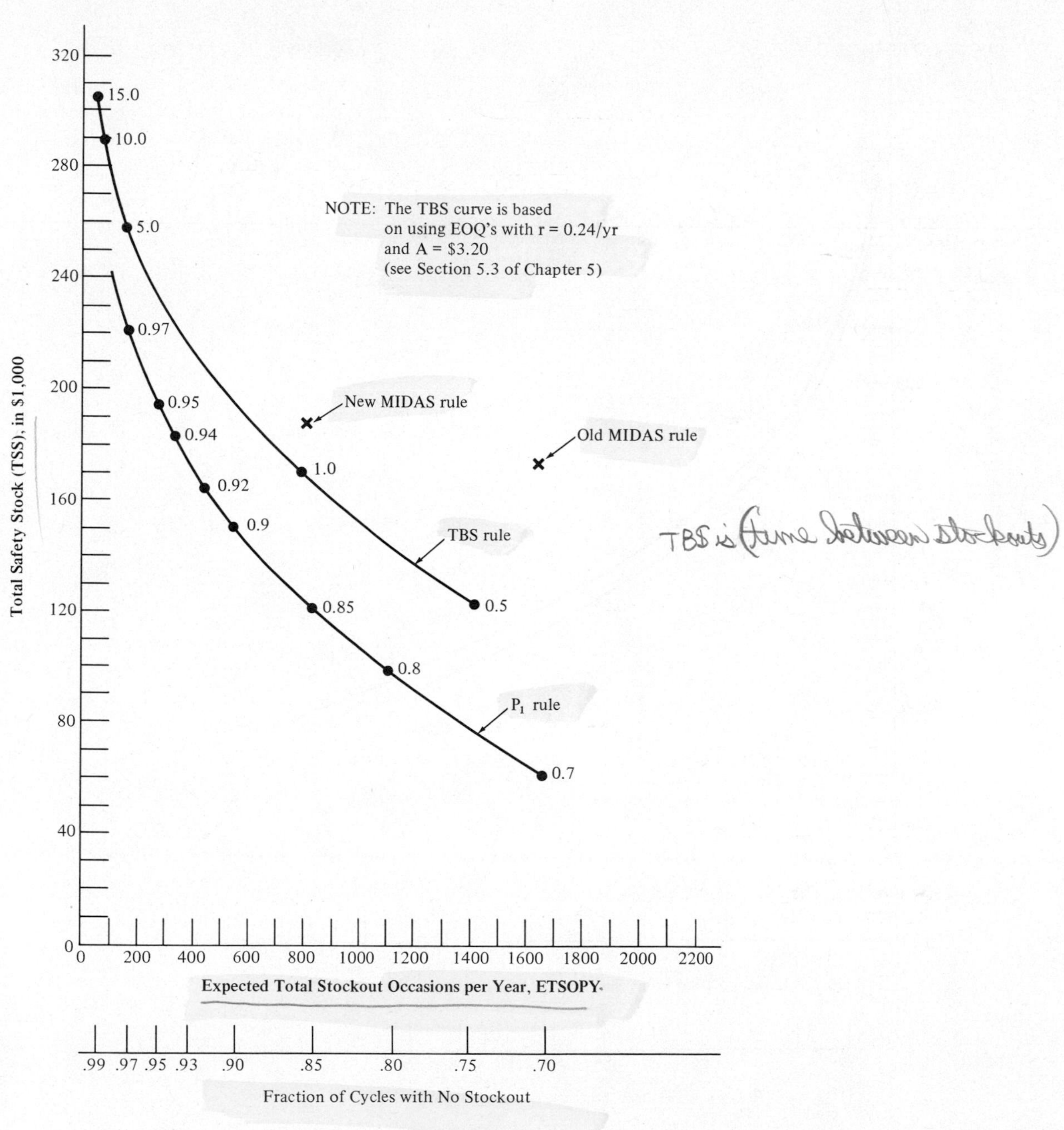

Figure 6.9b Exchange Curves of Safety Stock Versus Expected Value Short for the Professional Products Division of MIDAS.

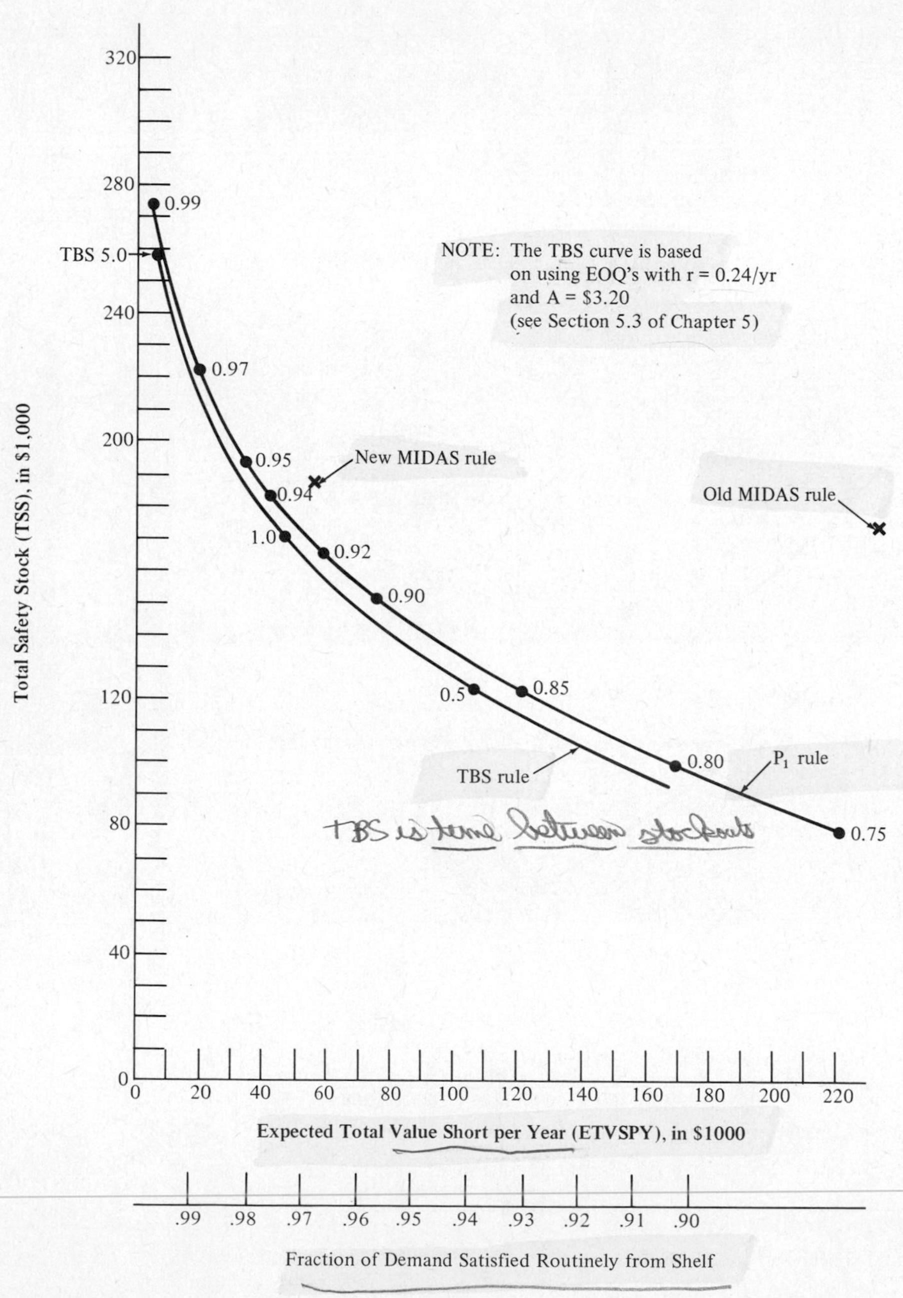

First of all, it is seen that with either measure of service the new MIDAS rule significantly improves service while only slightly raising total safety stock. Therefore, the comptroller's suggestion is a step in the right direction. However, it is seen that in either part of the figure we can simultaneously reduce total safety stock (in dollars) and improve service as compared with either of MIDAS' policies by using either the P_1 rule or the TBS rule provided P_1 (or TBS) is selected in a particular range. As an illustration, suppose we used the P_1 decision rule and decided to maintain the same total safety stock, namely $186,200, as that obtained under the new policy (that of the comptroller's office). In part a) of Figure 6.9 it is seen that the P_1 decision rule with $P_1 = 0.943$ achieves this while reducing the expected total stockout occasions per year to approximately 300 from 800. Similarly, in part b) of the figure the same P_1 value reduces the expected total value short per year to approximately $40,000 from $57,000.

The derivations of the exchange curves will be left to Chapter 7. However, it might be helpful to give an outline of the approach for one of the decision rules, namely the one using the P_1 service measure. For a given value of P_1 we can find, by Eq. 6.5, the value of k for any item. Knowing k we can then determine

i. The safety stock (in dollars) of the item

ii. The expected number of stockout occasions per year for the item

iii. The expected value short per year for the item

Each of these three quantities is summed across all items to obtain three numbers. These numbers are used to plot one point, corresponding to the given P_1 value, on each of the parts of Figure 6.9. This is repeated for a number of P_1 values tracing out two curves. Clearly, a computer routine is needed to accomplish this unless a small number of items are involved. Such a routine has been developed and will be referenced again in the appropriate part of Chapter 7.

6.7.2 *A Further Illustration of the Impact of Moving Away from Setting Reorder Points as Equal Time Supplies*

It is not uncommon for organizations to use the following type of rule for setting reorder points: reorder when the inventory position has dropped to a 2-month time supply. Without going into detail we wish to show the impact of moving away from this type of decision rule. To illustrate, let us consider three typical items produced and stocked by MIDAS International (the parent company, serving MIDAS Canada as well as other subsidiaries and direct customers in Germany, Australia, the U.S.A., England, etc.). Relevant characteristics of the items (three types of general purpose photographic papers) are given in Table 6.2.

Table 6.2

MIDAS Canada Identification	Demand Rate D units/year	Unit Value v \$/unit	Lead Time L months	σ_L units	Current order Quantity Q units	Current reorder Point s units
PSP-001	6,000	20.00	1.5	125	6,000	1,000
PSP-002	3,000	10.00	1.5	187.5	1,000	500
PSP-003	2,400	12.00	1.5	62.5	1,200	400

The order quantities, assumed as prespecified, are as shown. The current reorder points are each based on a 2-month time supply (that is, D/6).

Assuming normally distributed forecast errors for simplicity (any distribution could, in principle, be handled) it can be shown* that, under use of the current reorder points, the safety stocks, the expected stockout occasions per year, and the expected values short per year are as listed in columns (2), (3), and (4) of Table 6.3. If the total safety stock of \$7,450 is instead allocated among the items to give equal probabilities of stockout per replenishment cycle (that is, equal P_1 values), the resulting expected stockout occasions per year and the expected values short per year are as in columns (6) and (7) of the table. The reallocation has reduced both aggregate measures of service by over 50%. The reason for this is that the current equal-time supply strategy does not take account of the fact that PSP-002's forecast is considerably more uncertain (higher σ_L) than those of the other two items. Note the shift of additional safety stock to PSP-002 under the revised strategy. The marked service improvement for PSP-002 far outweighs the slight reduction in service of the other two items caused by the transfer of some of their safety stocks to PSP-002. The type of service improvement indicated here is typical of what can be achieved in most actual applications of logical decision rules for computing reorder points.

---

* *The details of such derivations will be left to Chapter* 7.

Table 6.3 Numerical Example of Shifting Away from Reorder Points as Equal Time Supplies

Item No.	Equal Time Supply Recorder Points			Reorder Points Based on Equal Probabilities of Stockout per Cycle		
	Safety Stock* $	Expected Stockout Occasions per Year	Expected Total value ($) Short per Year	Safety Stock $	Expected Stockout Occasions per Year	Expected Total Value Short per Year
(1)	(2)	(3)	(4)	(5)	(6)	(7)
1	5,000	0.023	21	3,630	0.074	82
2	1,250	0.754	845	2,730	0.221	185
3	1,200	0.110	35	1,090	0.147	49
Totals	$7,450	0.887	$901/yr.	$7,450	0.442	$316/yr.

* Under the given strategy

safety stock (in units) $= s - \bar{x}_L = s - DL$

Then,

safety stock (in \$) $= (s - DL)v$

6.8 Establishing the Values of the Control Parameters in a Periodic Review, Order-Up-To-Level (R, S) System

6.8.1 The Review Interval (R)

In computing the value of S we shall assume that a value of R has been predetermined. The nature of (R, S) control is such that a replenishment order is placed every R units of time. The determination of R is equivalent to the determination of an economic order quantity expressed as a time supply, except for two minor variations. First, the cost of reviewing the inventory status must be included as part of the fixed setup cost, A. Second, it is clear that it would be senseless to attempt to implement certain review intervals, for example, 2.36 days; that is, R is obviously restricted to a reasonably small number of feasible discrete values.

6.8.2 The Order-Up-To-Level (S)

The key time period over which protection is required is now of duration $R+L$, instead of just a replenishment lead time L. This is illustrated in

Figure 6.10 The Time Period of Protection in an (R, S) System.

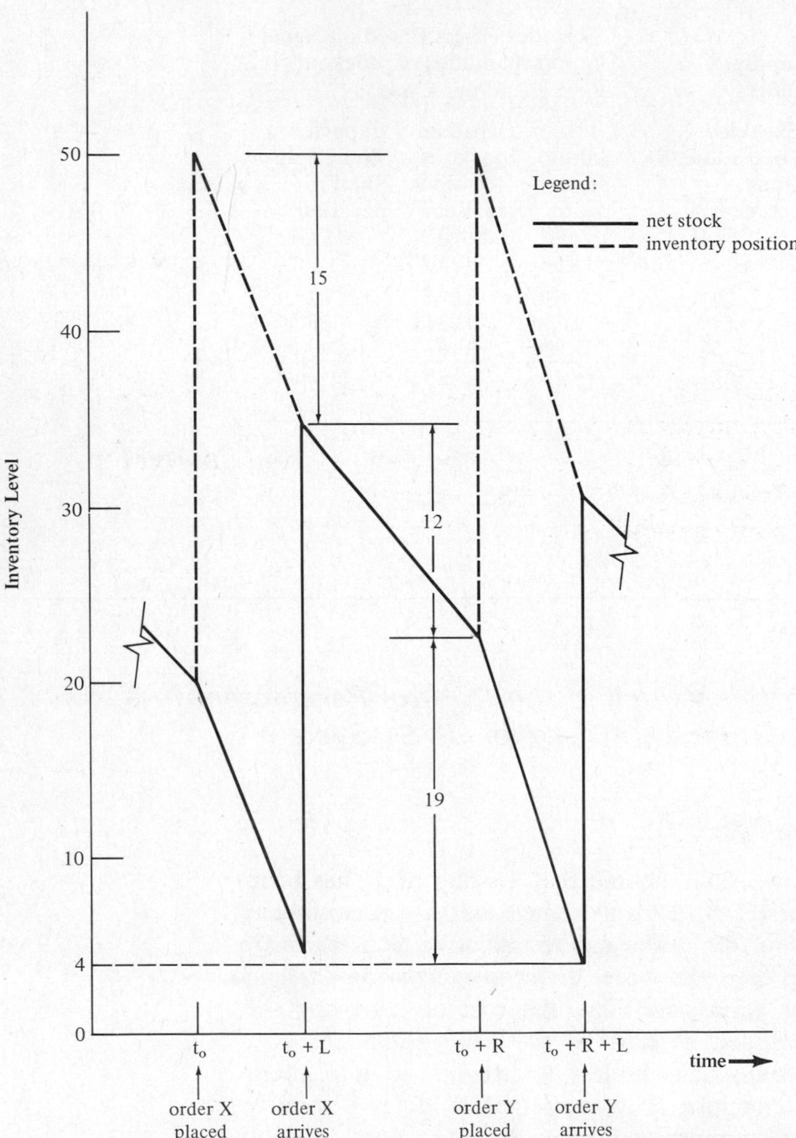

Figure 6.10 and Table 6.4 with an example where $S = 50$ units and where two consecutive orders (called X and Y) are placed at times t_0 and $t_0 + R$ respectively and arrive at $t_0 + L$ and $t_0 + R + L$ respectively. In selecting the order-up-to-level at time t_0 we must recognize that, once we've placed order X, no other later orders (in particular Y) can be received until time $t_0 + R + L$. Therefore, the order-up-to-level at time t_0 must be sufficient to

cover demand through a period of duration $R+L$. A stockout could occur in the early portion of the period (prior to t_0+L) but that would be a consequence of the setting of the order-up-to-level on the order preceding order X. What is of interest to us is that a stockout will occur towards the end of the period (after time t_0+L) if the total demand in an interval of length $R+L$ exceeds the order-up-to-level S. Another way of putting this is that any stockouts up to time t_0+L will not be influenced by our ordering decision at time t_0, however this decision certainly influences the likelihood of a stockout at time t_0+R+L. Of course, this does not mean that one would necessarily take no action if at time t_0 a stockout appeared likely by time t_0+L. Probably, one would expedite any already outstanding order or try to get the current order (that placed at time t_0) delivered as quickly as possible. Note however that this still does not influence the *size* of the current order.

Table 6.4 Illustration of Why (R+L) is the Crucial Time Interval in an (R, S) System (Illustrated for S = 50)

Event	Time or Interval[1]	Demand	(OH−BO)[2] Net Stock	On-Order	Inventory Position
	$t_0-\varepsilon$	—	20	—	20
place order for 30	$t_0-\varepsilon$ to $t_0+\varepsilon$	—	20	30	50[a]
	$t_0+\varepsilon$ to $t_0+L-\varepsilon$	15[b]	5	30	35
order of 30 arrives	$t_0+L-\varepsilon$ to $t_0+L+\varepsilon$	—	35	—	35
	$t_0+L+\varepsilon$ to $t_0+R-\varepsilon$	12[c]	23	—	23
place order for 27	$t_0+R-\varepsilon$ to $t_0+R+\varepsilon$	—	23	27	50
	$t_0+R+\varepsilon$ to $t_0+R+L-\varepsilon$	19[d]	4[e]	27	31
order of 27 arrives	$t_0+R+L-\varepsilon$ to $t_0+R+L+\varepsilon$	—	31	—	31

$$(e)=(a)-\underbrace{[(b)+(c)+(d)]}$$

- (e): net stock status just before a replenishment arrives at t_0+R+L
- (a): inventory position *after* order at t_0
- $[(b)+(c)+(d)]$: total demand in t_0 to t_0+R+L

(1) ε is a shorthand notation for a very small interval of time. Thus $t_0-\varepsilon$ represents a moment just prior to time t_0 while $t_0+\varepsilon$ represents a moment just after time t_0.

(2) (on-hand) − (backorders)

As mentioned above, a stockout will occur at the end of the current cycle (that is, at time t_0+R+L) if the total demand in an interval of duration $R+L$ exceeds S. A little reflection shows a very close analogy with the determination of s in the continuous review system. In fact, the only difference is the duration of the time period of concern, namely $R+L$ instead of just L. Therefore, for the case of normally distributed forecast errors and a specified probability, P_1, of no stockout per replenishment cycle we have the following decision rule:

Step 1 Select the safety factor k to satisfy

$$p_{u\geq}(k)=1-P_1 \tag{6.13}$$

where

$p_{u\geq}(k)=$ pr {unit normal variable takes on a value of k or larger}, a widely tabulated function (see Table C.1 in Appendix C).

Step 2 Safety stock,

$$SS=k\sigma_{R+L}$$

where σ_{R+L} is the standard deviation of forecast errors over a period of duration $R+L$.

Step 3 Order-up-to-level,

$$S=\hat{x}_{R+L}+SS$$

increased to the next higher integer (if not already exactly an integer) where $\hat{x}_{R+L}$ is the forecast value of total demand over a period of duration $R+L$.

For the TBS (average time between stockout occasions) service measure the only difference is that Eq. 6.13 is replaced by

$$p_{u\geq}(k)=\frac{R}{\text{TBS}} \tag{6.14}$$

where R is the prespecified value of the review interval, in the same units as TBS.

The extensions of either service measure to the case of Laplace distributed demand (slower moving items) are straightforward.

6.9 Variability in the Replenishment Lead Time Itself

In all the decision systems discussed in this chapter (and to be discussed in Chapter 7) the key variable in setting a reorder point or order-up-to-level is the total demand in an interval of length $R+L$ (which reduces to just L for the case of continuous review). So far our decisions have been based on a *known* replenishment lead time L with the only uncertain quantity being the demand *rate* during L or $R+L$. If L itself is not known with certainty it is apparent that increased safety stock is required to protect against this additional uncertainty.

Before discussing how to incorporate variability in L into the safety stock decision rules, we first emphasize that every reasonable effort should be made to eliminate such variability. One method would be by direct negotiation with suppliers. Quite often, the knowledge that you are monitoring his performance may be sufficient to induce a supplier to more dependable delivery. It should be noted that where the pattern of variability is known, for example, seasonally varying lead times, there is no problem because the lead time at any given calendar time is known and the safety stock (and reorder point) can be accordingly adjusted. Where lead times are increasing in a known fashion, such as in conditions of reduced availability of raw materials, again safety stocks (and reorder points) should be appropriately adjusted.

Where there is still some residual variability in the lead time two courses of action are possible:

i. Develop histograms of actual total demand over lead times (or review times plus lead times)—this has potential drawbacks for the reasons cited in Section 6.5.2, but may still be a reasonable approach.

ii. Use an approximate mathematical model to ascertain the standard deviation of total demand in a lead time.

This model assumes that the lead time (L) and the demand rate (D) are *independent* random variables. This is probably a reasonable approximation to reality (espccially when one recognizes how complex more realistic models become!) despite the fact that, in some cases, as discussed in Chapter 3, high demand is likely to be associated with long lead times (that is, positive correlation), because of the heavy workload placed on the supplier, or low demand can be associated with long lead times (that is, negative correlation) because the supplier has to wait longer to accumulate sufficient orders for his desired run size. If L and D are assumed to be independent random variables, then it can be shown (see, for example, pages 111–112 of Reference 8) that

$$E(x) = E(L)E(D) \tag{6.15}$$

and

$$\sigma_x = \sqrt{E(L)\,\mathrm{var}\,(D) + [E(D)]^2\,\mathrm{var}\,(L)} \tag{6.16}$$

where x, with mean $E(x)$ and standard deviation σ_x, is the total demand in a replenishment lead time, in units; L, with mean $E(L)$ and variance var (L), is the length of a lead time, in unit time periods; and D, with mean $E(D)$ and variance var (D), is the demand rate, in units per unit time period. Where variability in L exists, the $E(x)$ and σ_x quantities found from Eqs. 6.15 and 6.16 should be used in place of $\bar{x}_L$ and σ_L in all the decision rules of this chapter and Chapter 7.

Numerical Illustration—For the developing chemicals item XSC-023, used in Section 6.5.3, let us consider two situations:

Situation 1—No Uncertainty in the Lead Time Itself
(that is, var $(L) = 0$ in Eq. 6.16)

Suppose $E(L) = 3.5$ months

$$E(D) = 200 \text{ units/yr.} = \frac{200}{12} \text{ units/month}$$

and

$$\mathrm{var}\,(D) = 49 \text{ (units/month)}^2$$

Then Eqs. 6.15 and 6.16 give

$$E(x) = 58.3 \text{ units}$$

and

$$\sigma_x = 13.1 \text{ units}$$

which are the figures that were used in Section 6.5.3. There, to provide a desired probability (P_1) of no stockout per replenishment cycle equal to 0.90, we required a reorder point of 76 units.

Situation 2—Uncertainty in the Lead Time

Suppose that $E(L)$, $E(D)$, and var (D) are as above so that $E(x)$, the expected total demand over a lead time, is still 58.3 units. However, now we assume that L itself is random, in particular

$$\text{var}(L) = 0.3844 \text{ (months)}^2$$

(The standard deviation of L is $\sqrt{\text{var}(L)}$ or 0.62 months.) Then, Eq. 6.16 gives

$$\sigma_x = \sqrt{(3.5)(49) + \left(\frac{200}{12}\right)^2 (0.3844)}$$

$$= 16.7 \text{ units.}$$

Now, using the method of Section 6.5.3 we find that the reorder point must be 80 units. In other words, the uncertainty in L has increased the reorder point by 4 units.

6.10 *Summary*

In this chapter we have introduced the reader to the fundamentals of inventory control under probabilistic demand. Again the notion of an exchange curve was found to play a central role. We have deliberately kept the analysis as simple as possible, not an easy task when probabilistic concepts are involved. Sample decision rules have been shown for only two types of service measures. In the next chapter we lay out decision rules for two of the more important types of control systems under a variety of methods of measuring shortage costs or service levels.

The reader has a choice at this stage. He can plunge into the details of Chapter 7 to obtain a more complete understanding of operational control systems for coping with probabilistic demand or he can move directly to Chapter 8 where we return to a special case of deterministic demand where the known demand rate is permitted to vary with time (examples include seasonal effects and requirements of parts implied by an assembly master schedule). A by-pass of Chapter 7 is not likely to inhibit the understanding of any of the remaining chapters of the book.

Problems for Chapter 6

Problem 6.1

Consider MIDAS item ISF-086, a type of stabilization paper. It is reasonable to assume that demand over its replenishment lead time is normally distributed with $\bar{x}_L = 20$ units and $\sigma_L = 4.2$ units.

a. For a desired service level of $P_1 = 0.90$, compute the required safety factor, safety stock, and reorder point.

b. Repeat for $P_1 = 0.95$, 0.99, and 0.995.

c. Prepare a rough sketch of safety stock versus P_1. Is the curve linear? Discuss.

Problem 6.2

A film cassette carried by MIDAS is purchased from a domestic supplier, on the average, 10 times per year. It is reasonable to assume that demand over the replenishment lead time has a Laplace distribution with $\bar{x}_L = 8$ units and $\sigma_L = 4.1$ units. If the desired service level is a TBS value of 5 years, what must be the values of the safety factor, the safety stock, and the reorder point?

Problem 6.3

Consider the developing chemicals item XSC-023 discussed in Section 6.5.2. The histogram of historical lead times was shown in Table 6.1. If this histogram is representative of probabilities of total demands in future lead times and a reorder point of 51 is used, compute

a. The various possible shortage sizes and their probabilities of occurrence.

b. The expected (or average) shortage.

c. What reorder point would you use if the average shortage was to be no larger than 5 units? What is the associated probability of a stockout?

Problem 6.4

Cactus Grief's Music Shop sells 500 units of a particular musical instrument per year and, as a first approximation, demand is assumed to be deterministic. The owner, D. Grief, uses a purchase quantity of 100 units. The procurement lead time is 4 months.

a. What is the time between the placing of orders?

b. What is the reorder point based on the *on-hand* inventory level? (Hint: A diagram may be helpful).

c. How many orders are outstanding at any one time once the system is operating?

Problem 6.5

One of MIDAS' customers, a metropolitan Toronto hospital, controls its inventory of X-ray films by means of a periodic review, order-up-to-level (R, S) system. For a particular item $R = 1$ week, that is, reviews take place once a week. The replenishment lead time itself is of negligible duration because of the proximity of MIDAS' warehouse. The value of S is to be set so that the probability of a stockout in any particular week is only 0.005. The average demand for the item is 25 packages per week and the standard deviation of weekly demand is 6 packages.

a. What value of S should be used?

b. What is the expected time (TBS) between stockouts?

Problem 6.6

a. Consider the film cassette item of Problem 6.2. Suppose that σ_L has been inaccurately estimated and that the correct value is 5.0 units. What is the actual TBS achieved?

b. Repeat if the true σ_L was 3.0 units.

Problem 6.7

Consider two items with the following characteristics:

Item	Unit Value ($/unit)	D (units/yr.)	$\hat{x}_L$ (units)	σ_L (units)
1	10.00	300	100	10
2	1.00	300	100	35

Suppose that the inventory controller has set the safety stock of each of these items as a 1 month time supply.

a. What are the safety stocks in units? in dollars?

b. What is the P_1 value associated with each item?

c. Reallocate the same total safety stock (in dollars) so that the two items have the same value of P_1.

d. What reduction in total safety stock is possible if both items have $P_1 = 0.95$?

Problem 6.8

A supplier of a local distributor offers the following type of deal. If the unit purchase cost of a particular item is increased from v_1 to v_2, he will ensure a lead time of L_2 instead of the current value of $L_1 (L_2 < L_1)$. Indicate how you would perform a mathematical analysis to assist the distributor in deciding whether or not to accept the offer. Use a P_1 service measure.

Problem 6.9

Suppose you were a consultant to a company. The inventory manager likes the idea of a periodic review type system. However, he is faced with quantity discount opportunities on some of the individual items. What type of control system would you suggest using for such items? Discuss.

Problem 6.10

a. At the beginning of MIDAS Case D it was pointed out that the company's stated inventory control policy was "to have zero stockouts." Is this a realistic policy to pursue? In particular, discuss the implications in terms of various types of costs.

b. "On occasion MIDAS filled an important customer order by supplying a competitor's film at below retail price." What form of shortage costing would it be appropriate to apply under such circumstances? Does this type of strategy make sense?

REFERENCES FOR CHAPTER 6

1. Archibald, B., E. A. Silver, and R. Peterson. "Implementation Considerations in Selecting the Probability Distribution of Lead Time Demand." Working Paper No. 89, Department of Management Sciences, University of Waterloo, Waterloo, Ontario, Canada, July, 1974.

2. Bramson, M. "The Variable Lead-Time Problem in Inventory Control—A Survey of the Literature—Part 1." *Operational Research Quarterly*, Vol. 13, 1962, pp. 41–53.

3. Brooks, R., C. Gillen, and J. Lu. "Alternative Measures of Supply Performance: Fills, Backorders, Operational Rate, and NORS." RAND Memorandum Rm-6094-PR, Santa Monica, Calif., August, 1969.

4. Carlson, P. "On the Distribution of Lead Time Demand." *Journal of Industrial Engineering*, Vol. XV, No. 2, March–April, 1964, pp. 87–94.

5. Chang, Y. S. and P. Niland. "A Model for Measuring Stock Depletion Costs." *Operations Research*, Vol. 15, No. 3, May–June, 1967, pp. 427–447.

6. Cohen, G. "The Use of Service Rates in Evaluating Inventory Control Systems." *Journal of Industrial Engineering*, Vol. XV, No. 2, March–April, 1964, pp. 95–99.

7. Donaldson, W. "The Allocation of Inventory Items to Lot Size/Reorder Level (Q, r) and Periodic Review (T, Z) Control Systems." *Operational Research Quarterly*, Vol. 25, No. 3, September, 1974, pp. 481–5.

8. Drake, A. *Fundamentals of Applied Probability Theory.* McGraw–Hill, New York, 1967.

9. Eilon, S. "On the Cost of Runouts in Stock Control of Perishables." *Operations Research—Verfahren II*, edited by R. Henn, 1965, pp. 65–76.

10. Gross, D. and J. Ray. "Choosing a Spare Parts Inventory Operating Procedure—Bulk Control Versus Item Control." *Journal of Industrial Engineering*, Vol. XV, No. 6, November–December, 1964, pp. 310–315.

11. Hadley, G. and T. Whitin. *Analysis of Inventory Systems.* Prentice–Hall, Englewood Cliffs, N.J., 1963, Chap. 4–5.

12. Horodowich, P. "A Model for the Planning of Aggregate Finished Goods Inventory." *Production and Inventory Management*, Vol. 16, No. 2, June, 1975, pp. 27–40.

13. IBM. *Wholesale IMPACT—Advanced Principles and Implementation Reference Manual*, IBM Technical Publications Department, White Plains, New York, 1965, Chap. 3.

14. Lewis, C. D. "Generating a Continuous Trend Corrected, Exponentially Weighted Average on an Analogue Computer." *Opl. Res. Q.*, Vol. 17, No. 1, 1966, pp. 77–81.

15. Magee, J. F. and D. M. Boodman. *Production Planning and Inventory Control*, McGraw–Hill, New York, N.Y., 1967, Chap. 6.

16. Oral, M., M. Salvador, A. Reisman, and B. Dean. "On the Evaluation of Shortage Costs for Inventory Control of Finished Goods." *Management Science*, Vol. 18, No. 6, February, 1972, pp. B344–B351.

17. Plossl, G. W. and O. W. Wight. *Production and Inventory Control: Principles and Techniques*. Prentice–Hall, Englewood Cliffs, N.J., 1967, Chap. 5.

18. Presutti, V. and R. Trepp. "More Ado about EOQ." *Naval Research Logistics Quarterly*, Vol. 17, No. 2, June, 1970, pp. 243–251.

19. Pritchard, J. W. and R. H. Eagle. *Modern Inventory Management*. Wiley, New York, 1965, Chap. 7.

20. Scarf, H. "The Optimality of (S, s) Policies in the Dynamic Inventory Problem." Chapter 13 in *Mathematical Methods in the Social Sciences*. Editors Arrow, Karlin, and Suppes, Stanford University Press, 1960.

21. Schwartz, B. L. "A New Approach to Stockout Penalties." *Management Science*, Vol. 12, No. 2, August, 1966, pp. 538–544.

22. Vinson, C. "The Cost of Ignoring Lead Time Unreliability in Inventory Theory." *Decision Sciences*, Vol. 3, 1972, pp. 87–105.

CHAPTER SEVEN

Decision Systems for the Case of Probabilistic Demand

In the preceding chapter the basic concepts of control under probabilistic demand were laid out. Now we turn to a more detailed presentation of actual decision systems under several different possible options for costing shortages or measuring service. A wide variety of options (still by no means exhaustive) are presented simply because each is either appropriate for use or is actually being used under certain practical circumstances. We build on the developments of Chapter 6; therefore much of the basic material is not repeated.

It should be emphasized that, in every decision rule discussed, the fundamental problem is the determination of an appropriate value of the safety factor k. Once a value of k is found, the safety stock and the reorder point (or order-up-to-level) immediately follow from use of

$$s = \bar{x}_L + k\sigma_L$$

or

$$S = \bar{x}_{R+L} + k\sigma_{R+L}$$

The choice of methods of establishing safety stocks of individual items is discussed in Section 7.1. Because of the wide variety of options for establishing safety stocks it was felt desirable to prepare the summary guide shown in Table 7.1.

Table 7.1 Summary of Different Methods of Selecting the Safety Factor (k), Hence the Safety Stocks, etc. in Control Systems under Probabilistic Demand

Criterion	Discussed in Section	Sections in Which Decision Rules for (s, Q) System Can be Found[a]
Equal time supplies	7.1.1	—
Specified probability (P_1) of no stockout per replenishment cycle	7.1.2	7.2.3 (or 6.5.3 and 6.5.4)
Fixed safety factor, k	7.1.2	7.2.3
Specified average time (TBS) between stockout occasions	7.1.3	7.2.6 (or 6.6)
Specified fraction (P_2) of demand to be satisfied directly from shelf	7.1.4	7.2.4
Cost (B_1) per stockout occasion	7.1.5	7.2.5
Minimization of expected total stockout occasions per year subject to a specified total safety stock	7.1.6	7.2.5
Cost per unit short as a fraction (B_2) of unit value	7.1.7	7.2.6
Minimization of expected total value short per year subject to a specified total safety stock	7.1.8	7.2.6

[a] As will be shown in Section 7.4 the decision rules for (R, S) systems are easily obtained from those for (s, Q) systems.

Section 7.2 is concerned with continuous review, order point, order quantity (s, Q) systems. We again advocate a two-tier type of control. In Section 7.3 we return to the concept of exchange curves. Two types of exchange curves are presented for an assortment of decision rules applied to the MIDAS situation. One group shows the aggregate consequences of the different methods of establishing safety stocks; in each case, there is a policy variable whose value may be specified from aggregate considerations by management. The second type is of the composite variety, showing a three way tradeoff of total average stock versus total number of replenishments per year versus aggregate service.

Section 7.4 is briefly devoted to the two tiers of control for the other commonly used control system, namely the periodic review, order-up-to-level (R, S) system.

Derivations of some of the rules have been placed in the appendix of the current chapter. In addition, computer programmes have been developed for all of the decision rules and for the computations associated with the exchange curves.

7.1 *Choice of Methods of Establishing Safety Stocks of Individual Items*

In this section we consider a variety of criteria for establishing protection against the uncertainty of demand over the replenishment lead time (or review interval plus lead time), each criterion being an expression of management's attitude towards the balancing of two risks, the first being shortages caused by unusually large demands, the second being the carrying of excess stock caused by unusually low demands. In each case there is a variable whose value can be specified explicitly through cost considerations or implicitly through management's selection of a suitable operating point on an aggregate exchange curve.

7.1.1 *Equal Time Supplies*

This is a simple, commonly used approach. The safety stocks of a broad group of (if not all) items in an inventory population are set equal to the same time supply; for example, reorder any item when its inventory position minus the forecasted lead time demand drops to a 2-month supply or lower. This approach is seriously in error because it fails to take account of the difference in uncertainty of forecasts from item to item. The policy variable here is the common number of time periods of supply.

7.1.2 Specified Safety Factor (k) or Probability (P_1) of No Stockout per Replenishment Cycle

As was indicated in Section 6.5.3 of Chapter 6, for normally distributed forecast errors, if the safety stock of an item is expressed as the multiple of a safety factor (k) and the standard deviation of forecast errors over an interval of length L (or $R+L$), then

$$\text{prob}\{\text{stockout per replenishment cycle}\} = p_{u\geq}(k) \tag{7.1}$$

where $p_{u\geq}(k)$ is the probability that a unit normal variable takes on a value of k or larger.

Similarly, for the case of lead time demand having a Laplace distribution, we found that

$$\text{prob}\{\text{stockout per replenishment cycle}\} = \tfrac{1}{2}\exp(-\sqrt{2}k) \tag{7.2}$$

Both of Eqs. 7.1 and 7.2 reveal that specifying the same safety factor for two or more items is equivalent to specifying the same probability of no stockout per cycle for each of the items. This approach is based on a per cycle service measure; in particular, it ignores the frequency with which replenishment orders are placed. Therefore, it does not attempt to provide equal service on a per unit time basis. The policy variable is the common safety factor k or, equivalently, the probability, P_1, of no stockout per replenishment cycle

7.1.3 Specified Average Time (TBS) Between Stockout Occasions

This was the other service measure discussed in Chapter 6. Equivalently, one can specify the reciprocal of TBS which can be interpreted as the average number of stockout occasions (that is, replenishment cycles in which a stockout occurs) per year. Clearly, the policy variable here is TBS itself.

7.1.4 Specified Fraction (P_2) of Demand to be Satisfied Routinely from Shelf

A form of service measure which has considerable appeal to practitioners (particularly where a significant portion of the replenishment lead time is unalterable; for example, a branch warehouse where the major part of the lead time is the transit time by rail car) is the specification of a certain fraction of customer demand which is to be met routinely (without backorders or lost sales). To a good approximation, this fraction is equal to the ready rate, the fraction of time that the on-hand stock is positive. The policy variable is the common fraction, P_2, of demand to be satisfied directly from shelf.

7.1.5 *Specified Fixed Cost* (B_1) *per Stockout Occasion*

Here, it is assumed that the only cost associated with a stockout occasion is a fixed value B_1, independent of the magnitude and/or duration of the stockout. One possible interpretation would be the cost of an expediting action to avert an impending stockout. In general, it is difficult to explicitly ascertain this cost.

7.1.6 *Allocation of a Given Total Safety Stock Among Items so as to Minimize the Expected Total Stockout Occasions per Year*

As is shown in part 3 of the appendix of this chapter, allocating a fixed total safety stock among several items so as to minimize the expected total number of stockout occasions per year leads to a decision rule for selecting the safety factor of each item which is identical with that obtained by assuming a value (the same for all items) of the fixed cost B_1 and then selecting the safety factor to keep the total of carrying and stockout costs as low as possible (the latter approach was discussed in the preceding subsection). This allocation interpretation is probably more appealing to management. The policy variable in either case is B_1.

7.1.7 *Specified Fractional Charge* (B_2) *per Unit Short*

Here one assumes that a fraction B_2 of unit value is charged per unit short, that is, the cost per unit short of item i is $B_2 v_i$ where v_i is the unit variable cost of the item. Again, explicit determination of B_2 is not likely in most practical contexts.

7.1.8 *Allocation of a Given Total Safety Stock Among Items so as to Minimize the Expected Total Value of Shortages per Year*

Once more, one can show that allocating a fixed total safety stock among a group of items so as to minimize the expected total value (in dollars) of shortages per year leads to a decision rule for selecting the safety factor which is identical with either

i. that obtained by assuming a value (the same for all items) of the factor B_2 and then selecting the safety factor for each item to minimize the total of carrying and shortage costs, or

ii. That obtained by specifying the same average time (TBS) between stockout occasions for every item in the group.

Again, this aggregate view of allocating a limited resource may be considerably more appealing to management than the micro detail of attempting to explicitly ascertain a B_2 value from cost considerations or the somewhat arbitrary specification of a TBS value. If necessary, one can modify the criterion to include an essentiality-weighted value of backorders, that is, the backorders of item i in units would be multiplied by an essentiality factor instead of by the unit value of the item. In any event, the policy variable is either B_2 or TBS.

7.2 Decision Rules for Continuous Review, Order Point, Order Quantity (s, Q) Control Systems

As in Chapter 6 we advocate (based on the results of empirical tests) the use of a two-tier control system. The division of a population of items should be based on the $\bar{x}_L$ value. The normal distribution of lead time demand is most appropriate for $\bar{x}_L \geq 10$ units, the Laplace* for $\bar{x}_L < 10$ units. Again, if the practitioner wishes only a single tier, then we recommend use of the normal distribution for all B items.**

The reader may find Figure 7.1 helpful, in that it summarizes the general approach to selecting the safety factor and, hence, the safety stock and the reorder point for all of the decision rules in this section.

Recall that an (s, Q) system operates in the following manner: any time that the inventory position drops to s or lower, a replenishment order of size Q is placed. The assumptions, the notation, and the portion of the derivation of the rules common to all methods will be presented prior to showing the individual decision rules. Further details of some of the derivations can be found in the appendix of this chapter. A single computer programme, encompassing all of the decision rules, has been developed.

* *The Laplace distribution is discussed in Appendix B.*

** *An alternative, involving greater computational effort and/or use of more extensive tables, would be the Gamma distribution, which has intuitive appeal (as discussed by Burgin.*[4]*).*

Figure 7.1 General Decision Logic Used in Computing the Value of s.

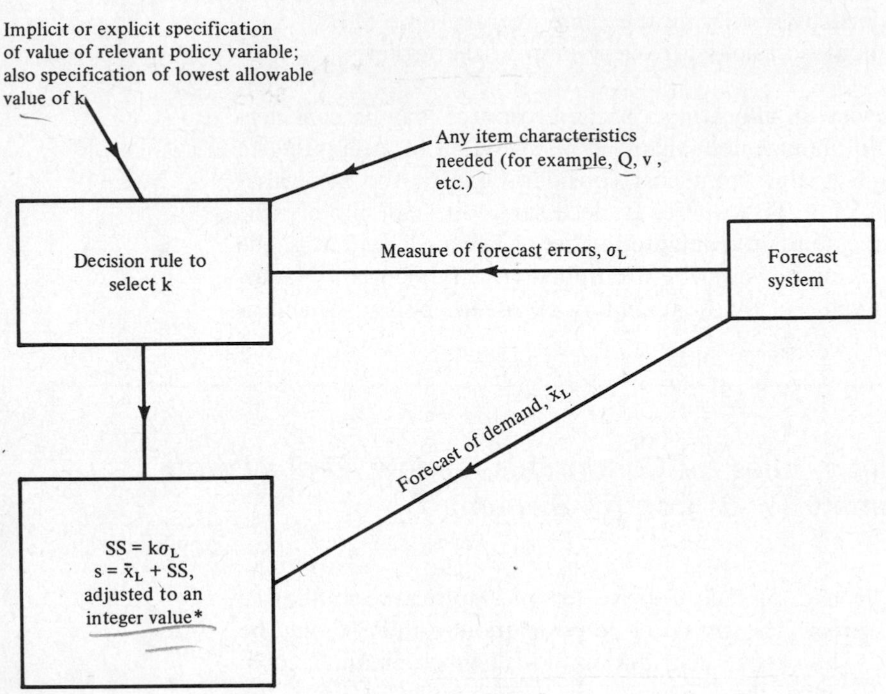

*If not already exactly an integer, we
i). raise to the next higher integer, if a service contraint is used.
ii). round to the nearest integer, if a shortage cost is used.

7.2.1 *Common Assumptions and Notation*

There are a number of assumptions which hold independent of the method of costing shortages or measuring service. These include:

a. Although demand is probabilistic, the *average* demand rate changes very little with time.

b. A replenishment order of size Q is placed when the inventory position is *exactly* at the order point s. This assumption is tantamount to assuming that all demand transactions are of unit size or else that the undershoots* of the order point are of negligible magnitude compared with the total lead time demand.

c. If two or more replenishment orders for the same item are simultaneously outstanding, then they must be received in the same order in which they were placed; that is, crossing of orders is not permitted. A special case satisfying this assumption is where the replenishment lead time is a constant.

d. Unit shortage costs (explicit or implicit) are so high that a practical operating procedure will always result in the average level of backorders being negligibly small when compared with the average level of the on-hand stock.

e. Forecast errors have a normal (or Laplace) distribution with no bias (that is, the average value of the error is zero).

f. Where a value of Q is needed, it is assumed to have been predetermined. In most situations, the effects of the two decision variables, s and Q, are not independent; that is, the best value of Q depends upon the s value and vice-versa. However, as will be shown in Chapter 9, where a closer look will be taken at the simultaneous determination of the two control parameters, the assumption of Q being predetermined without knowledge of s makes very good practical sense, particularly for B items.

g. The costs of the control system do not depend upon the specific value of s selected.

Common notation includes:

D–the demand rate in units/year.

$$G_u(k) = \int_k^{\infty} (u_0 - k) \frac{1}{\sqrt{2\pi}} \exp(-u_0^2/2)\, du_0$$

---

* *In a continuous review system an order is placed when a demand transaction reduces the inventory position to the order point or lower. The undershoot is the amount that the inventory position is below the order point when the order is placed. In Chapter 14 we shall consider a situation where the undershoots are not neglected.*

a special function of the unit normal (mean 0, standard deviation 1) variable*
k–safety factor.
L–the replenishment lead time, in years.
$p_{u\geq}(k)$–the probability that a unit normal (mean 0, standard deviation 1) variable takes on a value of k or larger.*
Q–the prespecified order quantity, in units.
r–the inventory carrying charge, in \$/\$/year.
s–the order point, in units.
SS–safety stock, in units.
v–the unit variable cost, in \$/unit.
$\bar{x}_L$–the forecast (or expected) demand over a replenishment lead time, in units.
σ_L–the standard deviation of errors of forecasts over a replenishment lead time, in units.

*7.2.2 *Common Derivation**

Because of the assumption of no crossing of orders, if an order is placed at some time t when the inventory position is at level s, then all previous orders outstanding at that time must have arrived prior to the moment (call it $t+L$) at which the current order arrives. Furthermore, any orders placed after the current one cannot arrive before $t+L$. In other words, all s of the inventory position at time t, and no other stock, must have reached the stocking shelf by time $t+L$. Therefore, the service impact of placing the current order when the inventory position is at the level s is determined by whether or not the total demand, x, in the replenishment lead time exceeds s. (If the on-hand level happens to be very low at time t, a stockout may be incurred early in the replenishment cycle before an earlier outstanding order arrives. However, this event is independent of the current replenishment, the one at time t, and should not be considered in evaluating the consequences of using an order point s for the current order.)

If the demand (x) in the replenishment lead time has a probability density function $f_x(x_0)$ defined such that

$$f_x(x_0)dx_0 = \text{prob}\,\{\text{total demand in the lead time lies between } x_0 \text{ and } x_0 + dx_0\},$$

---

* *$G_u(k)$ or $p_{u\geq}(k)$ can be obtained from k or vice-versa using a table lookup (a table of the unit normal distribution is shown in Appendix C) or a rational approximation (see, for example, p. 933 of Abramowitz and Stegun*[1] *or p. 93 of Brown*[2] *or Herron*[10] *or Parr*[14]*).*

then the above arguments lead to the following three important results:*

i. Safety stock (SS) = E (net stock just before the replenishment arrives)

$$= \int_0^\infty (s - x_0) f_x(x_0)\,dx_0$$

that is,

$$SS = s - \bar{x}_L \tag{7.3}$$

This has a particularly simple interpretation for the case where no more than one order is ever outstanding. In such a case Eq. 7.3 states that the average inventory level just before a replenishment arrives is equal to the inventory level when the replenishment is placed (all of this being on-hand inventory) reduced by the average demand during the lead time.

ii. prob {stockout in a replenishment lead time}

$$= \text{prob}\{x \geq s\}$$

$$= \int_s^\infty f_x(x_0)\,dx_0 \tag{7.4}$$

the probability that lead time demand is at least as large as the reorder point.

iii. Expected shortage per replenishment cycle,

$$\text{ESPRC} = \int_s^\infty (x_0 - s) f_x(x_0)\,dx_0 \tag{7.5}$$

Now, recall from the basic definition of Eq. 6.1 of Chapter 6 that

Net stock = (On-hand) − (Backorders),

that is,

$$NS = OH - BO$$

Therefore

$$E(NS) = E(OH) - E(BO) \tag{7.6}$$

---

* *$E(z)$ represents the expected or mean value of the random variable z.*

Because of the assumption of average backorders being very small relative to the average on-hand stock, we have

$$E(OH) \simeq E(NS) \tag{7.7}$$

Using Eqs. 7.3 and 7.7,

$$\begin{aligned} E(\text{OH just before a replenishment arrives}) &\simeq \text{Safety Stock (SS)} \\ &= s - \bar{x}_L \end{aligned}$$

and, because each replenishment is of size Q,

$$E(\text{OH just after a replenishment arrives}) \simeq s - \bar{x}_L + Q$$

Now, the mean rate of demand is constant with time. Therefore, on the average, the OH level drops linearly during a cycle from $(s - \bar{x}_L + Q)$ right after a replenishment arrives to $(s - \bar{x}_L)$ immediately before the next replenishment arrives. Thus,

$$E(OH) \simeq \frac{Q}{2} + (s - \bar{x}_L) = \frac{Q}{2} + k\sigma_L \tag{7.8}$$

where we have chosen to express the safety stock $(s - \bar{x}_L)$ as the multiple of two factors, viz.

$$SS = k\sigma_L \tag{7.9}$$

A useful graphical reminder of this equation is shown in Figure 7.2.

Figure 7.2 Average Behavior of On-Hand Stock in an (s, Q) System.

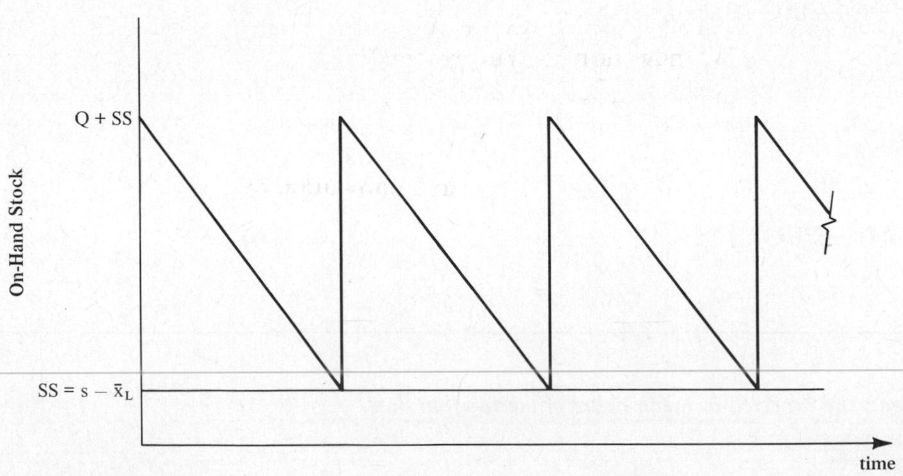

One other common feature, independent of the service measure used, is the expected number of replenishments per year. Each replenishment is of size Q and the mean rate of demand is D, as earlier. Therefore,

$$\text{Expected number of replenishments per year} = \frac{D}{Q} \qquad (7.10)$$

Normally Distributed Forecast Errors—As Shown in Appendix C, when forecast errors are normally distributed and the safety stock is expressed as in Eq. 7.9, then Eqs. 7.4 and 7.5 simplify to

$$\text{prob}\{\text{stockout in a replenishment lead time}\} = p_{u\geq}(k) \qquad (7.11)$$

and

$$\text{ESPRC} = \sigma_L G_u(k) \qquad (7.12)$$

Laplace Distributed Forecast Errors—As shown in Appendix B, when errors are Laplace distributed Eqs. 7.4 and 7.5 become

$$\text{prob}\{\text{stockout in a replenishment cycle}\} = \tfrac{1}{2}\exp(-\sqrt{2}k) \quad k \geq 0 \qquad (7.13)$$

and

$$\text{ESPRC} = \frac{\sigma_L}{2\sqrt{2}}\exp(-\sqrt{2}k) \quad k \geq 0 \qquad (7.14)$$

At this point, the safety factor derivations diverge based on the particular shortage cost or service measure used. Some illustrative details can be found in the appendix of this chapter. We now turn to the presentation of the individual decision rules. In each case we first present the rule (possibly including a graphical aid). In most cases this is followed by a numerical illustration of its use, then by a discussion of the behavior of the rule in terms of how the safety factor k varies from item to item in a population of items.

7.2.3 *Decision Rule for a Specified Safety Factor (k) or Probability (P_1) of No Stockout per Replenishment Cycle*

This decision rule was one of the cases discussed in Chapter 6, namely in Sections 6.5.3 and 6.5.4).

7.2.4 Decision Rule for a Specified Fraction (P_2) of Demand Satisfied Directly from Shelf

The Rule

Step 1 Select the safety factor k that satisfies*

$$G_u(k) = \frac{Q}{\sigma_L}(1-P_2) \qquad (\text{for } \bar{x}_L \geq 10 \text{ units}) \tag{7.15}$$

or

$$k = \frac{1}{\sqrt{2}} \ln\left[\frac{\sigma_L}{2\sqrt{2}Q(1-P_2)}\right] \qquad (\text{for } \bar{x}_L < 10 \text{ units}) \tag{7.16}$$

where Q has been predetermined, presumably by one of the procedures of Chapter 5 (and must be expressed in the same units as σ_L). The other relevant variables are defined in Section 7.2.1.

Make sure that the k value is at least as large as the lowest allowable (management specified) value (for example, zero) of the safety factor.

Step 2 Reorder point, $s = \bar{x}_L + k\sigma_L$, increased to the next higher integer (if not already *exactly* an integer).

Graphical Aids—Graphical aids for solving Eqs. 7.15 and 7.16 for k are shown in Figures 7.3 and 7.4. This avoids a table lookup, the use of a rational approximation or the taking of a logarithm. The graphs actually provide solutions to equations that are more exact than Eqs. 7.15 and 7.16, particularly for low values of Q/σ_L (see Reference 19). To illustrate, the equation for normally distributed errors is

$$G_u(k) - G_u(k + Q/\sigma_L) = \frac{Q}{\sigma_L}(1-P_2) \tag{7.18}$$

* *Equations 7.15 and 7.16 apply for the case of complete backordering. The only difference for the case of complete lost sales is that $(1-P_2)$ is replaced by $(1-P_2)/P_2$. For example, Eq. 7.16 becomes*

$$k = \frac{1}{\sqrt{2}} \ln\left[\frac{\sigma_L P_2}{2\sqrt{2}Q(1-P_2)}\right] \tag{7.17}$$

Numerical Illustration—Consider a particular type of developing liquid distributed by MIDAS. Management has specified that 99 percent of demand is to be satisfied without backordering. A replenishment quantity of 200 gallons has been predetermined and the forecast system provides us with $\bar{x}_L = 50$ gallons and $\sigma_L = 11.4$ gallons.

Figure 7.3 Graphical Aid for Faster Moving ($\bar{x}_L \geq$ 10 units) Items under the P_2 Service Measure.

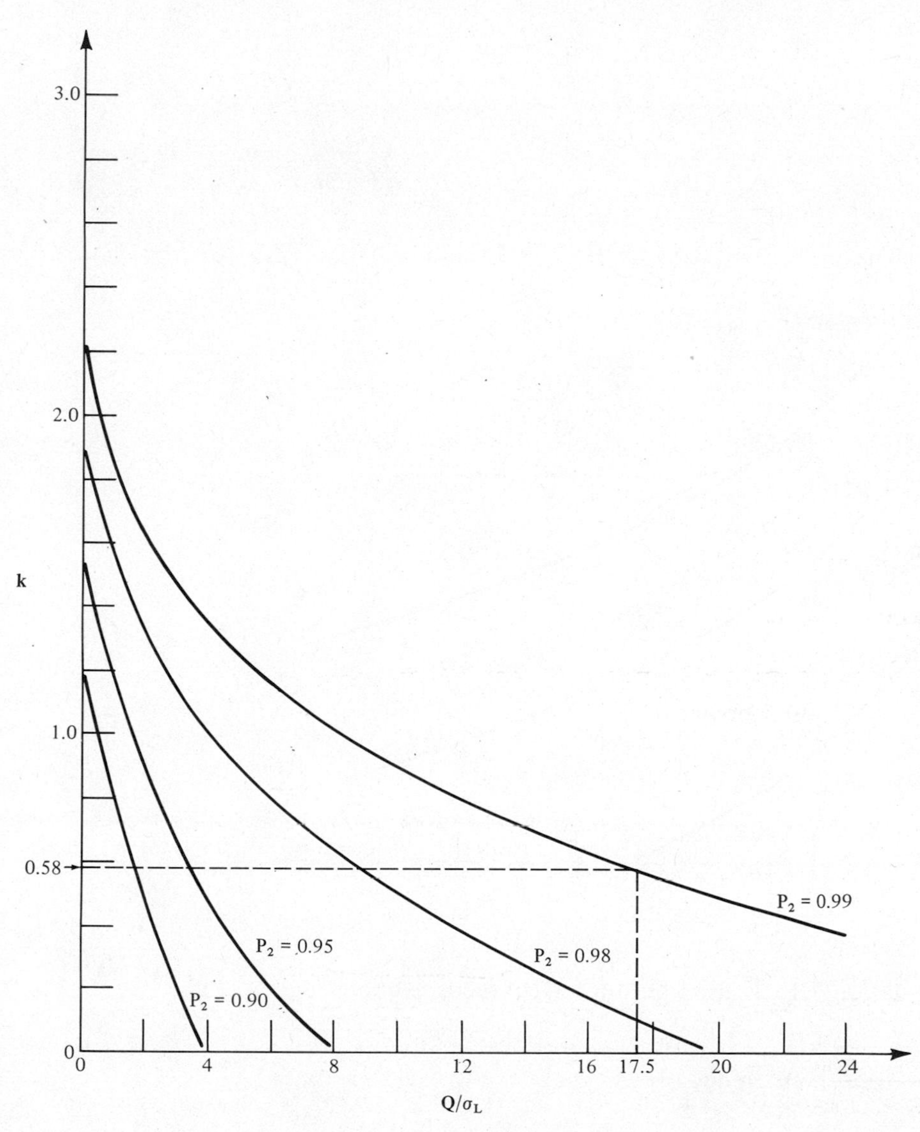

Figure 7.4 Graphical Aid for Slower Moving ($\bar{x}_L <$ 10 units) Items Under the P_2 Service Measure.

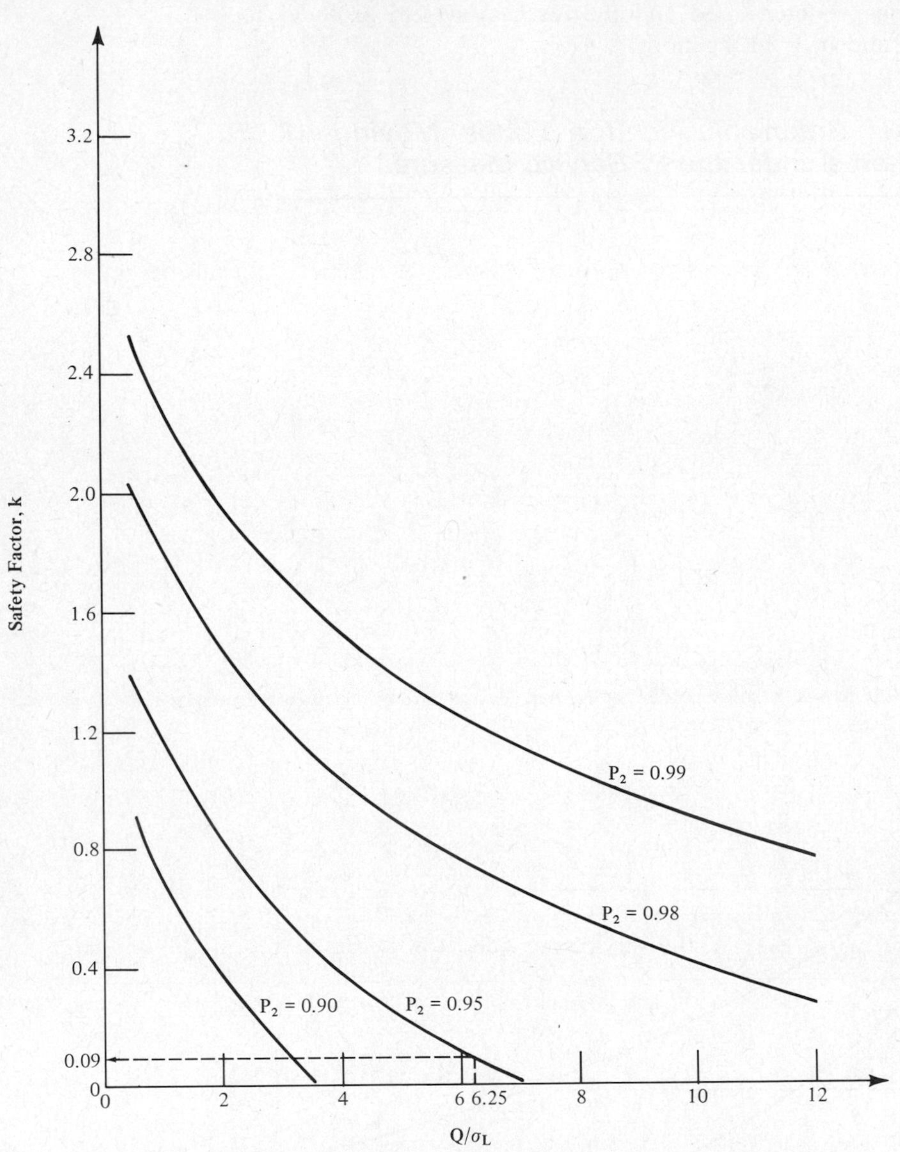

Step 1 Equation 7.15 is used because $\bar{x}_L$ exceeds 10 units. Thus,

$$G_u(k) = \frac{200}{11.4}(1 - 0.99) = 0.175$$

and Table C.1 in Appendix C gives

$$k = 0.58$$

The same result is obtained using Figure 7.3.

Step 2

$$s = 50 + 0.58(11.4) = 56.6 \rightarrow 57 \text{ gallons*}$$

For the case of complete lost sales (rather than backordering) use of Eq. 7.17 would lead us to the exact same value of the reorder point.

Discussion—Intuitively we would expect that the required safety stock would increase if i) Q decreased (more opportunities for stockouts), ii) σ_L increased (higher uncertainty of forecasts) or iii) P_2 increased (better service desired). This behavior is directly evident for the case of Eq. 7.16. The proof for Eq. 7.15 is a little less obvious. In that case, if any of the above-mentioned changes take place, $G_u(k)$ decreases, but as seen from the table in Appendix C, a decrease in $G_u(k)$ implies an increase in k, that is, exactly the desired behavior. The same conclusions can be reached by examining Figures 7.3 and 7.4.

In addition, on the average, σ_L tends to increase with D, therefore the increase in k with increasing σ_L says that, on the average under this decision rule, faster-moving items get higher safety factors than do the slower-moving items.

If the right hand side of Eq. 7.15 is large enough, a negative value of k is required to produce the equality; to give a service level as *poor* as P_2 one must deliberately plan to be short on the average when a replenishment arrives. Management may find this intolerable and, instead, set a lower limit on k (for example, zero). If k is set at zero when Eq. 7.15 or 7.16 calls for a negative value of k, the service provided will be better than P_2.

P_2 is usually quite close to unity. Therefore, Eqs. 7.15 and 7.17 normally give very similar values of $G_u(k)$, that is, of k itself. In other words, the value of the safety factor is little influenced by whether the model assumes complete backordering or complete lost sales (or any mix of these two extremes).

---

* *If the inventory can be monitored more finely than by integer gallons, the reorder point could be left at the non-integer value of* 56.6.

Use of a particular method of costing shortages, together with a cost minimization criterion, can be shown to be equivalent (see, for example, Hadley and Whitin[8]) to the use of the P_2 service measure. This shortage costing method assigns a cost of B_3 \$/\$ short/unit time (that is, the units of B_3 are identical to those of the carrying charge r). The equivalence between P_2 and B_3 is given by

$$P_2 = \frac{B_3}{B_3 + r}$$

7.2.5 *Decision Rule for i) a Specified Cost (B_1) per Stockout Occasion or for ii) Allocation of a Total Safety Stock so as to Minimize the Expected Total Stockout Occasions per Year*

The Rule

*Step 1**

For $\bar{x}_L \geq 10$ units (Normal Errors)

Is

$$\frac{DB_1}{\sqrt{2\pi}\, Qv\sigma_L r} < 1? \tag{7.19}$$

where Q has been predetermined, presumably by one of the methods of Chapter 5,

B_1 is expressed in dollars

and all the other variables (with units consistent such that the left-hand-side of the equation is dimensionless) are as defined in Section 7.2.1.

Yes, then go to step 2.

---

* *For the case of allocation of a total safety stock, B_1 is adjusted until the total implied safety stock is equal to the given quantity to be allocated.*

No, then continue with**

$$k=\sqrt{2\ln\left(\frac{DB_1}{\sqrt{2\pi}\,Qv\sigma_L r}\right)} \tag{7.20}$$

For $\bar{x}_L < 10$ units (Laplace Errors)

Evaluate

$$k=\frac{1}{\sqrt{2}}\ln\left[\frac{DB_1}{\sqrt{2}\,Qv\sigma_L r}\right] \tag{7.22}$$

If either of Eqs. 7.20 or 7.22 give a value of k lower than the minimum allowable value specified by management, then go to step 2. Otherwise, proceed directly to step 3.

Step 2 Set k at its lowest allowable value (specified by management).

Step 3 Reorder point $s=\bar{x}_L+k\sigma_L$, rounded to the nearest integer.

Numerical Illustration—Suppose an item is one of a number among which a certain amount of safety stock is to be allocated so as to keep the expected total stockout occasions per year as low as possible. An exchange curve analysis has led to a management specification of an aggregate operating point which implies a B_1 value of $300. Other relevant characteristics of the item are

$D=200$ units/year; $Q=80$ units

$v=\$2.00$/unit, $\bar{x}_L=50$ units, $\sigma_L=21.0$ units

$r=0.24$ $/$/year

** *An alternative to the use of Eq. 7.20 is to find by a table lookup, the k value that satisfies*

$$f_u(k)=\frac{Qv\sigma_L r}{DB_1} \tag{7.21}$$

where $f_u(k)$ is the probability density function of a unit normal variable evaluated at k. (see Table C.1 in Appendix C).

Step 1

$\bar{x}_L \geq 10$ units.

Therefore,

$$\frac{DB_1}{\sqrt{2\pi}\,Qv\sigma_L r} = \frac{200 \text{ units/yr.} \times \$300}{\sqrt{2\pi} \times 80 \text{ units} \times \$2.00/\text{unit} \times 21 \text{ units} \times 0.24/\text{yr.}}$$

$$= 29.7 > 1$$

Hence, from Eq. 7.20

$$k = \sqrt{2 \ln (29.7)} = 2.60$$

Step 3 (Step 2 is bypassed in this example.)

$$s = 50 + 2.60(21) = 104.6 \rightarrow 105 \text{ units}$$

The high implicit value of B_1 has led to a rather large safety factor.

Discussion—It is seen from either of Eqs. 7.20 and 7.22 that k decreases as σ_L or v goes up. Intuitively the behavior of k with v makes sense under the assumed stockout costing mechanism. If there is only a fixed cost per stockout occasion *which is the same for all items*, then it makes sense to allocate a greater proportional safety stock to the less expensive items where an adequate level of protection is achieved with relatively little investment. Furthermore, as shown in part 2 of the appendix of this chapter, it follows from Eq. 7.20 (or Eq. 7.22) that k decreases as Dv increases (this is not obvious from a quick look at the equations because both $\sigma_L v$ and Qv depend upon Dv). What this means is that higher safety factors are provided to the slower-moving items.

There is no solution to Eq. 7.20 when the condition of Eq. 7.19 is satisfied. In such a situation, as shown in the derivation in part 2 of the appendix, the best solution is the lowest allowable value of k.

Note that in establishing the reorder point in Step 3 we advocate rounding to the nearest integer rather than always going to the next highest integer. This is because, in contrast with the P_1, P_2 and TBS service measures, here we are not bound by a service constraint.

7.2.6 Decision Rule for i) a Common Fractional Charge (B_2) per Unit Short or ii) a Common Average Time (TBS) Between Stockout Occasions or for iii) Allocation of a Total Safety Stock so as to Minimize the Expected Total Value of Shortages per Year

The Rule

*Step 1**

For $\bar{x}_L \geq 10$ units (Normal Errors)

Is

$$\frac{Qr}{DB_2} > 1? \tag{7.23}$$

or is

$$\frac{Q}{D(\mathrm{TBS})} > 1? \tag{7.24}$$

where Q has been predetermined and the units of the variables are such that the left-hand-side of either equation is dimensionless (B_2 itself is dimensionless).

Yes, then go to step 2.
No, then continue with the following:
Select k so as to satisfy

$$p_{u\geq}(k) = \frac{Qr}{DB_2} \text{ or } \frac{Q}{D(\mathrm{TBS})} \tag{7.25}$$

For $\bar{x}_L < 10$ units (Laplace Errors)
Evaluate

$$k = \frac{1}{\sqrt{2}} \ln \frac{DB_2}{2Qr} \tag{7.26}$$

---

* *For the case of allocation of a total safety stock, B_2 or TBS is adjusted until the total implied safety stock is equal to the given quantity to be allocated.*

or

$$k = \frac{1}{\sqrt{2}} \ln \frac{D(\text{TBS})}{2Q} \tag{7.27}$$

If use of any of Eqs. 7.25 to 7.27 gives a k value lower than the minimum allowable safety factor specified by management, then go to step 2. Otherwise, move to step 3.

Step 2 Set k at its lowest allowable value (specified by management).

Step 3 Reorder point, $s = \hat{x}_L + k\sigma_L$, rounded to the nearest integer (raised to the next highest integer in the case of the service measure TBS, if not already *exactly* an integer).

Graphical Aids—Figures 7.5 and 7.6 display illustrative graphical aids for solving Eqs. 7.25 to 7.27, thus avoiding the use of a table lookup, rational approximation or logarithmic calculation.

Numerical Illustration—One of MIDAS' North American suppliers wishes to allocate a fixed amount of safety stock among a number of products so as to keep the total value of backorders per year as low as possible. The aggregate operating point selected by management implies a B_2 value of 0.25, that is, each unit short incurs an implicit cost equal to 25 percent of its unit value. The replenishment quantity of an item under consideration has been predetermined at 85 units. Other quantities of interest include

$\hat{x}_L = 50$ units, $\sigma_L = 10$ units

$r = 0.2$ \$/\$/yr., $D = 200$ units/yr.

Step 1

$\hat{x}_L \geq 10$ units,

therefore,

$$\frac{Qr}{DB_2} = \frac{85 \text{ units} \times 0.2/\text{yr.}}{200 \text{ units/yr.} \times 0.25} = 0.34 < 1$$

Then, Eq. 7.25 gives

$p_{u\geq}(k) = 0.34$

Figure 7.5 Graphical Aid for Faster Moving ($\bar{x}_L \geq$ 10 units) Items under i) the B_2 Shortage Cost Measure, ii) the TBS Service Measure or, iii) Allocation of a Total Safety Stock so as to Minimize the Expected Total Value of Shortages per Year.

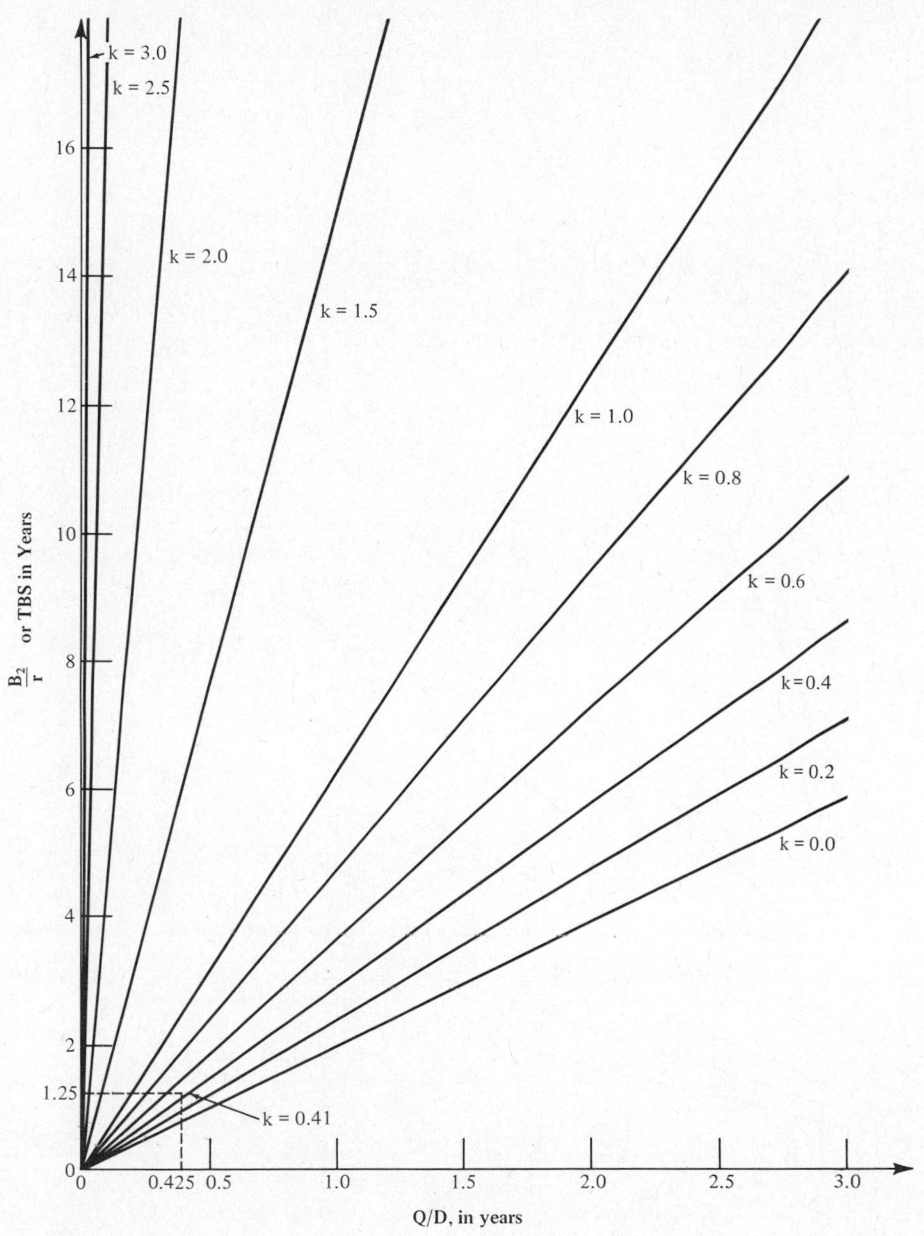

Figure 7.6 Graphical Aid for Slower Moving ($\bar{x}_L <$ 10 units) Items under i) the B_2 Shortage Cost Measure, ii) the TBS Service Measure or, iii) Allocation of a Total Safety Stock so as to Minimize the Expected Total Value of Shortages per Year.

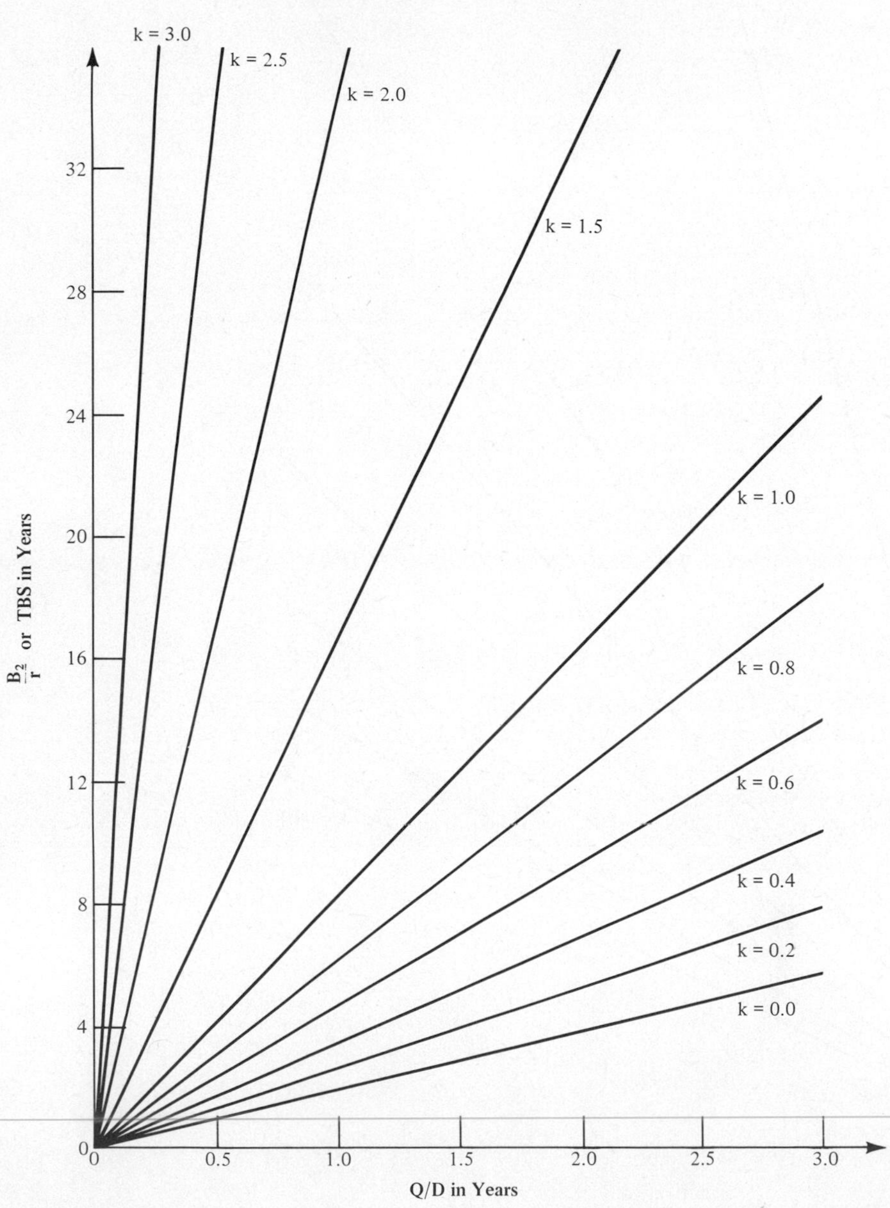

From Table C.1 in Appendix C, $k \simeq 0.41$ (presumably larger than the lowest allowable value).

Step 3

$s = 50 + 0.41\,(10) = 54.1 \rightarrow 54$ units.

Discussion—In contrast with the rules of the previous two sections Eqs. 7.25 to 7.27 show that here the selection of k does not depend upon σ_L. These equations also show that B_2/r is equivalent to TBS. Therefore, selection of a particular fractional charge B_2 per unit short is equivalent to the specification of a desired average time between stockout occasions equal to B_2/r. In the above numerical example the equivalent TBS is 0.25/0.2/yr. or 1.25 years. As seen in Figures 7.5 and 7.6, the safety factor k increases as B_2/r or TBS increases, as one would expect.

Under the use of economic order quantities we found that Q/D decreases as Dv increases. Therefore, at least under the use of EOQ's it is seen from any of Eqs. 7.25 to 7.27 that k increases as Dv increases, that is, under this decision rule larger safety factors are given to the faster-moving items, all other things being equal.

$p_{u\geq}(k)$ represents a probability; hence there is no solution to Eq. 7.25 when the right hand side of the equation exceeds unity, that is, when Eq. 7.23 or 7.24 is satisfied. It can be shown (in a manner paralleling the derivation in part 2 of the appendix of this chapter) that, when this happens, one should use the lowest permissible value of the safety factor.

7.3 *Exchange Curves Involving Safety Stocks for (s, Q) Systems*

In Section 6.7 of Chapter 6 we introduced the concept of exchange curves of total safety stock (in dollars) versus an aggregate measure of service. For prespecified order quantities, each safety stock decision rule traces out a single curve as a policy variable is varied.

In the derivation of the exchange curves, to be discussed in this section, we have made the assumption that *all* items in the population have normally distributed forecast errors. If a two-tier system of control is to be used, this then is an approximation. However, the items whose consequences would be erroneously computed would be those with $\hat{x}_L < 10$ units. Fortunately, the stocks, number of replenishments, and shortages of such slower moving items do not constitute appreciable components of the overall population totals of these quantities, hence the approximation should be quite reasonable. However, if desired, it would be a rather straightforward task to introduce branching logic into the exchange curve computer programmes that we have developed so that they could handle the Laplace distribution for slower-moving items.

7.3.1 Total Safety Stock Versus Aggregate Service for the Professional Products Division of MIDAS

For most of the methods discussed in Section 7.1 two exchange curves were developed for the 823 active items in the Professional Products Division. The two sets of curves, to be found in the two parts of Figure 7.7 show:

i. Total safety stock (in dollars) versus expected total stockout occasions per year

ii. Total safety stock (in dollars) versus expected total value of shortages per year

For each method the curves were generated by varying the appropriate policy variable. Also shown are the consequences of the old and new MIDAS decision rules (discussed in Case D and Section 6.7.1 of Chapter 6). In all cases the exchange curves were developed assuming an (s, Q) type system and where it was needed, the Q value was set equal to an economic order quantity (using $A = \$3.20$ and $r = 0.24$/yr. as found in Section 5.3 of Chapter 5).

Both parts of the figure show that a number of the decision rules of this chapter significantly outperform either of the MIDAS decision rules, in the sense that both the total safety stock and the expected total stockout occasions (or total value short) per year are simultaneously reduced. Under the "expected total stockout occasions per year" (Figure 7.7a) it is seen that no other rule does as well as the B_1 criterion. This is to be expected; as stated earlier, the B_1 decision rule is equivalent with minimizing the expected total stockout occasions per year for a given total safety stock. Similarly the B_2 or TBS rule does best in Figure 7.7b because of the equivalence of these rules with the rule implied by minimizing the expected total value of shortages per year for a given total safety stock. Interestingly enough, the simple P_1 (that is, equal k) rule does quite well in both graphs, that is, under either aggregate service measure. On the other hand, as expected, MIDAS' equal time supply rules do rather poorly.

7.3.2 Derivation of the Safety Stock Exchange Curves

In all cases, for a given value of the relevant policy variable, the corresponding point on each exchange curve is found in the following manner.

Figure 7.7a Exchange Curves of Safety Stock Versus Expected Stockout Occasions for the Professional Products Division of MIDAS.

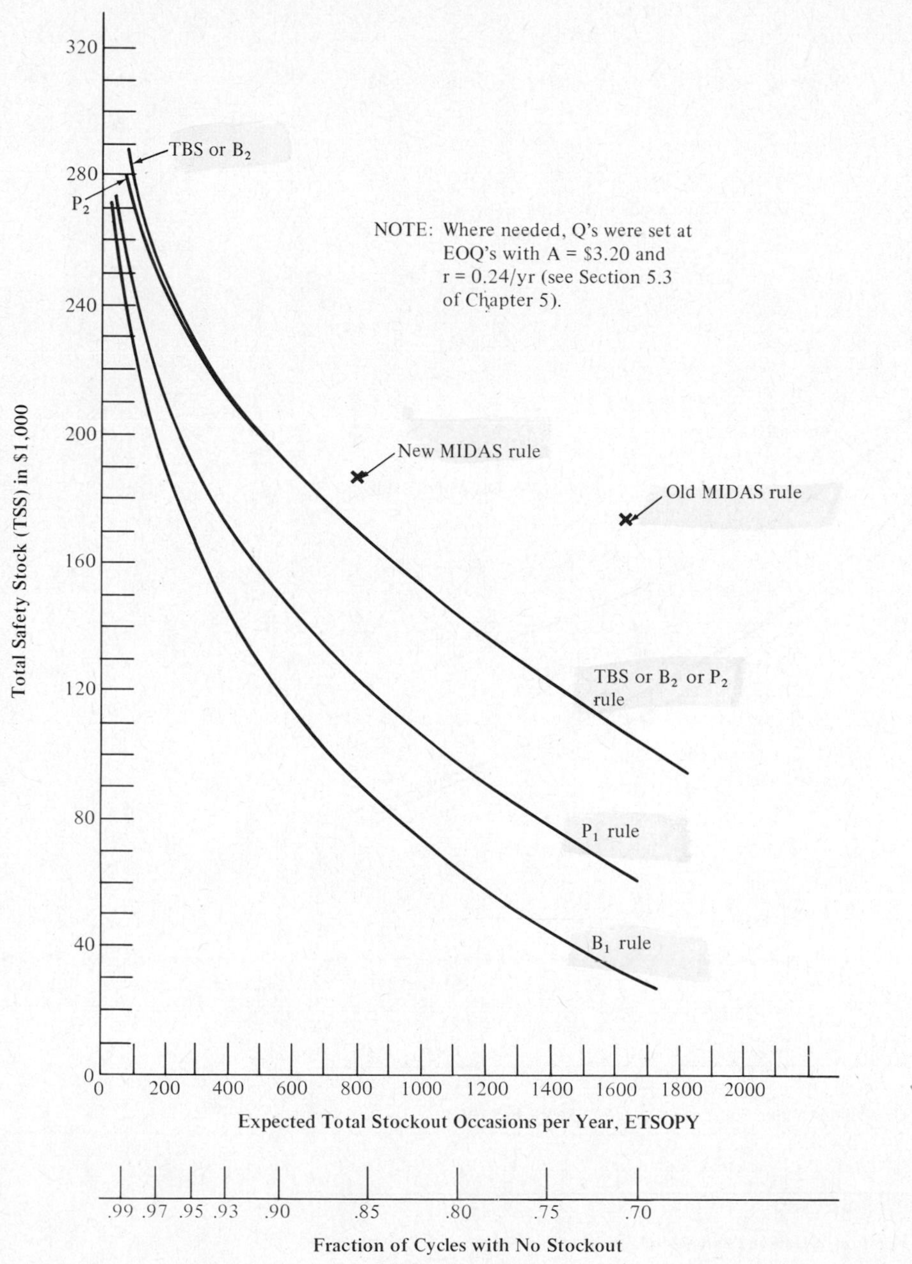

Figure 7.7b Exchange Curves of Safety Stock Versus Expected Value Short for the Professional Products Division of MIDAS.

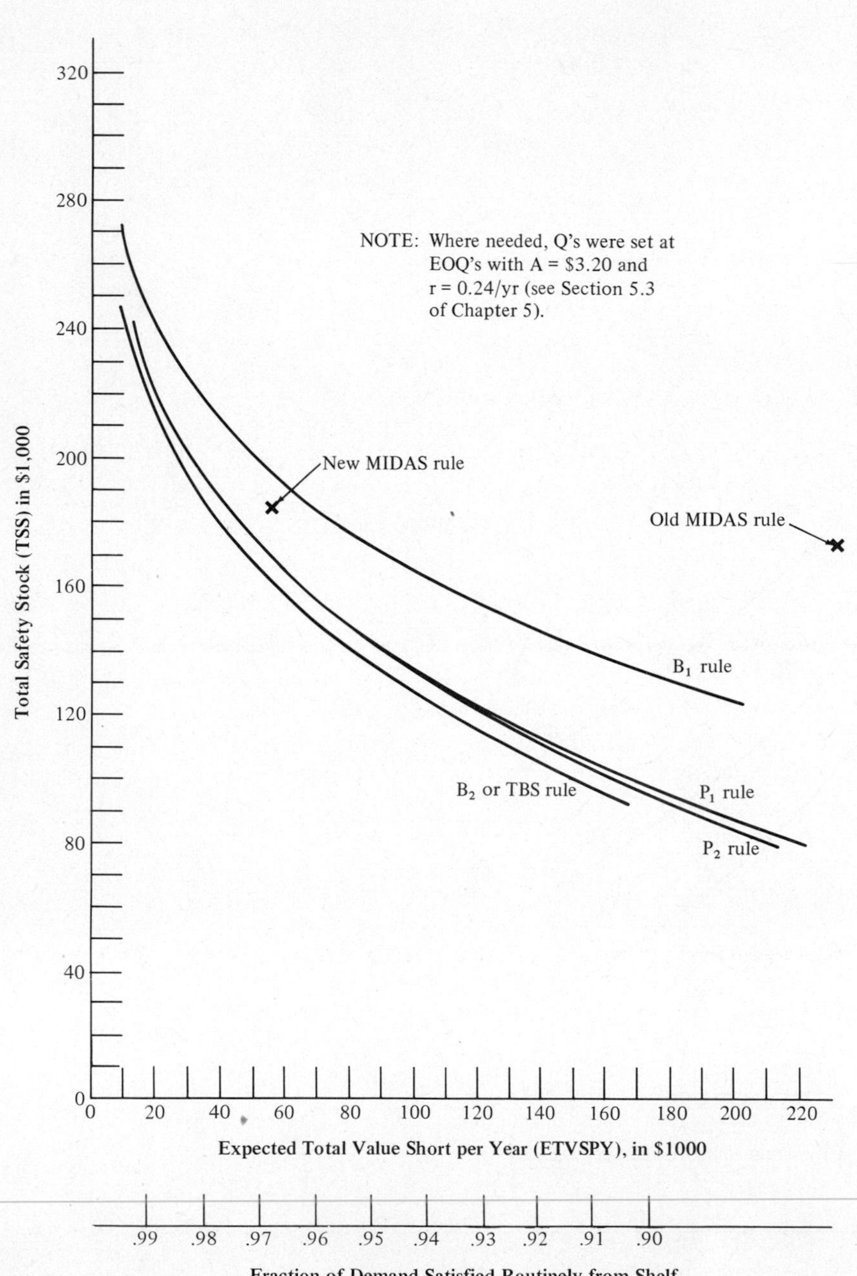

First, the value of the safety factor* k_i is ascertained for each item by use of the appropriate decision rule. Then three quantities are computed for each item, i:

$$\text{Safety stock (in dollars) of item } i = SS_i v_i = k_i \sigma_{Li} v_i \tag{7.28}$$

$$\text{Expected stockout occasions per year} = \frac{D_i}{Q_i} p_{u\geq}(k_i) \text{ for item } i \tag{7.29}$$

$$\text{Expected value of shortages per year} = \frac{D_i}{Q_i} \sigma_{Li} v_i G_u(k_i) \text{ for item } i^{**} \tag{7.30}$$

Equation 7.29 follows from multiplying the expected number of replenishment cycles per year (Eq. 7.10) by the probability of a stockout per cycle (Eq. 7.11). Similarly Eq. 7.30 is a result of the product of the expected number of replenishment cycles per year (Eq. 7.10) and the expected shortage per replenishment cycle, expressed in dollars (v_i times Eq. 7.12). Finally each of the three quantities (Eqs. 7.28, 7.29 and 7.30) is summed across all items, viz.:

$$\text{Total safety stock (in dollars)} = \sum_i k_i \sigma_{Li} v_i \tag{7.31}$$

$$\text{Expected total stockout occasions per year} = \sum_i \frac{D_i}{Q_i} p_{u\geq}(k_i) \tag{7.32}$$

---

* *The notation is the same as in Section 7.2.1 except a subscript i is used to denote that a particular item i is involved.*

** *Strictly speaking, as shown in Reference 19, Expected value of shortages per year for item i*

$$= \frac{D_i}{Q_i} \sigma_{Li} v_i \left[G_u(k_i) - G_u\left(k_i + \frac{Q_i}{\sigma_{Li}}\right) \right]$$

The approximation of Eq. 7.30 is quite accurate as long as $Q_i/\sigma_{Li} >$ 1, because then the additional term becomes negligible. When $Q_i/\sigma_{Li} < 1$, it is advisable to use the more accurate expression.

$$\text{Expected total value short per year*} = \sum_i \frac{D_i}{Q_i} \sigma_{Li} v_i G_u(k_i) \tag{7.33}$$

The results of Eq. 7.31 and 7.32 give a point on the first exchange curve (for example, Figure 7.7a) and those of Eq. 7.31 and 7.33 give a point on the second curve (for example, Figure 7.7b) for the particular safety stock decision rule. Repeating the whole process for several values of the policy variable generates a set of points for each of the two curves.

In some cases it is not necessary to go through all of the calculations of Eq. 7.31 to 7.33. To illustrate, for the case of a specified fraction (P_2) of demand to be satisfied directly from shelf for all items,

$$\text{Expected total value short per year} = (1 - P_2) \sum_i D_i v_i$$

provided of course, that no individual k_i has to be adjusted up to a minimum allowable value (thus providing a better level of service than P_2 for that particular item).

7.3.3 *Composite Exchange Curves*

For any decision rule for selecting safety stocks, we can combine the EOQ exchange curve (total cycle stock versus number of replenishments per year) with either of the safety stock exchange curves (total safety stock versus aggregate service level). The result is a set of composite exchange curves showing a three-way tradeoff of total average stock versus number of replenishments per year versus aggregate service level. A separate graph is required for each combination of decision rule and aggregate service measure. For the Professional Products Division of MIDAS we have shown an illustrative set of curves (for only one aggregate service measure) in Figure 7.8. They represent the use of the P_1 decision rule and an EOQ ordering strategy.

Each curve of Figure 7.8 clearly shows the behavior, for a given aggregate service level (value of ETSOPY), of the total average stock (TAS) as the number of replenishments per year (N) varies. For a while TAS decreases as N increases; this is a consequence of the cycle stock decreasing more quickly than the increase in the safety stock required to maintain the ETSOPY value. However, eventually as N gets larger, the increase in

---

* *See second footnote (footnote **) on previous page.*

Figure 7.8 Composite Exchange Curves for the Professional Products Division of MIDAS using EOQ and P_1 Decision Rules.

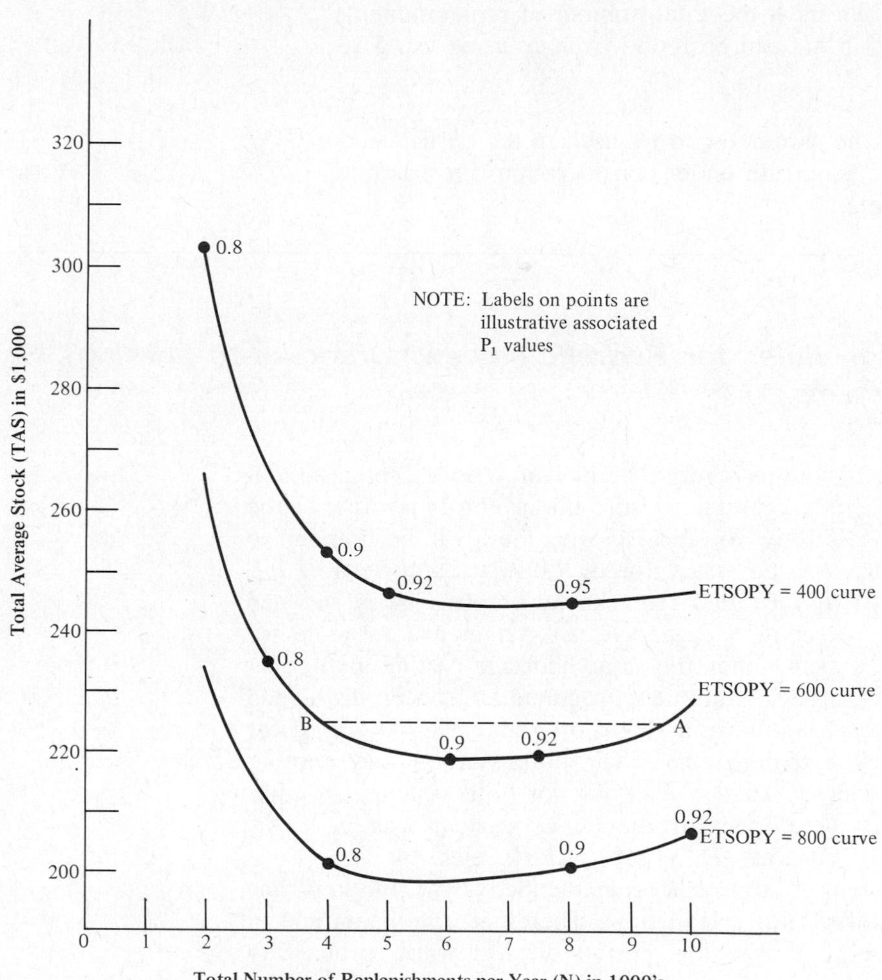

safety stock begins to dominate the decrease in cycle stock so that the TAS actually begins to increase. Operationally, for a given ETSOPY value, one would never operate at a point to the right of the low point of the corresponding curve (for example, point *A* on the middle curve). This is because there is another point (in this case *B*) to the left of the low point where the service and total average stock are unchanged while the replenishment load, *N*, is appreciably reduced.

Selection of a desired aggregate operating point on a composite exchange curve implies:

i. A value of r or A/r to be used in the economic order quantity decision rule (this is not shown directly on the graphs, rather we show the total number of replenishments per year, N. r or A/r can be found from N using Eq. 5.13 of Chapter 5).

ii. A value of the parameter to be used in the particular safety stock decision rule under consideration (for example, P_1, TBS, B_1, etc.)

7.4 Decision Rules for Periodic Review, Order-up-to-Level (R, S) Control Systems

Recall that in an (R, S) system every R units of time a replenishment order is placed of sufficient magnitude to raise the inventory position to the order-up-to-level S. Fortunately, for such systems there will be no need to repeat all the detail that was necessary for (s, Q) systems in Section 7.2, the reason being that there is a rather remarkable, simple analogy between each decision rule for selecting S in an (R, S) system and the rule for selecting s in a (s, Q) system under the same shortage costing method or service measure. In fact, a single computer programme has been developed that handles both systems. Similarly a single programme can be used for developing safety stock exchange curves for both systems and another programme for the composite exchange curves for both systems. In addition, the graphical aids developed for the (s, Q) systems can be easily modified to handle the analogous (R, S) safety stock rules.

Again a two-tier system of control is recommended. Now, the key time interval is a review interval plus a lead time. Therefore, the magnitude of the forecast demand $(\hat{x}_{R+L})$ over this period dictates which probability distribution to use for the demand (equivalently, the forecast errors) over the interval $R+L$.

7.4.1 Assumptions and Notation

The assumptions include:

a. Although demand is probabilistic the *average* demand rate changes very little with time.

b. There is a negligible chance of no demand between reviews; consequently, a replenishment order is placed at every review.

c. If two or more replenishment orders for the same item are simultaneously outstanding, then they must be received in the same order in which they were placed; that is, crossing of orders is not permitted. A special case satisfying this assumption is where the replenishment lead time is a constant.

d. Unit shortage costs (explicit or implicit) are so high that a practical operating procedure will always result in the average level of backorders being negligibly small when compared with the average level of the on-hand stock.

e. Forecast errors have a normal (or Laplace) distribution with no bias (that is, the average error is zero).

f. The value of R is assumed to be predetermined as was discussed in Section 6.8.1 of Chapter 6 (presumably based on one of the approaches of Chapter 5 but, of course, with an order quantity expressed as a time supply). In most situations, the effects of the two decision variables, R and S, are not independent, that is, the best value of R depends upon the S value and vice versa. However, as will be shown in Chapter 9, it is quite reasonable for practical purposes when dealing with B items to assume that R has been predetermined without knowledge of the S value.

g. The costs of the control system do not depend upon the specific value of S used.

Unlike in the (s, Q) situation the assumption of unit-sized demand transactions is not needed here.

The notation includes:

D—the demand rate, in units/year

$G_u(k) = \int_k^\infty (u_0 - k) \frac{1}{\sqrt{2\pi}} \exp(-u_0^2/2)\, du_0$, a special function of the unit normal (mean 0, standard deviation 1) variable.*

k—safety factor

L—the replenishment lead time, in years

$p_{u\geq}(k)$—the probability that a unit normal (mean 0, standard deviation 1) variable takes on a value of k or larger*

r—the inventory carrying charge, in \$/\$/year

R—the prespecified review interval, expressed in years

S—the order-up-to-level, in units

SS—safety stock, in units

v—the unit variable cost, in \$/unit

$\bar{x}_{R+L}$—the forecast (or expected) demand over a review interval plus a replenishment lead time, in units

σ_{R+L}—the standard deviation of errors of forecasts over a review interval plus a replenishment lead time, in units

*7.4.2 *Derivation**

Because of assumption b) we have

$$(\text{Number of reviews per year}) = 1/R$$

and

$$(\text{Number of replenishment orders placed per year}) = 1/R \tag{7.34}$$

In Section 6.8.2 of Chapter 6 we showed, by means of an example, that whether or not a stockout occurs in a particular cycle depends upon

---

* *$G_u(k)$ or $p_{u\geq}(k)$ can be obtained from k or vice versa using either a table lookup (a table of the unit normal distribution is shown in Appendix C) or a rational approximation (see, for example, p. 933 of Abramowitz and Stegun*[1] *or p. 93 of Brown*[2] *or Herron*[10] *or Parr*[14]).

whether or not the total demand in an interval of length $R+L$ exceeds the order-up-to-level S. We now develop the same result in a more rigorous fashion.

Consider a review instant (call it t_0) at which we place an order (call it order X) to raise the inventory position to the level S. The next order (Y) will not be placed until time t_0+R. Suppose that order Y arrives L later, that is, at time t_0+R+L. Because of the assumption of no crossing of orders, all previous orders, including order X, must have arrived prior to time t_0+R+L. Furthermore, no orders beyond order Y could have arrived. In other words, all S of the inventory position at time t_0, and no other stock, must have reached the stocking point by a time just before t_0+R+L. Therefore, the service impact of using an order-up-to-level of S in placing order X is determined by whether or not the total demand, x, in a review interval *plus* a replenishment lead time (that is, $R+L$) exceeds S.

If the demand (x) in $R+L$ has a probability density function $f_x(x_0)$ defined such that

$$f_x(x_0)dx_0 = \text{prob. \{total demand in } R+L \text{ lies between } x_0 \text{ and } x_0+dx_0\}$$

then the above reasoning leads to the following three important results*:

i. Safety stock (SS) = E (net stock just before order Y arrives)

$$= \int_0^\infty (S-x_0)f_x(x_0)dx_0$$

that is,

$$SS = S - \bar{x}_{R+L} \tag{7.35}$$

This has a particularly simple interpretation for the case where no more than one order is ever outstanding. In such a case Eq. 7.35 states that the average inventory level just before a replenishment arrives is equal to the inventory level when the replenishment order is placed (all of this being on-hand inventory) reduced by the average demand during a review interval plus lead time.

---

* *$E(z)$ again represents the expected or mean value of the random variable z.*

ii. prob {stockout in a replenishment cycle}

$$= \text{prob}\ \{x \geq S\}$$

$$= \int_S^\infty f_x(x_0)\, dx_0 \tag{7.36}$$

the probability that the total demand during a review interval plus lead time is at least as large as the order-up-to-level.

iii. expected shortage per replenishment cycle, ESPRC

$$= \int_S^\infty (x_0 - S) f_x(x_0)\, dx_0 \tag{7.37}$$

In a manner paralleling that of Section 7.2.2 we find that

$$E(\text{OH stock just before a replenishment arrives})$$
$$\simeq \text{Safety Stock (SS)}$$
$$= S - \bar{x}_{R+L}$$

Because there is a replenishment every R units of time, the average size of a replenishment is DR. Therefore,

$$E(\text{OH just after a replenishment arrives}) \simeq S - \bar{x}_{R+L} + DR$$

Now, the mean rate of demand is constant with time. Therefore, on the average, the OH level is half-way between these two extremes. Thus

$$E(\text{OH}) \simeq S - \bar{x}_{R+L} + DR/2 \tag{7.38}$$

It is convenient to again set

$$\text{SS} = k\sigma_{R+L} \tag{7.39}$$

Normally Distributed Forecast Errors—If forecast errors are normally distributed, then the results of Appendix C give that Eqs. 7.36 and 7.37 reduce to

$$\text{prob}\ \{\text{stockout in a replenishment cycle}\} = p_{u\geq}(k) \tag{7.40}$$

and

$$\text{ESPRC} = \sigma_{R+L} G_u(k) \tag{7.41}$$

Laplace Distributed Forecast Errors—As can be shown from Appendix B, when errors are Laplace distributed Eqs. 7.36 and 7.37 become

$$\text{prob}\,\{\text{stockout in a replenishment cycle}\} = \tfrac{1}{2}\exp(-\sqrt{2}k) \quad k \geq 0 \tag{7.42}$$

and

$$\text{ESPRC} = \frac{\sigma_{R+L}}{2\sqrt{2}}\exp(-\sqrt{2}k) \quad k \geq 0 \tag{7.43}$$

A comparison of pairs of equations follows.

Compare	With
7.35	7.3
7.38	7.8
7.39	7.9
7.34	7.10
7.40	7.11
7.41	7.12
7.42	7.13
7.43	7.14

The comparison reveals the validity of our earlier assertion (in Section 6.8 of Chapter 6) that the (R, S) situation is exactly equivalent to the (s, Q) situation if one makes the following transformations.

(s, Q)	(R, S)
s	S
Q	DR
L	$R+L$

It therefore follows that the decision rule for determining the S value in an (R, S) system for a particular selection of shortage cost or service measure is obtained from the corresponding rule for determining s in an (s, Q) system by simply making the above three substitutions. Furthermore, the development of exchange curves is directly analogous to that described for (s, Q) systems in Section 7.3.2.

7.5 Summary

In this chapter, under conditions of probabilistic demand and for a variety of shortage costs and service measures, we have shown the details of two common types of decisions systems:

i. (s, Q) systems

ii. (R, S) systems

The material presented included the actual decision rules, illustrative examples, graphical aids and a discussion of each of the rules. Again, aggregate exchange curve concepts turned out to be an important aspect of the analysis.

It should be apparent now to the reader that, even for the case of a single item considered in isolation at a single stocking point, it is no easy task to cope with uncertainty. It is little wonder that *very little usable theory has been developed for more complex probabilistic situations* (for example, coordinated control of related items at a single location, multi-echelon control of a single item, etc.). We shall have more to say on these issues in Chapters 12, 13, and 14.

Appendix to Chapter 7—Some Illustrative Derivations

1 *Laplace Errors and P_2 Service Measure*

Complete Backordering—Because each replenishment is of size Q we can argue as follows:

$$\text{Fraction backordered} = \frac{\text{expected shortage per replenishment cycle, ESPRC}}{Q}$$

$$\text{Fraction of demand satisfied directly from shelf} = 1 - (\text{Fraction backordered})$$

Therefore, we want

$$P_2 = 1 - \frac{\text{ESPRC}}{Q} \tag{7.44}$$

Substituting from Eq. 7.14, we have

$$P_2 = 1 - \frac{\sigma_L}{2\sqrt{2}Q} \exp(-\sqrt{2}k) \qquad k \geq 0 \tag{7.45}$$

or

$$\exp(-\sqrt{2}k) = \frac{2\sqrt{2}Q}{\sigma_L}(1 - P_2), \qquad k \geq 0$$

that is,

$$k = \frac{1}{\sqrt{2}} \ln \left[\frac{\sigma_L}{2\sqrt{2}Q(1 - P_2)}\right] \qquad k \geq 0 \tag{7.46}$$

which is Eq. 7.16.

As indicated, Eq. 7.46 really only holds for $k \geq 0$. This is because Eq. 7.14 is valid only for $k \geq 0$. As can be shown from the results of Appendix B, the equivalent of Eq. 7.14 for $k \leq 0$ is

$$\text{ESPRC} = \sigma_L\left[-k + \frac{1}{2\sqrt{2}} \exp(\sqrt{2}k)\right]$$

If one substitutes this into Eq. 7.44, then k must satisfy

$$-k+\frac{1}{2\sqrt{2}}\exp(\sqrt{2}k)=\frac{Q}{\sigma_L}(1-P_2) \qquad k\leq 0 \tag{7.47}$$

This is a difficult equation to solve for k. From an operational standpoint we instead use the result of Eq. 7.46 as long as it is larger than the lowest allowable k value (which often will be 0 in any event).

Strictly speaking, Eq. 7.45 is only an approximate result. The quantity

$$\frac{\sigma_L}{2\sqrt{2}Q}\exp(-\sqrt{2}k)$$

can certainly exceed unity which would give a meaningless negative service level. An exact, but more complicated, result has been developed elsewhere.[19]

Complete Lost Sales—If demands when out of stock are lost instead of backordered, then the expected demand per cycle is no longer just Q, but rather is increased by the expected shortage per replenishment cycle, ESPRC. Therefore, we now have

Fraction of demand satisfied directly from shelf

$$=1-\frac{\text{ESPRC}}{Q+\text{ESPRC}}$$

The derivation then carries through exactly as above, resulting in Eq. 7.17.

2 *Normal Errors and B_1 Costing*

The approach is to develop an expression for the expected total relevant costs per year as a function of the control parameter, k; let us denote this function by ETRC (k). There are three relevant components of costs: i) replenishment, ii) carrying and iii) stockout.

Using the result of Eq. 7.10, we have that the expected relevant replenishment costs per year are

$$C_r = AD/Q$$

As earlier, the expected carrying costs per year are

$$C_c = \bar{I}vr$$

Using Eq. 7.8, this gives

$$C_c = \left(\frac{Q}{2} + k\sigma_L\right) vr$$

The expected stockout costs, C_s, per year are obtained by multiplying three factors together, namely i) the expected number of replenishment cycles per year, ii) the probability of a stockout per cycle and iii) the cost per stockout. Thus, using Eqs. 7.10 and 7.11, we have

$$C_s = \frac{DB_1}{Q} p_{u\geq}(k)$$

Now,

$$\begin{aligned} \text{ETRC}\ (k) &= C_r + C_c + C_s \\ &= AD/Q + (Q/2 + k\sigma_L)vr + \frac{DB_1}{Q} p_{u\geq}(k) \end{aligned}$$

We wish to select the k value that minimizes ETRC (k). A convenient approach is to set

$$\frac{d\ \text{ETRC}\ (k)}{dk} = 0$$

that is,

$$\sigma_L vr + \frac{DB_1}{Q} \frac{dp_{u\geq}(k)}{dk} = 0 \tag{7.48}$$

But

$$\frac{dp_{u\geq}(k)}{dk} = -f_u(k)$$

(The derivative of the cumulative distribution function is the density function as shown in Section C.3 of Appendix C.) Therefore, Eq. 7.48 gives

$$f_u(k) = \frac{Qv\sigma_L r}{DB_1} \tag{7.49}$$

Now the density function of the unit normal is given by

$$f_u(k) = \frac{1}{\sqrt{2\pi}} \exp(-k^2/2)$$

Therefore, Eq. 7.49 gives

$$\frac{1}{\sqrt{2\pi}} \exp(-k^2/2) = \frac{Qv\sigma_L r}{DB_1}$$

which solves for

$$k = \sqrt{2 \ln \frac{DB_1}{\sqrt{2\pi}\, Qv\sigma_L r}} \tag{7.50}$$

However, one must proceed with caution. Setting the first derivative to zero does not guarantee a minimum. In fact Eq. 7.50 will have no solution if the expression inside the square root is negative. This will occur if the argument of the logarithm is less than unity. A case where this happens is shown in part b of Figure 7.9. In such a situation the model says that the lower k is, the lower the costs are. The model assumes a linear savings in carrying costs with decreasing k. Obviously this is not true indefinitely. The practical resolution is to set k at its lowest allowable value (usually zero).

Equation 7.50 shows that k increases as $D/Qv\sigma_L$ or $Dv/Qv\sigma_L v$ increases. Now, empirically (see discussion in Chapter 2) it has been found that, *on the average,*

$$\sigma_L v \simeq a_2 (Dv)^{b_2}$$

where a_2 and b_2 are constants which depend upon the particular company involved but, in all known cases, b_2 lies between 0.5 and 1. Also assuming an EOQ form for Qv we have

$$Qv = c\sqrt{Dv}$$

Therefore, we have that k increases as

$$\frac{Dv}{c\sqrt{Dv}\, a_2 (Dv)^{b_2}} \quad \text{or} \quad \frac{(Dv)^{1/2-b_2}}{a_2 c}$$

increases. But, because $b_2 > \frac{1}{2}$, the exponent of Dv in the above quantity is negative. Therefore, k goes down as Dv increases.

Figure 7.9 Behavior of Expected Total Relevant Costs for the Case of a Fixed Cost per Stockout.

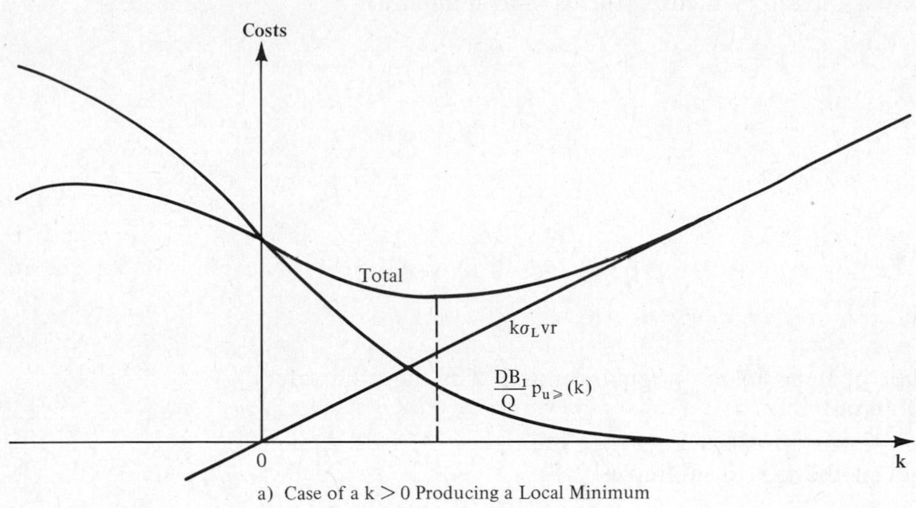

a) Case of a $k > 0$ Producing a Local Minimum

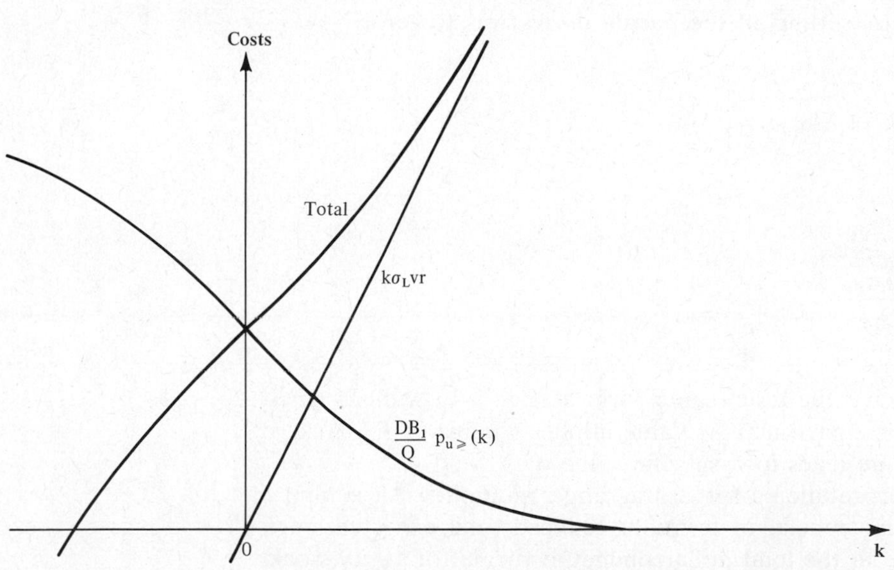

b) Case Where Lowest Possible k is Best

3 Normal Errors and Allocation of a Total Safety Stock so as to Minimize the Expected Total Stockout Occasions per Year

The problem is to select the safety factors, the k_i's, to minimize

$$\sum_{i=1}^{n} \frac{D_i}{Q_i} p_{u\geq}(k_i)$$

subject to

$$\sum_{i=1}^{n} k_i \sigma_{Li} v_i = Y$$

where n is the number of items in the population and Y is the total safety stock expressed in dollars.

One method of solution is to use a Lagrange multiplier, M (see Appendix A), that is, we select the k_i's to minimize

$$L(k_i\text{'s}, M) = \sum_{i=1}^{n} \frac{D_i}{Q_i} p_{u\geq}(k_i) - M\left(Y - \sum_{i=1}^{n} k_i \sigma_{Li} v_i\right)$$

This is accomplished by setting all the partial derivatives to zero. Now

$$\frac{\partial L}{\partial k_i} = -\frac{D_i}{Q_i} f_u(k_i) + M\sigma_{Li} v_i = 0$$

or

$$f_u(k_i) = M \frac{Q_i v_i \sigma_{Li}}{D_i}$$

But, this is seen to have the exact same form as Eq. 7.49 with $M \equiv r/B_1$. Therefore, selection of a particular M value implies a value of B_1. Also, of course, a given M value leads to a specific value of Y.

The economic interpretation of the Lagrange multiplier M is that it represents the marginal benefit, in terms of reduced total expected stockouts, per unit increase in the total dollar budget available for safety stocks. r is the cost to carry one dollar in safety stock for a year. B_1 is the cost associated with a stockout occasion. From a marginal viewpoint we wish to operate where

$$\text{(cost to carry last dollar of safety stock)} \\ = \text{(expected benefit of last dollar of safety stock)}$$

that is,

$$r = \text{(reduction in total expected stockouts per year)} \times \text{(cost per stockout)} \\ = MB_1$$

thus, $M = \dfrac{r}{B_1}$, as we found above.

Problems for Chapter 7

Problem 7.1

Consider an item with $A = \$25$, $Dv = \$4000/\text{yr.}$, $\sigma_L v = \$100$, $B_1 = \$30$, $r = 0.10$ \$/\$/yr.

a. Find i. the EOQ, in dollars
   ii. k, using the B_1 criterion
   iii. the safety stock, in \$
   iv. the annual cost of carrying safety stock
   v. the total average stock, in \$
   vi. the expected number of stockout occasions per year
   vii. the expected stockout costs per year.

b. The cost equation used to develop the rule for the B_1 criterion is

$$\text{ETRC } (k) = k\sigma_L vr + \frac{D}{Q} B_1 p_{u\geq}(k) \quad (1)$$

As seen in part a) the two components of Eq. 1 are not equal at the optimal k value. (This is in contrast to what we found for the EOQ analysis in Chapter 5.) Why are the two components not equal? What quantities are equal at the optimal k value?

c. By looking at the basic equations for the items requested in a) discuss how each would be affected (that is, whether it would be increased or decreased) by an increase in the r value.

Problem 7.2

Consider an item under (s, Q) control. Basic item information is as follows: $D = 40{,}000$ units/yr.; $A = \$20$; $r = 0.25$ \$/\$/yr.; $v = \$1.60$/unit. All demand when out of stock is backordered. The EOQ is used to establish the Q value. A service level of 0.95 (demand satisfied without backorder) is desired. The item is somewhat difficult to predict and two forecasting procedures are possible.

System	Cost to Operate per Year \$/yr.	σ_L units
A (complex)	200	1,000
B (simple)	35	2,300

Which forecasting system should be used? Discuss. *Note*: Forecast errors can be assumed to be normally distributed with zero bias for both models.

Problem 7.3

Canadian Wheel Ltd. establishes safety stocks so as to provide a fraction demand satisfied directly from stock at a level of 0.94. For a basic item with an essentially level average demand the demand rate is 1000 units/yr. and an order quantity of 200 units is used. The supplier of the item ensures a *constant* lead time of 4 weeks to Canadian Wheel. The current purchase price of the item from the supplier is \$0.80/unit. Receiving and handling costs add \$0.20/unit. The supplier offers to reduce the lead time to a new constant level of 1 week, but in so doing he will increase the selling price to Canadian by \$0.05/unit. Canadian management is faced with the decision of whether or not to accept the supplier's offer.

a. Qualtitatively discuss the economic tradeoff in the decision. (*Note*: Canadian would *not* increase the selling price of the item nor would they change the order quantity.)

b. Quantitatively assist management in the decision. (Assume that $\sigma_t = \sqrt{t}\sigma_1$ and $\sigma_4 = 100$ units where σ_4 is the standard deviation of forecast errors over the current lead time of 4 weeks. Also assume that forecast errors are normally distributed and that the carrying charge is 0.20 \$/\$/yr.)

Problem 7.4

The 4 N Company reacts to shortages at a particular branch warehouse in the following fashion: Any shortage is effectively eliminated by bringing material in from the plant by air freight at a cost of \$0.50/lb. Assume that the average demand rate of an item is essentially constant with time and that forecast errors are normally distributed. Assume that an (s, Q) system is to be used and that Q, if needed, is prespecified. To answer the following questions introduce whatever symbols are necessary:

a. What are the expected shortage costs per cycle?

b. What are the expected shortage costs per year?

c. What are the expected total relevant costs per year associated with the safety factor k?

d. Develop an equation that the best k must satisfy.

e. If we had two items with all characteristics identical except that item 1 weighed more (on a unit basis) than item 2, how do you intuitively think that the two safety factors would compare? Verify this using the result of part d).

Problem 7.5

Consider an item under (s, Q) control where lead time demand has a Laplace distribution. Suppose that the cost associated with a shortage of size z is $B_1 + B_2 vz$. Assume that the safety factor $k \geq 0$. Also assume that Q is prespecified.

a. Write an expression for the expected total relevant costs per year as a function of the safety factor k. (Introduce whatever variables you feel are appropriate, attempting to use the same notation as in the text.)

b. Find the equation that the best value of k must satisfy, in as simple a form as possible.

c. Verify that the best k varies in the appropriate way as each of the parameters involved changes.

d. Illustrate the use of the result of part b) for an item with $D = 60$ units/yr., $Q = 30$ units, $\sigma_L = 5$ units, $v = \$2.50$/unit, $B_1 = \$20$, $B_2 = 0.15$ and $r = 0.26$ \$/\$/yr.

Problem 7.6

One of MIDAS' customers, a retail photographic-supply outlet, orders from MIDAS once every 2 weeks. For a particular item with unit value (v) of \$3.00 it is felt that there is a cost of \$1.00 for each unit demanded when out of stock. Other characteristics of the item are

$L = 1$ wk. (MIDAS' promised delivery time)

$r = 0.30$/yr.

a. Consider a period of the year where $\bar{x}_1 = 30$ units and $\text{MAD}_1 = 6$ units (where the unit time period is 1 week). What order-up-to-level S should be used? (Assume $\sigma_t = \sqrt{t}\sigma_1$).

b. Suppose the average demand rate changed *slowly* throughout the year. Suggest a reasonable way for the retailer to cope with this situation.

Problem 7.7

a. Consider a group of n items that are each being independently controlled using an (R, S) type of system (periodic-review, order-up-to-level). Let R_i be the *prespecified* value (in months) of R for item i. Suppose that we wish to allocate a total given safety stock in dollars (call it W) among the n items so as to minimize the dollars of expected backorders per unit time summed across all n items. Develop the decision rule for selecting k_i, the safety factor for item i. Assume that forecast errors are normally distributed.

b. Illustrate for the following 2-item case ($r = 0.2$ \$/\$/yr., $W = \$1180$).

Item, i	v_i ($/unit)	A_i ($)	D_i (units/yr)	R_i (months)	L_i (months)	σ_{R_i} (units)	σ_{L_i} (units)	$\sigma_{L_i+R_i}$ (units)
1	1.00	2.00	3000	1	1	200	200	300
2	2.00	5.00	15000	0.5	1	500	300	700

Problem 7.8

As an internal consultant for a large distributor you have been asked to perform an analysis to develop a decision rule which will allow management to decide upon use of an (R, S) or an (s, Q) system for *each individual* item, that is, an (R, S) system can be used for some items and an (s, Q) system for other items. In your analysis you *should* ignore any interactions among the items (that is, joint setup costs, capacity restrictions, etc.). Introducing whatever symbols are necessary, *indicate* how you would go about developing the decision rule. In particular, identify relevant factors.

Problem 7.9

Why do non-unit-sized transactions significantly complicate the analysis of a continuous review inventory system?

Problem 7.10

Explain how the two exchange curves (Figures 7.7a and 7.7b) would be developed for the case of a fixed time supply of safety stock.

Problem 7.11

Consider three items with the following characteristics:

Item, i	D_i (units/yr.)	v_i ($/unit)	Q_i (units)	σ_{Li} (units)	$Q_i \cdot v_i$	$\sigma_{Li} \cdot v_i$	#cycles (D/Q)
1	1000	1.00	200	100		100.00	5
2	500	0.80	200	100		80.00	2.5
3	100	2.00	100	30		60.00	1.0

Suppose that a total safety stock of $120 is to be allocated among the three items. Consider the following service measures (shortage costing methods):

a. Same P_1 for the 3 items
b. Same P_2 for the 3 items (trial+error)
c. Same B_1 for the 3 items
d. Same B_2 for the 3 items
e. Same TBS for the 3 items
f. Minimization of total expected stockout occasions per year
g. Minimization of total expected value short occasions per year.
h. Equal time supply safety stocks

For each determine:

i. How the $120 is allocated among the three items
ii. ETSOPY
iii. ETVOPY

Note: Assume that forecast errors are normally distributed, that the same r value is applicable to all 3 items, and that negative safety factors are not permitted.

REFERENCES FOR CHAPTER 7

1. Abramowitz, M. and I. Stegun. *Handbook of Mathematical Functions.* Dover, New York, 1965, pp. 932–933.

2. Brown, R. G. *Decision Rules for Inventory Management.* Holt, Rinehart and Winston, New York, 1967, Chap. 13, 17, 26.

3. Burgin, T. "Backordering in Inventory Control." *Operational Research Quarterly*, Vol. 21, No. 4, December, 1970, pp. 453–461.

4. Burgin, T. "The Gamma Distribution and Inventory Control." *Operational Research Quarterly*, Vol. 26, No. 3i, September, 1975, pp. 507–525.

5. Das, C. "Effect of Lead Time on Inventory: A Static Analysis." *Operational Research Quarterly*, Vol. 26, No. 2i, June, 1975, pp. 273–282.

6. Das, C. "Explicit Formulas for the Order Size and Reorder Point in Certain Inventory Problems." *Naval Research Logistics Quarterly*, Vol. 23, No. 1, March, 1976, pp. 25–30.

7. Gerson, G. and R. G. Brown. "Decision Rules for Equal Shortage Policies." *Naval Research Logistics Quarterly*, Vol. 17, No. 3, September 1970, pp. 351–358.

8. Hadley, G. and T. M. Whitin. *Analysis of Inventory Systems.* Prentice-Hall, Englewood Cliffs, N.J., 1963, Chap. 4–5.

9. Hausman, W. "Minimizing Customer Line Items Backordered in Inventory Control." *Management Science*, Vol. 15, No. 12, August, 1969, pp. 628–634.

10. Herron, D. P. "Profit Oriented Techniques for Managing Independent Demand Inventories." *Production and Inventory Management*, Vol. 15, No. 4, 1974, pp. 57–74.

11. Kaplan, A. "Computing Expected Values of Customer Requests Backordered." *Management Science*, Vol. 17, No. 9, May, 1971, pp. 647–651.

12. Lu, T., J. Toellner and N. Kaufman. "A Practical Method for Calculating Reorder Points for Conditions of Stochastic Demand and Lead Time." *Journal of Industrial Engineering*, Vol. XIII, No. 6, November–December, 1962, pp. 503–505.

13. Montgomery, D., M. Bazaraa and A. Keswani. "Inventory Models with a Mixture of Backorders and Lost Sales." *NRLQ*, Vol. 20, No. 2, June, 1973, pp. 255–263.

14. Parr, J. O. "Formula Approximations to Brown's Service Function." *Production and Inventory Management*, Vol. 13, 1st Quarter 1972, pp. 84–86.

15. Peters, S. "Optimal Service Inventory Policies under Budgetary Constraints." in *Developments in Operations Research, Volume 1*, edited by B. Avi-Itzhak. Gordon & Breach, New York, N.Y., 1971.

16. Peterson, R., L. J. Thomas and A. J. Loiseau. "Operational Inventory Control with Stochastic,

Seasonal Demand." *INFOR*, Vol. 10, No. 1, February, 1972, pp. 81–93.

17. Schrady, D. and U. Choe. "Models for Multi-Item Continuous Review Inventory Policies Subject to Constraints." *Naval Research Logistics Quarterly*, Vol. 18, No. 4, December, 1971, pp. 451–463.

18. Schroeder, R. G. "Managerial Inventory Formulations with Stockout Objectives and Fiscal Constraints." *Naval Research Logistics Quarterly*, Vol. 21, No. 3, September, 1974, pp. 375–388.

19. Silver, E. A. "A Modified Formula for Calculating Service Under Continuous Inventory Review." *AIIE Transactions*, Vol. II, No. 3, September, 1970, pp. 241–245.

CHAPTER EIGHT

An Economic Order Quantity Based Decision System for the Case of a Time-Varying Demand Pattern

Recall that in Chapter 5 we developed the economic order quantity (and various modifications of it) by assuming essentially a *level, deterministic* demand rate. Chapters 6 and 7 were devoted to dealing with the important extension to where demand is probabilistic but the *average* demand rate is still level with time. In the current chapter we now relax this latter assumption and allow the average demand rate to vary with time, thus encompassing a broader range of practical situations, including:

i. Multi-echelon assembly operations where a firm schedule of finished products exploded back through the various assembly stages leads to production requirements at these earlier levels which are relatively deterministic but almost always vary appreciably with the time period. (This is a topic to which we shall return in Chapter 12 under the heading of Material Requirements Planning.)

ii. Production to contract where the contract requires that certain quantities have to be delivered to the customer on specified dates.

iii. Items having a seasonal demand pattern. (Artificial seasonality can be induced by pricing and/or promotion actions.)

iv. Replacement parts for an item that is being phased out of operation. Here, the demand rate drops off with time. (In some cases, particularly towards the end of its life, such an item is better treated by the Class C procedures to be discussed in Chapter 11.)

v. More generally, items with known trends in demand which are expected to continue.

vi. Parts for preventive maintenance where the maintenance schedule is accurately known.

Most of this chapter is concerned with the case where the demand varies with time but in an essentially deterministic fashion (more loosely speaking, the major component of variability can be predicted quite accurately as a function of time). This is the situation discussed in Sections 8.1 to 8.8.

In Section 8.1 we point out how much more complex the analysis becomes when we allow the demand rate to vary with time. Section 8.2 is concerned with the choice that we have among three different approaches, namely: i) straightforward use of the economic order quantity (even though one of the key assumptions upon which it is based is violated); ii) an exact optimal procedure; and iii) an approximate heuristic method. In Section 8.3 the assumptions common to all three approaches are laid out as well as a numerical example to be used for illustrative purposes throughout Sections 8.4 to 8.7. Further details on each of the three approaches are presented in Sections 8.4, 8.5, and 8.6, including a discussion of when to use each method. Two other approaches, sometimes used in practice, are briefly treated in Section 8.7. Then, in Section 8.8, we again focus attention on aggregate considerations by means of the exchange curve concept. Finally, in Section 8.9 we provide some suggestions for the case of probabilistic demand where the average rate varies with time. Because of the complexity of modelling such a situation the decision rules suggested are an attempt to achieve a workable solution and are certainly not meant to be optimal in any sense of the word.

8.1 *The Complexity of Time-Varying Demand*

Recall that we are first looking at a time-varying, but essentially deterministic, demand pattern. Nevertheless, as we shall now see, the analysis of such a situation is an order of magnitude more complex than what was possible in Chapter 5 under the assumption of a level demand pattern.

When the demand rate varies with time we can no longer assume that the best strategy is to always use the same replenishment quantity; in fact, this will seldom be the case. Moreover, an exact analysis becomes very complicated because the diagram of inventory level versus time, even for a constant replenishment quantity, is no longer the simple repeating sawtooth pattern that we saw in Figure 5.1 of Chapter 5. This prevents us from using simple average costs over a typical unit period of time as was possible in that chapter. Instead, we now have to use the demand information over a finite time period, extending from the present, when determining the appropriate value of the current replenishment quantity. This time period is known as the *planning horizon* and its length can have a substantial effect on the total relevant costs of the selected strategy. Moreover, all other factors being equal, we would prefer to have the planning horizon as short as possible because the farther into the future we look for demand information, the less accurate it is likely to be.

As indicated by the examples of time-varying demand discussed above, the demand can be either continuous with time or can occur only at discrete equi-spaced points in time. The former represents a stream of small-sized demands where the arrival rate varies with time, whereas the latter corresponds to something such as weekly shipments where a large demand quantity is satisfied at one time. The decision system which we shall propose is not affected by whether the demand is continuous or discrete with respect to time; all that will be needed is the total demand in each basic time period. A common case which can be handled is where the demand rate stays constant throughout a time period, only changing from one period to another. An illustration is shown in Figure 8.1. As discussed in Chapter 4, demand forecasts are usually developed in such a form, for example, a rate in January, another rate in February, etc.

Another element of the problem that is important in selecting appropriate replenishment quantities is whether replenishments must be scheduled at specified discrete points in time (for example, replenishments can only be scheduled at intervals that are integer multiples of a week) or whether

Figure 8.1 Demand Pattern When the Rate Stays Constant Through Each Period.

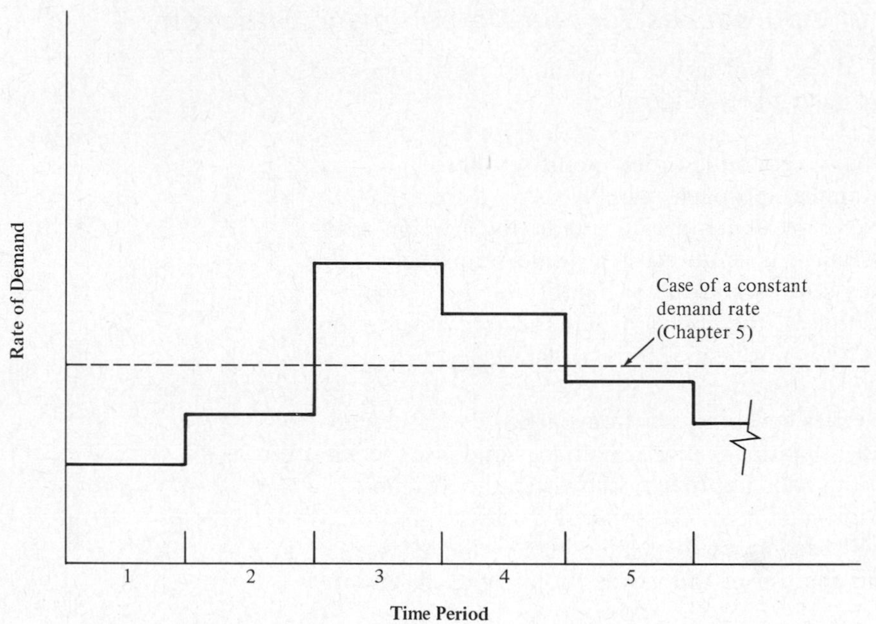

they can be scheduled at any point in continuous time. Considering a single item in isolation, the second case is probably more appropriate if the demand pattern is continuous with time. However, to ease scheduling coordination problems in multi-item situations, it usually makes sense to limit the opportunity times for replenishment of each item. Furthermore, if the demand pattern is such that all of the requirements for each time period must be available at the beginning of that time period, it is appropriate to restrict replenishment opportunities to the beginnings of periods. This latter assumption will be made in developing the logic of the decision system which we shall propose.

Still another factor that can materially influence the logic in selecting replenishment quantities is the duration of the demand pattern. A pattern with a clearly specified end resulting from a production contract is quite different from the demand situation where no well-defined end is in sight. In the former case it is important to plan to reach the end of the pattern with a low (if not zero) level of inventory. In contrast, for the continuing demand situation, if we use a finite planning horizon, there is no need to force the solution to include a low inventory level at the end of the horizon. Remaining inventory can be used in the interval beyond the horizon, where demand will continue (albeit, at a possibly different rate).

8.2 *The Choice of Approaches for the Deterministic Situation*

There are essentially three approaches to dealing with the case of a deterministic time-varying demand pattern:

i. Use of the basic economic order quantity—here one adopts a very simple approach, namely using a fixed EOQ, based on the average demand rate out to the horizon, anytime a replenishment is required. As would be expected, this approach makes sense when the variability of the demand pattern is low, that is, the constant demand rate assumption of the fixed EOQ is not significantly violated.

ii. Use of the exact best solution to a particular mathematical model of the situation—as we shall see, under a specific set of assumptions, this approach, known as the Wagner–Whitin algorithm, minimizes the total of certain costs (for reasons that will become evident later in the chapter, we purposely avoid the use of the words "total relevant costs" here).

iii. Use of an approximate or heuristic method—the idea here is to use an approach which captures the essence of the time-varying complexity but at the same time remains relatively simple for the practitioner to understand and does not require lengthy computations.

8.3 *General Assumptions and a Numerical Example*

8.3.1 *The Assumptions*

There are a number of assumptions that will be made (at least implicitly) in all three of the aforementioned approaches. We now lay these out rather than showing them three separate times later in the chapter. For two of the approaches certain of these assumptions can be relaxed by rather minor modifications of the decision methodology; such modifications will be demonstrated later in the chapter.

a. The demand rate is given in the form of $D(j)$ to be satisfied in period j ($j = 1, 2, \ldots, N$) where the planning horizon is at the end of period N. Of course, the demand rate may vary from one period to the next.

b. The entire requirements of each period must be available at the beginning of that period. Therefore, a replenishment arriving part-way through a period cannot be used to satisfy that period's requirements and it is cheaper, in terms of reduced carrying costs, to delay its arrival until the start of the next period. Thus, replenishments are constrained to arrive at the beginnings of periods.

c. The unit variable cost does not depend on the replenishment quantity; in particular, there are no discounts in either the unit purchase cost or the unit transportation cost.

d. The item is treated entirely independently of other items, that is, benefits from joint review and/or replenishments do not exist or are ignored.

e. The replenishment lead time is known with certainty (a special case being zero duration) so that delivery can be timed to occur right at the beginning of a period.

f. No shortages are allowed.

g. The entire order quantity is delivered at the same time.

h. For simplicity of exposition it is assumed that the carrying cost is only applicable to inventory which is carried over from one period to the next. It should be emphasized that all three approaches can easily handle the situation where carrying charges are included on the material during the period in which it is used to satisfy the demand requirements, but, for practical purposes, this is an unnecessary complication.

Reference to Section 5.1 of Chapter 5 reveals that, except for a, b, and h, these assumptions are identical with those required in the derivation of the basic economic order quantity. Assumption f, which is quite restrictive, will be relaxed in Section 8.9 when we shall consider the case of probabilistic demand.

Because of the assumption of deterministic demand, it is clear, from assumptions b, e, and f, that any method of selecting replenishment quantities should lead to the arrival of replenishments only at the beginning of periods when the inventory level is exactly zero.

8.3.2 *A Numerical Example*

The MIDAS International plant in Germany uses the following simple decision rule for ascertaining production run quantities: "Each time a production run is made, a quantity sufficient to satisfy the total demand in the next three months is produced." For the seasonal product PSF-007, a 10-inch by 12-inch lithographic film, MIDAS Canada is the only customer of MIDAS International. The basic unit of the product is a box of 50 sheets of film. MIDAS Canada requirements by month (shifted to take account of shipping time) in the upcoming year are:

Month	Sequential Number	Requirements (boxes)
January	1	10
February	2	62
March	3	12
April	4	130
May	5	154
June	6	129
July	7	88
August	8	52
September	9	124
October	10	160
November	11	238
December	12	41
		TOTAL = 1,200

It is seen that the demand pattern has two peaks, one in the late spring, the other in the autumn season.

The German plant estimates the fixed setup cost (A) per replenishment to be approximately \$54, and the carrying charge (r) has been set by management at 0.02 \$/\$/month. The unit variable cost (v) of the film is \$20.00/box.

The production planning department of MIDAS International would like to establish the size of the first production run (that needed by January 1) and also estimate the timing and sizes of future production quantities. The word "estimate" is used because MIDAS Canada could conceivably revise its requirements, particularly those late in the year, but still giving adequate time to permit adjustment of the later portions of the production schedule.

Use of the company's "three month" decision rule leads to the replenishment schedule and associated costs shown in Table 8.1. There are four

Table 8.1 Results of Using the Company's "Three Month" Rule on the Numerical Example

Month	1	2	3	4	5	6	7	8	9	10	11	12	Total
Starting Inventory	0	74	12	0	283	129	0	176	124	0	279	41	—
Replenishment	84	—	—	413	—	—	264	—	—	439	—	—	1,200
Requirements	10	62	12	130	154	129	88	52	124	160	238	41	1,200
Ending Inventory	74	12	0	283	129	0	176	124	0	279	41	0	1,118

Total replenishment costs = 4 × \$54 = \$216.00

Total carrying costs = 1,118 box-months × \$20.00/box × 0.02 \$/\$/month = \$447.20

Total replenishment plus carrying costs = \$663.20

replenishments covering the 12 months out to the horizon. The total relevant costs are \$663.20. The average month-ending inventory is 1118/12 or 93.17 boxes. Therefore, the turnover ratio is 1200/93.17 or 12.9.

8.4 *Use of a Fixed Economic Order Quantity*

When the demand rate is approximately constant we have advocated, in Chapter 5, the use of the basic economic order quantity. One possible approach to the case of a time-varying rate is to simply ignore the time variability, thus continuing to use the economic order quantity. To be more precise, the *average* demand rate ($\bar{D}$) out to the horizon (N periods), or to whatever point our forecast information extends, is evaluated and the economic order quantity

$$\text{EOQ} = \sqrt{\frac{2A\bar{D}}{vr}}$$

is used anytime a replenishment is needed. Actually $\bar{D}$ can simply be based on a relatively infrequent estimate of the average demand per period and need not necessarily be reevaluated at the time of each replenishment decision. To account for the discrete opportunities to replenish, at the time of a replenishment, the EOQ should be adjusted to exactly satisfy the requirements of an integer number of periods. A simple way to do this is to keep accumulating periods of requirements until the closest total to the EOQ is found.

To illustrate, for our numerical example,

$$\bar{D} = \frac{\text{Total requirements}}{12 \text{ months}} = 100 \text{ boxes/month}$$

Therefore,

$$\text{EOQ} = \sqrt{\frac{2 \times \$54 \times 100 \text{ boxes/month}}{\$20/\text{box} \times 0.02\ \$/\$/\text{month}}}$$

$$\simeq 164 \text{ boxes}$$

Consider the selection of the replenishment quantity at the beginning of January. The following table is helpful:

Month	January	February	March	April
Requirements	10	62	12	130
Cumulative Requirements to End of Month	10	72	84	214

The EOQ of 164 boxes lies between 84 and 214. 214 is closer to 164 than is 84. Therefore, the first replenishment quantity is 214 boxes, lasting through the end of April. The detailed results of applying the fixed EOQ approach to the numerical example are as shown in Table 8.2. It is seen from Tables 8.1 and 8.2 that the fixed EOQ approach, compared to the company's "three month" rule, reduces the total of replenishment and carrying costs from $663.20 to $643.20 or some 3.0 percent, a rather small saving. The turnover ratio has been increased from 12.9 to 1,200×12/528 or 27.3 but the replenishment costs have also increased.

8.5 The Wagner–Whitin Method: An "Optimal" Solution Under an Additional Assumption

Wagner and Whitin,[19] in a classic article, developed an algorithm which guarantees an optimal (in terms of minimizing the total costs of replenishment and carrying inventory) selection of replenishment quantities under the set of assumptions that were listed in Section 8.3.1 as well as one additional assumption that *may* be needed, namely that either the demand pattern terminates at the horizon or else the ending inventory must be pre-specified.

8.5.1 The Algorithm

The algorithm is an application of dynamic programming, a mathematical procedure for solving sequential decision problems.* The computational effort, often prohibitive in dynamic programming formulations, is significantly reduced because of the use of two key properties (derived by Wagner and Whitin) which the optimal solution must satisfy:

> *Property 1:* (already discussed in Section 8.3). A replenishment only takes place when the inventory level is zero.
> *Property 2:* There is an upper limit to how far before a period j we would include its requirements, $D(j)$, in a

* *The problem here is a sequential decision problem because the outcome of the replenishment quantity decision at one point in time has effects on the possible replenishment actions which can be taken at later decision times; for example, whether or not we should replenish at the beginning of November depends very much on how large the replenishment quantity at the beginning of October was.*

Table 8.2 Results of Using the Fixed EOQ Approach on the Numerical Example

Month	1	2	3	4	5	6	7	8	9	10	11	12	Total
Starting Inventory	0	204	142	130	0	0	0	52	0	0	0	0	—
Replenishment	214	—	—	—	154	129	140	—	124	160	238	41	1,200
Requirements	10	62	12	130	154	129	88	52	124	160	238	41	1,200
Ending Inventory	204	142	130	0	0	0	52	0	0	0	0	0	528

Total replenishment costs = 8 × \$54 = \$432.00
Total carrying costs = 528 box-months × \$20.00/box × 0.02 \$/\$/month = \$211.20
Total replenishment plus carrying costs = \$643.20

> replenishment quantity. Eventually, the carrying costs become so high that it is less expensive to have a replenishment arrive at the start of period j instead of including its requirements in a replenishment from many periods earlier.

To illustrate this second property, consider our numerical example where the setup cost (A) is \$54.00 and the cost (vr) to carry one unit in inventory forward a month is \$0.40/box/month. Consider the requirements of 88 boxes in the month of July. The carrying costs associated with these requirements if they were included in a replenishment at the beginning of June would be

$$88 \text{ boxes} \times \$0.40/\text{box/month} \times 1 \text{ month or } \$35.20.$$

Similarly, if the requirements were instead included in a replenishment at the beginning of May, the carrying costs associated with the 88 units would be

$$88 \text{ boxes} \times \$0.40/\text{box/month} \times 2 \text{ months or } \$70.40,$$

which is larger than \$54.00, the fixed cost of a replenishment. Therefore, the best solution could never have the requirements of July included in a replenishment at the beginning of May or earlier. It would be less expensive to have a replenishment arrive at the beginning of July.

The algorithm works backward in time, as is usually the case in dynamic programming, asking the following kind of question: "If we are now at the beginning of month j needing to replenish, what is the best size to make the replenishment?" To show how this question is answered, let us use the numerical example of Section 8.3.

Recall that the demand pattern is:

Month	Sequential Number	Requirements (boxes)
January	1	10
February	2	62
March	3	12
April	4	130
May	5	154
June	6	129
July	7	88
August	8	52
September	9	124
October	10	160
November	11	238
December	12	41
		Total = 1,200

If we're at the beginning of December (month 12) needing a replenishment, the answer is trivial: The replenishment should be 41 boxes (to meet December's requirements; shortages are not permitted) and the associated cost is the setup charge of \$54.00 (there is no carrying cost because the entire replenishment is depleted in the month at the beginning of which it is received).

If we're at the beginning of November (month 11) having zero inventory, we now have two options available:

> *Option* 1: Replenish enough (238 boxes) to cover only November's requirements; then proceed in the best way from the start of December with zero inventory.

> *Option* 2: Replenish enough (279 boxes) to cover the requirements of both November and December.

Costs of Option 1 = (Costs associated with November replenishment)
+ (Costs associated with the best plan from the start of December having zero inventory)
= \$54.00 + \$54.00
= \$108.00

Costs of Option 2 = (Setup cost for November replenishment)
+ (Carrying costs for December's requirements)
= \$54.00 + 41 boxes × \$0.40/box/month × 1 month
= \$54.00 + \$16.40
= \$70.40

The cost of the second option is less than that of the first. Therefore, the cost of the best strategy from now on, given that we're at the start of November (month 11) with zero inventory, is \$70.40.

If we're at the beginning of October (notice that we're going backwards through time) with zero inventory, we now have three options:

> *Option* 1: Replenish enough (160 boxes) to cover only October's requirements; then proceed in the best way from the start of November with zero inventory.

> *Option* 2: Replenish enough (398 boxes) to cover October's and November's requirements; then proceed in the best way from the start of December with zero inventory.

Option 3: Replenish enough (439 boxes) to cover the requirements of all three of October, November, and December.

Costs of Option 1 = (Costs associated with October replenishment)
+ (Costs associated with the best plan from the start of November having zero inventory)
= \$54.00 + \$70.40*
= \$124.40

Costs of Option 2 = (Setup cost for October replenishment)
+ (Carrying costs for November's requirements)
+ (Costs associated with the best plan from the start of December having zero inventory)
= \$54.00 + (\$238 × 0.40 × 1) + \$54.00
= \$203.20

Costs of Option 3 = (Setup cost for October replenishment)
+ (Carrying costs for November's requirements
+ (Carrying costs for December's requirements)
= \$54.00 + (\$238 × 0.40 × 1) + (\$41 × 0.40 × 2)
= \$182.00

Option 1 is seen to be preferable; that is, the best strategy, if we have to replenish at the beginning of October, is to have the replenishment cover the requirements of only October, then proceed in the best possible way from the start of November needing another replenishment at that time. Also the costs of this strategy through to the end of December (the horizon) are \$124.40.

One continues backward in this fashion month by month until the calculation is finally made for month 1; its result gives us the size of the first replenishment, which in this case is 84 boxes, that is, enough to cover the requirements through to the end of March. It is important to note that the method requires a starting point (somewhere in the future) where it is known that the inventory level is to be at zero or some other specified value.

---

* *Known from previous step (which dealt with November's replenishment).*

To illustrate the effect of property 2 discussed at the beginning of this section, consider the options open to us at the beginning of May if we have zero inventory and, for the moment disregard the property:

Option	Replenish enough to cover the requirements through the end of the month of	Then proceed in the best fashion having zero inventory at the start of the month of
1	May	June
2	June	July
3	July	August
4	August	September
5	September	October
6	October	November
7	November	December
8	December	—

All of options 3 to 8 include the requirements of July in the replenishment at the start of May, but earlier we found (because of property 2) that this cannot happen in the best solution. Therefore the choice is narrowed to only options 1 and 2.

If one is interested in computing the size of only the first replenishment quantity, then it may not be necessary to start all the way out at the horizon (month N). Use of property 2 shows that, if for a period j the requirements are so large that

$$D(j)vr > A$$

that is,

$$D(j) > A/vr,$$

then the optimal solution will have a replenishment at the beginning of period j; that is, the inventory *must* go to zero at the start of period j. Therefore, the earliest j where this happens can be used as an horizon for the calculation of the first replenishment. In the numerical example,

$$A/vr = \frac{\$54.00}{\$20/\text{box} \times 0.02\ \$/\$/\text{month}} = 135 \text{ box-months}$$

It is seen from the demand pattern that the earliest month with $D(j) > 135$ is May. Therefore, the end of April can be considered as an horizon in computing the replenishment quantity needed at the beginning of January. It should be emphasized that there may be no month out to the horizon where this happens.

The details of the best strategy for the whole 12-month period are shown in Table 8.3. There are seven replenishments and the total costs

Table 8.3 ***Results of Using the Wagner-Whitin Algorithm or the Silver-Meal Heuristic on the Numerical Example***

Month	1	2	3	4	5	6	7	8	9	10	11	12	Total
Starting Inventory	0	74	12	0	0	129	0	52	0	0	0	41	—
Replenishment	84	—	—	130	283	—	140	—	124	160	279	—	1,200
Requirements	10	62	12	130	154	129	88	52	124	160	238	41	1,200
Ending Inventory	74	12	0	0	129	0	52	0	0	0	41	0	308

Total replenishment costs = 7 × \$54 = \$378.00

Total carrying costs = 308 box-months × \$20.00/box × 0.02\$/\$/month = \$123.20

Total replenishment plus carrying costs = \$501.20

amount to \$501.20. Comparison with Tables 8.1 and 8.2 shows that the Wagner–Whitin algorithm produces total costs some 24.4 percent lower than those of the company's three-month rule and some 22.1 percent lower than those of a fixed EOQ strategy. Furthermore, the turnover ratio has been increased to $1200 \times 12/308$ or 46.8.

8.5.2 *Potential Drawbacks of the Algorithm*

As mentioned earlier, the Wagner–Whitin algorithm is guaranteed to provide a set of replenishment quantities that minimize the sum of replenishment plus carrying costs out to a specified horizon. However, the algorithm has received extremely limited acceptance in practice. The following are the primary reasons for this lack of acceptance:

a. The relatively complex nature of the algorithm which makes its understanding difficult for the practitioner.

b. The considerable computational effort required for each item handled by the algorithm, substantially more than for the fixed EOQ method or for the heuristic to be discussed in the next section.

c. The possible need for a well-defined ending point for the demand pattern (This would be artificial for the typical inventoried item where termination of demand is not expected in the near future). Such an ending point is not needed when there is at least one period whose requirements exceed A/vr. Moreover, all information out to the end point may be needed for computing even the initial replenishment quantity. In this connection considerable research effort (see References 2, 8, 12, 13, 14, and 21) has been devoted to ascertaining the minimum required length of the planning horizon to insure the selection of the optimal value of the initial replenishment.

d. The necessary assumption that replenishments can be made only at discrete intervals (namely at the beginning of each of the periods). This assumption can be relaxed by subdividing the periods; however, the computational requirements of the algorithm go up rapidly with the number of periods considered. (In contrast, the other two methods are easily modified to account for continuous opportunities to replenish.)

When one takes account of total relevant costs, particularly including system control costs, it is not at all surprising that the algorithm has received such limited acceptability. We do *not* advocate its use for B items (Let us not lose sight of the fact that in this chapter we are still talking about this class of items as opposed to Class A items where considerably more control expense is justified because of the higher potential savings per item.) Instead it is appropriate to resort to simpler heuristic methods that result in reduced control costs that more than offset any extra replenishment and/or carrying costs that their use may incur.

8.6 *The Silver–Meal Heuristic—A Recommended Approach for a Significantly Variable Demand Pattern*

As indicated by the results in the previous two sections, the Wagner–Whitin approach does substantially better than a fixed economic order quantity, at least for the illustrative numerical example. However, as mentioned in Section 8.5.2, the Wagner–Whitin approach has serious drawbacks from the practitioner's standpoint. Therefore, the natural question to ask is "is there a simpler approach that will capture most of the potential savings in the total of replenishment and carrying costs?" A number of individuals (see, for example, References 5, 7, 9, 10, 15, and 18) have suggested various decision rules, some of which have been widely used in practice. In particular, Silver and Meal[18] have developed a simple variation of the basic EOQ, which, as we shall see, accomplishes exactly what we desire. Moreover, in numerous test examples the Silver–Meal heuristic has performed extremely well when compared with the other rules encountered in the literature. Two of these other heuristics will be discussed in Section 8.7.

As mentioned earlier, the fixed EOQ approach should perform suitably when the demand pattern varies very little with time. For this reason we shall advocate use of the somewhat more complicated Silver–Meal heuristic only when the pattern is significantly variable. An operational definition of "significantly variable" will be given in Section 8.6.5.

8.6.1 *The Criterion Used for Selecting a Replenishment Quantity*

The heuristic selects the replenishment quantity so as to replicate a property which the basic economic order quantity possesses when the demand rate is constant with time, namely, the *total relevant costs per unit time for the duration of the replenishment quantity are minimized.* If a replenishment arrives at the beginning of the first period and it covers requirements through to the end of the Tth period, then the criterion function can be written as follows:

$$\frac{\text{(Setup cost)} + \text{(Total carrying costs to end of period T)}}{T}$$

This is a reasonable criterion and it has the desirable feature of not including, in the present replenishment, a large requirement well in the future (inclusion of such a requirement would make the "costs per unit time" measure too high). It is not difficult to develop numerical examples in which use of the criterion does not lead to the overall optimal solution, particularly for the case where the demand pattern has a well-defined ending point. Fortunately, this is not a major drawback because our primary concern is with demand patterns that do not have a clearly defined ending point in the near future. (This follows from our basic definition of Class B items.)

8.6.2 *The Essence of the Heuristic*

Because we are constrained to replenishing at the beginnings of periods the best strategy must involve replenishment quantities that last for an integer number of periods. Consequently, we can think of the decision variable for a particular replenishment as being the time T that the replenishment will last, with T constrained to integer values. The replenishment quantity Q, associated with a particular value of T, is

$$Q = \sum_{j=1}^{T} D(j) \tag{8.1}$$

provided we set the time origin so that the replenishment is needed and arrives at the beginning of period 1. According to the chosen criterion, we wish to pick the T value that minimizes the total relevant costs per unit time of replenishment and carrying inventory over the time period T.

Let the total relevant costs associated with a replenishment that lasts for T periods be denoted by $\text{TRC}(T)$. These costs are composed of the fixed replenishment cost A and the inventory carrying costs, that is,

$$\text{TRC}(T) = A + \text{carrying costs}$$

We wish to select T to minimize the total costs per unit time, $\text{TRCUT}(T)$, where

$$\text{TRCUT}(T) = \frac{\text{TRC}(T)}{T} = \frac{A + \text{carrying costs}}{T} \tag{8.2}$$

If $T=1$, there are no carrying costs (we only replenish enough to cover the requirements of period 1), that is,

$$\text{TRCUT}(1)=\frac{A}{1}=A$$

If the setup cost, A, is large, this may be unattractive when compared with including the second period's requirements in the replenishment, that is, using $T=2$.

With $T=2$ the carrying costs are $D(2)vr$, the cost of carrying the requirements $D(2)$ for one period. Therefore,

$$\text{TRCUT}(2)=\frac{A+D(2)vr}{2}$$

Now the setup cost is apportioned across two periods but a carrying cost is incurred.

With $T=3$ we still carry $D(2)$ for one period but now we also carry $D(3)$ for two periods. Thus,

$$\text{TRCUT}(3)=\frac{A+D(2)vr+2D(3)vr}{3}$$

In this case the setup charge is apportioned across three periods but this may not be attractive because of the added carrying costs.

The basic idea of the heuristic is to evaluate TRCUT(T) for increasing values of T until, for the first time,

$$\text{TRCUT}(T+1)>\text{TRCUT}(T)$$

that is, the total relevant costs per unit time start increasing. When this happens the associated T is selected as the number of periods that the replenishment should cover. The corresponding replenishment quantity Q is given by Eq. 8.1.

As evidenced by Figure 8.2, this method guarantees only a local minimum in the total relevant costs per unit time. It is possible that still larger values of T would yield still lower costs per unit time since we stop testing with the first increase in costs per unit time. We could protect against this eventuality by computing the ratio for a few more values of T, but the likelihood of improvement in most real cases is small. We shall return to this point in Section 8.6.5.

It is conceivable that the TRCUT(T) may continue to decrease all the way out to $T=N$. This says that it is appropriate to cover all requirements out to the horizon with the current replenishment. In such a case, it may

Figure 8.2 Graphical Portrayal of the Selection of T in the Silver-Meal Heuristic.

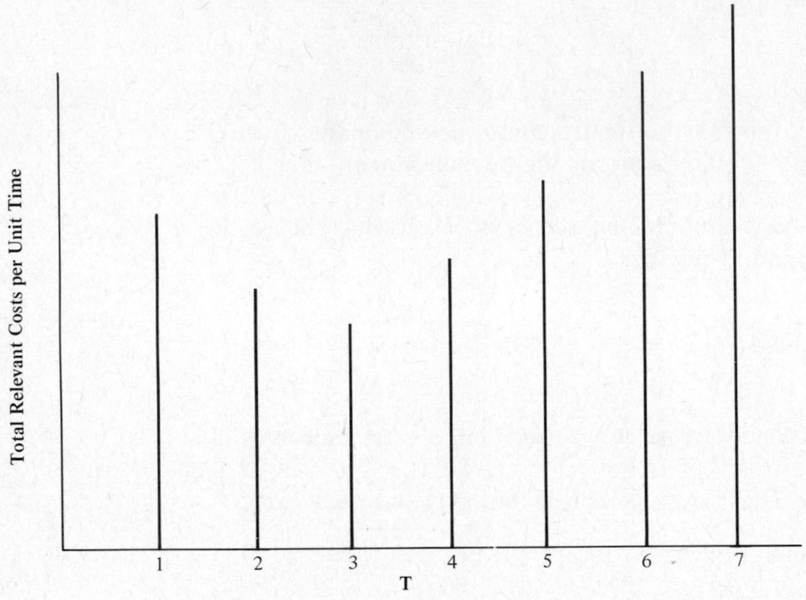

Case a – True Minimum Selected

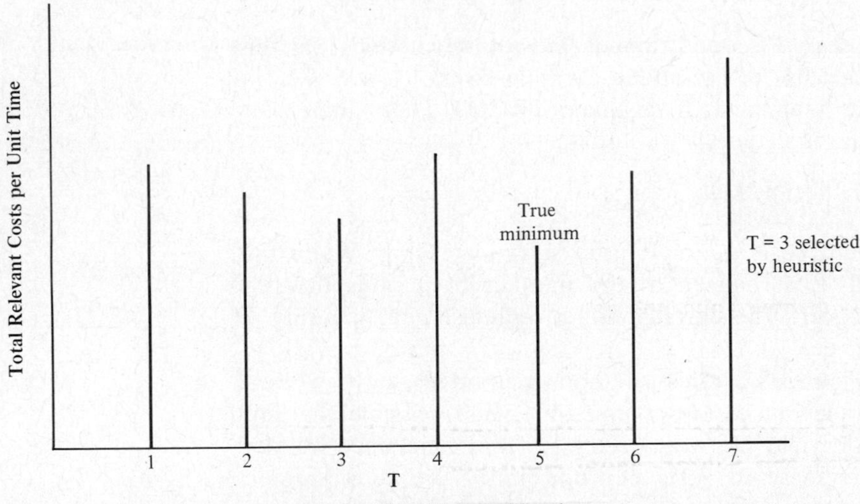

Case b – True Minimum Missed

be appropriate to cover an even longer time period but the heuristic is unable to provide the answer without forecast information beyond period N.

A streamlined version of the heuristic, shown in part 1 of the appendix of the current chapter, has been programmed. An interesting point is that in the streamlined version A, v, and r appear only in the form of a ratio,

A/vr; that is, only the value of the ratio and not the individual values of A, v, and r are crucial in the selection of T. Such is also the case in the Wagner–Whitin algorithm and in the basic EOQ. The latter is obvious in that

$$\text{EOQ} = \sqrt{\frac{2AD}{vr}} = \sqrt{2D}\sqrt{\frac{A}{vr}}$$

To illustrate the application of the heuristic let us again use the numerical example of Section 8.3. To refresh the reader's memory the values of A, v, and r and the first part of the requirements pattern are as follows:

$$A = \$54.00; \quad v = \$20.00/\text{box}; \quad r = 0.02\$/\$/\text{month}$$

Month, j	1	2	3	4	5	6	. . .
Requirements, $D(j)$	10	62	12	130	154	129	. . .

The calculations for the first replenishment quantity (assuming that the inventory is zero at the beginning of month 1) are shown in Table 8.4. The heuristic selects a T value of 3 with an associated Q, using Eq. 8.1, of

$$\begin{aligned} Q &= D(1) + D(2) + D(3) \\ &= 10 + 62 + 12 \\ &= 84 \text{ boxes} \end{aligned}$$

The table illustrates that the computations are simply multiplications, additions, divisions, and comparisons of numbers.

It turns out for this numerical example (and for a substantial portion of all others tested) that this simple heuristic gives the exact same solution as the Wagner–Whitin algorithm. Thus, the solution has already been shown in Table 8.3.

Table 8.4 Computations for the First Replenishment Quantity Using the Silver–Meal Heuristic

T	A	$D(2)vr$	$2D(3)vr$	$3D(4)vr$	Row Sum	Cumulative Sum	Cum. Sum. $\div T$
1	54.00				54.00	54.00	54.00
2		62(20)(0.02)			24.80	78.80	39.40
3			2(12)(0.4)[a]		9.60	88.40	29.47
4				3(130)(0.4)	156.00	244.40	61.10

[a] $vr = 20(0.02) = 0.4$

Figure 8.3 Continuous Demand Pattern.

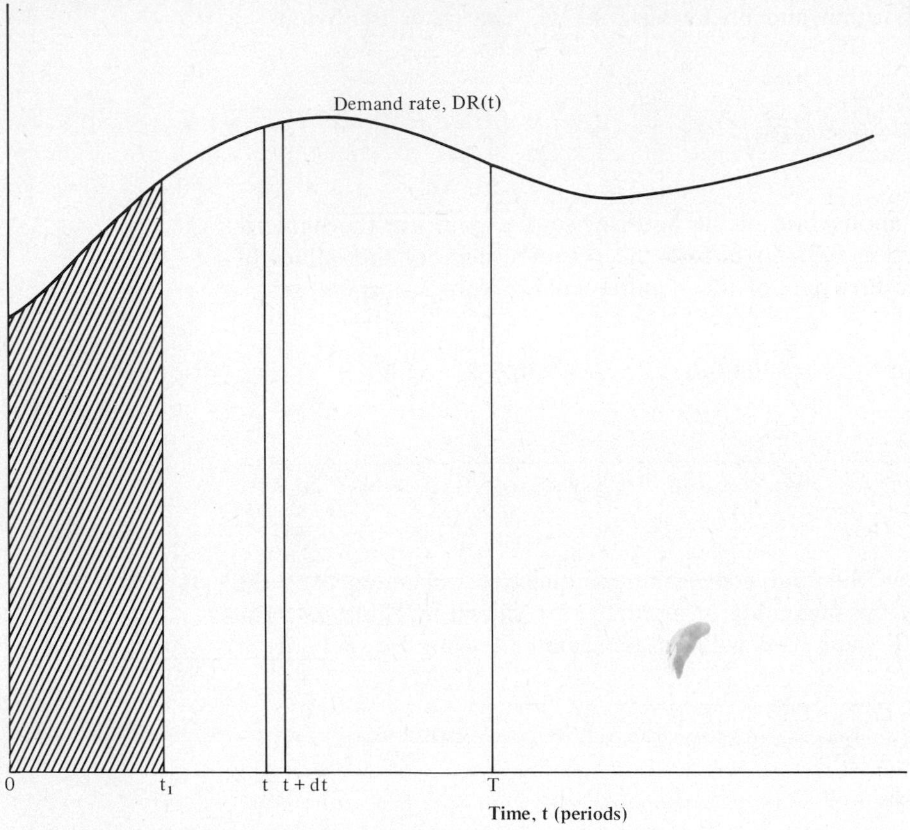

NOTE: The rate is defined such that the hatched area to the left of the vertical line at $t = t_1$ gives the total demand from time 0 to time t_1.

8.6.3 *An Interesting Property of the Continuous Time Version of the Heuristic*

A continuous time version of the heuristic has been presented in a paper by Silver and Meal.[17] By continuous time we mean that the assumptions of Section 8.3.1 are changed in two ways:

i. Demand is continuous with time at a *rate* $DR(t)$ which can depend upon time t. (This is illustrated in Figure 8.3.)

ii. A replenishment can be made at any point in time.

Consider the case where a replenishment is required at time 0. Then, as demonstrated in part 2 of the appendix to this chapter, for the limiting case where $DR(t) = D$, that is, the demand rate is constant with time, the heuristic's formula for computing the T to use reduces to

$$T = \sqrt{\frac{2A}{rDv}}$$

but this is the result found for the basic economic order quantity in Eq. 5.6 of Chapter 5. In other words, the limiting case of the continuous time version of the heuristic produces the basic economic order quantity, certainly a desirable characteristic.

In the discrete time version, because of the integer requirement on T, the limiting correspondence with the EOQ is more difficult to show.

8.6.4 *Performance of the Heuristic*

We know, from Section 5.2 of Chapter 5, that the basic economic order quantity is optimal under a set of assumptions which includes that the demand rate is constant and deterministic. As discussed earlier in the present chapter, when the demand rate varies with time there is no simply implementable "optimal" procedure. The justification for the use of the Silver–Meal heuristic must be made on a combination of simplicity and reasonable cost performance. The simplicity of the method has already been demonstrated.

The discrete version of the heuristic has been tested against the Wagner–Whitin algorithm, the basic economic order quantity, and other heuristics on a wide range of examples (some of which have been reported in reference 18). In all cases we reach the same conclusion, namely that anytime the Wagner–Whitin method significantly outperforms the fixed EOQ, so does the Silver–Meal heuristic. Moreover, in these examples, the average cost penalty for using the heuristic instead of the "optimal" Wagner–Whitin algorithm has been less than 1 percent; in many cases there is no penalty whatsoever.

8.6.5 *When to Use the Heuristic*

The heuristic, although quite simple, is still more involved than the determination of the basic economic order quantity. We know that the latter is the best replenishment quantity to use when there is no variability in the demand rate. In fact, the variability of the demand pattern should exceed some threshold value before it makes sense to use the heuristic.

A useful measure of the variability of a demand pattern is the variability coefficient. This statistic, denoted by VC, is given by

$$VC = \frac{\text{Variance of demand per period}}{\text{Square of average demand per period}}$$

As shown in part 3 of the appendix of this chapter, this simplifies to

$$VC = \frac{N \sum_{j=1}^{N} [D(j)]^2}{[\sum_{j=1}^{N} D(j)]^2} - 1 \tag{8.3}$$

where N is the number of periods of demand forecasts readily available. The aforementioned tests have shown that a threshold value of VC appears to be in the neighborhood of 0.25, that is,

If $VC < 0.25$, use a simple EOQ involving $\bar{D}$ as the demand estimate.

If $VC \geq 0.25$, use the Silver–Meal heuristic.

For the numerical example discussed in this chapter, Eq. 8.3 gives

$$VC = \frac{12(171094)}{(1200)^2} - 1 = 0.426$$

which is greater than the threshold value indicating that the heuristic, rather than the EOQ, should be used. (Recall from Tables 8.2 and 8.3 that the heuristic produced total relevant costs 22.1 percent below those resulting from use of the EOQ.)

In addition, one should worry about the absolute importance of the item, in terms of the potential savings in replenishment and carrying costs. A useful surrogate for this quantity is the total of these costs per unit time under use of the EOQ *in the EOQ cost model* (we know that the EOQ model is, strictly speaking, only an approximation for the case of time-varying demand, but it is simple to use), namely

$$\sqrt{2A\bar{D}vr}$$

If this quantity was very small, one would not be justified in departing from the simple EOQ decision rule. However, in this chapter we are concerned with B items, defined to be those with intermediate values of $\bar{D}v$. Thus, by definition, for such items the above test quantity will be large enough to ensure that we should not blindly remain with the basic EOQ when the demand rate varies enough.

A word of caution is in order. If the variability coefficient is very high and, at the same time, the EOQ expressed as a time supply, that is,

$$\sqrt{\frac{2A}{\bar{D}vr}}$$

is a large number of periods (on the order of at least 20), then it is possible that the first local minimum of the criterion function is not the overall minimum. In such circumstances we recommend that a user explore the possible benefits of evaluating larger T values, perhaps even out to the horizon. In such a case the T value to use would be the one giving the overall minimum of the criterion function (see Eq. 8.2).

If the Wagner–Whitin procedure is to be used at all, its use should be restricted to A items having highly variable demand patterns with a definite specified termination of the demand pattern at the horizon (such as in a fixed period contract).

8.6.6 *Sensitivity to Errors in Parameters*

In Section 5.4 of Chapter 5 it was illustrated that, for the case of the basic economic order quantity, the total cost curve is quite shallow in the neighborhood of the best order quantity. Thus, even substantial deviations of the order quantity away from its best value, tend to produce small percentage cost penalties. One case of such deviations is errors in the parameter (cost and/or demand) values. We concluded that the costs were relatively insensitive to errors in the input parameters for the case of the EOQ formulation.

Fortunately, tests have revealed that a similar phenomenon exists for the Silver–Meal heuristic. The results of one such test are shown in Figure 8.4. The basic data used (taken from Kaimann[11]) were:

$$A/vr = 150$$

Period	1	2	3	4	5	6	7	8	9	10	11	12
Requirements	10	10	15	20	70	180	250	270	230	40	0	10

A/vr was deliberately changed away from its correct value. For this incorrect value of A/vr the Silver–Meal heuristic was used to compute the replenishment quantities. The true value of A/vr was then employed to compute the costs associated with this sequence of replenishments. These costs were compared with those of the replenishment pattern resulting from using the correct value of A/vr. This was repeated for a number of different percentage errors in A/vr. To illustrate, in Figure 8.4 it is seen that if A/vr is erroneously set at a value 40 percent too high (that is, at a value of 210 instead of the correct level of 150), then the cost penalty is less than 2 percent. The plot is not a smooth curve (as was the case in Figure 5.4 of Chapter 5) because here the replenishment opportunities are discrete in nature. Nonetheless, in all cases tested, the percentage cost penalties, even for reasonable-sized errors in A/vr, were quite small.

Figure 8.4 Illustration of Insensitivity of Heuristic Results to Errors in Cost Parameters.

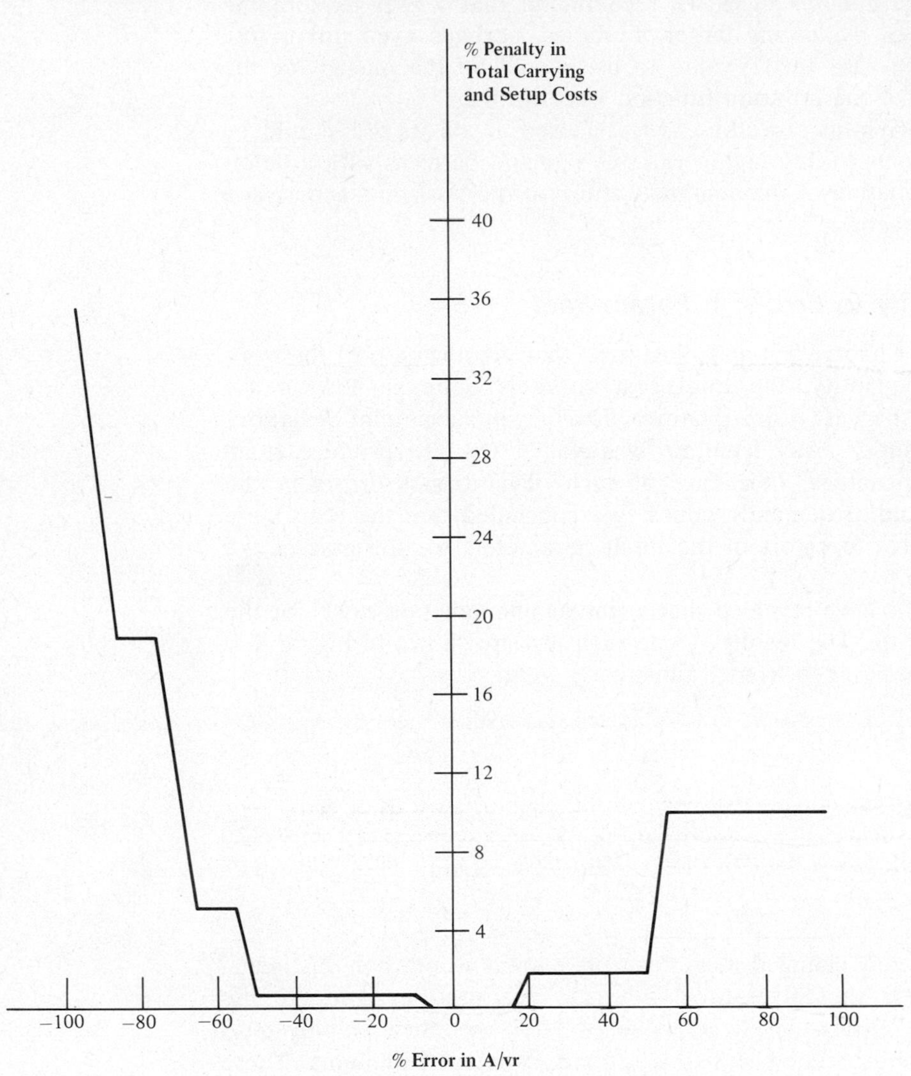

8.7 Two Other Heuristics Used in Practice

We now briefly cover two other heuristics, primarily because they have been used by practitioners. However, as mentioned earlier, the Silver–Meal heuristic, on a large number of tests, has compared very favorably with them. Moreover, we believe that the criterion (of minimization of costs per unit time), on which the Silver–Meal method is based, is more appealing than the logic underlying these other methods.

8.7.1 *The Economic Order Quantity Expressed as a Time Supply*

One approach described earlier (in Section 8.4) was to use a fixed order quantity, based on using the average demand rate $\bar{D}$ in the EOQ equation. Empirically, where there is significant variability in the demand pattern, better cost performance has been obtained by proceeding slightly differently. The EOQ is expressed as a time supply using $\bar{D}$, namely:

$$T_{\text{EOQ}} = \frac{\text{EOQ}}{\bar{D}} = \sqrt{\frac{2A}{\bar{D}vr}}$$

rounded to the nearest integer greater than zero. Then, any replenishment of the item is made large enough to cover exactly the requirements of this integer number of periods. Another name for this approach is the use of a *periodic order quantity.*

For the numerical example of Section 8.3.2, Eq. 8.4 gives

$$T_{\text{EOQ}} = \sqrt{\frac{2(54)}{(100)(20)(0.02)}} = 1.64$$

which rounds to 2.

8.7.2 *Part-Period Balancing*

The basic criterion used here is to select the number of periods covered by the replenishment such that the total carrying costs are made as close as possible to the setup cost, A. (Exact equality is usually not possible because of the discrete nature of the decision variable, *T*.) To illustrate, for the MIDAS numerical example of Section 8.3.2 we have

$$A = \$54.00; \qquad v = \$20.00/\text{box}; \qquad r = 0.02\ \$/\$/\text{month}$$

Month, j	1	2	3	4	5	6	...
Requirements, $D(j)$	10	62	12	130	154	129	...

The calculations for the first replenishment quantity (assuming that the inventory is zero at the beginning of month 1) are:

T	Carrying Costs
1	0
2	$D(2)vr = \$24.80 < \$54.00$
3	$24.80 + 2D(3)vr = \$34.40 < \$54.00$
4	$\$34.40 + 3D(4)vr = \$190.40 > \$54.0$

\$34.40 is closer to \$54.00 (the A value) than is \$190.40. Therefore, a T value of 3 is selected for the first replenishment.

Refinements of the above method, requiring more computational effort, have been developed (see Reference 5).

8.8 *Aggregate Exchange Curves*

As has been discussed earlier in the book, certain parameter values, such as r or A/r, may be selected implicitly by top management's specification of a reasonable operating situation from an aggregate standpoint. In Chapter 5, for the case of the basic economic order quantity, it was relatively easy to develop an exchange curve because of the analytic relationships between (i) total cycle stock and r or A/r (see Eqs. 5.8 and 5.12) and (ii) total number (or costs) of replenishments per unit time and r or A/r (see Eqs. 5.9 and 5.13).

For the case of time-varying demand no such simple results exist because of the discrete nature of the decision variable T, the number of periods of requirements to be included in a replenishment. Therefore, in this case, in order to develop an exchange curve, we must proceed as follows.

A representative sample of items is selected from the population of items under consideration. As will be discussed in a general way in Chapter 19, the exact sample size to select depends upon the number and characteristics of items in the population which are to be controlled by the Silver–Meal heuristic (that is, have a variability coefficient exceeding 0.25).

A value of A/r or r is selected. Then, for each item in the sample the Silver–Meal heuristic is used to determine the replenishment quantities over a reasonable time period such as 12 months. This implies a certain number of replenishments and an average inventory level (in dollars) for the item. Summing these quantities across the items of the sample produces the total number of replenishments and the total average inventory of the sample. These figures must be appropriately scaled up to correspond with the total group of items to be controlled by the Silver–Meal procedure. This must be repeated for several values of A/r or r to develop the tradeoff curve.

An additional point is worth mentioning here. One often wants an exchange curve for all of the items in the population. In such a case, the results for the Silver–Meal items must be added to those for the items to be replenished according to the basic economic order quantity (Section 5.3 of Chapter 5) to produce one composite curve as a function of A/r or r.

8.9 *The Case of a Time-Varying Probabilistic Demand Pattern*

The methods developed earlier in this chapter, for the case of deterministic demand, included as an assumption that replenishments can be made only at the beginning of each period (for example, a week or a month). Effectively, this says that we are dealing with a periodic review system. The review instances would be located exactly one replenishment lead time (L) before the start of each period so as to ensure receipt of a replenishment at the beginning of a time period.

Consistent with our reasoning in Chapters 6 and 7, when a periodic review is used (rather than continuous monitoring) it is reasonable to simultaneously use an order-up-to-level, the level to which the inventory position is raised when an order is placed. However, as evidenced by the logic earlier in the current chapter, often a replenishment can be expected to last for several review periods. Thus, it would be inappropriate to restrict attention to an (R, S) system where an order *must* be placed at every review. Instead we resort to an (R, s, S) system of control in which an order is placed at a review only if the inventory position is low enough (at s or lower). The selection of the values of the control parameters (R, s, and S) in such a system is difficult enough when the average demand rate does not vary with time. Here, we have it varying with time, thus, we would expect that both s and S will change with time. An optimal solution is out of the question. Instead, we shall outline a rather simple "first-generation" heuristic decision system. (A more elaborate heuristic system, that is based on somewhat more realistic assumptions, has been developed in Reference 16, but requires further operational testing.)

We shall only consider the P_1 (probability of no stockout per replenishment cycle) service measure. Reference 16 also treats the P_2 (fraction of demand to be satisfied routinely from shelf) service measure.

We shall first lay out the underlying assumptions. Then the decision rules will be presented.

8.9.1 *Assumptions*

a. The review interval R is prespecified.

b. The replenishment lead time L is known.

c. At a review instant, which we shall denote* by time ($-L$), demand forecasts $D(1), D(2), D(3), \ldots, D(N)$ are known for N basic time periods where period 1 begins L after the review. Also assumed given is the forecast of demand over the interval L immediately following the review, that is, from time ($-L$) to time 0.

d. Forecast errors over an interval of length $R+L$ are normally distributed with no bias (that is, an average value of

---

* *The reason for the selection of the particular time origin is that an order, if placed at this review instant, will arrive at time* 0, *that is, at the beginning of time period* 1.

zero). The standard deviation of errors over such an interval now can depend upon calender time (because the average level changes with time). In particular, we assume that

$$\sigma_{(t,u)} = c\bar{x}_{(t,u)} \tag{8.5}$$

where

$\bar{x}_{(t,u)}$ is the forecast demand, in units, over the interval from time t to time u.*

$\sigma_{(t,u)}$ is the standard deviation of forecast errors, in units, over the same time interval.*

c is a coefficient of variation that must be estimated for the population of items under consideration (that is, the same value would ordinarily be reasonable for a large group of items).

e. The decision to place an order, that is, the specification of an s value, does not depend upon the S value to be used.

f. The costs of the control system itself do not depend upon the specific values of s and S used.

8.9.2 *The Decision Rules*

We shall sequentially discuss the decisions of

i. When to place an order

ii. How many periods the replenishment should be *expected* to cover

iii. The size of the replenishment

Deciding When to Place an Order—Because of the aforementioned varying nature of both s and S the replenishment cycles will tend to

---

* *It is necessary to use the notation* $\bar{x}_{(t,u)}$ and $\sigma_{(t,u)}$ *instead of* $\bar{x}_{u-t}$ *and* σ_{u-t} *because, owing to the time variability of the demand pattern, the forecast and anticipated errors over an interval of length* $u-t$ *now depend upon the exact calendar location of the interval.*

look quite different from one another. Therefore, in attempting to ascertain when to make a replenishment we only look at the consequences within the present cycle of not placing a replenishment order at the particular review instant in question. In particular, the key question is "will adequate service be provided if we delay ordering until at least the next review instant?"

As mentioned earlier, let the time origin (time 0) be the moment at which a replenishment would arrive if an order was placed at the current review instant. Consequently, the time of the current review must be $(-L)$, that is, a replenishment lead time prior to time 0.

As discussed in Section 6.8 of Chapter 6, the important time period in deciding on whether or not to replenish at a particular review instant is a review interval (R) plus a replenishment lead time (L), here from time $(-L)$ to time (R).

We evaluate the actual safety factor, k_a, if we were to not place an order and then compare it with the safety factor, k_r, required to provide the desired service level. If k_a is less than k_r, an order must be placed now, that is, at time $(-L)$; if k_a is larger than k_r, no order need be placed until at least the next review instant (time $R-L$).

The formula for computing k_a follows from the assumption of normally distributed errors. It is given by

$$k_a = \frac{w - \bar{x}_{(-L,R)}}{\sigma_{(-L,R)}} \tag{8.6}$$

where w is the inventory position at the time of the review, in units.

For the P_1 service measure k_r must satisfy

$$p_{u\geq}(k_r) = 1 - P_1 \tag{8.7}$$

where $p_{u\geq}(k)$, a function used repeatedly in Chapter 7, is the probability that a unit normal (mean 0, standard deviation 1) variable takes on a value of k or larger.

The actual service provided will tend to be somewhat higher than P_1, the primary reason being that an order placed now will arrive only L time units in the future, whereas the required safety factor k_r is based on a period of duration $R+L$. In practice, one could reduce k_r by trial-and-error in an effort to compensate for this effect (there is no obvious analytic correction).

Deciding on the Number of Periods to be Covered by the Replenishment—Our philosophy here parallels that advocated in Chapters 6 and 7, namely that the order quantity and safety stock decisions are made sequentially. The argument in the preceding subsection concerned the selection of the reorder point (hence, the safety stock).

As for the order quantity, we work indirectly through the choice of the number of periods to be covered by the replenishment. Suppose that it is decided to place an order at time $(-L)$ to arrive at time 0. Let T be the integer number of periods (of length R) that the order is to cover from the moment of its arrival *if the demand rates follow their forecast values exactly*. When demand is assumed deterministic but time-varying (at the forecast values), it is appropriate to use the procedure shown in Section 8.6.2 for selecting the appropriate value of T. Note that the forecast demand $\bar{x}_{(0,R)}$ is $D(1)$, $\bar{x}_{(R,2R)}$ is $D(2)$, etc.

Selecting the Size of the Replenishment—In Section 8.6.2 the replenishment size, Q, was very simply related to the period of coverage, T. Here, the uncertainty in forecasts complicates things somewhat. We take a pragmatic approach and suggest that the Q value should be selected so as to achieve an order-up-to-level, S, given by

$$S = \bar{x}_{(-L,TR)} + k_r c \bar{D}(R+L) \tag{8.8}$$

where $\bar{x}_{(-L,TR)}$ is the expected demand from the current review until the next order is expected to arrive, and $\bar{D}$ is the average demand per period of length R. Thus, the second term in Eq. 8.8 is a rough estimate of the safety stock to cover the last $R+L$ of the cycle now being initiated (a more elaborate procedure is prescribed in Reference 16).

Finally Q is given by

$$Q = S - w \tag{8.9}$$

where w, as earlier, is the current inventory position.

8.9.3 *Omitting Some Reviews*

If a T value greater than 1 is selected, then we do not expect to have to place another replenishment order at the next review instant. In fact, if the T value selected is quite large, then it is unlikely that an order will be required at any of the next several review instants. Consequently, if the cost of a review is high, it makes sense to omit some reviews entirely. Again, there is an economic tradeoff involved. Omitting reviews saves review costs but increases the chances of a stockout. An exact economic analysis is probably not warranted. A reasonable rule of thumb is to omit reviews for the first $T/2$ intervals after an order to cover T periods has been placed. This can be used in conjunction with a monitoring of actual demand and changes in forecasts. As long as cumulative demand from the time that the order is placed does not significantly exceed the cumulative forecast and, furthermore, no appreciable increases have been made in the forecasts for the next $(R+L)$ interval, there is no need, before most of T elapses, to go through a formal review of whether or not to place an order.

8.10 *Summary*

In this chapter we have provided a decision system for coping with the relaxation of another of the key assumptions inherent in the use of the basic economic order quantity. The system permits the practitioner to deal, in a realistic way, with *time-varying* demand patterns. The Silver-Meal Heuristic, through extensive testing, has been found to be robust. A guideline has been provided as to when one should consider the EOQ-based approaches as no longer being valid.

With this chapter we complete our discussion of systems for controlling B items. In the next part of the book we turn our attention to other special classes of items.

Appendix to Chapter 8

1 A Streamlined Version of the Silver–Meal Heuristic

The details of the derivation can be found in Reference 18. As mentioned in the text, the basic idea is to evaluate TRCUT(T) for increasing values of T until, for the first time,

$$\text{TRCUT}(T+1) > \text{TRCUT}(T) \tag{8.10}$$

If we define a counter $F(T)$ by

$$F(1) = \frac{A}{vr}$$

and

$$F(T) = F(T-1) + (T-1)D(T) \qquad T = 2, 3, \ldots$$

then Eq. 8.10 simplifies to

$$T^2 D(T+1) > F(T)$$

the condition for T to be used if none of 1, 2, 3, . . . , $T-1$ are used.

2 A Property of the Continuous Time Version of the Silver–Meal Heuristic

Recall that in this version of the heuristic two assumptions are changed as follows:

i. Demand is continuous with time at a rate $DR(t)$ which depends upon the time t (see Figure 8.3).

ii. A replenishment can be made at any point in time.

Suppose that a replenishment is made at time 0 and lasts for T periods (T need not be an integer anymore). The total relevant costs, TRC(T), associated with the replenishment are composed of the fixed replenishment cost A and the inventory carrying costs. The latter are conveniently computed by defining the carrying costs CCR(t)dt associated with the requirements $DR(t)dt$ in a small interval t to $t+dt$ (see Figure 8.3) if the current replenishment satisfies these requirements. Because, the stock to satisfy these requirements is carried for a time period t, we have

$$\mathrm{CCR}(t)\,dt = [DR(t)\,dt]tvr$$

Thus, the total relevant costs associated with the replenishment are

$$\begin{aligned}\mathrm{TRC}(T) &= A + \int_0^T \mathrm{CCR}(t)\,dt \\ &= A + vr\int_0^T tDR(t)\,dt\end{aligned}$$

We wish to minimize $\mathrm{TRC}(T)/T$. This is done by setting $d[\mathrm{TRC}(T)/T]/dT = 0$, that is,

$$\frac{d}{dT}\left[\frac{A + vr\int_0^T tDR(t)\,dt}{T}\right] = 0$$

The result is

$$T^2DR(T) - \int_0^T tDR(t)\,dt = \frac{A}{vr} \tag{8.11}$$

For our purposes here we only wish to explore the limiting case of a constant demand rate, that is,

$$DR(t) = D \quad \text{independent of } t$$

In this case, Eq. 8.11 reduces to

$$T^2D - \frac{T^2D}{2} = \frac{A}{vr}$$

that is,

$$T = \sqrt{\frac{2A}{rDv}}$$

3 An Expression for the Variability Coefficient

The variability coefficient, VC, is defined as

$$VC = \frac{\text{Variance of demand per period}}{\text{Square of average demand per period}} \tag{8.12}$$

Here the demand per period can be thought of as a discrete variable taking on the values $D(1)$, $D(2), \ldots, D(N)$, each with probability $1/N$. Then we have that the average demand per period

$$\bar{D} \text{ or } E(D) = \frac{1}{N}[D(1) + D(2) + \ldots + D(N)]$$

$$= \frac{1}{N}\sum_{j=1}^{N} D(j) \tag{8.13}$$

and the variance of demand per period

$$\text{Var}(D) = \frac{1}{N}[D(1)]^2 + \frac{1}{N}[D(2)]^2 + \ldots + \frac{1}{N}[D(N)]^2 - [E(D)]^2$$

$$= \frac{1}{N}\sum_{j=1}^{N} [D(j)]^2 - [E(D)]^2 \tag{8.14}$$

Substitution of Eqs. 8.13 and 8.14 into Eq. 8.12 gives

$$VC = \frac{\frac{1}{N}\sum_{j=1}^{N} [D(j)]^2 - [E(D)]^2}{[E(D)]^2}$$

$$= \frac{\frac{1}{N}\sum_{j=1}^{N} [D(j)]^2}{\frac{1}{N^2}[\sum_{j=1}^{N} D(j)]^2} - 1$$

$$= \frac{N\sum_{j=1}^{N} [D(j)]^2}{[\sum_{j=1}^{N} D(j)]^2} - 1$$

Problems for Chapter 8

Problem 8.1

A sale of polarizing filters is held twice annually by MIDAS. The demand pattern for a particular size of filter for the past year is as follows:

J	F	M	A	M	J
21	29	24	86	31	38

J	A	S	O	N	D
45	39	31	78	29	32

It is anticipated that demand for the next year will follow this pattern, hence these figures are being used as the "best estimates" of forthcoming sales. Demand will also continue in future years. The cost of these filters is \$8.65, ordering costs are approximately \$35.00, and the carrying cost is 0.24 \$/\$/yr.

Calculate the variability coefficient and select the appropriate order quantities.

Problem 8.2

The demand pattern for another type of MIDAS filter is:

J	F	M	A	M	J
18	31	23	95	29	37

J	A	S	O	N	D
50	39	30	88	22	36

These filters cost the company \$4.75 each; ordering and carrying costs are as in Problem 8.1. The variability coefficient equals 0.33. Use the Silver–Meal Heuristic to determine the sizes and timing of replenishments of stock.

Problem 8.3

In this chapter for the case of deterministic time-varying demand we developed the Silver–Meal Heuristic. It selects a value of T which minimizes the relevant costs per unit time over the duration (T) of the replenishment.

The result we developed was to select the integer T to minimize

$$\frac{A + vr\sum_{j=1}^{T}(j-1)D(j)}{T} \tag{1}$$

Another heuristic proposed in the literature is the so-called "least unit cost" method. In it a value of T is selected so as to minimize the *relevant costs per unit* included in the replenishment quantity.

a. Develop an expression similar to Eq. 1 that the best (according to this criterion) T value must satisfy.

b. For the following item having zero inventory at the beginning of period 1 develop the magnitude of the *first* replenishment *only*:

Item characteristics:

$$A = \$50 \qquad v = \$2.00/\text{unit}$$
$$r = 0.05\ \$/\$/\text{period}$$

Period j	1	2	3	4	5	6	7
D(j)	200	300	500	500	400	400	300

c. A marked difference between this method and that of Silver–Meal exists in the dependence on $D(1)$. Briefly discuss. In particular, suppose $D(1)$ was much larger than any of the other $D(j)$'s. What effect would this have on the best T for

i. Silver–Meal?
ii. Least unit cost?

Problem 8.4

Consider an item with the following properties:

$A = \$20 \qquad v = \$2.00/\text{unit}$
$r = 0.24\ \$/\$/\text{yr}.$

At time 0 the inventory has dropped to zero and a replenishment (with negligible lead time) must be made. The demand pattern for the next 12 months is:

Month, j	1	2	3	4	5	6
Demand (units) $D(j)$	50	70	100	120	110	100

Month, j	7	8	9	10	11	12
Demand (units) $D(j)$	100	80	120	70	60	40

All the requirements of each month must be available at the beginning of the month. Replenishments are restricted to the beginnings of the months. No shortages are allowed. Using each of the following methods develop the pattern of replenishments to cover the 12 months and the associated total costs of each pattern (do *not* bother to count the costs of carrying $D(j)$ during its period of consumption, namely period j). In each case, the size of the last replenishment should be selected so as to end month 12 with no inventory.

a. Fixed economic order quantity (rounded to the nearest integer number of months of supply; that is, each time the EOQ, based on the average demand through the entire 12 months, is adjusted so that it will last for exactly an integer number of months).

b. A fixed time supply (an integer number of periods) based on the EOQ expressed as a time supply, using the average demand rate for the 12 months.

c. On each replenishment, selection of Q (or, equivalently, the integer T) which minimizes the costs *per unit of quantity* ordered to cover demand through T.

d. The Silver–Meal Heuristic.

e. One replenishment at the start of month 1 to cover all the requirements to the end of month 12.

f. A replenishment at the beginning of every month.

Note: For each case it would be helpful to develop a table with at least the following columns: i). Month, ii). Replenishment Quantity, iii). Starting Inventory, iv). Demand, v). Ending Inventory

Problem 8.5

Consider an item with the following deterministic time-varying demand pattern:

Week	1	2	3	4	5	6
Demand	50	80	180	80	0	0

Week	7	8	9	10	11	12
Demand	180	150	10	100	180	130

Suppose that the pattern terminates at week 12. Let other relevant characteristics of the item be:

Inventory carrying cost per week (incurred only on units carried over from one week to the next) is \$0.20/unit.

Fixed cost per replenishment is \$30.

Initial inventory and replenishment lead time are both zero. Perform an analysis similar to that of Problem 8.4 (of course, substituting "week" for "month")

Problem 8.6

Consider an item with the following declining demand pattern:

Period	1	2	3	4	5	6	7	8	9	10
Demand	600	420	294	206	145	101	71	50	35	25

Period	11	12	13	14	15	16	17	18	19	20
Demand	17	12	9	6	5	3	2	2	1	1

There is no further demand after period 20.

$$A = \$50 \qquad v = \$2.50/\text{unit}$$
$$r = 0.02/\text{period}$$

Perform an analysis similar to that of Problem 8.4.

Problem 8.7

A manager likes the Silver–Meal Heuristic but feels that it is inapplicable for his company's conditions because of the presence of quantity discounts.

a. Suggest a modified version of the heuristic that might satisfy his needs.

b. Illustrate for the following example, computing the timing and magnitude of order quantities out to the horizon of 6 months.

$$A = \$40 \qquad r = 0.02/\text{month}$$
$$v_0 = \$5.00/\text{unit}$$
$$d = 0.10 \quad \text{if} \quad Q \geq 1000 \text{ units}$$

Month, j	1	2	3	4	5	6
$D(j)$	200	400	600	700	200	100

Problem 8.8

Consider a population of items having essentially deterministic but time-varying demand patterns. Suppose that one was interested in developing an exchange curve of total cycle stock (in dollars) versus total number of replenishments per year as a function of A/r (the latter being unknown, but constant for all items). An analyst has suggested using the approach of Section 5.3 of Chapter 5 with

$$D_i = \text{annual demand for item } i.$$

Discuss whether or not this is a reasonable suggestion.

Problem 8.9

Suppose you were a supplier for a single customer having a deterministic, but time-varying demand pattern. Interestingly enough, the time-varying nature is actually of benefit to you!

a. Making use of the Silver–Meal Heuristic, indicate how you would decide on the maximum discount that you would be willing to give the customer in return for him maintaining his current pattern instead of providing a perfectly level demand pattern. Assume that replenishments can take place only at the beginnings of periods.

b. Illustrate for the numerical example of Problem 8.5. Suppose that the current selling price is \$60/unit.

REFERENCES FOR CHAPTER 8

1. Berry, W. L. "Lot Sizing Procedures for Requirements Planning Systems: A Framework for Analysis." *Production and Inventory Management*, Vol. 13, No. 2, 1972, pp. 19–34.

2. Blackburn, J. and H. Kunreuther. "Planning and Forecast Horizons for the Dynamic Lot Size Model with Backlogging." *Management Science*, Vol. 21, No. 3, November, 1974, pp. 215–255.

3. Brown, R. G. "Replenishment Lot Quantities for Time-Varying Demand." private communication, March 1971, 35 pages.

4. Cantellow, D., S. Burton and R. Laing. "An Automatic Model for Purchase Decisions." *Operational Research Quarterly*, Vol. 20, Special Issue, 1969, pp. 25–42.

5. De Matteis, J. J. and A. G. Mendoza. "An Economic Lot-Sizing Technique." *IBM Systems Journal*, Vol. 7, 1968, pp. 30–46.

6. Diegel, A. "A Linear Approach to the Dynamic Inventory Problem." *Management Science*, Vol. 12, No. 7, March, 1966, pp. 530–540.

7. Diegel, A. "Seven Alternatives to Dynamic Programming for Dynamic Lots." Paper presented to the 39th National Meeting, Operations Research Society of America, May, 1971, 19 pages.

8. Eppen, G. D., F. J. Gould, and B. P. Pashigian. "Extensions of the Planning Horizon Theorem in the Dynamic Lot Size Model." *Management Science*, Vol. 15, No. 5, January, 1969, pp. 268–277.

9. Gorham, T. "Dynamic Order Quantities." *Production and Inventory Management*, Vol. 9, No. 1, 1968, pp. 75–79.

10. IBM. *The Production Information and Control System, E20-0280-1.* International Business Machines Corporation, Data Processing Division, White Plains, New York, 1967.

11. Kaimann, R. A. "E.O.Q. vs. Dynamic Programming—Which One to Use for Inventory Ordering?" *Production and Inventory Management*, Vol. 10, No. 4, 1969, pp. 66–74.

12. Kunreuther, H. and T. Morton. "Planning Horizons for Production Smoothing with Deterministic Demands: I." *Management Science*, Vol. 20, No. 1, September, 1973, pp. 110–125.

13. Kunreuther, H. and T. Morton. "Planning Horizons for Production Smoothing with Deterministic Demands: II." *Management Science*, Vol. 20, No. 7, March, 1974, pp. 1037–1046.

14. Lundin, R. and T. Morton. "Planning Horizons for the Dynamic Lot Size Model: Zabel vs Protective Procedures and Computational Results." *Operations Research*, Vol. 23, No. 4, July–August, 1975, pp. 711–734.

15. Sanderson, G. A. "Determining the Economic Lot Size Under Conditions of Non-Linear Demand." paper presented at the

14th Annual International Conference of APICS, November, 1971.

16. Silver, E. A. "A Probabilistic Demand Version of the Silver–Meal Heuristic." OR Report 28, Département de Mathématiques, Ecole Polytechnique Fédérale de Lausanne, Switzerland, 1976.

17. Silver, E. A. and H. C. Meal. "A Simple Modification of the EOQ for the Case of a Varying Demand Rate." *Production and Inventory Management,* Vol. 10, No. 4, 1969, pp. 52–65.

18. Silver, E. A. and H. C. Meal. "A Heuristic for Selecting Lot Size Requirements for the Case of a Deterministic Time-Varying Demand Rate and Discrete Opportunities for Replenishment." *Production and Inventory Management,* Vol. 14, No. 2, 1973, pp. 64–74.

19. Wagner, H. M. and T. M. Whitin. "Dynamic Version of the Economic Lot Size Model." *Management Science,* Vol. 5, October, 1958, pp. 89–96.

20. Woolsey, R. E., E. A. Silver and H. Swanson. "Effect of Forecast Errors on an Inventory Model with Variations in the Demand Rate." *Production and Inventory Management,* Vol. 14, No. 2, 1973, pp. 10–14.

21. Zabel, E. "Some Generalizations of an Inventory Planning Horizon Theorem." *Management Science,* Vol. 10, No. 3, April, 1964, pp. 465–471.

PART 3

Decision Rules and Systems for Special Classes of Items

Part 2 of the book was concerned with decision systems for the routine control of B items, that is, the bulk of the items in a typical population of stockkeeping units. Now we turn our attention to special items, those at the ends of the Dv spectrum, namely the A and C groups, as well as those items not having a well-defined continuing demand pattern (the latter having been assumed in the development of the decision systems for B items). The most important items, the A group, are handled in Chapter 9. Then, in Chapter 10, we deal with so-called single period models, applicable for items possessing the characteristic of not being storable from one period to the next. Chapter 11 is concerned with the low dollar movement items, the C group. The presentation of this portion of the book continues in the same vein as Part 2, namely we are concerned primarily with decision rules for managing *individual* item inventories.

CHAPTER NINE

Decision Systems for Managing the Most Important (Class A) Inventories

In this chapter we devote our attention to the relatively small number of items classified in the A group. Section 9.1 presents a brief review of the nature of A items. This is followed, in Section 9.2, by some general guidelines for the control of such items. Then, in Sections 9.3 and 9.4 the basic decision rules are presented; Section 9.3 is concerned with the faster moving A items (that is, high D values) and Section 9.4 with the slower moving ones (that is, low D values). Section 9.5 deals with a more elaborate set of decision rules which, in an (s, Q) system, take account of the service (shortage) related effects of Q in selecting its value.* Finally, in Section 9.6

* *Equivalently, R in an (R, S) system.*

we discuss a modelling and solution procedure, simulation, which, although rather costly to use, has potential merit in some A item situations.

9.1 The Nature of Class A Items

Recall from Chapter 3 that class A items are defined to be those at the upper end of the spectrum of importance; that is, the total costs of replenishment, carrying stock, and shortages associated with such an item are high enough to justify a more sophisticated control system than those proposed for the less important B items in Chapters 5 to 8. This usually means a high annual dollar usage (that is, a high value of Dv). However, one or more other factors may dictate that an item be placed in the A category. For example, an item, although its sales are relatively low, may be essential to round out the product line; to illustrate, MIDAS carries SUPER-CHROME for its prestige value. Poor customer service on such an item may have adverse effects on customers who buy large amounts of other products in the line. In essence, the important issue is a tradeoff between control system costs (such as the costs of collecting required data, performing the computations, providing action reports, etc.) and the other three categories of costs mentioned above (for simplicity, let us call this latter group "other" costs). By definition, these "other" costs for an A item will be appreciably higher than for a B item. On the other hand, *given that the same control system is used* for an A and a B item the control costs will be essentially the same for the two items. A numerical example is in order:

Consider two types of control systems, one simple, one complex. Suppose we have an A and a B item with estimated "other" costs under use of the simple system being \$900/year and \$70/year respectively. It is estimated that use of the complex control system will reduce these "other" costs by 10 percent. However, the control costs of this complex system are estimated to be \$40/year/item higher than those incurred in using the simple system. The following table illustrates that the complex system should be used for the A, but not for the B item.

Using Complex System

Item	Increase in Control Costs	Reduction in Other Costs	Net Increase in Costs
A	40	0.1(900) = 90	−50
B	40	0.1(70) = 7	+33

As mentioned above, the factor Dv is important in deciding on whether or not to put an item in the A category. However, the type of control to use within the A category should definitely depend upon the magnitudes of the individual components, D and v. As we shall see later in this chapter, a high Dv resulting from a low D and a high v value (low unit sales of a high value item) implies different control from a high Dv resulting from a high D and a low v value (high unit sales of a low value item). To illustrate, we would certainly control the inventories of the following two items in different ways:

Item 1: a MIDAMATIC film processor, valued at \$30,000, which sells at a rate of 2 per year. *Item* 2: a developing chemical, valued at \$2.00/gallon, which sells at a rate of 30,000 gallons per year.

9.2 *Guidelines for Control of A Items*

In Part 2, which was concerned primarily with B items, we advocated a management by exception approach; that is, most decisions would be made by routine (computerized or manual) rules. Such should not be the case with A items; the potential high payoff warrants frequent managerial attention to (vigilance of) the replenishment decisions of individual items. Nonetheless, decision rules, based on mathematical models, do have a place in aiding the manager. Normally these models cannot incorporate all the important factors; in such cases the manager must modify the suggested (by the model) action through the subjective incorporation of any important omitted factors. The art of management is very evident in this type of activity.

We now list a number of suggested guidelines for the control of A items; these are above and beyond what can normally be incorporated in a *usable* mathematical decision rule:

1. *Inventory records* should be maintained on a *perpetual* (transactions recording) basis, particularly for the more expensive items. This need not be through the use of a computer; the relatively small number of A items makes the use of a manual system (for example, Kardex or VISI-Record) quite attractive.

2. *Keep top management informed*—Frequent reports, (for example, monthly), should be prepared for at least a portion of the A items. These should be made available to senior management for careful review.

3. *Estimating and influencing demand.*

a. Manual input to forecasts (for example, knowledge of intentions of important customers) is likely advisable.

b. Mitchell[40] has pointed out that for expensive, slow moving items it is particularly important to ascertain the predictability of the demand. Where the demand is of a special planned nature (for example, scheduled overhaul of a piece of equipment) or where adequate warning of the need for a replacement part is given (for example, a machine part fails but can be rapidly and inexpensively repaired to last for sufficient time to requisition and receive a new part from the supplier), there is no need to carry protection stock. On the other hand, where the demand occurs without warning (that is, a random breakdown) some protective stock may be in order. We shall devote our attention to this latter kind of item in Section 9.4.

Forecasting demand for a *slow moving* item is not an easy matter. Very few transactions occur over a reasonable historical time period so that a purely *objective* estimate of a demand rate is usually not feasible. Instead, one must take advantage of the subjective knowledge of experts, such as design engineers in the case of spare parts for a relatively new piece of equipment. A sensitivity analysis should be undertaken; in some cases the stocking decision is not particularly sensitive to errors in estimating the demand rate. Also, more sophisticated Bayesian approaches, which combine subjective prior knowledge about a class of similar items with actual demand data for a single member of the class, may be in order. We shall return to this advanced topic in Chapter 14.

c. One need not live with a given demand pattern. Seasonal and/or erratic fluctuations can sometimes be reduced by altering price structures, negotiating with customers, smoothing shipments, etc. (a topic also discussed in Chapters 2 and 15).

4. *Estimating and influencing supply*—Again, it may not be advisable to passively accept a given pattern of supply. Negotiations (for example, establishing blanket orders) with suppliers may reduce the average replenishment lead time,

its variability or both. Taking a supplier to lunch may be far more effective than using a complicated decision rule that attempts to incorporate lead time variability. In the same vein, it is important to coordinate A item inventory requirements in-house with the production scheduling department.

5. *Frequent review of decision parameters*—In Chapter 19 we shall discuss the importance of appropriate monitoring of parameter values. Suffice it to say for now that frequent review, (as often as monthly or bi-monthly) of such quantities as the order points and order quantities, is advisable for A items.

6. *Precise Determination of Values of Control Quantities*—In Chapter 5 we advocated the use of tabular aids in establishing order quantities for B items. It was argued that restricting attention to a limited number of possible time supples (for example, $\frac{1}{2}$, 1, 2, 3, 6, and 12 months) results in small cost penalties. Such is not the case for A items; the percentage penalties may still be small, but even small percentage penalties represent sizable absolute costs for such items. Therefore, order quantities of A items should be based on the most exact analysis possible.

7. *Shortages and Service*—In Chapter 6 we pointed out that it is often very difficult to estimate the cost of shortages; an alternative suggested was to instead specify a desired level of customer service. We do not advocate this approach for A items because of the typical management behavior in the short run in coping with potential or actual shortages of such items. One does not sit back passively and accept shortages of A items. Rather expediting actions (both in and out of house), emergency air freight shipments, etc. are undertaken, that is, the shortages are avoided or eliminated quickly. Such actions, with associated costs which can be reasonably estimated, should be recognized when establishing safety stocks to prevent them. On the other hand, it should be pointed out that, in certain situations, customers are willing to wait a short time for delivery. Because A items are replenished frequently, it may be satisfactory to operate with very little on-hand stock (that is, low safety stock) and instead backorder and satisfy such demands from the next order due in very soon.

9.3 *Basic Decision Rules for Faster-Moving A Items (Defined by $\bar{x}_L \geq 10$ Units)**

As discussed in Chapter 3 we recommend the use of a two-tier type of control within each of the A, B, and C classes of items. Within each class the boundary between the two tiers is given by a value of the average demand (forecast) over a replenishment lead time, $\bar{x}_L$. Empirical tests have indicated that $\bar{x}_L = 10$ units is a reasonable threshold value. A handy summary of the two-tier system, to be discussed in this section and Section 9.4, is shown in Figure 9.1.

For items with $\bar{x}_L \geq 10$ units a normal distribution is appropriate for the forecast errors. As mentioned in the previous section, we advocate use of explicit (or implicit) costing of shortages. Therefore, the decision rules of Sections 7.2.5 and 7.2.6 of Chapter 7 (with $\bar{x}_L \geq 10$ units) should be used.

Figure 9.1 The Suggested Two-Tier Control System for A Items.

Fast movers $\bar{x}_L \geq 10$ units	Use Normal forecast errors and methods of Sections 7.2.5 and 7.2.6 of Chapter 7	
	Relation between $\bar{x}_L$ and σ_L	
	$0.9\sqrt{\bar{x}_L} \leq \sigma_L \leq 1.1\sqrt{\bar{x}_L}$	σ_L outside $(1 \pm 0.1)\sqrt{\bar{x}_L}$
Slow movers $\bar{x}_L < 10$ units	Use Poisson models of Section 9.4.1	Use Laplace models of Sections 7.2.5 and 7.2.6 of Chapter 7

Note: $\bar{x}_L$ is the average (forecast) demand over the replenishment lead time and
σ_L is the standard deviation of forecast errors over the same interval of time.

* *In an (R, S) system $\bar{x}_L$, the average demand in a lead time, is replaced by $\bar{x}_{R+L}$, the average demand in a review interval plus a lead time.*

It should be noted that σ_L must be obtained from the actual MAD of forecast errors of the item under consideration. In some cases it may be appropriate to consider the more elaborate decision rules to be discussed in Section 9.5.

9.4 Basic Decision Rules for Slower-Moving A Items (Defined by $\bar{x}_L < 10$ units)*

Empirically the Poisson distribution (see Appendix B for a discussion of the properties of the distribution) has been found to provide a reasonable fit to the distribution of demand for an s.k.u. when the average demand rate is low. In any event, more elaborate models of the demand distribution would be intractable to implement; from our experience it is clear that most practitioners hesitate to use a Poisson model, let alone a more complex probabilistic structure. The Poisson distribution has but a single parameter, namely the average demand (in this case, $\bar{x}_L$). Once $\bar{x}_L$ is specified, a value of the standard deviation of forecast errors, σ_L, follows from the Poisson relation

$$\sigma_L = \sqrt{\bar{x}_L} \tag{9.1}$$

Therefore, the Poisson is appropriate to use only when the actually observed σ_L (for the item under consideration) is quite close to $\sqrt{\bar{x}_L}$. An operational definition of quite close, based on tests which we have carried out (Archibald et al.[1]), is use the Poisson with parameter $\bar{x}_L$ if

$$0.9\sqrt{\bar{x}_L} \leq \sigma_L \leq 1.1\sqrt{\bar{x}_L} \tag{9.2}$$

that is, if σ_L is within 10% of $\sqrt{\bar{x}_L}$.

The discrete nature of the Poisson distribution (in contrast, the Normal and Laplace distributions deal with continuous variables) is both a blessing and a curse. For slow-moving items, it is important to be able to deal with discrete units. On the other hand, discrete mathematics create problems in implementation as we shall see.

* *In an (R, S) system $\bar{x}_L$, the average demand in a lead time, is replaced by $\bar{x}_{R+L}$, the average demand in a review interval plus a lead time.*

When the expression 9.2 is not satisfied, the Poisson model is inappropriate and, in such a case, we recommend (based upon the findings reported in Reference 1) use of the decision rules based on the Laplace distribution (as was the case for *all* slow-moving B items).

Now let us look at the details of the decision rules.

9.4.1 *Decision Rules Based on a Poisson Model (for items with $\bar{x}_L < 10$ units and $0.9\sqrt{\bar{x}_L} \leq \sigma_L \leq 1.1\sqrt{\bar{x}_L}$)*

9.4.1.1 *The B_2 Cost Measure in the Special Case of Very Slow-Moving, Expensive Items ($Q=1$)*—As mentioned above, the discrete nature of the Poisson distribution causes problems in obtaining an operational decision rule. For one important situation, namely where the replenishment quantity $Q=1$, an analysis (based on the work of Melese et al.[39]) leads to a decision rule quite easy to implement.

First, let us see under what conditions $Q=1$ makes sense. From Eq. 5.3 of Chapter 5 the total relevant costs, if an order quantity of size Q is used, are

$$\text{TRC}(Q) = Qvr/2 + AD/Q$$

We are indifferent between $Q=1$ and $Q=2$ where

$$\text{TRC}(1) = \text{TRC}(2)$$

that is,

$$vr/2 + AD = vr + AD/2$$

or

$$D = vr/A$$

For any lower value of D we prefer the use of $Q=1$. To illustrate, for the Professional Products Division of MIDAS, we found in Chapter 5 that $A/r \simeq 13.11$. Therefore, we have

$$\text{use} \quad Q=1 \quad \text{if} \quad D < 0.0763v$$

The line $D = 0.0763v$ is shown on Figure 9.2 as well as the boundary line for A items in MIDAS ($Dv > 6{,}000$ dollars/year). The two inequalities define a region in the figure where it is appropriate to use $Q=1$ for A items. It is a simple matter to locate on the figure the (D, v) point corresponding to any item under consideration. The location immediately tells us if the use of $Q=1$ is correct.

Figure 9.2 A Items with $Q = 1$ for the Professional Products Division of MIDAS.

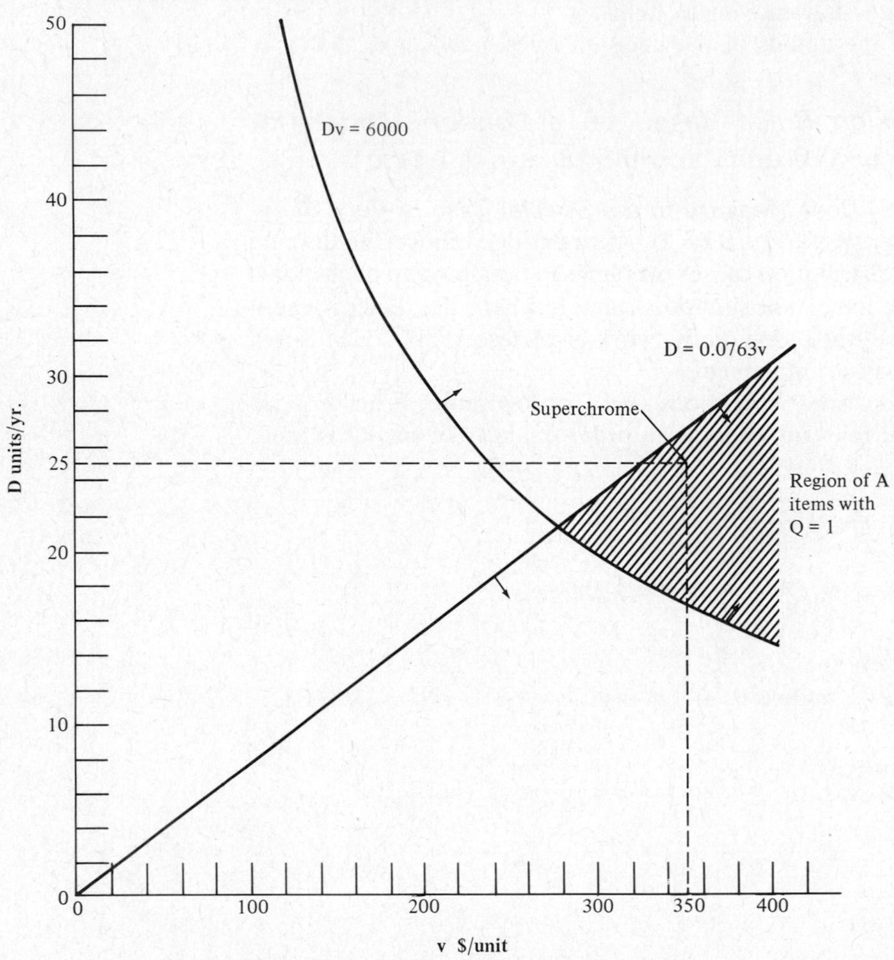

Assumptions behind the Derivation of the Decision Rule—The assumptions include:

i. Continuous review, order point, order quantity system with $Q = 1$ (the remaining decision variable is the order point, s, or the order-up-to-level, $S = s + 1$).

ii. Poisson demand.

iii. The replenishment lead time is a constant, L time periods (the results still hold if L has a probability distribution as long as we use its mean value, $E(L)$; however, the derivation is considerably more complicated in this more general case).

iv. There is complete backordering of demands when out of stock. (Karush[34] and Mitchell[40] have investigated the case of complete lost sales; the results differ very little from the complete backordering situation.)

v. There is a fixed cost, $B_2 v$, per unit backordered (that is, a fixed fraction, B_2, of the unit value is charged for each unit backordered).

Graphical Portrayal of the Decision Rule—As shown in part 1a of the appendix of the current chapter we are indifferent between reorder points s and $s+1$ when

$$\frac{p_{po}(s+1 \mid \bar{x}_L)}{p_{po\leq}(s+1 \mid \bar{x}_L)} = \frac{r}{DB_2} \tag{9.3}$$

where*

$p_{po}(s+1 \mid \bar{x}_L)$ = probability that a Poisson variable with mean $\bar{x}_L$ takes on the value $s+1$,

$p_{po\leq}(s+1 \mid \bar{x}_L)$ = probability that a Poisson variable with mean $\bar{x}_L$ takes on a value less than or equal to $s+1$,

and, as earlier,

r is the carrying charge, in \$/\$/unit time.

D is the demand rate, in units/unit time.

B_2 is the fraction of unit value charged per unit short.

$\bar{x}_L$ is the average (forecast) demand in a replenishment lead time.

---

* $p_{po}(x_o \mid \bar{x}_L) = \dfrac{(\bar{x}_L)^{x_0} \exp(-\bar{x}_L)}{x_0!}$ $\quad x_0 = 0, 1, 2, \ldots$

For a value of each of s and $\bar{x}_L$ Eq. 9.3 is solved for r/B_2D. For a given value of s, this is repeated for a number of values of $\bar{x}_L$ to produce a curve representing indifference between s and $s+1$ as a function of $\bar{x}_L$ and r/B_2. This is illustrated in Figure 9.3. The computations are lengthy but they need only be done once-and-for-all to set up the curves. Note that $\bar{x}_L = DL$. These curves define regions on a graph of r/B_2D versus $\bar{x}_L$ where we prefer one s value to others.

For a given item, values of r, D, and B_2 are used to evaluate the quantity r/DB_2. The point in Figure 9.3, corresponding to this value of r/DB_2 and the appropriate $\bar{x}_L$ indicates the best value of the order point, s, to use.

Numerical Illustration—Consider the case of SUPERCHROME with

$$v = \$350/\text{unit}$$

$$D = 25 \text{ units/year}$$

$$r = 0.24 \ \$/\$/\text{year}$$

$$L = 3 \text{ wks.} = \tfrac{1}{14} \text{ year}$$

and B_2 is estimated to be $\frac{1}{5}$ (that is, 350/5 or \$70 per unit backordered).

First of all, it is seen from Figure 9.2 that this is an A item with $Q=1$ being appropriate. Now

$$\frac{r}{DB_2} = \frac{0.24}{25(\frac{1}{5})} = 0.048/\text{unit}$$

and

$$\bar{x}_L = DL = 25(\tfrac{1}{14}) \simeq 1.8 \text{ units}$$

Use of Figure 9.3 shows that the best order point is 4, that is, we order one-for-one each time a demand drops the inventory position to 4. Another way of saying this is that the inventory position should always be maintained at the level of 5.

Sensitivity to Value of B_2—A precise value of B_2 is not easy to ascertain. Fortunately the indifference curves can be used in a different way to alleviate this difficulty. To illustrate, consider the item (SUPERCHROME) in the above numerical illustration. Assume that D, r, and $\bar{x}_L$ are all known at the indicated values. The indifference curves identify the following regions where each s value shown is best for the given value of $\bar{x}_L$.

Figure 9.3 Indifference Curves for the Reorder Point under the B_2 Cost Measure When $Q = 1$.

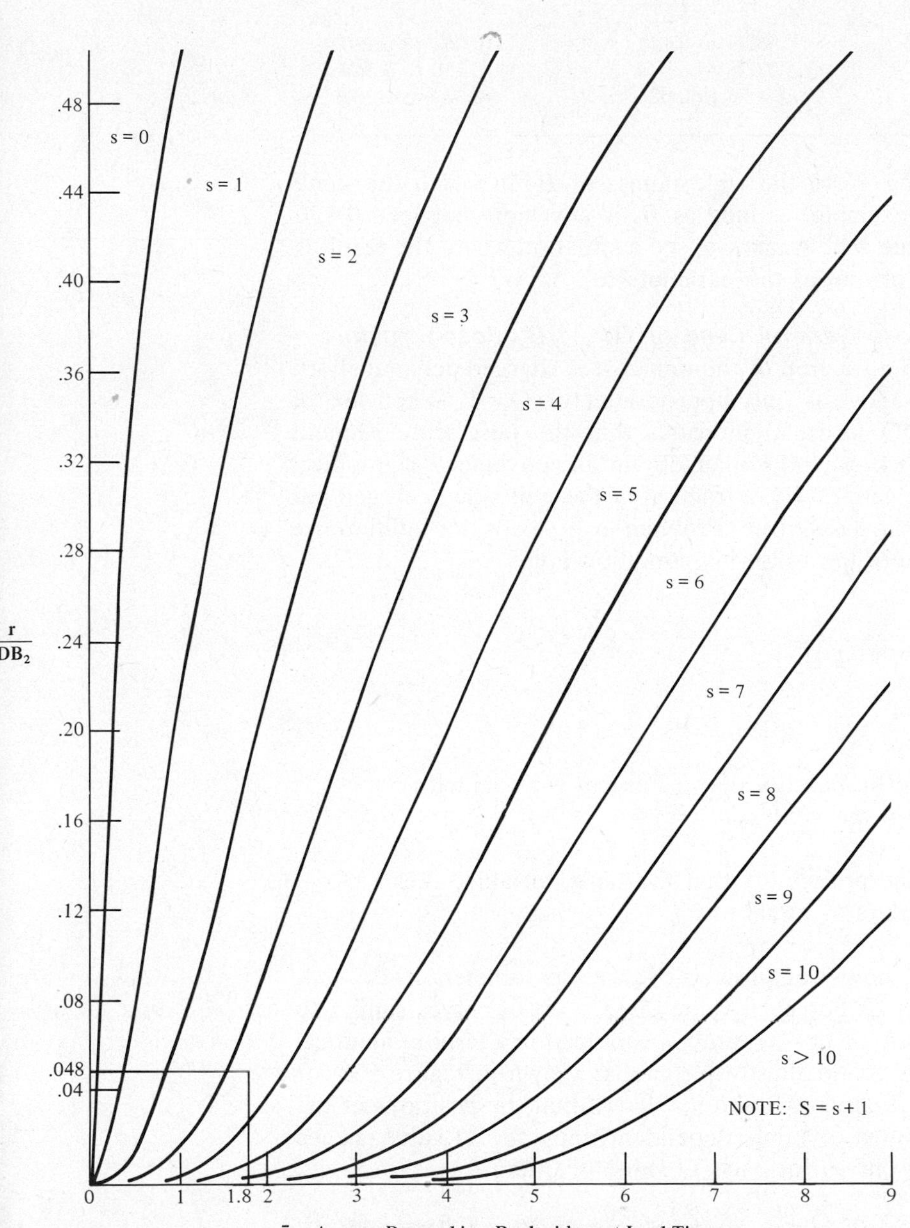

s Value	Range of r/DB_2	Corresponding Range of B_2
3	0.074 to 0.178	0.054 to 0.130
4	0.026 to 0.074	0.130 to 0.369
5	0.0076 to 0.026	0.369 to 1.263

These results are striking. Note the wide ranges of B_2 in which the same value of s is used. For example, as long as B_2 is anywhere between 0.130 and 0.369 the best s value is 4. Again, we see a situation where the result is insensitive to the value of one of the parameters.

9.4.1.2 *The More General Case of $Q>1$; B_2 Cost Structure*—This is the case in which a fraction of the unit cost is charged per unit short. The solution discussed above is only appropriate for $Q=1$. When use of Figure 9.2 (or the EOQ formula) indicates that the best replenishment quantity is 2 or larger we can no longer obtain as convenient a graphical solution, at least for the case of B_2 (a fraction of the unit value charged per unit short). An exact analysis, (see Problem 9.7) leads to indifference between s and $s+1$ where the following condition holds

$$\frac{\sum_{j=1}^{Q} p_{po}(s+j \mid \bar{x}_L)}{\sum_{j=1}^{Q} p_{po\leq}(s+j \mid \bar{x}_L)} = \frac{r}{DB_2}. \tag{9.4}$$

where

$p_{po}(x_0 \mid \bar{x}_L)$ is the probability that a Poisson variable with mean $\bar{x}_L$ takes on the value x_0.

$p_{po\leq}(x_0 \mid \bar{x}_L)$ is the probability that the same variable takes on a value less than or equal to x_0.

Unfortunately, there are now four (instead of three) parameters in Eq. 9.4, namely $\bar{x}_L$, s, r/DB_2, and Q. For each value of Q, a set of curves similar to Figure 9.3 (the special case of $Q=1$) can be developed in a fashion identical to that used for Figure 9.3. An illustrative case is shown in Figure 9.4 for $Q=5$. A comparison of Figures 9.3 and 9.4 shows that the positions of the indifference curves are most certainly dependent upon the Q value, hence the necessity of a set of curves for each Q value of interest.

9.4.1.3 *The Case of $Q \geq 1$, B_1 Cost Structure*—A fixed cost B_1 occurs per stockout occasion. In some cases it may be more appropriate to assume a fixed cost B_1 per (impending) stockout occasion as opposed to a cost

Figure 9.4 Indifference Curves for the Reorder Point under the B_2 Cost Measure When $Q = 5$.

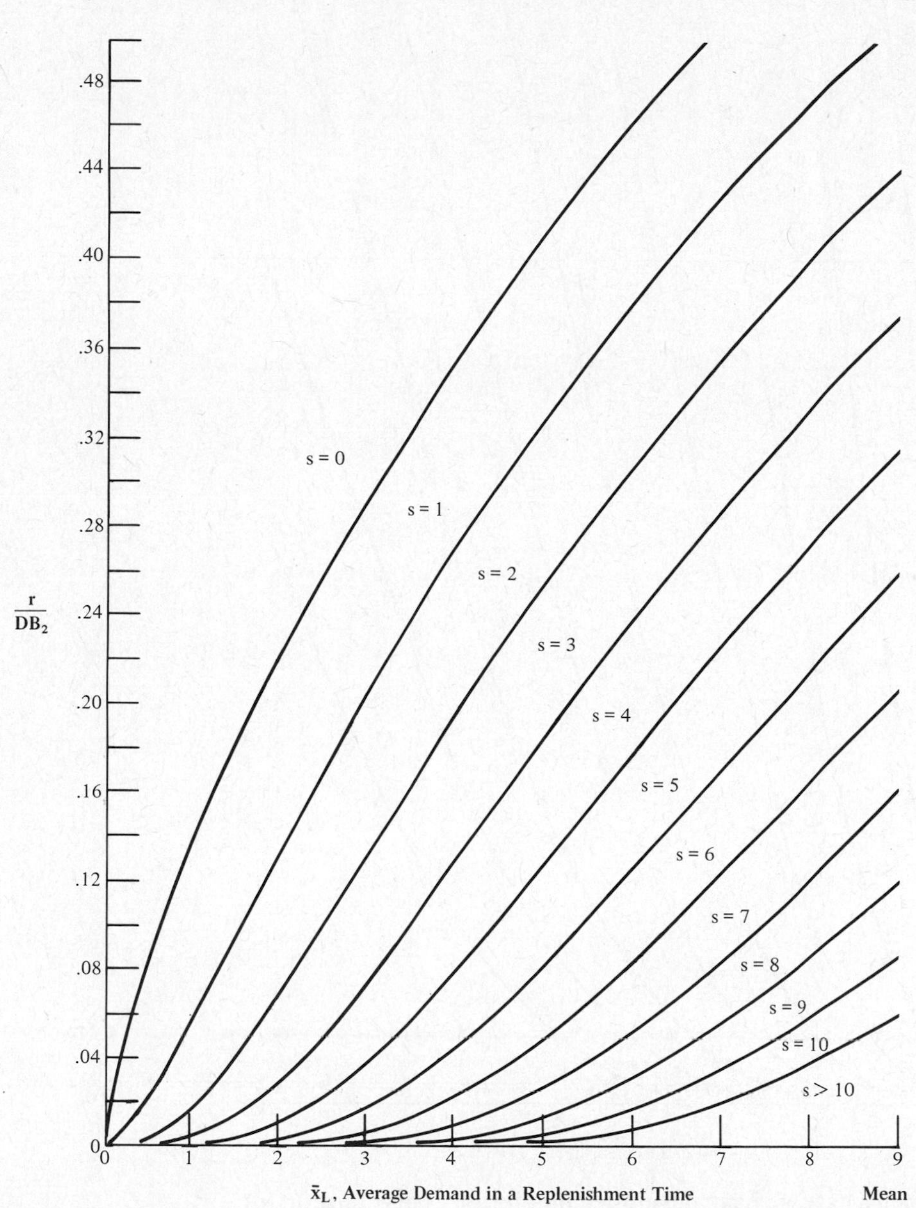

Figure 9.5 Indifference Curves for the Reorder Point under the B_1 Cost Measure.

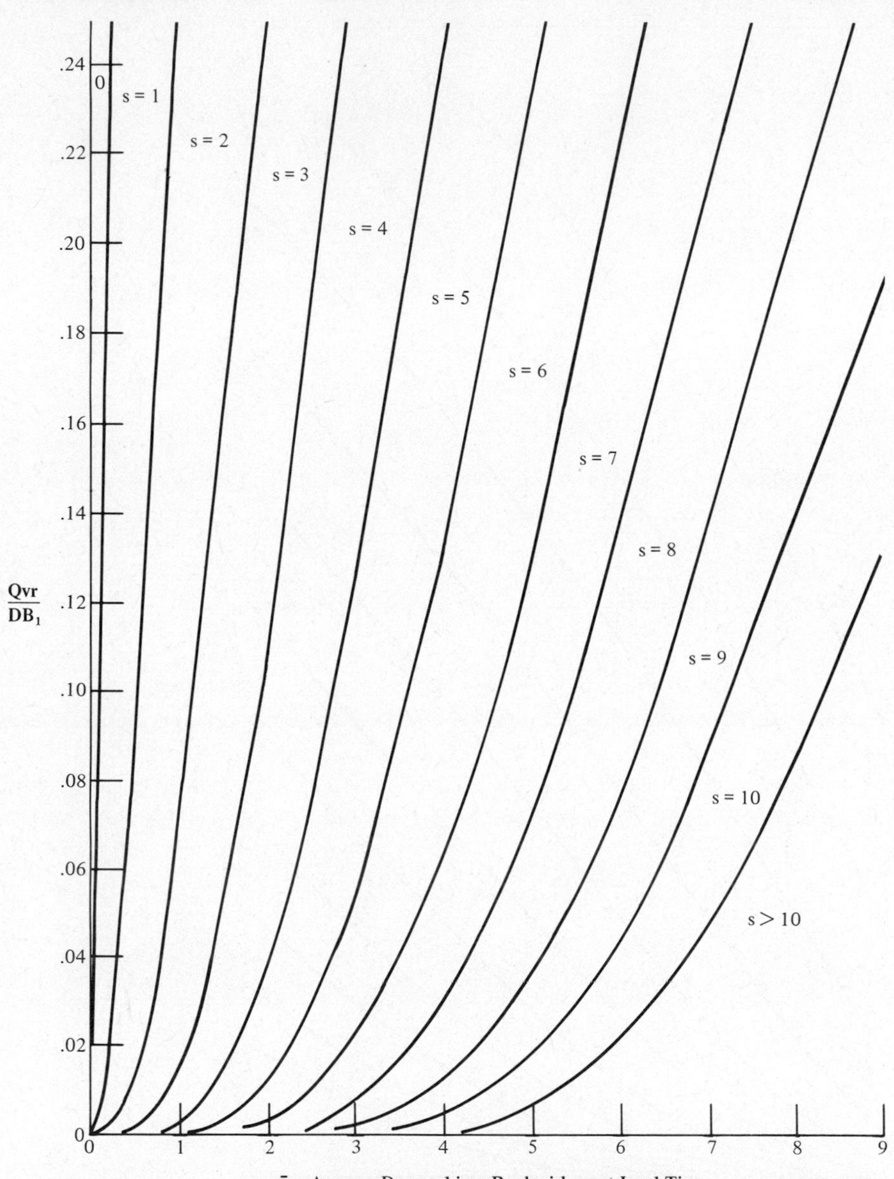

per unit short. For such a case we have developed indifference curves useful for selecting the appropriate reorder point. As shown in part 1b of the appendix of this chapter, we are indifferent between s and $s+1$ as reorder points when

$$\frac{p_{po}(s+1 \mid \bar{x}_L)}{p_{po\leq}(s \mid \bar{x}_L)} = \frac{Qvr}{DB_1} \tag{9.5}$$

where all the variables have been defined above. Again, the indifference curves of Figure 9.5 are developed and used in the same fashion as those of Figure 9.3.

9.4.2 *Decision Rules for Slow-Movers Where the Poisson Assumption is Inappropriate (that is $\bar{x}_L < 10$ units but σ_L does not satisfy $0.9\sqrt{\bar{x}_L} \leq \sigma_L \leq 1.1\sqrt{\bar{x}_L}$)*

As mentioned earlier, when σ_L deviates too far from $\sqrt{\bar{x}_L}$ this indicates that the Poisson assumption would be too far in error. In such cases we suggest reverting to the procedures advocated for slow-moving B items, namely involving the Laplace distribution. Nevertheless, we still recommend restriction to one of the two cases (B_1 and B_2) involving costing of shortages. Therefore, the methods of Sections 7.2.5 and 7.2.6 of Chapter 7 (with $\bar{x}_L < 10$ units) should be used.

9.5 *Simultaneous Versus Sequential Determination of Two Control Parameters of an Individual Item*

In most of our discussions in Chapters 6 and 7 there were two control parameters per item, viz:

s and Q in an (s, Q) system

R and S in an (R, S) system

Our approach was to first determine one of the parameters, namely Q or R, then (sequentially) find the best value of the second parameter, s or S, conditional upon the value of Q or R respectively. The derivation of the value of Q or R ignored the effect that this parameter has on the service level or shortage costs per unit time. To illustrate, consider the (s, Q) control system with a fixed cost B_1 per stockout occasion. From part 2 of the appendix of Chapter 7 we have

$$\text{ETRC}(k, Q) = AD/Q + (Q/2 + k\sigma_L)vr + \frac{DB_1}{Q} p_{u\geq}(k) \tag{9.6}$$

where, as earlier,

$$s = \bar{x}_L + k\sigma_L$$

and $p_{u\geq}(k)$ is a tabulated function giving the probability that a unit normal variable takes on a value of k or larger.

The approach advocated in Chapter 7 was to first pick the Q value which minimizes the first two terms, ignoring the last term. But clearly, the selection of Q influences the shortage costs (the last term); the larger Q is, the smaller these costs become. The exact approach, of simultaneously determining k and Q would involve finding the (k, Q) pair that minimize the ETRC (k, Q) expression of Eq. 9.6. As we shall see, this exact approach is considerably more involved from a computational standpoint. Furthermore, the order quantity is no longer the simple, well-understood economic order quantity, hence is likely to be more difficult to implement. Fortunately, as we shall show, the percentage penalty in the total of replenishment, carrying and shortage costs using the simpler sequential approach tends to be quite small. Thus, in most situations, we were justified in advocating its use for B items. However, even small percentage savings may be attractive for A items. For this reason, we now take a closer look at the simultaneous determination of the two control parameters.

Again, because we are dealing with A items, we restrict attention to the two cases where shortages are costed (B_1 and B_2) rather than those situations where a service level is specified. We shall restrict our attention to (s, Q) systems. Similar results apply for (R, S) systems and can be found in Silver and Wilson.[50] Graphs will be presented showing the percentage penalty in costs (excluding those of the control system) resulting from using the simpler sequential procedure in lieu of the sophisticated simultaneous approach, that is,

$$\mathrm{PCP} = \frac{[\mathrm{ETRC(sequential\ parameter\ values)} - \mathrm{ETRC(simultaneous\ parameter\ values)}]}{\mathrm{ETRC(simultaneous\ parameter\ values)}} \times 100 \tag{9.7}$$

where PCP is the percentage cost penalty and ETRC $(\cdot)$ are the expected total relevant costs (excluding system control costs) per unit time using the parameter values in the parentheses.

For one case (namely, B_1 costing) we also show a summary of the decision logic for simultaneously selecting the values of the two control parameters. The derivation has been relegated to part 2 of the appendix of the current chapter with additional details being available in Silver and Wilson.[50] In the development of the "simultaneous" decision rules all of the assumptions discussed in Section 7.2.1 of Chapter 7 still apply except a value of Q is no longer prespecified.

9.5.1 Fixed Cost per Stockout Occasion, B_1 (analogous with Section 7.2.5)

The two equations (derived in part 2a of the appendix of the current chapter), in the two unknowns Q/σ_L and k (the latter being the safety factor) are

$$\frac{Q}{\sigma_L}=\frac{\text{EOQ}}{\sigma_L}\sqrt{\left[1+\frac{B_1}{A}p_{u\geq}(k)\right]}. \tag{9.8}$$

and

$$k=\sqrt{2\ln\left[\frac{1}{2\sqrt{2\pi}}\left(\frac{B_1}{A}\right)\left(\frac{\sigma_L}{Q}\right)\left(\frac{\text{EOQ}}{\sigma_L}\right)^2\right]} \tag{9.9}$$

where $\text{EOQ}=\sqrt{\dfrac{2AD}{vr}}$ is the basic economic order quantity

A is the fixed cost component incurred with each replenishment

D is the demand rate.

v is the unit variable cost of the item.

r is the carrying charge.

σ_L is the standard deviation of lead time demand.

$p_{u\geq}(k)$ is a function of the unit normal variable. (It is tabulated in Appendix C and a rational approximation for it is also available, as discussed earlier.)

A suggested iterative solution procedure is to initially set $Q=\text{EOQ}$, then solve for a corresponding k value in Eq. 9.9, then use this value in Eq. 9.8 to find a new Q value, etc. In certain cases, Eq. 9.9 will have the square root of a negative number; in such a case, k is set at its lowest allowable value as previously discussed in Section 7.2.5 and then Q is obtained using this k value in Eq. 9.8. Because of the convex nature of the functions involved, convergence to the true simultaneous solution pair (Q and k) is ensured. For further details concerning convexity, when the solution converges, etc. the reader should refer to Hadley and Whitin[24] (see also Problem 9.8).

From Eq. 9.8 it is seen that the simultaneous Q is always larger than the EOQ. This makes sense when one views Eq. 9.6. The EOQ is the Q value that minimizes the sum of the first two cost components. However, at that value the last term in Eq. 9.6 is still decreasing as Q increases. Thus it pays to go somewhat above the EOQ.

Once we have ascertained that the simultaneous Q is larger than the EOQ, it follows from Eq. 9.9 that the simultaneous k is smaller than or equal to the sequential k (they may be equal because of the boundary condition of a lowest allowable k). Again, this is intuitively appealing—the larger Q value makes stockout opportunities less frequent, hence we can afford to carry less safety stock.

Numerical Illustration—For illustrative purposes suppose that MIDAS was considering the use of a B_1 shortage cost rule for certain items with a B_1 value of \$32 per shortage occasion. One of these items, XSC-012, a liquid fixer, has the following characteristics:

$$D = 220 \text{ containers/yr.}$$

$$v = \$12.00/\text{container}$$

$$\bar{x}_L = 30 \text{ containers}$$

$$\sigma_L = 10.5 \text{ containers}$$

Using the MIDAS values of $A = \$3.20$ and $r = 0.24/\text{yr.}$ we have that the EOQ is

$$\text{EOQ} = \sqrt{\frac{2 \times 3.20 \times 220}{12.00 \times 0.24}} \simeq 22$$

Therefore,

$$\text{EOQ}/\sigma_L = 22/10.5 \simeq 2.1$$

Also

$$B_1/A = 32/3.20 = 10$$

The iterative procedure gives

Iteration Number	1	2	3	4	5
Q/σ_L	2.1	2.53	2.625	2.655	2.665
k	1.69	1.58	1.55	1.54	1.54

The order quantity (Q) is given by

$$Q = \sigma_L \times (\text{final value of } Q/\sigma_L) \simeq 30 \text{ containers}$$

and the reorder point (s) by

$$s = \bar{x}_L + k\sigma_L = 30 + 1.54(10.5) \simeq 46 \text{ containers}$$

Figure 9.6 % Cost Penalty Associated with Using the Sequential Approach for an (s, Q) System for the Case of a Fixed Cost per Stockout Occasion, B_1.

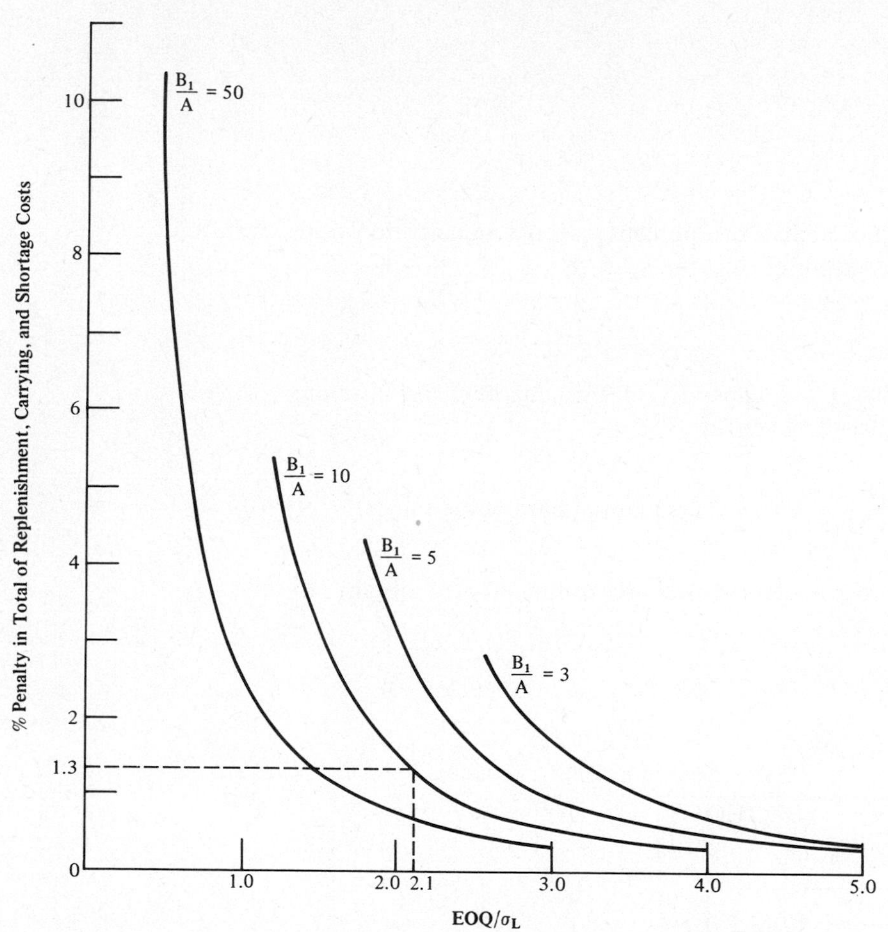

We certainly do not recommend hand solution of the two equations. Either a nomograph should be developed or the solution should be computerized.

The cost penalties of using the simpler sequential approach of Section 7.2.5 are shown in Figure 9.6 as a function of the two dimensionless parameters, EOQ/σ_L and B_1/A. The curves have been terminated to the left where the simultaneous solution first gives $k = 0$. It is seen that the percentage cost penalty, for a fixed value of B_1/A, increases as EOQ/σ_L decreases; that is, as the variability of demand increases relative to the EOQ. This is to be expected in that the sequential approach computes the order quantity, ignoring the variability. Further general comments will be made after the results for the other (B_2) case are presented.

Numerical Illustration of the Cost Penalty—For the item shown above

$$B_1/A = 10$$

and

$$EOQ/\sigma_L = 2.1$$

Use of Figure 9.6 shows that the percentage cost penalty for using the simple sequential procedure of Section 7.2.5. is

$$PCP \simeq 1.3\%$$

As shown in part 2b of the appendix of this chapter, the absolute cost penalty (ACP) in dollars is given by

$$ACP = \frac{PCP}{PCP + 100} \cdot ETRC \quad \text{(sequential parameter values)} \tag{9.10}$$

Now the sequential parameter values are quite easy to obtain. By the method of Section 7.2.5

$$Q = EOQ = 22$$

and k is selected to satisfy

$$k = \sqrt{2 \ln \left[\frac{1}{2\sqrt{2\pi}}\left(\frac{B_1}{A}\right)\left(\frac{EOQ}{\sigma_L}\right)\right]}$$

$$= \sqrt{2 \ln \left[\frac{1}{2\sqrt{2\pi}}(10)(2.1)\right]}$$

$$= 1.69$$

Now

$$ETRC\,(k, Q) = \left(\frac{Q}{2} + k\sigma_L\right)vr + \frac{D}{Q}[A + B_1 p_{u\geq}(k)]$$

$$ETRC\,(1.69, 22) = \left[\frac{22}{2} + (1.69)(10.5)\right](12.00)(0.24)$$

$$+ \frac{220}{22}[3.20 + 32(0.0455)]$$

$$= \$129.35/\text{yr.}$$

Thus, from Eq. 9.10 we have

$$\text{ACP} = \frac{1.3}{1.3+100}(129.35)$$
$$= \$1.66/\text{yr}.$$

an extremely small penalty despite the fact that the item has an annual usage of \$2,640.

9.5.2 *Fixed Fraction B_2 of Unit Value Charged per Unit Short*

The cost penalties of using the simpler sequential approach of section 7.2.6 are shown in Figure 9.7 as a function of the two dimensionless parameters, EOQ/σ_L and $B_2 v\sigma_L/A$. Note the strange shapes of the curves. Consider the curve for a particular value of $B_2 v\sigma_L/A$ (say 5). For very large EOQ/σ_L the cost penalty is negligible. One can show this as a consequence of the fact that, as EOQ/σ_L tends to infinity, the simultaneous k value (denoted by k_{sim}) tends to the sequential k value (denoted by k_{seq}); also the simultaneous Q (denoted by Q_{sim}) becomes equal to the EOQ. As EOQ/σ_L decreases (moving to the left) the percentage cost penalty increases as a consequence of Q_{sim} becoming farther and farther above the EOQ and k_{sim} becoming farther and farther below k_{seq}. However, eventually the unconstrained k_{sim} becomes smaller than the lowest allowable k and must be set to that value. As EOQ/σ_L gets small enough k_{seq} also has to be set equal to the lowest allowable k value. This also drives Q_{sim} back towards the EOQ and the cost penalty drops back to 0 as EOQ/σ_L becomes extremely small. It should be emphasized, as previously discussed in Chapter 7, that when EOQ/σ_L is very small the term for the expected shortage costs per year must be

$$\frac{D}{Q} B_2 v\sigma_L [G_u(k) - G_u(k + Q/\sigma_L)]$$

and not just

$$\frac{D}{Q} B_2 v\sigma_L G_u(k)$$

This behavior of the cost penalty reaching a maximum and then dropping back to 0 as EOQ/σ_L continues to decrease did not occur in Figure 9.6 for two reasons. First of all, we terminated the plots where k_{sim} first became 0 (the lowest allowable value). However, even if we continued plotting the results for lower EOQ/σ_L values, the curves would not turn back down. This is because in the B_1 model Q_{sim} always stays larger than the EOQ (as is evident from Eq. 9.8).

*Figure 9.7 % Cost Penalty Associated with Using the Sequential Approach for an (s, Q) System for the Case of **a Fixed Fraction B_2 of Unit Value Charged per Unit Short.***

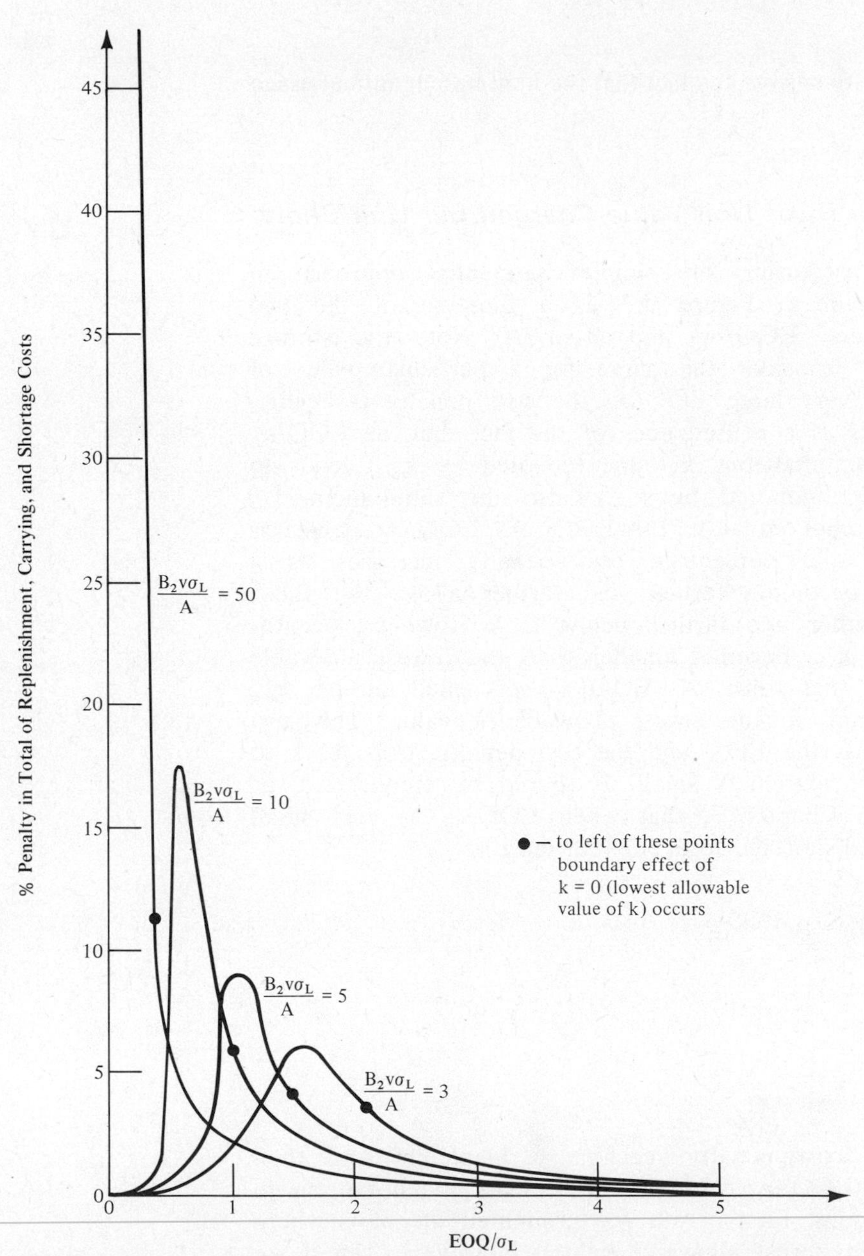

9.5.3 *Further Comments on the Results*

It is seen that in both cases only two dimensionless parameters influence the cost penalty.* In both cases one of the dimensionless parameters is EOQ/σ_L. Again, we see the appearance of the basic economic order quantity.

As illustrated by the case where the decision rules were explicitly shown, the simultaneous approach requires an iterative solution of two complicated equations in two unknowns. (The situation is even more complicated for (R, S) systems. There we can obtain only one equation that the two unknowns must satisfy. The solution procedure is to perform a one-dimensional search on R values. For each R value the single equation implies an associated value of k. This R, k pair is then substituted in the cost equation. The R value, and associated k, giving the lowest cost are selected.) Furthermore, although not explicitly shown here, in the B_2 case a table lookup or use of a rational approximation of a function of the unit normal variable is required at each iteration. This amount of complexity should not be taken lightly when considering the possible use of a simultaneous solution.

There is one common finding in both of Figures 9.6 and 9.7**. The percentage penalties are quite low as long as EOQ/σ_L does not become too small. Now, let us look more closely at the factor EOQ/σ_L.

$$\frac{\mathrm{EOQ}}{\sigma_L}=\sqrt{\frac{2AD}{vr\sigma_L^2}}=\sqrt{\frac{2ADv}{r(\sigma_L v)^2}} \tag{9.11}$$

As discussed in Chapter 2, some investigators (for example, see Reference 32) have found evidence that, *on the average*, $\sigma_L v$ tends to increase with Dv in the following manner:

$$\sigma_L v \simeq a_2 (Dv)^{b_2}$$

where b_2 is greater than 0.5. Substituting this in Eq. 9.11 yields

$$\frac{\mathrm{EOQ}}{\sigma_L}\simeq\sqrt{\frac{2ADv}{ra_2^2(Dv)^{2b_2}}}=C(Dv)^{0.5-b_2}$$

Because b_2 is larger than 0.5, this says that, on the average, EOQ/σ_L decreases as Dv increases, that is, low values of EOQ/σ_L are more likely

---

* *In (R, S) systems there is a third parameter, namely $\sigma_L/\bar{x}_L$.*

** *This finding also holds for (R, S) systems and for other service measures; in fact, the cost penalties are lower for the other service measures analyzed. (See Reference 50).*

with A items than with B or C items. From above, this implies that the larger percentage errors in using the sequential approach are more likely to occur with A items. This, together with the fact that the absolute costs associated with A items are high, indicates that the sophisticated simultaneous procedures *may* be justified, for some A items. A corollary is that the absolute savings of a simultaneous approach are not likely to be justified for B items; hence, the suggested use of the simpler sequential approach in Chapters 6 and 7 was appropriate.

To summarize, the purpose of this section has been to provide the practitioner with a guide as to when the sophisticated simultaneous derivation is justified. Furthermore, if enough items are involved, it may be appropriate to develop tables or curves (similar in concept to Figures 9.6 and 9.7) that give the best simultaneous values of k and Q as a function of the two dimensionless parameters involved. Buckland,[5] Christinsen et al,[9] Das,[14] Herron,[27,28] and Psoinos[44] have done this.

9.6 *Simulation in Production Planning and Inventory Control*

A manager, faced with a choice among two or more control systems or among values of a control parameter (for example, the reorder point) within a single control system, would ideally like to test out the effects, on the real system, of the two or more alternatives before making a decision. This is usually not practical because of the associated disruptive, and possibly disastrous (if one of the alternatives turns out to be really bad), effects of such experimentation. One method of predicting the effects of the different alternatives is through the use of mathematical models; in fact, this is certainly a major thrust of this book. However, particularly when there are dynamic and/or sequential* effects with uncertainty present (for example, forecast errors), it may not be possible to analytically develop (through deductive mathematical reasoning) the best choice among the alternatives. In such a case, one can turn to the use of simulation. Simulation still involves a model of the system. However, now, instead of using deductive mathematical reasoning, one instead, through the model, simulates through time the behavior of the real system under each alternative of interest. Conceptually, the approach is identical with that of using a physical simulation model of a prototype system, for example, the use of a small-scale hydraulic model of a

* *An example of a sequential effect would be the following: if A occurs before B, then C results, but if B occurs before A, then D takes place.*

series of reservoirs on a river system. More basically, prior to even considering possible courses of action, simulation can be used to simply obtain a better understanding of the system under study (perhaps via the development of a descriptive analytic model of the system).

In the next subsection we discuss other reasons for using simulation models in the areas of production planning and inventory control. This is followed by a discussion of some specific problems which are candidates for simulation. Finally, we provide some general comments concerning simulation, including references for those readers not familiar with the subject.

Simulation is a powerful but expensive tool. Therefore, it is natural to think of its use for problems involving class A items because of the high potential cost savings through improved decision rules for this group of items.

9.6.1 *Reasons for Simulation*

As discussed above, a major reason for using simulation is that *realistic* models of certain complex situations cannot be solved by deductive mathematical reasoning. Two other important reasons include

i. Verification of a mathematical solution—Most analytic models make certain assumptions which may affect the validity of the solution. In some situations incorrect solutions may be so costly when implemented that it makes good sense to first test the analytic solution by means of a simulation of the real system.

ii. Better understanding of the system—A simulation, by its nature, is much easier to understand than is a more abstract analytic solution. In fact, a simulation can be quite valuable as a teaching device (and not just within an academic environment). Also, in developing the micro-detail of a simulation the individuals involved are forced to closely examine the existing system. This close examination may lead to side benefits which turn out to be more rewarding than the results of the primary intent of the simulation.

9.6.2 *Production/Inventory Problems Which are Candidates for Simulation*

Illustrative problems which are candidates for solution by simulation methods include:

i. Products with interdependent demand—one example is where two products tend to be purchased together (for example, hot dogs and rolls in a supermarket), a second is where products may be substitutable (for example, two different colored dresses of the exact same size and style). A sample use of simulation within this latter context is provided by McGillivray and Silver.[38]

ii. Coordinated control—in Chapter 13 we shall discuss problems where two or more items are coordinated for replenishment purposes. Although the decision rules will be based on mathematical models not explicitly involving simulation, the latter was certainly used in the research phase in validating some of the assumptions which were made in developing the decision rules (see, for example, Reference 48). Other analytic approaches to determining the control parameters in a coordinated control context have required simulation (for example, Curry and Hartfiel[13] and Schaack and Silver[46]).

iii. Multi-echelon systems—it will become clear in Chapter 12 that analytical decision rules for multi-echelon systems involving probabilistic demand are out of the question, at least for the present. Therefore, simulation models have and will continue to be used to develop control guidelines for such situations. (see, for example, Connors et al.[10]).

iv. Transient effects of changes—almost all usable analytic models are appropriate for the so-called steady state situation, that is, far enough away from a starting point so that the initial conditions are not important. For example, Eqs. 5.8 and 5.9 of Chapter 5 show the total cycle stock and the total annual costs of replenishments as functions of the carrying charge r for steady state conditions. However, a manager might be vitally interested in the transient behavior of the cycle stock away from an initial position if the r value is suddenly changed. In particular, although the steady state cycle stock may be appreciably lower than the current stock level, this steady state value may not be achieved for some time out into the future. If the manager is counting on the released capital for other purposes, he certainly would like to know approximately how it will be released with time. In more complex situations where decision rules (as opposed to only parameter values) are changed, the transient situation can be worse than the present state of affairs even though in the steady state the new system will be better than the present one.

v. Job-shop scheduling—the very nature of a job shop, namely that many different orders are handled, each going through various work centres in different patterns, rules out an analytic solution to sequencing and other scheduling problems. Simulation is a valuable tool under these circumstances (see, for example, Buffa and Taubert[6]).

vi. Aggregate scheduling—as will be discussed in Chapter 17, the more realistic models of the costs and constraints of work force balancing and production smoothing to meet a seasonal demand pattern do not permit the analytic deduction of the best strategy to use. Consequently, with such models a type of simulation is used in that one evaluates the expected costs under a wide variety of options, searching for an alternative which has an associated, acceptably low, cost figure.

Other complex problems where simulation may be helpful will be discussed in Chapter 14. Undoubtedly, the reader can furnish additional examples from production/inventory environments with which he is familiar.

9.6.3 *General Comments on Simulation*

Simulation is a topic to which one could easily devote an entire book. Thus, we can, at best, briefly discuss only some of the key concepts. Somewhat more detail is provided in the tutorial exposition of Reference 49. In addition, there are a number of excellent texts on the subject including Hammersley and Handscomb,[25] Kleijnen,[35] Naylor et al.[41] and Tocher.[51]

Strategic Planning (Statistical Design)—The concern here is with what experiments to conduct. An interesting reference on this topic is Hunter and Naylor.[31] The discussion will be directed to two distinct types of uses of simulation models:

i. *Development of a descriptive analytic model of the system.* This involves the determination of exactly what variables have major impacts on the measure(s) of effectiveness. The context is very similar to that of physical experimentation where extensive guidelines have been developed for the design of experiments. An example of a physical context where experimentation has been useful is in the determination of what factors (e.g., supplier, worker, lighting level) affect the quality of output of a production process. However, there is one important difference between simulation and physical experimentation. In the latter there is very little control on the residual variability; in contrast, in simulation this variability can be markedly reduced by using the same sequence of random numbers for more than one experiment. This reduction in the residual variance in turn reduces the length of run required to achieve a specified accuracy. Of course, the use of the same set of random numbers causes the results to be statistically dependent; the statistical testing must take proper account of this dependence.

ii. *Selection of the best of a number of alternative control actions.* This is a situation not very common in physical experimentation. More commonly one is interested in the following type of question: Is one type of drug more effective than another in combatting a particular virus? The usual test criterion involves an hypothesis that the two drugs are not significantly different. This is not very helpful when trying to select from among several alternatives. Here, the experimental design should be sequential in nature (for example, as the results of the first runs are seen, the less attractive alternatives should be quickly discarded). Furthermore, statistical analyses should involve ordering procedures, that is, ranking of alternatives.

Some Tactical Considerations—Tactical planning follows the strategic considerations of the previous section. It determines how each of the runs specified in the experimental design is to be run, that is, it is concerned with efficiency of execution. A particularly good reference on this topic is the article by Conway.[11]

There are three fundamental tactical problems:

i. Equilibrium (or steady state)—it takes some time for the model to reach equilibrium, that is, behavior independent of starting conditions. We should not measure performance during this transient period unless it is the startup period which is of critical interest in the actual situation. An analogy where we would be interested in the transient period would be the testing of an automobile engine with cold morning starting conditions.

ii. As much reduction as possible of the variability of the measure of effectiveness—relative to most of the analytic solution procedures described elsewhere in this book, simulation is rather straightforward. Unfortunately, it is deceptively straightforward; using the most obvious approach of employing the true probability distributions may be a very inefficient way of proceeding, inefficient in the sense that the required simulation run length to achieve a desired level of accuracy in a measure of effectiveness could be materially reduced (equivalently, for a given run length, the accuracy could be substantially improved). One situation where this is likely to happen is where a rather rare event has a major impact on the measure of effectiveness. Modifications away from straightforward probability sampling are known as variance reducing techniques in that they are designed so as to reduce the variability in the measure of effectiveness for a given run length. Lucid discussions of variance reducing procedures are provided by Carter and Ignall[8] and Hammersley and Handscomb.[25]

iii. Variability and sample sizes—even when variance reduction techniques are properly utilized, some inherent variability will remain in the measure of effectiveness. The problem here is to ascertain how long a simulation run is required to achieve a desired accuracy in the measure of effectiveness, or more broadly speaking, we wish to select the run length so as to minimize the sum of the simulation costs and the expected costs of incorrect decisions made because of inaccurate results generated by the simulation. The statistical analysis is rather complicated. A relevant reference is the work of Fishman.[18]

Drawbacks of Simulation—As mentioned earlier, there are several appealing reasons for using simulation in place of an analytic model. As a counterbalance, we leave the reader with brief comments on some of the drawbacks of the approach.

Simulation tends to be expensive in terms of development (including programming) and, particularly, computer running time. It does not give a general solution to a problem; rather a separate run is required for each set of parameter values. This is in contrast to an analytic model, such as the economic order quantity of Eq. 5.4, where the one expression holds for a wide range of parameter values. Of course, the results of a simulation can be plotted as a function of an input parameter and interpolation then used to ascertain approximate results for intermediate values of the parameter.

A serious drawback of a simulation is that it compares only the set of alternatives input by the analyst or manager. At best, it provides evidence permitting the decision maker to select the preferred of the tested alternatives. However, the set selected for testing in the first place may only include rather poor solutions. To illustrate, consider a simulation designed to evaluate inventory control strategies for a high volume item. If the only two alternatives tested were to (i) use an order quantity of 1, versus (ii) use an order quantity of 2, the simulation would probably correctly say that 2 was preferable to 1. However, the most preferred quantity, likely in the hundreds or thousands, would not even be tested.

As mentioned earlier, simulation is very effective as a teaching device. In fact, after a while the user tends to accept some of the results without proper questioning. Obviously, this over-convincing property can be dangerous if the underlying model and/or the input data are in error.

9.7 *Summary*

In this chapter we have provided approaches for coping with the most important group of items, the Class A items. The methods of Sections 9.3 and 9.4 allow for control similar to that suggested for B items in earlier chapters, except for the use, in some cases, of the Poisson distribution. More elaborate methods of analysis and associated decision rules were shown in Sections 9.5 and 9.6. Above all else, the subjective guidelines of Section 9.2 should be carefully considered.

It is worth noting that A items most certainly play an important role in the multi-echelon and coordinated control situations to be discussed in Chapters 12 and 13. Finally, they are prime candidates for the single period models to be presented in the next chapter.

Appendix for Chapter 9—Derivations

1. *Indifference Curves for Poisson Demand*

a. *The Case of $Q=1$ and a B_2 Penalty*—Suppose an order-up-to-level S is used, or equivalently, an order for one unit is placed when the inventory position drops to the level $S-1$. In this system the inventory position is effectively always at the level S. All outstanding orders at a time t must arrive by time $t+L$ and no order placed after t can arrive by $t+L$. Therefore, the net (on-hand minus backorders) stock at time $t+L$ must be equal to the inventory position at time t minus any demand in t to $t+L$, that is,

$$(\text{Net stock at time } t+L) = S - (\text{demand in } L)$$

or

$$p_{NS}(n_0) = \text{prob}\,\{x = S - n_0\} \tag{9.12}$$

where

$p_{NS}(n_0)$ is the probability that the net stock at a random point in time takes on the value n_0.
x is the total demand in the replenishment lead time.

The expected on-hand inventory ($\bar{I}$) is the expected *positive* net stock, that is,

$$\begin{aligned}\bar{I} &= \sum_{n_0=0}^{S} n_0 p_{NS}(n_0) \\ &= \sum_{n_0=0}^{S} n_0 p_x(S-n_0)\end{aligned}$$

where

$p_x(x_0)$ is the probability that total lead time demand is x_0.

Substituting, $j = S - n_0$, we have

$$\bar{I} = \sum_{j=0}^{S} (S-j)p_x(j)$$

Furthermore, with Poisson demand, the probability that a particular demand requires backordering is equal to the probability that the net stock is zero or less,
that is,

$$\text{prob}\,\{\text{a demand is not satisfied}\} = p_{NS\leq}(0)$$

Using, Eq. 9.12 we have

$$\text{prob}\,\{\text{a demand is not satisfied}\} = p_{x\geq}(S)$$

The expected shortage costs per unit time (C_s) are

$$\begin{aligned} C_s &= (\text{cost per shortage}) \times (\text{expected demand per unit time}) \\ &\quad \times \text{prob}\,\{\text{a demand is not satisfied}\} \\ &= B_2 v D p_{x\geq}(S) \end{aligned}$$

Expected total relevant costs per unit time, as a function of S, are

$$\begin{aligned} \text{ETRC}(S) &= \bar{I}vr + C_s \\ &= vr \sum_{j=0}^{S} (S-j)p_x(j) + B_2 v D p_{x\geq}(S) \end{aligned}$$

A convenient method of solution is the use of indifference curves. These are obtained by equating ETRC(S) to ETRC($S+1$) for a given value of S. In general, this gives, after simplification,

$$\frac{p_x(S)}{p_{x\leq}(S)} = \frac{r}{DB_2} \tag{9.13}$$

However, because $Q = 1$, we have that

$$s = S - 1$$

Therefore, Eq. 9.13 can be written as

$$\frac{p_x(s+1)}{p_{x\leq}(s+1)} = \frac{r}{DB_2}$$

Equation 9.3 follows by recognizing that the lead time demand (x) has a Poisson distribution with mean $\bar{x}_L$.

b. *The Case of a B_1 Cost Penalty*—We assume that the cost B_1 is incurred only if the demand in the lead time *exceeds* the reorder point s.

The expected total relevant costs per unit time associated with using a reorder point s are

$$\text{ETRC}(s) = vr \sum_{x_0=0}^{s} (s - x_0)p_x(x_0) + \frac{D}{Q} B_1 p_{x>}(s)$$

Equating $\text{ETRC}(s) = \text{ETRC}(s+1)$ for indifference between s and $s+1$ leads to

$$\frac{p_x(s+1)}{p_{x\leq}(s)} = \frac{Qvr}{DB_1}$$

Again, Eq. 9.5 follows by recognizing that the lead time demand (x) has a Poisson distribution with mean $\bar{x}_L$.

2. *Simultaneous Solutions for Two Control Parameters*

a. *(s, Q) System with B_1 Cost Penalty*—We let

$$s = \bar{x}_L + k\sigma_L$$

From Eq. 9.6 the expected total relevant costs per unit time under use of a safety factor k and an order quantity Q are given by

$$\text{ETRC}(k, Q) = AD/Q + (Q/2 + k\sigma_L)vr + \frac{DB_1}{Q} p_{u\geq}(k)$$

To reduce the number of separate parameters that have to be considered we normalize by multiplying both sides by the constant term $2/vr\sigma_L$. We refer to the result as the normalized total relevant costs, NTRC(k, Q). Thus

$$\text{NTRC}(k, Q) = \frac{2AD}{vrQ\sigma_L} + \frac{Q}{\sigma_L} + 2k + \frac{2AD}{vrQ\sigma_L}\frac{B_1}{A} p_{u\geq}(k)$$

Recall that

$$\text{EOQ} = \sqrt{\frac{2AD}{vr}}$$

Therefore,

$$\text{NTRC}(k, Q) = \left(\frac{\text{EOQ}}{\sigma_L}\right)^2 \frac{\sigma_L}{Q}\left[1 + \frac{B_1}{A} p_{u\geq}(k)\right] + \frac{Q}{\sigma_L} + 2k$$

A necessary condition (unless we are at a boundary) for the minimization of a function of two variables is that the partial derivative with respect to each variable be set to zero.

$$\frac{\partial \text{NTRC}(k, Q)}{\partial Q} = -\left(\frac{\text{EOQ}}{\sigma_L}\right)^2 \frac{\sigma_L}{Q^2}\left[1+\frac{B_1}{A}\, p_{u\geq}(k)\right]+\frac{1}{\sigma_L}=0$$

or

$$\frac{Q}{\sigma_L}=\frac{\text{EOQ}}{\sigma_L}\sqrt{\left[1+\frac{B_1}{A}\, p_{u\geq}(k)\right]}$$

$$\frac{\partial \text{NTRC}(k, Q)}{\partial k}=2-\left(\frac{\text{EOQ}}{\sigma_L}\right)^2 \frac{\sigma_L}{Q}\frac{B_1}{A} f_u(k)=0$$

or

$$f_u(k)=2\frac{A}{B_1}\frac{Q}{\sigma_L}\left(\frac{\sigma_L}{\text{EOQ}}\right)^2$$

(*Note:* We have used the fact that

$$\frac{dp_{u\geq}(k)}{dk}=-f_u(k))$$

that is,

$$\frac{1}{\sqrt{2\pi}}\exp\left(-k^2/2\right)=2\frac{A}{B_1}\frac{Q}{\sigma_L}\left(\frac{\sigma_L}{\text{EOQ}}\right)^2$$

This simplifies to Eq. 9.9.

b. *Absolute Cost Penalty (ACP) for Using Sequential Approach*—From Eq. 9.7 we have that the *percentage* cost penalty (PCP) for using the sequential approach is

$$\text{PCP}=\frac{\begin{array}{l}[\text{ETRC (sequential parameter values)}\\ -\text{ETRC (simultaneous parameter values)}]\end{array}}{\text{ETRC (simultaneous parameter values)}}\times 100 \tag{9.14}$$

Now, the absolute cost penalty (ACP) is defined as

$$\text{ACP}=\text{ETRC(sequential parameter values)} - \text{ETRC(simultaneous parameter values)} \tag{9.15}$$

Therefore,

$$\text{ETRC(simultaneous parameter values)} = \text{ETRC(sequential parameter values)} - \text{ACP} \quad (9.16)$$

Substitution of Eqs. 9.15 and 9.16 into Eq. 9.14 gives

$$\text{PCP} = \frac{100(\text{ACP})}{\text{ETRC(sequential parameter values)} - \text{ACP}}$$

This can be solved for ACP to give

$$\text{ACP} = \frac{\text{PCP}}{\text{PCP} + 100} \cdot \text{ETRC(sequential parameter values)}$$

Problems for Chapter 9

Problem 9.1

Consider an (s, Q) system of control for a single item and with normally distributed forecast errors.

a. Find an expression that k must satisfy *given a Q value* if we wish to have an expected number of stockout occasions per year equal to N.

b. Derive the two simultaneous equations which Q and k must satisfy if we wish to minimize the total expected costs of replenishment and carrying inventory subject to the expected number of stockout occasions per year being N.

c. For the following example develop Q, k and the associated total relevant costs per year for two strategies:

i. $Q = \text{EOQ}$ and corresponding k.
ii. Simultaneous best (Q, k) pair.
Item characteristics:

$A = \$5$ $\quad v = \$2.00/\text{unit}$

$r = 0.16/\text{yr.}$ $\quad D = 1000 \text{ units/yr.}$

$\sigma_L = 80 \text{ units}$ $\quad N = 0.5/\text{yr.}$

Problem 9.2

Ceiling Drug is concerned about the inventory control of an important item. Currently they are using an (s, Q) system where Q is the EOQ and the safety factor k is selected based on a B_2v shortage costing method. Relevant parameter values are estimated to be:

$D = 2500 \text{ units/yr.}$
$v = \$10/\textit{unit}$
$A = \$5$
$r = 0.25/\text{yr.}$
$B_2 = 0.6$
$\bar{x}_L = 500 \text{ units}$
$\sigma_L = 100 \text{ units}$

a. What are the Q and s values currently in use?

b. Determine the simultaneous best values of Q and s.

c. What is the percent penalty (in the total of replenishment, carrying and shortage costs) of using the simpler sequential approach?

Problem 9.3

Consider the item in problem 9.2 and assume that the sequential approach is used. Suppose that, through improved forecasting, σ_L can be reduced to 70 units. Up to what extra amount per year should the company be willing to pay to achieve this improved forecasting?

Problem 9.4

Suppose that the Laplace distribution of lead time demand was appropriate for an item. For the B_1 shortage cost measure

a. Develop a method for *simultaneously* finding the Q and k values that minimize expected total costs in an (s, Q) system, where, as usual, $s = \bar{x}_L + k\sigma_L$.

b. Illustrate for the following item:

$D = 100 \text{ units/yr.}$
$A = \$20$
$v = \$8.00/\text{unit}$
$r = 0.2/\text{yr.}$
$\bar{x}_L = 7.5 \text{ units}$
$\sigma_L = 2.5 \text{ units}$
$B_1 = \$60$

c. For the item of part (b) what is the cost penalty for using $Q = \text{EOQ}$ followed by the best k given $Q = \text{EOQ}$?

Problem 9.5

Company X has an A item which it controls by an (s, S) system. The item has only a few customers. According to the (s, S) policy, if a large order drives the inventory position to or below s, enough is ordered to raise the position to S. Discuss the implicit cost tradeoff that the company is making in still raising the position to S even after a large demand has just occurred.

Problem 9.6

In relation to an (s, Q) inventory control system an operations analyst has made the following observation:

> *Suppose we determine Q from the EOQ, then find the safety factor from the "fraction demand satisfied routinely from shelf" criterion. Suppose that through explicit cost considerations we estimate r to be a particular value r_1. Now if we deliberately set r at a lower value r_2 when determining Q and s, we can reduce actual total relevant costs.*

a. Could the analyst be telling the truth? Attempt to develop an analytic proof.

b. Illustrate with an item having the following characteristics:

$$Dv = \$4{,}000/\text{yr.}$$
$$A = \$100$$
$$r_1 = 0.2/\text{yr.}$$
$$\sigma_L v = \$500$$
$$P_2 = 0.975$$

Problem 9.7

In an (s, Q) system it can be shown that the inventory position has a uniform distribution with probability 1/Q at each of the integers $s+1, s+2, \ldots, s+Q-1, s+Q$.

a. Using this result show, for Poisson demand and the B_2 shortage cost measure, that

$$\text{ETRC}(s) = vr\sum_{j=1}^{Q}\frac{1}{Q}\sum_{x_0=0}^{s+j}(s+j-x_0)p_{po}(x_0 \mid \bar{x}_L)$$
$$+B_2 vD\sum_{j=1}^{Q}\frac{1}{Q}\sum_{x_0=s+j}^{\infty}p_{po}(x_0 \mid \bar{x}_L)$$

b. Show that indifference between s and $s+1$ exists when

$$\frac{\sum_{j=1}^{Q} p_{po}(s+j \mid \bar{x}_L)}{\sum_{j=1}^{Q} p_{po\leq}(s+j \mid \bar{x}_L)} = \frac{r}{DB_2}$$

(*Note:* $p_{po}(x_0 \mid \bar{x}_L)$ is the p.m.f. of a Poisson variable with mean $\bar{x}_L$.)

Problem 9.8

Consider a situation where the lowest allowable k value is 0. The B_1 shortage costing method is appropriate.

a. On a plot of k versus Q/σ_L sketch each of Eqs. 9.8 and 9.9. (Hint: For each evaluate $dk/d(Q/\sigma_L)$. Also look at the behavior of each for limiting values of k and/or Q/σ_L.)

b. Attempt to ascertain under precisely what conditions there will be no simultaneous solution of the two equations.

c. Verify, using Eq. 9.6, that under such circumstances the cost minimizing solution is to set $k=0$ and

$$Q/\sigma_L = \text{EOQ}/\sigma_L\sqrt{1+0.5B_1/A}$$

Problem 9.9

Consider a perishable commodity that is outdated in exactly three basic periods. Suppose that an ordering decision is made at the beginning of each period and the replenishment arrives instantaneously. An order-up-to-level (R, S) system is used. The perishability of the item means that any units procured at the start of period t and still on-hand at the end of period $t+2$ must be discarded. Any demand not satisfied is lost (that is, there is no backordering). Simulate the behavior of such a system for 20 periods assuming $S=30$ units and the demands in the 20 consecutive periods are 11, 9, 3, 4, 14, 11, 7, 9, 11, 10, 12, 15, 8, 11, 8, 8, 14, 15, 5, 11. In particular, what is the average of each of the following?

i. inventory carried forward to the next period
ii. number of units discarded per period
iii. lost sales per period

Assume that at the start of period 1 (before an order is placed) there is no older stock, that is, we place an order for 30 units.

Problem 9.10
MIDAS Case D included a discussion on how the Inventory Control Manager placed orders for very expensive items. Comment on

a. "He tried to order only enough items to meet actual sales for the one month period, one lead time period ahead," in particular the choice of a one month period.
b. "To meet unexpected demand he usually ordered ten to twenty percent more than the number of units he was able to identify through purchase orders or commitments."

REFERENCES FOR CHAPTER 9

1. Archibald, B., E. A. Silver and R. Peterson. "Selecting the Probability Distribution of Demand in a Replenishment Lead Time." Working Paper No. 89, Department of Management Sciences, University of Waterloo, Waterloo, Ontario, Canada, August 1974.

2. Boothroyd, H. and R. Tomlinson. "The Stock Control of Engineering Spares—A Case Study." *Operational Research Quarterly*, Vol. 14, 1963, pp. 317–332.

3. Brenner, M. "A Cost Model for Determining the Sample Size in the Simulation of Inventory Systems." *Journal of Industrial Engineering*, Vol. XVII, No. 3, March, 1966, pp. 141–144.

4. Buchan, J. and E. Koenigsberg. *Scientific Inventory Management.* Prentice-Hall, Englewood Cliffs, N.J., 1963, pp. 349–353.

5. Buckland, J. C. L. "A Nomogram for Stock Control." *Operational Research Quarterly*, Vol. 20, No. 4, 1970, pp. 445–450.

6. Buffa, E. S. and W. H. Taubert. *Production-Inventory Systems: Planning and Control.* Irwin, 1972, Chap. 11–12.

7. Burton, R. and S. Jaquettc. "The Initial Provisioning Decision for Insurance Type Items." *Naval Research Logistics Quarterly*, Vol. 20, No. 1, March, 1973, pp. 123–146.

8. Carter, G. and E. Ignall. "Virtual Measures: A Variance Reduction Technique for Simulation." *Management Science*, Vol. 21, No. 6, February, 1975, pp. 607–616.

9. Christinsen, R. S., B. B. Rosenman and H. P. Galliher. *Recommendations on Implementation of Massachusetts Institute of Technology Research in Secondary Item Supply Control.* AD 268 372, Clearinghouse, U.S. Department of Commerce, 1959.

10. Connors, M., C. Coray, C. Cuccaro, W. Green, D. Low and H. Markowitz. "The Distribution System Simulator." *Management Science*, Vol. 18, No. 8, April, 1972, pp. B425–B453.

11. Conway, R. "Some Tactical Problems in Digital Simulation." *Management Science*, Vol. 10, No. 1, October, 1963, pp. 47–61.

12. Croston, J. D. "Stock Levels for Slow-Moving Items." *Operational Research Quarterly*, Vol. 25, No. 1, March, 1974, pp. 123–130.

13. Curry, D. and D. Hartfiel. "A Constrained Joint Setup Cost Inventory Model." *INFOR*, Vol. 13, No. 3, October, 1975, pp. 316–327.

14. Das, C. "Some Aids for Lot-Size Inventory Control under Normal Lead Time Demand." *AIIE Transactions*, Vol. 7, No. 1, March, 1975, pp. 77–79.

15. Das, C. "Approximate Solutions to the (Q, r) Inventory Model for Gamma Lead Time Demand." *Management Science*, Vol. 22, No. 9, May, 1976, pp. 1043–1047.

16. Dickson, G. and P. Mailandt. "Some Pitfalls of Solving Inventory

Problems by Simulation." *Production and Inventory Management,* Vol. 13, No. 2, June, 1972, pp. 74–86.

17. Feeney, G. J. and C. C. Sherbrooke. "The $(S-1, S)$ Inventory Policy Under Compound Poisson Demand." *Management Science,* Vol. 12, No. 5, January, 1966, pp. 391–411.

18. Fishman, G. "Digital Computer Simulation: Estimating Sample Size." RAND Publication RM-5866-PR, Santa Monica, Calif., 1969.

19. Foster, F., J. Rosenhead and V. Siskind. "The Effect of the Demand Distribution in Inventory Models Combining Holding, Stockout and Re-order Costs." *Journal of Royal Statistical Society,* Series B. Vol. 33:2, 1971, pp. 312–325.

20. Galliher, H., P. Morse and M. Simond. "Dynamics of Two Classes of Continuous Review Inventory Systems." *Operations Research,* Vol. 7, No. 3, June, 1959, pp. 362–384.

21. Geisler, M. "A Test of a Statistical Method for Computing Selected Inventory Model Characteristics by Simulation." *Management Science,* Vol. 10, No. 4, July, 1964, pp. 709–715.

22. Gross, D. and J. Ince. "A Comparison and Evaluation of Approximate Continuous Review Inventory Models." *International Journal of Production Research,* Vol. 13, No. 1, 1975, pp. 9–23.

23. Gross, D. and A. Soriano. "The Effects of Reducing Leadtime on Inventory Levels—Simulation Analysis." *Management Science,* Vol. 16, No. 2, October, 1969, pp. 61–76.

24. Hadley, G. and T. Whitin. *Analysis of Inventory Systems.* Prentice-Hall, Englewood Cliffs, N.J., 1963, Chapter 4.

25. Hammersley, J. M. and D. C. Handscomb. *Monte Carlo Methods.* Methuen & Co. Ltd., London, England, 1964.

26. Herron, D. P. "Use of Dimensionless Ratios to Determine Minimum-Cost Inventory Quantities." *Naval Research Logistics Quarterly,* Vol. 13, 1966, pp. 167–176.

27. Herron, D. P. "Inventory Management for Minimum Cost." *Management Science,* Vol. 14, No. 4, December, 1967, pp. B219–B235.

28. Herron, D. P. "A Manager's Guide to Setting Inventory Policies." *Production and Inventory Management,* Vol. 11, No. 4, 1970, pp. 66–78.

29. Heyvaert, A. C. and A. Hurt. "Inventory Management of Slow-Moving Parts." *Operations Research,* Vol. 4, No. 5, October, 1956, pp. 572–580.

30. Hunt, J. "Balancing Accuracy and Simplicity in Determining Reorder Points." *Management Science,* Vol. 12, No. 4, December, 1965, pp. 94–103.

31. Hunter, J. S. and T. H. Naylor. "Experimental Designs for Computer Simulation Experiments." *Management Science,* Vol. 16, No. 7, March, 1970, pp. 422–434.

32. IBM. *Wholesale IMPACT—Advanced Principles and Implementation Reference Manual.* IBM Technical Publications Department, White Plains, New York, 1965, Chapter 2.

33. Ignall, E. "On Experimental Designs for Computer Simulation Experiments." *Management Science*, Vol. 18, No. 7, March, 1972, pp. 384–388.

34. Karush, W. "A Queueing Model for an Inventory Problem." *Operations Research*, Vol. 5, No. 5, October, 1957, pp. 693–703.

35. Kleijnen, J. P. C. *Statistics and Simulation.* Marcel Dekker Inc., New York, N.Y., 1975.

36. Lampkin, W. "A Review of Inventory Control Theory." *The Production Engineer*, Vol. 46, No. 2, 1967, pp. 57–66.

37. Lampkin, W. and A. Flowerdew. "Computation of Optimum Re-order Levels and Quantities for a Re-order Level Stock Control System." *Operational Research Quarterly*, Vol. 14, 1963, pp. 263–278.

38. McGillivray, A. R. and E. A. Silver. "Accounting for Substitutable Demand in Inventory Control." Working Paper 101, Department of Management Sciences, University of Waterloo, Waterloo, Ontario, Canada, 1976.

39. Melese, M., Barache, Comes, Elina et Hestaux. "La Gestion des Stocks de Pieces de Rechange dans la Siderurgie." ("Inventory Control of Spare Parts in the French Steel Industry.") *Proceedings of the Second International Conference on Operational Research*, 1960, English Universities Press, pp. 309–323.

40. Mitchell, G. H. "Problems of Controlling Slow-Moving Engineering Spares." *Operational Research Quarterly*, Vol. 13, 1962, pp. 23–39.

41. Naylor, T. H., J. L. Balintfy, D. S. Burdick and K. Chu. *Computer Simulation Techniques.* Wiley, New York, N.Y., 1968.

42. Nemhauser, G. "A Note on Lot Sizes and Safety Stock Level." *Journal of Industrial Engineering*, Vol. XVII, No. 7, July, 1966, pp. 389–390.

43. Parker, L. L. "Economical Order Quantities and Reorder Points with Uncertain Demand." *Naval Research Logistics Quarterly*, Vol. 11, No. 4, December, 1964, pp. 351–358.

44. Psoinos, D. "On the Joint Calculation of Safety Stocks and Replenishment Order Quantities." *Operational Research Quarterly*, Vol. 25, No. 1, March, 1974, pp. 173–177.

45. THE RAND CORPORATION. *One Million Random Digits and 100,000 Normal Deviates.* The Free Press, Glencoe, Illinois, 1955.

46. Schaack, J. P. and E. A. Silver. "A Procedure, Involving Simulation, for Selecting the Control Variables of an (s, c, S) Joint Ordering Strategy." *INFOR*, Vol. 10, No. 2, June, 1972, pp. 154–170.

47. Silver, E. A. "A Modified Formula for Calculating Customer Service Under Continuous Inventory Review." *AIIE Transactions*, Vol. II, No. 3, September, 1970, pp. 241–245.

48. Silver, E. A. "A Control System for Coordinated Inventory Replenishment." *International Journal of Production Research*, Vol. 12, No. 6, 1974, pp. 647–671.

49. Silver, E. A. "A Tutorial on Simulation." OR Report 32, Département de Mathématiques, Ecole Polytechnique Fédérale de Lausanne, Switzerland, 1977.

50. Silver, E. A. and T. G. Wilson. "Cost Penalities of Simplified Procedures for Selecting Reorder

Points and Order Quantities." *Proceedings of the Fifteenth Annual International Conference of the American Production and Inventory Control Society*, October, 1972, pp. 219–234.

51. Tocher, K. D. *The Art of Simulation.* English Universities Press Ltd., London, England, 1963.

52. Vazsonyi, A. "Comments on a Paper by Karush." *Operations Research*, Vol. 8, No. 3, May–June, 1960, pp. 418–420.

53. Wagner, H., M. O'Hagan and B. Lundh. "An Empirical Study of Exactly and Approximately Optimal Inventory Policies." *Management Science*, Vol. 11, No. 7, May, 1965, pp. 690–723.

54. Whitin T. and J. Youngs. "A Method for Calculating Optimal Inventory Levels and Delivery Time." *Naval Research Logistics Quarterly*, Vol. 2, No. 3, September, 1955, pp. 157–173.

CHAPTER TEN

Decision Rules for the Case of a Single Relevant Period

The developments in Chapters 5 to 9 were all based on the assumption of a demand pattern for an item continuing well into the future (possibly on a time-varying basis), that is, "a going concern" with the opportunity to store inventory from one selling period to the next. In the present chapter we remove this ability to store inventory from one period to the next; hence, the problem that we study is known as the single period problem. Decision situations where this framework is relevant include:

i. The newsboy—how many copies of a particular issue of a newspaper to stock?

ii. The Christmas tree vendor—how many trees should he purchase to put on sale in his lot?

iii. The cafeteria manager—how many hot meals of a particular type should he prepare prior to the arrival of his customers?

iv. The supplies manager in a remote region (for example, medical and welfare work in northern Canada)—what quantity of supplies should be brought in by boat prior to the long winter freezeup?

v. The farmer—what quantity of a particular crop should he plant in a specific season?

vi. The toy manufacturer—a particular product shows significant potential sales as a "fad" item. How many units should be produced on the one major production run to be made?

vii. The garment manufacturer—what quantity of a particular style good should he produce prior to the short selling season?

The decoupling property of a single period being relevant for each replenishment decision significantly simplifies the analysis in contrast with the more general case where inventory is storable from one period to the next and, hence, the effects of a replenishment action can last for several periods, interacting with later replenishment actions. Nonetheless, particularly in the style goods context where demand is rather unpredictable and there may be production constraints involved, managers find the single period problem quite difficult to handle. The main objective of this chapter is to present some decision rules which will help cope with such situations.

In Section 10.1 we spell out in more detail the characteristics (and associated complexity) of the style goods version of the single period problem. The models presented in Sections 10.2 through 10.4 deal with progressively more realistic, but more complicated, versions of the problem. In Section 10.2 we are concerned with the case of a single product with but one replenishment (procurement or production) opportunity and with no constraint on the allowable replenishment quantity. This is followed in Section 10.3 by a similar situation except that now there is an upper limit on the replenishment quantity. Section 10.4 deals with the important generalization to more than one product. Again, an exchange curve is an important by-product of the analysis. Next, in Section 10.5 we provide some brief comments concerning the situation where there are several production periods prior to the selling season and forecasts of demand are revised as one moves through the production phase. The chapter is completed by a discussion in Section 10.6 of several other research findings relevant to the single period problem.

10.1 *The Style Goods Problem*

The main features of the style goods problem are:

i. There is a relatively short (no longer than 3 or 4 months) selling season with a well defined beginning and end.

ii. The buyer (at the stocking point) or producer has to commit himself to a large extent, in terms of how much of each stockkeeping unit to order or produce, prior to the start of the selling season. However,

iii. There may be one or more opportunities for replenishment after the initial order is placed. Such replenishment actions may be taken prior to the selling season (if the forecast of demand has risen appreciably) or during the early part of the selling season itself (if actual demand to date indicates that the original forecast was considerably low).

iv. Forecasts prior to the season include considerable uncertainty stemming from the long period of inactivity (no sales) between seasons. During this inactive period, the economic conditions and/or style considerations may have changed appreciably. Consequently, forecast revisions tend to be heavily influenced by firm orders or sales to date in the current season, far more than in the case of reasonably stable items (as discussed in Chapter 4).

v. When the total demand in the season exceeds the stock made available, there are associated underage costs. These may simply be lost profit if the sales are foregone. On the other hand, they may represent the added costs of expediting (for example, a special order by air freight) or acquiring the material from a competitor at a high unit value.

vi. When the total demand in the season turns out to be less than the stock made available, overage costs result. The unit salvage value of leftover inventory at the end of a season is likely to be quite low (well below the unit acquisition cost). It is quite expensive to carry stock over to the next season; moreover, there is no guarantee that such leftover stock will even sell at that time. Markdowns (that is, reduced selling prices) and/or transfers (between locations) may be used to avoid leftover stock.

vii. Style good products are often substitutable. Depending upon how finely one defines a "style," a stockout in one s.k.u. does not necessarily mean a lost sale, because the demand may be satisfied by another product.

viii. Sales of style goods are usually influenced by promotional activities, space allocation in the store, etc.

In the simplest form of the style goods problem, wherein we ignore the last two points made above as well as markdowns and transfers, the remaining decision variables are the timing and magnitudes of the replenishment quantities. To illustrate the complexity of even this simplified version one need only refer to the work of Wadsworth[23] who considered the case of a style good sold in a fall season with raw material acquisition required in the spring, summer production of unlimited capacity, and a limited amount of fall production (after the total season demand is known exactly) being possible but at a higher unit cost than the summer production. The complex nature of Wadsworth's solution to this problem indicates that an *exact* analysis of a more realistic style goods problem is out of the question. For this reason, as elsewhere in this book, we advocate the use of heuristic methods designed to generate *reasonable* solutions.

10.2 *The Simplest Case: The Unconstrained, Single Item, Newsboy Problem*

10.2.1 *Determination of the Best Order Quantity*

Let us consider the situation faced by the owner of a newstand. Each day he has to decide on the number of copies of a particular paper to stock. There is an underage cost, c_u, associated with each demand which he cannot meet and an overage cost, c_o, associated with each copy that he is not able to sell. Suppose the underage cost was exactly equal to the overage cost. Then it seems intuitively reasonable that he would want to select the number (Q) of copies to purchase such that there was a 50 percent chance of the total demand being below Q and a 50 percent chance of it being above Q. But what about the case where $c_u = 2c_o$ or $c_u = 3c_o$? It turns out that his decision rule should be to select the Q^* value which satisfies

$$p_{x<}(Q^*) = \frac{c_u}{c_u + c_o} \tag{10.1}$$

where $p_{x<}(x_0)$ is the probability that the total demand x is less than the value x_0.

Notice that when $c_u = c_o$ Eq. 10.1 gives

$$p_{x<}(Q^*) = 0.5$$

which is the intuitive result discussed above.

When $c_u = 2c_o$, we have from Eq. 10.1

$$p_{x<}(Q^*) = \frac{2c_o}{2c_o + c_o} = \frac{2}{3}$$

that is, he should select the order quantity such that the probability of the total demand being smaller than it is $\frac{2}{3}$.

Now let us reflect on how Eq. 10.1 is developed. It is simplest to use an approach, namely marginal analysis, which is different conceptually from the usual approach, namely total cost analysis, which we have been using earlier in the book. The argument proceeds as follows:

Consider the Qth unit purchased. It will be sold if, and only if, the total demand x equals or exceeds Q, otherwise an overage cost will be incurred for this Qth unit. However, if the demand equals or exceeds Q, we have avoided an underage cost by having the Qth unit available. In other words, we have

Specific Cost Element	Probability that the specific cost element is incurred (or avoided) by the acquisition of the Qth unit	Expected value of the specific cost element associated with the Qth unit (product of previous two columns)
Overage, c_o	prob {demand is less than Q} $= p_{x<}(Q)$	$c_o p_{x<}(Q)$
Underage, c_u	prob {demand is greater than or equal to Q} $= 1 - p_{x<}(Q)$	$c_u[1 - p_{x<}(Q)]$

Consider a particular Qth unit. If the expected overage cost associated with acquiring it exceeded the expected saving in underage costs, we would not want to acquire that unit. In fact, we might not want to acquire the $(Q-1)$st, the $(Q-2)$nd, etc. On the other hand, if the expected saving in underage costs exceeded the expected overage cost associated with acquiring the Qth unit, we would want to acquire it. However, we might also wish to acquire the $(Q+1)$st, the $(Q+2)$nd, etc. The last unit (Q^*) we would want to acquire is that one where the expected overage cost incurred exactly equalled the expected underage cost saved, that is, Q^* must satisfy

$$c_o p_{x<}(Q^*) = c_u[1 - p_{x<}(Q^*)]$$

or

$$p_{x<}(Q^*) = \frac{c_u}{c_u + c_o}$$

which is Eq. 10.1.

The solution of Eq. 10.1 is shown graphically in Figure 10.1 where we have plotted the cumulative distribution of demand, $p_{x<}(x_0)$. One locates the value of $c_u/(c_u + c_o)$ on the vertical axis, comes across horizontally to the curve, then down vertically to read the corresponding x_0 which is the Q^*

Figure 10.1 Graphical Solution of the Newsboy Problem.

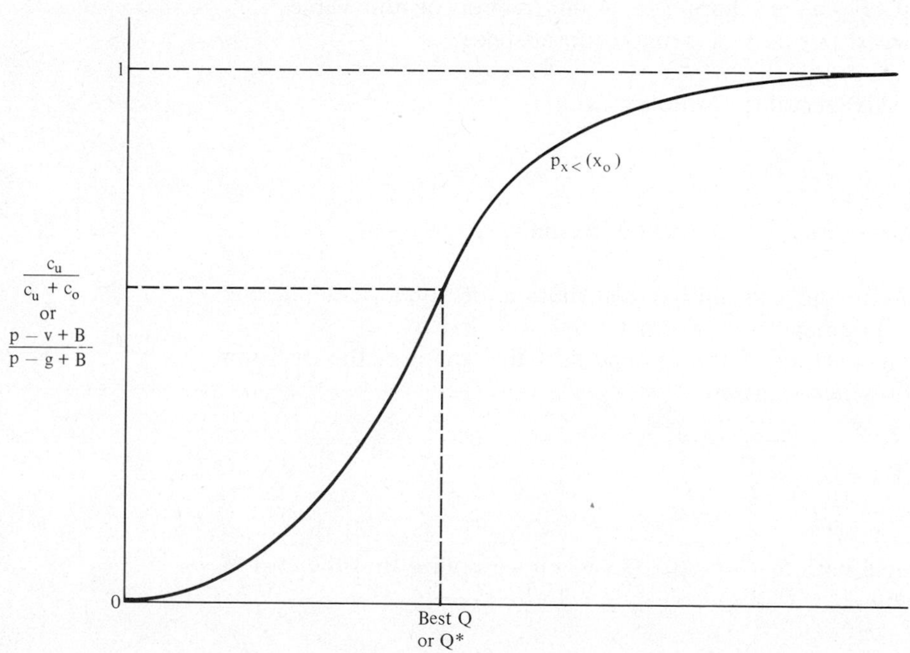

value. There is always a solution because the fraction lies between zero and unity which is the range covered by the cumulative distribution.

We have just seen that the marginal cost analysis approach leads to the decision rule of Eq. 10.1 in a rather straight-forward fashion. However, it does not give us an expression for evaluating the expected costs when any particular Q value is used. The alternative approach of minimizing total cost does, but the analysis is considerably more complicated as is demonstrated for the analogous case of total profit maximization in part 1a of the appendix of this chapter.

10.2.2 *An Equivalent Result Obtained through Profit Maximization*

The above discussion has centred on cost minimization. Instead, let us now approach the problem from a profit maximization standpoint. Let

v be the acquisition cost, in dollars/unit

p be the revenue per sale (that is, the selling price), in dollars/unit

B (or $B_2 v$) be the penalty for not satisfying demand, in dollars/unit (B_2, as in Chapter 7, is the fraction of unit value that is charged per unit of demand unsatisfied)

g be the salvage value, in dollars/unit

As earlier, we let

Q be the quantity to be stocked, in units

and $p_{x<}(x_0)$ represent the cumulative distribution of total demand, the probability that total demand x takes on a value less than x_0.

Then, as shown in part 1a of the appendix of this chapter, the decision rule is to select Q^* which satisfies

$$p_{x<}(Q^*) = \frac{p - v + B}{p - g + B} \tag{10.2}$$

This result is identical with that of Eq. 10.1 when we realize that the cost of underage is given by

$$c_u = p - v + B$$

and the cost of overage is

$$c_o = v - g$$

Because the cumulative distribution function is non-decreasing as its argument increases, we can make the following intuitively appealing deductions from Eq. 10.2.

i. If the sales price, cost per unit short, or salvage value increases, the best Q increases.

ii. If the acquisition cost per unit increases, the best Q decreases.

10.2.3 *The Case of Discrete Demand*

Strictly speaking, when we are dealing with discrete (integer) units of demand and purchase quantity, it is unlikely that there is an integer Q value which exactly satisfies Eq. 10.1 or Eq. 10.2. To illustrate, suppose we have an item where

$$\frac{c_u}{c_u + c_o} = 0.68$$

and the probability distribution of demand is as shown in the second row of the following table (the third row is derived from the second row):

no. of units, x_0	1	2	3	4	5	Total
$p_x(x_0) = \text{prob}\,(x = x_0)$	0.2	0.3	0.2	0.2	0.1	1
$p_{x<}(x_0) = \text{prob}\,(x < x_0)$	0	0.2	0.5	0.7	0.9	—

It is seen from the third row that there is no Q that would give $p_{x<}(Q) = 0.68$, the nearest values are $p_{x<}(3) = 0.5$ and $p_{x<}(4) = 0.7$. As shown in part 1b of the appendix of this chapter, when discrete units are used, the best value of Q is the smallest Q value which satisfies

$$p_{x\leq}(Q) > \frac{c_u}{c_u + c_o} = \frac{p - v + B}{p - g + B} \tag{10.3}$$

Numerical Illustration—Consider the case of a Mennonite farmer who raises cattle and sells the beef at the weekly farmer's market in Kitchener–Waterloo, Ontario. He is particularly concerned about a specific expensive cut of meat. He sells it in a uniform size of 5 kilograms at a price of \$30. He wants to know how many 5 kg. units to take to market. Demand is not known with certainty, rather all that he has available are frequency counts of the total 5 kg. units demanded in each of the last 20 market sessions. These are chronologically as follows: 1, 3, 3, 2, 2, 5, 1, 2, 4, 4, 2, 3, 4, 1, 5, 2, 2, 3, 1, and 4. Frequency counts of how many 1's, how many 2's, etc. occurred in the 20 weeks are shown in the second row of Table 10.1. The third row is a set of estimates of the probabilities of the various sized demands based upon the assumption that the historical occurrences are representative of the probabilities, for example, in 6 out of 20 weeks the total demand has been 2 units, therefore the probability of a total demand of 2 units is approximately 6/20 or 0.3.

Table 10.1 *Demand Distribution for Farmer's Meat Example*

i. Demand in a session x_0	1	2	3	4	5	Total
ii. Frequency count $N(x_0)$	4	6	4	4	2	20
iii. $p_x(x_0) \simeq \dfrac{N(x_0)}{20}$	0.2	0.3	0.2	0.2	0.1	1.0
iv. $p_{x\leq}(x_0)$	0.2	0.5	0.7	0.9	1.0	—

The farmer stores the processed beef in a freezer on his farm. He estimates the value of a 5 kg. unit to be $19 after he removes it from the freezer and gets it to the market. Once the beef is brought to market he chooses not to take it home and refreeze it. Therefore, any leftover beef at the market he sells to a local butcher at a discount price of $15 per 5 kg. unit. Finally, other than the foregone profit, he feels that there is no additional cost (for example, loss of good will) associated with not satisfying a demand.

According to our notation

$$p = \$30/\text{unit}$$

$$v = \$19/\text{unit}$$

$$B = 0$$

$$g = \$15/\text{unit}$$

Therefore

$$\frac{p-v+B}{p-g+B} = \frac{30-19+0}{30-15+0} = 0.734$$

Use of the fourth row of Table 10.1, together with the decision rule of Eq. 10.3, shows that he should bring four 5 kg. units to market. It is interesting to note that the average or expected demand is

$$\bar{x} = \sum_{x_0} x_0 p_x(x_0) = (1)\,(0.2) + 2\,(0.3) + 3\,(0.2) + 4\,(0.2) + 5\,(0.1)$$
$$= 2.7 \text{ units}$$

Therefore, because of the economics, the best strategy is to take (4−2.7) or 1.3 units above the average demand.

10.2.4 *The Case of Normally Distributed Demand*

The result of Eq. 10.1 or 10.2 is applicable for any distribution of total demand. Again, it is worthwhile, as in Chapters 6 and 7, to look at the special case of normally distributed demand. First of all, such a distribution tends to be applicable in a significant number of situations. Secondly, as we shall see, sensitivity analysis (effects of incorrectly specifying the order quantity Q) can be performed rather easily when demand is normal, in contrast with the case of a general probability distribution.

Suppose the demand x is normally distributed with a mean of $\bar{x}$ and a standard deviation of σ_x and we define

$$k = \frac{Q - \bar{x}}{\sigma_x} \tag{10.4}$$

This is analogous to what we did in Chapters 6 and 7. Then, as shown in part 1c of the appendix of this chapter, the decision rule of Eq. 10.2 transforms to

Select k such that

$$p_{u\geq}(k) = \frac{v - g}{p - g + B} \tag{10.5}$$

where $p_{u\geq}(k)$ is the probability that a unit normal variable takes on a value of k or larger; this is a widely tabulated function (see, for example, Table C.1 of Appendix C) first introduced in Chapter 6. Then, from Eq. 10.4, set

$$Q = \bar{x} + k\sigma_x \tag{10.6}$$

Furthermore, in this case, as shown in the appendix, we obtain a relatively simple expression for expected profit as a function of Q, namely

$$E[P(Q)] = (p - g)\bar{x} - (v - g)Q - (p - g + B)\sigma_x G_u\left(\frac{Q - \bar{x}}{\sigma_x}\right) \tag{10.7}$$

where $G_u(u_0)$ is a tabulated function of the unit normal variable (see Table C.1 of Appendix C) first introduced in Chapter 7; in fact, Schlaifer[19] defines the $G_u(\cdot)$ function through consideration of a problem of this type.

Numerical Illustration—MIDAS supplies several products to the Canadian Federal Government through a "National Standing Offer Contract" until March 31, 1978. Unfortunately from MIDAS' standpoint, such a contract does not specify a fixed amount of each product. The case of product PMF-198 poses a serious problem. This product, which is sold to the Government only, is 100 foot rolls of 24 inch wide lithographic film. For technological reasons the plant in Germany is discontinuing the product as of June 15, 1977. The issue is one of deciding on how many rolls to buy before the line is discontinued. The selling price is \$50.30 per roll whereas the unit cost to MIDAS is \$35.10. Should the need arise the product could be bought from competitors at a retail price of approximately \$60.00 per roll. Any material not sold to the Government could be disposed of at a special price of \$25.00 per roll.

Through an analysis of historical buying behavior of the Government on this and similar products, MIDAS' inventory manager is willing to assume that the total demand through March 31, 1978, is approximately normally distributed with a mean of 900 rolls and a standard deviation of 122 rolls.*

---

* *One way of arriving at an estimate of the standard deviation would be to specify the probability that total demand exceeded a certain value (other than the mean), for example, prob* $(x \geq 1100) = 0.05$ *leads to the standard deviation of* 122 *rolls, viz:*

For x normally distributed,

$$\text{prob}\,(x \geq 1100) = p_{u\geq}\left(\frac{1100 - \bar{x}}{\sigma_x}\right) = p_{u\geq}\left(\frac{200}{\sigma_x}\right)$$

But from the table in Appendix C

$$p_{u\geq}(1.645) = 0.05$$

Therefore

$$\frac{200}{\sigma_x} = 1.645$$

or

$$\sigma_x = 122.$$

Using our notation

$$p = \$50.30/\text{roll}$$

$$v = \$35.10/\text{roll}$$

$$g = \$25.00/\text{roll}$$

$$B = (\$60.00 - 50.30) \text{ or } \$9.70/\text{roll}$$

From Eq. 10.5 we want

$$p_{u\geq}(k) = \frac{35.10 - 25}{50.30 - 25 + 9.70} = 0.288$$

From the table in Appendix C we have

$$k = 0.56$$

Therefore, Eq. 10.6 gives

$$Q = 900 + 0.56(122) = 968.3, \text{ say } 968 \text{ rolls.}$$

Use of Eq. 10.7 gives the expected profit for various values of Q; the results are shown in Table 10.2 and in Figure 10.2. Again, the curve is quite shallow around the best Q value. It is interesting to note that following the temptation of ordering the expected demand, namely $Q = 900$, would lead to a 2.0 percent reduction in expected profit.

Table 10.2 Sensitivity of Expected Profit to Q Value Selected in Film Example

Q	% Deviation from Best Q (namely 968)	$E[P(Q)]$	% of Best Possible Profit
700	27.7	8670	71.0
800	17.4	10690	87.5
900	7.0	11980	98.0
930	3.9	12150	99.4
968	0	12220	100
1000	3.3	12170	99.6
1030	6.4	12050	98.6
1100	13.6	11570	94.7
1200	24.0	10640	87.1

Figure 10.2 Typical Sensitivity to Errors in Q in the Newsboy Context.

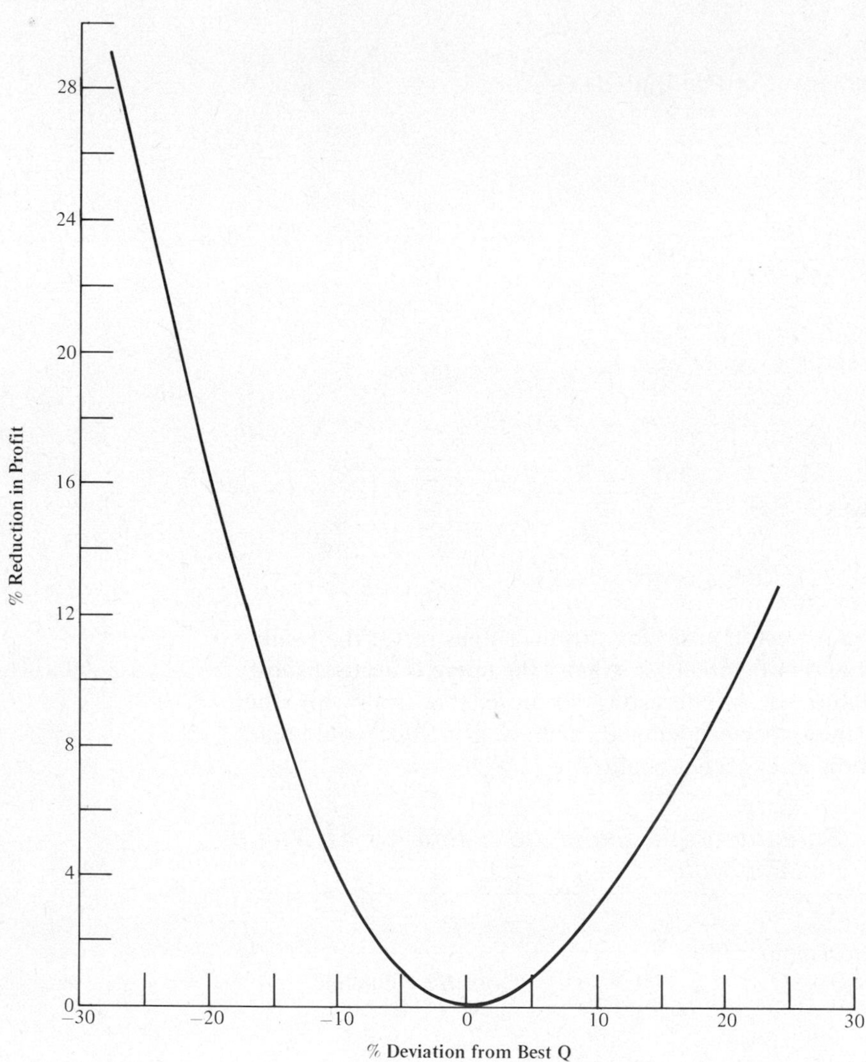

10.2.5 *The Case of a Fixed Charge to Place the Order*

Where there is a high enough fixed setup cost to place any size order the best strategy may be to not order anything at all. The decision would be based upon comparing the cost of not ordering at all with the expected profit (ignoring the fixed cost as we did earlier) under use of the Q^* value, viz.:

If $E[P(Q^*)] > A - B\bar{x}$, order Q^*.

If $E[P(Q^*)] < A - B\bar{x}$, order nothing.

In general, $E[P(Q^*)]$ is quite difficult to evaluate. In the case of normally distributed demand Eq. 10.7 is of considerable help in this direction.

10.2.6 *Developing the Probability Distribution of Demand*

In certain single-period contexts (illustrated by the newsboy and farmer examples), where conditions tend to change slowly with time, it is not unreasonable to think that an historically observed histogram of total demands can be used as a direct estimate of the probability distribution of demand in a future period; for example, if in 2 out of 20 historical periods the total demand was 6, then the probability that a 6 will occur in a future period is $\frac{2}{20}$ or 0.10.

However, there are other contexts of the single period problem where historical data are lacking or are, at best, not likely to be representative of future conditions. This is particularly true in the style goods context. In such situations one can turn to the use of Bayesian approaches. As these will be discussed in detail in Chapter 14 we shall present here only the basic ideas. The essence of the Bayesian approach is the encoding, into a probability distribution, of the subjective knowledge of humans involved in the decision making context. To illustrate, we consider the case of the introduction of a *new* style item. The inventory manager involved in the decision of how much to procure knows that the item is similar in some respects to other items for which he has historical sales information. Suppose that the possible total demands (in a selling season) for the item are $0, 1, 2, \ldots, N$ where N is the largest conceivable demand (actually these may be in units of 10's, 100's or even 1000's). There are $(N+1)$ unknown probabilities $q_0, q_1, \ldots, q_N$, where

$$q_i = \text{prob}\,\{\text{total demand will be } i\}$$

The inventory manager may be able to provide estimates of these probabilities, call them $\hat{q}_0, \hat{q}_1, \ldots, \hat{q}_N$. However, one other piece of information is needed to use the Bayesian approach, namely how certain the manager is of his estimates. Two suggested tacks for eliciting this information are:

i. Ask the manager the following question: "Starting from knowing *absolutely nothing* about the probability distribution of total demand, how many periods would you have to observe to place you at your current state of certainty about the values of the q_i's?" The higher the answer, the more confident he is about his estimates.

ii. Ask the manager the following type of question: "If we observed 5 periods and in 2 of them the total demand was 6, what would then be your best estimate of q_6?"

The details of this type of approach can be found in Reference 20.

10.3 *The Constrained, Single Item Situation*

In the previous section the model did not include any limit on the size of the order quantity. Such a limit is illustrated in the problem of selecting how many copies of a newspaper should be placed in one of the street corner, self-service stands. The size of the stand imposes an upper limit on the number of copies. The limit may also be expressed as a maximum number of dollars that can be invested in the stock. For illustrative purposes, we choose to use this second approach.

Suppose that the upper limit on investment is W dollars. Then the approach is as follows:

Step 1 Use Eq. 10.2 to ascertain the unconstrained best value, Q^*.

Step 2 If $Q^*v < W$, then the constraint is not binding and Q^* is indeed the best order quantity. On the other hand, if $Q^*v > W$, the best Q to use is that value right at the constraint, namely

$$Q = \frac{W}{v} \text{ (truncated, if necessary, to the next lowest integer).}$$

10.4 *The Constrained Multi-Item Situation*

Now we consider the situation of more than one type of stock keeping unit to be stocked for a single period's demand. It should be emphasized that the model to be developed here is based upon the assumption of independent demands for the various products. However, now the space or budget constraint takes on more practical significance than in the context of the previous section.

We need some notation before presenting the solution procedure. Let

n = number of different items (s.k.u.'s) involved (numbered $1, 2, 3, \ldots, n$)

${}_ip_{x<}(x_0)$ = prob {total demand for item i is less than x_0}

v_i = acquisition cost of item i, in \$/unit

p_i = selling price of item i, in \$/unit

B_i = penalty for not satisfying demand of item i, in \$/unit

g_i = salvage value of item i, in \$/unit

W = budget available for allocation among the stocks of the n items, in dollars

Suppose that a manager wishes to use up the total budget* so as to maximize the total expected profit of the n items. As shown in part 2 of the appendix of this chapter, a convenient way to solve this problem is through the use of a Lagrange multiplier. The resulting decision procedure is:**

Step 1 Select an initial positive value of the multiplier, M.

Step 2 Determine each Q_i ($i = 1, 2, 3, \ldots, n$) so as to satisfy

$${}_ip_{x<}(Q_i) = \frac{p_i - (M+1)v_i + B_i}{p_i - g_i + B_i} \tag{10.8}$$

---

* *We are assuming that the total budget is to be allocated. If such is not necessarily the case, each item i's unconstrained optimal Q_i^* should be ascertained independently using Eq. 10.2. If the total $\sum Q_i^* v_i < W$, then the Q_i^*'s should be used. If not, the constrained approach must be used to find the Q_i's.*

** *If the constraint is, instead, of a production nature such that no more than W units can be produced, then the decision procedure is modified in two ways:*

i. Equation 10.8 is changed to

$${}_ip_{x<}(Q_i) = \frac{p_i - v_i - M + B_i}{p_i - g_i + B_i} \tag{10.9}$$

ii. In step 3 we compare

$$\sum_{i=1}^{n} Q_i$$

with W.

Step 3 Compare

$$\sum_{i=1}^{n} Q_i v_i$$

with W.
If $\sum Q_i v_i \simeq W$, we're through.
If $\sum Q_i v_i < W$, return to step 2 with a smaller value of M.
If $\sum Q_i v_i > W$, return to step 2 with a larger value of M.

The multiplier has an interesting economic interpretation; it is the value (in terms of increased total expected profit) of adding one more dollar to the available budget, W.

It is important to recognize that as different values of M are used, one is actually tracing out an exchange curve of total expected profit versus total allowed budget (investment in stock) as illustrated in Figure 10.3 which is an exchange curve for the following numerical illustration.

Figure 10.3 Exchange Curve for the Multi-Item, Single Period Situation.

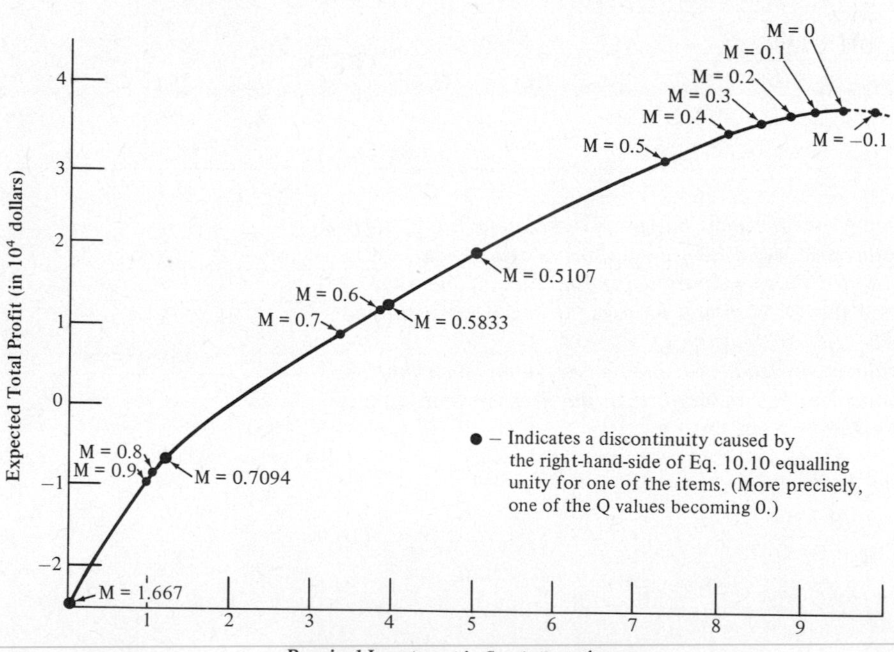

Numerical Illustration—Suppose MIDAS was faced with decisions on four items rather than just the one illustrated in Section 10.2.4. The manager is willing to accept that in each case total demand is normally distributed. For the case of normally distributed demand Eq. 10.8 becomes

$$p_{u\geq}(k_i)=\frac{(M+1)v_i-g_i}{p_i-g_i+B_i} \tag{10.10}$$

where, as earlier, $p_{u\geq}(k_i)$ is the probability that a unit normal variable takes on a value of k_i or larger (tabulated in Appendix C) and

$$Q_i=\bar{x}_i+k_i\sigma_i \tag{10.11}$$

where

$\bar{x}_i$ is the forecast demand for item i.

σ_i is the standard deviation of the demand for item i (here we have simplified the notation somewhat to avoid a sub-subscript).

The relevant parameter values are estimated to be as shown in the top six rows of Table 10.3. The manager has a budget of $70,000 to allocate among these four items. He would like to know how to do this. Also, he is quite interested in the profit impact if the budget is changed somewhat. The calculations for several values of the multiplier M are shown in the lower part of Table 10.3 and the results are shown graphically in Figure 10.3. It is seen that the expected total profit is approximately $28,800 when the proposed budget of $70,000 is used. However, increasing the budget could lead to a substantial improvement in the total profit, a useful piece of information for top management. The dotted part (on the far right) of the curve shows that the total expected profit would start to decrease if the budget was too high and *one was required to invest the whole amount in stocks of the four items* (a negative value of M applies in this region). In actuality, once a budget of approximately $94,900 was reached, no further investment would be made as this is the budget needed for the best solution with no budget restriction (the case of $M=0$).

Table 10.3 Numerical Illustration of Multi-Item Single Period Problem

	Item 1	Item 2	Item 3	Item 4	Total
p_i \$/unit	50.30	40.00	32.00	6.10	—
v_i \$/unit	35.10	15.00	28.00	4.80	—
g_i \$/unit	25.00	12.50	15.10	2.00	—
B_i \$/unit	9.70	0	10.30	1.50	—
$\bar{x}_i$ units	900	800	1200	2300	—
σ_i units	122	200	170	200	—
Using $M=0$ (that is, no budget restriction)					
Q_i from Eqs. 10.10 and 10.11	968	1066	1211	2300	—
$E[P(Q_i)]$ from Eq. 10.7	12220	19100	2960	2540	\$36,820
$Q_i v_i$ \$	33977	15990	33908	11040	\$94,915
Using $M=0.4$					
Q_i	840	900	995	2101	—
$E[P(Q_i)]$	11340	18660	1610	2340	\$33,950
$Q_i v_i$	29484	13500	27864	10085	\$80,933
Using $M=0.6$					
Q_i	750	842	0[a]	0[a]	—
$E[P(Q_i)]$	9720	18230	−12360	−3450	\$12,140
$Q_i v_i$	26325	12630	0	0	\$38,955
Using $M=0.5093$[b]					
Q_i	797	866	695	1995	—
$E[P(Q_i)]$	10660	18430	−2420	2110	\$28,780
$Q_i v_i$	27992	12990	19460	9577	\$70,019

[a] The right-hand-side of Eq. 10.10 exceeds unity, implying that k_i (or equivalently Q_i) should be set at its lowest possible value. The lowest value for Q_i is zero.

[b] By trial and error, it was found that this value of M was required to produce a total used budget of approximately \$70,000.

10.5 More than One Period in Which to Prepare for the Selling Season

Particularly in a production context (for example, style goods in the garment industry) there may be an extended length of time (divided, for convenience, into several time periods) in which replenishment commitments are made before the actual selling season begins. There are likely to be production constraints on the total amounts that can be acquired in each time period. Furthermore, forecasts of total demand are almost certain to change during these pre-season periods, perhaps as a consequence of firm customer orders being received. We would like to be able to modify the decision rule of the previous section so as to effectively cope with these new complexities.

For multi-period production/inventory problems Ignall and Veinott[14] have developed conditions under which a relatively simple policy, known as a myopic policy, is optimal for the sequence of periods. A myopic policy is one that selects the production quantities for the current period so as to minimize expected costs *in the current period alone.* Obviously, a myopic policy is much simpler to compute than is a more general multiperiod policy. However, the multi-period style goods problem discussed above does not satisfy the conditions for which a myopic policy is optimal.

Furthermore, Hausman and Peterson[11] have shown that an "optimal" solution to the problem is out of the question. However, they have proposed two heuristic decision rules which appear to perform quite well, at least on the numerical examples tested. The heuristics are closely related to the single period procedure of Section 10.4 but allowance is made for production capability in all remaining periods.

10.6 *Other Issues Relevant to the Control of Style Goods*

In this section we provide the highlights of other investigations which have been conducted relevant to the control of style goods. It should be emphasized that this type of research is in its infancy so that considerably more verification or modification of the proposed decision rules is necessary before routine applications are possible. Nevertheless, the interested reader is encouraged to seek out the details in the referenced literature.

10.6.1 *Updating of Forecasts*

This topic has been covered in Chapter 4 but we now re-mention those aspects of particular relevance to the style goods problem. In a multi-period problem opportunities exist to update forecasts. Several alternative methods exist including

i. Exploitation of the properties of the forecasts made by decision makers—Hausman[10] has found that under certain circumstances ratios of successive forecasts turn out to be independent variables with a specific form of probability distribution.

ii. Taking advantage of the observation that sales at the retail level tend to be proportional to inventory displayed—Wolfe,[24] in particular, has used this approach to revise forecasts based on demands observed early in the selling period.

iii. Simple extrapolation methods using a normal-shaped cumulative sales curve for wholesale demands (see Hertz and Schaffir[13]).

iv. Bayesian procedures—in the Bayesian approach one or more parameters of the probability distribution of demand are assumed unknown. Prior knowledge is encoded in the form of probability distributions over the possible values of these parameters. As demands are observed in the early part of the season, these probability distributions are appropriately modified to take account of the additional information. An example of this type of approach is the work of Murray and Silver[16] who consider the situation where the numbers of potential customers for a particular style good are known by time period during the selling season. For each such customer there is a probability p that he makes a purchase of the item. p is not known exactly, rather a probability distribution is placed over its possible values ($0 \leq p \leq 1$). There are opportunities for replenishment at the end of each period. The authors formulate a dynamic programming model, involving Bayesian updating, and indicate certain reasonable approximations to make the solution computationally feasible when the numbers of potential customers are large. Another example of a Bayesian approach is the work of Riter.[18]

10.6.2 *Reorders and Markdowns*

Wolfe,[24] using the aforementioned assumption about sales being proportional to the inventory level, develops methods of determining each of the following:

i. The expected time T_F, to sell a fraction F of the initial inventory if a fraction f has been sold by time t ($f<F$). A style can be tentatively identified as a fast-mover (with associated possible reorder) or slow-mover (with associated possible markdown) depending upon the value of T_F for a particular selected F value.

ii. The associated order-up-to-level if a reorder is to be placed at a specific time.

iii. The timing of a markdown as a function of the fraction of initial inventory sold to date, the current price, the markdown price, the salvage value of leftover material and the *assumed known* ratio of the sales rate after the markdown to that before it.

10.6.3 *Multi-stage Production with Non-Zero Lead Times*

Crowston et al.[3] deal with a multi-stage production process with non-zero lead times. The demand process is assumed to follow a seasonal pattern with *known* seasonal coefficients. However, a prior probability distribution is placed on the total demand in the season. The Bayesian updating used is an extension of work earlier proposed by Chang and Fyffe.[2] *Exact* analysis of the decision problem (how much to initiate through each stage of production at the beginning of each period) is shown to be computationally infeasible. However, a heuristic decision rule which is a sophisticated off-shoot of the decision rule of the basic newsboy problem, is shown to perform very well.

10.6.4 *Relating Future Demand to Service Provided*

As was mentioned briefly in Chapter 6, one of the ways of modelling the effects of shortages is to explicitly make the demand level depend upon the service provided. Eilon[5] has done exactly this for the newsboy problem. He deals with the case of normally distributed demand where the mean, $\bar{x}$, depends upon the probability, P_1, of stockout per period, that is,

$$\bar{x} = F(P_1) \quad \text{where } F \text{ is a function} \tag{10.12}$$

He assumes that the demand distribution is stationary, that is, it does not change from period to period for a given service level. Also it is assumed that the standard deviation of demand, σ_x, is not influenced by the value of P_1.

We know from Section 10.2.4 that the best Q to select depends upon $\bar{x}$. However, the selection of a specific Q implies a given probability of stockout per cycle, P_1, which, in turn, from Eq. 10.12 implies an $\bar{x}$ value, etc. Eilon shows how the problem can be reduced to the selection of a single variable, namely the safety factor k. There are different ways, depending upon the nature of the F function, of finding the best value of k.

A non-trivial aspect of this approach is the determination of the function F; in other words, how does one ascertain the relationship between the service provided and the demand rate? Field tests with differing service levels might be a partial answer. However, note that the impact on the demand rate of a change in the service level would likely not reveal itself for a few periods beyond the moment of the change.

10.7 *Summary*

In this chapter we have presented some decision logic for coping with the style goods problem. This logic exploited the property of not being able (for economic reasons) to carry stock over from one selling season to the next. The sophistication of the decision rules developed restricts their use to A items and, perhaps, some of the more important members of the B category. One fact is certain; such sophistication is completely unwarranted for individual C items, the topic of the next chapter.

Appendix to Chapter 10—Derivations

1. *Basic Newsboy Results*

a. Profit Maximization—Each unit purchased costs v, each unit sold produces a revenue of p, each unit disposed as salvage gives a revenue of g, and there is an additional cost B associated with each unit of demand not satisfied. If a quantity Q is stocked and a demand x_0 occurs, the profit is

$$P(Q, x_0) = \begin{cases} -Qv + px_0 + g(Q - x_0) & \text{if } x_0 \leq Q \quad (10.13) \\ -Qv + pQ - B(x_0 - Q) & \text{if } x_0 \geq Q \quad (10.14) \end{cases}$$

The expected value of the profit as a function of Q, is given by

$$E[P(Q)] = \int_0^\infty P(Q, x_0) f_x(x_0)\,dx_0$$

Substituting from Eqs. 10.13 and 10.14 gives

$$\begin{aligned} E[P(Q)] &= \int_0^Q [-Qv + px_0 + g(Q - x_0)] f_x(x_0)\,dx_0 \\ &\quad + \int_Q^\infty [-Qv + pQ - B(x_0 - Q)] f_x(x_0)\,dx_0 \\ &= -Qv \int_0^\infty f_x(x_0)\,dx_0 + (p - g) \int_0^Q x_0 f_x(x_0)\,dx_0 \\ &\quad + gQ \int_0^Q f_x(x_0)\,dx_0 - B \int_Q^\infty x_0 f_x(x_0)\,dx_0 \\ &\quad + (p + B)Q \int_Q^\infty f_x(x_0)\,dx_0 \end{aligned} \tag{10.15}$$

To find the maximizing value of Q we set

$$\frac{dE[P(Q)]}{dQ} = 0 \tag{10.16}$$

In doing this we make use of the following theorem of calculus (for a proof see, for example, Sokolnikoff and Redheffer[21]):

Theorem: Consider a definite integral, denoted by $I(x)$, which is a function of a variable x in two ways. First, the integrand $f(x, y)$ is a function of x (and the variable y which is integrated). Second, both of the limits denoted by $y_1(x)$ and $y_2(x)$ are functions of x. Mathematically we have

$$I(x) = \int_{y_1(x)}^{y_2(x)} f(x, y)\,dy$$

Then, the derivative is given by

$$\frac{dI(x)}{dx} = \int_{y_1(x)}^{y_2(x)} \frac{\partial f(x, y)}{\partial x}\,dy + f(x, y_2)\frac{dy_2(x)}{dx} - f(x, y_1)\frac{dy_1(x)}{dx} \tag{10.17}$$

Use of Equations 10.15, 10.16, and 10.17 (and also recognizing that

$\int_0^\infty f_x(x_0)\,dx_0 = 1$) gives

$$-v + (p-g)Qf_x(Q) + g\int_0^Q f_x(x_0)\,dx_0 + gQf_x(Q)$$
$$+ BQf_x(Q) + (p+B)\int_Q^\infty f_x(x_0)\,dx_0 - (p+B)Qf_x(Q) = 0$$

Several terms cancel to give

$$-v + g\int_0^Q f_x(x_0)\,dx_0 + (p+B)\int_Q^\infty f_x(x_0)\,dx_0 = 0$$
$$-v + gp_{x<}(Q) + (p+B)[1 - p_{x<}(Q)] = 0$$

or

$$p_{x<}(Q) = \frac{p - v + B}{p - g + B} \tag{10.18}$$

In addition, one can show that the second derivative

$$\frac{d^2E[P(Q)]}{dQ^2}$$

is negative, thus ensuring that we have found a profit maximizing (and not minimizing) value of Q.

b. Discrete Case—The expected total cost in the discrete case is

$$\mathrm{ETC}(Q) = \sum_{x_0=0}^{Q-1} c_o(Q - x_0)p_x(x_0) + \sum_{x_0=Q}^{\infty} c_u(x_0 - Q)p_x(x_0) \qquad (10.19)$$

where

$$p_x(x_0) = \mathrm{prob}\,\{x = x_0\}$$

Let

$$\Delta\mathrm{ETC}(Q) = \mathrm{ETC}(Q+1) - \mathrm{ETC}(Q) \qquad (10.20)$$

Then, $\Delta\mathrm{ETC}(Q)$ is the change in expected total cost when we switch from Q to $Q+1$. For a convex cost function (the case here) the best Q (or one of the best Q values) will be the lowest Q where $\Delta\mathrm{ETC}(Q)$ is greater than zero. Therefore, we select the smallest Q for which

$$\Delta\mathrm{ETC}(Q) > 0$$

Substituting from Eqs. 10.19 and 10.20 we have

$$\sum_{x_0=0}^{Q} c_o(Q+1-x_0)p_x(x_0) + \sum_{x_0=Q+1}^{\infty} c_u(x_0 - Q - 1)p_x(x_0)$$
$$-\sum_{x_0=0}^{Q-1} c_o(Q - x_0)p_x(x_0) - \sum_{x_0=Q}^{\infty} c_u(x_0 - Q)p_x(x_0) > 0$$

We split each of the first two summations into two separate parts, introduce the $x_0 = Q$ term (having zero value) into the third summation, and take away the $x_0 = Q$ term (also having zero value) from the fourth summation. The result is

$$\sum_{x_0=0}^{Q} c_o(Q - x_0)p_x(x_0) + c_o \sum_{x_0=0}^{Q} p_x(x_0) + \sum_{x_0=Q+1}^{\infty} c_u(x_0 - Q)p_x(x_0)$$
$$- c_u \sum_{x_0=Q+1}^{\infty} p_x(x_0) - \sum_{x_0=0}^{Q} c_o(Q - x_0)p_x(x_0)$$
$$- \sum_{x_0=Q+1}^{\infty} c_u(x_0 - Q)p_x(x_0) > 0$$

Thus

$$c_o \sum_{x_0=0}^{Q} p_x(x_0) - c_u \sum_{x_0=Q+1}^{\infty} p_x(x_0) > 0$$

$$c_o p_{x\leq}(Q) - c_u[1 - p_{x\leq}(Q)] > 0$$

This simplifies to: use the smallest Q that satisfies

$$p_{x\leq}(Q) > \frac{c_u}{c_u + c_o}$$

c. *Normally Distributed Demand*—If we set

$$k = \frac{Q - \bar{x}}{\sigma_x} \tag{10.21}$$

then, as shown in part C.5 of Appendix C, Eq. 10.18 simplifies to

$$p_{u<}(k) = \frac{p - v + B}{p - g + B} \tag{10.22}$$

where

$$p_{u<}(k) = \text{prob}\,\{\text{a unit normal variable takes on a value less than } k\}$$

Using the fact that

$$p_{u\geq}(k) = 1 - p_{u<}(k),$$

Eq. 10.22 reduces to

$$p_{u\geq}(k) = \frac{v - g}{p - g + B}$$

Next, we wish to show the simplification in Eq. 10.15 which results for the case of normally distributed demand. To do this we need to recognize that, under the use of Eq. 10.21, it is shown in Section C.5 of Appendix C that

i. $\int_Q^{\infty} f_x(x_0)\,dx_0 = p_{u\geq}(k)$

ii. $\displaystyle\int_Q^\infty x_0 f_x(x_0)\,dx_0 = \int_Q^\infty (x_0 - Q) f_x(x_0)\,dx_0 + Q\int_Q^\infty f_x(x_0)\,dx_0$

$$= \sigma_x G_u(k) + Qp_{u\geq}(k)$$

iii. $\displaystyle\int_0^Q x_0 f_x(x_0)\,dx_0 = \int_0^\infty x_0 f_x(x_0)\,dx_0 - \int_Q^\infty x_0 f_x(x_0)\,dx_0$

$$\simeq \bar{x} - \sigma_x G_u(k) - Qp_{u\geq}(k)$$

Therefore, Eq. 10.15 becomes

$$\begin{aligned} E[P(Q)] = {} & -Qv + (p-g)[\bar{x} - \sigma_x G_u(k) - Qp_{u\geq}(k)] \\ & + gQ[1 - p_{u\geq}(k)] - B[\sigma_x G_u(k) + Qp_{u\geq}(k)] \\ & + (p+B)Qp_{u\geq}(k) \end{aligned}$$

or

$$E[P(Q)] = (p-g)\bar{x} - (v-g)Q - (p-g+B)\sigma_x G_u(k)$$

2. *The Constrained Multi-Item Situation*

The problem is to select the Q_i's $(i = 1, 2, \ldots, n)$ to maximize

$$\sum_{i=1}^{n} E[P(Q_i)]$$

subject to

$$\sum_{i=1}^{n} Q_i v_i = W \qquad (10.23)$$

where, from Eq. 10.15

$$\begin{aligned} E[P(Q_i)] = {} & -Q_i v_i + \int_0^{Q_i} [p_i x_0 + g_i(Q_i - x_0)]_i f_x(x_0)\,dx_0 \\ & + \int_{Q_i}^\infty [p_i Q_i - B_i(x_0 - Q_i)]_i f_x(x_0)\,dx_0 \end{aligned} \qquad (10.24)$$

and

${}_i f_x(x_0)\,dx_0 =$ prob {total demand for product i lies between x_0 and $x_0 + dx_0$}

The Lagrangian approach (see Appendix A) is to select the multiplier M and Q_i's to maximize

$$L(Q_i\text{'s}, M) = \sum_{i=1}^{n} E[P(Q_i)] - M\left[\sum_{i=1}^{n} Q_i v_i - W\right] \tag{10.25}$$

This is accomplished by setting partial derivatives to zero.

$$\frac{\partial L}{\partial M} = 0$$

simply produces Eq. 10.23. Substituting Eq. 10.24 into Eq. 10.25 we have

$$L(Q_i\text{'s}, M) = \sum_{i=1}^{n} (-Q_i v_i + I_1 + I_2) - M\left[\sum_{i=1}^{n} Q_i v_i - W\right] \tag{10.26}$$

where I_1 and I_2 are the two integrals in Eq. 10.24. The key point is that I_1 and I_2 do not involve the v_i's.

Now Eq. 10.26 can be rewritten as

$$L(Q_i\text{'s}, M) = \sum_{i=1}^{n} [-Q_i(M+1)v_i + I_1 + I_2] + MW$$

The expression in square brackets is the same as $E[P(Q_i)]$ except v_i is replaced by $(M+1)v_i$. Therefore, when we set

$$\frac{\partial L}{\partial Q_i} = 0$$

we obtain the same result as the independent Q^* for item i except that v_i is replaced by $(M+1)v_i$, that is, select Q_i to satisfy

$${}_ip_{x<}(Q_i) = \frac{p_i - (M+1)v_i + B_i}{p_i - g_i + B_i} \tag{10.27}$$

A given value of M implies a value for each Q_i which in turn implies a value of

$$\sum_{i=1}^{n} Q_i v_i$$

Equation 10.27 shows that the higher the value of M, the lower must be ${}_ip_{x<}(Q_i)$, that is, the lower must be Q_i.

Problems for Chapter 10

Problem 10.1

Alexander Norman owns several retail fur stores in a large North American city. In the spring of each year he must decide on the number of each type of fur coat to order from his manufacturing supplier for the upcoming winter season. For a particular muskrat line his cost per coat is \$150 and the retail selling price is \$210. He estimates an average sales of 100 coats but with considerable uncertainty which he is willing to express as a uniform distribution between 75 and 125. Any coat not sold at the end of the winter can be disposed of at cost (\$150) to a discount house. However, Norman feels that on any such coat he has lost money because of the capital tied up in the inventory for the whole season. He estimates a loss of \$0.15 for every dollar tied up in a coat that must be sold off at the end of the season.

a. How many coats should he order?

b. One of the factors contributing to the uncertainty in sales is the unknown level of retail luxury tax on coats that will be established by the government early in the fall. Norman has connections in the government and manages to learn the tax level prior to his buying decision. This changes his probability distribution to a normal form with a mean of 110 and a standard deviation of 15. Now what is his best order quantity? How much was the inside information concerning the tax worth to him?

Problem 10.2

Plante, Fillion, Nettoyer, Tremblay, and Beausejour Lte. (PFNTB), a Montreal department store, sells a certain type of wrapping paper for the Christmas season. The basic unit is a package that sells for \$1.00. The supplier offers a quantity discount structure as follows: the unit cost is \$0.50/package if less than 300 packages are acquired but is \$0.45/package (for all packages) if at least 300 packages are acquired. Any packages unsold by Christmas are cleared by the store in January at a special price of \$0.30/package. The buyer of PFNTB estimates that sales are Laplace distributed with a mean of 250 packages and a probability of 0.1 that sales will exceed 300 packages. What amount should the buyer acquire from the supplier?

Problem 10.3

Consider the situation where tooling is set up to make a major piece of equipment and spare parts can be made relatively inexpensively. After this one production run of the product and its spares, the dyes, etc., will be discarded. Discuss the relationship between the problem of how many spares to run and the single period problem.

Problem 10.4

Mr. Jones, a recent M.B.A. graduate, the only entrepreneur in his graduating class, will establish a distinctive newspaper concession on the corner of two busy streets near his alma mater. After conducting in-depth interviews, he has decided to stock three daily newspapers: the *Hong Kong Chronicle*, the *New York Times*, and the *Barrie Bugle*. Having successfully avoided all courses requiring arithmetic during his academic career, he has contacted you to advise him on the kind of ordering policy that he should follow.

a. You first make the assumption that the daily demand for each of the three papers is normally distributed. The mean number of papers sold during the first 4 days of the week appears to be 50 percent greater than on Fridays and Saturdays. Mr. Jones has a small kiosk (acquired through a student loan from the bank) that can stock only 500 papers each day. In keeping with analytic modelling tradition, you assume, for mathematical convenience, that the cost of being short of any of the three papers on any particular day is \$0.06 and the cost of not selling a paper on any particular day is \$0.02. Recommend inventory stocking rules for Mr. Jones.

b. Illustrate with the following numerical example for a typical Tuesday:

Paper	Mean Daily Demand	Variance of Daily Demand
Chronicle	400	10,000
Times	200	8,100
Bugle	300	10,000

c. After collecting your exorbitant consulting fee, you confess to your bartender, explaining the shortcomings of the numerical example and ordering policy above. Criticize your answers to (a) and (b) in the light of reality.

d. How would you ascertain whether it was worthwhile for Jones to go deeper into debt to buy a larger kiosk (capable of holding 1000 copies)?

Problem 10.5

A local vendor of newspapers feels that dissatisfaction of customers leads to future lost sales. In fact, he feels that the average demand for a particular newspaper is related to the service level as follows

$$\bar{x} = 1000 + 500P$$

where $\bar{x}$ is the average demand in copies/period and P is the fraction of demand that is satisfied.

Demands are normally distributed and the standard deviation (per period) is equal to 200, independent of the service level. Other (possibly) relevant factors are:

Fixed cost per day to get any papers in = \$2

Cost per paper (for vendor) = \$0.07

Selling price per paper = \$0.15

Salvage value per paper = \$0.02

a. Ignoring the effect of disservice on demand, what is the best number of papers to acquire per period?

b. Taking account of the effect, now what is the best number to acquire?

c. What average profit is the vendor losing if he proceeds as in (a) instead of as in (b)?

Problem 10.6

Neighborhood Hardware Ltd. acts as a central buying agent and distributor for a large number of retail hardware outlets in Canada. The product line is divided into six major categories with a different buyer being responsible for each single category. One category is miscellaneous equipment for outdoor work around the home. The buyer for this group, Mr. Harry Lock, seeks assistance from a recently hired analyst, J. D. Smith, in the computer division of the company. In particular, he is concerned with the acquisition of a particular type of small snowblower which must be ordered several months before the winter. Smith, after considerable discussions with Lock, has the latter's agreement with the following data:

Unit acquisition cost is \$60.00/unit.

Selling price is \$100.00/unit.

Any units unsold towards the end of the winter will be marked down to \$51.00/unit ensuring a complete clearance, thus avoiding the prohibitive expense of storage until the next season. The probability distribution of regular demand is estimated to be:

Hundreds of Units, j_0	3	4	5	6	7	8
$p_j(j_0)$	0.1	0.1	0.4	0.2	0.1	0.1

a. What is the expected demand?

b. What is the standard deviation of demand?

c. To maximize expected profit how many units should Smith (using a discrete demand model) tell Lock to acquire?

d. What is the expected profit under the strategy of part c?

e. Suppose Smith instead decides to fit a normal distribution, having the same mean and standard deviation, to the above discrete distribution. With this normal model what is the recommended order quantity, rounded to the nearest hundred units?

f. If the discrete distribution is the true one, what cost penalty is incurred by the use of the somewhat simpler normal model?

Problem 10.7

Suppose the supplier in Problem 10.6 offers a discount such that the unit cost is $55.00 if an order of at least 750 units is placed? Should Neighborhood take advantage of this offer?

Problem 10.8

In reality, Mr. Lock of Neighborhood Hardware, has to order three different snowblowers from the same supplier. He tells the analyst, Smith, that he'll go along with his normal model (whatever that is!) but, in no event, will he allocate more than $70,000 for the acquisition of snowblowers. In addition to item SB-1, described in Problem 10.6, characteristics of the other two items are:

Item	Unit Acquisition Cost	Selling Price	Clearance Price
	$/unit	$/unit	$/unit
SB-2	80	110	70
SB-3	130	200	120

Item	Demand Mean	Demand Standard Deviation
	units	units
SB-2	300	50
SB-3	200	40

a. What should Smith suggest as the order quantities of the three items?

b. What would be the approximate change in expected profit if Lock agreed to a $5,000 increase in the budget allocated for snowblowers?

Note: Assume in this problem that there are no quantity discounts available.

Problem 10.9

Consider a company with N warehouses and a certain amount (W units) of stock of a particular s.k.u. to allocate among the warehouses. The next allocation will not be made until one period from now. Let

$_if_x(x_0)$ be the probability density of demand in a period for warehouse i $(i = 1, 2, \ldots, N)$

Develop a rule for allocating the W units of stock under each of the following costing assumptions (treated separately).

a. A cost H_i incurred at warehouse i if any shortage occurs.

b. A cost B_i is charged per unit short at warehouse i.

Problem 10.10

Jack G. Gold, the manager of the bookstore at Lawson College, must decide on how many copies of a particular text to order in connection with an elective course to be offered by Professor Patrick Dunphy of the college's Department of Philosophy. Gold decides to seek the assistance of Professor William F. Jennings of the Department of Industrial Engineering who has some familiarity with inventory models. Jennings ascertains from Gold that historically there has been considerable variance between the number of books that Dunphy says he needs for a course and the actual number purchased by the students. The particular text under consideration is supplied by a publisher that allows up to 20 percent returns from the bookstore, with the latter only incurring the shipping costs (that is, the wholesale purchase price is completely refunded). To illustrate, up to 20 copies could be handled in this fashion if the original order was for 100 copies. No refund is possible on any amount beyond the 20 percent. Gold indicates that any copies that could not be returned would be marked down to 50 percent of his cost (the wholesale price) which would clear them out. Gold points out that his permitted markup on all books is 15 percent of his wholesale price. Suppose that, through analysis of historical records and discussions with Gold and Dunphy, Jennings is able to develop a reasonable probability distribution of total demand for the text.

a. Outline how Jennings might develop a decision rule for Gold to use in deciding on how many copies of Dunphy's text to order.

b. Mention some complexities ignored in your analysis.

REFERENCES FOR CHAPTER 10

1. Baker, K. "On the Relation of Stockout Probability to the Optimum Reorder Mechanism in Complex Production-Inventory Systems." *Operational Research Quarterly*, Vol. 21, No. 3, September, 1970, pp. 335–340.

2. Chang, S. H. and D. E. Fyffe. "Estimation of Forecast Errors for Seasonal-Style-Goods Sales." *Management Science*, Vol. 18, No. 2, October, 1971, pp. B-89–B-96.

3. Crowston, W. B., W. H. Hausman and W. R. Kampe II. "Multistage Production for Stochastic Seasonal Demand." *Management Science*, Vol. 19, No. 8, April, 1973, pp. 924–935.

4. Denicoff, M., J. Fennell, S. Haber, W. Marlow and H. Solomon. "A Polaris Logistics Model." *Naval Research Logistics Quarterly*, Vol. 11, 1964, pp. 259–272.

5. Eilon, S. "On the Cost of Runouts in Stock Control of Perishables." *Operations Research—Verfahren II* edited by R. Henn, pp. 65–76, 1965.

6. Goyal, S. "Optimal Decision Rules for Producing Greeting Cards." *Operational Research Quarterly*, Vol. 24, No. 3, September, 1973, pp. 391–401.

7. Hadley, G. "Generalizations of the Optimal Final Inventory Model." *Management Science*, Vol. 8, No. 4, July, 1962, pp. 454–457.

8. Hadley, G. and T. M. Whitin. "An Optimal Final Inventory Model." *Management Science*, Vol. 7, No. 2, January, 1961, pp. 179–183.

9. Hartung, P. "A Simple Style Goods Inventory Model." *Management Science*, Vol. 19, No. 12, August, 1973, pp. 1452–1458.

10. Hausman, W. H. "Sequential Decision Problems: A Model to Exploit Existing Forecasters." *Management Science*, Vol. 16, No. 2, October, 1969, pp. 93–111.

11. Hausman, W. H. and R. Peterson. "Multiproduct Production Scheduling for Style Goods with Limited Capacity, Forecast Revisions and Terminal Delivery." *Management Science*, Vol. 18, No. 7, March, 1972, pp. 370–383.

12. Hausman, W. H. and R. St. G. Sides. "Mail-order Demands for Style Goods: Theory and Data Analysis." *Management Science*, Vol. 20, No. 2, October, 1973, pp. 191–202.

13. Hertz, D. B. and K. H. Schaffir. "A Forecasting Method for Management of Seasonal Style-Goods Inventories." *Operations Research*, Vol. 8, No. 1, January–February, 1960, pp. 45–52.

14. Ignall, E. and A. Veinott. "Optimality of Myopic Inventory Policies for Several Substitute Products." *Management Science*, Vol. 15, No. 5, January, 1969, pp. 284–304.

15. Magee, J. F. "Guides to Inventory Policy." *Harvard Business Review*, May–June, 1956, p. 58.

16. Murray, G. R., Jr. and E. A.

Silver. "A Bayesian Analysis of the Style Goods Inventory Problem." *Management Science*, Vol. 12, No. 11, July, 1966, pp. 785–797.

17. Ravindran, A. "Management of Seasonal Style-Goods Inventories." *Operations Research*, Vol. 20, No. 2, March–April, 1972, pp. 265–275.

18. Riter, C. "The Merchandising Decision under Uncertainty." *Journal of Marketing*, Vol. 31, January, 1967, pp. 44–47.

19. Schlaifer, R. *Introduction to Statistics for Business Decisions.* McGraw-Hill, New York, 1961, p. 320.

20. Silver, E. A. "Bayesian Determination of the Reorder Point of a Slow Moving Item." *Operations Research*, Vol. 13, No. 6, November–December, 1965, pp. 989–997.

21. Sokolnikoff, I. S. and R. M. Redheffer. *Mathematics of Physics and Modern Engineering*. McGraw-Hill, New York, 1958, pp. 261–2.

22. Spurrell, D. J. "A Simple Method of Production Planning in Multi-item Situations." *Operational Research Quarterly*, Vol. 18, No. 2, 1967, pp. 149–159.

23. Wadsworth, G. P. "Probability," Chapter 1 in *Notes on Operations Research.* Technology Press, Cambridge, Mass., 1959, pp. 26–29.

24. Wolfe, H. B. "A Model for Control of Style Merchandise." *Industrial Management Review.* Vol. 9, No. 2, 1968, pp. 69–82.

25. Wollaston, J. "Retail Inventory Control—A Progress Report." *Production and Inventory Management.* Vol. 12, No. 1, 1971, pp. 1–14.

CHAPTER ELEVEN

Decision Systems for Managing Routine (Class C) Inventories

The C category or so-called "cats and dogs" usually represents an appreciable percentage of the total number of distinct s.k.u. but a very small fraction of the total dollar investment in the inventory of a typical company. Each such item taken singly is relatively unimportant, but, because of their large numbers, appropriate simple control procedures must be utilized. In this chapter we discuss such methods. Section 11.1 spells out in greater detail the nature of C items and the primary objectives in designing methods for controlling them. In Section 11.2 we propose control procedures by considering, in order, the type of inventory records to use, the selection of the reorder quantity (or reorder interval), and the choice of the reorder point (or order-up-to-level). Section 11.3 is concerned with the important issue of removing totally (or relatively) inactive items from the company's inventory. Finally, in Section 11.4 we address the related question of whether demands for a particular item should be purchased (made) to order or met from stock.

11.1 *The Nature of C Items*

The categorization of items for control purposes was first discussed in Chapter 3. To refresh the reader's memory we repeat some of the important points here.

The primary factor which indicates that an item should be placed in the C category is a low dollar usage (Dv value). The exact cut-off value between the B and C categories should be selected so that somewhere on the order of 30 to 50 percent of all the items are classified in the C category. (For the MIDAS Professional Products Division a cut-off value of \$240/yr. was selected, resulting in a somewhat low 26.1 percent of all the items being in the C category). A low Dv value alone is not sufficient to dictate that an item should be placed in the C category. The real requirement is that the annual total of replenishment, carrying, and shortage costs be quite low under any reasonable control strategy. Normally, Dv is a useful surrogate for this total. However, a low dollar-usage item may have potentially severe shortage penalties associated with it. Some typical examples come to mind:

> i. A slow-moving product which rounds out a service line provided to an important customer—shortages on this item can cause severe reductions in the usage of several faster-moving items.
>
> ii. A product which is the "pride and joy" of the president because he was instrumental in its development—here there is a high "implicit" cost associated with a shortage.
>
> iii. The authors vividly remember the case of an electronics manufacturer whose limited manufacturing area was clogged with five expensive pieces of custom-made equipment, each the size of two large refrigerators, because the company had once again run out of the plastic control knobs worth 7 cents each.

For a true C type item the low total of replenishment, carrying, and shortage costs implies that, regardless of the type of control system used, we cannot achieve a sizable *absolute* saving in these costs. Therefore, the guiding principle should be to use simple procedures which keep the control costs per s.k.u. quite low, that is, we wish to keep the labor and paperwork per item to a minimum.

11.2 *Control of Active C Items*

In this section we assume that it makes sense to actually stock the C item under consideration. In Section 11.4 we shall address the more fundamental question of stocking an item versus making or buying it to each customer order.

11.2.1 *Inventory Records*

As a consequence of the primary objective mentioned above, in most cases it may be most appropriate to not maintain any inventory record of a C item, but instead simply rely on an administrative mechanism for reordering such as placing an order when the last box in a bin is opened. If an inventory record is maintained, it should certainly not require the recording of each transaction; instead a rather long review interval, such as six months, should be considered. Of course, for demand estimation and order control purposes a record should be kept of the dates of placement and receipt of replenishment orders.

Stated another way, we are saying that there are two choices in relation to the selection of a review interval for a C item:

i. Periodic review with a relatively long interval.

ii. Continuous review but with a mechanism for triggering orders which requires neither a physical stock count nor the updating (in a ledger) of the stock status—an example is a two bin system of control.

11.2.2 *Selecting the Reorder Quantity (or Reorder Interval)*

Stated bluntly, the frills of the economic order quantity, Silver–Meal Heuristic, etc., are completely unwarranted for Class C items. Instead, one should make use of a simple offshoot of the basic EOQ developed in Chapter 5, namely that one of at most a few possible time supplies should be assigned to each class C item. The time supply to use should be based as much on shelf-life and obsolescence considerations as on the setup, unit cost and carrying charge factors. It is usually reasonable to use a single value of the ratio A/r for all C items (one convenient way of estimating this value is through the exchange curve notions of Chapter 5). To illustrate, consider the MIDAS situation. The value of r was found to be 0.24/year and a reasonable average value of A is \$3.20. Furthermore, for C items management has decided that only three possible time supplies, namely 6, 12, and 18 months, are worth considering. Using the approach suggested in Section 5.5.2 of Chapter 5 we develop the particularly simple decision rule shown in Table 11.1. D would not be estimated through a forecasting system but rather through knowledge of the starting and ending inventory as well as the total replenishments received in a period of say 6 months or 1 year duration. For a 6 month period,

$$\underset{\text{(units/yr.)}}{\text{estimate of } D} = 2 \times [(\text{starting inventory}) + (\text{total replenishments}) - (\text{ending inventory})]$$

Of course, if pilferage losses are significant, an overly high estimate of D would result. Needless to say, rather than taking account of these losses, the preferable approach is to reduce the losses themselves.

Table 11.1 Suggested Reorder Time Supplies for MIDAS C Items

For annual dollar movement (Dv) in this range (\$/yr.)	Use this number of months of supply
$53 \leq Dv$	6
$18 \leq Dv < 53$	12
$Dv < 18$	18

11.2.3 *Selecting the Reorder Point (or Order-up-to-Level)*

As with A and B items it is probably advisable to distinguish between low lead time demand (that is, low $\bar{x}_L$) and high lead time demand (that is, high $\bar{x}_L$) C items. The threshold $\bar{x}_L$ value of 10 units suggested for B items (as first discussed in Section 6.5.3, Chapter 6) should be used for C items as well. The reason for the split into "slow" and "fast" categories is that the Laplace and normal distributions provide the best fits to forecast errors in these two ranges respectively. Naturally, most C items will be in the slow category. This is fortunate because the Laplace distribution is somewhat simpler to use than is the normal. Furthermore, for the case of very high service levels (which, as we shall discuss, are typical for C items) the Laplace, for a given desired service level, leads to a larger safety factor than does the normal; thus the actual service provided using the Laplace distribution is higher than that provided through use of the normal. Of course, the carrying costs increase somewhat. This conservative, in terms of service, behavior of the Laplace is probably desirable for C items where the associated added carrying costs per item are very small.

One could choose any of the criteria, discussed in Chapters 6 and 7, for selecting the safety factor. However, we advocate the use of a specific criterion, namely "selecting the safety factor to provide a specified expected time, TBS, between stockout occasions," which we have found to be particularly appealing to management in most C item contexts. This appears to be a method of expressing their risk aversion with which they feel comfortable. Thinking in terms of an average time between stockouts is apparently more straightforward than dealing with probabilities or fractions. Quite often many C items are involved in a single customer order. Therefore, to assure a reasonable chance of satisfying the complete customer order, a very high level of service must be used for each C item. Therefore, large values of TBS (for example, 5 years to 100 years) are not unreasonable when one recognizes the small added expense of carrying a high safety stock. The decision rule for the TBS criterion (derived in Section 6.6 of Chapter 6) is to select the reorder point* so that

$$\text{(probability of a stockout per cycle)} = \frac{Q}{D(\text{TBS})} \tag{11.1}$$

If we set

$$s = \bar{x}_L + k\sigma_L \tag{11.2}$$

where**

$$\bar{x}_L = LD \tag{11.3}$$

is the expected demand (in units) in the replenishment lead time of length

---

* *If a periodic review, order-up-to-level (R, S) system is to be used, then throughout this section the decision rules should be modified as follows:*

i. replace L by R+L
ii. replace Q/D by R
iii. replace s by S

** *Note:* $\bar{x}_L$ *is not an output of the forecast system (as mentioned earlier, we are advocating not forecasting C items). D is estimated as discussed in the preceding subsection.*

L (years), and σ_L is the estimate of the standard deviation (in units) of forecast errors over L (we shall return shortly to a discussion of how σ_L is estimated). The results for the two types of forecast error distributions are shown below.

Normal Forecast Errors ($\bar{x}_L \geq 10$ units)—Select the safety factor k to satisfy*

$$p_{u\geq}(k) = \frac{Q}{D(\text{TBS})} \tag{11.4}$$

where

$p_{u\geq}(k)$ = prob {unit normal variable (mean 0, standard deviation 1) takes on a value of k or larger},

a widely tabulated function (see Table C.1 in Appendix C).

Laplace Forecast Errors ($\bar{x}_L < 10$ units)—Select the safety factor k to satisfy*

$$k = \frac{1}{\sqrt{2}} \ln \left[\frac{D(\text{TBS})}{2Q}\right] \tag{11.5}$$

Now at this stage the alert reader surely must be wondering, "Who needs all this aggravation, especially for C items?" Such a viewpoint is indeed correct. Equations 11.4 and 11.5 hold for general values of Q/D and TBS. In the context of any company only a few values of each of these two parameters would be specified. For these few combinations, the equations could be used once-and-for-all to develop a simple table. We illustrate this for the MIDAS case in Table 11.2 using the earlier selected Q/D values of 6, 12, and 18 months and also management specified values of 10, 20, and 50 years for TBS.

Once k is selected, then the reorder point follows from Eq. 11.2. However, for this purpose an estimate of σ_L is required. One point is certain: σ_L should *not* be developed from observing forecast errors of the specific C item under consideration. Instead, we suggest the use of either

---

* *In Eq.* 11.4 *or* 11.5 *a negative k results if Q/D*(TBS)$>$0.5. *Usually, management would set k* $=0$ *in such a case.*

Table 11.2 Table to Select Safety Factor, k, for MIDAS Situation

A. *Laplace Case* ($\bar{x}_L < 10$ units)

TBS Value (years)	Order quantity expressed as a time supply in months ($12Q/D$)		
	6	12	18
10	1.62	1.14	0.85
20	2.12	1.62	1.34
50	2.76	2.28	1.99

B. *Normal Case* ($\bar{x}_L \geq 10$ units)

TBS Value (years)	Order quantity expressed as a time supply in months ($12Q/D$)		
	6	12	18
10	1.64	1.23	1.04
20	1.96	1.64	1.44
50	2.33	2.05	1.88

of the following methods of developing an estimate of σ_L:

i. Use an aggregate relationship of the form*

$$\sigma_L = a_1(D/12)^{b_1}L^{c_1} \tag{11.6}$$

where L is expressed in months and D is in units/yr.

ii. Assume that the lead time demand of a C item is approximately Poisson distributed. For such a distribution (see Appendix B) we have the simple relation

$$\sigma_L = \sqrt{\bar{x}_L} = \sqrt{DL} \tag{11.7}$$

Numerical Illustration—Consider item XSC-037, a slow moving X-ray developing chemical, with $D = 48$ units/year, $L = 2$ months, an order

---

* *As discussed in Chapters* 2 *and* 4, a_1, b_1, *and* c_1 *are parameters estimated from a sample of items from the population under consideration; in the case of MIDAS their values were found to be:*

$a_1 = 1.3 \quad b_1 = 0.65 \quad c_1 = 0.5$

quantity time supply of 12 months, and a specified TBS of 20 years.

$$\bar{x}_L = DL = 48 \text{ units/year} \times 1/6 \text{ yr.} = 8 \text{ units}$$

We use the top portion of the Table (because $\bar{x}_L$ is less than the threshold value) and read that the safety factor k should be set at 1.62. Suppose we make the Poisson assumption. Then Eq. 11.7 gives

$$\sigma_L \simeq \sqrt{8} = 2.83 \text{ units}$$

From Eq. 11.2 we have that the reorder point is

$$s = 8 + 1.62(2.83) = 12.6, \text{ say } 13 \text{ units.}$$

11.2.4 *The Two-Bin System Revisited*

In Section 6.4 of Chapter 6 we described a particularly simple physical form of an (s, Q) system, namely what is called a two-bin system. To review, in a two-bin system the on-hand inventory is segregated into two distinct sections (generically called bins). The capacity of one of the bins (called the reserve bin) is set equal to the reorder point. Demands are satisfied from the other bin until its stock is depleted. When it becomes necessary to open the reserve bin this is a signal to place a replenishment order. When the order arrives the reserve bin is refilled and sealed. The remainder of the order is placed in the other bin.

The authors have seen some rather clever forms of the bins concept. Examples include:

i. The use of "baggies" in the case of small electronic components

ii. Color coding of the end of an appropriate bar in steel stacked in a distribution warehouse

To facilitate proper initiation of an order a bin reserve tag should be attached to the reserve bin such that when the latter is opened the clerk now has the tag which serves as a reminder to report the opening of the bin. In fact, in many cases, the tag itself can be used as an order form. At the very least, dates and order quantities can be recorded on it (permitting an estimate of D when it is needed).

Obviously, for satisfactory performance of such a system it is imperative that a tag be promptly submitted to purchasing (or production scheduling) whenever a reserve bin is opened. Foremen, assemblers, salesmen, etc., must be motivated to follow this procedure while they meet their own objectives in the rush of daily activities.

11.2.5 *Grouping of Items*

In some cases it may be advantageous to group C items for control purposes. In particular, if a group of items (including some from the A and B categories) are provided by the same supplier, or produced in-house on the same equipment, then coordinated control (to be discussed in Chapter 13) may very well be in order to reduce replenishment costs; that is, when one item in the group needs reordering several others should likely be included in the order. This is particularly appealing for a C item; by including it in an order initiated by another item we avoid incurring a full setup cost (A) for the replenishment of the C item.

Coordination does not rule out the use of a two-bin system of control for the individual C item. Rather, reserve tags of opened reserve bins are held centrally between designated periodic times at which the group under consideration is ordered. Of course, the reserve stock must be appropriately scaled up to provide protection over a length of time equal to the sum of the periodic ordering interval plus the replenishment lead time.

11.3 *Reducing the Number of Items Stocked*

When a study of the inventory control situation of a company is undertaken it is not uncommon to find a significant percentage of the stocked items which have had absolutely no sales (or internal usage) in the last one or more years of time. Dyer[5] reports that for the distribution industry the percentage of stocked items that have had no usage in the previous 52 weeks has been found to lie anywhere from 16 to 47 percent. We shall refer to such s.k.u. as dead items.

There are a number of possible causes for the death of an item. Obsolescence is certainly a factor. Deliberate changes in sales/marketing efforts may leave a residual of unused items. An acquisition error (for example, ordering 1,000 instead of 100 units) may lead to a supply of an item that cannot possibly be depleted in the lifetime of the s.k.u.

Whatever the cause(s) of the dead items it is important to be able to (i) identify such items (as well as those having extremely low, but non-zero , movement) and (ii) decide on what remedial action(s) to take. Of course, ideally one would like to be able to anticipate the death of an item and take appropriate action(s) to avoid being caught with a large surplus stock. It should be noted that this general problem area is likely to increase in importance as the rate of technological change increases, causing the life cycle of the typical product to shorten.

11.3.1 *Review of the Distribution by Value*

Again, we make use of a simple, but powerful, tool of analysis, the distribution by value (DBV) list. Recall from earlier (see Table 2.5 in Chapter 2) that the DBV is a listing of items in decreasing order of annual dollar usage (Dv value). At the bottom of the table will be all of the items which had no sales (or internal usage) over the period from which D was estimated (normally the most recent full year). Furthermore, moving up the table we immediately encounter the items which have had very low usage.

To establish the DBV, values of D_i and v_i are required for each item i. If, at the same time, a reading on the inventory level, I_i, of item i can be obtained, then a very useful additional table can be developed as follows:

For each item the expected time at which the current stock level will be depleted, also called the "coverage", is computed by the formula,

$$CO = \frac{12I}{D} \tag{11.8}$$

where

CO is the coverage, in months.
I is the on-hand inventory, in units.
D is the expected usage rate, in units/year.

The items are then shown in a table (see Table 11.3) in decreasing order of coverage. Also shown is the inventory (in dollars) of each item and the cumulative percentage of the total inventory as one proceeds down the table. In Table 11.3 (involving a population of 200 items with a total inventory valued at $7,863) it is seen that 4.2 percent of the total inventory is tied up in stock of zero-movers and some 6.9 percent is included in items having a coverage of 5 years (60 months) or more. Such information would be of use to management in deciding on the seriousness of the overstock situation and on what remedial course(s) of action to take.

Individual item usage values (D_i's) are needed to construct the distribution by value table. Where these are not readily available a practical alternative is to simply tour the storage facilities applying a so-called "dust" test: any stock that looks overly dusty (or its equivalent) is a candidate for identification as a dead or very slow-moving item.

11.3.2 *Disposal of Dead (and Dying) Stock*

A coverage analysis, as discussed above, will almost certainly identify some stock which will not be depleted by normal sales in the foreseeable future. Unpleasant as this fact may be, it is not enough to bewail the situation.

Table 11.3 Items Listed by Coverage

Rank Order	Cumulative Percent of Items	Item Identification	I units	D units/ year	v \$/unit	CO months	Iv \$	Cumulative Inventory \$	as percent of total
1	0.5	—	150	0	1.80	infinite	270	270	3.4[a]
2	1.0	—	60	0	0.50	infinite	30	300	3.8
3	1.5	—	10	0	1.10	infinite	11	311	4.0
4	2.0	—	5	0	3.20	infinite	16	327	4.2
5	2.5	—	53	2	1.00	318	53	380	4.8
6	3.0	—	40	3	0.90	160	36	416	5.3
7	3.5	—	64	12	2.00	64	128	544	6.9
8	4.0	—	180	37	0.35	58.4	63	607	7.7
.	.	.	.	.	.	.	.	.	.
.	.	.	.	.	.	.	.	.	.
.	.	.	.	.	.	.	.	.	.
								7,861	100.0
199	99.5	—	2	1,000	1.00	0.024	2.00	7,863	100.0
200	100.0	—	0	463	0.20	0	0	7,863	100.0

[a] 3.4 = (270/7,863) × 100

Furthermore, the fact that the unit value (raw material, labor, etc.) of the inventory is high should not prevent disposal at a much lower unit price if this is all that the market will bear. In particular, one should recognize that often the most costly aspect of "dead" inventory is that it is taking up significant space in a storage area of limited capacity. In addition, there is often a nuisance cost associated with dead stock that has physically deteriorated. Examples include the presence of rats and vermin, excessive rusting, etc. The authors recall the case of manufactured, large, metal piping that was stored in an open yard. One particular item, left standing for a number of years, had slowly sunk into the mud with each spring thaw until it stabilized in a semi-submerged state. Excavation equipment, with associated high usage cost, was required to remove the dead stock in order to free up the space that it was occupying. Possible courses of action for disposing of dead stock include:

i. Returns to suppliers at a unit value likely lower than the initial acquisition cost: a good example is that of a college bookstore returning extra copies of a book to the publishing company's distributor.

ii. Shipment of the material to another location: where an item is stocked at more than one location it may be dead at one location but still experience demand elsewhere. The transfer of stock not only frees up space at the "dead" location, but it also helps avoid the costly setup (or acquisition) costs associated with satisfying the likely infrequent demands at the "live" location(s).

iii. Mark-downs or special sales: the unit price is reduced sufficiently to generate demand for the product; an example would be the reduced price of wrapping paper, decorations, etc., immediately following the Christmas season.

iv. Use of stock for promotional purposes: dead stock may be converted to a revenue generator by providing free samples of it when customers purchase other products; for example, an appliance store with an overstock situation of an inexpensive table lamp might offer it free as a bonus to each customer buying a color television set. The extreme case of this action is donation of the stock to some charitable cause.

v. Auctions: these should not be overlooked as a possible means of salvaging some value from dead stock.

vi. Disposal for scrap value: the best course of action may be to sell the material directly to a scrap dealer, a common transaction when there is a significant metallic component of the item.

Whatever the course of action that is selected, the dead stock will not disappear overnight. Therefore, it is important to lay out an approximate timetable for disposal and to subsequently insure that appropriate followup effort is provided.

11.3.3 *Items with Very Low Sales*

As mentioned earlier, increased technological change tends to proliferate the number of products and shorten product life cycles. Therefore, it is not surprising to find many C items with extremely low, albeit non-zero, sales. Many of these items may be minor variations of faster-moving products. In such a case, it can be attractive to eliminate the slow-moving special versions. Of course, decisions of this type, as well as those where there is no substitute product, go beyond the area of production planning/inventory management. Marketing considerations, including customer relations (for example, the slow-mover may be carried as a service item for an important customer) are obviously relevant. Furthermore, the appropriate course of action may not be to discontinue selling the item, but rather to make or buy it to order as opposed to stocking it, an issue to which we next turn.

11.4 *Stocking Versus Not Stocking an Item*

Given that we have decided to satisfy customer demands for a given s.k.u. the question we now face is, *Should we make a special purchase from the supplier (or production run) to satisfy each individual customer-demand transaction or should we purchase (or produce) to stock?* It should be emphasized that this question is not just restricted to C items. As we shall see, a low demand rate tends to favor non-stocking but there are a number of other factors that also influence the decision.

Earlier in the book we have seen that, *given that an item is stocked*, its total relevant costs per year are quite insensitive to the precise settings of the control variables (for example, the reorder point and the order quantity). Interestingly enough, more substantial savings can often be achieved through the appropriate answer to the question of whether or not the item should even be stocked.

11.4.1 *The Relevant Factors*

For simplicity we shall talk in terms of a purchased item; the concepts are readily adaptable to the in-house production context. There are a number of factors that can influence the decision to stock or not stock the item. These include:

i. The system cost (file maintenance, forecasting, etc.) per unit time of stocking an item.

ii. The unit variable cost of the item both when it is bought for stock and when it is purchased to meet each demand transaction: a more favorable price may be achieved by the regular larger buys associated with stocking. In addition, a premium per unit may be necessary if the non-stocking purchases are made from a competitor.

iii. The cost of a temporary backorder associated with each demand in the non-stocking situation.

iv. The fixed setup cost associated with each replenishment in both contexts. Account should be taken of possible coordination with other items, in that setup costs are reduced by such coordination.

v. The carrying charge (including the effects of obsolescence) which, together with the unit variable cost, determines the cost of carrying each unit of inventory per unit time.

vi. The frequency and magnitudes of demand transactions.

vii. The replenishment lead time.

11.4.2 A Simple Decision Rule

A general model to handle all of the above factors would be, because of its complexity, of limited value to the typical practitioner. Therefore, in this subsection we present a simple rule (based on work by Popp[12]), valid under specific assumptions. Even when these assumptions are violated the rule should still be useful as a guideline. In any event, in the next subsection some extensions will be discussed.

Assumptions

i. The unit variable cost is the same under stocking and non-stocking.

ii. The fixed setup cost is the same under stocking and non-stocking.

iii. In deriving the decision rule to decide on whether to stock the item or not we allow the order quantity to be non-integer (of course, if the item was actually stocked and demands were in integer units, we would certainly use an integer value for the order quantity).

iv. The replenishment lead time is negligible; consequently there is no backordering cost.

*The Decision Rule**—Do *not* stock the item if *either* of the following two conditions holds (otherwise stock the item):

$$c_s > A/E(i) \tag{11.9}$$

or

$$E(t)vr > \frac{E(i)}{2A}\left[\frac{A}{E(i)} - c_s\right]^2 \tag{11.10}$$

where

c_s is the system cost, in dollars per unit time, of having the item stocked.

* *The derivation of this rule is given in the appendix of this chapter.*

A is the fixed setup cost, in dollars, associated with a replenishment.

$E(i)$ is the expected (or average) interval (or time) between demand transactions.

$E(t)$ is the expected (or average) size of a demand transaction in units.

v is the unit variable cost of the item, in \$/unit.

r is the carrying charge, in \$/\$/unit time.

A graphical representation of the decision rule is shown in Figure 11.1.

Figure 11.1 A Rule for the Stock–No Stock Decision.

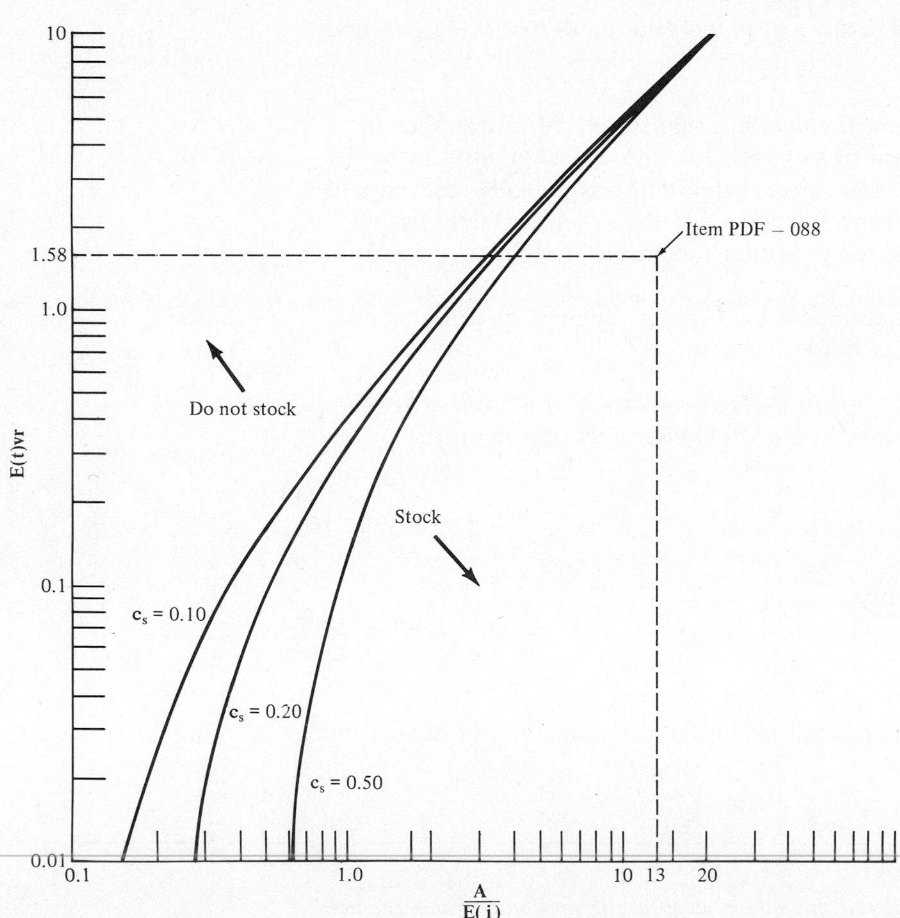

For a given c_s value we use the associated curve. If the $E(t)vr$ and $A/E(i)$ values are such that the corresponding point falls to the left or above the curve, the item should not be stocked. If, on the other hand, the point falls to the right or below the curve, then the item should be stocked using the economic order quantity

$$\text{EOQ} = \sqrt{\frac{2AD}{vr}} \tag{11.11}$$

where

$$D = E(t)/E(i) \tag{11.12}$$

is the demand rate, in units per unit time.

The behavior of the rule (best illustrated by Figure 11.1) as a function of the factors involved makes intuitive sense. As the setup cost A goes up we move to the right in the graph, thus tending to the stocking situation. In the same way, as the expected time between transactions decreases we move to the region where stocking is preferred. Considering the vertical axis, as v or r increase, we tend to the non-stocking situation; it becomes too expensive to carry the item in inventory. It is seen that as c_s increases we are less likely to prefer stocking of the item. Finally, the larger the expected transaction size, $E(t)$, the more likely we are to be in the region of non-stocking. Larger transaction sizes tend to support non-stocking in that now the individual special orders satisfy a relatively large demand.

Numerical Illustration—MIDAS Canada has been purchasing a specialty film item PDF-088 from a competitor each time that a customer demand has been encountered. The manager of purchasing feels that it would be attractive to make less frequent, larger purchases. Relevant parameter values have been estimated as follows:

$$v = \$4.70/\text{roll}$$

$$E(t) = 1.4 \text{ rolls}$$

$$E(i) = 10 \text{ weeks or } 10/52 \text{ years}$$

$$A = \$2.50$$

$$r = 0.24\ \$/\$/\text{yr.}$$

$$c_s = 0.20\ \$/\text{yr.}$$

We have

$$E(t)vr = (1.4)(4.70)(0.24) = 1.58\ \$/\text{yr.}$$

$$A/E(i) = 2.50/10/52 = 13.00\ \$/\text{yr.}$$

Use of Eqs. 11.9 and 11.10 or Figure 11.1 reveals that the item should indeed be purchased for stock with the best order quantity, from Eqs. 11.11 and 11.12, being 6 rolls.

11.4.3 *Some Extensions*

It is rather straightforward (see Problem 11.9) to generalize the decision rule of the previous subsection to allow the unit variable cost and the fixed setup cost to each depend upon whether or not the item is purchased for stock. In place of Eqs. 11.9 and 11.10 we have:

Do *not* stock the item if *either* of the following conditions hold (otherwise stock the item):

$$c_s > \frac{A_{ns}}{E(i)} + \frac{E(t)}{E(i)}(v_{ns} - v_s) \tag{11.13}$$

or

$$E(t)v_s r > \frac{E(i)}{2A_s}\left[\frac{A_{ns}}{E(i)} + \frac{E(t)}{E(i)}(v_{ns} - v_s) - c_s\right]^2 \tag{11.14}$$

where

v_s is the unit variable cost, in \$/unit, if the item is stocked.

v_{ns} is the unit variable cost, in \$/unit, if the item is not stocked.

A_s is the fixed setup cost, in dollars, if the item is stocked.

A_{ns} is the fixed setup cost, in dollars, if the item is not stocked (the cost of backordering and extra paperwork would be included in A_{ns}).

and all the other variables are as defined after Eqs. 11.9 and 11.10.

Equations 11.13 and 11.14 cannot be represented in a simple graphical fashion because of the large number of variables present.

Croston[2] has developed a decision rule, including a graphical aid, for the case of a periodic review, order-up-to-level (R, S) system. His model assumes a negligible replenishment lead time, at most one demand transaction in each review interval, and a normal distribution of transaction sizes.

It should be emphasized that the two quantities, $E(t)$ and $E(i)$, needed in Eqs. 11.9 and 11.10 or Eqs. 11.13 and 11.14, would be estimated from rather sparse data, sparse because of the low usage nature of the items under consideration. The statistical fluctuations of such limited data could cause an item, whose underlying parameters had really not changed, to pass the stocking test one year and fail it in the next. Johnson[7] has proposed the useful idea of two threshold values, one to discontinue stocking an item, the other to institute stocking. The intermediate or buffer area helps prevent an item from flipping back and forth between stocking and non-stocking as time passes.

11.5 *Summary*

In this chapter we have discussed procedures for controlling the inventories of the large number of items with low annual dollar usage. Simplicity of control was stressed because of the low annual total of replenishment, carrying, and shortage costs associated with such items. Said another way, if the total of replenishment, carrying, and shortage costs for an item is on the order of but a few dollars per year, we must use for that item a control system that costs only pennies per year.

A final point worth mentioning is that with C items, in particular, the best method of control may be ascertained from the warehouseman or production foreman who knows, for example, that a lot size of 10 units fits conveniently into a storage bin or into the usual production schedule. Using a decision rule that provides a different quantity (with a likely trivial annual difference in costs) is hardly worth the risk of alienating the warehouseman or foreman.

Appendix to Chapter 11—Derivation of Eqs. 11.9 and 11.10

The demand rate per unit time, D, is given by

$$D = E(t)/E(i) \tag{11.15}$$

Ignoring the minor effects of thc non-unit sized transactions, we have the same setting as in the derivation of the economic order quantity (Section 5.2 of Chapter 5). Therefore, from Eq. 5.4 of Chapter 5 and Eq. 11.15 the best order quantity, if the item is stocked, is

$$\text{EOQ} = \sqrt{\frac{2AE(t)}{vrE(i)}}$$

Moreover, from Eq. 5.5 of Chapter 5 and including the c_s system cost, the best total relevant costs per unit time, if the item is stocked, are

$$\text{TRC}_s(\text{EOQ}) = \sqrt{2AE(t)vr/E(i)} + c_s \tag{11.16}$$

If the item is not stocked, there is a cost A associated with each transaction which occurs, on the average, every $E(i)$ units of time. Therefore, the total relevant costs per unit time, if the item is not stocked, are

$$\text{TRC}_{ns} = A/E(i) \tag{11.17}$$

Clearly, if c_s itself is larger than $A/E(i)$, then $\text{TRC}_{ns} < \text{TRC}_s$. This gives the condition of Eq. 11.9. More generally, requiring

$$\text{TRC}_{ns} < \text{TRC}_s$$

and using Eqs. 11.16 and 11.17, leads to

$$A/E(i) < \sqrt{2AE(t)vr/E(i)} + c_s$$

or

$$2AE(t)vr/E(i) > \left[\frac{A}{E(i)} - c_s\right]^2$$

that is,

$$E(t)vr > \frac{E(i)}{2A}\left[\frac{A}{E(i)} - c_s\right]^2$$

Problems for Chapter 11

Problem 11.1

Consider a MIDAS item with the following characteristics

$D = 50$ units/yr.; $v = \$0.40$/unit;
$L = 3$ months.

In establishing a value of σ it is reasonable to assume that demand for the item is adequately approximated by a Poisson process. For an (s, Q) control system

a. find the appropriate Q value using Table 11.1,

b. find the s value assuming a desired TBS of 20 years and using Table 11.2.

Problem 11.2

Suppose for the item in Problem 11.1 we instead decided to use an (R, S) system of control. What should be the values of R and S?

Problem 11.3

Suppose a company is using the following rule for controlling the stock of C items. Whenever the inventory position drops to 2 months or lower, order a 6 month supply. For each of the following items, what is the implied value of TBS? (Use Eq. 11.6 with $a_1 = 1.2$, $b_1 = 0.62$ and $c_1 = 0.5$.)

a. Item 372: $D = 60$ units/yr., $L = 1.5$ months.

b. Item 373: $D = 60$ units/yr., $L = 3$ months.

C. Item 374: $D = 30$ units/yr., $L = 1.5$ months.

Problem 11.4

For the specialty film item discussed in Section 11.4.2, how large would c_s have to be to make it unattractive to stock the item?

Problem 11.5

Consider a company with $A = \$4.00$, $r =$ 0.30/yr. and cost of stocking, $c_s = \$0.50$/yr. There are two items (X and Y) having the same annual demand rate, $D = 10$ units/yr. and unit value $v = \$6.00$/unit. However, the transactions for item X tend to be larger than those for item Y, namely the average transaction size for X is 5 units while that for Y is only 2 units.

a. Show, using Figure 11.1, that X should not be stocked and Y should be stocked.

b. Why are the decisions different for the two items?

Problem 11.6

A C item is often purchased from the same supplier as a B or A item. Suppose that such is the case and, based upon an EOQ analysis for the B (or A) item involved, an order is placed for the B (or A) item every 2 months. Assume that demand for the C item is essentially constant with time at a rate of 18 units/yr. Assume that the item has a unit value of \$3.00/unit. The *additional* fixed cost of including the C item in an order of the B (or A) item is \$1.20. The carrying charge is 0.24/yr. It is reasonable to restrict attention to ordering the C item in a quantity that will last for 2 months, 4 months, 6 months, etc. (that is, an integer multiple of the time supply of the other item). Which of these time supplies is preferred?

Problem 11.7

In Section 11.2.3 two possible methods were suggested for estimating σ_L for a C item. The Poisson approach of Eq. 11.7 is certainly simpler than use of the regression result of Eq. 11.6.

a. For the numerical illustration of item XSC-037 obtain σ_L and s using Eq. 11.6.

b. For the MIDAS values of a_1, b_1, and c_1 show that under most values of D and L the simple Poisson approach will give a lower σ_L than the aggregate relationship. Is this desirable?

Problem 11.8

Suppose you have been hired as an inventory control consultant by a client having thousands of inventoried items. The client feels that there is merit in each of the (R, S) and two-bin (s, Q) systems of control and is willing to have some C items under each of the two types of control. Using whatever symbols you feel are appropriate, develop as simple a decision rule as possible for deciding on which type of control to use for each specific item.

Problem 11.9

Develop Eqs. 11.13 and 11.14.

Problem 11.10

In the first part of MIDAS Case D a description was presented of the Inventory Control Manager's method of dealing with slow-moving items. Review his method, suggesting possible improvements.

References for Chapter 11

1. Brown, R. G. *Management Decisions for Production Operations.* Dryden Press, Hinsdale, Illinois, 1971, Chapter 4.

2. Croston, J. D. "Stock Levels for Slow-Moving Items." *Operational Research Quarterly,* Vol. 25, No. 1, March, 1974, pp. 123–130.

3. Dyer, D. "To Stock or Not to Stock? That is the Question." *Modern Distribution Management,* Vol. 7, No. 5, March 23, 1973, pp. 3–7.

4. Dyer, D. "How to Make a Profit on Non-Stock Shipments." *Modern Distribution Management,* Vol. 7, No. 14, July 27, 1973, pp. 3–7.

5. Dyer, D. "Manufacturers! Dead Items are Killing You." *Modern Distribution Management,* Vol. 7, No. 16, August 31, 1973, pp. 3–6.

6. Hart, A. "Determination of Excess Stock Quantities." *Management Science,* Vol. 19, No. 12, August, 1973, pp. 1444–1451.

7. Johnson, J. "On Stock Selection at Spare Parts Stores Sections." *Naval Research Logistics Quarterly,* Vol. 9, No. 1, March, 1962, pp. 49–59.

8. Mohan, C. and R. Garg. "Decision on Retention of Excess Stock." *Operations Research,* Vol. 9, No. 4, July–August, 1961, pp. 496–499.

9. Naddor, E. "Inventory Returns and Special Sales." *Journal of Industrial Engineering,* Vol. XVIII, No. 9, September, 1967, pp. 560–561.

10. Orr, D. and A. Kaplan. "The Economic Stockage Model." Inventory Research Office, U.S. Army Logistics Management Center, Fort Lee, Virginia, June, 1971.

11. Plossl, G. W. and O. W. Wight. *Production and Inventory Control: Principles and Techniques.* Prentice-Hall, Englewood Cliffs, N.J., 1967, pp. 56–61.

12. Popp, W. "Simple and Combined Inventory Policies, Production to Stock or to Order." *Management Science,* Vol. 11, No. 9, July, 1965, pp. 868–873.

13. Wulff, P. "Don't Need It? Scrap It." *Purchasing,* June 5, 1973, pp. 37–39.

PART 4

Decision Systems for Coordinated Control of Individual Items

In Parts 2 and 3 we have been concerned with the control of individual items. The rules and systems developed have treated the individual items in isolation, the one exception being where we were concerned with aggregate consequences of a particular decision rule. Examples of the latter were all the exchange curve considerations and situations (such as the multi-item newsboy problem of Chapter 10) where there was a constraint on the total value of the order quantities.

In Part 4 we now turn to explicit consideration of coordinated control in two important contexts where such coordination often leads to substantial cost savings. First, in Chapter 12, we deal with the multi-stage or multi-echelon situation. In the multi-stage manufacturing context the products are developed by a number of manufacturing operations from raw materials through components, subassemblies, etc., to the finished s.k.u. It is clear that replenishment decisions at different stages should not be made independently because of the intimate interdependence of the different stages of the same product. In a multi-echelon setting material is stored at more than one geographical location with one or more central stores feeding the stock to branch locations. Again, replenishment decisions at the central and branch warehouses should be coordinated because the branches draw on the stock at the central location.

Chapter 13 is concerned with a different type of coordination. Here we return to the single stocking point context but now consider coordination of replenishments of a group of items to reduce replenishment costs. Such coordination makes sense if one of the following conditions occurs:

i. Several items are purchased from the same supplier

ii. Several items share the same mode of transportation

iii. Several items are produced on the same piece of equipment and setup costs depend upon the sequencing of the items

The above-mentioned coordination issues make *exact* analyses an order-of-magnitude more complex than those of earlier chapters. Therefore, we are frequently forced to resort to heuristic decision rules.

Chapter 14 differs somewhat from the rest of the book. It is devoted to the discussion of a potpourri of individual item problems that are complex in nature, but where substantial progress towards practical solutions has been made. In the last chapter of the book (Chapter 20) we shall briefly return to related complex problems which remain as challenging topics for further research.

Midas Canada Corporation (E)*

Inter-office Memorandum (translated from German)

TO: Mr. Wolfgang Gatzke, Manager of Manufacturing, MIDAS International
FROM: Mr. Otto Felker, Vice-President of Operations, MIDAS International
TOPIC: Inventory Control in the Manufacturing of Film Processors

I have recently received feedback from two individuals. Mr. Klaus Reiner, Vice-President of Marketing, informs me that most promised due dates for customer deliveries are not being met. In fact, he states: "The only way we can get something delivered anywhere near the promised date is to expedite like crazy." At the same time, Mr. Dieter Schwaban, the Comptroller, states that raw material and in-process inventories have increased markedly in the past year. How is it possible that simultaneously customer service is decreasing while inventories are rising?

I have scanned the shift reports of a number of production foremen. Perhaps some of their typical comments may provide some insight:

> *We don't seem to ever know our needs in terms of components. For example, there were 50 units of the wash tank for the assembly W53688 in inventory for several months. This week, when we finally received an order release for assembling the tanks into the larger processing units, 75 of them were needed!*
>
> *Production order V7145 could not be completed today. As usual, one of the five needed components was out of stock.*
>
> *Production was below standard because a rush order forced us to tear down lot V7286 which was partially completed.*

* *The MIDAS cases describe actual decision systems which are based on consulting experiences of the authors. They do not describe the situation at any single company, but are in fact a compendium of actual situations which have been compressed into the environment of a single firm and industry for illustrative purposes. The cases are not intended as presentations of either effective or ineffective ways of handling administrative problems.*

> *These order quantities and reorder points, based on mathematics, are useless! I don't care what they suggest. This week I needed components for the assembly of* 30 *tube and pivot assemblies and I won't need any more for several weeks as no further assemblies are planned in that period.*

Didn't you state at the last scheduling meeting that we now had item inventory records on the computer and that forecasting procedures for usage of each component item had been developed? Clearly, something is wrong with the procedures. Are they appropriate for our type of manufacturing environment? In particular, I recall that Rudy Ertle, who attended an international meeting of a production and inventory control society last year, was enthusiastic about a recently developed approach (MPR, MRP, PMR or something like that) that he thought was particularly well suited for our situation. I suggest that you talk with Rudy.

CHAPTER TWELVE

Planning and Control in Multi-echelon Stocking Situations

In Chapters 5 through 11 we have dealt with a stocking point in isolation. In particular, the order-point or order-up-to-level systems of Chapters 6 through 8 (here we shall refer to them as stock replenishment systems) assume reasonably smooth demand whose residual variability can be predicted by statistical procedures. Furthermore, these methods assume that the inventory of an item should be replenished as soon as its level drops below a prescribed value (order point) or on a regular basis (periodic review, order-up-to-level). In a multi-stage production process (for example, primary, secondary, assembly, and packaging operations) or in a multi-echelon distribution system (for example, central warehouse, regional warehouses,

and retail outlets) these assumptions are normally not valid. In particular, the demand at one level is clearly dependent upon the production or ordering behavior of the next level closer to the ultimate customer. In such a situation the requirements at a level other than that of the end item should probably not be forecast by statistical extrapolation of the historical demand observed at that level; instead one can usually take advantage of the fact that the requirements of a particular level are, at least to a large extent, implied by the replenishment schedule of the level one step closer to the end item. To illustrate, consider an assembly made up of two components (A and B) with a negligible assembly time. Suppose component A is used only in this particular assembly. If it is ascertained that 500 assemblies are required in the month of June, then clearly we need 500 units of component A by the assembly time for June. In such a situation it would be inappropriate to estimate A's requirements by means of statistical forecasting. Furthermore, it is quite conceivable that the next batch of assemblies would not be needed until several months later. In such a case there would be no need to replenish the inventory of component A *immediately* after the 500 units were used to satisfy June's assembly requirements.

In this chapter we discuss methods of coping with such multi-echelon production/inventory problems. Section 12.1 begins with the relatively simple multi-echelon distribution (non-production) context and introduces the important notion of a base stock control system. In Sections 12.2 to 12.4 we turn explicitly to the production (manufacturing) setting. Section 12.2 amplifies the complexities of planning and control in a multi-stage manufacturing process. In Section 12.3 we point out the problems of using stock replenishment systems in such an environment. Then, in Section 12.4, we present a radically different approach for coping with such a situation, namely the important topic of material requirements planning. In Section 12.5, the rather simple situation of *deterministic* constant end-item demand in a serial* production system is handled; here an analytic model is quite useful in specifying the interrelationship of run quantities at the various stages of production. Finally, Section 12.6 is concerned with one important *probabilistic* multi-echelon situation where mathematical modelling has proved to be of significant value.

---

* *By serial we mean that there is no convergence (that is, assembly) or divergence (that is, splitting of an item into two or more items); rather the product simply goes through a sequence of conversion operations from raw material to a finished item.*

12.1 *The Base Stock Control System*

For illustrative purposes let us consider the simplified multi-echelon situation depicted in Figure 12.1, namely a single product being supplied from a central warehouse through a branch warehouse and a retail outlet to the ultimate customers. The replenishment lead times between adjacent levels (in each case assuming that the feeding level has adequate stock) are as follows:

Branch to retailer—1 week

Central to branch—1 week

Supplier to central—3 weeks

Straightforward use of the methods of Chapters 5 through 8 would dictate that each stocking level (retailer, branch warehouse, and central warehouse) would *independently* make replenishment decisions based upon its own

i. Cost factors and service considerations

ii. Predicted demand—presumably forecasts based upon historical demand that it has observed *from the next stocking point down the line*

iii. Replenishment lead time from the next stocking point up the line

Such a system of control tends to have two serious flaws. First of all, even if end-customer demand is fairly smooth, the orders placed farther and farther up the line become progressively larger and less frequent; for example, the central warehouse is now faced with a "demand" pattern made up of infrequent transactions equal in size to the replenishment orders generated at the branch warehouse. Under an order point type system of control, the central warehouse would thus have to carry a large safety stock to protect against these infrequent demands, even when end-item usage possessed relatively little variability. In an example in Chapter 2, with lead times neglected (non-zero lead times would make matters worse), it was shown that a 20 percent transient change in retail sales had a dramatic effect at the distributor level (referred to here as the branch warehouse). As mentioned in Chapter 2 this is consistent with Forrester's[14] findings that small changes in end-item demand can lead to large

Figure 12.1 A Multi-echelon Situation with Single Stage Information Flow.

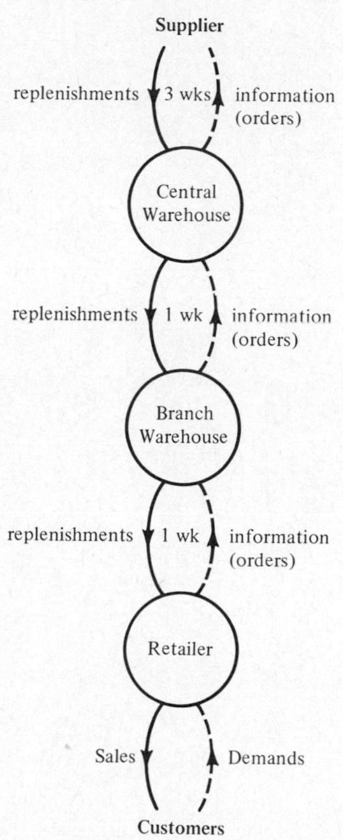

oscillations in the replenishment sizes and inventory levels upstream in such a system. A second problem is that independent control of stocking points does not allow one to properly take account of the cost implications at one level of using certain ordering logic at another level, for example, reducing replenishment quantities from the central warehouse to the branch warehouse may appear unattractive to the latter (when analysed by means of a *single level* EOQ type approach), where, in fact, the benefits caused by smoother demand at the central warehouse could more than compensate for the increased total setup costs at the branch level.

The base stock system is a response to at least the first of the above difficulties. The key change is to make end-item demand information available for decision making at *all* stocking points as illustrated in Figure 12.2. This necessitates the use of an effective communication system, for example, telex or a remote input computer linkage. *Each stocking point makes replenishments based on actual end-item customer demands* rather

Figure 12.2 Information and Stock Flow in a Base Stock System.

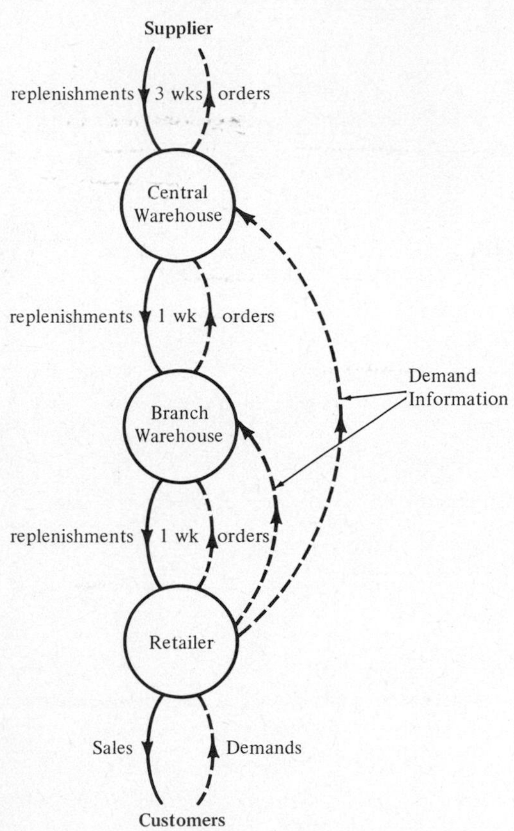

than on replenishment orders from the next level downstream. With this modification the procedures of Chapters 5 through 8 are now more appropriate to use. In particular, the most common type of base stock system is one where an order point and an order-up-to-level are used for each stocking point, that is, an (s, S) system. For each stocking point treated independently an order quantity (Q) is established (using end-item demand forecasts) by one of the methods of Chapters 5 and 8. Next, a reorder point s is established by one of the procedures of Chapters 6 and 7, using end-item demand forecasts over the replenishment lead time appropriate to the level under consideration (for example, the central warehouse would use a lead time of 3 weeks). Then *the order-up-to-level, S, also called the base stock level*, is determined through the relation

$$S = s + Q \tag{12.1}$$

In terms of physical operation, the inventory position at each level is monitored according to the following relation:

$$\text{Inventory position} = (\text{On-hand}) + (\text{On-order}) - (\text{Committed}) \quad (12.2)$$

where it is important to recognize that:

i. The "on-hand" for a particular stocking point includes all of the on-hand stock at that point and at all stocking points closer to the customer as well as any stock in transit beyond the stocking point under consideration (closer to the customer). In the case of a production assembly process the on-hand of a component in Eq. 12.2 would include all units of the component from its point of manufacture (or acquisition) right through to and including those in the finished product.

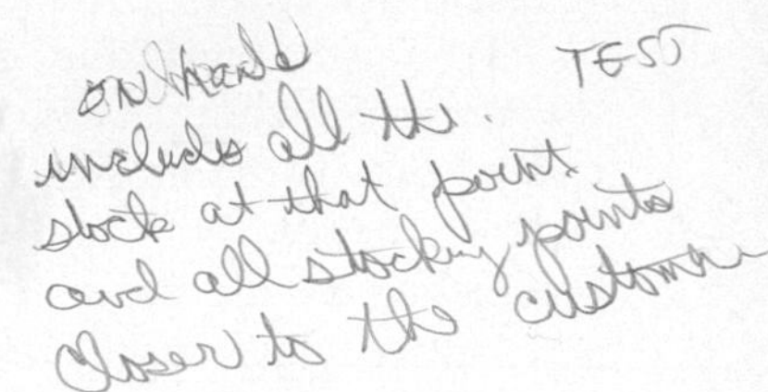

ii. The "committed" includes all customer demand received but not yet satisfied at the end-item point (this is important when there is an appreciable delay in satisfying customer demand, for example, when there is a stockout, with associated backorders, at the end-item storage point).

To illustrate, suppose that at a point in time the physical stocks of our example (Figure 12.2) are:

Branch warehouse—50 units

Retail outlet—20 units

Also suppose that 5 units of known customer demand have not yet been satisfied. Furthermore, assume that there is no order outstanding from the branch on the central warehouse and nothing in transit between the branch and the retail outlet. Then, the inventory position for the branch level would be

$$\text{Inventory position} = (50+20) + (0) - (5) = 65 \text{ units}$$

Clark and Scarf[6] have defined a quantity called the echelon stock as follows: "echelon stock of stage j is the number of units in the system which are in or have passed through stage j but have as yet not been sold." It is seen from the above discussion that Eq. 12.2 can also be expressed as

$$\text{Inventory position} = (\text{Echelon stock}) + (\text{On-order})$$

Once the inventory position is known (after each transaction or on a periodic basis; in the latter case the replenishment lead time for safety stock calculations at each level must be increased by the review interval), it is compared with the reorder point, s. Whenever it is at or lower than s, enough is ordered (from the preceding level) to raise the position to the base stock level, S.

To repeat, ordering decisions at any stocking point in the base stock system are made as a result of *end-item* demand, not orders from the next level downstream. There is much less variability in the former than in the latter, hence significantly lower safety stocks (reduced carrying costs) are achieved by the base stock system.

Notice, that in the base stock system each level is still permitted to "pull" requisitions from the next higher level. For illustrative purposes let us consider a slightly different multi-echelon situation as depicted in Figure 12.3. A more sophisticated type of control system, referred to as a "push" system would operate in the following manner. Rather than each branch warehouse "pulling" stock from the central warehouse, instead the central warehouse "pushes" stock out to the branches. How much to push to each depends upon the stock status at the central warehouse and at each branch warehouse. This type of system has been analyzed by Brown[4] among others.

Figure 12.3 A Multi-echelon System with More than One Stocking Point at the Same Level.

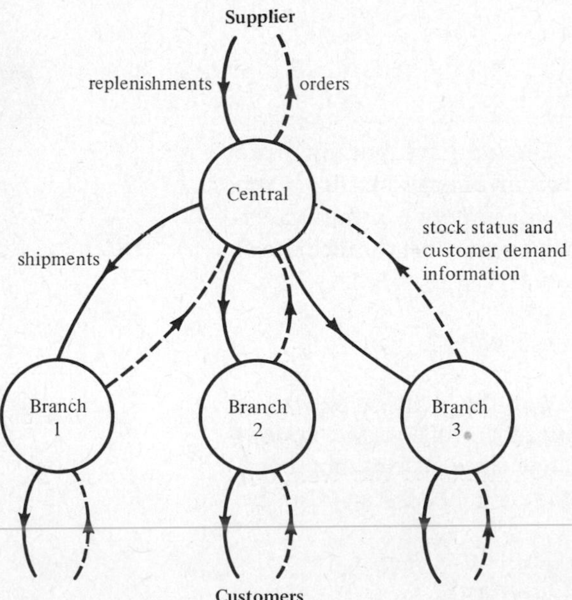

12.2 The Complexity of Multi-stage Manufacturing Processes

In the terminology introduced earlier in the book, in the preceding section we were still dealing with the situation of a merchant. Now we turn to the more complicated context of a producer. Let us consider a manufacturing facility with a number of different work centres. To achieve each finished product (in the form of an assembly of several components) processing through several of these centres is required. Inventories can exist in the following forms:

i. Raw materials

ii. Work-in-process raw materials to component parts

iii. Component parts

iv. Work-in-process component parts to subassemblies

v. Subassemblies

vi. Work-in-process subassemblies to assemblies

vii. Assemblies

As mentioned earlier, the requirements through time of a particular component are influenced (in fact, primarily dictated) by the production schedules of the next (closer-to-the-end-items) level of components in which this element is used, that is, there are complicated interactions between the production schedules (and associated inventories) of the various level items. Furthermore, relatively smooth demand for end-products can produce erratic requirements through time for a particular component because of the batching of assemblies, subassemblies, etc. This is illustrated in the example of Table 12.1 where the same subassembly A is used in three different assemblies. Notice that the end usage of each assembly is uniform with time, yet the requirements for subassembly A are highly erratic with time because the assemblies (for setup cost reasons) are made in lots covering more than a single period of demand.

An added complexity in a manufacturing environment is the frequent need for many components to achieve a single finished item. Inadequate supplies of any of the components will lead to delays as well as excess in-process stock of the other components. To make matters worse there are capacity constraints at the work centers (only so many machine-hours of

Table 12.1 An Illustration of Erratic Requirements for a Subassembly[a]

Time Period	1	2	3	4	5	6	7	8	9	10
Assembly *X*										
Demand	10	10	10	10	10	10	10	10	10	10
Production	30	—	—	30	—	—	30	—	—	30
Assembly *Y*										
Demand	5	5	5	5	5	5	5	5	5	5
Production	20	—	—	—	20	—	—	—	20	—
Assembly *Z*										
Demand	7	7	7	7	7	7	7	7	7	7
Production	14	—	14	—	14	—	14	—	14	—
Subassembly *A*										
Requirements	64	—	14	30	34	—	44	—	34	30

[a] Each of assemblies *X*, *Y*, and *Z* requires one unit of subassembly *A*. For simplicity, we assume negligible assembly times.

production can be achieved at a particular work centre in a shift of operation).

The cost components involved include setup and value added costs at machine centers (or replenishment costs for raw materials), inventory carrying costs, production overtime costs, shortage costs, and system control costs. Ideally, given forecasts of usage of end-items by time period, one would like to establish production run (purchase) quantities through time at the various levels of manufacturing so as to keep the total relevant costs as low as possible while at the same time not violating any of the constraints. The complexity of the problem clearly rules out the determination of "optimum" production and procurement quantities. Rather the best for which we can hope is a feasible solution which produces reasonable costs. This is the philosophy underlying the material requirements planning method to be discussed in Section 12.4. However, before that discussion we now emphasize the weaknesses of using stock replenishment systems in a manufacturing environment.

12.3 The Weaknesses of Stock Replenishment Systems in a Manufacturing Setting

Recall that by the terms "stock replenishment" we mean decision rules that employ order points or order-up-to-levels based on *safety stocks* developed through analysis of errors of *forecasting* the needs of individual components treated *independently*, precisely the approach presented in Chapters 6 and 7. The weaknesses of such an approach in a manufacturing environment include:

i. There is no need to statistically forecast the requirements of a component. Once the production plans for all items in which it is used have been established, then the requirements of the component follow, as *dependent* demand, by simple arithmetic. (This is illustrated by the example of Table 12.1.)

ii. The procedures for establishing safety stocks are usually based on reasonably smooth demand. As discussed above (and illustrated in Table 12.1) this is usually unrealistic in the case of component items.

iii. As mentioned earlier in this chapter, replenishment systems are geared to replenish stocks immediately following large demands that drive inventories to low levels. Again, in an erratic demand situation, a large demand may be followed by several *known* periods of inactivity. In such a situation it makes no sense to immediately replenish the stock—unnecessary carrying costs would be incurred by such an action.

iv. Where several components are needed for a single assembly the inventories of these individual components should not be treated in isolation. To illustrate, consider the case where twenty different components are required for a particular assembly. Suppose, under *independent* control of the components, that for each component there is a 95 percent chance that it is in stock. Then the probability of being able to build a complete assembly is only $(0.95)^{20}$ or 0.36, that is, 64 percent of the time at least one of the components would be unavailable, thus delaying the completion of an assembly.

12.4 *Material Requirements Planning (MRP)*

The basic concepts of material requirements planning (MRP) have been known for many years. However, the associated data-processing requirements were prohibitive until the advent of the random access computer—prohibitive primarily in the sense that the time required to develop or modify a production schedule was so long as to not allow the production schedule to be available when it was needed. The other major factor in the recent marked increase of MRP has been the effective efforts by the American Production and Inventory Control Society to encourage adoption of the method.

There are a number of excellent writings on the subject (see, for example, References 36 to 39). Also, software packages are in existence (see, for example, Reference 23). Therefore, we have chosen to omit many of the finer details of MRP.

12.4.1 *Objectives of MRP*

MRP, recognizing the distinct differences of the manufacturing (producer) environment from that of distribution (merchant), is specifically geared to satisfy the basic needs of the manufacturing setting. In particular, account is taken of the fact that, in such a setting, inventory management is inseparable from production planning. The needs of the manufacturer include:

i. Planned and controlled inventories, in particular having items available at the time of usage (and not much earlier).

ii. Generation and revision of replenishment actions both in terms of procurement and production, that is, item by item, what is to be purchased (manufactured) and when. Priorities, particularly for shop scheduling and control purposes, should be based on up-to-date information on due dates and availability of components.

iii. Capacity planning by means of projection of planned order requirements. From the suppliers' standpoint this also gives a projection of order workload which can help reduce supply lead times and costs of production.

12.4.2 *Some Important Terminology*

Before describing the MRP approach it is first necessary to discuss some concepts that will be utilized in such a description.

Bill of Materials—To properly take account of the dependent nature of demand we must have a means of projecting the needs, in terms of components, for a production lot of a particular assembly or subassembly. The bill of materials helps us achieve this goal. In the more common modular form, which we shall use, a bill of materials for a particular inventory item (termed the parent) shows all of its *immediate* components and their numbers per unit of the parent. This is illustrated in Figure 12.4 for the dryer roll assembly (which is itself only a rather minor component

Figure 12.4 The Dryer Roll Assembly of an Automatic Film Processor.

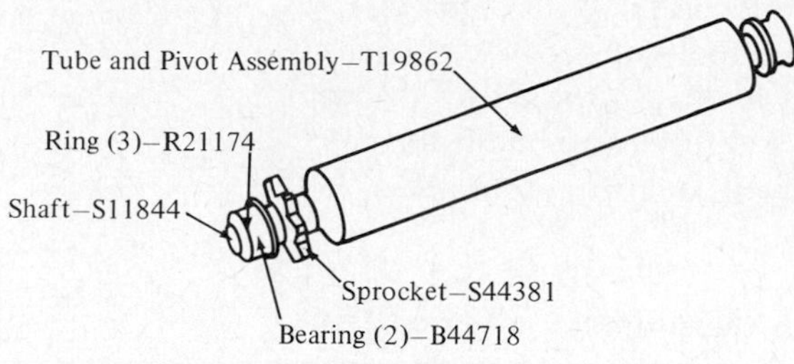

Bill of Materials:

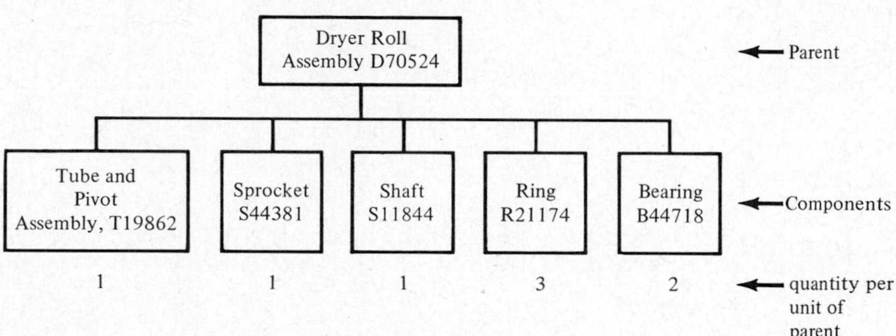

of several options of MIDAS International's automatic film processors). The meaning of the word "immediate" becomes clear when it is seen that in Figure 12.4 we do not subdivide the tube and pivot assembly, T19862, into its components. This would be done on a separate bill of materials for that item.

Where there is a wide diversity of end items (because of a number of optional choices available to the customer) one would not bother to develop a bill of materials for each end-item, rather the first level would be that of the major subassemblies.

Level Coding—To provide a systematic framework for exploding back the implications on all components of a given schedule of final assembly operations it is convenient to use a particular method of coding the bills of materials. Each bill of materials is assigned a level code according to the following logic:

> Level 0—a finished product (or end-item) not used as a component of any other product.

Level 1—the most removed (from the ultimate consumer) level of usage of the item under consideration is as a direct component of a level 0 item. At the same time the level 1 item could also be a finished product in itself. To illustrate, consider the example of an automobile and tires. A particular type of tire could be sold as a finished product in its own right. However, if it was used as a direct component in the manufacture of one or more types of level 0 automobiles, it would be classified as a level 1 item.

Level 2—the most removed (from the ultimate consumer) level of usage is as a direct component of a level 1 item.

Figure 12.5 Level Coding.

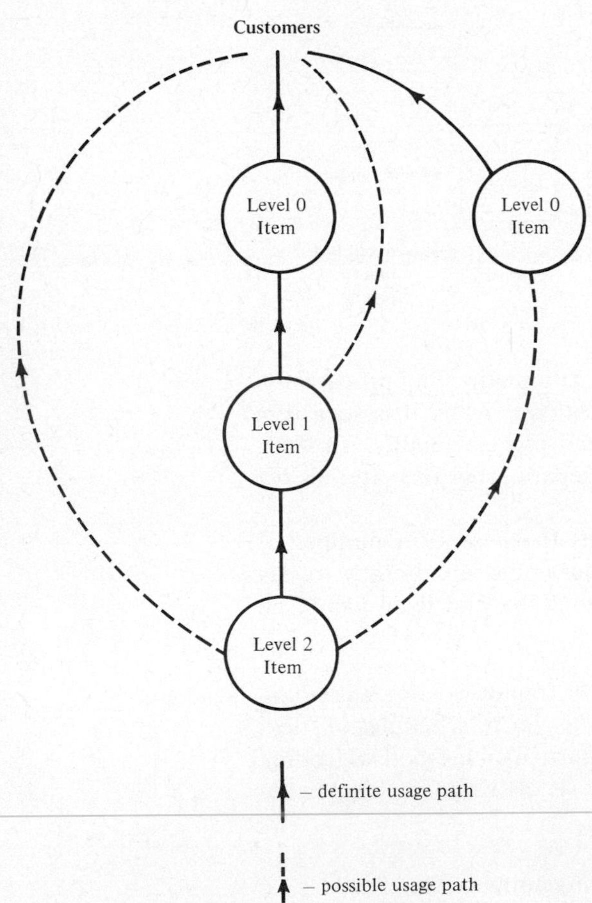

> Again, as shown by the dotted lines in Figure 12.5, a level 2 item could be used as a direct component of a level 0 item or could even itself be a finished product.

> Level n—the most removed level of usage is as a direct component of a level $(n-1)$ item, that is, as a component on a bill of materials with level code $(n-1)$.

This coding process is continued all the way back to raw materials which are themselves given appropriate level codes.

Figure 12.6 illustrates a portion (only a small fraction of the components are shown) of such a coding for one particular model of MIDAS' automatic film processors. Note the position of the dryer roll assembly (of Figure

Figure 12.6 A Portion of the Level-by-Level Coding for a MIDAS Automatic Film Processor.

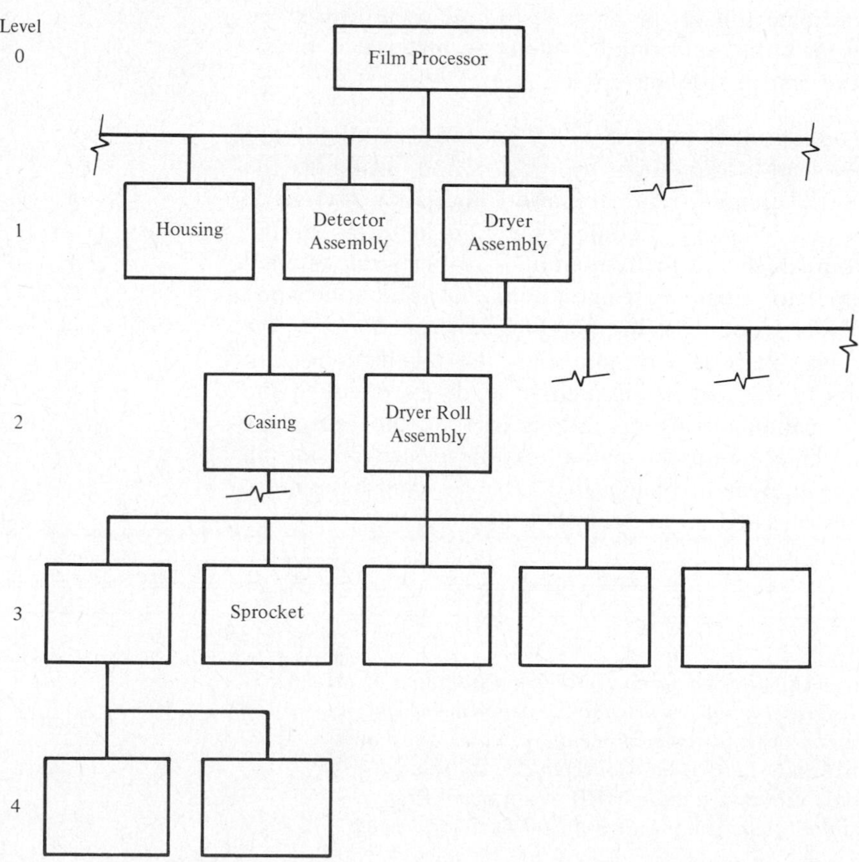

12.4) which, incidentally, is also used to satisfy direct demand as a service part.

Lead Times (Offsetting)—The manufacturing operation represented by a particular bill of materials, for example, combining components *B* and *C* in a complicated machining activity to produce subassembly *A*, may require a considerable length of time, particularly when one recognizes that such operations tend to be performed on batches of items. In such a case, if certain requirements of item A are specified for a particular date (the due date), then we must properly offset (or phase in time) the order release date for the machining operation; in other words, the corresponding units of parts *B* and *C* must be available at a suitably earlier time. To illustrate, suppose that the dryer assembly (Figure 12.6) operation is performed in a batch size such that approximately one week is required from order release to completion date. Therefore, if 100 dryer assemblies were required by, for example, June 26th, then 100 of the components, namely the casing, dryer roll assembly, etc., would be needed by June 19th. (In actuality one might be able to start assembling the 100 dryer units before all 100 of each of the components were available.) In the case of a raw material the lead time (offset) is the time that elapses from when we send the purchase order until the moment when the material is physically present ready for the first processing operation.

The Master Production Schedule—The master schedule shows the planned (or firm) production quantities by time period* out into the future for every end-(level 0) item. In the case where there is a myriad of possible final assemblies, the master schedule would be in terms of the level 1 subassemblies from which the final assemblies would be developed (in a relatively short time) to satisfy customer demands. The total time period covered by the master schedule is the planning horizon. To properly anticipate needs all the way back to raw materials the planning horizon should be at least as long as the *largest* cumulative lead time through the various procurement and manufacturing operations (that is, the longest in terms of cumulative lead time, of all the paths possible in progressing all the way down through the equivalent of Figure 12.6). We shall have more to say concerning the master schedule in Section 12.4.10.

---

* *MRP, in its usual computerized form, requires the handling of scheduling on a discrete time basis, the normal period being one week, that is, requirements and replenishment quantities are shown no finer than on a weekly time basis. Conceptually, as pointed out by Rhodes*[41]*, one could certainly handle MRP on an event (transaction) basis rather than by the somewhat artificial basis of discrete time slots.*

12.4.3 *Information Required for MRP*

To carry out material requirements planning the following input information is essential:

i. The master production schedule out to the planning horizon.

ii. The inventory status of each item (including possible backorders).

iii. The timing of and quantities involved in any outstanding or planned replenishment orders.

iv. Forecasts (which can be partially or entirely firm customer orders) of demand for each component, *subject to direct customer demand*, by time period out to the planning horizon.

v. All relevants bills of materials and associated level codes.

vi. Production or procurement lead times (offsets) for each operation.

vii. Possible scrap allowances for some operations (for example, to convert item B to item A we require, because of losses, on the average, 105 units of B to obtain 100 units of A).

As will be discussed later, additional information may be needed in order to determine the production quantities (lot sizes) for any specific item.

12.4.4 *The General Approach of MRP*

In this subsection, to provide an overview, we present only an outline of the general approach used in MRP, purposely omitting details that we shall subsequently discuss in the following subsection.

MRP seeks to achieve the objectives outlined in Section 12.4.1, which include overcoming the weaknesses of stock replenishment systems in a manufacturing environment, the latter as discussed in Section 12.3. In particular MRP makes specific use of the dependent nature of demands for components. Also account is taken of the time-varying (erratic) nature of the requirements for components. Moreover, the inventories of different components needed for the same operation are coordinated so as to avoid the situation of a shortage of one element delaying the operation as well as tying up the other components in inventory.

MRP begins with the master production schedule which provides the timing (order release dates) and quantities of production (normally assembly) of all end-(level 0) items. The product files (bills of materials) indicate the immediate component items and their quantities per unit of each parent item. Thus, a time series of requirements (at each order release date of the level 0 items) is generated for the level 1 items. For each level 1 item one must add to this time series of *dependent* requirements any requirements for externally generated direct independent demand (for example, as service parts). The result is a new series of requirements by time period, known as the *gross requirements* of the item.

Next, for each level 1 item, existing inventories (quantities on hand plus already on order) are allocated against the gross requirements to produce a modified series of requirements by time period, known as the *net requirements* of the item. Then appropriate coverage is provided for this level 1 item by adjusting previously scheduled replenishment actions and/or by initiating new replenishment actions. Adjustments include:

i. Increasing (or decreasing) a replenishment quantity

ii. Advancing (or delaying) the order due date

iii. Cancelling the order

A new action involves specification of the item involved, the order quantity, the order release date and the order due date. In selecting the timing and sizes of replenishments we are faced with a deterministic, time-varying pattern of demands, precisely the situation encountered in Chapter 8. Therefore, the Silver–Meal heuristic (the details are in Section 8.6 of Chapter 8) could certainly be used for selecting the lot sizes. However, quite often a very simple solution (which would be found by the heuristic) is appropriate, namely to cover only a single time period with a replenishment quantity. This is the case when

i. The requirements pattern is very erratic, that is, the only requirements are large occasional quantities, or

ii. The production operation involved has a very low setup cost, usually the case in an assembly operation.

The part-period balancing heuristic (discussed in Section 8.7.2 of Chapter 8) has also been frequently used in MRP systems. If an analytic procedure such as the Silver–Meal or part-period balancing heuristic is used, provision must be made for manual override—the scheduler likely possesses information not included in the model, for example, "Georges Roy, the foreman at a particular work center, will never accept a small lot size late in a month." In addition, it should be emphasized that lot-sizing decisions at the level under consideration have ramifications back through all the component levels. However, the usual lot-sizing procedures consider carrying and setup costs only at the level being scheduled. Thus, at best, a suboptimization is being achieved.

Once coverage is completed for the level 1 item the associated bill of materials indicates which level 2 items are used as components. The order release dates and quantities of the level 1 item thus imply requirements through time of level 2 items. This is done for all level 1 items. Again, any direct external demand for a level 2 item, as well as any usage as a *direct* component of any level 0 items, must then be included to obtain the gross requirements of that item. These requirements are then netted, covered, etc.

The above process is continued all the way back to all raw materials which, in turn, have their requirements properly covered by purchasing actions. Note that all items having a given level code are processed before any items on the next (higher numbered) level. It is clear that a computer is indispensable for the step-by-step explosion of requirements at the next level implied by each individual item coverage pattern.

12.4.5 *A Numerical Illustration of the MRP Procedure*

We use the context of the MIDAS International automatic film processors to illustrate the MRP procedure. Reference is made to the product structure depicted in Figures 12.4 and 12.6. In particular, let us focus in on the dryer roll assembly, D70524. It is used in two different dryer assemblies (D63321 and D63322) which, in turn, appear in several different options of the end item automatic film processors. Suppose that through the first stages of application of MRP we have arrived at the order release patterns for the two dryer assemblies shown in Table 12.2. These patterns, together with direct external demand, imply the gross requirements pattern for the dryer roll assembly, shown at the bottom of the table. The gross requirement in a period is the total number of units in the order releases of the two parents planned for that period (we can simply take the total here because precisely 1 unit of the component is needed for each unit of either parent) plus any anticipated direct external demand in the period.

Next, net requirements for item D70524 are determined by taking account of any on-hand inventory and any released or planned orders. Suppose that

i. The offset (production lead time) for this item is 1 period

ii. The current on-hand inventory is 10 units

iii. An order for 30 units had been tentatively planned for release in period 1 (offset to be available in period 2)

The sixth row of Table 12.3 shows the resulting net requirements.

Table 12.2 Derivation of Gross Requirements for the Dryer Roll Assembly, D70524[a]

Time Period	1	2	3	4	5	6	7	8
Dryer Assembly, D63321 planned order releases		50		20		40		60
Dryer Assembly, D63322 planned order releases			30			30		
Dryer Roll Assembly, D70524 direct external demand (dealer requests for spare parts)			10				10	
Dryer Roll Assembly, D70524 gross requirements	–	50	40	20	–	70	10	60

[a] 1 unit of D70524 is used in each of D63321 and D63322.

It is seen that the tentatively planned order of 30 units is inadequate to meet the requirements in period 2. Therefore this order quantity must be revised upwards. In fact, it might be attractive to order enough to also cover the requirements in later periods (particularly periods 3 and 4). If a logical analysis is to be used, one important point is worth mentioning. As will become apparent in Section 12.5, if we wish to select lot sizes so as to keep the total of setup and inventory carrying costs of the item under consideration as low as possible (certainly a reasonable objective), then the appropriate factor for converting units of the item to dollars for inventory costing purposes is only the variable cost *added* at the operation under consideration, that is, it should not include the variable costs of the components which are merged or modified in some other way. To illustrate, for the dryer roll assembly the actual unit value is $27.50, but all except $8 of this is simply the total value of the eight component parts (see Figure 12.4). Therefore, the appropriate v value to use is $8. This type of reasoning applies to all level codes. In the case of the most extreme level code, namely the purchase of a raw material, the unit variable purchase cost itself is used because, prior to the purchase of the material, the company under consideration has no resources tied up in the material, that is, the prior unit variable cost is zero.

Suppose that the setup cost for the dryer roll assembly operation is $7.50 and the inventory carrying charge has been set at 0.005 $/$/period (if the period was 1 week, this would correspond to an r value of 0.26 $/$/yr). If the Silver–Meal heuristic was used, then the logic of Section 8.6.2 of Chapter 8 gives the production schedule (in terms of planned *initiation* of assemblies of dryer rolls) shown in the bottom row of Table 12.3. Only the order in period 1 would be released, the later quantities are tentative for planning purposes.

Table 12.3 Determination of Net Requirements for the Dryer Roll Assembly, D70524 (offset = 1 week)

Time Period	1	2	3	4	5	6	7	8
Gross requirements	–	50	40	20	–	70	10	60
Inventory at start of period	10	10	–					
Order release	30							
Order due		30						
Inventory at end of period	10							
Net requirements	–	10[a]	40	20	–	70	10	60
Net requirements without the period 1 order	–	40	40	20	–	70	10	60
Coverage (by Silver–Meal heuristic)–order due dates	–	100	–	–	–	80	–	60
Coverage-order release dates	100	–	–	–	80	–	60	–

[a] (10) = (50) – (10) – (30)

To show one further level of the MRP computations consider the ring item, R21174, used in the assembly of the dryer roll, D70524 (see Figure 12.4). Part of the gross requirements for the ring are implied by the dates and quantities of the order releases for the dryer roll, D70524, shown in the last row of Table 12.3. Recognizing that 3 rings are required for each dryer roll assembly, the associated ring requirements are shown in the first row of Table 12.4. The rings are used in a number of other assemblies. MRP would first be used to determine the order release patterns of these other assemblies. Suppose this has already been done and the combined order releases, expressed in terms of numbers of rings required, are as shown in the second row of Table 12.4. Suppose further that the current inventory, material on order, and planned purchase orders are as shown in the table. The purchase lead time is 3 periods. One can then easily develop the net requirements row of the table. To illustrate:

i. In period 1,

$$\begin{aligned}(\text{ending inventory}) &= (\text{starting inventory}) + (\text{order due})\\ &\quad - (\text{gross requirements})\\ &= 1200 + 0 - 1000\\ &= 200\end{aligned}$$

a positive quantity, hence there are no net requirements.

Table 12.4 Determination of Gross and Net Requirements for the Ring, R21174 (offset = 3 weeks)

Time Period	1	2	3	4	5	6	7	8
Dryer Roll Assembly D70524 planned order releases[a]	300				240		180	
Other dryer roll assemblies planned order releases	700	500	300	700	300	200	600	100
Gross requirements of Ring	1,000	500	300	700	540	200	780	100
Inventory of Ring at start of period	1,200	200	800	500	−200	660	460	−320
Order release of Ring		1,400						
Order due		1,100[b]			1400			
Inventory of Ring at end of period	200	800	500	−200	660	460	−320	−420
Net requirements of Ring	—	—	—	200	—	—	320	100

[a] All entries in the table are expressed in terms of rings (for example, 3 rings are required for 1 dryer roll assembly, D70524).
[b] This order was released in time period (−1).

ii. In period 4,

$$(\text{ending inventory}) = 500 + 0 - 700$$
$$= -200$$

a negative quantity, hence net requirements are the 200 units unfilled in that period.

In this example there are no net requirements for the first 3 periods. This is fortunate in that this is the procurement lead time; any net requirements in this period would have required expediting of an outstanding order or a crash new order. There are net requirements in period 4. One simple way of covering these would be to advance the due date of the second order by one period. This means that the order would be released in period 1 instead of period 2. Of course, one might also consider increasing the size of this order and/or planning additional future orders to cover the net requirements in the later periods.

12.4.6 *Outputs of MRP*

MRP provides a number of outputs of use to management. These include:

i. Actual and projected inventory status of every item.

ii. Listing of released and planned orders by time period—this document is particularly useful for planning required capacity by period (for example, is overtime required in a particular period?). The planning of required capacity will be covered in considerably more detail in Part V of this book.

iii. Rescheduling and cancellation notices—these are particularly helpful in establishing and adjusting order priorities in a job shop context.

12.4.7 *Low Value, Common Usage Items*

There is one exception to the rule of using MRP level-by-level explosion to ascertain the requirements of all items, namely the case of low value items having high usage rates, that is, basic components of many items (for example, bolts, washers, nuts, etc.) The costs of precise physical control and the computer processing time required to ascertain the requirements are likely to be prohibitive when one recognizes the low cost of carrying safety stocks of such items. Therefore, for such items it is preferable to use one of the control systems suggested in Chapter 6, namely a continuous review, order point, order quantity system (that is, a two-bin system) or a periodic review, order-up-to-level system.

12.4.8 *Pegging*

Consider an item which is used as a component of several other items. Straightforward use of MRP, as discussed above, leads to gross requirements on this item which are generated from a number of sources. In some circumstances, it may be important to know which items generated which amounts of these requirements. In particular, if a shortage of the item under consideration is imminent, it would be helpful to know which subassemblies, assemblies, finished products and, ultimately, customer orders would be affected. To achieve this we proceed as follows: When the production (procurement) schedule of an item is exploded to generate gross requirements on the next (higher numbered) level items these requirements are "pegged" with an identification of the item generating them.

It is clear that considerable file space and data-processing effort are required in connection with pegging. Therefore, this procedure should be used only when the information so generated is of paramount importance.

12.4.9 *Handling Changes*

Our discussions so far have implicitly dealt with MRP as a process carried out once per basic time period. However, changes in various inputs are certainly not restricted to occurring only once per period. These possible changes include:

i. Changes in the master schedule or in direct external demand for components

ii. Identified discrepancies in inventory records

iii. Actual completion time or quantity different from planned

iv. Changes in product structure (bill of materials)

v. Changes in costs, lead times, etc.

MRP must be able to effectively cope with such changes. There are two very different options available, namely regeneration and net change.

In the regeneration method the entire MRP process, as discussed in Sections 12.4.4 and 12.4.5, is carried out once per period (typically the period is of one week duration) using batch-processing computer techniques. All changes that have taken place since the previous regeneration are incorporated in the new run. In the net change approach, one does not wait until the next period to incorporate a change and replan coverage. Replanning takes place on essentially a continuous time basis. For a particular change the possible effects are limited to components of the item causing the change. Therefore, the modification of the previous schedule tends to be much more limited than under regeneration; in effect, only a partial explosion of requirements is undertaken each time a change is processed. Orlicky[36] presents the details of how a net change system operates.

In a regenerative system between regenerations only the on-hand and on-order inventory levels of each item are updated according to the standard inventory transactions such as demands, receipts, quality losses, etc. The possible associated changes in requirements for component items are not updated until the next regeneration, hence these requirements become less reliable as the period between regenerations progresses. In contrast, these requirements (and associated priorities, etc.) are kept up to date in a net change system as changes are incorporated on a frequent basis.

Obviously this up-to-date, rapid response capability of a net change system is desirable. Furthermore, the data processing load is more evenly spread through time than in a regenerative arrangement. Primarily for the first of these reasons it appears that most users will eventually switch to a net change system. However, there are potential problems that should not be overlooked. First of all, net change tends to promulgate any earlier errors. Therefore, on an occasional basis a regeneration is necessary to purge the system of errors. Second, some judgment must be used in deciding on how quickly to process the different changes. Too frequent processing can lead to unnecessary instability, for example, the size of an order jumping up and down several times prior to the actual production. Finally, net change is somewhat less efficient from a data-processing standpoint.

12.4.10 *The Master Production Schedule*

Everything in MRP is predicated upon the existence of a master production schedule. Viewed another way, the master schedule drives the MRP system, implying inventory investments, manufacturing schedules of components, patterns of acquisition of raw materials, etc.

The master schedule serves as an interface between marketing and manufacturing, converting customer orders and forecasted demand into production requirements by time period. Thus its development cannot be accomplished in isolation by manfacturing personnel. Inputs include not only firm customer orders (in the near future) and forecasted demand (more toward the end of the planning horizon) but also inventory status and production capacity data (the latter by time period).

Knowing these inputs, ideally one would like to establish a master production schedule that minimizes total relevant costs while staying within the capacity constraints. However, as mentioned earlier, the relevant costs are not restricted to those at the master level. The complicated nature of a manufacturing environment rules out cost minimization. Instead, one strives for a feasible master schedule that appears to keep costs at a reasonable level.

Over the longer horizon, the resources need not be firmly established. Thus, over this type of horizon the master scheduling procedure can be viewed as a tool for determining desirable changes in resources (for example, acquisition of additional machinery of a particular type).*

The process of developing a master schedule is essentially one of trial-and-error. A useful construct to employ is the load profile. It gives the approximate needs in terms of various resources by time period associated with 1 unit of a particular end-item being put in the master schedule in a base period. Such load profiles are developed for each end-product, but need only be done once in a lifetime for a product (except, of course, if engineering changes take place). The MRP system is used to develop these load profiles (for details, see Chapter 11 of Orlicky[37]). Once the load

---

* *We shall return to related issues in Part 5 of the book.*

profiles are available, they are used to project the likely resource requirements by time period of a particular trial master schedule. In effect, MRP is used in a simulation mode to show the likely consequences of a proposed master schedule. From experimentation (that is, trying out several different master schedules) and/or through actual scheduling experience an effective scheduling committee can select a master schedule that will indeed give a reasonable, feasible solution to the problem.

The master schedule, to be really useful, must be seen as being realistic from the viewpoints of both manufacturing and marketing. If, because of changed conditions, it appears that actual production will not meet the master schedule, then every effort must be made to remove the discrepancy. First, if possible, actual production should be brought in line with the master plan by working overtime, allocating extra manpower to a bottleneck operation, etc. If this still cannot reconcile the difference, then it is necessary to modify the master schedule.

To summarize, it is clear that the master production schedule plays a vital role in the production/inventory function of a manufacturing organization. A mathematically optimal selection of a schedule is clearly beyond the state of the art. A more prudent approach is a committee selection of a feasible schedule, using the above mentioned aids. Because of the major importance of the problem area, this committee should involve top management representatives from each of marketing, manufacturing and finance.

12.4.11 *Coping with Uncertainty in MRP*

To this point our discussions on MRP have essentially ignored the effects of uncertainty (in end-item usage, in lead times, etc.). In Chapters 6 and 7 we coped with uncertainty by the introduction of safety stocks. This is *not* the predominant approach in MRP. Aside from some possible safety stocks in end-items, those components subject to direct external demand and, perhaps, some raw materials, no safety stocks are included in MRP. *The philosophy is that safety stocks are not really appropriate in a dependent demand situation.* Rather, one can more effectively avoid shortages and excess inventories through the adjustment of (production) lead times, these adjustments being accomplished by expediting or, more generally, shifting priorities of shop orders.

Outright elimination of safety stocks or safety times (the latter meaning that orders are scheduled for completion slightly ahead of the requirements time) for the dependent demand items may not be the final answer in MRP; in particular, it would appear attractive in some cases to maintain safety stocks in common semi-finished material rather than in a myriad of finished items. An exact analysis of how much safety stock to include in which items would be very complicated because of the erratic time-varying nature of the demand patterns at the dependent levels.

12.5 *The Case of Deterministic Constant Demand with a Serial Production Process*

In this section we show that an analytic model is helpful in gaining insight in a particular type of multi-echelon supply situation. We restrict attention to the case of a serial production process (see Figure 12.7) where an item progresses serially through a series of operations, none of which are of an assembly or splitting nature, that is, each operation has only one predecessor and only one successor operation. In fact, for exposition purposes, we shall restrict ourselves to the most simple case of but two operations, denoted by primary (p) and finishing (f). Primary could correspond to simply the purchase of raw material.

Figure 12.7 A Serial Production Process.

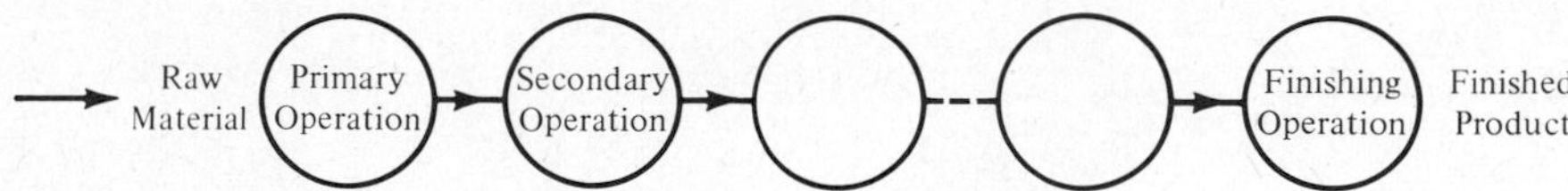

12.5.1 *Two Serial Operations*

First let us lay out some notation:

D—deterministic, constant demand rate for the finished product, in units/unit time (normally one year)

A_p—fixed (setup) cost associated with a replenishment at the primary stage, in dollars

A_f—fixed (setup) cost associated with a replenishment at the finishing stage, in dollars

v_p—the unit variable cost or value (raw material plus processing) of the item immediately *after* the primary operation, in \$/unit

v_f—the unit variable cost or value (raw material plus processing) of the item immediately *after* the finishing operation, in \$/unit

r—the carrying charge, the cost of having one dollar of the item tied up in inventory for a unit time interval, that is, the dimensions are \$/\$/unit time

Q_p—the replenishment quantity at the primary stage, in units

Q_f—the replenishment quantity at the finishing stage, in units

The two controllable (or decision) variables are the replenishment sizes Q_p and Q_f. Figure 12.8 shows the behavior of the two levels of inventory with the passage of time for the particular case where $Q_p = 3Q_f$. A little

Figure 12.8 Behavior of the Inventory Levels in a Deterministic Two Stage Process.

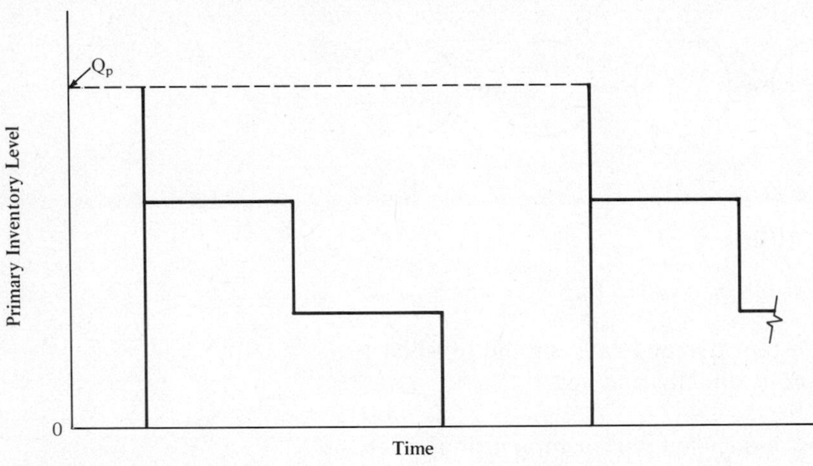

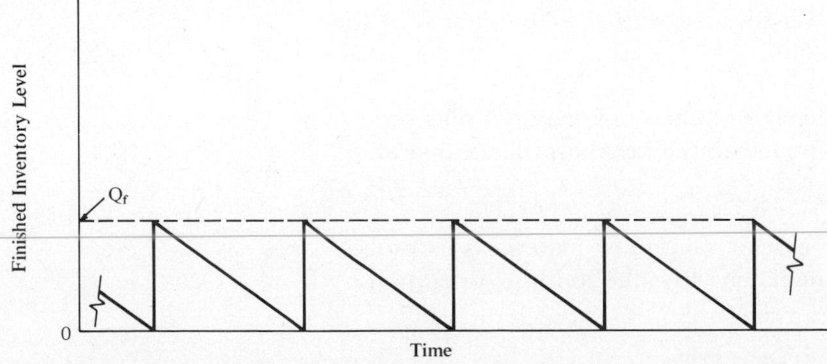

reflection shows that (at least for the case of deterministic demand) it never would make sense to have Q_p anything but an integer multiple of Q_f. Therefore we can think of two alternative decision variables Q_f and n where

$$Q_p = nQ_f \qquad n = 1, 2, 3, \ldots \tag{12.3}$$

that is, n is a positive integer.

The logic (proved in the appendix of this chapter) for computing the best values of Q_f and n, hence Q_p from Eq. 12.3, is as follows:

Step 1 Compute

$$n^* = \sqrt{\frac{A_p(v_f - v_p)}{A_f v_p}} \tag{12.4}$$

If n^* is exactly an integer, go to step 4 with $n = n^*$. Also, if $n^* < 1$, go to step 4 with $n = 1$. Otherwise, proceed to step 2.

Step 2 Ascertain the two integer values, n_1 and n_2, which surround n^*.

Step 3 Evaluate

$$F(n_1) = \left[A_f + \frac{A_p}{n_1}\right][(n_1 - 1)v_p + v_f]$$

and

$$F(n_2) = \left[A_f + \frac{A_p}{n_2}\right][(n_2 - 1)v_p + v_f] \tag{12.5}$$

If $F(n_1) \le F(n_2)$, use $n = n_1$

If $F(n_1) > F(n_2)$, use $n = n_2$

Step 4 Evaluate

$$Q_f = \sqrt{\frac{2\left[A_f + \frac{A_p}{n}\right]D}{[(n-1)v_p + v_f]r}} \tag{12.6}$$

Step 5 Calculate

$$Q_p = nQ_f$$

It should be pointed out that in Eq. 12.4 $(v_f - v_p)$ and not v_f itself appears. At the same time the term of the form $[(n-1)v_p + v_f]$ which appears in Eqs. 12.5 and 12.6 can be rewritten as $[nv_p + (v_f - v_p)]$ so that again what matters is $(v_f - v_p)$ and not v_f itself. This supports a statement, made earlier in the chapter, that the added unit value at an operation, and not the unit value after the operation, is what should determine the replenishment quantity.

Numerical Illustration of the Logic—Let us consider a particular liquid developer, product XSC-444, which MIDAS buys in bulk, then breaks down and repackages. The demand for this item can be assumed to be essentially deterministic and level at a rate of 1,000 gallons per year. The unit value of the bulk material (v_p) is \$1.00/gallon while the value added by the transforming (break and package) operation $(v_f - v_p)$ is \$4.00/gallon. The fixed component of the purchase charge (A_p) is \$10.00 while the setup cost for the break and repackage operation (A_f) is \$15.00. Finally the estimated carrying charge is 0.24 \$/\$/yr.

Step 1

$$n^* = \sqrt{\frac{(10)\,(4)}{(15)\,(1)}}$$
$$= 1.66$$

Step 2

$n_1 = 1$

$n_2 = 2$

Step 3

$F(1) = [15 + \tfrac{10}{1}][0 + 5] = 125$

$F(2) = [15 + \tfrac{10}{2}][(1)\,(1) + 5] = 120$

that is, $F(1) > F(2)$.

Thus, use $n = 2$.

Step 4

$$Q_f = \sqrt{\frac{2[15 + \tfrac{10}{2}]1{,}000}{[(1)(1) + 5]0.24}} \simeq 167 \text{ gallons}$$

Step 5

$Q_p = (2)\,(167) = 334$ gallons

In words, we purchase 334 gallons* at a time; one-half of these or 167 gallons are immediately broken and repackaged. When these 167 (finished) gallons are depleted, a second break and repackage run of 167 gallons is made. When these are depleted, we start a new cycle by again purchasing 334 gallons of raw material.

12.5.2 *Extensions to Other Deterministic Multi-stage Processes*

Schwarz[44] has extended the analysis to a more general two-stage process, which he calls a one-warehouse, n-retailer situation (depicted in Fig. 12.9 for $n=4$). For $n \geq 3$ he shows that the form of the optimal policy can be very complex; in particular, requiring that the order quantity at one or more of the locations vary with time even though all relevant demand and cost factors are time-invariant. He rightfully argues for restricting attention to a simpler class of strategies (where each location's order quantity does not change with time) and develops an effective heuristic for finding quite good solutions.

Schwarz and Schrage[45] adopt essentially the same approach for another type of deterministic situation, namely "pure" assembly (each node feeds

Figure 12.9 A One-Warehouse, 4-Retailer System.

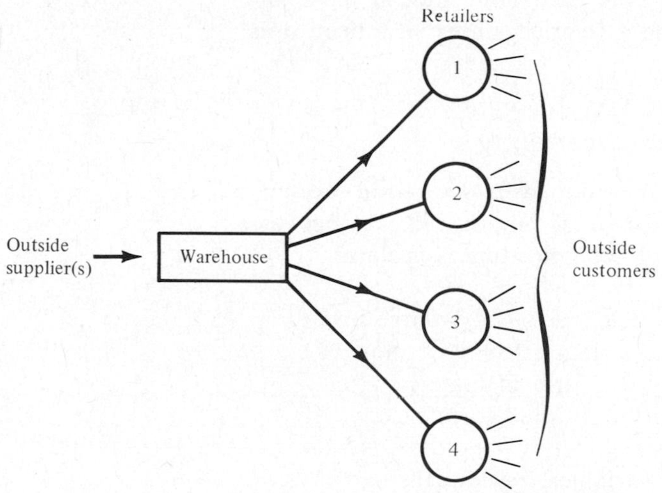

* *Of course, it may make sense to round this quantity to a convenient shipment size such as 350 gallons. In such a case Q_f would also be adjusted (to 175 gallons).*

Figure 12.10 A "Pure" Assembly System.

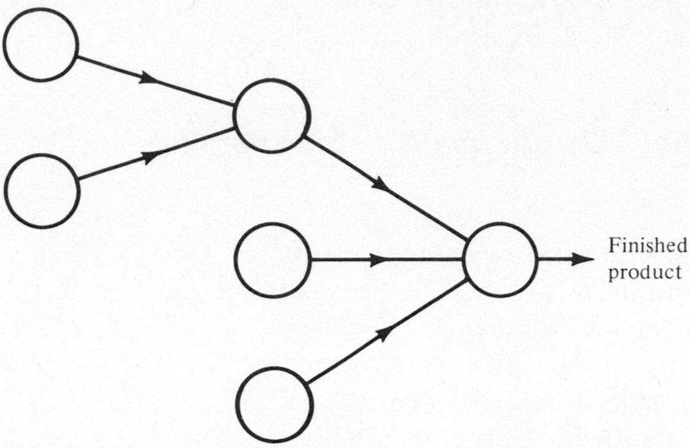

into, at most, one other node; a simple illustration is portrayed in Figure 12.10). They make use of a "myopic" strategy where each node and its successor are treated in isolation by much the same procedure as for the two-stage serial case discussed in the preceding section. Graves and Schwarz[18] do a similar type of analysis for arborescent systems (just the opposite of a "pure" assembly system; now each node has, at most, one node feeding *into* it). Other work in the assembly context has been done by Crowston et al.[8,9]

12.5.3 The Difficulties Caused by Uncertainty

When the demand pattern is no longer assumed known with certainty, even the two-stage, serial process (the case of Section 12.5.1) becomes very complicated to analyze. The principle complicating issues are:

i. Where should safety stock be held? If $v_f - v_p$ is large and the finishing operation lead time is small, it may be more attractive to keep safety stock in the form of material after the primary stage rather than in the finished form.

ii. There are now four decision variables. Besides the two replenishment quantities there are also the two reorder points.

iii. What do we do when an order for Q_f is placed on the primary inventory and less than Q_f is on hand? In particular, are partial shipments allowed?

Consequently, it is not surprising that very little in the way of usable theory has been developed for the multi-echelon situation with probabilistic demand. One exception is the case that we show in the next section. Also, specialized results for particular company situations have been developed through the use of simulation (see, for example, Berman[1] and Connors et al.[7]), a topic discussed in Chapter 9.

12.6 Allocation of Stock Among Assemblies and Repairable Subassemblies (the Father—Sons Problem)

Useful models have been developed for a specific type of probabilistic multi-echelon situation which is of particular interest within the military supply context. Consider an organization (for example, the government) which owns a group of end-items (for example, a fleet of trucks) which are composed of subassemblies (for example, engines, tires, etc.) which in turn may be made up of components, etc. A diagram, depicting the situation for the case of only assemblies and subassemblies, is shown in Figure 12.11. With an on-going system there are inventories of spare assemblies, subassemblies, etc., some of which may be at a zero level.

Figure 12.11 The Father-Sons Problem Setting.

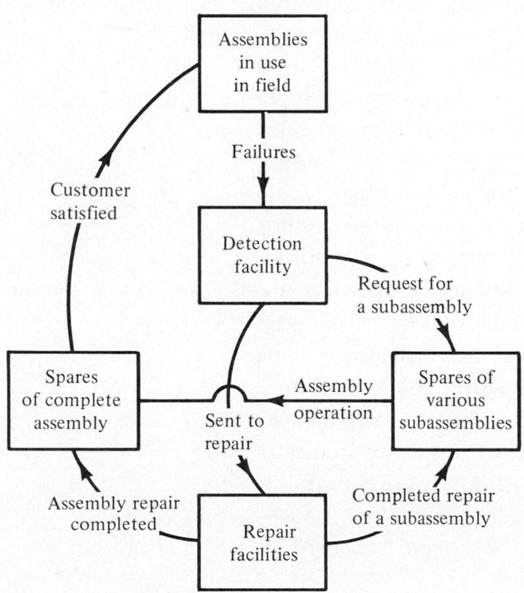

The breakdown of an assembly causes it to arrive at the stocking location. If a complete assembly is available, it is exchanged for the failed one and the customer waits a negligible length of time. If a complete spare assembly is not available, the customer must wait. The failed assembly goes to a checkout or detection station where the failed subassembly is detected (the detection time being a random variable). Once the failed subassembly is identified, it is removed and replaced if a spare is available (with cannibalization, this spare can be cannibalized from another assembly waiting for some other component to be repaired). If such a replacement is possible, the customer (or possibly an earlier one that generated the other assembly involved in the cannibalization) is satisfied. Naturally, replacement must be preceded by removal of the failed component. Also, as soon as the failed unit is removed, it is sent off for repair or replacement. Such repair may be at either a local or a remote location. A model, developed by Sherbrooke[47] and extended by Silver[48] and Mason,[30] allows a probabilistic assignment of each repair to one of two or more repair locations. The repair time is a random variable which can depend upon both the unit involved and the location at which the repair takes place. There is a possibility that the local detection facility cannot identify the failed component. Therefore, the model allows for a certain percent of the assemblies having to be sent off for repair as whole units.

The completion of repair of a particular subassembly adds an extra unit to the spares inventory. This unit may immediately trigger the preparation of a complete assembly. Furthermore, the arrival of a complete assembly into its inventory location may immediately lead to the satisfying of an outstanding customer backorder.

Incidentally, the model allows for an assembly requiring more than one unit of a particular subassembly, for example, a truck requiring four tires.

The decision problem is the allocation of a specified budget among spares of the assembly and subassemblies so as to provide as high a level of customer service as possible. More generally, repetition of the solution for different size budgets would produce an exchange curve of budget available versus the best possible service achievable with each budget level.

Sherbrooke[47] developed equations which give the service level (either as a ready rate or as the expected number of back-orders at a random point in time) for a given number of spares of each type. However, he did not develop a normative model (how to decide on best numbers of spares) because of the mathematical complexity of the equations. Silver's[48] contribution was the establishment of a heuristic decision rule, which, although not guaranteed optimal, appeared to generate an allocation quite close to the best possible. Mason[30] subsequently devised a more accurate heuristic but one requiring non-trivial computional effort. Both of these heuristics have been successfully utilized by the Defence Research Analysis Establishment of Canada. Further important related work has been reported by Muckstadt.[32]

12.7 Summary

In this chapter we have dealt with the important topic of "dependent" demand, that is, the situation where the requirements at one stocking point are heavily dependent upon the production (or procurement) pattern of the next stage closer to the ultimate consumer. We saw that an approach, radically different from that of earlier chapters, was required, namely material requirements planning. This approach provides a practial means of controlling inventories, scheduling orders, etc. in a manufacturing environment. The multi-echelon situation with significantly probabilistic demand requires considerable research effort before appreciable results generalizable to many companies are likely to be achieved. For those interested in further readings in the multi-echelon inventory area, Clark[5] provides an extensive bibliography.

Appendix to Chapter 12—Derivation of the Logic for Computing the Best Replenishment Quantities in a Deterministic, Two Stage Process

It is seen from Figure 12.8 that the average level of the finished inventory (I_f) is still $Q_f/2$ but the average level of the primary inventory ($\bar{I}_p$) is not $Q_p/2$ because of the discrete nature of the withdrawals by the finishing operation. In a typical (repeating) cycle the primary inventory is at each of the levels $2Q_p/3$, $Q_p/3$, and 0 for $\frac{1}{3}$ of the cycle. Therefore

$$\bar{I}_p = \tfrac{1}{3}[2Q_p/3 + Q_p/3 + 0] = \frac{Q_p}{3}$$

By similar reasoning, for the general case of $Q_p = nQ_f$, rather than $Q_p = 3Q_f$, one can show that

$$\bar{I}_p = \left(\frac{n-1}{2n}\right) Q_p \tag{12.7}$$

Now, as in the derivation of the basic economic order quantity in Chapter 5, the two relevant types of costs are the setup costs and inventory carrying costs. Let TRC (Q_p, Q_f) be the total relevant costs per unit time. Then

$$\text{TRC}(Q_p, Q_f) = \frac{A_pD}{Q_p} + \bar{I}_p v_p r + \frac{A_fD}{Q_f} + \bar{I}_f v_f r$$

Substituting from Eqs. 12.3 and 12.7 we have

$$\text{TRC}(Q_p, Q_f) = \frac{A_pD}{nQ_f} + (n-1)\frac{Q_f v_p r}{2} + \frac{A_fD}{Q_f} + \frac{Q_f v_f r}{2} \tag{12.8}$$

We must find the values of n (an integer) and Q_f which minimize this expression. A convenient approach is to first set the partial derivative of TRC with respect to Q_f equal to zero and solve for the associated $Q_f^*(n)$, which is the best Q_f given the particular n value, viz.:

$$\frac{\partial \text{TRC}}{\partial Q_f} = -\frac{A_pD}{nQ_f^2} + \frac{(n-1)v_p r}{2} - \frac{A_fD}{Q_f^2} + \frac{v_f r}{2} = 0$$

which solves for

$$Q_f{}^*(n) = \sqrt{\frac{2\left[A_f + \dfrac{A_p}{n}\right]D}{[(n-1)v_p + v_f]r}} \tag{12.9}$$

This expression is then substituted back into Eq. 12.8 to give TRC* (n), the lowest cost possible for the given value of n. The resulting equation is

$$\text{TRC}^*\,(n) = \sqrt{2\left[A_f + \frac{A_p}{n}\right]D[(n-1)v_p + v_f]r}$$

Finally, we must find the integer value of n which minimizes TRC* (n). First, we recognize that the n which minimizes the simpler expression

$$F(n) = \left[A_f + \frac{A_p}{n}\right][(n-1)v_p + v_f] \tag{12.10}$$

will also minimize TRC* (n).
A convenient way to find the minimizing n value is to first set

$$\frac{dF(n)}{dn} = 0$$

which gives

$$[(n-1)v_p + v_f]\left[-\frac{A_p}{n^2}\right] + \left[A_f + \frac{A_p}{n}\right]v_p = 0$$

This solves for

$$n^* = \sqrt{\frac{A_p(v_f - v_p)}{A_f v_p}} \tag{12.11}$$

which in general will not be an integer. The next step is to ascertain $F(n_1)$ and $F(n_2)$ from Eq. 12.10 where n_1 and n_2 are the two integers surrounding the n^* of Eq. 12.11. Whichever gives the lower value of F is the appropriate n to use. Finally the corresponding Q_f and Q_p values are found by using this n value in Eqs, 12.9 and 12.3 respectively.

Graves and Schwarz[18] use the concept of echelon stock (introduced in Section 12.1) to avoid the problem of having to evaluate the average inventory at the primary level (Eq. 12.7). Recall that the echelon stock for the primary level would be all the stock at both the primary and finishing levels, while the echelon stock for the finishing level would simply be the physical stock at that level. The *average* echelon stock for the primary level would be $Q_p/2$ while that for the finishing level would be $Q_f/2$. Now, the tricky aspect is that, when determining inventory carrying costs, the echelon stock for a given level must be valued at only the value added at that level, that is, we have

$$\text{Carrying costs} = \left[\frac{Q_p}{2}v_p + \frac{Q_f}{2}(v_f - v_p)\right]r \tag{12.12}$$

It can be shown (see Problem 12.5) that these costs are equivalent with the carrying costs shown in Eq. 12.8.

Problems for Chapter 12

Problem 12.1

For the base stock system shown in Figure 12.2 suppose that replenishment quantities for the three stocking levels have been predetermined as

(retailer from branch) $Q_r = 50$ units

(branch from central) $Q_b = 100$ units

(central from supplier) $Q_c = 300$ units

Suppose that customer demand is normally distributed with weekly figures being

$\bar{x}_1 = 25$ units

and

$\sigma_1 = 8$ units

Determine the reorder points and base stock levels at each of the three stocking points, assuming a desired probability of no stockout per replenishment cycle at each level of 0.95.

Problem 12.2

In the procedure, described in Section 12.1, for selecting the base stock level what implicit assumption is made about the availability of stock at the next (further removed from the customer) level? Can you suggest a correction factor that might allow relaxation of this assumption.

Problem 12.3

A company assembles three distinct finished s.k.u., items F1, F2, and F3. The bills of materials for these items, their components, etc. are as follows:

Item F1—composed of 1 unit of Al, A2, and A3 and 2 units of A4.

Item F2—composed of 1 unit of A1, A2, and A4

Item F3—composed of 1 unit of A1 and A4

Item A1—composed of 1 unit of A2 and B1

Item A2—composed of 1 unit of A4, B1, and B2

Item A3—composed of 1 unit of B1 and B2 and 3 units of B3

Item A4—composed of 2 units of B3

Item B1—composed of 1 unit of B3 and C1

Item B2—composed of 1 unit of C1 and C2

Item B3—composed of 1 unit of C1, C2 and C3

Items C1, C2, and C3 are purchased parts. In addition items A1 and A2 are sold directly to customers as spare parts.

Develop a level by level coding for the 13 items.

Problem 12.4

Consider a two-stage serial process where the second stage is a rather minor operation adding little extra value to the product. To be more specific, suppose we have an item with these characteristics:

$D = 1000$ units/yr. $\quad v_p = \$5.00$/unit

$v_f = \$6.00$/unit $\quad r = 0.24$/yr.

$A_p = \$20.00$ $\quad A_f = \$10.00$

Use the procedure of Section 12.5 to obtain Q_p, Q_f, and n. Do your results make intuitive sense?

Problem 12.5

Verify that the carrying costs of Eq. 12.12, arrived at by echelon stock reasoning, are equal to those in Eq. 12.8.

Problem 12.6

Starting with the result of Eq. 12.10 (in the appendix of this chapter) find an expression, involving A_f, A_p, v_p, v_f, and n, that must be satisfied for indifference between n and $n+1$. Sketch the curves (for different n values) with suitable horizontal and vertical axes.

Problem 12.7

In the "two serial" setting of Section 12.5.1 a simpler approach would be to establish the economic order quantity of the finished item *viewed in isolation*, then pick the best value of Q_p, given this value of Q_f. For the numerical illustration (MIDAS item XSC-444) of Section 12.5.1 answer the following:

a. Find the Q_f and Q_p by this procedure.
b. What is the percent cost penalty compared with the solution found by the method described in Section 12.5.1?
c. Repeat parts (a) and (b) for the following example:

$$A_p = \$10 \quad A_f = \$3$$

$$v_p = \$5.00/\text{unit} \quad v_f = \$7.00/\text{unit}$$

$$D = 1{,}000 \text{ units/yr} \quad r = 0.24 \ \$/\$/\text{yr}.$$

d. Discuss under what conditions you would expect an appreciable cost penalty.
e. How does all this relate to the level-by-level selection of lot sizes in MRP?

Problem 12.8

Consider a two-level inventory system where both levels are owned by the same organization. The structure is shown in Figure 12.12.

Figure 12.12

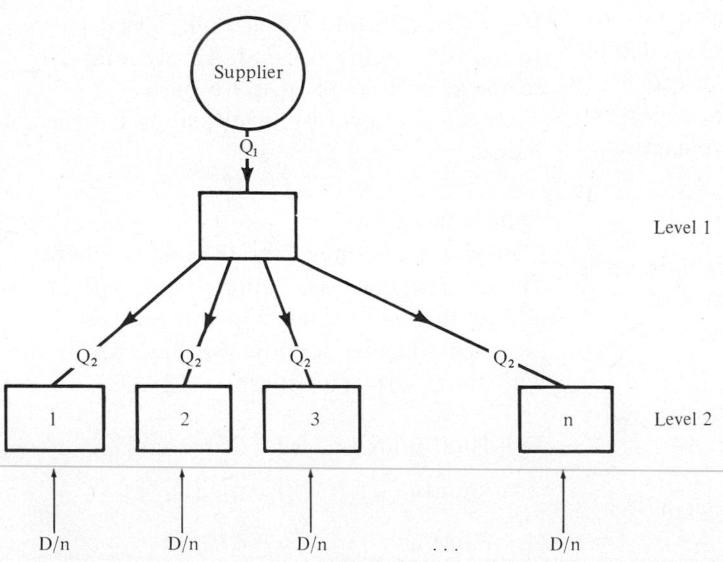

Demand is deterministic and at a constant rate. Moreover, the demand is the same at each of the level 2 installations. Replenishment lead times are negligible at both levels. There are no quantity discounts. Let us define a few parameters:

n—number of level 2 installations

D—total demand rate, units/yr.

Q_1—replenishment quantity for level 1, in units

Q_2—replenishment quantity for a level 2 location, in units

A_1—fixed cost of a replenishment at level 1, in \$

A_2—fixed cost of a replenishment at a level 2 location, in \$

v_1—value of inventory stored at level 1, \$/unit

v_2—value of inventory stored at level 2, \$/unit

a. Write the appropriate expression for the total costs per year.

b. Outline a procedure for determining the optimal values of Q_1 and Q_2. Proceed as far as possible in developing an explicit algorithm.

c. Illustrate your answer to part (b) with the following numerical example:

$n = 3$
$D = 90{,}000$ units/yr.
$A_1 = \$110$
$A_2 = \$25$
$v_1 = \$1.00/\text{unit}$
$v_2 = \$4.00/\text{unit}$
$r = 0.13$ \$/\$/yr.

d. What should your answer be in part (b) for the case of $v_2 = v_1$? Discuss.

e. Suppose replenishment lead times were non-zero. Could you handle this situation? Discuss.

Problem 12.9

In MIDAS Case D the Inventory Control Manager described his method of separating MIDAMATICS (and PROCESSORS) parts into two physically separate storage areas, one for assembly parts, the other for spare parts. His last comment was "I've often wondered whether there was any way of combining the inventory for both types of parts so that there would be enough safety stock to meet emergencies from either of the two sources." What suggestions would you have in this regard? Include a discussion of some of the less tangible factors.

Problem 12.10

MIDAS Case E shows that the Manager of Manufacturing, Mr. Wolfgang Gatzke, is on the firing line. Briefly indicate what suggestions you would make to him.

REFERENCES FOR CHAPTER 12

1. Berman, E. B. "Monte Carlo Determination of Stock Redistributions." *Operations Research*, Vol. 10, No. 4, July–August, 1962, pp. 500–506.

2. Berry, W. and D. C. Whybark. "Research Perspectives for Material Requirements Planning Systems." *Production and Inventory Management*, Vol. 16, No. 2, June, 1975, pp. 19–25.

3. Brooks, R. B. S., C. A. Gillen and J. Y. Lu. *Alternative Measures of Supply Performance: Fills, Backorders, Operational Rate, and NORS*. RM–6094–PR, The RAND Corporation, Santa Monica, Calif., August 1969.

4. Brown, R. G. *Decision Rules for Inventory Management*. Holt, Rinehart and Winston, New York, N.Y., 1967, Chapters 20–21.

5. Clark, A. "An Informal Survey of Multi-Echelon Inventory Theory." *Naval Research Logistics Quarterly*, Vol. 19, No. 4, December, 1972, pp. 621–650.

6. Clark, A. J. and H. Scarf. "Optimal Policies for a Multi-Echelon Inventory Problem." *Management Science*, Vol. 6, July 1960, pp. 475–490.

7. Connors, M., C. Coray, C. Cuccaro, W. Green, D. Low and H. Markowitz. "The Distribution System Simulator." *Management Science*, Vol. 18, No. 8, April, 1972, pp. B425–453.

8. Crowston, W., M. Wagner and A. Henshaw. "A Comparison of Exact and Heuristic Routines for Lot-Size Determination in Multi-Stage Assembly Systems." *AIIE Trans.*, Vol. 4, No. 4, December, 1972, pp. 313–317.

9. Crowston, W., M. Wagner and J. Williams. "Economic Lot Size Determination in Multi-Stage Assembly Systems." *Management Science*, Vol. 19, No. 5, January, 1973, pp. 517–527.

10. Demmy, W. S. *Allocation of Spares and Repair Resources to a Multi-Component System*. Air Force Logistics Command Report 70–17, Wright-Patterson AFB, Ohio, November, 1970.

11. Elmaghraby, S. "A Note on the 'Explosion' and 'Netting' Problems in the Planning of Material Requirements." *Operations Research*, Vol. 11, No. 4, July-August, 1963, pp. 530–535.

12. Everdell, R. "Master Scheduling: Its New Importance in the Management of Materials." *Modern Materials Handling*, October, 1972, pp. 33–40.

13. Fabrycky, W. and J. Banks. "A Hierarchy of Deterministic Procurement Inventory Systems." *Operations Research*, Vol. 14, No. 5, September-October, 1966, pp. 888–901.

14. Forrester, J. *Industrial Dynamics*. M.I.T. Press, Cambridge, Mass., 1961.

15. Garwood, D, "Stop, Before You Use the Bill Processor." *Production and Inventory Management*, Vol. 11, No. 2, 1970, pp. 73–79.

16. Giffler, B. "Mathematical

Solution of Parts Requirements Problems." *Management Science*, Vol. 11, No. 9, July, 1965, pp. 847–867.

17. Gleiberman, L. "The Engineering Change of the Total Requirements Matrix for a Bill of Materials." *Management Science*, Vol. 10, No. 3, April, 1964, pp. 488–493.

18. Graves, S. and L. Schwarz. "Single Cycle Continuous Review Policies for Arborescent Production/Inventory Systems." Working Paper Series No. 7544, Graduate School of Management, University of Rochester, Rochester, N.Y., October 1975, 25 pp.

19. Gross, D. "Centralized Inventory Control in Multilocation Supply Systems." *Multistage Inventory Models and Techniques*, edited by H. Scarf, D. Gilford and M. Shelly, Chapter 3, Stanford University Press, Stanford, Calif., 1963.

20. Haber, S. and R. Sitgreaves. "An Optimal Inventory Model for the Intermediate Echelon When Repair is Possible." *Management Science*, Vol. 21, No. 6, Feburary, 1975, pp. 638–648.

21. Haehling von Lanzenauer, C. "Optimale Lagerhaltung bei Mehrstufigen Produktions Prozessen (Optimal Inventory Policies in Multistage Production Processes)." *Unternehmensforschung* (Germany), Vol. 11, 1967, pp. 33–48.

22. Hanson, S. "The Synergistic Effects of Master Scheduling." *Production and Inventory Management*, Vol. 14, No. 3, 1973, pp. 75–77.

23. IBM, *System/3 Inventory and Requirements Planning Program Description.* IBM Technical Publications Department, White Plains, N.Y., 1972, pp. 87–122.

24. Iglehart, D. L. and A. Lalchandani "An Allocation Model." *SIAM Journal Appl. Math.*, Vol. XV, No. 2, March, 1967, pp. 303–323.

25. Kaplan, A. "A Stock Redistribution Model." *Naval Research Logistics Quarterly*, Vol. 20, No. 2, June. 1973, pp. 231–239.

26. Kaplan, A. and R. Deemer. "Stock Allocation in a Multi-Echelon System." *Final Report*, Inventory Research Office, Institute for Logistics Research, US Army Logistics Management Center, April, 1971, 31 pp.

27. Ling, R. and K. Widmer. "Master Scheduling in a Make-to-Order Plant." *Proceedings of the Seventeenth Annual International Conference of the American Production and Inventory Control Society*, 1974, pp. 320–334.

28. Lowerre, W. M. "Miracle Requirements Planning." *Production and Inventory Management*, Vol. 15, No. 1, 1974, pp. 50–54.

29. Magee, J. F. and D. M. Boodman. *Production Planning and Inventory Control.* McGraw-Hill, New York, N.Y., 1967, Chapter 6.

30. Mason, D. W. "The Fatso (*Father-Son*) Sparing Model and Computer Program." D. Log A Working Paper No. 8/75, Defence Research Analysis Establishment, Ottawa, Canada, 1975.

31. Miller, B. L. "Dispatching from Depot Repair in a Recoverable Item Inventory System: On the Optimality of a Heuristic Rule." *Management Science*, Vol. 21, No. 3, November, 1974, pp. 316–325.

32. Muckstadt, J. A. "A Model for a Multi-Item, Multi-Echelon, Multi-Indenture Inventory System." *Management Science*, Vol. 20, No. 4, December, 1973, pp. 472–481.

33. New, C. *Requirements Planning*. Gower Press, Essex, England, 1974.

34. New, C. "Lot-Sizing in Multi-Level Requirements Planning Systems." *Production and Inventory Management*, Vol. 15, No. 4, 1974, pp. 57–71.

35. New, C. "Safety Stocks for Requirements Planning." *Production and Inventory Management*, Vol. 16, No. 2, June, 1975, pp. 1–18.

36. Orlicky, J. A. "Net Change Material Requirements Planning." *IBM Systems Journal*, Vol. 12, No. 1, 1973, pp. 2–29.

37. Orlicky, J. A. *Material Requirements Planning*. McGraw Hill, New York, N.Y., 1975.

38. Orlicky, J., G. Plossl and O. Wight. "Structuring the Bill of Material for MRP." *Production and Inventory Management*, Vol. 13, No. 4, 1972, pp. 19–42.

39. Plossl, G. and O. Wight. *Material Requirements Planning by Computer. Special Report of the American Production and Inventory Control Society*, Washington, D.C., 1971.

40. Porter, R. "Management of Multiple Warehouse Systems." *Automation*, January, 1972, pp. 52–56.

41. Rhodes, P. "Lot Allocation Planning—A Fresh Approach to Material Requirements Planning." *Proceedings of the Seventeenth Annual International Conference of the American Production and Inventory Control Society*, November 1974, pp. 14–19.

42. Rhodes, P. and S. Wilson. "A Decentralized Inventory Control System for Distribution Warehouses." *Production and Inventory Management*, Vol. 13, No. 4, 1972, pp. 73–93.

43. Roberts, P. and M. Bramson. "The Commonality Problem in Stock Control for Complex Assemblies." *Operational Research Quarterly*, Vol. 20, Special Issue, 1969, pp. 71–85.

44. Schwarz, L. "A Simple Continuous Review, Deterministic One-Warehouse, N-Retailer, Inventory Problem." *Management Science*, Vol. 19, No. 5, January, 1973, pp. 555–566.

45. Schwarz, L. and L. Schrage. "Optimal and System Myopic Policies for Multi-Echelon Production/Inventory Assembly Systems." *Management Science*, Vol. 21, No. 11, July, 1975, pp. 1285–1294.

46. Sherbrooke, C. C. "METRIC: A Multi-Echelon Technique for Recoverable Item Control." *Operations Research*, Vol. 16, No. 1, January-February, 1968, pp. 122–141.

47. Sherbrooke, C. C. "An Evaluator for the Number of Operationally Ready Aircraft in a Multilevel Supply System." *Operations Research*, Vol. 19, No. 3, May-June, 1971, pp. 618–635.

48. Silver, E. A. "Inventory Allocation Among an Assembly and its Repairable Subassemblies." *Naval Research Logistics Quarterly*, Vol. 19, No. 2, June, 1972, pp. 261–280.

49. Szendrovits, A. "Manufacturing Cycle Time Determination for a Multi-Stage Economic Production Quantity Model." *Management Science*, Vol. 22, No. 3, November, 1975, pp. 298–308.

50. Taha, H. and R. Skeith. "The Economic Lot Sizes in Multistage Production Systems." *AIIE Trans.*, Vol. II, No. 2, June 1970, pp. 157–162.

51. Thomas, A. "Optimizing a Multi-Stage Production Process." *Operational Research Quarterly*, Vol. 14, 1963, pp. 201–213.

52. Thompson, G. "On the Parts Requirements Problem." *Operations Research*, Vol. 13, No. 3, May-June, 1965, pp. 453–461.

53. Wight, O. "To Order Point or Not to Order Point." *Production and Inventory Management*, Vol. 9, No. 3, 1968, pp. 13–28.

54. Williams, J. F. "Multi-Echelon Production Scheduling When Demand is Stochastic." *Management Science*, Vol. 20, No. 9, May, 1974. pp. 1253–1263.

55. Zacks, S. "A Two-Echelon Multi-Station Inventory Model for Naval Applications." *Naval Research Logistics Quarterly*, Vol. 17, No. 1, March, 1970, pp. 79–85.

56. Zangwill, W. "A Backlogging Model and a Multi-Echelon Model of a Dynamic Economic Lot Size Production System—A Network Approach." *Management Science*, Vol. 15, No. 9, 1969, pp. 506–527.

CHAPTER THIRTEEN

Coordinated Replenishments at a Single Echelon

In the preceding chapter we discussed control procedures in a multi-echelon (or multi-stage) situation where the replenishment quantities at the different echelons were coordinated. Now we turn to a somewhat different case where coordination is appropriate, namely where all the items involved are stored at the same stocking point and the interrelationship is caused by

i. a common supplier,

ii. a common mode of transportation, or

iii. a common production facility on which the items are produced.

As we shall see in Section 13.1 there are several possible advantages in coordinating the replenishments of such a group of interrelated items. The potential disadvantages will also be discussed. In Section 13.2, for the case of deterministic demand, the economic order quantity analysis of Chapter 5 (which there assumed *independent* control of items) is extended to the situation where there is a major setup cost associated with a replenishment of a family of coordinated items and a minor setup cost for each item involved in the particular replenishment. Section 13.3 extends the quantity discount arguments of Chapter 5 to the case where the discount is based on the magnitude of the total replenishment of a group of items, for example, a freight ratc reduction if a carload size replenishment is achieved. Then in Sections 13.4 and 13.5 we turn to the complex situation where items are to be coordinated but demand is probabilistic. Essentially, two approaches are discussed. Section 13.4 deals with so-called "can-order" systems which normally are of a continuous review nature and are not concerned with attaining a specified total replenishment size. In this type of system when the inventory of any item of a coordinated group drops low enough, a replenishment is triggered. Whether or not each other item is included in the replenishment is dictated by how low its inventory level happens to be at that moment. In contrast, the "service-point" approach of Section 13.5 involves periodic review, and the decision of whether or not to place a replenishment order at a particular review is dictated by the group service implications of waiting until the next review. Furthermore, the total replenishment size is normally established to achieve a quantity discount.

It should be noted that in the literature the terminology "joint replenishment" is sometimes used in lieu of "coordinated replenishment."

13.1 *Advantages and Disadvantages of Coordination*

There are a number of reasons for coordinating items when making replenishment decisions. These include:

i. Savings on unit purchase costs: When a group of items is ordered from the same vendor a quantity discount in purchase cost may be realized if the total order is greater than some breakpoint quantity. It may be uneconomical to order this much of a single item, but it could certainly make sense to coordinate several items so as to achieve a total order size as large as the breakpoint. An example of such a situation would be the acquistion by a distributor of a line of steel products from a particular manufacturer. In some cases a vendor-imposed minimum order quantity may dictate the same sort of joint consideration.

ii. Savings on unit transportation costs: The discussion is basically the same as above. Now a grouping of individual item orders may be advisable to achieve a quantity such as a carload. A good example, observed by the authors, is the shipment of cereal products from a supplier to the regional warehouses of a supermarket chain. The MIDAS situation (Case A) provides another example—several items from the parent company in Germany are simultaneously shipped to Canada in the same container.

iii. Savings on ordering costs: In some cases where the fixed (setup) cost of placing a replenishment order is high, it might make sense to put several items on a single order so as to reduce the annual total of these fixed costs. This is likely most relevant where the replenishment is by in-house production. In such a case the major component of the fixed ordering cost is the manufacturing setup cost. An illustration would be in the bottling of beer products. There are major changeover costs in converting the production line from one quality of beer to another. In contrast, the costs of changing from one container type to another are rather minor.

iv. Ease of scheduling: Coordinated handling of a vendor group can facilitate scheduling of buyer time, receiving (and inspection) workload, etc. In fact, we have found that, by and large, managers and purchasing agents alike tend to think and deal in terms of vendors or suppliers rather than individual s.k.u.

On the other hand, there are possible disadvantages of using coordinated replenishment procedures. These include:

i. An increase in the average inventory level: When items are coordinated some will be reordered earlier than if they were treated independently.

ii. An increase in system control costs: By the very nature of the problem, coordinated control is more complex than independent control of individual items. Therefore, under coordinated control review costs, computational costs, etc., are likely to be higher.

iii. Reduced flexibility: Not being able to work with items independently reduces our flexibility in dealing with unusual situations. One possible result is reduced stability of customer service on an individual item basis.

13.2 *The Deterministic Case—Selection of Replenishment Quantities in a Family of Items*

In this section we consider the case (discussed above) where there is a family of coordinated items defined in the following manner. There is a major setup cost (A) associated with a replenishment of the family. In the procurement context this is the fixed (or header) cost of placing an order, independent of the number of distinct items involved in the order. In the production environment this is the changeover cost associated with converting the facility from the production of some other family to production within the family of interest. Then there is a minor setup cost (a_i) associated with including item i in a replenishment of the family. In the procurement context a_i is often called the line cost, the cost of adding one more item or line to the requisition. From a production standpoint a_i represents the relatively minor cost of switching to production of item i from production of some other item within the same family.

13.2.1 *Assumptions*

All of the assumptions behind the derivation of the economic order quantity (Section 5.2 of Chapter 5) are retained except that now coordination of items is allowed in an effort to reduce setup costs. We recapitulate the assumptions:

a. The demand rate of each item is constant and deterministic, (this assumption will be relaxed in Sections 13.4 and 13.5).

b. The replenishment quantity of an item need not be an integral number of units (the extension to integral units is as discussed for a single item in Chapter 5).

c. The unit variable cost of any of the items does not depend upon the replenishment quantity; in particular, there are no discounts in either the unit purchase cost or the unit transportation cost (we shall relax this assumption in Section 13.3).

d. The replenishment lead time is of zero duration (the extension to a fixed, known, non-zero duration, independent of the magnitude of the replenishment, is straightforward).

e. No shortages are allowed. (Sections 13.4 and 13.5 will deal with the situation where shortages can occur.)

f. The entire order quantity is delivered at the same time (relaxation of this assumption creates problems, particularly in the production setting where capacity considerations may make certain desirable schedules infeasible; an excellent reference on this aspect is Maxwell[22]).

13.2.2 *The Decision Rule*

In the independent EOQ analysis of Chapter 5 we showed that the EOQ expressed as a time supply was given by

$$T_{\mathrm{EOQ}} = \sqrt{\frac{2A}{Dvr}}$$

Note that T_{EOQ} increases as the ratio A/Dv increases. Within our present context this indicates than an item i with a high set up cost a_i and a low dollar usage rate $D_i v_i$ should probably be replenished less frequently (higher time supply) than an item j having a low a_j and a high $D_j v_j$. Because of the assumptions of deterministic demand, no shortages permitted and instantaneous delivery, it makes sense to include an item in a replenishment only when its inventory drops to the zero level. Therefore, a reasonable type of policy to consider is the use of a time interval (T) between replenishments of the family and a set of m_i's where m_i, an integer, is the number of T intervals that the replenishment quantity of item i will last, that is, item i will be included in every m_ith replenishment of the family; for example, if $m_{17} = 3$, this says that item 17 will only be included in every third replenishment of the family with a replenishment quantity sufficient to last a time interval of duration $3T$ (each time it will be replenished just as its stock hits the zero level). We wish to select the values of T and the m_i's to keep the total relevant costs as low as possible.

As shown in the appendix of this chapter the integer m_i's must be selected so as to minimize

$$\left(A + \sum_{i=1}^{n} \frac{a_i}{m_i}\right) \sum_{i=1}^{n} m_i D_i v_i \tag{13.1}$$

where

A = major setup cost for the family, in dollars

a_i = minor setup cost for item i, in dollars

D_i = demand rate of item i, in units/unit time

v_i = unit variable cost of item i, in \$/unit

n = number of items in the family (the items are numbered $1, 2, 3, \ldots, n-1, n$).

Also, once the best m_i's are known, the corresponding appropriate value of T is given by

$$T^*(m_i\text{'s}) = \sqrt{\frac{2(A + \sum a_i/m_i)}{r \sum m_i D_i v_i}} \tag{13.2}$$

It is worth noting that r does not appear in Eq. 13.1, that is, the best values of the m_i's do not depend upon the carrying charge.

Goyal,[15] among others, (see the reference list at the end of this chapter) has proposed a search procedure for finding the best set of m_i's. We suggest instead use of the following much simpler (non-iterative) procedure which is derived in the appendix of this chapter:

Step 1 Number the items such that

$$\frac{a_i}{D_i v_i}$$

is smallest for item 1. Set $m_1 = 1$.

Step 2 Evaluate

$$m_i = \sqrt{\frac{a_i}{D_i v_i} \frac{D_1 v_1}{A + a_1}}$$

rounded to the nearest integer greater than zero. (13.3)

Step 3 Evaluate T^* using the m_i's of step 2 in Eq. 13.2.

Step 4 Determine

$$Q_i v_i = m_i D_i v_i T^* \qquad i = 1, 2, \ldots, n \tag{13.4}$$

In numerous tests (see Reference 32) this procedure has produced results at or near the best possible solution. A computerized version of the method has also been developed.

13.2.3 A Graphical Aid

The square root computations of Eq. 13.3 can be avoided through the use of a simple graphical aid. Because of the rounding rule of Eq. 13.3, we are indifferent between the integer values m_i and m_i+1 when

$$\sqrt{\frac{a_i}{D_i v_i}\frac{D_1 v_1}{A+a_1}}$$

is halfway between m_i and m_i+1, that is

$$m_i+\tfrac{1}{2}=\sqrt{\frac{a_i}{D_i v_i}\frac{D_1 v_1}{A+a_1}}$$

This leads to

$$\frac{a_i}{D_i v_i}=(m_i+\tfrac{1}{2})^2\frac{A+a_1}{D_1 v_1}$$

which is a straight line in a plot of $a_i/D_i v_i$ versus $(A+a_1)/D_1 v_1$. Thus, the indifference curves are a set of straight lines as shown in Figure 13.1.* Multiplication of both of $a_i/D_i v_i$ and $(A+a_1)/D_1 v_1$ by the same constant does not affect the solution of Eq. 13.3. This provides us with considerable flexibility in using the graph (for example, if both ratios are extremely small, we can multiply each by the same large number and only then ascertain the location on the graph of the corresponding point).

---

* *A somewhat more rigorous (rather than simply rounding) argument (see Reference 33) leads to indifference between m_i and m_i+1 where*

$$\frac{a_i}{D_i v_i}=m_i(m_i+1)\frac{A+a_1}{D_1 v_1}$$

which again gives straight lines (albeit with slopes slightly differing from those found above) on Figure 13.1. The cost effects of this more sophisticated version are likely to be minimal.

Figure 13.1 Implementation Aid for the Determination of the m_i's.

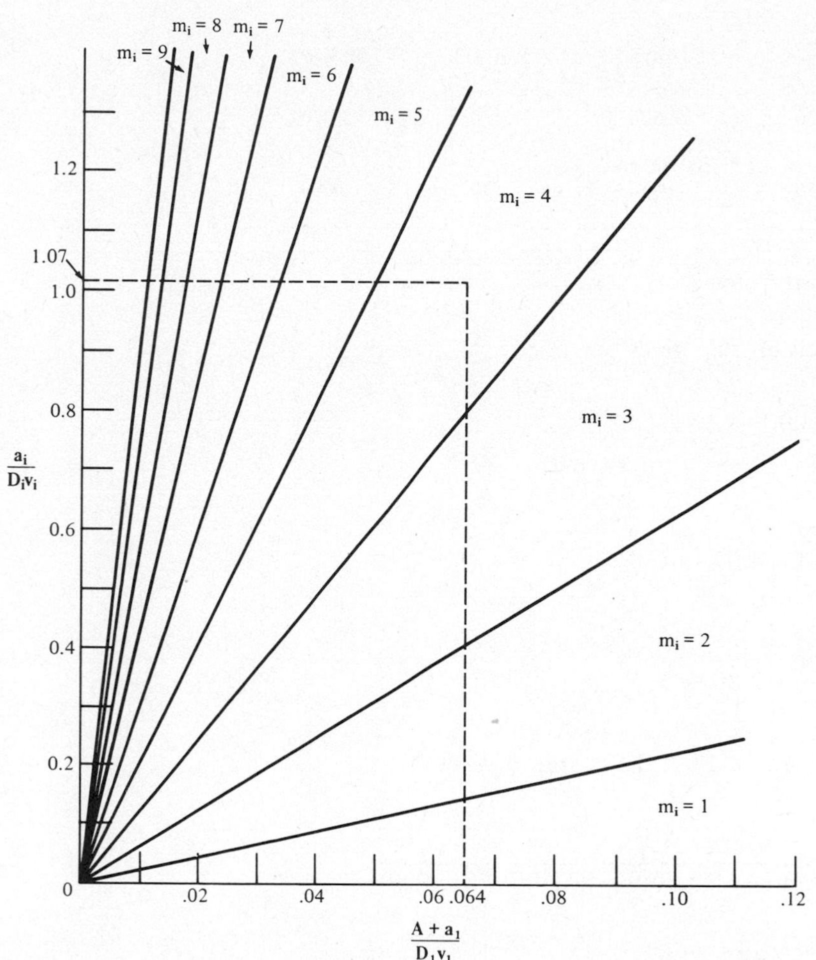

Numerical Illustration—The MIDAS International plant (in West Germany) uses the same machinery to place three different developing liquids into assorted container sizes. One of these liquids (known as product XSC in MIDAS Canada) is packaged in four different sized containers, namely 1, 5, 10, and 50 litres. The major setup cost to convert to this type of liquid is estimated to be $40. It costs $15 to switch from one container size to another. The demand rates of this family of items are shown in Table 13.1. The carrying charge has been established as 0.24 $/$/year.

Table 13.1 The MIDAS Family of Items Problem $A=\$40$, $a_i=\$15$ (doesn't depend on i), $r=0.24$ \$/\$/yr.

Item, i	1[a]	2	3	4
Description	10 litres	1 litre	5 litres	50 litres
D_iv_i(\$/yr.)	86,000	12,500	1,400	3,000
m_i	1	1	4	3
		$T^*=0.0762$ yrs.		
Q_iv_i(\$)	6,550	950	430	690

[a] As discussed in the decision logic the items have been numbered such that item 1 has the smallest value of a_i/D_iv_i. (Here the largest value of D_iv_i because all the a_i's are the same.)

Use of step 2 of the decision rule gives

$$m_2=\sqrt{\frac{15}{12{,}500}\,\frac{86{,}000}{55}}=1.37\rightarrow 1$$

$$m_3=\sqrt{\frac{15}{1{,}400}\,\frac{86{,}000}{55}}=4.09\rightarrow 4$$

$$m_4=\sqrt{\frac{15}{3{,}000}\,\frac{86{,}000}{55}}=2.80\rightarrow 3$$

These entries are shown in Table 13.1. Then step 3 gives

$$T^*=\sqrt{\frac{2(40+\frac{15}{1}+\frac{15}{1}+\frac{15}{4}+\frac{15}{3})}{0.24[1(86{,}000)+1(12{,}500)+4(1{,}400)+3(3{,}000)]}}$$

$$=0.0762 \text{ yrs.}\simeq 4 \text{ weeks.}$$

Step 4 gives that the run quantities are

$$Q_1v_1=(1)(86{,}000)(0.0762)=\$6{,}550$$ (run quantity in dollars of 10 litre container)

$$Q_2v_2=(1)(12{,}500)(0.0762)\simeq\$950$$

$$Q_3v_3=(4)(1{,}400)(0.0762)\simeq\$430$$

$$Q_4v_4=(3)(3{,}000)(0.0762)\simeq\$690$$

To convert these run quantities to units we would have to divide by the v_i values.

To illustrate the use of the graphical aid consider item 3:

$$\frac{a_3}{D_3 v_3} = \frac{15}{1,400} = 0.0107$$

and

$$\frac{A + a_1}{D_1 v_1} = \frac{55}{86,000} = 0.000640$$

We multiply both ratios by 100; the resulting point is shown in Figure 13.1. The associated m_3 is seen to be 4 which, of course, agrees with the result found above through direct use of Eq. 13.3.

13.3 *The Deterministic Case—Group Discounts*

As mentioned earlier, unit price or freight rate discounts may be offered on the total dollar value or the total volume of a replenishment made up of several items (for example, the use of containers for MIDAS shipments from Germany to Canada). Consequently, the inventory control manager would like to ascertain when to take advantage of such a discount. Therefore, knowing the discount structure, the major setup cost (A) of a group of items, the item characteristics (a_i's, D_i's, and v_i's) and the carrying charge (r), we want to develop decision logic for selecting the appropriate individual order quantities, which imply a group quantity and, hence, whether or not a particular discount is achieved.

As in the case of a single item, treated in Chapter 5, taking advantage of an offered discount reduces the replenishment costs (both the fixed and unit costs) but increases the inventory carrying costs. At first glance, it would appear that the analysis for multiple items should not be much more difficult than that for a single item. Such would be the case if every item was included in every replenishment. However, we know from the preceding section that an $m_i > 1$ is likely for an item having a high value of $a_i/D_i v_i$, that is, such items should not necessarily be included in every replenishment, even to help achieve a quantity discount level. Therefore, it is conceivable that the best strategy might be one where on certain replenishments a discount was achieved, while on others it was not (even though all demand rates are assumed known and at constant levels). The analysis of such a strategy would be quite complex because the replenishment cycles would no longer all be of the same duration, T (the ones where quantity discounts were achieved would be longer than the others). Rather than attempting to explicitly model such complex possibilities we suggest the following reasonable compromise solution (illustrated for the case of a single possible discount based on the total replenishment size, in units).

Our approach parallels that used in Section 5.6 of Chapter 5. We consider three possible solutions. The first (and if it is feasible, it is the best to use) is where a coordinated analysis assuming a quantity discount leads to total replenishment quantities which are *always* sufficient to achieve the discount. The second case is where the best result is achieved right at the breakpoint. Finally the third possibility is the coordinated solution without a quantity discount. Therefore, first, the method of Section 13.2 is used to ascertain the m_i's and T assuming that the discount is achieved. The *smallest** replenishment quantity is computed and compared with the breakpoint quantity (Q_b) required. If it exceeds Q_b, we use the m_i's and T developed. If it is less than Q_b, then we must compare the cost of the best solution without a discount to the cost of the solution where the smallest replenishment quantity is right at the breakpoint. Whichever of these has the lower cost is then the solution to use. The details are as follows (again, a computerized version has been developed):

Step 1 Compute the m_i's and T as in Section 13.2 but assuming that each

$$v_i = v_{oi}(1-d)$$

where

v_{oi} is the basic unit cost of item i without a discount.

d is the fractional discount when the *total* replenishment equals or exceeds the breakpoint quantity, Q_b.

It should be noted that the set of m_i's does not depend upon the size of the discount as long as the unit cost of each item is reduced by the same percentage discount (which is typically the case). This can be seen from Eq. 13.3, where, if we use $v_i = v_{oi}(1-d)$ for all i, the $(1-\text{d})$

---

* *What we are assuming here is that if a discount is to be achieved, it must be achieved by every replenishment, that is, we are ignoring the more complex possibility of achieving a discount on only some of the replenishments. The smallest replenishments are those where only the items with $m_i = 1$ are included.*

terms in the numerator and denominator cancel.

Compute the size of the smallest family replenishment

$$Q_{\mathrm{sm}} = \begin{array}{l}\text{(summation of order quantities}\\ \text{of all items having } m_i = 1)\end{array} \tag{13.5}$$

If $Q_{\mathrm{sm}} \geq Q_b$, use the m_i's, T, and Q_i's found above. If not, we proceed to step 2.

Step 2 We scale up the family cycle time T (found in step 1) until the smallest replenishment size equals the quantity breakpoint. This is achieved at

$$T_b = \frac{Q_b}{\text{(summation of } D_i\text{'s of all items having } m_i = 1)} \tag{13.6}$$

The m_i's found in step 1 are maintained. The cost of this breakpoint solution is evaluated using the following total relevant cost expression:

$$\mathrm{TRC}(T_b, m_i\text{'s}) = (1-d)\sum_{i=1}^{n} D_i v_{oi} + \frac{A + \sum_{i=1}^{n} \frac{a_i}{m_i}}{T_b} + \frac{r(1-d)T_b}{2}\sum_{i=1}^{n} m_i D_i v_{oi} \tag{13.7}$$

Step 3 The procedure of Section 13.2 is used to find the m_i's, T, and Q_i's without a discount (as mentioned earlier, the best m_i's here must be the same as those found in step 1). As shown in the appendix to this chapter, the total relevant costs of this solution are given by a somewhat simpler expression than Eq. 13.7, namely

$$\mathrm{TRC}(\text{best } T \text{ and } m_i\text{'s}) = \sum_{i=1}^{n} D_i v_{oi} + \sqrt{2\left(A + \sum_{i=1}^{n} \frac{a_i}{m_i}\right) r \sum_{i=1}^{n} m_i D_i v_{oi}} \tag{13.8}$$

Step 4 The TRC values found in steps 2 and 3 are compared. The m_i's, T, and Q_i's associated with the lower of these are to be used. If the solution right at the breakpoint is used, care must be taken (because of the likely required integer nature of the Q's) to ensure that the breakpoint is actually achieved. Adjustment of one or more Q values to the next higher integers may be necessary.

Numerical Illustration—Consider three parts, EDS-031, EDS-032, and EDS-033, used in the assembly of the MIDAS STABILIZATION PROCESSOR. These three products are purchased from the same domestic supplier who offers a discount of 5 percent if the value of the total replenishment quantity is at least \$600. We use \$1.50 as the basic cost of placing an order with one item involved. The inclusion of each additional item costs \$0.50. It therefore follows that

$$A = \$1.50 - \$0.50 = \$1.00$$

and

$$a_i = \$0.50 \quad \text{for all} \quad i$$

An r value of 0.24 \$/\$year is to be used and the D_i's and v_{oi}'s are shown in columns (1) and (2) of Table 13.2.

Table 13.2 *MIDAS Example with Group Quantity Discount, $A = \$1.00$; $a_i = a = \$0.50$; $r = 0.24$ \$/\$/yr.*

Results of Step 1

Item i	Code	D_i (units/yr.) (1)	v_{oi} (\$/unit) (2)	$D_i v_{oi}$ (\$/yr.) (3)	m_i (4)	T (yrs.) (5)	$Q_i v_{oi}$ (\$) (6)
1	EDS-001	12,000	0.50	6,000	1		275 } 385
2	EDS-002	8,000	0.30	2,400	1	0.0459	110 }
3	EDS-003	700	0.10	70	5		16
				8,470			

$385 < 600$
Therefore go to step 2 (see text).

Final solution

$T = 0.0715$ yrs.

Item i	m_i	Q_i (units)	$Q_i v_i$ (\$)
1	1	858	429.00 } \$600.60
2	1	572	171.60 }
3	5	250	25.00

Following the above procedure step 1 produces the results shown in columns (4) through (6) of the table. It is seen from Eq. 13.5 that

$$Q_{sm} \text{ in dollars} = 275 + 110 = \$385$$

which is below the quantity breakpoint of \$600. Therefore, we proceed to step 2. Use of Eq. 13.6, suitably modified because the breakpoint is expressed in dollars, gives

$$T_b = \frac{\$600}{\$6{,}000/\text{yr.} + \$2{,}400/\text{yr.}}$$

$$= 0.07143 \text{ yr.}$$

The cost of the breakpoint solution is from Eq. 13.7

$$\text{TRC}(T_b, m_i\text{'s}) = 0.95(8{,}470) + \frac{1.00 + 0.50 + 0.50 + 0.10}{0.07143}$$

$$+ \frac{0.24(0.95)}{2}(0.07143)(6{,}000 + 2{,}400 + 350)$$

$$= 8{,}047 + 29 + 71$$

$$= \$8{,}147/\text{yr.}$$

In step 3 we know that the set of best m_i's is $m_1 = m_2 = 1$ and $m_3 = 5$ (from step 1). Using Eq. 13.8 we have

$$\text{TRC(best } T \text{ and } m_i\text{'s}) = 8{,}470 + \sqrt{2(2.10)0.24(8{,}750)}$$

$$= 8{,}470 + 94$$

$$= \$8{,}564/\text{yr.} > \$8{,}147/\text{yr.}$$

Therefore, we should use the solution of step 2, namely that which assures that the smallest replenishment quantity is at the breakpoint. This is achieved by using*

$$T = 0.0715 \text{ yr.}$$

---

* *The T and Q values have been adjusted upwards slightly to ensure that $Q_1 v_{01} + Q_2 v_{02}$ is at least as large as the breakpoint value of* \$600.

$Q_1 = 858$ units (D_1T) every group replenishment

$Q_2 = 572$ units (D_2T) every group replenishment

$Q_3 = 250$ units $(5D_3T)$ every fifth group replenishment

It is seen that a sizable saving of (8,564 − 8,147) or \$417/yr. is achieved by taking the discount.

13.4 *Probabilistic Demand: Can-Order Systems*

For the moment we shall discuss two distinct ways of coping with probabilistic demand when coordinating the replenishments of a family of items. The first of these, the so-called "can-order" system, which will be discussed in this section, is specifically geared to the situation where savings in setup costs are of primary concern (for example, where several products are run on the same piece of equipment) as opposed to achieving a specified total replenishment size (for quantity discount purposes). It involves continuous review (transactions recording). The second type of system, to be discussed in Section 13.5, uses the so-called "service-point" approach. It involves periodic review and is particularly suited to the situation where the primary concern is with achieving a specified total replenishment size (for quantity discount purposes). A third intermediate type of system is possible, where each item has a periodic review, order point, order-up-to-level (R, s, S) type of control but with all items of the group having the same review interval. The method of computing appropriate values of R, the s's and S's hinges upon an approximate procedure (Ehrhardt[11] or Naddor[24]) developed for the case of a single item (R, s, S) system, an advanced topic to be covered in Chapter 14. Therefore, we shall return to this third type of system at that time.

As one would expect from earlier comments, the development of decision rules for coordinated items under probabilistic demand is anything but a simple task—the logic is quite involved. For this reason, in both this section and Section 13.5 we attempt to present only the basic concepts of each system. The reader interested in further details is encouraged to make use of the references provided.

13.4.1 *The Physical Operation of an (S, c, s) System*

Balintfy[3] was the first to propose the use of an (S, c, s) system, a special type of continuous review system for controlling coordinated items. In such a system, whenever item *i*'s inventory position drops to s_i (called its must-order point) or lower, it triggers a replenishment action so as to raise item *i*'s level to its order-up-to-level S_i. At the same time any other item *j* (within the associated family) with inventory position at or below its can-order point c_j is included in the replenishment. If item *j* is included, a quantity is ordered sufficient to raise its level to S_j. The idea of having a can-order point is to allow an item *j*, whose inventory position is low enough (at c_j or lower), to be included in the order triggered by item *i*, thus eliminating an extra major setup cost that would likely occur in the near future due to item *j* reaching its must-order point. On the other hand, inclusion of item *j* in the order is not worthwhile if its inventory position is high enough above its must-order point (that is, above c_j). The behavior of a typical item under such a system of control is shown in Figure 13.2.

Ignall[18] has shown that an (*S*, *c*, *s*) policy does not necessarily minimize the sum of replenishment, inventory carrying, and shortage costs. However, the policy that would minimize these costs would be considerably more

Figure 13.2 Behavior of an Item Under (S, c, s) Control.

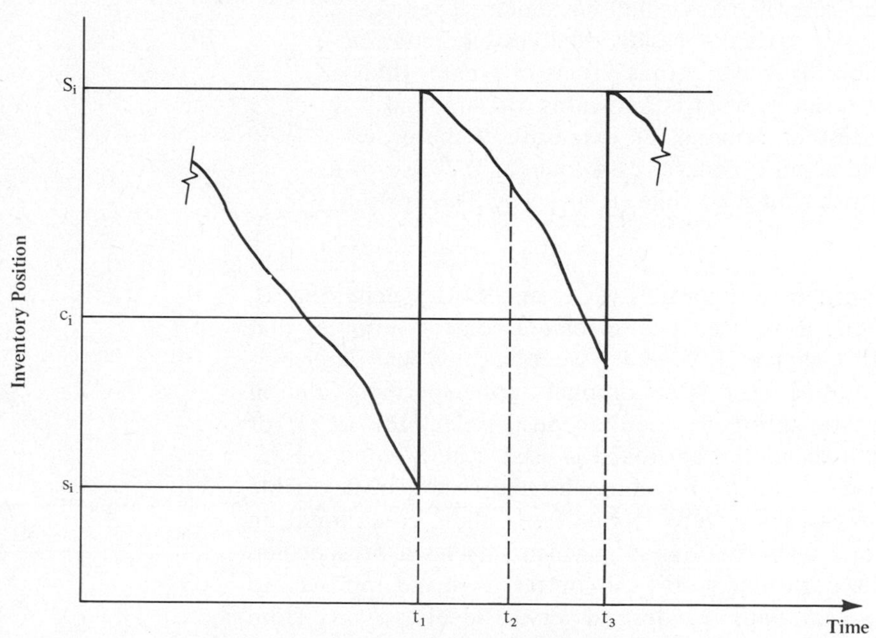

At time t_1 this item triggers a replenishment.

At time t_2 some other item in the group triggers a replenishment, but this item is not included because its inventory position is above its can-order point.

At time t_3 some other item in the group triggers a replenishment in which this item is now included.

complex than the (S, c, s) strategy. Therefore, when one properly takes account of the system control costs, it is felt that an (S, c, s) approach achieves a solution which is close to the best attainable.

13.4.2 *The Essence of a Suggested Procedure for Computing Values of the Order-up-to-Levels (S_i's), Can-Order Points (c_i's) and Must-Order Points (s_i's)*

One of the authors (Reference 31) has developed a reasonable procedure for ascertaining values of the S's, c's, and s's. The derivation is based on a set of assumptions, the most severe of which are:

i. The replenishment lead time is of constant known length. Furthermore, its length does not depend upon which subset of the items of the family are involved in the replenishment.

ii. Demand for each item is of a Poisson nature where, of course, each item can have a different demand rate. The Poisson distribution is an approximation to reality, most appropriate for the case of many small customers. The assumption of Poisson arrivals of individual customer transactions is reasonable. However, transactions of greater than unit size would result in what is known as a compound Poisson distribution of demand (an extension of the procedure to handle this more general case, but for the case of a negligible replenishment lead time, is given by Thompstone and Silver[36]).

For each item i there are three quantities (S_i, c_i, and s_i) to specify, that is, if the family has 10 items, there are 30 interrelated control variables that must be given values. In Chapters 5, 6, and 7 we advocated first determining Q (or R) and then finding s (or S) conditional on the specified value of Q (or R) rather than attempting to simultaneously select the (s, Q) or (R, S) pair. Again here a sequential approach is used. The S's and c's are found, by an approximate iterative procedure, for the case of a negligible replenishment lead time (each s is zero in this case), then, conditional on these S and c values, one finds the lowest s_i which satisfies a prespecified service constraint for the particular item i (in contrast with the approach to be discussed in Section 13.5, here the desired service level can vary from item to item). As earlier we know that the S's, c's, and s's so obtained will not strictly minimize the sum of replenishment and carrying costs. However, the cost penalty is likely to be low and we are willing to absorb it in order to have a computationally feasible scheme for evaluating the control parameters.

13.4.3 *Effects of (S, c, s) Control*

A Numerical Illustration—To indicate the effects of coordinated control on the control parameter settings and the expected total relevant costs we present the four-item example of Table 13.3. No details of the derivation of the parameter settings are given. (These are available in Reference 31.) Examination of Table 13.3 reveals the following points (typical of all examples tested):

i. Coordination tends to substantially lower the order-up-to-levels (the S's). This is because under coordination the average setup cost associated with the replenishment of an item tends to be lower, thus we need not order as much each time we replenish.
ii. Coordination, to a lesser extent, lowers the must-order points (the s's). Under coordination, an item i is often reordered when its inventory level is substantially above s_i, hence s_i can be lowered (compared with the case of independent control) while still providing adequate service.
iii. The major impact of coordination is on the lower dollar usage items (items 2, 3, and 4 in the example).
iv. The cost saving is substantial (here approximately 15 percent).

Table 13.3 A Numerical Example of Coordinated Control $A = \$50$, $a_i = a = \$10$, $r = 0.2$/yr., $L = 1$ month. Service level, $P_1 = 0.95$ for all items

			Independent Control			Coordinated Control			
Item, i	D_i (units/yr.)	v_i ($/unit)	s_i	S_i	EC_i^a ($/yr.)	s_i	c_i	S_i	EC_i^a ($/yr.)
1	290	6.90	33	192	232.03	32	119	184	221.74
2	41	1.20	7	150	35.34	4	41	100	23.26
3	77	3.90	11	120	88.86	9	52	97	70.93
4	122	2.30	16	194	84.98	13	82	156	67.19
					Total = $441.21/yr.				Total = $383.12/yr.

[a] EC_i—the expected costs (replenishment plus carrying) per year associated with item i.

Cost Savings of Several Examples—Based on a number of test examples performed (see References 31 and 36) the following conclusions can be drawn (at least for the cases of Poisson and compound Poisson demand) concerning the cost savings possible through the use of the (S, c, s) procedure discussed in the preceding subsection:

i For typical values of the input factors (A, a_i's, D's, v's, number of items, etc.) the average cost savings over independent control are in the neighborhood of 15 to 20 percent.

ii. The cost savings increase as the a/A ratios decrease, certainly intuitively appealing.

iii. The cost savings improve as n increases; the more items there are in the group, the more attractive coordinated replenishment becomes.

iv. The *percent* cost savings tend to diminish as the required service level increases (a large safety stock dominates either type of control).

v. Somewhat surprisingly, for a fixed level of service, the cost savings are quite insensitive to the length of the replenishment lead time.

13.5 *Probabilistic Demand: Prespecified Total Replenishment Size*

In contrast with the situation in the previous section, now, to achieve a group quantity discount, we have a prespecified group replenishment size (probably developed by a method such as described in Section 13.3). The two remaining issues are:

i. When to place a group order

ii. How to allocate the prespecified group replenishment quantity among the members of the involved family?

Unless stated otherwise, we shall restrict attention to situations where the following assumptions are satisfied:

a. The inventory levels are reviewed every R units of time (that is, periodic review) and replenishment *decisions* can be made only at those times.

b. The replenishment lead time is of a fixed duration of L time units, which does not depend upon the makeup of the family replenishment.

c. The demand for each item i in a period of duration (R+ L) is normally distributed (that is, forecast errors are normally distributed) with known mean, $\hat{x}_{R+L,i}$, and standard deviation, $\sigma_{R+L,i}$.

13.5.1 *Deciding When to Order*

The first inclination would be to simply extend the logic of one of the basic single item systems studied in Chapter 6, namely the (R, S) system where every R units of time enough of the item is ordered to raise its inventory position to S, that is, now we would have an S_i for each item. The problem is that such a system would generate total replenishments of variable size, that is, it would not ensure a total replenishment of a prespecified size.

Instead, one could suggest generating a total order of the prescribed size every R units of time. However, this system would not operate effectively because the total inventory would tend to get out of line (build up or drop off) if the average total demand in R was not equal to the prespecified replenishment size. In the case of changing demand rates this could be avoided only by frequently altering the total replenishment size (which might not be possible if one wished to achieve a group discount).

Alternatively, a reorder point system could be used, that is, at a review the inventory level of each item i would be compared with its reorder point to ascertain whether or not it should be included in a replenishment at that time. In Chapter 6 we indicated that, even for a single item, determination of the appropriate values of the control parameters in a periodic review, order point system is very complicated. Here the situation would be even worse because of the following problem: If a group of items was controlled by an order point system, an order would usually be placed when only one of them had dropped to its reorder point. The other items would still have inventory above their reorder points; this means that, on the average, they would be above their safety stocks when the order arrives. This excess inventory is known as remnant stock. A mathematical representation of expected remnant stock (and its effect on service) has defied closed-form representation. Therefore, there is no simple logical way to set the reorder points so as to achieve a prescribed service level.

A compromise solution is achieved by placing a group replenishment of the prespecified total size, not at every review time, but only at those where further delay would produce unsatisfactory customer service. This approach, first documented in the Wholesale IMPACT System (Reference 17) is known as the "service point" method. The basic idea (which is similar to that mentioned in Section 8.9.3 of Chapter 8) is as follows:

At a review time we calculate the expected shortages (of the various items of a group) that will occur if we wait until at least the next review time to place an order. Associated with the group of items are allowable average shortages per cycle, if we are to provide desired levels of service. If the expected shortage (ESPRC)* is less than the allowed average shortage (ASPRC), then no order is placed at this time. However, when

$$\text{ESPRC} > \text{ASPRC}$$

a reorder action must be taken (this will, in general, lead to a higher than desired service level, the primary reason being that the order will arrive only a lead time, L, from now hence the actual expected shortage will be considerably lower than ESPRC which is based on an interval of length $R+L$). If delaying the arrival of a replenishment for various fractions (f) of a review interval is permissible, then we find the largest value of f such that

$$\text{ESPRC} \leq \text{ASPRC}$$

Exactly as in Section 7.4.2 of Chapter 7, we find that the equation for ESPRC for a single item** for a delay of fR is

$$\text{ESPRC}(fR) = \sigma_{fR+L} G_u\left(\frac{w - \bar{x}_{fR+L}}{\sigma_{fR+L}}\right) \tag{13.9}$$

where

$\bar{x}_{fR+L}$ is the forecast demand over an interval of duration $fR+L$.

σ_{fR+L} is the standard deviation of forecast errors over the same interval.

---

* *Consistent with the notation earlier in the book,* PRC *stands for "per replenishment cycle."*

** *For simplicity in notation we omit the subscript i's that would normally be shown for item i.*

w is the current inventory position.

$G_u(\cdot)$ is a function of the unit normal variable, introduced in earlier chapters and tabulated in Appendix C.

$$\text{ASPRC} = \bar{x}_c(1 - P_2) \tag{13.10}$$

where

P_2 is the desired service level (fraction of demand to be satisfied directly from shelf).

$\bar{x}_c$ is the average demand for the item between orders (that is, per cycle), the demand rate multiplied by the expected time between orders (a rough approximation for the latter is the group order size divided by the total demand rate for the group) between orders.

For a group of n items, for a given delay (fR), we compare

$$\sum_{i=1}^{n} \text{ESPRC}(fR)$$

with

$$\sum_{i=1}^{n} \text{ASPRC}$$

to make our decision. It is clear that a particular delay could satisfy this criterion while still giving very poor service to one or more individual items.

The unmodified "service point" procedure requires the calculation of Eq. 13.9 at least once* for each item at every review time. There are two ways of reducing this heavy computational load:

i. Through the use of so-called "peek-points." The idea here is that, if none of the items are below their peek-points, we don't even bother calculating the ESPRC's at this review instant. If a peek-point is set too high, unnecessary

---

* *More than once if a delay of R cannot be tolerated and delays for fractions of R are permissible.*

computations will be performed. On the other hand, if it is set too low, excessive shortages of the item will tend to occur. Unfortunately, there is no simple way of specifying the appropriate peek-points. Hence, we advocate a trial and error adjustment of the peek-points until the user is reasonably satisfied with the operation of the system.

ii. Through the use of a look-ahead procedure. Here, when we place an order or test for the placing of an order we calculate the number of review intervals (T) that are likely to elapse before another order will be required. Then we select some number (T') less than T and decide not to recalculate the ESPRC's until T' periods have elapsed. The larger T' is, the smaller the overall computational load is, but the greater the chance of not placing an order when we should do so.

13.5.2 *Allocating an Order Among Items*

When it is time to place an order we must decide on how much to order of each item subject to:

i. The total replenishment size being equal to a prespecified value

ii. Stock being allocated among the items so as to best achieve service objectives

Again we concentrate on the IMPACT (Reference 17) approach. When we have a fixed total quantity to allocate among several items we really have two basic choices. First, we can hold the desired service objectives fixed and vary the time for which the order is to last (this is known as variable allocation). Second, we can hold the time fixed and vary the service objectives (this is known as fixed allocation).

When it is time to place an order we use the following equation to determine the quantity of an item i that is included in every replenishment of the group (in the notation of Section 13.2 it has $m_i = 1$).

$$Q_i = D_i U + k_i \sigma_U - w_i \tag{13.11}$$

with

$$U = \text{Delay} + L + T, \quad \text{in years} \tag{13.12}$$

where

Q_i is the quantity to order, in units.

D_i is the demand rate, in units/yr.

σ_U is the standard deviation of forecast errors over a time interval U, in units.

w_i is the current inventory position, in units.

"Delay" is any deliberate delay before the present order is placed (the fR idea of Section 13.5.1), in years.

T is the expected time between joint replenishments, in years.

the safety factor k_i satisfies

$$G_u(k_i) = \frac{D_i T(1-P_2)}{\sigma_U} \tag{13.13}$$

P_2 is the desired fraction of demand to be satisfied directly from the shelf.

For an item not necessarily included in every replenishment (that is, its $m_i > 1$) the IMPACT suggested order size is

$$Q_i = m_i D_i T + k_i \sigma_T - w_i \tag{13.14}$$

where all of the symbols are as defined above.

The use of the factor σ_T in the safety stock term is difficult to justify. A more reasonable period of uncertainty would be either U or "Delay$+L+m_iT$."

The steps in the allocation procedure are as follows:

i. Assume values for item service (P_2's) and for the joint-order interval (T), the latter likely being an output of Section 13.3.

ii. For these values calculate the Q_i's as shown above.

iii. Convert these quantities to the units in which the joint order quantity is to be specified and total them. Let this total be Q_{TOT}.

iv. Check to see if Q_{TOT} is close enough to the desired group replenishment quantity.

v. If Q_{TOT} is unacceptable, select a new value for service, P_2, (fixed allocation) or order interval, T, (variable allocation) and repeat the above steps. In altering the service objectives under fixed allocation IMPACT multiplies every $(1-P_2)$ by the same factor. In this manner the disservice for all items is adjusted by the same proportion.

13.5.3 *Other Approaches to Allocation*

To review, allocation is concerned with the following situation. We have a number of coordinated items* with given inventory positions. A total order of a prescribed size is given. The problem is how to divide the order among the various items. A fixed time until the next replenishment may be prescribed or the time may be variable.

The selection of an appropriate criterion is no simple matter. Ideally one would like to minimize costs but some costs, such as those associated with shortages, are difficult to measure. One possible criterion is to minimize inventory carrying costs; this is achieved by allocating so as to have remnant stocks as low as possible (which also is equivalent to maximizing the expected time until the next replenishment). Another criterion is to minimize total shortages (in a fixed interval). In general, these two criteria will give quite different results.

Low and Waddington's Procedure—In their article Low and Waddington[19] use the criterion of minimizing expected remnant stock. They deal with Poisson demands for individual items. The exact solution of the allocation problem involves the solution of a dynamic programming model. Routine use of this model would be computationally prohibitive. However, the authors make use of empirical relationships developed from the results of the model. Letting the sales rate of item i be D_i (where the D's have been normalized to add to unity) they have developed a workable procedure for obtaining the allocation quantities as a function of the D_i's and the number of items in the group. In fact, the results have been converted to an easily-usable tabular form.

Brown's Procedure—Brown[4] also uses the criterion of minimizing remnant stock. (His discussion is in the context of the same item at several

---

* *An analogous situation is a single item stocked at several different locations.*

locations.) He shows that the criterion is satisfied by allocating such that the probability that item i is the first to run out (trigger) is equal to the fraction of the group's sales that item i contributes. However, putting this result to practical use is another matter. The mathematical representation of the probability that item i is the first to run out is extremely complex. Therefore, Brown argues that we should use a slightly different relationship, namely select a time period T and make the probability that an item runs out in that period proportional to the fraction of the group's sales that the item contributes. He develops a simple scheme for doing this for the case of normally distributed forecast errors.

13.6 *Summary*

In this chapter we first showed the details of coordinated control under deterministic demand, both with and without quantity discounts. Then we developed an appreciation of the complexity of the probabilistic demand situation. For the latter we discussed two quite different types of coordinated control.

The can-order system of Section 13.4 is specifically geared to the situation where the primary concern is with reducing the total setup costs per unit time. To make the analysis more tractable we again advocated a sequential approach in the selection of the control parameters (the S's and c's, then the s's). Nevertheless, a Poisson demand assumption was required and the associated algorithm definitely requires a computer for solution.

The second approach, the service point, allocation system of Section 13.5 is designed specifically for the situation where the dominant concern is with achieving a group quantity discount. We saw that adequate service could be guaranteed only on the average for the whole group of items, with possibly poor service for individual items. Again the resulting decision system really requires a computer for successful implementation.

To summarize, the procedures discussed in Sections 13.4 and 13.5 are not simple enough for routine use by practitioners. Research, currently on-going, is needed to develop simpler heuristic rules that allow the setting of reasonable values of the control parameters. In the next chapter we shall report further on one promising avenue under exploration by Naddor.[24]. We shall also return to a discussion of families of coordinated items in the medium range aggregate scheduling procedures of Chapter 18.

Appendix to Chapter 13—Derivation of Results in Section 13.2.2

If a time interval T between replenishments of the family and a set of m_i's are used, where m_i, an integer, is the number of T intervals that the replenishment quantity of item i will last, then this replenishment quantity (Q_i) is given by

$$Q_i = D_i m_i T \tag{13.15}$$

The typical saw-tooth diagram of inventory is applicable so that the average inventory of item $i(\bar{I}_i)$ is

$$\bar{I}_i = \frac{Q_i}{2} = \frac{D_i m_i T}{2}$$

A group setup cost (A) is incurred every T units of time whereas the cost a_i is incurred only once in every $m_i T$ units of time. Therefore, the total relevant costs per unit time are given by

$$\text{TRC}(T, m_i\text{'s}) = \frac{A + \sum_{i=1}^{n} a_i/m_i}{T} + \sum_{i=1}^{n} \frac{D_i m_i T v_i r}{2} \tag{13.16}$$

Setting

$$\frac{\partial \text{TRC}}{\partial T} = 0$$

gives the best T for the particular set of m_i's, that is,

$$-\frac{A + \sum_i a_i/m_i}{T^2} + \frac{r}{2} \sum_i m_i D_i v_i = 0$$

or

$$T^*(m_i\text{'s}) = \sqrt{\frac{2(A + \sum a_i/m_i)}{r \sum m_i D_i v_i}} \tag{13.17}$$

which is Eq. 13.2.

Substitution of Eq. 13.17 back into Eq. 13.6 gives the best cost for a given set of m_i's, viz:

$$\text{TRC}^*(m_i\text{'s}) = \frac{A+\sum a_i/m_i}{\sqrt{\dfrac{2(A+\sum a_i/m_i)}{r\sum m_iD_iv_i}}} + \sqrt{\frac{2(A+\sum a_i/m_i}{r\sum m_iD_iv_i}}\,\frac{r\sum m_iD_iv_i}{2}$$

which simplifies to

$$\text{TRC}^*(m_i\text{'s}) = \sqrt{2(A+\sum a_i/m_i)r\sum m_iD_iv_i} \qquad (13.18)$$

(This equation was used to directly produce Eq. 13.8.)

We wish to select the m_i's to minimize TRC*(m_i's). From an inspection of Eq. 13.18 this is achieved by selecting the m_i's to minimize

$$F(m_i\text{'s}) = (A+\sum a_i/m_i)\sum m_iD_iv_i \qquad (13.19)$$

The minimization of Eq. 13.19 is no simple matter because of two facts: (i) the m_i's interact (that is, the effects of one m_i value depend upon the values of the other m_j's), (ii) the m_i's must be integers.

If we choose to ignore the integer constraints on the m_i's and set partial derivatives of $F(m_i$'s) equal to zero (necessary conditions for a minimum), then

$$\frac{\partial F(m_i\text{'s})}{\partial m_j} = -\frac{a_j}{m_j^2}\sum_i m_iD_iv_i + D_jv_j(A+\sum a_i/m_i) = 0$$

or

$$m_j^2 = \frac{a_j\sum m_iD_iv_i}{D_jv_j(A+\sum a_i/m_i)} \qquad j=1,2,\ldots,n \qquad (13.20)$$

For $j \neq k$, we have

$$m_k^2 = \frac{a_k}{D_kv_k}\,\frac{\sum m_iD_iv_i}{(A+\sum a_i/m_i)}$$

Dividing gives

$$\frac{m_j^2}{m_k^2} = \frac{a_j}{D_jv_j}\,\frac{D_kv_k}{a_k}$$

or

$$\frac{m_j}{m_k} = \sqrt{\frac{a_j}{D_j v_j} \frac{D_k v_k}{a_k}} \qquad j \neq k$$

It is seen that if

$$\frac{a_j}{D_j v_j} < \frac{a_k}{D_k v_k}$$

then (the continuous solution) m_j is less than (the continuous solution) m_k. Therefore, the item i having the smallest value of $a_i/D_i v_i$ should have the lowest value of m_i, namely 1. It is reasonable to assume that this will hold even when the m_j's are restricted to being integers; of course, in this case, more than one item could have $m_j = 1$.

If the items are numbered such that item 1 has the smallest value of $a_i/D_i v_i$, then

$$m_1 = 1 \tag{13.21}$$

and, from Eq. 13.20,

$$m_j = \sqrt{\frac{a_j}{D_j v_j}} \sqrt{\frac{\sum m_i D_i v_i}{(A + \sum a_i/m_i)}} \qquad j = 2, 3, \ldots, n \tag{13.22}$$

Suppose that there is a solution to these equations which results in

$$\sqrt{\frac{\sum m_i D_i v_i}{(A + \sum a_i/m_i)}} = C \tag{13.23}$$

Then, from Eq. 13.22 we have

$$m_j = C\sqrt{\frac{a_j}{D_j v_j}} \qquad j = 2, 3, \ldots, n \tag{13.24}$$

Therefore,

$$\sum_{i=1}^{n} m_i D_i v_i = D_1 v_1 + \sum_{i=2}^{n} C\sqrt{\frac{a_i}{D_i v_i}}\, D_i v_i$$

$$= D_1 v_1 + C \sum_{i=2}^{n} \sqrt{a_i D_i v_i} \tag{13.25}$$

Similarly

$$\sum_{i=1}^{n} a_i/m_i = a_1 + \frac{1}{C}\sum_{i=2}^{n} \sqrt{a_i D_i v_i} \tag{13.26}$$

Substituting Eqs. 13.25 and 13.26 back into the left hand side of Eq. 13.23 and squaring we obtain

$$\frac{D_1 v_1 + C\sum_{i=2}^{n}\sqrt{a_i D_i v_i}}{A + a_1 + \frac{1}{C}\sum_{i=2}^{n}\sqrt{a_i D_i v_i}} = C^2$$

Cross-multiplication gives

$$D_1 v_1 + C\sum_{i=2}^{n}\sqrt{a_i D_i v_i} = C^2(A + a_1) + C\sum_{i=2}^{n}\sqrt{a_i D_i v_i}$$

or

$$C = \sqrt{\frac{D_1 v_1}{A + a_1}}$$

Substitution of this expression back into Eq. 13.24 gives

$$m_j = \sqrt{\frac{a_j}{D_j v_j}\frac{D_1 v_1}{A + a_1}} \tag{13.27}$$

which is Eq. 13.3.

It should be pointed out, that throughout we could have normalized as follows:

i. Use

$$\frac{D_i v_i}{\sum D_j v_j}$$

instead of $D_i v_i$.

ii. Use a_i/A instead of a_i.

This would reduce the number of parameters involved and also make everything dimensionless.

Problems for Chapter 13

Problem 13.1

Consider a family of 4 items with the following characteristics:

$A = \$100 \qquad r = 0.2/\text{yr.}$

Item i	$D_i v_i$ (\$/yr.)	a_i (\$)
1	100,000	5
2	20,000	5
3	1,000	21.5
4	300	5

a. Use the procedure of Section 13.2.2 to find appropriate values of the family cycle time T and the integer m_i's.

b. Suppose that we restricted attention to the case where every item is included in each replenishment of the family. What does this say about the m_i's? Now find the best value of T.

c. Using Eq. 13.16 (in the appendix), find the cost difference in the answers to parts (a) and (b).

Problem 13.2

The Ptomaine Tavern, a famous fast lunch spot near an institute of higher learning, procures three basic cooking ingredients from the same supplier. H. Fishman, one of the co-owners, estimates that the fixed cost associated with placing an order is \$10.00. In addition, there is a fixed "aggravation" charge of \$1.00 for each s.k.u. included in the order. Usage of each of the three ingredients is relatively stable with time. The usages and basic unit values are as follows:

Item *ID*	usage rate (units/wk.)	unit value (\$/unit)
CO-1	300	1.00
CO-2	80	0.50
CO-3	10	0.40

a. If a coordinated replenishment strategy is to be used, what should be the values of the m_i's?

b. When pressed by a consulting analyst for a value of the carrying charge, r (needed to compute the family cycle time T), Fishman replies: "I don't know from nothing concerning a carrying charge! All I know is that I'm satisfied with placing an order every two weeks." How would you use this answer to impute an approximate value of r? Discuss why it is likely to be only an approximation.

c. What quantities of the three items should the Tavern order?

d. Suppose that the supplier offers Ptomaine a 3 percent discount on any order totalling at least \$1,350 in value (before the discount). Fishman's partner, L. Talks, likes the idea of saving on the purchase price. Fishman is not so sure about the advisability of tieing up so much money in inventory. Should Ptomaine take advantage of the quantity discount offer?

Problem 13.3

Suppose you wished to estimate the annual costs of treating the members of a family independently in setting up run quantities. Under independent treatment some major setups would be avoided, simply by the chance happening of two items of the same family being run one right after the other. How would you estimate the fraction of setups where this would happen?

Problem 13.4

A certain large manufacturing company has just hired a new member of its industrial engineering department, a Mr. V. G. Rickson. Rickson, knowing all about coordinated control, selects a family of 2 items with the following properties:

Item, i	D_i (units/yr.)	v_i ($/unit)
1	10,000	0.50
2	1,000	0.40

From accounting records and discussions with operating personnel he estimates that $A = \$5.00$, $a_1 = \$1.00$, $a_2 = \$4.00$, and $r = 0.2/\text{yr}$.

a. He computes the best values of T, m_1, and m_2. What are these values?

b. The production supervisor, Mr. C. W. Donrath, is skeptical of the value of coordination and argues that independent control is less costly, at least for this family of 2 items. Is he correct?

Problem 13.5

For the A, a_i's deterministic demand context consider a special coordinated strategy, namely where all $m_i = 1$.

a. Determine the optimal value of T.

b. Determine the associated minimum total relevant costs per unit time.

c. Find the best independent and coordinated (the latter with all $m_i = 1$ as above) strategies for each of the following 2 examples:

Example 1

$A = \$10 \quad r = 0.2/\text{yr.}$

Item, i	D_i (units/yr.)	v_i ($/unit)	a_i ($)
1	800	1	2
2	400	0.5	4

Example 2

$A = \$10 \quad r = 0.2/\text{yr.}$

Item, i	D_i (units/yr.)	v_i ($/unit)	a_i ($)
1	900	1	2
2	20	0.5	4

d. Determine as simple a relationship as possible that must be satisfied in order for the above special case of coordinated control (every $m_i = 1$) to be preferable to completely independent control. Ignore any system costs in your analysis. Normalize where possible to reduce the number of parameters.

Problem 13.6

a. Obtain a lower bound on the minimum costs achievable within the A, a_i's deterministic demand context of Section 13.2. *Hint:* One way is to substitute the *non-integer* m_i's of Eq. 13.3 into the cost expression of Eq. 13.18 (remembering that $m_1 = 1$).

b. Determine this lower bound for the 4 item example of Problem 13.1. How far above this bound is the integer m_i's solution found in that problem?

Problem 13.7

The Steady–Milver Corporation produces ball bearings. It has a family of three items which, run consecutively, do not take much time for changeovers. The characteristics of the items are as follows:

Item, i	*ID*	D_i (units/yr.)	raw material ($/unit)
1	BB1	2,000	2.50
2	BB2	1,000	2.50
3	BB3	500	1.60

Item, i	value added ($/unit)	value after production, v_i ($/unit)	a_i ($)
1	0.50	3.00	5
2	0.50	3.00	2
3	0.40	2.00	1

The initial setup cost for the family is \$30.00. Management has agreed upon an r value of 0.10 \$/\$/yr. Production rates are substantially larger than the demand rates.

a. What are the preferred run quantities of the three items?

b. Raw material for product BB1 is acquired from a supplier distinct from that for the other two products. Suppose that the BB1 supplier offers an 8 percent discount on all units if an order for 700 or more is placed. Should Steady–Milver take the discount offer?

Problem 13.8

In Section 13.5.1, under periodic review, a "service point" approach was suggested for deciding when to place a group replenishment.

a. Illustrate the approach for the case of a single item with the following characteristics:

$Q = 300$ units $\quad D = 80$ units/period

$\sigma_1 = 20$ units (and demand is normally distributed)

$R = 1$ period

$L = 2.5$ periods

desired $P_2 = 0.99$

In particular, find the threshold value w_{th} such that if

$$w \le w_{th}$$

we must place an order at the current review (where w is the inventory position). Assume that

$$\sigma_t = \sqrt{t}\,\sigma_1$$

b. Consider an item with an erratic demand pattern (that is, the only demands that occur are infrequent very large demands). What danger is there in using the above system for an erratic item?

Problem 13.9

In Section 13.5.3 mention was made of an allocation procedure suggested by R. G. Brown. To recount, a total order of a prescribed size (say W dollars) is to be allocated among n items ($i = 1, 2, \ldots, n$). For a time period of specified duration T we wish to make the probability that item i runs out during T proportional to the fraction of the group's sales that item i contributes. Suppose that it is reasonable to assume that demand in period T for item i is normally distributed with mean $\bar{x}_i$ and standard deviation σ_{Ti}.

a. Introducing whatever symbols are necessary, develop a routine for allocating the order among the items according to the above criterion.

b. Illustrate for the following 3 item example, in which $W = \$900$:

Item i	$\bar{x}_i$ (units)	σ_{Ti} (units)	v_i (\$/unit)	Initial (before allocation) inventory, I_i (units)
1	100	40	1.00	50
2	300	70	2.00	100
3	250	100	1.20	250

c. Repeat part b) but with

$$I_1 = 250 \qquad I_2 = 150 \qquad I_3 = 0$$

REFERENCES FOR CHAPTER 13

1. Andres, F. and H. Emmons. "A Multiproduct Inventory System with Interactive Set-up Costs." *Management Science*, Vol. 21, No. 9, May, 1975, pp. 1055–1063.

2. Baker, K. R. "On Madigan's Approach to the Deterministic Multi-Product Production and Inventory Problem." *Management Science*, Vol. 12, No. 9, May, 1970, pp. 636–638.

3. Balintfy, J. L. "On a Basic Class of Multi-Item Inventory Problems." *Management Science*, Vol. 10, No. 2, January, 1964, pp. 287–297.

4. Brown, R. G. *Decision Rules for Inventory Management.* Holt, Rinehart, and Winston, New York, N.Y., 1967, Chapters 5, 20.

5. Cahen, J. F. "Stock Policy in Case of Simultaneous Ordering." *International Journal of Production Research*, Vol. 10, No. 4, October, 1972, pp. 301–312.

6. Chern, C. M. "A Multi-Product Joint Ordering Model with Dependent Set-Up Cost." *Management Science*, Vol. 20, No. 7, March, 1974, pp. 1081–1091.

7. Cox, D. and W. Jessop. "The Theory of a Method of Production Scheduling When There are Many Products." *Operational Research Quarterly*, Vol. 13, 1962, pp. 309–328.

8. Curry, G. L. and D. Hartfiel. "A Constrained Joint Setup Cost Inventory Model." *INFOR*, Vol. 13, No. 3, October, 1975, pp. 316–327.

9. Curry, G. L., R. W. Skeith and R. G. Harper. "A Multi-product Dependent Inventory Model." *AIIE Transactions*, Vol. II, No. 3, September, 1970, pp. 263–267.

10. Doll, C. L. and D. C. Whybark. "An Iterative Procedure for the Single-Machine, Multi-Product, Lot Scheduling Problem." *Management Science*, Vol. 20, No. 1, September, 1973, pp. 50–55.

11. Ehrhardt, R. *The Power Approximation: Inventory Policies Based on Limited Demand Information. Technical Report #7*, School of Organization and Management, Yale University, 1976.

12. Eilon, S. "Multi-Product Scheduling in a Chemical Plant." *Management Science*, Vol. 15, No. 6, February, 1969, pp. 267–279.

13. Evans, R. "Inventory Control of a Multiproduct System with a Limited Production Resource." *Naval Research Logistics Quarterly*, Vol. 14, 1967, pp. 173–184.

14. Friend, J. "Stock Control with Random Opportunities for Replenishment." *Operational Research Quarterly*, Vol. 11, No. 3, 1961, pp. 130–136.

15. Goyal, S. K. "Determination of Optimum Packaging Frequency of Items Jointly Replenished." *Management Science*, Vol. 21, No. 4, December, 1974, pp. 436–443.

16. Goyal, S. K. "Analysis of Joint Replenishment Inventory Systems with Resource Restrictions." *Operational Research Quarterly*,

Vol. 26, No. 1 ii, April, 1975, pp. 197–203.

17. IBM. *Wholesale IMPACT—Advanced Principles and Implementation Reference Manual,* E20-0174-1. White Plains, N.Y., 1971.

18. Ignall, E. "Optimal Continuous Review Policies for Two Product Inventory Systems with Joint Set-up Costs." *Management Science,* Vol. 15, No. 5, January, 1969, pp. 278–283.

19. Low, R. and J. Waddington. "The Determination of the Optimum Joint Replenishment Policy for a group of Discount—Connected Stock Lines." *Operational Research Quarterly,* Vol. 18, No. 4, Dec., 1967, pp. 443–462.

20. Madigan, J. G. "Scheduling a Multi-Product, Single Machine System for an Infinite Planning Period." *Management Science,* Vol. 14, No. 11, July, 1968, pp. 713–719.

21. Maher, M., J. Gittins, and R. Morgan. "An Analysis of a Multi-Line Re-Order System Using a Can-Order Policy." *Management Science,* Vol. 19, No. 7, March, 1973, pp. 800–808.

22. Maxwell, W. L. "The Scheduling of Economic Lot Sizes." *Naval Research Logistics Quarterly,* Vol. 11, 1964, pp. 89–124.

23. Naddor, E. "Production Scheduling: Analysis and Time-Sharing Applications." *Research Publication GRM*-917, General Motors Corporation, Warren, Michigan, 1969.

24. Naddor, E. "Optimal and Heuristic Decisions in Single and Multi-Item Inventory Systems." *Management Science,* Vol. 21, No. 11, July, 1975, pp. 1234–1249.

25. Naddor, E. and S. Saltzman. "Optimal Reorder Periods for an Inventory System with Variable Costs of Ordering." *Operations Research,* Vol. 6, September–October, 1958, pp. 676–685.

26. Nocturne, D. "Economic Ordering Frequency for Several Items Jointly Replenished." *Management Science,* Vol. 19, No. 9, May, 1973, pp. 1093–1096.

27. Renburg, B. and R. Planche. "Un Modele pour la Gestion Simultanée des *n* Articles d'un Stock." *Revue Francaise d'Informatique et de Recherche Operationnelle,* Serie Bleue, Vol. 6, 1967, pp. 47–59.

28. Schaack, J. P. and E. A. Silver. "A Procedure, Involving Simulation, for Selecting the Control Variables of an (S, c, s) Joint Ordering Strategy." *INFOR,* Vol. 10, No. 2, June, 1972, pp. 154–170.

29. Silver, E. A. "Some Characteristics of a Special Joint Order Inventory Model." *Operations Research,* Vol. 13, No. 2, March–April, 1965, pp. 319–322.

30. Silver, E. A. "Three Ways of Obtaining the Average Cost Expression in a Problem Related to Joint Replenishment Inventory Control." *Naval Research Logistics Quarterly,* Vol. 20, No. 2, June, 1973, pp. 241–254.

31. Silver, E. A. "A Control System for Coordinated Inventory Replenishment." *International Journal of Production Research,* Vol. 12, No. 6, 1974, pp. 647–671.

32. Silver, E. A. "Modifying the

Economic Order Quantity (EOQ) to Handle Coordinated Replenishments of Two or More Items." *Production and Inventory Management*, Vol. 16, No. 3, 1975, pp. 26–38.

33. Silver, E. A. "A Simple Method of Determining Order Quantities in Joint Replenishments Under Deterministic Demand." *Management Science*, Vol. 22, No. 12, August 1976, pp. 1351–1361.

34. Simmons, D. "Optimal Inventory Policies Under a Hierarchy of Setup Costs." *Management Science*, Vol. 18, No. 10, June, 1972, pp. B591–B599.

35. Sivazlian, B. "Stationary Analysis of a Multicommodity Inventory System with Interacting Set-up Costs." *SIAM J. Appl. Math*, Vol. 20. No. 2, March, 1971, pp. 264–278.

36. Thompstone, R. M. and E. A. Silver. "A Coordinated Inventory Control System for Compound Poisson Demand and Zero Lead Time." *International Journal of Production Research*, Vol. 13, No. 6, 1975, pp. 581–602.

CHAPTER FOURTEEN

Reasonable Approaches to Some Challenging Problems

Introduction of some of the real world complexities, ignored in earlier chapters, makes the analysis of production/inventory problems considerably more complex. Recognizing this fact, there are two purposes that this chapter is meant to serve. First, in Section 14.1 various aspects of modelling, particularly in relation to complex problems, not explicitly discussed elsewhere in the book, will be presented. Second, in Section 14.2, we shall indicate some of the more complex aspects of inventory management/production planning where substantial headway towards solution has been made; in fact, in some cases operational control systems have been developed. It should be emphasized that in *only* this chapter we do not restrict our presentation exclusively to operational systems. A rather extensive bibliography is provided at the end of the chapter.

We now briefly outline the specific areas to be discussed in Section 14.2. Sections 14.2.1 and 14.2.2 deal with reasonable approaches to selecting the values of the control variables in individual item (s, S) and (R, s, S) control systems. In Section 14.2.3 we discuss the logic of (R, s, S) coordinated control of a group of items, where a common review interval (R value) is used for the group. Section 14.2.4 deals with a special demand situation, namely the case of rather infrequent customer transactions. Then, in Section 14.2.5 we turn to Bayesian forecasting methods, a topic of interest for items with rather limited historical information. Next, the control of items, subject to perishability, is discussed in Section 14.2.6. Finally, in Section 14.2.7 we present a decision problem illustrating an interaction between inventory management and another functional area of the firm, the problem being the simultaneous selection of pricing and inventory policies.

14.1 *The Art of Modelling*

In developing a mathematical model to aid in decision making one is faced with the difficult task of incorporating the important factors, yet keeping the model as simple as possible. This is especially true for the more complex problem areas where ineffective modelling can lead to either incorrect decisions or higher than necessary computational and data collection costs. In this section we present some modelling approaches which the reader may find helpful in dealing with complex problem situations. There are some excellent references (see, for example Ackoff and Sasieni[1] and Morris[42]) on the general topic of modelling.

A useful guideline is to start with as simple a model as possible, only adding complexities as necessary. The initial simpler versions of the model, if nothing else, provide useful insights into the form of the solution. We have found it helpful in multi-item problems to first consider the simplest cases of 2 items, then 3 items, etc. In the same vein, it is worthwhile to analyse the special case of a zero lead time before generalizing to a non-zero lead time. We recall the incident of an overzealous mathematician who was employed by a consulting firm. Given a problem to solve involving just two items, he proceeded to wipe out the study budget by first solving the problem for the general case of n items and then substituting $n=2$ in the very last step.

14.1.1 *Use of a Projected Property of the Solution*

Where it is known a priori that the solution to a problem will possess a certain property, this information should be used, if possible, to simplify the modelling and/or solution process. One good example of this is the restricting of attention to a particular type of solution, for example an (s, S) policy rather than modelling a situation where any order quantity can be requisitioned when we are at any inventory level. Of course, this is contingent upon knowing that the best solution in the subset considered will be close to the overall best solution, a point to which we shall return in Section 14.1.4. White[76] cites the desirability of using the fact that a very costly event will only occur on an infrequent basis in any reasonable solution to a problem. Neglecting these infrequent occurrences simplifies the modelling, leading to a straightforward trial solution of the problem. Once this trial solution is found, the above assumption is tested. If it turns out to be reasonable, as is often the case, the trial solution becomes the final solution. A good example of this approach was illustrated in Chapter 7 where it was assumed that in any reasonable inventory control policy the average level of backorders would be negligibly small when compared with the average level of the on-hand stock.

14.1.2 *Equivalent Problems*

One important aspect of the art of modelling when facing a new problem is to attempt to show an equivalence with a different problem for which a solution method is already known. Naddor[43] has effectively demonstrated this approach in the context of inventory control systems.

As a simple illustration consider a periodic review, order-up-to-level system with a negligible lead time ($L=0$). Assume that a review is made after every unit time period. Suppose that the unit value of the item is v, there is a carrying charge r and a cost B_3v per unit short *per unit time.* We shall consider two different types of demand patterns and show that the two problems are entirely equivalent.

Case 1, Instantaneous Demand—Consider first the case where demand in a unit time period all occurs right at the beginning of the interval (just after the order is placed). Let $f_x(x_0)$ represent the probability density function of the total demand in a unit period. The expected total relevant costs per unit period as a function of the order-up-to-level S are

$$\mathrm{ETRC}_1(S) = vr\int_0^S (S-x_0)f_x(x_0)\,dx_0 + B_3v\int_S^\infty (x_0-S)f_x(x_0)\,dx_0 \qquad (14.1)$$

where r and B_3 are assumed to have units of \$/\$/unit period. This has a structure similar to that of the newsboy problem (Chapter 10). As done there, we set

$$\frac{d\,\mathrm{ETRC}\,(S)}{dS} = 0$$

for a minimum, which leads to the result that the S to use must satisfy the following equation:

$$p_{x<}(S) = \int_0^S f_x(x_0)\,dx_0 = \frac{B_3}{r + B_3} \tag{14.2}$$

Because of the demand all being at the beginning of the period, $p_{x<}(S)$ represents the probability that there will be some on-hand inventory in a period, or equivalently, the fraction of time when the on-hand inventory is positive.

For the case of normally distributed demand, if we set

$$S = \bar{x}_1 + k\sigma_1 \tag{14.3}$$

where $\bar{x}_1$ is the average demand per unit time period and σ_1 is the standard deviation of the demand per unit time period, then Eq. 14.2 reduces to selecting the k_0 that satisfies

$$p_{u\geq}(k_0) = \frac{r}{r + B_3} \tag{14.4}$$

where $p_{u\geq}(k_0)$ is the probability that a unit normal variable takes on a value of k_0 or greater (see Appendix C). Furthermore, the associated minimum total relevant costs are

$$\text{ETRC}_1(S_{\text{opt}}) = v(r + B_3)\sigma_1 \frac{1}{\sqrt{2\pi}} \exp\left(-k_0^2/2\right) \tag{14.5}$$

Case 2, Continuous Demand—In this second case we assume that the total demand y in a unit period occurs at a uniform rate throughout the interval. Let $f_y(y_0)$ be the probability density function of y. There are two distinct patterns of net inventory with time as shown in Figure 14.1. In the first situation where $y < S$ there is no shortage and the average on-hand level throughout the unit period is $S - y/2$. In the second situation $(y > S)$ a shortage occurs and there are two types of costs:

$$\begin{aligned}
\text{carrying costs} &= (\text{average on-hand level}) \\
&\quad \times (\text{period it is carried}) \times (vr) \\
&= \frac{S}{2}\left(\frac{S}{y}\right) vr \\
&= \frac{S^2 vr}{2y}
\end{aligned}$$

Figure 14.1 Net Inventory for Case 2.

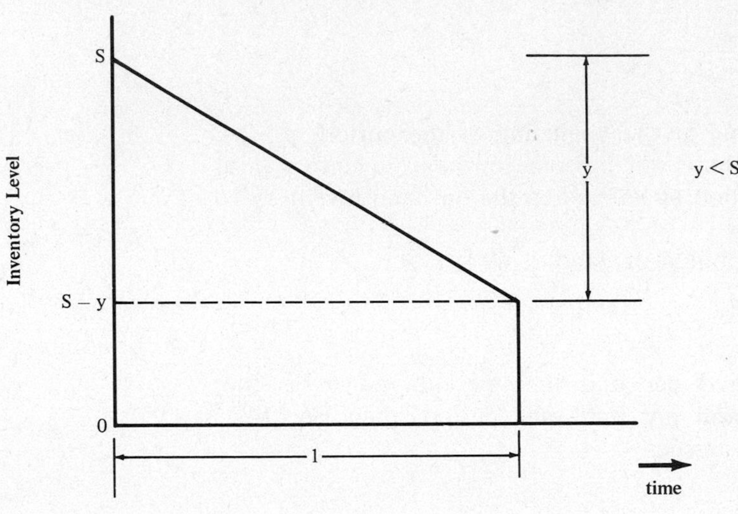

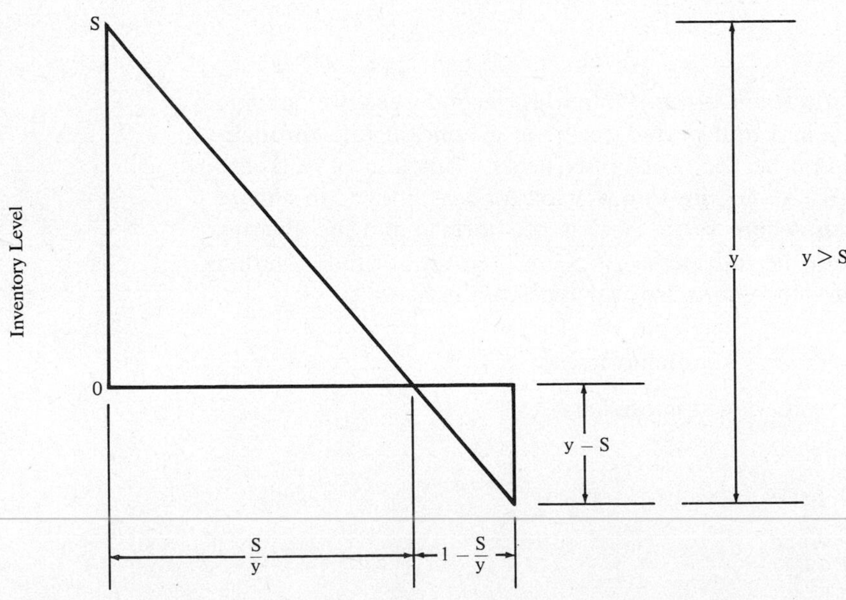

$$\begin{aligned}\text{shortage costs} &= (\text{average backordered})\\ &\quad \times (\text{period of backorder}) \times (B_3 v)\\ &= \frac{y-S}{2}\left(1-\frac{S}{y}\right)B_3 v\\ &= \frac{(y-S)^2 B_3 v}{2y}\end{aligned}$$

The expected total relevant costs per period are thus

$$\begin{aligned}\text{ETRC}_2(S) = &\int_0^S \left(S - \frac{y_0}{2}\right) vr\, f_y(y_0)\,dy_0\\ &+ \int_S^\infty \left[\frac{S^2 vr}{2y_0} + \frac{(y_0-S)^2 B_3 v}{2y_0}\right] f_y(y_0)\,dy_0 \qquad (14.6)\end{aligned}$$

This cost expression is certainly more complicated than Eq. 14.1. However, it can be shown (see pages 167–8 of Reference 43) that Eq. 14.6 reduces to Eq. 14.1 through the transformation

$$f_x(x_0) = \int_{x_0}^\infty \frac{f_y(y_0)}{y_0}\,dy_0$$

that is, the two problems are equivalent with this relationship between the probability density functions. Thus the simple solution procedure of Case 1 can be used to solve the more difficult problem of Case 2. This type of equivalence will play a key role in the treatment of (R, s, S) systems to be presented in Section 14.2.2.

14.1.3 *Use of Renewal Processes*

Throughout the book the basic approach in establishing the expected total relevant costs per unit time has been to trace the following steps:

i. Determine the average inventory level $(\bar{I})$, in units

ii. Carrying costs per year $= \bar{I}\, vr$

iii. Determine the average number of replenishments per year (N)

iv. Replenishment costs per year $= NA$

v. Determine the expected shortage costs per replenishment cycle, say W

vi. Expected shortage costs per year $= NW$

vii. Total expected costs per year = sum of ii, iv, and vi

If the inventory process has a natural regenerative point where the same state repeats periodically, then a different approach, using a key result of renewal theory, is possible. A good example of a regenerative point is immediately after each order in an (R, S) system, at which time the inventory position is at precisely the level S. Each time that the regenerative point is reached a cycle of the process is said to begin. The time between consecutive regenerative points is known as the length of the cycle, which we shall denote by T_c. In the (R, S) system example T_c is always equal to R. In other processes T_c can be a random variable (an example is shown in Silver[59]).

There is a set of costs (carrying, replenishment, and shortage) associated with each cycle. Let us denote the total of these costs by C_c. This quantity is almost certainly a random variable because its value depends upon the demand process which is usually random in nature.

A fundamental result of renewal theory (see, for example, Ross[55]) which holds under very general conditions, is:

$$\begin{matrix}\text{expected total relevant costs} \\ \text{per unit time}\end{matrix} = \frac{E(C_c)}{E(T_c)} \tag{14.7}$$

The key point is that in a complicated process it may be easier to evaluate each of $E(C_c)$ and $E(T_c)$ instead of the left hand side of Eq. 14.7 directly.

14.1.4 *Bounding to Test a Heuristic*

One of the major reasons for advocating the use of a heuristic solution to a problem is the difficulty of obtaining the optimal solution. In fact, often it may be computationally prohibitive to find the optimal solutions even for a few realistic test examples. To evaluate the effectiveness of a heuristic one must be able to estimate how close it comes to the optimal solution. Where one cannot obtain the solution, an attractive alternative may exist, namely to find the cost performance of the best solution to a less constrained (hence, possibly easier to solve) version of the problem. Clearly, the optimum solution to the original problem cannot produce a lower cost than this best solution to the less constrained problem. Thus, the cost of the latter is a lower bound on the cost of the optimal solution. Hence, if the heuristic's solution has a cost only slightly above this bound, it must be very close (in cost performance) to the optimum solution. On the other hand, if the cost of the heuristic solution is well above the bound, this does not necessarily mean that the heuristic leads to a poor solution. After all, the cost of the optimal solution may also be well above the bounding value.

We illustrate (another good illustration is provided by Schwarz[57]) with the heuristic for the case of deterministic coordinated control, first discussed in Section 13.2 of Chapter 13. Recall that there are n items in a family with a major setup cost A associated with any replenishment for the family and a minor setup cost a_i if item i is included in a family replenishment. Attention was restricted to the type of policy where a family setup is made every T years and, when item i is replenished, the quantity obtained is sufficient to last for an integer multiple, m_i, of the family cycle (the latter of length T). The basic cost equation is (from Eq. 13.16 of Chapter 13)

$$\text{TRC}(T, m_i\text{'s}) = \frac{A + \sum_{i=1}^{n} a_i/m_i}{T} + \sum_{i=1}^{n} \frac{D_i m_i T v_i r}{2} \tag{14.8}$$

Furthermore we know from Chapter 13 that by setting

$$\frac{\partial \text{TRC}}{\partial T} = 0$$

and substituting the resulting T value in Eq. 14.8 we find the minimum costs for a given set of m_i's, namely (from Eq. 13.18 of Chapter 13)

$$\text{TRC}^*(m_i\text{'s}) = \sqrt{2(A + \sum a_i/m_i) r \sum m_i D_i v_i} \tag{14.9}$$

Now, in developing a lower bound on the optimal cost we shall use much the same approach as in the derivation of the heuristic, namely recognizing that $m_1 = 1$ (where item 1 is defined as the item with the lowest value of $a_i/D_i v_i$) and setting

$$\frac{\partial \text{TRC}^*}{\partial m_i} = 0 \qquad i = 2, 3, \ldots, n$$

Proceeding exactly as in the appendix of Chapter 13 we find that the optimal *non-integer* values of the m_i's are (from Eq. 13.27 of Chapter 13)

$$m_i = \sqrt{\frac{a_i}{D_i v_i} \frac{D_1 v_1}{A + a_1}} \qquad i = 2, 3, \ldots n \tag{14.10}$$

Substitution of Eq. 14.10 and $m_1 = 1$ back into Eq. 14.9 provides, after considerable algebra, a lower bound on the total costs of the optimal (T, m_i's) policy namely

$$\text{TRC}_{\text{bound}} = \sqrt{2(A+a_1)D_1v_1r} + \sum_{j=2}^{n}\sqrt{2a_jD_jv_jr_j} \tag{14.11}$$

There is an interesting interpretation of the bound when one remembers that an optimal policy must have item 1 included in every replenishment of the family. The first term is the total relevant cost per unit time of an EOQ strategy (see Eq. 5.5 of Chapter 5) for item 1 considered alone, if one associates the full cost $A+a_1$ with each replenishment of item 1. The second term represents a summation of the total relevant costs per unit time of an EOQ strategy of each of the other items, where a cost of only a_j is associated with a replenishment of item j ($j \neq 1$).

For the numerical illustration of Section 13.2 of Chapter 13, the value of this bound works out to be \$2054.15/yr. The solution developed by the heuristic of Section 13.2 has a cost of \$2067.65/yr. (evaluated by substituting the *integer* m_i values, found by the heuristic, into Eq. 14.9). The bound clearly indicates that the heuristic solution is very close to (if not right at) the optimum for the particular example.

14.2 *Results for Some Complicated Situations*

This section is devoted to the presentation of results, some of them in the form of operational decision rules, for situations where we take account of some important real world complexities beyond those considered in earlier chapters.

14.2.1 *Approximate Decision Rules for (s, S) Systems*

Recall from Chapter 6 that in an (s, S) system we have a continuous review situation. Whenever the inventory position drops to the reorder point s or lower an order is placed of sufficient magnitude to raise the position to the order-up-to-level S. When all transactions are of unit size then every order is of size $(S-s)$ and is placed when the inventory position is exactly at the level s. We can thus think of an order quantity

$$Q = S - s \tag{14.12}$$

and then the assumptions of an (s, Q) system (see Section 7.2.1 of Chapter 7) hold. *Non unit-sized transactions are what complicate the analysis.*

Furthermore, in contrast with an (R, S) system where each cycle of *fixed* length R starts with the inventory position at the level S, here we have a cycle of random length (how long it takes for the inventory position to drop from S to s or lower).

For one type of shortage costing measure (cost of B_1 per stockout occasion) and normally distributed forecast errors we now discuss three approaches, of increasing complexity, for selecting s and S under conditions of non unit-sized transactions.

Method 1 (Simple Sequential Determination of s and S)— Here, we choose to neglect the undershoots (how far below s the inventory position is located when an order is placed). In addition, S and s are computed in a sequential fashion as follows. The Q expression of Eq. 14.12 is set equal to the economic order quantity as in Chapter 5. Then, *given this value of* Q we find s by the procedure of Section 7.2.5 of Chapter 7. Finally, from Eq. 14.12, the S value is given by

$$S = s + Q \tag{14.13}$$

Numerical Illustration

Consider MIDAS item XMF-014, a 1000 sheet box of 8 in. × 10 in. rapid process X-ray film. For illustrative purposes suppose that MIDAS' X-Ray Film Division was considering using an (s, S) control system for this item. Relevant given characteristics of the item include

$$D = 1400 \text{ boxes/yr.}$$

$$v = \$5.90/\text{box}$$

$$A = \$3.20$$

$$r = 0.24/\text{yr.}$$

$$B_1 = \$150$$

$$\hat{x}_L = 270 \text{ boxes}$$

$$\sigma_L = 51.3 \text{ boxes}$$

Use of the above outlined procedure leads to

$$Q = 80 \text{ boxes}$$

$$s = 389 \text{ boxes}$$

$$S = 469 \text{ boxes}$$

Method 2 (Simultaneous Determination of s and S)—Here we continue to ignore the undershoots but we do take account of the interaction of the best values of s and S. In fact, the approach is identical with that of Section 9.5.1 of Chapter 9 for finding the simultaneous best values of s and Q. Then the final step is to set $S = s + Q$. In comparison with method 1, the current approach is more difficult computationally but *may* reduce the total of replenishment, carrying and shortage costs.

Numerical Illustration

For the same item *XMF*-014 the results are

$$Q = 102 \text{ boxes}$$

$$s = 383 \text{ boxes}$$

$$S = 485 \text{ boxes}$$

Method 3 (Use of Undershoot Distribution)—Here we attempt to take account of the non-zero undershoots. A stockout occurs if the sum of the undershoot plus the total lead time demand exceeds s. Thus, the variable in which we are interested is

$$x' = z + x$$

where z is the undershoot and x is the total lead time demand.

We know the distribution of x (assumed to be normal). The distribution of z is quite complex, depending in general upon the distance $S - s$ and the probability distribution of transaction sizes. However, when $S - s$ is considerably larger than the average transaction size, then we can make use of a result developed by Karlin[34], namely

$$p_z(z_0) = \frac{1}{E(t)} \sum_{t_0 = z_0 + 1}^{\infty} p_t(t_0) \tag{14.14}$$

where

$p_z(z_0)$ = probability that the undershoot is of size z_0

$p_t(t_0)$ = probability that a demand transaction is of size t_0

$E(t)$ = the average transaction size

Equation 14.14 can be used to compute the mean and variance of the undershoot variable z. The results are

$$E(z) = \frac{1}{2}\left[\frac{E(t^2)}{E(t)} - 1\right]$$

and

$$\text{var}(z) = \frac{1}{12}\left\{\frac{4E(t^3)}{E(t)} - 3\left[\frac{E(t^2)}{E(t)}\right]^2 - 1\right\}$$

The two variables z and x can be assumed to be independent. Therefore

$$E(x') = E(z) + E(x) = \left[\frac{1}{2}\frac{E(t^2)}{E(t)} - 1\right] + \bar{x}_L \tag{14.15}$$

and

$$\text{var}(x') = (\text{var})(z) + \text{var}(x)$$

$$= \frac{1}{12}\left\{\frac{4E(t^3)}{E(t)} - 3\left[\frac{E(t^2)}{E(t)}\right]^2 - 1\right\} + \sigma_L^2 \tag{14.16}$$

For convenience, we assume that x' has a normal distribution* with the above shown mean and variance. With this assumption, the method, as derived in the appendix of this chapter, is as follows:

Step 1 Select k and Q to simultaneously satisfy the following two equations:

$$Q = \text{EOQ}\sqrt{1 + \frac{B_1}{A} p_{u\geq}(k)} - E(z), \text{ rounded to an integer} \tag{14.17}$$

and

$$k = \sqrt{2 \ln\left[\frac{1}{2\sqrt{2\pi}}\left(\frac{B_1}{A}\right)\frac{(EOQ)^2}{(Q + E(z))\sigma_{x'}}\right]} \tag{14.18}$$

where

$p_{u\geq}(k)$ is the probability that a unit normal variable takes on

---

* *x is normally distributed but z is certainly not, in that Eq.* 14.14 *reveals that $p_z(z_0)$ is monotonically decreasing with z_0. Hence, the assumption of $(z+x)$ having a normal distribution is only an approximation.*

a value greater than or equal to k

$$\text{EOQ} = \sqrt{\frac{2AD}{vr}}$$

$$\sigma_{x'} = \sqrt{\text{var}\ (x')}$$

Step 2

$s = E(x') + k\sigma_{x'}$, rounded to the nearest integer.

Step 3

$$S = s + Q$$

Numerical Illustration

Again we use the same item, XMF-014. Now, of course, we need a probability distribution of transaction sizes (or, alternatively, the first three moments $E(t)$, $E(t^2)$, and $E(t^3)$). Suppose for illustrative purposes that the distribution is

t_0	1	2	3	6	12	24	36	72
$p_t(t_0)$	0.25	0.05	0.05	0.1	0.25	0.15	0.1	0.05

Then

$$E(t) = \sum_{t_0} t_0 p_t(t_0) = 14.9$$

$$E(t^2) = \sum_{t_0} t_0^2 p_t(t_0) = 515.7$$

$$E(t^3) = \sum_{t_0} t_0^3 p_t(t_0) = 25857.2$$

From Eqs. 14.15 and 14.16

$$\begin{aligned} E(x') &= \frac{1}{2}\left[\frac{515.7}{14.9} - 1\right] + 270 \\ &= 16.81 + 270 \\ &= 286.81 \end{aligned}$$

$$\begin{aligned} \text{Var}\ (x') &= \frac{1}{12}\left\{\frac{4(25857.2)}{14.9} - 3\left[\frac{515.7}{14.9}\right]^2 - 1\right\} + (51.3)^2 \\ &= 278.90 + 2631.69 \\ &= 2910.59 \end{aligned}$$

Step 1 Equations 14.17 and 14.18 give that k and Q must satisfy

$$Q = 79.5\sqrt{1 + 46.875 p_{u\geq}(k)} - 16.81$$

and

$$k = \sqrt{2 \ln \left[\frac{1}{2\sqrt{2\pi}} (46.875) \frac{(79.5)^2}{(Q + 16.81)(53.95)} \right]}$$

The solution is

$$Q = 87 \text{ boxes}$$

$$k = 2.17$$

Step 2

$$s = 286.81 + 2.17\sqrt{2910.59}$$

$$= 404 \text{ boxes}$$

Step 3

$$S = 404 + 87 = 491 \text{ boxes}$$

Comparison of the Three Methods—It is interesting to compare the results of the three methods for the numerical illustration of item XMF-014. Archibald[2] has developed a search procedure that finds the optimal (s, S) pair for an arbitrary discrete distribution of transaction sizes and also gives the expected total relevant costs for any (s, S) pair used. Utilizing his procedure we found the results shown in Table 14.1. It is seen that Method 3, which takes account of the undershoot effects, leads to a solution negligibly close to the optimum. Note that method 2, which finds s and Q simultaneously, actually does slightly worse than method 1 which finds them in a simpler sequential fashion. The reason for this bizarre behavior is that method 1 makes two somewhat counter-balancing assumptions. First, ignoring the undershoot effect (both of methods 1 and 2 do this) tends to make s somewhat lower than desirable. Second, the sequential, rather than simultaneous, determination of the two parameters tends to cause s to be larger than in method 2, in this case offsetting the first effect somewhat. It is worth noting that, even with the significant departure from unit-sized transactions shown in the numerical illustration, the simplistic approach of Chapter 7 still gives a cost penalty of only 3.5 percent.

Table 14.1 Illustrative Comparison of the Three Methods of Finding Values of s and S, Item XMF-014

Method	Description	s	S	ETRC $/yr.	Percent above best value
1	Sequential, ignoring undershoot	389	469	350.82	3.5
2	Simultaneous, ignoring undershoot	383	485	351.95	3.8
3	Simultaneous and using undershoot	404	491	339.01	0.0
	Optimal solution	406	493	339.00	—

14.2.2 *Approximate Decision Rules for Single Item (R, s, S) Systems*

As mentioned in Chapter 6, several authors have shown that, under quite general conditions, the system that minimizes the total of review, replenishment, carrying and shortage costs will be a member of the (R, s, S) family. However, the determination of the exact best values of the three parameters is extremely difficult. The problem results partly from the fact that undershoots of the reorder point s are present even if all transactions are unit-sized. This is because we only observe the inventory level every R units of time. Another aspect of the difficulty (see Wagner et al.[74]) is that, if as earlier we set $Q = S - s$, then the optimal value of Q is not a unimodal function of the demand rate, that is, as the demand rate increases, the optimal Q may first increase, then decrease, etc. Because of the complexity of exact analyses we shall again advocate the use of a heuristic approach developed by Naddor.[44] (Other heuristic methods are discussed by Ehrhardt,[16] Snyder,[63] Wagner,[73] and Wagner et al.[74])

Naddor's method deals with one particular service measure, namely a specified fraction (P_3) of time that there is some positive on-hand inventory,* or the equivalent specified cost (B_3) per dollar short per unit time. Through analysis of a number of numerical examples, he makes the

* *The fraction of time that the on-hand inventory is positive is sometimes called the ready rate or availability index. As discussed in Chapter 6, P_3 is often a very good approximation to the fraction (P_2) of demand satisfied routinely from the shelf.*

following observations concerning the optimal policies in* (T, S), (R, s, Q), and (R, s, S) systems:

> *Observation 1*—The best replenishment interval (T) in a (T, S) system is essentially the same as that in a corresponding deterministic situation.
>
> *Observation 2*—The best order quantity (Q) in a (R, s, Q) system is approximately the same as that in the corresponding deterministic system.
>
> *Observation 3*—The best order-up-to-levels in (T, S) and (R, s, S) systems are essentially the same.
>
> *Observation 4*—The best reorder points in (R, s, Q) and (R, s, S) systems are essentially the same.

He also points out a well-known result (see pages 364-374 of Reference 27) discussed in Chapter 6, namely

> *Observation 5*—The minimum cost for an† (R, S) policy is at least as large as that for the best (R, s, Q) policy which, in turn, is at least as large as that for the best (R, s, S) policy.

It is interesting that observations 1 and 2 are essentially the same findings as were made in Chapter 9, namely that for most items selection of Q (or T) through a deterministic analysis followed sequentially by the best s (or S) given the Q (or T) value produces results very similar to the simultaneous selection of Q and s (or T and S).

Naddor also makes use of a *fundamental problem* where the total demand in each basic discrete time period‡ occurs at the beginning of the period and there is a negligible replenishment lead time. This is the exact situation discussed in Case 1 of Section 14.1.2. For such a setting we have, from Eq. 14.2 and the discussion immediately following it,

$$P_3 = \frac{B_3}{r + B_3} \tag{14.19}$$

---

* *We use the notation (T, S) because he starts with a basic review interval R and in the (T, S) system he allows T (the time interval between consecutive order placements) to be an integer multiple of R, a generalization of the (R, S) systems we have presented earlier.*

† *Here an (R, S) policy is the special case where $T = R$.*

‡ *R is an integer multiple of this basic time period.*

where

P_3 is the fraction of time that the on-hand inventory is greater than zero.

B_3 is the cost per dollar short per unit time.

Thus there is an equivalence between a B_3 value and a value of P_3.

Using the notion of equivalent problems (discussed in Section 14.1.2) as well as the above listed five observations, Naddor's heuristic is as follows (the reader may find Figure 14.2 helpful in tracing the logic; also a

Figure 14.2 Logic of Naddor's Heuristic for Selecting Values of s and S in an (R, s, S) System.

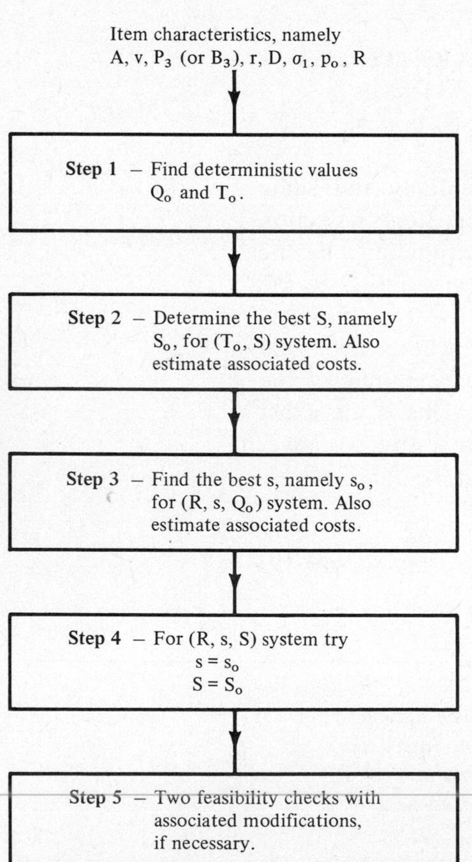
Item characteristics, namely
A, v, P3 (or B3), r, D, σ1, po, R
Step 1 – Find deterministic values Qo and To.
Step 2 – Determine the best S, namely So, for (To, S) system. Also estimate associated costs.
Step 3 – Find the best s, namely so, for (R, s, Qo) system. Also estimate associated costs.
Step 4 – For (R, s, S) system try s = so S = So
Step 5 – Two feasibility checks with associated modifications, if necessary.

numerical example follows the heuristic):

Step 1—Finding the Best Q and T for the Associated Deterministic System

When demand is deterministic and deliberate backorders at a cost of B_3 dollars per dollar short per unit time are permitted, it can be shown (see, for example, page 46 of Reference 27) that the modified version of the EOQ is

$$Q_0 = \sqrt{\frac{2AD(r+B_3)}{vrB_3}} \tag{14.20}$$

rounded to the nearest integer, and, expressed as a time supply, this gives

$$T_0 = \sqrt{\frac{2A(r+B_3)}{DvrB_3}} \tag{14.21}$$

rounded to the nearest integer multiple of R.

Step 2—Finding the Best S for a (T, S) System

First, observation 1 reveals that the T_0 of Eq. 14.21 can be used as the best T of a (T, S) system. Then for this given value of T, as well as the known value of the lead time L, we find the best value of S, namely S_0. This involves showing an equivalence with the fundamental problem (Case 1 of Section 14.1.2) and also assumes normality of demand.* Naddor shows, through lengthy algebra and calculus, that the probability distribution of demand in the equivalent fundamental problem is such that†

$$\bar{x}_1(T_0; L) = (T_0/2 + L)D \tag{14.22}$$

and

$$\sigma_1(T_0; L) = \sqrt{(L + T_0/3)\sigma_1^2 + (TD)^2/12 + (1 - p_0^{T_0})/6} \tag{14.23}$$

---

* *Naddor's results indicate that the assumption of normal demand (both here and in Step 3) is quite reasonable for a wide range of actual demand distributions.*

† *The notation $\bar{x}_1(T_0; L)$ and $\sigma_1(T_0; L)$ emphasizes the dependence upon T_0 and L of $\bar{x}_1$ and σ_1 in the fundamental problem.*

where

D is the expected demand per unit time period,

σ_1 is the standard deviation of the actual demand in a unit time period.

p_0 is the probability that no demand occurs in a unit time period.

From Eqs. 14.3 and 14.4 we thus have that S_0 must satisfy

$$S_0 = \bar{x}_1(T_0; L) + k_0\sigma_1(T_0; L) \tag{14.24}$$

rounded to the nearest integer, where

$$p_{u\geq}(k_0) = \frac{r}{r+B_3} \tag{14.25}$$

Furthermore, the associated total relevant costs per unit time (*possibly* needed in Step 5) are

$$\text{ETRC (best } T \text{ and } S) = v(r+B_3)\sigma_1(T_0; L)f_u(k_0) + A\frac{(1-p_0^{T_0})}{T_0} \tag{14.26}$$

where $f_u(k_0)$ is the unit normal density function evaluated at k_0 (see Table C.1 of Appendix C).

This last equation follows from Eq. 14.5 with the inclusion of the last term which represents the setup costs per unit time. ($p_0^{T_0}$ is the probability that no demand occurs throughout T_0, hence that no order is required at a particular review.)

Step 3—Finding the Best s for an (R, s, Q) System

Observation 2 is used to ascertain that the best Q, call it Q_0, for the (R, s, Q) system is given by the result of Eq. 14.20. Then for this given value of Q as well as the known values of R and L, we find the best value of s, namely s_0. This is done by finding an equivalent fundamental problem and assuming that the equivalent demand is normal (Case 1 of Section 14.1.2). With the order-up-to-level S in the fundamental problem being related to the reorder point s by the expression

$$S = s + Q_0 \tag{14.27}$$

Naddor demonstrates that the probability distribution of demand in the equivalent problem is such that

$$\bar{x}_1(Q_0; R; L) = (R/2 + L)D + Q_0/2 \tag{14.28}$$

and

$$\sigma_1(Q_0; R; L) = \sqrt{(L + R/3)\sigma_1^2 + (RD)^2/12 + (1 - p_0^R)/6 + Q_0^2/12} \tag{14.29}$$

where D, σ_1, and p_0 are as defined after Eq. 14.23.

The fundamental problem's solution involves the selection of an order-up-to-level S. The best value, namely S_0, is chosen to satisfy

$$S_0 = \bar{x}_1(Q_0; R; L) + k_0\sigma_1(Q_0; R; L), \tag{14.30}$$

rounded to the nearest integer, where

$$p_{u\geq}(k_0) = \frac{r}{r + B_3} \tag{14.31}$$

Finally, from Eq. 14.27 we have that

$$s_0 = S_0 - Q_0 \tag{14.32}$$

Also, Naddor shows that the expected total relevant costs per unit time of the best s and Q pair (again *possibly* needed in Step 5) are given by

$$\text{ETRC (best } s \text{ and } Q) = v(r + B_3)\sigma_1(Q_0; R; L)f_u(k_0) + AN \tag{14.33}$$

where N, the expected number of orders per unit time, is approximated by

$$N = \text{minimum of } [D/Q_0; (1 - p_0^R/R] \tag{14.34}$$

Step 4—Finding the Best s and S Values for an (R, s, S) System

Based on observation 3, the S_0 found in step 2 is the likely best S in an (R, s, S) system. Similarly, observation 4 indicates that the s_0 found in step 3 is likely to be the best s in an (R, s, S) system.

Step 5—Two Feasibility Checks on the Results of Step 4

First, it is possible that the s_0 found exceeds the S_0 value. Clearly this is infeasible; in such a case s_0 is reduced to the S_0 value.

Second, for the case where $T_0 = R$ in the result of step 1, we compare* ETRC (R and best S) from Eq. 14.26 of step 2 with ETRC (best s and Q) from Eq. 14.33 of step 3. If the lower of these is ETRC (R and best S), then observation 5 is violated and we should use the (R, S_0) policy, that is, we set $s_0 = S_0$.

Numerical Illustration—Consider an item with the following characteristics:

The unit time period is 1 week.

The review interval R is 2 weeks.

The lead time L is 1 week.

$D = 20$ units/wk.

$p_0 = 0.15$

$\sigma_1 = 7.1$ units/wk.

$v = \$2.80/\text{unit}$

$A = \$5.00$

$r = 0.208$ \$/\$/yr. $= 0.004$ \$/\$/wk.

$B_3 = 0.832$ \$/\$/yr. $= 0.016$ \$/\$/wk.

Note that, from Eq. 14.19, we have that the equivalent ready rate is

$$P_3 = \frac{0.016}{0.004 + 0.016} = 0.80$$

Step 1

$$Q_0 = \sqrt{\frac{2(5.00)(20)(0.020)}{(2.80)(0.004)(0.016)}}$$

$$\simeq 149 \text{ units}$$

---

* *Eq.* 14.26 *gives* ETRC (*best* T *and* S) *but here we know that best* $T = R$.

and

$$T_0 = \frac{Q_0}{D} = \frac{149}{20} = 7.45 \text{ wks.}$$

which rounds to 8 wks (the nearest integer multiple of 2 wks, the R value).

Step 2 Equations 14.22 and 14.23 give

$$\bar{x}_1(T_0; L) = \bar{x}_1(8; 1) = (8/2+1)20 = 100 \text{ units}$$

and

$$\sigma_1(T_0; L) = \sqrt{(1+8/3)(7.1)^2 + (160)^2/12 + [1-(0.15)^8]/6}$$
$$= 48.1 \text{ units}$$

Equation 14.25 gives

$$p_{u\geq}(k_0) = \frac{0.004}{0.004+0.016} = 0.2$$

From Table C.1 in appendix C we thus have

$$k_0 = 0.84$$

Then, from Eq. 14.24 there follows

$$S_0 = 100 + 0.84\ (48.1)$$
$$\simeq 140 \text{ units}$$

Step 3 From Eqs. 14.28 and 14.29 we have

$$\bar{x}_1(Q_0; R; L) = \bar{x}_1(149; 2; 1) = (2/2+1)20$$
$$+ 149/2 = 114.5 \text{ units}$$

and

$$\sigma_1(Q_0; R; L)$$

$$= \sqrt{[(1+2/3)(7.1)^2 + (40)^2/12 + [1-(0.15)^2]/6 + (149)^2/12]}$$

$$= 44.1 \text{ units}$$

From Eq. 14.31 there follows

$$p_{u\geq}(k_0) = 0.2$$

Hence, $k_0 = 0.84$. Thus, Eq. 14.30 gives

$$S_0 = 114.5 + 0.84(44.1)$$

$$\simeq 152 \text{ units}$$

Next, Eq. 14.32 leads to

$$s_0 = 152 - 149 = 3 \text{ units}$$

Step 4

$S_0 = 141$ units, from step 2

and

$s_0 = 3$ units, from step 3

Step 5 First, $S > s_0$, therefore the solution is feasible. Second, $T_0 \neq R$, therefore the second check is not required. Thus our choice for an (R, s, S) system is

$R = 2$ weeks (prespecified)

$s = 3$ units

$S = 141$ units

Again a search procedure (due to Archibald[2]) was used to find the optimal (s, S) pair and to cost out the above solution as well as the optimal one. The results are as shown in Table 14.2. It is seen that, although the heuristic gives control parameter values differing somewhat from the optimal settings (particularly in the case of s), the cost penalty is negligible.

Table 14.2 Naddor's Heuristic for the Numerical Example

Approach	s	S	costs per unit time (\$/period)	percent above best value
Naddor's heuristic	3	141	1.376	0.36
Optimal solution (by search)	9	142	1.371	—

14.2.3 *Coordinated* (R, s, S) *Control*

Two types of coordinated control systems under probabilistic demand were discussed in Sections 13.4 and 13.5 of Chapter 13. Now, we turn to a third possibility whose explanation follows rather naturally from that of the individual (R, s, S) control system of the previous subsection. In addition to the assumptions made there, here we also assume that the setup cost structure is as in Section 13.4 of Chapter 13, namely that for a specific group (or family) of items (numbered $i = 1, 2, \ldots, n$) there is a major setup cost A for any replenishment of the group and a minor setup cost a_i whenever item i is involved in the group replenishment. The objective is to keep total relevant costs as low as possible. Note that there are no quantity discounts available, hence there is no pressing need to achieve a group replenishment quantity of a certain size. Again the logic is based on the work of Naddor.[44]

For a given value of the review interval R, the *lowest* achievable expected total relevant costs per unit time are estimated to be

$$\mathrm{ETRC}^*(R) = \sum_{i=1}^{n} \mathrm{ETRC}_i^*(R) + N_G(R)A \tag{14.35}$$

where $\mathrm{ETRC}_i^*(R)$ is the lowest expected total relevant costs per year for item i when a review interval R is used (these are found by determining s_i and S_i through the heuristic of Section 14.2.2 with a setup cost of only a_i for a replenishment and are given by Eq. 14.26 or Eq. 14.33, depending upon which is appropriate); also $N_G(R)$ is the expected number of group replenishments per unit time (when a review interval R is used) and is approximated by

$$N_G = \left(1 - \prod_{i=1}^{n} [1 - RN_i(R)]\right) / R \tag{14.36}$$

where $N_i(R)$, the expected number of replenishments per unit time of item i, is a by-product of the above determination of $\mathrm{ETRC}_i^*(R)$ and is given by Eq. 14.34.

The approximation in Eq. 14.36 is the use of the term $RN_i(R)$ for the probability that item i requires a replenishment at a particular review time. Actually, for n not too small a simpler approximation is that

$$N_G \simeq 1/R \tag{14.37}$$

that is, there is a group replenishment at each review.

Essentially the approach involves a search on the control parameter R. For each value of R, Eq. 14.35 gives the lowest achievable costs. The R value corresponding to the first minimum of $\mathrm{ETRC}^*(R)$ as we increase R

is selected as the review interval. (This assumes unimodality of Eq. 14.35 as a function of R, quite reasonable from an intuitive standpoint.) The s_i's and S_i's (associated with the chosen R value) are used for the individual item order points and order-up-to-levels.

14.2.4 *Intermittent Demand*

Most of the analyses that we have conducted earlier in the book, at least for the case of continuous review systems, have assumed reasonably smooth demand patterns including relatively small transaction sizes. There are two troublesome situations where these kinds of assumptions are inappropriate: first, where demand transactions simply occur on a very infrequent basis, second, where occasional very large transactions are intermingled with mostly small-sized transactions. In this section we examine the first of these two complicating circumstances; the second will be briefly discussed, as a promising research area, in Chapter 20.

The exponential smoothing forecast methods described in Chapter 4 have been found to be rather ineffective where transactions (not necessarily unit-sized) occur on a rather infrequent basis. To illustrate this point, let us consider a particularly simple situation where only transactions of a single size j occur exactly every n periods of time. Suppose that simple exponential smoothing (level only) with a smoothing constant a is used and the updating is done every unit time period, that is,

$$\bar{d}_t = ad_t + (1-a)\bar{d}_{t-1} \tag{14.38}$$

where $\bar{d}_t$ is the forecast of demand made at the end of period t and d_t is the actual demand in period t.

In the context of our special case we have

$$d_t = \begin{cases} j & t = 1,\ n+1,\ 2n+1,\ 3n+1\ldots \\ 0 & \text{otherwise} \end{cases}$$

where we have rather arbitrarily said that the first demand occurs in period 1. For low values of t the forecasts depend upon the initial forecast, $\bar{d}_0$. However, as t gets larger and larger, the effect of this initial term dies out. Therefore, we would expect that for large t the forecasts would settle into a pattern repeating every n units of time (where n is the cycle time of the simple demand pattern).* Suppose we have reached this stable situation

---

**There are more rigorous methods, than the one we use, for developing the pattern of forecasts. One involves the use of transform methods (see Croston*[13]).

and we let $\hat{d}_0$ represent the forecast just before a period in which a transaction occurs. The transaction is of size j and no other transaction occurs for the next $n-1$ periods. Updating according to Eq. 14.38 we obtain the forecast just before the next transaction occurs as

$$(1-a)^n \hat{d}_0 + a(1-a)^{n-1} j$$

But this must again equal $\hat{d}_0$. Therefore,

$$\hat{d}_0 = (1-a)^n \hat{d}_0 + a(1-a)^{n-1} j$$

or

$$\hat{d}_0 = \frac{a(1-a)^{n-1} j}{1-(1-a)^n} \tag{14.39}$$

Furthermore, the forecast u periods later (where $0<u<n$) is

$$\hat{d}_u = a(1-a)^{u-1} j + (1-a)^u \hat{d}_0$$

Using Eq. 14.39, this becomes

$$\hat{d}_u = \frac{a(1-a)^{u-1} j}{1-(1-a)^n} \qquad u = 1, 2, 3, \ldots, n-1 \tag{14.40}$$

The forecasts in a typical n period cycle are shown in Figure 14.3 (illustrated for $n=6$ and $a=0.2$). It is seen that immediately after the demand transaction the forecast exceeds the average demand per period, thereafter throughout the cycle the forecast decreases, dropping below the average demand by the end of the cycle. In other words, for a deterministic demand pattern exponential smoothing produces a saw-tooth type forecast.

This illustration is a symptom of undesirable performance of exponential smoothing under the more general situation of infrequent* transactions, not necessarily all of the same size. For such a situation it is preferable to forecast two separate components of the demand process, namely the time between consecutive transactions and the magnitude of individual transactions, that is, we let

$$d_t = x_t z_t \tag{14.41}$$

---

* *Infrequent in the sense that the average time between transactions is considerably larger than the unit time period, the latter being the interval of forecast updating.*

Figure 14.3 Typical Behavior of Exponential Smoothing for a Deterministic Intermittent Demand.

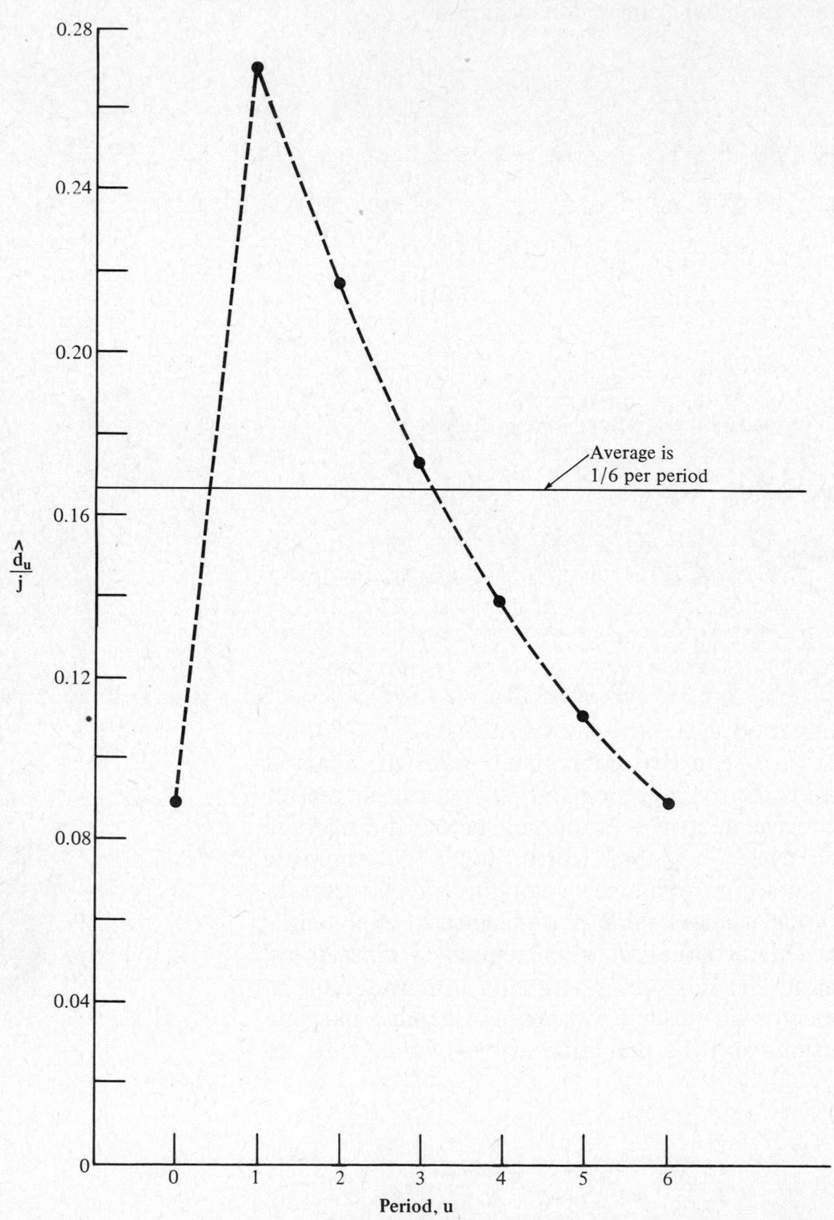

NOTE: Demand is $d_u = \begin{cases} j & u = 1, 7, 13 \ldots \\ 0 & \text{otherwise} \end{cases}$

where

$$x_t = \begin{cases} 1 & \text{if a transaction occurs} \\ 0 & \text{otherwise} \end{cases}$$

and z_t is the size of the transaction.

If we define a quantity n as the number of periods between transactions and if demands in separate periods are considered independent, then the occurrence or non-occurrence of a transaction in a period can be considered as a Bernoulli process with probability of occurrence being $1/n$, that is

$$\text{prob}\,\{x_t = 1\} = 1/n$$

and

$$\text{prob}\,\{x_t = 0\} = 1 - 1/n$$

Within this framework and assuming that transaction sizes are normally distributed Croston[13] recommends the following reasonable updating procedure: If $d_t = 0$ (that is, no demand occurs),

i. Transaction size estimates are not updated

ii. $\hat{n}_t = \hat{n}_{t-1}$

If $d_t > 0$ (that is, a transaction occurs),

i. $\hat{z}_t = ad_t + (1-a)\hat{z}_{t-1}$

ii. $\hat{n}_t = an_t + (1-a)\hat{n}_{t-1}$

where

n_t is the number of periods since the last transaction.

$\hat{n}_t$ is the estimated value of n at the end of period t.

$\hat{z}_t$ is the estimate, at the end of period t, of the average transaction size.

Croston argues that forecasts for replenishment purposes will usually be needed immediately after a transaction. He shows that the forecast at that time, namely

$$\hat{d}_t = \hat{z}_t / \hat{n}_t$$

is preferable to that obtained by simple exponential smoothing for two reasons:

i. It is unbiased, whereas the simple smoothing forecast is not.

ii. It has a lower variance than does the simple smoothing forecast.

However, Croston warns that the infrequent updating (only when a transaction occurs) introduces a marked lag in responding to actual changes in the underlying parameters. Therefore he rightfully stresses the importance of control signals to identify deviations.

A key quantity to use in establishing an order-up-to-level for an intermittently demanded item is MAD (z), the mean absolute deviation of the sizes of *non-zero* sized transactions. This quantity is only updated each time that a transaction occurs. The updating equation is of the form

$$\text{new MAD}(z) = a\,|d_t - \hat{z}_{t-1}| + (1-a) \text{ old MAD}(z) \qquad d_t > 0 \tag{14.42}$$

In establishing the order-up-to-level, account is also taken of the fact that there is a non-zero chance of no transaction occurring in a time period.

To illustrate, consider the simple situation where replenishment is instantaneous and we wish to provide a specified probability (P_1) of no stockout per period. Denote the order-up-to-level by S. A stockout will occur only if a transaction occurs and it is of at least size S. Suppose transaction sizes are normally distributed with mean $\hat{z}$ and mean absolute deviation MAD (z) and we let*

$$S = \hat{z} + k(1.25) \text{ MAD}(z) \tag{14.43}$$

---

* *For a normal distribution* $\sigma \simeq 1.25$ *MAD.*

then

$$\text{prob}\{\text{stockout}\} = \text{prob}\{\text{demand occurs}\} \times \text{prob}\{\text{demand} \geq S\}$$

$$= \frac{1}{\hat{n}} p_{u\geq}(k) \tag{14.44}$$

Therefore, we want

$$1 - P_1 = \frac{1}{\hat{n}} p_{u\geq}(k)$$

or

$$p_{u\geq}(k) = \hat{n}(1 - P_1) \tag{14.45}$$

where, as usual, $p_{u\geq}(k)$ is the probability that a unit normal variable takes on a value of at least k (see Table C.1 of Appendix C).

Numerical Illustration—A particular Toronto-based customer of MIDAS Canada, namely a retailer of photographic supplies, reviews the stock of a specific high-priced film (MIDAS code PSF-074) each day. Because of the proximity of MIDAS' warehouse any order placed in the late afternoon is delivered to the retailer first thing the next morning. The sales of this film are such that it is extremely rare for two or more customers to demand it in a day, however a customer transaction can be for several units. Suppose that an intermittent forecasting system, as discussed above, has led, on the day that a transaction has occurred, to the following updated estimates:

$$\hat{n} = 5.2 \text{ days (between transactions)}$$

$$\hat{z} = 10.2 \text{ units}$$

$$\text{MAD}(z) = 2.4 \text{ units}$$

Let us suppose that the retailer desires a probability 0.98 of no stockout per day. Equation 14.45 gives

$$p_{u>}(k) = 5.2(1 - 0.98) = 0.104$$

or, from Table C.1 of Appendix C,

$$k = 1.26$$

Then, Eq. 14.43 leads to

$$S = 10.2 + (1.26)(1.25)(2.4)$$

$$= 14 \text{ units}$$

Thus, the retailer should plan to use an order-up-to-level of 14 units (equivalently, have 14 units in stock at the beginning of each day).

If instead of using the above procedure, we simply considered the demand per day d (including 0 values of d) as being approximately normally distributed (our usual approach in earlier chapters), then d, for the above example, would have*

$$E(d) = \frac{1}{5.2}(10.2) = 1.96 \text{ units/day}$$

and

$$E(d^2) = \frac{1}{5.2}E(z^2) = \frac{1}{5.2}[\text{var}(z) + (E(z))^2]$$

$$= \frac{1}{5.2}[(1.25)^2(2.4)^2 + (10.2)^2]$$

$$= 21.74$$

Therefore,

$$\text{var}(d) = 21.74 - (1.96)^2 = 17.90$$

or

$$\sigma_d = 4.23$$

To give a probability 0.02 of a stockout we would use

$$s = E(d) + k\sigma_d$$

where k satisfies

$$p_{u\geq}(k) = 0.02$$

From Table C.1 of Appendix C

$$k \simeq 2.05$$

Thus, $S = 1.96 + 2.05(4.23) = 10.6$, say 11 units, which is less than the more

---

* *Here we are using results for the sum of a random number (the number of transactions per day) of random variables (each transaction size). See, for example, pages* 111–112 *of Reference* 15.

appropriate result of 14 units found above. In other words, the simple approach (ignoring the intermittent nature of the demand) gives inadequate protection. In fact, the service actually provided (found by computing the actual k implied in Eq. 14.43 through use of $S = 11$ and then substituting that k value in Eq. 14.44) would be a P_1 value of only 0.924 instead of the desired 0.98.

14.2.5 *Bayesian Forecasting*

As discussed in Chapter 4 one can model a demand process by one or more parameters (for example, level, trend and seasonality factors). Normally these parameters are not known with certainty. In smoothing operations, such as moving averages and exponential smoothing, *point estimates* of these uncertain parameters are updated. No indication of the uncertainty in these estimates is shown. In addition, these methods normally require considerable historical data for initialization purposes.

A fundamentally different method of estimating the values of unknown parameters is the so-called Bayesian updating procedure. In its simplest form, a probability distribution is placed over the possible values of an unknown parameter. As actual demand data are observed, Bayes' Rule of conditional probability is used to modify the probability distribution, the modification being based on the amount and nature of the data. Mathematically, consider an unknown parameter θ. For simplicity, we restrict attention to the case where θ can take on only a finite number of discrete values. We also assume that the same restriction applies for the demand d in a particular period. Bayes' Rule says that

$$p_{\theta \mid d}(\theta_0 \mid d_0) = \frac{p_\theta(\theta_0) p_{d \mid \theta}(d_0 \mid \theta_0)}{\sum_{\theta_0} p_\theta(\theta_0) p_{d \mid \theta}(d_0 \mid \theta_0)} \tag{14.46}$$

where

$p_\theta(\theta_0)$ is the a priori (before the particular demand d_0 is observed) probability that $\theta = \theta_0$,

$p_{\theta \mid d}(\theta_o \mid d_0)$ is the a posteriori probability (after the demand d_0 is observed) that $\theta = \theta_0$ given that $d = d_0$ was observed,

$p_{d \mid \theta}(d_0 \mid \theta_0)$ is the so-called likelihood function, the probability of observing a demand of d_0 given that the underlying parameter value is θ_0.

For a given type of likelihood function, the a priori distribution $p_\theta(\theta_0)$ can be selected from a particular family so that the updating of Eq. 14.46 is very simple to carry out, resulting in $p_{\theta|d}(\theta_0 | d_0)$ being another member of the same family.

There are two very different types of situations (which we shall subsequently discuss separately) where Bayesian forecasting has proved fruitful:

i. A parameter (or parameters) is (are) not known with certainty *but* its (their) value(s) do *not* change with time; this allows a much simpler updating procedure but is much more restrictive than the second case to be discussed. It is primarily applicable in the early life of a product when limited history is available.

ii. A parameter (or parameters) is (are) not known with certainty *and* its (their) value(s) are allowed to change in a probabilistic fashion with time.

Unchanging Parameters for a Slow Moving (that is, Low Usage) Item—Let us consider a slow moving item for which we are attempting to establish a reorder point in an (s, Q) system of control. From Chapter 6 we know that the key quantity is the total demand, call it x, in a replenishment lead time. With a slow moving item, particularly early in its life, we have inadequate data to accurately estimate the probability distribution of lead time demand. In other words,

$$\text{if} \quad q_j = \text{prob}\{x = j\}, \qquad j = 0, 1, 2, \ldots, N$$

where N is the largest conceivable total demand in a lead time, then we don't really know the q_j values with certainty. Rather we express our uncertainty about the q_j's in terms of a probability distribution over their values (in Section 10.2.6 of Chapter 10 we briefly discussed a similar situation in the context of a style goods item). One of the authors (Reference 58) has shown that a convenient distribution to use is a member of the multidimensional Beta family. It has $N+1$ parameters, denoted by m_0, $m_1, \ldots, m_j, \ldots, m_N$. With this as the prior distribution, if a demand of size i is observed in a lead time, Bayes' Rule gives that the posterior distribution is a member of the same family having the same set of parameters except m_i is increased to $m_i + 1$. Reference 58 shows how to establish the reorder point for P_1 and P_2 service measures when the q_j's have such a multidimensional Beta distribution (instead of being exactly known). Also discussed are methods for obtaining the initial m values from subjective prior information, for example, similarity to an already existing set of products.

Allowing for Transient Perturbations, Changes in the Level and Changes in the Trend—Harrison and Stevens[28] have developed a Bayesian procedure which allows us to incorporate possible transient and permanent changes in the parameters of the demand process. Closely paralleling the notation of Chapter 4 the basic demand process is

$$d_t = \bar{d}_t F_t + \varepsilon_t \tag{14.47}$$

with

$$\bar{d}_t = \bar{d}_{t-1} + G_{t-1} + \gamma_t \tag{14.48}$$

and

$$G_t = G_{t-1} + \delta_t \tag{14.49}$$

where

d_t is the demand rate in period t.
$\bar{d}_t$ is the level value in period t.
G_t is the slope (gradient) value in period t.
F_t is the seasonal factor for period t (here assumed known and not changing).
ε_t is observational noise for period t.
γ_t is the level perturbation in period t.
δ_t is the slope perturbation in period t.

The random elements ε_t, γ_t, and δ_t are assumed to be independently and normally distributed with zero means and variances σ_ε^2, σ_γ^2, and σ_δ^2, where these variances can change, but in a known fashion, with time.

Note that a large value of ε_t would produce a strictly transient effect, whereas a large value of γ_t (δ_t) would cause a permanent change in the level (trend). Within an actual time series of demand data these types of events tend to occur with rather low probability. Harrison and Stevens model their occurrence by allowing a choice of a number of possible distributions from which the values ε_t, γ_t, and δ_t are generated at each observation. They call each set of three distributions (one for each of the three variables) a possible state of the system. If the system is in state j at time t, then ε_t, γ_t, and δ_t are generated independently from normal distributions with zero means and variances $\sigma_\varepsilon^2(j)$, $\sigma_\gamma^2(j)$, and $\sigma_\delta^2(j)$. If there are N such states, then the parameters of the system are

π_j – the probability of being in state j $\quad (j = 1, 2, \ldots, N)$

and

$\sigma_\varepsilon^2(j)$, $\sigma_\gamma^2(j)$, and $\sigma_\delta^2(j)$ $\quad (j = 1, 2, \ldots, N)$

From empirical testing it has been found that $N=4$ states is perfectly adequate. The four states and the associated variances are as follows:

State	σ_ε^2	σ_γ^2	σ_δ^2
no change	standard	0	0
transient	large	0	0
step change	standard	large	0
slope change	standard	0	large

Reference 28 also provides suggested numerical values of the variances as well as probabilities of the four states (the π_j's).

From a Bayesian standpoint the two uncertain parameters in Eqs. 14.47 to 14.49 are $\bar{d}_t$ and G_t. The convenient prior distribution to use is a member of the bivariate normal family (see, for example, page 272 of Reference 15). Where there is but a single possible state j (that is, $N=1$) the posterior distribution, after observing a value of the demand d_t, is still a member of the same family. However, where there is more than one state possible (four, in our case), Bayes' Rule gives a mix of bivariate normal distributions as the posterior distribution. For data storage and computational considerations Harrison and Stevens approximate this mix by a single bivariate normal distribution having the same set of first and second moments (means, variances and covariances).

Results using this updating procedure have been particularly encouraging, including a robustness of the method, in terms of an insensitivity to the assumed values of σ_ε^2, σ_γ^2, σ_δ^2 and the π_j's. In particular, the behavior of the state of knowledge as demand values occur is intuitively very appealing. To illustrate, suppose that suddently in period t a demand value was observed well above what was expected. The Bayesian procedure then says that we're quite uncertain as to what state the process is in, that is, there is one of three possibilities, namely: (i) a transient perturbation has occurred (a large positive ε in Eq. 14.47); or (ii) the level has shifted (a positive γ in Eq. 14.48); or (iii) the trend has increased (a positive δ in Eq. 14.49). However, after the next demand value (in period $t+1$) is observed, the uncertainty is largely resolved by the Bayesian updating. If the demand value is back near where the old parameter values would have suggested, then a transient perturbation has occurred. If the value continues well above that predicted, then either the level has shifted (indicated by the demand in period $t+1$ being close to the one in period t) or the trend has increased (indicated by the demand in period $t+1$ being appreciably above that in period t). But, this is precisely how a human decision maker would interpret this sequence of events.

14.2.6 *Inventory Control of a Perishable Item*

In earlier parts of the book we have not *explicitly* dealt with the issue of perishability except in Chapter 10 where, for style goods, a type of perishability was recognized in that any items remaining at the end of the season could only be disposed of at a salvage value below the unit acquisition cost. More generally, a rather crude allowance for the risk of perishability could be built into the inventory carrying charge. In the recent few years considerable work has been done on a more explicit treatment of perishability in inventory control.

Types of Perishable Items—As mentioned above, one type of perishable item is a style good where the utility of each unit stays essentially constant throughout the selling season, then the utilities of all units drop appreciably at the end of the season. In contrast there are items where the utility of a unit decreases throughout its lifetime, independent of the status of the other units. Within this second category we can further subdivide perishable items by whether or not the rate of decrease is age-dependent. Examples of items having age-dependent decay are human blood, certain drugs, meats and fresh produce, etc. Illustrative items, having essentially age-independent decay, are radioactive chemicals and certain volatile liquids (see Cohen,[9] Emmons,[20] Ghare and Schrader,[24] and Van Zyl[69]).

In the subsequent discussion we shall treat only a special case of age-dependent deterioration, namely an item with a fixed known lifetime with constant utility during the life and zero utility thereafter. This case (and a major portion of the research that has been carried out on the control of perishable items) is motivated by the problem of blood banking (see extensive bibliographies in Cohen and Pierskalla[11] and Elston[19]).

The Optimal Policy for an Item Having a Constant Utility During Its Known Lifetime of m Periods—A number of authors (including Bulinskaya,[6] Fries,[22] Nahmias and Pierskalla,[50,51] Pierskalla and Roach,[54] and Van Zyl[69]) have addressed this type of problem. One of the more comprehensive treatments is afforded by Nahmias;[45–49] our discussion will parallel his work.

Assumptions made include:

i. A periodic review system is used.

ii. All orders are placed at the beginnings of periods and the replenishment lead time is negligible.

iii. All stock arrives in a "new" state.

iv. Demands in successive periods are independent random variables with the same known probability distribution (Nahmias handles a slightly more general case).

v. Inventory is depleted according to a first-in-first-out (FIFO) policy, that is, the oldest inventory is issued first—

FIFO is an optimal issuing policy over a wide range of assumptions (see, for example, Pierskalla and Roach[54]).

vi. If a unit has not been used by the time it has been on-hand for m periods, then it deteriorates (is outdated) and must be discarded.

vii. There is complete backordering of unsatisfied demand (the case of complete lost sales can also be handled).

viii. Costs (all assumed linear) include acquisition, holding, shortages and out-dates (again a somewhat more general cost structure can be handled). Note that there is no fixed cost (A) associated with a replenishment.

At the beginning of each period we know the numbers of units on hand of each age. It is convenient to let x_i = number of units on hand that will end their lifetime (outdate) exactly i periods in the future. Thus, a vector

$$\mathbf{x} = (x_{m-1}, x_{m-2}, \ldots, x_2, x_1)$$

represents the state of the system at the start of a period (prior to the placement of an order). We let y represent the amount of new units to be ordered. The problem is to develop a decision rule for y as a function of $\mathbf{x}$, the demand distribution and all the unit costs.

To begin with, if m is large, we know that any decision rule that depends on all the m separate components of $\mathbf{x}$ will be unwieldy to implement. Unfortunately, Nahmias[46] shows that the optimal policy is of the form:

$$\begin{aligned} &\text{If } \mathbf{x} \text{ is such that } \sum_{i=1}^{m-1} x_i \le x_c, \text{ then order } y(\mathbf{x}). \\ &\text{If } \mathbf{x} \text{ is such that } \sum_{i=1}^{m-1} x_i > x_c, \text{ then } y = 0. \end{aligned} \tag{14.50}$$

where the critical level x_c depends on the unit costs and the probability distribution of demand.

Thus, whether or not to order and how much to order both depend upon the vector $\mathbf{x}$. To make matters worse, the computation of $y(\mathbf{x})$ is extremely complex. A primary reason for this is the complicated way in which the vector state of the process changes from period to period. Any units in state i (that is, x_i) at the start of a particular period that are not used to satisfy demand in that period will move into state $i-1$ at the start of the next period (that is, will become the x_{i-1} value at that time). Unfortunately, how many (call the number z_i) of the x_i units are used to satisfy demand in the single period depends, not only on the demand value d, but also on the values $x_1, x_2, \ldots, x_{i-1}$, namely as follows (using the FIFO assumption):

$$z_i = \begin{cases} 0 & \text{if} \quad d \leq \sum_{j=1}^{i-1} x_j \\ d - \sum_{j=1}^{i-1} x_j & \text{if} \quad \sum_{j=1}^{i-1} x_j < d \leq \sum_{j=1}^{i} x_j \\ x_i & \text{if} \quad \sum_{j=1}^{i} x_j < d \end{cases} \tag{14.51}$$

Thus, the x_{i-1} value at the start of the next period (which is the current x_i minus the z_i value) depends in a complicated way on d and all of $x_1, x_2, \ldots, x_i$ in the current period.

A Heuristic Policy for an Item Having a Constant Utility During Its Known Lifetime of m Periods—The above-indicated unwieldy nature of the optimal solution identifies the need for a simpler, heuristic, inventory control policy. Nahmias,[45] using simulation, looked at three plausible heuristics and found a "single critical number" policy to be preferable from the viewpoint of a combination of simplicity and low cost performance.

A "single critical number" policy operates as follows: We collapse the state of the system into a single dimension, using

$$x = \sum_{i=1}^{m-1} x_i \tag{14.52}$$

that is, the total on-hand inventory, regardless of its age. Then, the order quantity y is given by

$$y = \begin{cases} x_c' - x & x < x_c' \\ 0 & \text{otherwise} \end{cases} \tag{14.53}$$

where x_c' is the critical number (order-up-to-level). This type of policy is appealing for at least three reasons. First, the rule used to decide on whether to order anything at all, namely

$$\sum_{i=1}^{m-1} x_i < x_c'$$

is of essentially the same form as in the optimal policy (see Eq. 14.50). Second, for non-perishable items earlier in the book one of our basic control systems was an (R, S) system, which is precisely what the heuristic is advocating. Third, a fixed order-up-to-level represents a relatively easy policy to implement.

Having decided to pursue a "single critical number" policy, our worries would not necessarily be over. Again, primarily because of the complex nature of the change in inventory status from period to period, it is very difficult to find the optimal "single critical number" policy. Fortunately, Nahmias[49] has, if you like, developed a heuristic within a heuristic, namely a simple myopic approach for finding a single critical number close to the optimal one. The word myopic, meaning near-sighted, implies that the critical number (the order-up-to-level) is selected only taking account of the approximate costs in the very next period, neglecting costs beyond that point. For small values of m (namely $m=2$ and 3), where it is possible (although extremely time-consuming) to compute the optimal policy, he has found that use of the much simpler, myopic, single critical number policy results in an average cost penalty of less than 1 percent, an extremely encouraging result.

Other individuals who have explored "single critical number" policies include Cohen[10] and Chazan and Gal.[7]

14.2.7 *Explicit Recognition of Interactions of Production Planning/Inventory Management with Other Functional Areas of the Firm*

As indicated to some extent in Chapter 3, decisions in the inventory management/production planning area interact with decisions in other functional areas of the firm. Where such is the case, it may make sense to consider these interactions in deciding upon the decision alternative to select. We purposely use the word "may" because an analysis which includes the interactive effects is certainly more complicated than separate analyses of the distinct functional areas. Thus, the more sophisticated modelling is only justified if appreciable savings result from the coordinated decision making.

To illustrate an interactive situation we choose the problem of pricing and inventory decisions. Pricing of a commodity affects its demand rate. The inventory strategy (for example, when and how much to order) in turn, depends upon the demand pattern. But then, in turn, the pricing policy really should be a function of the ordering strategy (because the latter influences costs), etc. Quite often the pricing and ordering decisions are made in a sequential fashion, that is, the sales department first selects a price (or set of prices as a function of time), these imply a demand pattern, then the production/inventory department chooses an ordering strategy based on this given demand pattern. The key point in this sequence of decisions is that, in choosing the pricing strategy, no attempt is made to anticipate its interactive effects with the inventory decision.

Several authors have considered the interactive problem. Wagner and Whitin,[75] Wagner,[72] and Thomas[66] have all analyzed the situation where price is allowed to vary from period to period in an unrestricted fashion. The solution procedure in each case is a modified version of the Wagner–Whitin algorithm for the case of deterministic time-varying demand, outlined in Section 8.5 of Chapter 8. Smith[62] has considered the case of a perishable commodity where the price fluctuation from one period to the next is constrained. His solution method involves dynamic programming. Kunreuther and Schrage[38] have analyzed the situation where a single price is established for an entire season, the most obvious case being the pricing of an item in a telephone or mail-order catalogue. For illustrative purposes we shall elaborate on the method proposed by Kunreuther and Schrage.

The demand rate in period j is assumed to be a known function of the price p, that is

$$D(j;p) = \text{demand rate in period } j \text{ given a selling price } p \qquad j = 1, 2, \ldots, N$$

where N is the horizon.

The fixed setup cost, the unit variable cost and the carrying charge all can depend upon the particular time period, viz.:

$A(j)$–fixed setup cost in period j
$v(j)$–unit variable cost of material acquired in period j
$r(j)$–carrying charge in period j, in \$/\$/period

There are two types of decisions to be made: (i) the selection of a fixed price, and (ii) the choice of the periods in which to replenish. Essentially, an iterative solution procedure is advocated. An initial price is selected. This implies a demand pattern through time. For this given pattern the ordering strategy that minimizes costs is selected, again through a modified version of the Wagner–Whitin algorithm. Next, for this given ordering pattern (that is, specified periods in which replenishments are made) the best price is selected. Dependent upon the exact demand/price relationship this may be accomplished through the use of calculus. With this new price, we return to the selection of a best ordering strategy, etc. This is continued until the ordering strategy remains the same on two consecutive iterations. Unfortunately, as Kunreuther and Schrage show, convergence may not occur at the true optimum price. Moreover, in several cases tested the simultaneous iterative solution provides rather minimal improvement over the simpler sequential approach, a finding consistent with results of Chapter 9 where simultaneous selection of s and Q (or S and R) tended to give small cost savings over sequential selection of the parameters.

Repeating our viewpoint expressed in Chapter 8 all of the methods of the references listed above are probably too sophisticated for routine use by most companies, particularly when the potential benefits seem so limited. What is needed are clearer guidelines as to when the simultaneous decisions are necessary, as well as implementation aids, particularly in the form of heuristic decision rules.

In closing this section we mention that a similar finding of a rather limited improvement through simultaneous decision making has been reported by Constable and Whybark.[12] The interactive problem they have considered involves the functional areas of transportation and inventory. The selection of a transportation mode (more generally, a supplier-transportation mode combination) affects unit transportation (more generally, unit variable) costs, but also directly affects the inventory decision through the implied value of the replenishment lead time. Other studies on simultaneous decision making in production planning/inventory management and other functional areas have been conducted by Baker and Damon,[3] Damon and Schramm,[14] Haber and Sitgreaves,[26] Herron,[29] and Ladany and Sternlieb.[39]

14.3 *Summary*

In this chapter we have diverged from one of our primary objectives, namely to provide only *operational* decision rules for inventory management and production planning. This was done so as to be able to display some of the more interesting, complex problems of individual item control where, in some cases, additional applied research is needed to develop truly operational decision systems. In the last chapter of the book we shall return to a brief discussion of additional fruitful problem areas where considerable research is needed to provide practical results.

With this chapter we have completed the discussion of detailed individual item decision rules. In the next part of the book attention will be shifted to a more aggregate type of planning and with a longer planning horizon.

Appendix to Chapter 14—Derivation of Method of Computing s and S Taking Account of Undershoots (Section 14.2.1)

Recall that

$$x' = z + x$$

where

z is the undershoot.
x is the total lead time demand.

Also, $S = s + Q$ (Step 3 of the decision rule).

The average inventory is

$$\bar{I} \simeq \frac{Q}{2} + s - E(x') \qquad (14.54)$$

The average replenishment quantity is $(S - s) + E(z)$, that is, $Q + E(z)$. x' is assumed to be normally distributed and the safety stock is expressed as

$$SS = k\sigma_{x'}$$

Therefore,

$$s = E(x') + k\sigma_{x'}$$

(which is Step 2 of the decision rule). Also, the probability of a stockout per cycle is $p_{u\geq}(k)$. Moreover, Eq. 14.54 becomes

$$\bar{I} \simeq \frac{Q}{2} + k\sigma_{x'}$$

Thus, the expected total relevant costs per year are

$$\mathrm{ETRC}(k, Q) = \frac{AD}{Q + E(z)} + \frac{D}{Q + E(z)} \times B_1 p_{u\geq}(k) + \left(\frac{Q}{2} + k\sigma_{x'}\right) vr$$

$$= \frac{D}{Q + E(z)}[A + B_1 p_{u\geq}(k)] + \left(\frac{Q}{2} + k\sigma_{x'}\right) vr \qquad (14.55)$$

For a minimum we require

$$\frac{\partial \mathrm{ETRC}}{\partial Q} = 0 = \frac{\partial \mathrm{ETRC}}{\partial k}$$

These two conditions directly lead to Eqs. 14.17 and 14.18.

Problems for Chapter 14

Problem 14.1

Repeat the numerical illustration of Section 14.2.2 but with B_3 instead being 0.036 \$/\$/wk. Do the changes in s and S make sense?

Problem 14.2

Consider the retail customer of MIDAS Canada described in the numerical illustration of Section 14.2.4. However, now, instead of a desired probability of stockout per day, the retailer wishes to explicitly use a cost per unit short, namely \$9/unit. In addition, assume that the cost of the film (MIDAS code PSF-074) is \$15/unit and the carrying charge is 0.001 \$/\$/day.

a. What order-up-to-level S should the retailer use?
b. If the intermittent nature of the demand was ignored, what S value would be selected? What would be the approximate cost penalty?

Problem 14.3

Yagar Construction Supplies carries a certain type of steel rod. The rod is available in two lengths, namely 1 and 2 metres. Any customer request is for one of these two lengths. In fact, historical data show that in 1,000 customer requests 770 of them have been for the 1 metre length. The owner has two options open to him:

Option 1: Carry both (1 metre and 2 metre) items in stock and consider them as independent items.
Option 2: Order only 2 metre items and cut them into two 1-metre pieces as needed to satisfy requests for 1 metre lengths.

Indicate in some detail an analysis that you would suggest to assist Yagar in selecting an option. Assume that the company wishes to use the service criterion of specifying a maximum probability of stockout per replenishment occasion. Numerically illustrate your answer.

Problem 14.4

Consider a situation in which all of the assumptions inherent in the derivation of the EOQ (see Section 5.1 of Chapter 5) hold except for one change: now the amount (Y) actually received when we order Q is a random variable with probability density function $f_Y(Y_0; Q)$, where the "semi-colon Q" is included to emphasize that the probability distribution of Y depends upon the Q value used.

a. Discuss reasons for Y being a random variable.

Introducing whatever symbols you feel are appropriate, answer the following:

b. What is the cost in the current cycle (that is, in the time until just before the next order is placed) if an order is now placed and $Y = Y_0$ is observed? (Include the cost of placing the current order.)
c. What is the time until the next order in part (b)?
d. Find an expression for the expected value of the cost in the current cycle if an order of size Q is requested.
e. Find an expression for the expected duration of the current cycle if an order of size Q is requested.
f. Using the results of parts (d) and (e), outline how you would go about selecting the value of Q that minimizes costs per unit time. (Hint: You might wish to make use of the result of Eq. 14.7.)

g. Obtain a closed form expression for the best Q value for the case where $f_Y(Y_0; Q)$ has an expected value of Q and a variance σ^2.

h. Consider an item with an EOQ value of 100 units and a σ value (as defined in part (g)) of 40 units. What is the best Q value? What is the percent cost penalty of simply using the EOQ?

i. Repeat part (g) when the expected value is bQ and the variance is $\sigma_1^2 Q^2$, that is, (i) there is a bias, unless $b = 1$, and (ii) the standard deviation is proportional to Q.

j. Consider an item with an EOQ value of 100 units, a σ_1 value (as defined in part (i)) of 0.4 units and a b value of 0.5. What is the best Q value? What is the percent cost penalty of simply using the EOQ?

Problem 14.5

Many companies, in practice, initiate an expediting action when the stock level becomes dangerously low. Suppose that there is a cost B_1 associated with such an action. Consider an item with a fixed lead time L_1. An expediting action is only considered at the moment when we are L_2 units from the end of a regular lead time. The expediting action causes the outstanding order (of fixed size Q) to arrive in L_3 time units (where $L_3 < L_2$ and L_3 is a known quantity). In addition, there is a cost $B_2 v$ per unit short and a carrying charge r. Develop a model that would be helpful in the selection of

s—the regular order point
w—the expedite level (if the *net stock* is less than or equal to w at a time L_2 from the end of the regular lead time, an expediting action is taken).

Assume that demands in non-overlapping periods are independent, normally distributed variables with an annual demand rate D and a standard deviation of annual demand, σ_1. Also, for simplicity, assume that, at most, one order is outstanding at any point in time.

Problem 14.6

A company has available two modes of transportation for supplying demand at a branch warehouse:

i. Surface mode at a transit time of L_s days and a cost of p_s \$/lb.

ii. Air freight mode at a negligible transit time and a cost of p_a \$/lb. (assume $p_a > p_s$)

If the surface mode is used, then emergency air shipments can be made, as necessary, to ensure that a fraction, P_2, of demand is met without appreciable delay.

a. Introducing whatever symbols you feel are appropriate, develop a decision rule for deciding on what portion, if any, of the demand should be routinely satisfied by air freight (assume that continuous review and a fixed order quantity will be used). First discuss the key factors involved.

b. Discuss some complexities ignored in your analysis.

REFERENCES FOR CHAPTER 14

1. Ackoff, R. and M. Sasieni. *Fundamentals of Operations Research.* John Wiley, New York, N.Y., 1968, Chapters 1–4.

2. Archibald, B. "Continuous Review (*s*, *S*) Policies for Discrete, Compound Poisson, Demand Processes." unpublished Ph.D. dissertation, Department of Management Sciences, University of Waterloo, Waterloo, Ontario, Canada, 1976.

3. Baker, K. R. and W. Damon. "A Simultaneous Planning Model for Production and Working Capital." Paper No. 132, Graduate School of Business Administration, Duke University, Durham, North Carolina, September, 1975.

4. Brown, G., J. Lu and R. Wolfson. "Dynamic Modeling of Inventories Subject to Obsolescence." *Management Science*, Vol. 11, No. 1, September, 1964, pp. 51–63.

5. Brown, G. and W. Rogers. "A Bayesian Approach to Demand Estimation and Inventory Provisioning." *Naval Research Logistics Quarterly*, Vol. 20, No. 4, December, 1973, pp. 607–624.

6. Bulinskaya, E. "Some Results Concerning Optimum Inventory Policies." *Theory of Probability and Its Applications*, Vol. 9, 1964, pp. 389–403.

7. Chazan, D. and S. Gal. "A Markovian Model for a Central Blood Bank." Technical Report 022, IBM Israel Scientific Center, Haifa, Israel, 1975.

8. Cohen, G. "Bayesian Adjustments of Sales Forecasts in Multi-Item Inventory Control Systems." *Journal of Industrial Engineering*, Vol. XVII, No. 9, September, 1966, pp. 474–479.

9. Cohen, M. "Pricing Policy for the Perishable Product—I: Age Independent Decay." Technical Report No. 75-11-11, Department of Decision Sciences, The Wharton School, University of Pennsylvania, Philadelphia Pa., 1975.

10. Cohen, M. "Analysis of Single Critical Number Ordering Policies for Perishable Inventories." *Operations Research*, Vol. 24, No. 4, July–August 1976, pp. 726–741.

11. Cohen, M. and W. Pierskalla. "The Application of Perishable Inventory Theory to Blood Bank Management." Technical Report, Department of Decision Sciences, The Wharton School, University of Pennsylvania, Philadelphia Pa., June, 1975.

12. Constable, G. K. and D. C. Whybark. "The Combined Transportation and Inventory Policy Decision." Paper No. 454, Krannert Graduate School of Industrial Administration, Purdue University, West Lafayette, Indiana, April, 1974.

13. Croston, J. D. "Forecasting and Stock Control for Intermittent Demands." *Operational Research Quarterly*, Vol. 23, No. 3, September, 1972, pp. 289–303.

14. Damon, W. and R. Schramm. "A Simultaneous Deci-

sion Model for Production, Marketing and Finance." *Management Science* Vol. 19, No. 2, October, 1972, pp. 161–172.

15. Drake, A. *Fundamentals of Applied Probability Theory.* McGraw-Hill, New York, 1967.

16. Ehrhardt, R. *The Power Approximation: Inventory Policies Based on Limited Demand Information.* Technical Report #7, School of Organization and Management, Yale University, 1976.

17. Eilon, S. and J. Elmaleh. "An Evaluation of Alternative Inventory Control Policies." *International Journal of Production Research,* Vol. 7, No. 1, 1968, pp. 3–14.

18. Eilon, S. and J. Elmaleh. "Adaptive Limits in Inventory Control." *Management Science,* Vol. 16, No. 8, April, 1970, pp. 533–548.

19. Elston, R. "Blood Bank Inventories." *CRC Critical Reviews in Clinical Laboratory Sciences,* Vol. 1, 1970, pp. 528–548.

20. Emmons, H. "A Replenishment Model for Radioactive Nuclide Generators." *Management Science,* Vol. 14, No. 5, January, 1968, pp. 263–274.

21. Feeney, G. J. and C. C. Sherbrooke. "An Objective Bayes Approach for Inventory Decisions." RAND Corp., Santa Monica Calif., U.S.G.R. & D.R. AD-613 470 Clearinghouse, March, 1965.

22. Fries, B. "Optimal Ordering Policy for a Perishable Commodity with Fixed Lifetime." *Operations Research,* Vol. 23, No. 1, January–February, 1975, pp. 46–61.

23. Geisler, M. "Application of the 'Excess Distribution' to an Inventory Study." *Operations Research,* Vol. 12, No. 4, July–August, 1964, pp. 620–623.

24. Ghare, P. and G. Schrader. "Model for an Exponentially Decaying Inventory." *Journal of Industrial Engineering,* Vol. XIV, No. 5, September–October, 1963, pp. 238–243.

25. Haber, S. and R. Sitgreaves. "A Methodology for Estimating Expected Usage of Repair Parts with Application to Parts with No Usage History." *Naval Research Logistics Quarterly,* Vol. 17, No. 4, December, 1970, pp. 535–546.

26. Haber, S. and R. Sitgreaves. "An Optimal Inventory Model for the Intermediate Echelon When Repair is Possible." *Management Science,* Vol. 21, No. 6, February, 1975, pp. 638–648.

27. Hadley, G. and T. Whitin. *Analysis of Inventory Systems.* Prentice-Hall, Englewood Cliffs, N.J., 1963.

28. Harrison, P. and C. Stevens. "A Bayesian Approach to Short-Term Forecasting." *Operational Research Quarterly,* Vol. 22, No. 4, December, 1971, pp. 341–362.

29. Herron, D. P. "Expanding Air Freight Horizons by Use of the Airfreight Profitability Factor." P-54, *Proceedings of the Seventh International Forum for Air Cargo,* Society of Automotive Engineers Inc., Warrendale, Pa., 1974.

30. Hunt, J. A. "Balancing Accuracy and Simplicity in Determining Reorder Points." *Management Science,* Vol. 12, No. 4, December, 1965, pp. B94-B103.

31. Jennings, J. "Blood Bank Inventory Control." *Management Science*, Vol. 19, No. 6, February, 1973, pp. 637–645.

32. Jennings, J. "Comments on Blood Bank Inventory Model of Pegels and Jelmert." *Operations Research*, Vol. 21, No. 3, May–June, 1973, pp. 855–856.

33. Kaplan, A. "Stock Rationing." *Management Science*, Vol. 15, No. 5, January, 1969, pp. 260–267.

34. Karlin, S. "The Application of Renewal Theory to the Study of Inventory Policies." Chapter 15 in Arrow, K., S. Karlin and H. Scarf. *Studies in the Mathematical Theory of Inventory and Production.* Stanford University Press, Stanford, Calif., 1958.

35. Karlin, S. and C. Carr. "Prices and Optimal Inventory Policies." Chapter 10 in Arrow, K., S. Karlin and H. Scarf. *Studies in Applied Probability and Management Science.* Stanford University Press, Stanford, Calif., 1962.

36. Kolesar, P. "Comments on a Blood-Bank Inventory Model of Pegels and Jelmert." *Operations Research*, Vol. 21, No. 3, May–June, 1973, pp. 856–858.

37. Kunreuther, H. and J. F. Richard. "Optimal Pricing and Inventory Decisions for Retail Stores." *Econometrica*, Vol. 39, January, 1971, pp. 173–175.

38. Kunreuther, H. and L. Schrage. "Joint Pricing and Inventory Decisions for Constant Priced Items." *Management Science*, Vol. 19, No. 7, March, 1973, pp. 732–738.

39. Ladany, S. and A. Sternlieb. "The Interactions of Economic Ordering Quantities and Marketing Policies." *AIIE Transactions*, Vol. 6, No. 1, March, 1974, pp. 35–40.

40. Lampkin, W. "The Expected Size of an Order in an (s, S, T) Policy with Poisson Demand." *Operational Research Quarterly*, Vol. 17, No. 1, March, 1966, pp. 91–93.

41. Leneman, O. and F. Beutler. "On a New Approach to the Analysis of Stationary Inventory Problems." *Naval Research Logistics Quarterly*, Vol. 16, No. 1, March, 1969, pp. 1–15.

42. Morris, W. T. "On the Art of Modelling." *Management Science*, Vol. 13, No. 12, August, 1967, pp. 707–717.

43. Naddor, E. *Inventory Systems.* John Wiley, New York, N.Y., 1966, Chapter 10.

44. Naddor, E. "Optimal and Heuristic Decisions in Single- and Multi-Item Inventory Systems." *Management Science*, Vol. 21, No. 11, July, 1975, pp. 1234–1249.

45. Nahmias, S. "A Comparison of Alternative Approximations for Ordering Perishable Inventory." *INFOR*, Vol. 13, No. 2, June, 1975, pp. 175–184.

46. Nahmias, S. "Optimal Ordering Policies for Perishable Inventory—II." *Operations Research*, Vol. 23, No. 4, July–August, 1975, pp. 735–749.

47. Nahmias, S. "On Ordering Perishable Inventory When Both the Demand and the Leadtime are Random." *Technical Report No. 29,* Department of Industrial Engineering, University of Pittsburgh, Pittsburgh Pa., October, 1975.

48. Nahmias, S. "The Fixed Charge Perishable Inventory Problem." *Technical Report No. 30*, Department of Industrial Engineering, University of Pittsburgh, Pittsburgh, Pa., December, 1975.

49. Nahmias, S. "Myopic Approximations for the Perishable Inventory Problem." *Management Science*, Vol. 22, No. 9, May, 1976, pp. 1002–1008.

50. Nahmias, S. and W. Pierskalla. "Optimal Ordering Policies for a Product that Perishes in Two Periods Subject to Stochastic Demand." *Naval Research Logistics Quarterly*, Vol. 20, No. 2, June, 1973, pp. 207–229.

51. Nahmias, S. and W. Pierskalla. "Optimal Ordering Policies for Perishable Inventory—I." *Proceedings of the Twentieth International Meeting, The Institute of Management Sciences*, Vol. II, Jerusalem Academic Press, Jerusalem, Israel 1973, pp. 485–492.

52. Pegels, C. and A. Jelmert. "An Evaluation of Blood Inventory Policies: A Markov Chain Application." *Operations Research*, Vol. 18, No. 6, November–December, 1970, pp. 1087–1098.

53. Pekelman, D. "Simultaneous Price-Production Decisions." *Operations Research*, Vol. 22, No. 4, July–August, 1974, pp. 788–794.

54. Pierskalla, W. and C. Roach. "Optimal Issuing Policies for Perishable Inventory." *Management Science*, Vol. 18, No. 11, July, 1972, pp. 603–614.

55. Ross, S. *Applied Probability Models with Optimization Applications*. Holden-Day, San Francisco, 1970, pp. 52–53.

56. Sargent, R. and H. Bradley. "A 'Variable S' Inventory Model." *Management Science*, Vol. 15, No. 11, July, 1969, pp. 716–727.

57. Schwarz, L. "A Simple, Continuous Review, Deterministic, One-Warehouse, N-Retailer Inventory Problem." *Management Science*, Vol. 19, No. 5, January, 1973, pp. 555–566.

58. Silver, E. A. "Bayesian Determination of the Reorder Point of a Slow Moving Item." *Operations Research*, Vol. 13, No. 6, November–December, 1965, pp. 989–997.

59. Silver, E. A. "Establishing the Order Quantity When the Amount Received is Uncertain." *INFOR*, Vol. 14, No. 1, February, 1976, pp. 32–39.

60. Sivazlian, B. "Dimensional and Computational Analysis in Stationary (s, S) Inventory Problems with Gamma Distributed Demand." *Management Science*, Vol. 17, No. 6, February, 1971, pp. B307–B311.

61. Smith, B. and R. Vemuganti. "A Learning Model for Inventory of Slow-Moving Items." *AIIE Transactions*, Vol. 1, No. 3, September, 1970, pp. 274–277.

62. Smith, L. A. "Simultaneous Inventory and Pricing Decisions for Perishable Commodities with Price Fluctuation Constraints." *INFOR*, Vol. 13, No. 1, February, 1975, pp. 82–87.

63. Snyder, R. "Computation of (S, s) Ordering Policy Parameters." *Management Science*, Vol. 21, No. 2, October, 1974, pp. 223–229.

64. Snyder, R. "A Note on Fixed and Minimum Order Quan-

tity Stock Systems." *Operational Research Quarterly*, Vol. 25, No. 4, December, 1974, pp. 635–639.

65. Thatcher, A. "Some Results on Inventory Problems." *Journal of Royal Statistical Society*, Series B, Vol. 24, No. 1, 1962, pp. 1–33.

66. Thomas, L. J. "Price-Production Decisions with Deterministic Demand." *Management Science*, Vol. 16, No. 11, July, 1970, pp. 747–750.

67. Thomas, L. J. "Price and Production Decisions with Random Demand." *Operations Research*, Vol. 22, No. 3, May–June, 1974, pp. 513–518.

68. Tijms, H. C. "The Transient Behaviour and the Limiting Distribution of the Stock Level in a Continuous Time (s, S) Inventory Model." Report 13/71, Afdeling Mathematische Besliskunde, Amsterdam, July, 1971.

69. Van Zyl, G. "Inventory Control for Perishable Commodities." unpublished Ph.D. dissertation, University of North Carolina, Chapel Hill, N.C. 1964.

70. Veinott, A. F. "On the Optimality of (s, S) Inventory Policies; New Conditions and a New Proof." *SIAM Journal of Applied Mathematics*, Vol. 14, September, 1966, pp. 1067–1083.

71. Veinott, A. F. and H. M. Wagner. "Computing Optimal (s, S) Inventory Policies." *Management Science*, Vol. 11, No. 5, March, 1965, pp. 525–552.

72. Wagner, H. "A Postscript to 'Dynamic Problems in the Theory of the Firm'." *Naval Research Logistics Quarterly*, Vol. VII, No. 1, 1960, pp. 7–12.

73. Wagner, H. M. *Principles of Operations Research*. Second Edition, Prentice-Hall, Englewood Cliffs, N.J., 1975, pp. 831–836.

74. Wagner, H. M., M. O'Hagan and B. Lundh. "An Empirical Study of Exactly and Approximately Optimal Inventory Policies." *Management Science*, Vol. 11, No. 7, May, 1965, pp. 690–723.

75. Wagner, H. M. and T. Whitin. "Dynamic Problems in the Theory of the Firm." *Naval Research Logistics Quarterly*, Vol. V, No. 1, 1958, pp. 53–74.

76. White, D. J. "Problems Involving Infrequent but Significant Contingencies." *Operational Research Quarterly*, Vol. 20, No. 1, March, 1969, pp. 45–57.

*Midas Canada Corporation (F)**

The Assembly Department in 1976 consisted of a total of 17 employees and a manager who was responsible for scheduling the day to day assembly of MIDAMATICS and STABILIZATION PROCESSORS, the installation of Takashi Camera Systems, the repairs of all three types of equipment and the breaking and packaging of bulk shipments of processing chemicals. He also helped out on the assembly lines during emergencies.

In preparing by hand the overall Master Plan for his department, the Assembly Manager stated that his goal was to provide employment for all 17 employees at an approximately constant rate throughout the year, subject to some policy constraints. He was not allowed to carry finished MIDAMATICS or Takashi Camera Systems in inventory and he was to avoid working overtime whenever possible. On the basis of the Master Plan more detailed daily schedules were prepared by him once a week and revised daily. The Assembly Manager described his job as follows:

> *Recently I read an article in the Harvard Business Review** which rather nicely described what I do. The author used an analogy from space. A space rocket, if it is to hit the moon, must be launched within a "window" of a few hours and miles per hour. The limits on the window at launching are much rougher than they are at the other end, when the rocket nears the moon; if the launch falls outside the window, the target will be missed. This is exactly what I try to do. My objective is to plan for an actual daily work load in the department two and three months from now which will fall within the limits of the workforce capability that will be available to me at that time.*

* *The MIDAS cases describe actual decision systems which are based on consulting experiences of the authors. They do not describe the situation at any single company, but are in fact a compendium of actual situations which have been compressed into the environment of a single firm and industry for illustrative purposes. The cases are not intended as presentations of either effective or ineffective ways of handling administrative problems.*

** *See William K. Holstein. "Production Planning and Control Integrated."* Harvard Business Review, *May–June, 1968, p. 125.*

The Scheduling Committee

A Master plan for the coming year was prepared during the latter part of December and revised normally only once in July. The Scheduling Committee consisted of the Sales Manager of the Equipment Division, the Inventory Control Manager, the Comptroller and the President, the latter acting as chairman. The Assembly Department Manager acted as secretary and prepared draft Master Plans for the Committee's consideration and approval.

The scheduling process started with a consideration of projected sales estimates for each of the next 12 months initiated by the respective sales managers and reviewed by the Inventory Control Manager. Usually only estimates which deviated by more than 10 percent from last year's experience were challenged by the Committee and had to be defended by the orginators who were often asked to prepare written presentations of their reasons. Once a concensus was reached these Sales Forecasts became the basis for all subsequent planning in the Assembly Department (see Table 1).

Table 1. Midas Canada Corporation; 1977 Sales Forecasts

Month	Midamatics (units)	Stab. Processors (Units)	Install (Units)	Repairs (Hrs.)	Bulk (lbs.)	Bulk (Gals.)
Jan.	0	40	0	800	800	560
Feb.	8	60	0	600	2,400	1,680
March	5	120	1	300	1,600	1,120
April	10	240	2	200	1,400	980
May	15	300	2	200	1,800	1,260
June	7	100	0	500	1,600	1,120
July	2	100	0	500	1,000	700
August	5	100	0	500	1,200	840
September	10	200	1	300	2,400	1,680
October	15	300	1	300	2,000	1,400
November	20	400	3	200	3,000	2,100
December	3	40	0	600	800	560
TOTALS	100	2,000	10	5,000	20,000	14,000

The Master Plan

1. *Determination of Work Force Size*

The Assembly Department Manager converted the forecasts in Table 1 into equivalent labor hours as shown in Table 2. He allowed 100 hours for the assembly of MIDAMATICS, 4 hours for the assembly of PROCÉSSORS, and 32 hours for each expected installation of a Takashi camera system. The conversion factors were based on experience gained over the years. Actual times varied from these average figures depending on circumstances and somewhat on the exact specification of the equipment involved. On the same basis he allowed two minutes per pound or gallon of chemical that was repackaged into smaller quantities. The Assembly Manager stated:

> *I can make no defense of these factors other than saying that they have worked in the past. We haven't done any studies to actually check them.*

Table 2. Midas Canada Corporation; 1977 Manpower Forecasts (In Man Hours)

Month	Midamatics (1)	Stab. Processors (2)	Install. (3)	Repairs (4)	Bulk (5)	Totals (6)
Jan.	0	160	0	800	45	1,005
Feb.	800	240	0	600	136	1,776
March	500	480	32	300	91	1,403
April	1,000	960	64	200	79	2,303
May	1,500	1,200	64	200	102	3,066
June	700	400	0	500	91	1,691
July	200	400	0	500	57	1,157
August	500	400	0	500	68	1,468
September	1,000	800	32	300	136	2,268
October	1,500	1,200	32	300	113	3,145
November	2,000	1,600	96	200	170	4,066
December	300	160	0	600	45	1,105
TOTALS	10,000	8,000	320	5,000	1,133	24,453

Over the years we have come to accept these factors as being reasonable. For example, we feel that it is not worth our while to differentiate between gallons and pounds of chemicals packed—so we add the expected sales quantities for liquids and solids together and treat them as one and the same from an overall planning point of view.

The next step was the determination of how large a total workforce would be required. Each employee received 2 weeks holidays in July when the Assembly Department was shut down. In addition, 5 statutory holidays were granted to the non-unionized employees who normally worked a 35 hour week. On this basis the Assembly Manager calculated that the 245 working days available in 1977 would be distributed as given in columns 1 and 2 of Table 3. During January, the available 21 working days were equivalent to 8.6 percent (column 2, Table 3) of the 245 working days of capacity available for the whole year. Theoretically speaking, if the Assembly Manager hired exactly enough employees to produce the forecasted 24,453 man-hours of required output, then 8.6 percent of the production would have to be carried out in January.

Column 3 of Table 3 lists the percent of total expected sales, as given in Table 2, that must be met each month.

Table 3. Midas Canada Corporation, 1977 Stabilized Monthly Production Rates

Month	No. of Working Days (1)	Percent of Production Capacity (%) (2)	Expected Sales Rate (%) (3)	Planned Production Capacity (%) (4)	Available Slack (%) (5)
Jan.	21	8.6	4.1	10.2	6.1
Feb.	20	8.2	7.4	9.8	2.4
March	22	9.0	5.7	10.7	5.0
April	22	9.0	9.4	10.7	1.3
May	22	9.0	12.5	10.7	−1.8
June	21	8.6	6.9	10.2	3.3
July	13	5.3	4.7	6.3	1.6
Ausust	21	8.6	6.0	10.2	4.2
September	22	9.0	9.3	10.7	1.4
October	21	8.6	12.9	10.2	−2.7
November	21	8.6	16.6	10.2	−6.4
December	19	7.8	4.5	9.3	4.8
TOTALS	245	100.3[a]	100.0	119.2	19.2

[a] This column does not add up to 100.0 percent because of rounding inaccuracies.

For example, in January, 1,005 man-hours were being forecast as being required (column 6, Table 2) which amounted to 4.1 percent (column 3, Table 3) of expected annual sales of 24,453.

Conceivably a theoretical minimum of only 14.26 employees would be required to handle the expected annual workload of 24,453 man-hours:

$$\frac{24{,}453 \text{ man-hours}}{7 \text{ hrs/day} \times 245 \text{ days/man}} = 14.26$$

The Assembly Manager normally proposed the hiring of approximately 20 percent more employees than the theoretical minimum, in this case 17 men, to provide for flexibility in his planning. The work force of 17 represented, in terms of total annual man-hours, 119.2 percent of expected annual demand:

$$\frac{17 \text{ men} \times 7 \text{ hrs/day} \times 245 \text{ days/man} \times 100}{24{,}453 \text{ hours}} = 119.2\%$$

That is, in terms of work force capacity, 19.2 percent of over-capacity or slack was available for scheduling the production of the six product lines and for meeting unforeseen contingencies. The 119.2 percent of planned capacity was distributed by month as given in column 4 of Table 3. For example, the planned production capacity for January with 17 men was calculated to be 10.2 percent of expected annual demand:

$$\frac{17 \text{ men} \times 7 \text{ hr/day} \times 21 \text{ days}}{24{,}453 \text{ man-hours}} \times 100 = 10.2\%$$

As a result $(10.2 - 4.1)$ or 6.1 percent of slack was available for production planning in January (column 5, Table 3).

2. *Planning the Production of Major Product Lines*

The Scheduling Committee had in 1976, once again, debated the wisdom of hiring a work force that could produce 20 percent more output than forecasted sales. They reluctantly approved the Assembly Manager's proposal only after the latter had explained that historically he had found it necessary "to allow for 1 to 3 percent slack per month in order to have some flexibility to meet unexpected deviations from forecasted sales patterns, schedule disruptions brought about by the unavailability of materials, machine breakdowns, illness in the workforce . . ." He also stated that he had found it difficult to completely smooth out all seasonal fluctuation in expected sales and to compile weekly and daily schedules within the constraints of a Master Plan unless this amount of slack was available to him.

It was company policy not to carry any finished MIDAMATICS or Takashi Camera systems in inventory. Therefore the Assembly Manager first allocated exactly the amount of capacity required per month to produce the forecasted units as in Table 4. All allocations were made in terms of percent of total forecasted 1977 sales of 24,453 man-hours.*

Table 4. ***Midas Canada Corporation; 1977 Master Plan—Phase I (All figures in percent of total forecasted sales of 24,453)***

Month	Midamatics Exp. Sales (1)	Midamatics Cap. Alloc. (2)	Takashi Exp. Sales (3)	Takashi Cap. Alloc. (4)	Total Cap. Alloc. (5)	Total Planned Capacity (6)	Available Slack (7)
Jan.	0	0	0	0	0	10.2	10.2
Feb.	3.3	3.3	0	0	3.3	9.8	6.5
March	2.0	2.0	0.1	0.1	2.1	10.7	8.6
April	4.1	4.1	0.3	0.3	4.4	10.7	6.3
May	6.1	6.1	0.3	0.3	6.4	10.7	4.3
June	2.9	2.9	0	0	2.9	10.2	7.3
July	0.8	0.8	0	0	0.8	6.3	5.5
August	2.0	2.0	0	0	2.0	10.2	8.2
September	4.1	4.1	0.1	0.1	4.2	10.7	6.5
October	6.1	6.1	0.1	0.1	6.2	10.2	4.0
November	8.2	8.2	0.4	0.4	8.6	10.2	1.6
December	1.2	1.2	0	0	1.2	9.3	8.1
TOTALS	40.8	40.8	1.3	1.3	42.1	119.2	77.1

In Phase II of developing the Master Plan the Assembly Manager allocated some of the "Available Slack" (column 7, Table 4) to the breaking of bulk and to repairs. From experience, the Assembly Manager had found it not worthwhile to plan more than six months ahead. He felt that the extra effort needed produced minimal benefits because of the many changes that usually occurred during a six month period. Therefore, in December he prepared a plan which did not extend beyond June 30, by which time a new revised schedule would have been prepared by the Scheduling Committee for the second half of the year.

* *The production smoothing system which the Assembly Manager used had been installed at MIDAS-CANADA by a management consulting firm from New York City in* 1971.

The easiest thing to smooth was the breaking of bulk shipments of chemicals. The Inventory Control Manager agreed to combine the forecasted orders for chemicals for January, February and March, a total of 1.2 percent of annual sales for disassembly in January (see Table 5, columns 5 and 6). Similarly the expected orders for April, May, and June (1.1%) were also grouped for disassembly in March. The Comptroller approved these temporary increases of total dollar investment in production smoothing inventories.

With the cooperation of his salesmen the Equipment Division Manager agreed to compile a list of customers whose equipment could be serviced in January rather than in the month predicted according to column 3 of Figure 5. The list would include both customers who would likely need repairs or who had maintenance contracts that stipulated service in either February or March and who agreed to receiving repair service earlier. In this manner the Assembly Manager hoped to shift the repair work load as indicated in Table 5, column 4.

The final step, Phase III, in the development of the Master Plan consisted of the smoothing of the assembly rate of MIDAS STABILIZATION PROCESSORS. This always proved to be a contentious issue and often required the intervention of the President for resolution. In 1977, for example, the Assembly Manager proposed the capacity allocation outlined in column 6 of Table 6. This proposed production schedule would result in the production smoothing inventories calculated in the sixth column of Table 7.

The Comptroller objected vigorously to this last aspect of the proposed plan. The Assembly Manager responded by pointing out that it was company policy not to carry any finished goods inventory in MIDAMATICS and to install Takashi Camera Systems on demand. As a result, he pointed out, he had no other option but to smooth the assembly rate of PROCESSORS if the overall production rate was to be stabilized.

The Committee then discussed the possible merits of keeping limited numbers of subassemblies of MIDAMATICS and PROCESSORS in inventory in order to give more options and flexibility to the Assembly Manager. The advisability of carrying some Takashi equipment in inventory, as proposed by the Vice-president of Sales, was rejected on the basis that the limited amount of sales did not justify the stocking of any inventories. The Assembly Manager commented saying,

> *My major concern is providing flexibility for the months ahead so that I can avoid getting myself into a bind and having to use overtime because I do not have enough experienced skilled repairmen or installers when needed. I do have some additional flexibility that is not reflected in the Master Plan. The warehouse can lend me a man now and then to help out, and I of course in turn help them out when I can. Sometimes I get the salesman to part ship, or to delay their sale by a month or so.*

Table 5. Midas Canada Corporation; 1977 Master Plan—Phase II (All figures in percent of total forecasted sales of 24,453)

Month	Mida. Cap. Alloc. (1)	Taka Cap. Alloc. (2)	Repairs Exp. Sales (3)	Repairs Cap. Alloc. (4)	Bulk Exp. Sales (5)	Bulk Cap. Alloc. (6)	Total Cap. Alloc. (7)	Planned Capacity (8)	Available Slack (9)
Jan.	0	0	3.3	5.3	0.2	1.2	6.5	10.2	3.7
Feb.	3.3	0	2.5	1.5	0.6	0	4.8	9.8	5.0
March	2.0	0.1	1.2	0.6	0.4	1.1	3.8	10.7	6.9
April	4.1	0.3	0.8	0.8	0.3	0	5.2	10.7	5.5
May	6.1	0.3	0.8	0.4	0.4	0	6.8	10.7	3.9
June	2.9	0	2.0	2.0	0.4	0	4.9	10.2	5.3

Table 6. Midas Canada Corporation; 1977 Master Plan—Phase III (All figures in percent of total forecasted sales of 24,453)

Month	Mida. Cap. Alloc. (1)	Taka Cap. Alloc. (2)	Rep. Cap. Alloc. (3)	Bulk Cap. Alloc. (4)	Processor Exp. Sales (5)	Processor Cap. Alloc. (6)	Total Cap. Alloc. (7)	Planned Cap. (8)	Available Slack (9)
Jan.	0	0	5.3	1.2	0.7	1.2	7.7	10.2	2.5
Feb.	3.3	0	1.5	0	1.0	2.5	7.3	9.8	2.5
Mar.	2.0	0.1	0.6	1.1	2.0	4.4	8.2	10.7	2.5
April	4.1	0.3	0.8	0	3.9	3.0	8.2	10.7	2.5
May	6.1	0.3	0.4	0	4.9	1.9	8.7	10.7	2.0
June	2.9	0	2.0	0	1.6	2.3	7.2	10.2	3.0

Table 7. Midas Canada Corporation; 1977 Production Smoothing Inventories: Stabilization Processors

Month	Exp. Sales (1)	Prod. Rate (2)	Cum. Sales (3)	Cum. Prod. (4)	Invent. (%) (5)	Invent.[a] (Units) (6)
Dec.	—	—	—	—	—	10
Jan.	0.7	1.2	0.7	1.2	0.5	41
Feb.	1.0	2.5	1.7	3.7	2.0	132
Mar.	2.0	4.4	3.7	8.1	4.4	279
Apr.	3.9	3.0	7.6	11.1	3.5	224
May	4.9	1.9	12.5	13.0	0.5	41
June	1.6	2.3	14.1	15.3	1.2	83

[a] All of columns 1 to 5 are in percentages of annual sales expressed in hours. To convert inventory from percentages to units the following calculation is necessary: For example in January:

$$\text{Ending Inventory} = \left(24{,}453\,\frac{\text{Hrs}}{\text{Yr}} \times 0.005\right) \Big/ 4 \text{ hrs/unit} + 10 = 41 \text{ units}$$

The 10 units added on in the above equation refer to the amount of inventory on hand at the beginning of January.

The Assembly Manager then expressed concern about whether he could schedule his work load daily within the constraints of the Master Plan so as to meet the daily shipment requirements of each of the sales divisions. In particular he was unsure about the mix of assemblers, repairmen and installers that should constitute the 17 employees for the year ahead.

Since no other proposals were put forward, the President suggested that the Master Plan, as proposed by the Assembly Manager be accepted. (See Tables 8 and 9.)

Table 8 Midas Canada Corporation; The 1977 Master Plan[a] (as of Dec. 31, 1976)

	Mida-matics	Stabil. Processor		Takashi Install.	Repairs		Bulk		Totals			Total Production	
	Exp. Sales (1)	Exp. Sales (2)	Alloc. Cap. (3)	Exp. Sales (4)	Exp. Sales (5)	Alloc. Cap. (6)	Exp. Sales (7)	Alloc. Cap. (8)	Exp. Sales (9)	Planned Prod'n (10)	Cap. (11)	Available Slack (12)	Planned Slack (13)
Jan.	0	0.7	1.2	0	3.3	5.3	0.2	1.2	4.2	7.7	10.2	6.0	2.5
Feb.	3.3	1.0	2.5	0	2.5	1.5	0.6	0	7.4	7.3	9.8	2.4	2.5
Mar.	2.0	2.0	4.4	0.1	1.2	0.6	0.4	1.1	5.7	8.2	10.7	5.0	2.5
Apr.	4.1	3.9	3.0	0.3	0.8	0.8	0.3	0	9.4	8.2	10.7	1.3	2.5
May	6.1	4.9	1.9	0.3	0.8	0.4	0.4	0	12.5	8.7	10.7	−1.8	2.0
June	2.9	1.6	2.3	0	2.0	2.0	0.4	0	6.9	7.2	10.2	3.3	3.0
July	0.8	1.6	—	0	2.0	—	0.2	—	4.6	—	6.3	1.7	—
Aug.	2.0	1.6	—	0	2.0	—	0.3	—	5.9	—	10.2	4.3	—
Sept.	4.1	3.3	—	0.1	1.2	—	0.6	—	9.3	—	10.7	1.4	—
Oct.	6.1	4.9	—	0.1	1.2	—	0.5	—	12.8	—	10.2	−2.6	—
Nov.	8.2	6.5	—	0.4	0.8	—	0.7	—	16.6	—	10.2	−6.4	—
Dec.	1.2	0.7	—	0	2.5	—	0.2	—	4.6	—	9.3	4.7	—
	40.8	32.7		1.3	20.3		4.8		99.9		119.2		

[a] Note that because of rounding errors some of the figures in the Exhibits do not match exactly. For example, columns 3 and 5, Table 3, should be identical to columns 9 and 12 of Table 8, respectively.

Table 9. Midas Canada Corporation; 1977 Production Smoothing Inventories: The Assembly Department

	Dec.	Jan.	Feb.	Mar.	Apr.	May	June
MIDAMATICS[a] (units)	0	0	0	0	0	0	0
PROCESSORS[b] (units)	10	41	132	279	224	41	83
TAKASHI[a] (units)	0	0	0	0	0	0	0
REPAIRS[c] (hours)	0	489	244	98	98	0	0
BULK[d] (lbs & gals.)	0	7336	2934	8069	5869	2934	0

[a] As a matter of policy no MIDAMATICS were allowed to be carried in inventory as a means of production smoothing.
[b] Includes total inventory of Processors. Ten were left in inventory at end of 1976.
[c] "Inventory" here indicated the number of hours of repair business that salesmen were asked to solicit over and above that which was expected to result during the normal course of events during that month. It was assumed that the amount of business solicited in this manner would reduce next month's expected repairs accordingly. This amounted to a planned maintenance programme that resulted from a desire to smooth workload.
[d] Only inventory over and above normal stocks that resulted from production smoothing is listed here.

PART 5

Operational Decision Systems for Planning Aggregate Inventories, Production Rates, and Work Force Sizes

In the next four chapters we present an evaluative overview of a selection of operational models. It will not be our purpose to survey in detail all theoretical approaches that have been proposed or developed. Excellent surveys of this nature already exist and we see no purpose in duplication.[1]*

While a rich selection of decision systems that could be used in corporate planning exists, modelling has progressed much faster than application in practice. More careful consideration needs to be given to the *process and strategy* of introducing aggregate planning technology. This is why we will emphasize in our overview the implementability and practicability of existing methodology. The design of relatively simple (manual) decision systems tailored to existing conditions will be emphasized in Chapters 15 and 16. In Chapters 17 and 18 more complex (computer-oriented), proven-in-practice, decision systems will be considered.

Merchants, as defined in this book, are not generally concerned with the determination and allocation of physical *productive* capability to the same extent as producers. One could choose to define warehousing and merchandising facilities as being the equivalent of a merchant's fixed productive capacity. But, in the context of Part 5 of this book, such a definition would gain us little. Formal aggregate planning models and systems suitable for merchants have received relatively little attention in the management science literature.[13,20] Strictly speaking, Chapters 15, 16, and 17 of this part of the book are more directly applicable to producers. Subsequently, in Chapter 18, we do describe a four level hierarchical production planning decision system that does have implications for *both* merchants and producers.

In Table 1 we present a cross-section of generally available methods for planning aggregate production, workforce, and inventory levels. Most *feasible solution methods* make only a limited effort towards achieving some form of *explicit* tradeoff between the competing costs we will discuss at the beginning of Chapter 15. The apparent overriding objective for these approaches is the achievement of *any* feasible allocation of available resources which guarantees that daily sales orders will be met. In a competitive, uncertain, sometimes personally hostile, environment the achievement of a feasible aggregate plan by trial and error, consultation and compromise can be a truly notable feat. Such events are especially notable if achieved, as is often the case, without the benefit of decision making aids, rules, or data-processing technology.

In practice, the corporate planning process can at times resort to straight *barter.* "You support my production plan for our division in England and I

---

* *All references for the Introduction to Part 5 appear at the end of Chapter* 15.

Table 1 A Classification of Selected Aggregate Production Planning Methods and Models

Classification	Type of Model	Type of Cost Structure	Discussed in
A. Feasible Solution Methods	1. Barter 2. Tabular/Graphical	General/Not Explicit Linear/Discrete	Intro. 15.3.1 Chapter 16
B. Mathematically Optimal Models	3. Transportation Models	Linear/Continuous	15.4, Chapter 16
	4. Mathematical Linear Programming Models	Linear/Non-Linear	17.1
	5. Linear Decision Rules	Linear/Quadratic/ Continuous	17.5
C. Near-Optimal Decision Procedures	6. Management Coefficients	Not Explicit	17.3
	7. Parametric Production Planning	Quadratic/ not specified	17.5
	8. Search Decision Rules	General/Explicit	17.2.1
D. Multiechelon Decision Systems	9. Hax and Meal (A series of models)	Linear/Continuous/ Discrete/Quadratic	Chapter 18

will support your request in Argentina."* However, in many situations a tabular approach similar to that used by the Assembly Manager in MIDAS (F) may be used to focus the attention of barterers or a Scheduling Committee on specifics. Recall that the scheduling committee at MIDAS, while concerned about costs, made no attempt at explicitly measuring the cost of proposed plans. Their major goal was to achieve a feasible production plan which satisfied the Assembly Manager, within the overall financial constraints agreed to by the President and Comptroller. The degree to which cost data explicitly enter the decisions varies from situation to situation, but the MIDAS approach is not atypical. In this connection Harrison[12] has advocated the use of a deterministic simulation program that traces out the likely pattern of physical effects of a given aggregate strategy without the introduction of any cost parameters in the explicit model.

* *Donald B. McCaskill former executive vice-president of Warner–Lambert Company, as quoted in "Management Science in Canada." Management Science, Vol. 20, No. 4, December,* 1973, *Special Edition, (edited by Rein Peterson, David W. Conrath, and C. T. L. Janssen.), p.* 571.

It should not be surprising that, in practice, Feasible Production Plans always represent (to varying degrees) a very "personal" accomplishment to those who become involved in the political process of corporate planning. Personal, in the sense that any aggregate plan is in part the result of historical accidents, deals, and organization compromises in which the decision makers have a stake. Personal, also in the sense that every feasible schedule in practice will include such details as John Doe, the best tool and die maker in your plant, being on vacation in August. It may even reflect such unquantifiable hunches as allowing for the possible breakdown of some important piece of equipment because the operator has recently been drinking more heavily due to family problems.

Many analysts, in the past, intent on implementing *their own brand of mathematical optimality*, have neglected to deal seriously with the personal stakes held by incumbents operating within extant decision procedures. In our opinion, this neglect is one major reason for the lack of a larger number of implementations of aggregate planning models to date. The importance of politically feasible solutions is part of a larger rationale and reality that must always be considered a part of the aggregate production planning decision making environment.

Of the mathematically optimal models, linear programming models have received widest acceptance because they have proven to be relatively easy to design and implement. The assumption of linearity in the costs involved has proven to be less of a problem than originally thought, doing relatively little harm to the overall value of the technique when applied in practice.[1]

Buffa and Taubert have concluded that "one could just about flip a coin" in comparing the total cost advantages of linear and quadratic models. They also point out that in practice cost functions are probably neither all linear nor all quadratic, but a mixture of the two including, in particular, *a variety of discontinuities which are difficult to model mathematically.** They recommend and have developed a computer-based near optimal methodology called Search Decision Rules which is not as dependent on the assumption of a limited set of continuous mathematical forms.

In Chapter 18, we consider a comprehensive multi-level, yet flexible, aggregate planning system, which in our opinion represents the direction in which future development in aggregate planning must move. We agree with Hax[13] that it would be a serious mistake to attempt to deal with all the hierarchical decisions at once, via a single mathematical model as advocated by some management scientists.[7] Instead we advocate the partitioning of the total production planning system so that adequate decision models could be selected to deal with individual decisions at each hierarchical level. We also advocate the design of linking mechanisms between

---

* *Elwood S. Buffa and William H. Taubert,*[1] *pp.* 251–299.

these partitions for transferring of higher level results to lower decision levels in the hierarchy to yield an overall decision system that is both responsive to managerial opinion and to rational tradeoffs between competing measures of performance at all levels of an organization. The total decision system presented in Chapter 18 is only one specific example of a possible tailored hierarchical planning system.

CHAPTER FIFTEEN

The Medium Range Aggregate Production Planning Decision

In this chapter we examine the structure of the aggregate planning problem. A feasible solution method using a graphical-tabular decision procedure is presented as an illustrative example. Subsequently a simple extension to such feasible solution approaches is discussed, utilizing ideas based on the transportation method of linear programming. All decision procedures in this chapter can be used manually and require little knowledge of the mathematics of management science.

We decided to present the material in this chapter and in Chapter 16 in this way for two reasons. First, there is a need in many organizations to demonstrate to management that the aggregate planning problem can be structured rationally and resolved with the assistance of relatively simple, yet powerful, concepts and models. Secondly, many analysts do not seem to be aware of the current low state of implemented aggregate planning theory. The procedures described in this chapter are rudimentary in technique, but, if implemented, would represent a significant improvement in the level of rational decision making practiced in many organizations. Before attempting to implement more complex analytical models an analyst should consider, as a first step, the introduction of tabular-graphical procedures such as described in this chapter.

15.1 *The Aggregate Planning Problem*

The aggregate production planning problem, in its most general form as treated by analysts to date, can be stated as follows: Given a set of (usually 12 monthly) forecasts of demand for a *single* product, or for some measure of output that is common across several products, what should be for each period:

a. The size of the work force, W_t

b. The rate of production, P_t

c. The quantity shipped, S_t

The problem is usually resolved *analytically* by minimizing the expected total cost over a given planning interval consisting of some or all of the following cost components:

a. The cost of regular payroll and overtime

b. The cost of changing the production rate from one period to the next (including such items as costs of layoffs, hiring, firing, training, learning, etc.)

c. The cost of carrying inventory

d. Cost of shortages resulting from not meeting demand inadvertently (or on purpose)

In the above definition only three decision variables need to be determined: the required workforce size, W_t, (number of man-hours per month, *t*); the required production rate per period, P_t, (units of product per month, *t*); *and the number of units to be shipped per month*, S_t. The resulting inventory per month, I_t, can then be determined from the three decision variables by:

$$I_t = I_{t-1} + P_t - S_t \tag{15.1}$$

Workforce per period, W_t, does not appear directly in the identity Eq. 15.1 because any set level of W_t in turn determines the possible range of values that P_t can assume. That is, the size of the workforce is always *one* of the important determinants of the feasible rate of production per period.

Note that the solution to the problem posed is greatly simplified *if average demand over the planning interval is expected to be constant.* Under such a circumstance there would be no need to consider changing the level of the production rate, nor the size of the workforce, nor the planned quantity to be shipped from period to period.* One would need only carry sufficient inventory (safety stock) to balance the risk of running out using one of the many methods described in Chapters 6 and 7. The appropriate size of regular payroll would be given by:

$$W_t = \frac{\text{Average Sales Rate per period}}{\text{Productivity per worker}} \tag{15.2}$$

We would have to consider using overtime only to replenish safety stock on occasion or if Eq. 15.2 resulted in a non-integer number of workers (e.g., 16.2) so that it might be worthwhile to round down and make up the shortfall through working overtime.

The complexity in the aggregate production planning problem therefore arises from the fact that in most situations demand per period is not constant but varies from month to month according to some *known* (seasonal) pattern. Only then, do the following questions need to be answered:*

a. Should inventory investment be used to absorb the fluctuation in demand over the planning period by accumulating inventories during slack periods to meet demand in peak periods?

---

* *We are also assuming implicitly that there are no problems in receiving a constant supply of raw materials and labor at a fixed wage rate. If the supply of raw materials, or labor is seasonal, then these statements need to be modified.*

b. Why not absorb the fluctuations in demand by varying the size of the workforce by hiring, firing, or laying off workers?

c. Why not keep the size of the workforce constant and absorb fluctuations in demand by changing the rate of production per period by working shorter or longer hours as necessary, including the payment of overtime?

d. Why not keep the size of the workforce constant and meet the fluctuation in demand through planned backlogs or by subcontracting excess demand?

e. Is it always profitable to meet all fluctuations in demand or should some orders not be accepted?

To develop decision models to analyse these questions a number of logical conditions and data requirements have to be met. First, as is obvious from the above, management must be able to forecast reasonably accurately the *fluctuating* demand over an appropriately long planning interval (horizon). The degree to which the different models that we will discuss are affected by forecast errors will vary, but they will all require that a reasonable forecast of demand be made (e.g., by using the regression methods referred to in Chapter 4).

Secondly, to apply any one of the analytical approaches in practice, management must be able to develop a single overall *surrogate* measure of output and sales for all the different products to be scheduled by an aggregate production plan. This can prove to be quite difficult in practice. Some examples of units used in past applications include gallons of paint or beer, man-hours of assembly labor as in the MIDAS (F) Case, machine hours in some job shop situations, cases of cans packed (regardless of size) by a cannery, or dollars of sales, if each dollar of sales represents approximately the same amount of productive effort to be allocated.

Thirdly, management must be able to identify and measure the costs associated with the various options raised above and discussed in greater detail in the next section.

15.2 Costs Involved

There are essentially six categories of costs involved in the aggregate planning problem:

a. Regular time costs: The variable cost of producing a unit of output during regular working hours, including direct and indirect labor, materials, and manufacturing expenses.

b. Overtime costs: The costs associated with using manpower beyond normal working hours.

c. Production rate change costs: The expenses incurred in altering the production rate substantially from one period to the next.

d. Inventory associated costs: The costs associated with carrying any level of inventory, conveniently subdivided as follows:

i. Out of pocket expenses: Including the cost of running the warehouse, depreciation, taxes, insurance, etc.

ii. Lost opportunity: The cost of tieing up capital that could be invested elsewhere if inventory was not needed.

e. Costs of insufficient capacity in the short run: The costs incurred when demands occur while an item is out of stock. Such costs can be a result of backordering, lost sales revenue, and loss of good will. Also included in this category are the costs of actions initiated to prevent shortages, e.g., split lots and expediting.

f. Control system costs: The costs associated with operating the control system. They include the costs of acquiring the data required by analytical decision rules, the costs of computational effort exerted per time period, and any implementation costs which depend upon the particular control system chosen.

15.2.1 *Costs of Regular Time Production*

A typical relation of cost versus production rate is shown in Figure 15.1. Usually some form of monotonic increasing behavior is assumed (i.e., the costs associated with any production rate must be at least as high as those associated with any lower production rate). The near vertical rises in Figure 15.1 occur because additional pieces of equipment are required at increasingly higher rates of production. The shape of the cost curve may also depend upon the particular time period under consideration.

A major portion of regular time production costs in Figure 15.1 is the regular time wage bill paid to the full time workforce. When such costs are identified separately they are usually assumed to increase linearly with the size of the workforce as in Figure 15.2. It is becoming more difficult in practice to reduce the size of the workforce from one month to the next

Figure 15.1 Typical Costs of Regular Time Production

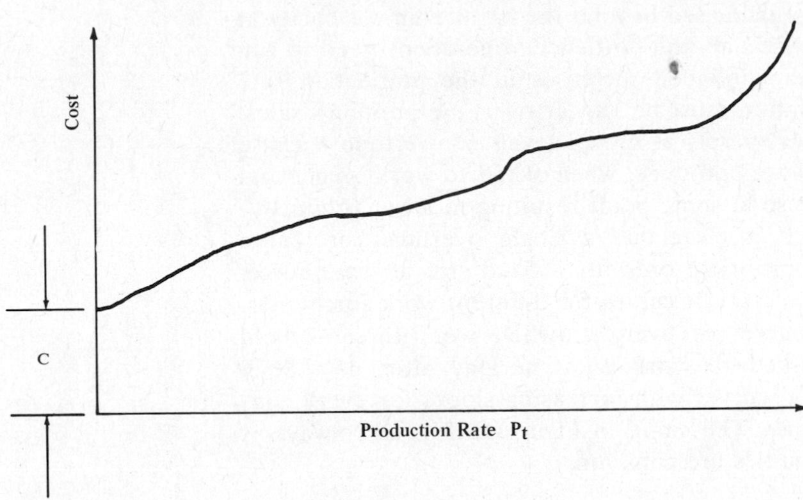

because of social pressures, public opinion and union contracts. As a result, W_t, the size of the workforce in many situations, is in effect a constant and not a decision variable that can be altered at will. Under such a circumstance the regular wage bill becomes a fixed cost, as shown by the dotted line in Figure 15.2 and the size of the intercept "C" on Figure 15.1 would have to be adjusted upward accordingly.

Figure 15.2 Typical Cost of Regular Time Labour

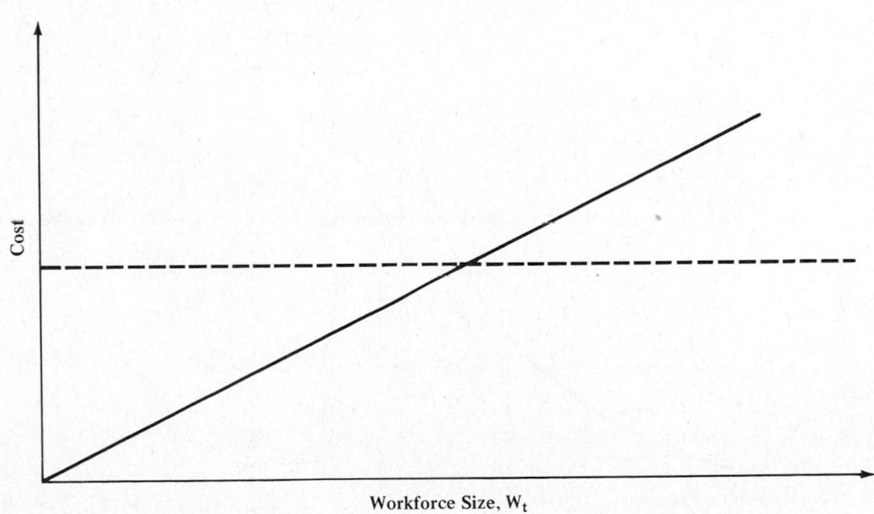

15.2.2 *Overtime Costs*

The general graphical form of overtime costs is illustrated in Figure 15.3. The production rate is at first increased beyond the regular time capacity at little extra cost. This is because only the bottleneck operations need to run on overtime. However, with continued increases in the production rate more and more of the operation must be run at overtime premium rates. The overtime cost curve rises sharply at higher levels of overtime because the efficiency with which workers produce, when asked to work longer and longer hours, starts to decrease at some point resulting in lower productivity per man-hour worked. It is clear that a single overtime cost curve versus production rate is appropriate only for a fixed size of work force, that is, there really are a whole set of curves for different work force sizes. There is also a different curve for every t (when work force is held constant) if workers are asked to work overtime day after day. Such *cumulative tiredness* results in curves with increasing slopes for every consecutive t worked on overtime. The curve in Figure 15.3 is not always as smooth as shown. Discontinuities are common.

Figure 15.3 Typical Shape of Overtime Costs for a Given Work Force Size

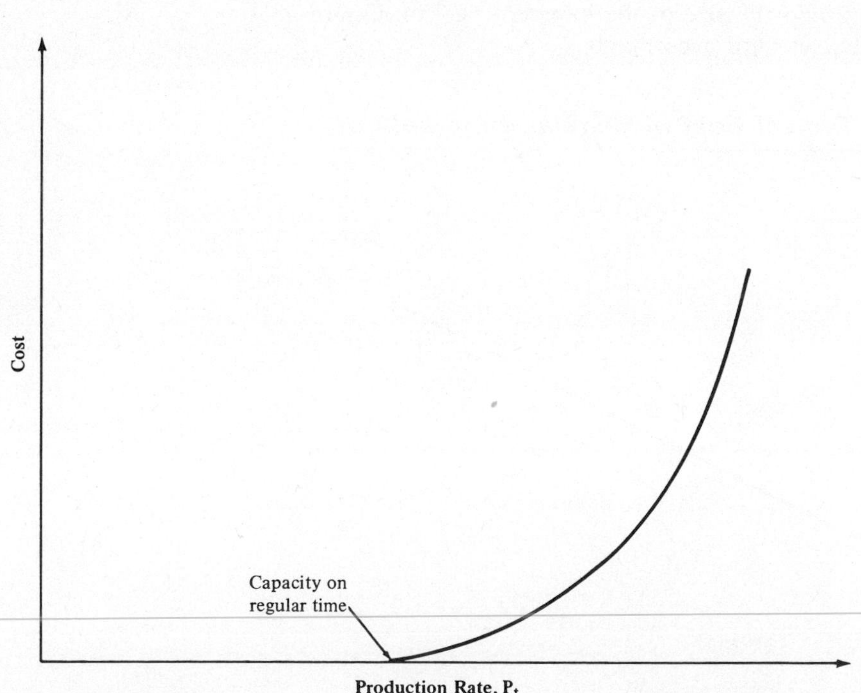

15.2.3 *Costs of Changing the Production Rate*

These costs consist primarily of production rate changes brought on by changes in the size of the work force. Such changes incur costs of training, reorganization, terminal pay, loss of morale, and decreased interim productivity. Decreased productivity results in part from the learning process when new labor and/or equipment must be started up. Another source of changeover costs is a common union requirement that specifies that when a man is laid off, his job can revert to any other union member according to seniority. As a result, the layoff of a few workers can result in "bumping", a series of shifts in job responsibilities.

A typical behavior of the costs as a function of the change in rates is shown in Figure 15.4. Two points are worth mentioning: First, the curve is usually asymmetric about the vertical axis, that is, a unit increase does not necessarily cost the same as a unit decrease. Second, ideally there should be a separate curve for each starting rate P_{t-1}. This is because a change from 90 percent to 95 percent of production capacity has an appreciably different cost than going from 30 percent to 35 percent.

Figure 15.4 Cost of Production Rate Changes.

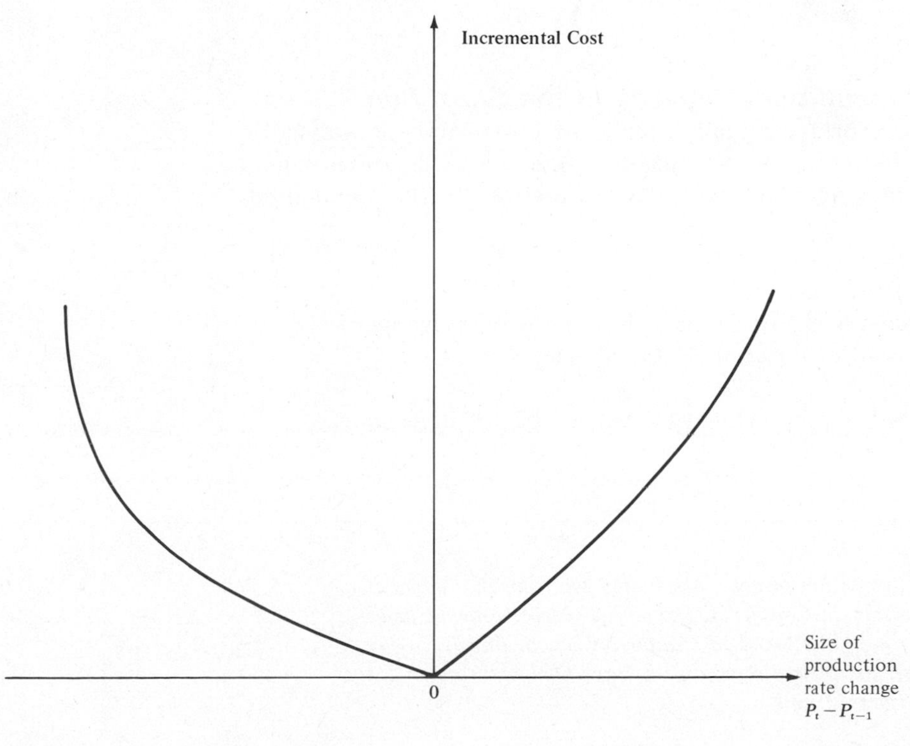

Some decision models do not include a cost for changing production rates. Instead they may specify that the change from one period to the next can be no greater than a certain value or simply that the rate itself must stay within certain bounds. As we will see the inclusion of this particular type of cost becomes an important issue in the evaluation of alternative analytical models.

15.2.4 *Inventory Associated Costs*

As discussed in Chapter 3 there is a cost associated with tieing up funds invested in inventory. The standard approach is to say that the costs for T periods are given by

$$\text{Costs for } T \text{ periods} = \bar{I}_1 r + \bar{I}_2 r + \bar{I}_3 r + \ldots + \bar{I}_T r$$

$$= r \sum_{k=1}^{T} \bar{I}_k, \tag{15.3}$$

where $\bar{I}_k$ is the average inventory (in dollars) in period k, often approximated by the starting or ending inventory, and r is the carrying rate in \$/\$/period. The parameter r reflects all the costs of carrying inventory mentioned above. Typically its value lies in the range 0.05/year to over 0.50/year depending partly on the tradeoff point selected by management on Exchange Curves.*

15.2.5 *Costs of Insufficient Capacity in the Short Run*

When an unplanned shortage actually occurs the costs can be expressed in a number of different ways; which to use is a function of the environment of the particular stocking point under consideration.** The possibilities include:

a. A fixed cost each time that a shortage occurs, independent of the size or duration of the shortage

b. A cost that is proportional to the number of units short

---

* *Recall the discussion of costs associated with the individual item inventory decision in Chapter 3. Exchange Curves and the determination of r were discussed in Chapters 3, 5, 6, and 7.*

** *For a more complete discussion on ways of measuring shortage costs see Chapters 6 and 7.*

c. A cost that is proportional to the time duration of the shortage

d. Combinations of a, b, and c

In general, the actual costs of a shortage, as well as those associated with avoiding a stockout, are quite difficult to estimate.

Many aggregate planning models look at the combined costs of inventory and insufficient short run capacity in a slightly different and more aggregate fashion. From fundamental economic arguments which we presented in Chapter 5 the best inventory level in period t can be shown to be proportional to the square root of O_t, where O_t is the forecasted sales(orders) for period t. Over a narrow range any square root function can be approximated reasonably well by a straight line, i.e.,

$$\text{Optimal inventory in period } t \simeq a + bO_t \tag{15.4}$$

where a and b are constants.

Deviations from the optimal inventory result in extra costs; too high an inventory results in excessive carrying costs, too low an inventory leads to inordinate shortage costs. For a given value of O_t the typical curve of costs versus inventory is shown in Figure 15.5. There is actually a whole set of such curves, one for each value of O_t, the current aggregate rate of demand. See Holt et al.[15] for a complete discussion.

Figure 15.5 Inventory and Shortage Costs.

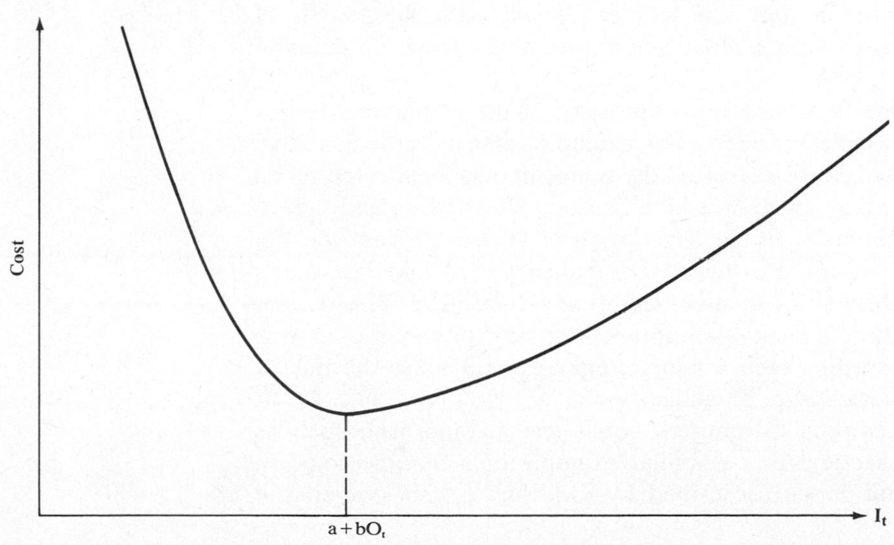

Management also can resort to *planned* backlogs, short shipments and subcontracting to meet peak demands. In general, it is not profitable to always try to meet all demands. Accentuated seasonal periods of high demands may lead to unreasonably high total costs no matter which of the methods one selects from those discussed above. Specifically, in practice it is usually true that

$$S_t \neq O_t, \qquad \text{for all } t. \tag{15.5}$$

That is, the quantity shipped is not identical to the quantity ordered in every period, nor should it be as has been pointed out by Peterson.[20] For other discussions of costs relevant to the aggregate production planning problem see Holt et al.[15] or McGarrah.[18]

15.3 *Feasible Solution Methods*

15.3.1 *General Comments*

Each group within an organization approaches the determination of appropriate inventory investment (and thereby production smoothing and workforce balancing) with somewhat different motives. Top management, along with financial managers, are pleased if inventory investment can be successfully kept at a "minimum." Operating management prefers long production runs, smooth production and workforce levels, and thereby also fluctuating inventory investment. Marketing managers usually elect for a larger inventory investment, but are less concerned with the length of production runs than with having most finished items available on demand off the shelf.

It is common practice to achieve a compromise of the conflicting desires through a bargaining (barter) process. For example, many companies have a Scheduling Committee, consisting of all the senior managers affected by an aggregate production plan, which considers various alternatives and agrees on a feasible set of tradeoffs. For a description of such a process see the MIDAS (F) Case. An approach often used in industry is to take last year's plan and adjust it slightly so as to meet this year's conditions. The danger in doing this lies in the implicit assumption that any previous plan was close to optimal; by pursuing such a course, management takes the risk of getting locked into a series of poor plans.

Alternatively a Scheduling Committee could use an approach such as discussed in the next section. For a similar example of a feasible solution method see the tabular model described by Gordon[11] who studied the

Chain Brewing Company* located in the Eastern U.S.A. Close[6] reports on a graphical feasible solution method that considers linear costs explicitly.

15.3.2 *An Example of a Graphical-Tabular Method*

The most useful and rudimentary analytical extensions from bartering are graphical-tabular in nature. Such procedures, while not mathematically optimal, always guarantee a feasible solution. Such methods are surprisingly effective and difficult to improve on.

Consider the forecasted demand pattern in Table 15.1 and its plot as cumulative sales in Figure 15.6. The straight line a–e represents a level (constant) production plan of 30 hours of production per month which meets the *expected* cumulative forecast of 360 production hours for the 12 month period.** Other cumulative production plan lines can be drawn on Figure 15.6 (for example, a–b–c–d–e) which may be more desirable because they cost less or because they take better account of the uncertainty of the forecasts.

Table 15.1 Cumulative Forecasts (In Production Hours)

Period, t	Forecast Usage, S_t	Cumulative Usage
1. Sept–Oct	30	30
2. Nov–Dec	30	60
3. Jan–Feb	120	180
4. Mar–Apr	90	270
5. May–Jun	60	330
6. Jul–Aug	30	360

The dotted lines above and below the solid black line o–g–f represent the maximum and minimum forecasted cumulative sales that could reasonably occur. For example, by the end of month six, cumulative sales could be as much as 240 production hours or as little as 120 production hours,

* *This is a disguised name.*

** *The single surrogate measure of output in which all variables are measured is assumed to be production hours. A single hour of production may require several man-hours to achieve.*

Figure 15.6 Graphs of Cumulative Forecasts and Alternative Production Plans.

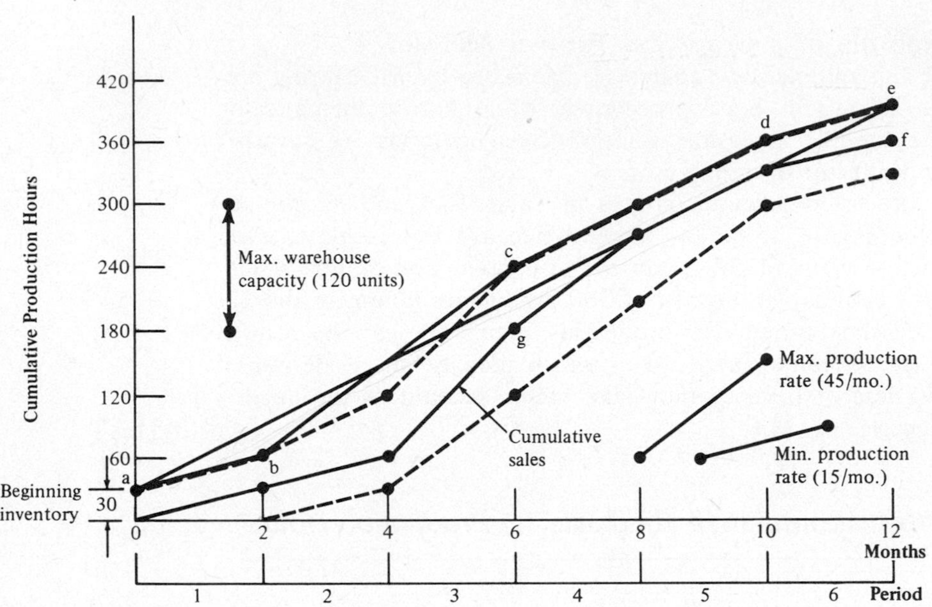

rather than the expected 180 hours forecasted, which will be used as the basis for planning.* In Table 15.2 part of the relevant information from the graph is presented in tabular form for the case of a constant production plan.

Note from Figure 15.6 and Table 15.2, *if forecasted sales materialize as expected, then a constant production plan is feasible,* although during the months 8 to 10 inclusive, inventory would be drawn down to zero. (In Figure 15.6 we have assumed that 30 hours of production were in inventory at the beginning of period zero. The same 30 hours of production are available at the end of the 12 month planning horizon.) Any cumulative production plan that ends up at point f or higher on Figure 15.6 without violating any exogenous constraints would be *feasible.* This is a very powerful and useful result, quite easily achieved graphically! The selection of a low cost, feasible production plan graphically, from among the infinite numbers possible, will be somewhat more difficult, as we shall see.

* *In practice a number of possible future scenarios such as in Figure* 15.6 *are usually explored.*

Table 15.2 Constant Production Plan (30 Hours of Production/mo.)

End of Period	Cum. Avail.	Expected Cum. Sales	Expected Invent.	Max. Cum. Sales	Min. Invent.	Min. Cum. Sales	Max. Invent.
1	90	30	60	60	30	0	90
2	150	60	90	120	30	30	120
3	210	180	30	240	−30	120	90
4	270	270	0	300	−30	210	60
5	330	330	0	360	−30	300	30
6	390	360	30	390	0	330	60

In Figure 15.6 any vertical distance between a cumulative sales line and a cumulative production line represents the amount of inventory on hand at that point in time. For example, at the end of month 2 we *expect* to have 60 hours of production on hand. At the end of month 8, if sales are *higher* than expected, we could be 30 production hours short. On the other hand, if *lower* than expected sales materialize, then we could have a maximum of 120 hours of production on hand at the end of month 4. The possibility of running out of inventory in months 8 to 10 inclusive could render the constant production plan infeasible. Company policy could dictate that such a possibility should not be tolerated in any production plan considered. In addition there is usually a maximum level of inventory that is allowed by management policy. This could represent either the maximum space available in the warehouse for storage or alternatively the maximum investment risk that management is willing to undertake. (In Figure 15.6 warehouse capacity is assumed to be 120 production hours.) Such constraints are called *exogenous*, that is, such constraints are imposed externally on the decision problem.*

Other exogenous constraints are possible. For example, in Figure 15.6 we have assumed that the manufacturing facility can support a maximum production rate of 45 production hours/month and that management is unwilling to take the chance of losing key personnel which a production rate of less than 15 production hours/month would entail.

---

* *To keep the exposition simple we have assumed that the cumulative production lines are achievable with certainty. Note that it is possible under this procedure to draw on Figure 15.6 dotted cumulative production lines above and below the expected production shown to represent any uncertainty involved.*

All exogenous constraints are shown graphically on Figure 15.6 and can be used graphically as follows. When drawing alternate *feasible* production plans in Figure 15.6 the slopes of production lines drawn must always lie between the maximum (45 p.h./mo.) and minimum (15 p.h./mo.) extremes allowed. Furthermore, the vertical distance between any cumulative production plan and any cumulative sales forecast must be *greater* than zero and less than 120 production hours (because of top management policy). Under these exogenous constraints the constant production plan is *infeasible*, as is clear from Table 15.2. On the other hand, the other production plan a–b–c–d–e on Figure 15.6 and summarized in Table 15.3 is feasible.

Table 15.3 Production Plan a–b–c–d–e

End of Period	Cum. Avail.	Expected Cum. Sales	Expected Invent.	Max. Cum. Sales	Min. Invent.	Min. Cum. Sales	Max. Invent.
1	60	30	30	60	0	0	60
2	150	60	90	120	30	30	120
3	240	180	60	240	0	120	120
4	300	270	30	300	0	210	90
5	360	330	30	360	0	300	60
6	390	360	30	390	0	330	60

To this point we have not considered costs in our discussion of the production plans that are possible. This would in practice be the next level of sophistication that is attempted. By assuming the data in Table 15.4 the *expected* cost of production plan a–b–c–d–e can be computed as in Table 15.5.

Having found one feasible production plan and its expected cost there remains the task of trying to find a better feasible production plan that is lower in cost to that in Table 15.5. This could involve a further *ad hoc* trial and error search or alternatively one could introduce an analytic technique as discussed in the next section.

Table 15.4 Cost Structure and Initial Conditions

Cost of Regular Time (R/T) Labor = \$200/production hour
Cost of Overtime (O/T) Labor = \$300/production hour
Cost of Hiring = \$120/production hour
Cost of Firing = \$70/production hour
Cost of Carrying Inventory = \$40/production hour/2 month period
Initial Inventory = 30 production hours
Initial Workforce = 30 production hours/2 month period

Table 15.5 Expected Cost of Production Plan a–b–c–d–e

		Work Force			Production		Expected	
t	W_{t-1}	Hired	Fired	W_t	R/T	O/T	S_t	I_t
0	—	—	—	(30)	—	—	—	(30)
1	30	0	0	30	30	0	30	30
2	30	60	0	90	90	0	30	90
3	90	0	0	90	90	0	120	60
4	90	0	30	60	60	0	90	30
5	60	0	0	60	60	0	60	30
6	60		30	30	30	0	30	30
Totals	—	60	60	360	360	0	360	270
Costs	—	$7,200	$4,200	$72,000	—	0	—	$10,800
Total Cost = $94,200								

Before proceeding, let us summarize the steps that are required in using the graphical-tabular procedure we have been discussing:

1. Plot the cumulative expected forecasts and the attendant maximum and minimum extremes on a graph (as in Figure 15.6).

2. Consider first a plan involving a constant production rate (i.e., a–e on Fig. 15.6) which involves *zero changeover costs.* Check to see if a constant production plan is feasible, given exogenous constraints. Determine the total cost of this plan.

3. Consider next a plan tailored to match the forecast fluctuations as exactly as *feasible* (i.e., a–b–c–d–e on Figure 15.6). This will result in a plan with *minimum inventory holding costs.* Determine the total cost of this plan as in Table 15.5.

4. After examining the plans derived in steps 2 and 3, investigate plans intermediate in position.* These plans should

* *Note that plans a–e and a–b–c–d–e in Figure* 15.6 *do not bound the large number of alternatives possible. That is, the optimal plan does not necessarily lie on a line drawn between them. Nevertheless the two graphs from steps* 2 *and* 3 *usually greatly delimit the number of alternatives one would want to consider evaluating.*

attempt to trade-off inventory holding (and shortage) costs versus changeover, regular time and overtime costs. The Land Algorithm, discussed in the next section, which calculates the *optimal* allocation of exogenously determined production capacity may be useful at this stage. For each plan devised determine the total cost.

5. Select the feasible plan found by the steps above that is considered to be most desirable by a Scheduling Committee or its equivalent. (Hopefully total cost would be one of the relevant criteria.)

Note that the best one can hope for is to design a mathematically near-optimal plan, by this procedure. One shortcoming of our heuristic method is that it does not usually yield mathematically optimal trade-offs between the costs of regular time and overtime production, carrying costs and changeover costs. What is worse, one is never quite sure how near or far from a mathematical optimum any particular plan is. Close[6] claims that experienced production planners can, by trial and error, design feasible production plans that are surprisingly close to the mathematically optimal trade-offs possible. This appears to be the case because (as we saw in Chapter 5) the total cost equation of most inventory decision models tends to be u-shaped with a shallow bottom around the optimal point. It is, of course, possible that mathematical optimality is an irrelevant criterion to the managers on a Scheduling Committee who strive to "optimize" far more complex objectives.

15.4 *The Land Algorithm*

The simplest optimization technique that could be used to help deal with the problem discussed in this chapter was originally proposed by Bowman[4] in 1956. In this section we shall examine another form of the more general linear programming (transportation) model, proposed almost simultaneously by Beale and Morton,[2] and Land.[17] Land's version is suitable for manual computations. Subsequently in Chapter 16 we shall apply this method to the MIDAS (F) case. By doing this we hope to demonstrate that the transportation optimization methodology has many features which make it very practical. These features, we believe, have not received their rightful recognition by analysts and acceptance by managers.

What a transportation optimization technique offers to a tabular-graphical procedure such as we have been discussing is summarized by the diagram of Figure 15.7. That is, for a set of exogenously determined *ad hoc* inputs (chosen by a decision maker using his own biases, insights and

Figure 15.7 Aggregate Planning Involving the Land Algorithm.

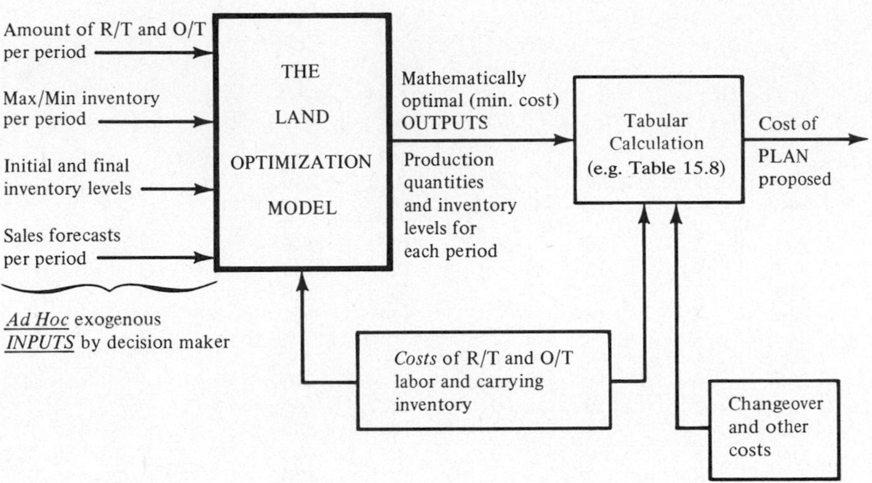

creativity) a mathematically optimal production plan is routinely calculated.* We shall present the Land Algorithm verbally. Some additional information on technical aspects appears in an appendix at the end of this chapter.

The transportation tableau, as suggested by Land, for manually solving the aggregate planning problem that we have been discussing, is given in Table 15.6. Columns 1 and 2 are self explanatory. I_{max} is the maximum inventory (90 production hours) that may be carried from one period to the next and is the upper limit allowed to the sum of the figures for any single period in column 8. The beginning inventory of 30 production hours is subtracted from the 120 production hours of warehouse capacity because it is expected that at least this amount will always be on hand at the end of each period and it is also the amount of inventory that is expected to be on hand at the end of period 6.

Column 3 lists the two sources of production available in period 1: regular time (1, 1) and overtime (1, 2). The cost of each source in column 4 is derived from Table 15.4. In column 5 a rank is assigned to each source starting with the least expensive source. Column 6 records the

* *While we have shown the use of the Land algorithm and the tabular-graphical methodology in a manual mode, there is, of course, no reason why it cannot be computerized using visual displays, etc.*

Table 15.6 The Land Algorithm Applied to the Aggregate Planning Problem

Period	$I_{max} = 120$ -30 90	Source	Cost at t	Rank	CAPACITY Avail at t	Used in t	Avail in $t+1$	Cost at $t+1$
(1)	(2)	(3)	(4)	(5)	(6)	(7)	(8)	(9)
1	Sept–Oct	1 1	200	1	60	30	30	240
	$S_1 = 30$	1 2	300	2	18		18	340
2	Nov.–Dec.	2 1	200	1	60	30	30	240
	$S_2 = 30$	2 2	300	3	18		18	340
		1 1	240	2	30		30	280
		1 2	340	4	18		12[a]	380
3	Jan.–Feb.	3 1	200	1	60	60	0	—
	$S_3 = 120$	3 2	300	4	18		18	340
		2 1	240	2	30	30	0	—
		2 2	340	5	18		18	380
		1 1	280	3	30	30	0	—
		1 2	380	6	12		12	420
4	Mar.–Apr.	4 1	200	1	60	60	0	—
	$S_4 = 90$	4 2	300	2	18	18	0	—
		3 2	340	3	18	12	6	380
		2 2	380	4	18		18	420
		1 2	420	5	12		12	460
5	May–June	5 1	200	1	60	60	0	—
	$S_5 = 60$	5 2	300	2	18		18	340
		3 2	380	3	6		6	420
		2 2	420	4	18		18	460
		1 2	460	5	12		12	500
6	July–Aug.	6 1	200	1	30	30	0	—
	$S_6 = 30$	6 2	300	2	9		9	340
		5 2	340	3	18		18	400
		3 2	420	4	6		6	460
		2 2	460	5	18		18	500
		1 2	500	6	12		12	540

[a] Reduced from 18 to 12 to satisfy the inventory capacity constraint.

capacity available from each source for each period. These capacity figures have to be determined exogenously by the decision maker. In Table 15.6 the regular time capacity was set at 60 production hours/period based on insights garnered by the authors from the constant production plan we examined in Table 15.2. In particular, by allowing overtime to a maximum of 30 percent of regular time capacity, the undesirable (infeasible) zero expected inventory position calculated in Table 15.2 could now be overcome. The 30 production hour regular time capacity for period 6 was chosen to make the ending condition of period 6 the same as that at the beginning of period 1.

In column 7 are recorded the actual amounts of production scheduled in each period. The Land Algorithm instructs us to use the sources available in column 6 in order of rank given in column 5 until the forecasted requirements in column 2 (S_i) have been met. The remaining capacity is then available for use in $t+1$ (column 8) as long as the total capacity carried forward in any one period is less than 90 production hours (I_{max}).

For example, in period 3 expected demand is $S_3 = 120$. The least expensive source is (3, 1). The total capacity of 60 production hours is used up leaving none for period 4 (column 8). The next lowest cost source is (2, 1) and all of its capacity of 30 production hours is scheduled. (This means that 30 production hours of regular time are scheduled in period 2 to meet demand in period 3.) The remaining 30 man-hours of expected demand are then scheduled using the third lowest cost source (1, 1), regular time production in period 1 carried forward in inventory for two periods for use in period 3.

From column 7 of Table 15.6 we can derive the production plan given in Table 15.7. Note that the production quantities for each period *cannot* be read directly off Table 15.6.

The production plan in Table 15.7 is not feasible since there is a chance that in period 3, if sales are higher than expected, we could run out of inventory. (That is, safety stock is less than the 60 shown on Figure 15.6.) To overcome this deficiency we must increase the inventory level at the end of period 3 by 18 production hours. From Table 15.6 we see that this increase in inventory can be best achieved by producing 6 man hours on (3, 2) (because at the end of period 6 there were only that many man-hours left in this source) and the remaining 12 man-hours on (2, 2). To make the ending inventory at the end of period 6 equal to 30 we must compensate for these increases in inventory by reducing the production in period 4 from source (4, 2) to zero, from 18. Such minor adjustments will often be necessary with the Land Algorithm when applied in our context. Note that these minor adjustments did not alter the mathematical optimality of the solution we had achieved in Table 15.6. These minor adjustments do not appear in Table 15.6, but are included in the cost calculations of Table 15.8.

Note that the total cost of the plan in Table 15.8 is only 1 percent lower than plan a–b–c–d–e (see Table 15.5). That is, the graphical-tabular procedure seems to have yielded a reasonably good plan right off the bat. Close reports similar kinds of findings in his research. In his paper he compared graphically designed plans with mathematically optimal plans derived through techniques such as linear programming.*

---

* *See Close,*[6] *Table* 2, *page* 456.

Table 15.7 Production Plan Derived in Table 15.6

Period	R/T Prodn.	O/T Prodn.	Expect Sales	Expect Invent.	Max Sales	Min Invent.	Min Sales	Max Invent
0	—	—	—	30	—	30	—	30
1	30 + 30 = 60	0	30	60	60	30	0	90
2	30 + 30 = 60	0	30	90	60	30	30	120
3	60	12	120	42	120	−18	90	102
4	60	18	90	30	60	0	90	90
5	60	0	60	30	60	0	90	60
6	30	0	30	30	30	0	30	60

Table 15.8 Expected Cost of Production Plan

Period		Work Force			Production		Expected	
t	W_{t-1}	Hired	Fired	W_t	R/T	O/T	S_t	I_t
0	—	—	—	(30)	—	—	—	(30)
1	30	30	0	60	60	0	30	60
2	60	0	0	60	60	12	30	102
3	60	0	0	60	60	18	120	60
4	60	0	0	60	60	0	90	30
5	60	0	0	60	60	0	60	30
6	60	0	30	30	30	0	30	30
Totals	—	30	30	330	330	30	360	312
Cost	—	\$3,600	\$2,100	\$66,000	—	\$9,000	—	\$12,480
Total Cost = \$93,180								

One would in general continue to design plans and find the mathematically optimal allocation of sources by repeatedly using the Land Algorithm. Since the main conceptual points that we wished to make with this example have been made, we shall terminate our search for further production plans at this point.

15.5 *Conclusions*

We have presented a graphical-tabular Method and the Land Algorithm in detail to illustrate the basic tradeoffs involved in the aggregate planning problem. This example also provides us with some other insights which we believe to hold in a large number of cases. First of all, we were able to derive a plan by simple graphical and tabular methods which was hard to beat as we saw in Table 15.8. In his article Close[6] also compared graphical solutions to those derived by more complex methods. Under two different cost structures his plans were within 3 and 0.4 percent, of mathematically optimal solutions which required considerably more effort and time to compile. Such small gains are of little practical significance since most cost data is probably not accurate within 3 percent, and forecast errors can wipe out most or all of such small differences.

We must of course be careful not to over-generalize on the basis of a simple example. One reason that we were able to quickly derive a good solution is the fact that the cost and demand structure made it relatively easy to make the tradeoffs required. Basically the example required only the trading off of hiring/firing costs, costs of regular production and the costs of carrying an appropriate level of inventories. We felt that *the cost of* *overtime was so prohibitive that it never really entered into consideration in our graphical phase* (yet some overtime was used in the final Land solution).*

If the tradeoffs had not been so obvious, and if other variables in addition had to be considered, it would have been much more difficult to derive a good solution. Under such circumstances the Land Algorithm would have proven to be much more valuable than it actually was in the example we considered. This is one of the basic advantages of any algorithm which results in a mathematically optimal solution. It can make tradeoffs between more variables, more efficiently than a heuristic procedure that depends on an analyst to make the necessary tradeoffs using his own judgment.

The second insight suggested by the example, therefore, concerns the need to always select decision models for aggregate planning whose sophistication matches the complexity demanded by the specific situation faced in different organizations. Shycon has pointed out the fact that management scientists can get carried away in their search for generality and optimality. They "tend, at times, to over-agonize about the entire analytical process. In short, sometimes they make more of a big deal of the routines of analysis than is justified by the type of result required and the management need."[22] We believe that aggregate planning theory is one area where management scientists have gotten somewhat carried away.

The sparse number of applications in this area is therefore in large part due to two related reasons. First, some management scientists have tried to construct more and more complex models, which are not easy to adapt to changing real world conditions. Secondly, the manager is too often isolated from the process of achieving a "solution." It is possible that every time we claim we have invented a more complex model that includes more decision variables than ever before, or when we claim that some computerized algorithms can achieve an "optimal solution" faster than ever before, we are actually progressively alienating more and more managers from ever considering using decision models for aggregate planning. The manager does not necessarily want quick and easy answers. Nor does he want to delegate too much of the analysis to an inanimate process. He may well want to agonize, to make deals and compromises, and to derive "personalized" alternative plans—even at the expense of *mathematical* optimality. To a manager, the aggregate plan is too important a decision for him *not* to spend a considerable amount of time in developing it.

---

* *Perhaps this is one of the reasons that many managers intuitively are reluctant in practice to plan for the use of overtime in their aggregate schedules.*

It is for this reason that we devote the next chapter to considering the *process* of achieving a good operational solution to the MIDAS (F) case. The decision process we shall develop in Chapter 16 builds on the ideas presented in this chapter. In sum, the arguments in Chapters 15 and 16 boil down to suggesting that in the interest of implementability we should "go back to basics," not unlike the strategy adopted by some coaches of losing football teams.

Appendix to Chapter 15—Technical Aspects of the Land Algorithm

Aside from providing a simple visual and manual solution technique, the Land Algorithm also allows the specification of monthly inventory constraints, something that was not possible under the Bowman Transportation Model.

The form of the problem considered by Land can be stated as:

$$\text{Min } C_n = \sum_{i=1}^{n} \sum_{j=1}^{k} \sum_{t=1}^{n} c_{ijt} p_{ijt} + \sum_{t=1}^{n-1} r_t I_t$$

Subject to:

$$0 \leq p_{ijt} \leq P_{ijt} \qquad (t = 1, 2, \ldots, n;\ i = 1, 2, \ldots, n;\ j = 1, 2, \ldots, k)$$

$$\sum_{t} p_{ijt} \leq P_{ij} \qquad (i = 1, 2, \ldots, n;\ j = 1, 2, \ldots, k)$$

$$0 \leq I_t \leq I_{t\max} \qquad (t = 1, 2, \ldots, n)$$

$$(I_0, I_n \text{ specified outside model})$$

$$I_{i-1} + \sum_{t=1}^{n} \sum_{j=1}^{k} p_{ijt} = S_i + I_i; \qquad (i = 1, 2, \ldots, n)$$

where

p_{ijt} is the amount produced in source (e.g., shift) j of period i to satisfy demand in period t.

c_{ijt} is the production cost per unit of p_{ijt}.

P_{ijt} is a capacity limit on each p_{ijt}.

P_{ij} is the production capacity in source j of period i.

I_t is the inventory at the end of period t.

$I_{t\max}$ is the capacity limit on I_t.

S_t are the requirements (demand) in period t.

r_t is the charge per unit carried in inventory at the end of period t.

Problems for Chapter 15

Problem 15.1

Given the description of the problem in Case F, how would you go about formulating the MIDAS situation in a Land Transportation format? (See Table 15.6.) Do you have all the information you need?

Problem 15.2

The president of MIDAS-Canada suspected that the Inventory Control Manager was building too much slack into his Master Plan. Do you agree and what action (if any) would you recommend?

Problem 15.3

In Case F the Inventory Control Manager described how he planned to inventory "man-hours of repairs." Explain how this can be done. Do you see any problems in doing this?

Problem 15.4

In Case F the Master Plan is prepared only 6 months ahead. Is this advisable in this case? Under what circumstances would you recommend a longer decision horizon?

Problem 15.5

In Chapter 15 we discussed the concept of "cumulative tiredness." Can this concept be included into the Land Transportation model of the aggregate scheduling decision?

Problem 15.6

Why does it usually cost a different amount to change the rate of production from 90 to 95 percent of capacity than from 30 to 35 percent of capacity? Which of the two is likely to cost more? How would your answer differ if the change were from 95 to 90 percent of capacity versus 35 to 30 percent of capacity?

Problem 15.7

Clarke Manufacturing Co. makes 30 types of transformers. Sales forecasts for 1977, for type CT-OIM are as below:

Month	Demand (Units)
Jan.	600
Feb.	500
Mar.	700
Apr.	900
May	1000
June	1200
July	900
Aug.	700
Sept.	700
Oct.	600
Nov.	600
Dec.	600

A maximum of 24 transformers of this type can be produced at one time. The company works one shift of 8 hrs/day. Each worker can handle only one machine at a time and produces on the average 2 units per 8-hour shift.

Regular time pay is $4/hr. and the overtime rate is $6/hr. Cost of carrying inventory is set at 0.02$/$/month. Costs of hiring and firing a worker are estimated at $360 and $180 respectively. Union contract stipulates that at least 14 workers have to be employed at all times. On Dec. 31, 1976 there were 15 workers on the payroll and inventory on hand was 300 units. The desired minimum level of inventory was set at 300 units with each unit costed at $50. Normally a worker can work a max. of 56 hours in a week. Assume each month is 20 working days in length.

Formulate the least cost production plan for 1977 using a graphical approach. (No back ordering is allowed and inventory level should not go too far below 300 units.)

Problem 15.8

For the Clarke Manufacturing Co. example in Problem 15.7 assume that in addition to the data already given:

i. Cumulative tiredness reduces daily production by 5 percent per day for each 10 hours of overtime worked in a month

ii. Sales forecasts are expected to be within ±25 percent of actual sales

iii. Backlogging is allowed at a penalty of $30 per unit

Instead of the data given in problem 15.7 assume that the company has only a choice of working either one or two shifts throughout a year (that is, they cannot hire and fire during their fiscal year). A maximum of 16 transformers can be produced at a time on either shift, although the productivity on the second shift tends to be about 30 percent lower. Recommend a production plan for Clarke Manufacturing under these revised assumptions.

Problem 15.9

Starship Ltd. manufactures boats and distributes them across the U.S.A. Part C-212 (Motor) is the most expensive single part. The table below shows the sales forecast for this part for the next 12 months.

Months	Forecast (units)
1	300
2	600
3	300
4	400
5	800
6	900
7	1600
8	1800
9	1600
10	800
11	500
12	400

Labor cost is $40 per unit at regular time and $60 per unit at overtime. Carrying cost is $2 per month per unit.

A maximum of 20 men can work at any time. The monthly output on regular time per man is 50 units. Overtime production can be up to 40 percent of regular time production. Maximum monthly inventory is set at 1000 units. There is no constraint on the minimum number of workers per month.

a. Develop an optimal production schedule for the next 12 months. Indicate

i. The total cost of production (i.e., labor and carrying costs)

ii. The total production every month

iii. The total number of workers required in each of the 12 months

b. Draw the cumulative production and demand curves.

Problem 15.10

In problem 15.9 if the maximum inventory limit is raised to 1300 units, how much is the increased storage capacity worth?

Problem 15.11

Refer to problem 15.9. If at least 12 workers have to be employed at all times, how does this constraint affect total cost?

REFERENCES FOR CHAPTER 15

1. Buffa, Elwood S. and Taubert, William H. *Production Inventory Systems: Planning and Control.* Richard D. Irwin Inc., Homewood Illinois, 1972.

2. Beale, E. M. L. and Morton, G. "Solution of A Purchase-Storage Programme: Part I." *Operational Research Quarterly,* Vol. 9, No. 3, 1958, pp. 174–187.

3. Bishop, George T. "On a Problem of Production Scheduling." *Operations Research,* Vol. 5, No. 1, February, 1957.

4. Bowman, E. H. "Production Scheduling by the Transportation Method of Linear Programming." *Operations Research,* Vol. 4, No. 1, February, 1956.

5. Bowersox, Donald J. *Readings in Physical Distribution Management.* The MacMillan Company, London, 1969.

6. Close, J. F. C. "A Simplified Planning Scheme for the Manufacturer with Seasonal Demand." *The Journal of Industrial Engineering,* Vol XIX, September, 1968.

7. Connors, M. M., Coray, C., Cuccaro, C. J., Green, W. K., Low, D. W., Markowitz, H. M. "The Distribution System Simulator." *Management Science,* Vol. 18, No. 8, April, 1972.

8. Eilon, S. *Elements of Production Planning and Control.* MacMillan, 1962.

9. Feltham, G. A. "Some Quantitative Approaches to Planning for Multiproduct Production Systems." *The Accounting Review,* Vol. 45 No. 1, January, 1970, pp. 11–36.

10. Galbraith, J. "Solving Production Smoothing Problems." *Management Science,* Vol. 15, No. 12, August, 1969, pp. 665–674.

11. Gordon, J. R. M. "A Multi-Model Analysis of an Aggregate Scheduling Decision." Unpublished Ph.D. dissertation, Sloan School of Management, Massachusetts Institute of Technology, 1966.

12. Harrison, F. L. "Production Planning in Practice." *OMEGA,* Vol. 4, No. 4, 1976, pp. 447–454.

13. Hax, Arnoldo C. *Aggregate Capacity Planning: A Review.* Technical Report No. 85, Operations Research Center, M.I.T., Boston, Mass. September, 1973.

14. Hillier F. and Lieberman, G. *Introduction to Operations Research.* Holden Day, San Fransisco, 1967, pp. 191–193.

15. Holt, C., Modigliani, F., Muth, J., and Simon, H. *Planning Production, Inventories and Work Force.* Prentice-Hall, 1960.

16. Kolenda, J. F. "A Comparison of Two Aggregate Planning Models." Unpublished Master's Thesis. Wharton School of Finance and Commerce, 1970.

17. Land, A. H. "Solution of A Purchase-Storage Programme: Part II." *Operational Research Quarterly,* Vol. 9. No. 3, 1958, pp. 188–197.

18. McGarrah, R. E. *Production and Logistics Management.* Wiley, New York, 1963.

19. Moskowitz, Herbert, "The Value of Information in Aggregate Production Planning—A Behavioral

Experiment." Paper No. 347. Institute for Research in the Behavioral, Economic and Management Science, Purdue University, April, 1972.

20. Peterson, R. "Optimal Smoothing of Shipments in Response to Orders." *Management Science*, Vol. 17, No. 9, May, 1971.

21. Sadlier, C. David. "Use of the Transportation Method of Linear Programming in Production Planning: A Case Study." *Operational Research Quarterly*, Vol. 21, No. 4, 1970, pp. 393–402.

22. Shycon, Harvey N. "Perspectives on MS Applications." *INTERFACES*, May, 1974, p. 23.

23. Starr, Martin K. *Systems Management of Operations.* Prentice-Hall, Englewood Cliffs, 1971.

24. Van De Mark, R. L. *Wholesale Inventory Control.* Brodrax Printing Co. Dallas, Texas, 1966.

25. Wagner, Harvey M. *Principles of Operations Research.* Prentice-Hall, Englewood Cliffs, 1969.

26. Zoller, K. "Optimal Disaggregation of Aggregate Production Plans." *Management Science*, Vol. 17, No. 8, April, 1971, pp. 553–579.

CHAPTER SIXTEEN

A Manual Approach to the Aggregate Production Planning Decision

In Chapter 15 we explored the aggregate planning decision in detail and examined a selection of analytical methods which have been proposed for the solution of segments of the aggregate scheduling problem. In this chapter we present a comprehensive *manual* decision system applicable in the MIDAS Canada Corporation context (see Case F). The decision procedures developed for MIDAS were tailored to the needs and capabilities of existing management personnel. The MIDAS decision system yields only near-optimal results, mathematically speaking, and is presented here to demonstrate how operational systems of this kind can be designed in practice to *extend and meld into extant procedures.*

16.1 The MIDAS Problem

MIDAS represents a relatively typical situation. Management did not know how to incorporate the uncertainty of their forecasts into the decision procedures used for developing a Master Plan. As a result, they maintained a large work force to meet contingencies. They also were reticent to include the use of overtime in their plans. Overtime was considered too expensive, something to be used only in case of emergencies, even though they had actually never explicitly determined any of the costs associated with the production planning decision. Their existing decision

Figure 16.1 An Overview of the New MIDAS Decision System.

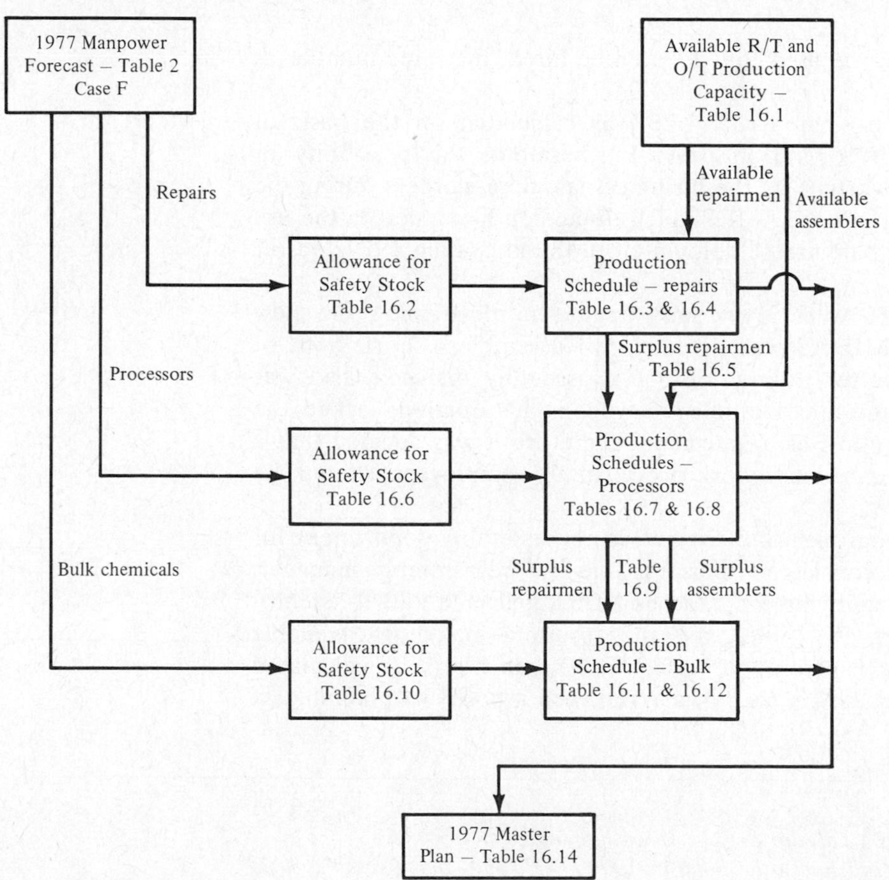

procedures could be classified as emphasizing only feasible strategies, with almost no attempt being made at explicit cost tradeoffs. The decision system which we designed for MIDAS tried to correct these shortcomings by explicitly considering uncertainty, cost tradeoffs and employment policies. An overview of the system is presented in Figure 16.1.

16.2 *Determination of Overall Capacity Constraints*

The assembly manager at MIDAS wished to allow for "1 to 3 percent slack per month" in his Master Plan. He also wanted to hire 20 percent more employees than the "theoretical minimum" number required which he calculated to be 14.26 men:*

$$\frac{24{,}453 \text{ man hours}}{7 \text{ hours/day} \times 245 \text{ days/man}} = 14.26$$

For 1977 he therefore proposed that 17 men be hired, the same number as were hired in 1976.

It was pointed out to him that 14.26 was calculated on the basis of regular time, one shift operation only. Furthermore, the possibility of working extra shifts, overtime or the hiring of part time workers during the peak season was being ignored. After much discussion he agreed to the use of some overtime and part time employment in the upcoming 1977 Master Plan.

In December, 1976, when work was begun on developing the new decision procedures, MIDAS was actually two assemblers short, both of whom had quit for better paying jobs. The assembly manager also was considering terminating a third employee who, in his opinion, lacked the level of skill he required of his repairmen. Therefore it was decided that a Master Plan involving a total work force of 14 employees should be attempted.

Five experienced repairmen had worked in the assembly department for many years and were considered indispensable by the assembly manager. Therefore an overall work force composed of 5 repairmen and 9 assemblers was agreed upon. In Table 16.1 the resulting maximum available regular and overtime (30 percent of regular time) man-hours are calculated for each month. The company had always followed a policy of planning six

* *See MIDAS (F) case for details. It was estimated that* 24,453 *man-hours of work had to be done in* 1977. *See Table* 2 *of Case F.*

Table 16.1 Available Regular and Overtime Production Capacity (After allowing for Takashi and Midamatic forecasted sales)

Month (1)	No. Days (2)	Total Man-hours per Man per Month (3)	5 Repairmen R/T (4)	Less Instal. (5)	Available R/T (6)	Available O/T (7)	9 Assemblers R/T (8)	Less Mida. (9)	Available R/T (10)	Available O/T (11)
Jan.	21	140	698	0	698	210	1257	0	1257	377
Feb.	20	133	665	0	665	200	1197	800	397	359
Mar.	22	146	732	32	700	220	1317	500	817	395
Apr.	22	146	732	64	668	220	1317	1000	317	395
May.	22	146	732	64	485[a]	220	1317	1500	0[a]	395
Jun.	21	140	698	0	698	210	1257	700	557	377

[a] 183 man-hours of Midamatic assembly scheduled on R/T with Repairmen.

months ahead and it was decided not to deviate from this time horizon at this point in time.

Columns 3 and 4 of Table 16.1 were calculated as follows (illustrated foı January):

$$\text{Column 3: } 21 \text{ days} \times 7 \text{ hours/day} \times 0.95 = 140 \text{ Hrs./month}$$

$$\text{Column 4: } 21 \text{ days} \times 7 \text{ hours/day} \times 5 \text{ repairmen} \times 0.95 \doteqdot 698 \text{ man hours} \qquad (16.1)$$

In each case, the available total man-hours was multiplied by 0.95 to allow for expected production inefficiencies. Since repairmen were the only employees who could install Takashi systems, the total available man-hours, in column 4, was reduced each month by the forecasted man hours of Takashi installations expected on column 5 (see also Figure 2, Case F), to give the regular timc man-hours available for repairs in column 6. Available overtime in column 7 was calculated as being 30 percent of column 4.

For assemblers, regular time capacity was calculated in Table 16.1 as follows. The forecasted man-hours to assemble Midamatics was subtracted in column 9 to give the regular time available for Processer Assembly in column 10. Since it was company policy not to carry inventory in Midamatics, any Midamatics to be installed in a month had to be assembled to order during that month. Note that in May, the forecasted man hours required to assemble Midamatics was greater than the available regular time capacity from the 9 assemblers. As a result, 183 man hours were "borrowed" from the regular time capacity available that month from repairmen. Because the assembly of Midamatics required considerably less technical skill than the installation of Takashi systems and repairs of all types of equipment sold by MIDAS, available regular time capacity from repairmen was first utilized for Takashi installations and repairs. Then surplus repairmen man-hours and assembler capacity were used to schedule processors and ultimately to break bulk.

16.3 *Scheduling Manpower Requirements for Repairs*

The first step in planning the manpower required for repairs consisted of the introduction of an allowance for uncertainty into the forecasts given in Table 2 of the MIDAS Canada corporation Case F. It was decided that because of company policy to build Midamatics and to install Takashi systems to order, no safety factors which took account of forecast uncertainty in these products would be introduced in this, the initial design stage of the new decision system. (Note that this could be easily done by methods similar to those described below.)

The members of the Scheduling Committee agreed that the uncertainty in the demand for repairs could be taken into consideration by adding to the forecasted manpower requirements given in Table 2, Case F, twice the standard deviation of each month's demand during the last 5 years. The five past sales figures for each month were corrected for trend before the standard deviations were calculated.

Table 16.2 Modification to Forecasted Manpower Requirements Resulting From Adding Safety Stock-Repairs

Month (1)	Starting Inventory (2)	Closing Inventory (Safety Stock) (3)	Increase Demand (4)	Inventory Available (5)
Jan.	0	15	15	
Feb.	15	57	42	
Mar.	57	26		31
Apr.	26	25		1
May	25	42	17	
June	42	93	51	

In Table 16.2 the resulting modifications to forecasted manpower requirements were then calculated as follows. Since under existing decision procedures no "safety stock" in repair time was maintained explicitly, in January (under column 2) 0 man-hours was entered. Two standard deviations of the last 5 years demand amounted to 15 man-hours for January, and as a result (column 4) planned man-hours for repairs in January were increased by 15. "Safety stock" necessary for February was estimated at 57 man-hours, therefore the forecasted demand in February had to be increased by a further 42 man-hours.* However in March a lower "safety stock" requirement meant that a surplus of 31-man hours was available for use during the month. The figures in columns 4 and 5 of Table 16.2 were used to either augment the demand (taken from Table 1, Case F) each month in column 5 of Table 16.3 or make "inventory" available in each month under source (1, 0) or (2, 0) . . . , or (6, 0) in column 2.

The worksheet in Table 16.3 is a modified version of the Land algorithm discussed in detail in section 15.4 of the previous chapter. In January demand for repairs was forecasted in Case F, Table 2 to be 800 man-hours. In Table 16.4 we decided to increase this demand by 15 man-hours to allow for some safety stock. In column 2 the available sources to meet the forecasted demand in January are identified as inventory (1, 0), regular time production (1, 1) and overtime production (1, 2). Similar definitions hold for all other months.

In column 3 the cost per man-hour of each source utilized are given. Repairmen were paid $6.00 per man-hour (9.00 on over time) and assemblers received $4.00 per man-hour ($6.00 on overtime). The company guaranteed each repairman a year around work week of at least 35 hours. As a result, the discretionary (marginal) cost of repairmen per regular time man-hour in column 3 is given as 0. Similarly, the cost of any surplus inventory utilized during the period is given also as 0. Overtime man-hours are costed at $9.00 reflecting the fact that these costs would be incurred over and above the *guaranteed* weekly wage paid to repair-men. The cost of carrying one man-hour of repair time from one month to the next was estimated at $1.00. This reflected the cost of arranging with clients the rescheduling of planned maintenance earlier than stipulated in

---

* *"Inventory" of man-hours to do repairs was created by carrying out scheduled maintenance on Takashi and Midamatic equipment earlier than stipulated in service contracts sold by MIDAS. Special permission to do so had to be solicited from clients. Two standard deviations of safety stock were selected because, in the opinion of the Inventory Control Manager, this yielded sufficient coverage against contingencies in most cases.*

Table 16.3 Worksheet For Six Months Production Schedule-Repairs

Month (1)	Source (2)	Cost (3)	Available at t (4)	Demand at t (5)	Production (6)	Available at $t+1$ (7)	Remarks (8)
Jan.	1 0	0	0	~~800~~ 815	0	0	Inventory
	1 1	0	698		698	0	Regular Time
	1 2	9	210		117	93	Overtime
Feb.	2 0	0	0	~~600~~ 642	0	0	It was mana-
	2 1	0	665		642	23	gement policy
	2 2	9	200			200	to limit inven-
	1 2	10	93			77	tory to 300 Hrs.
Mar.	3 0	0	31	300	31	0	
	3 1	0	700		269	300	
	3 2	9	220			0	
	2 1	1	23			0	
	2 2	10	200			0	
	1 2	11	77			0	
Apr.	4 0	0	1	200	1	0	
	4 1	0	668		199	300	
	4 2	9	220			0	
	3 1	1	300			0	
May	5 0	0	0	~~200~~ 217	0	0	
	5 1	0	485		217	268	
	5 2	9	220			0	
	4 1	1	300			32	
June	6 0	0	0	~~500~~ 551	0	0	
	6 1	0	698		551	147	
	6 2	9	210			0	
	5 1	1	268			153	
	4 1	2	32			0	

contracts. These costs included the cost of telephone enquiries, formal letters agreeing to earlier maintenance, etc.

According to the Land algorithm discussed in Chapter 15, all available sources in each month should be ranked (and subsequently exhausted until all demand is met) in order of increasing cost. For January, this resulted in utilization of all of the 698 man-hours of regular time available (from Table 16.1). In addition 117 man-hours of overtime were also required. Note that we could not utilize assembler time here because these workers lack the necessary skills. A total of 93 man-hours of overtime was carried forward to February. Table 16.3 also reflects the decision by senior management to limit the maximum "inventory" of repair time from one month

Table 16.4 Six Month Production Plan-Repairs

Month (1)	Starting Inventory (2)	Production (3)	Demand (4)	Closing Inventory (5)	Safety Stock (6)	Anticip. Stock (7)
Jan.	0	815	800	15	15	0
Feb.	15	642	600	57	57	0
Mar.	57	269	300	26	26	0
Apr.	26	199	200	25	25	0
May	25	217	200	42	42	0
June	42	551	500	93	93	0

to the next to 300 man-hours, to avoid large disruptions in planned maintenance contracts (see column 7).

Table 16.4 summarizes the resulting production plan for repairs calculated in Table 16.3. Table 16.5 gives the surplus man-hours of repairman time that was left over and could be transferred for use in assembling processors (see columns 4 and 7). Note the order in which repairman time is being allocated: first to the installation of Takashi systems; then to repairs; now all surplus is being transferred to assemble Midamatics. As we shall see later, the breaking of bulk which receives the lowest priority of all, has the last call on repairman time (if there is any left).

Table 16.5 Surplus Man Hours—Repairmen

	Regular Time			Overtime		
Month (1)	Available[a] (2)	Sched. (3)	Transfer to Proc. (4)	Available[a] (5)	Sched. (6)	Transfer to Proc. (7)
Jan.	698	698	0	210	117	93
Feb.	665	642	23	200	0	200
Mar.	732	301	431	220	0	220
Apr.	732	263	469	220	0	220
May	732	464	268	220	0	220
June	698	551	147	210	0	210
Totals	4257	2919	1338	1280	117	1163

[a] From columns 6 and 7 of Table 16.1, respectively.

16.4 *Scheduling Manpower Requirements for the Assembly of Stabilization Processors*

For the scheduling of Processors a decision procedure similar to the scheduling of repairman time was utilized. Once again, forecasted manpower requirements were modified by adding two times the standard deviation of the past 5 years demand, as shown in Table 16.6.

Table 16.6 Modifications Resulting from Adding Safety Stock—Processors

Month	Starting Inventory	Closing Inventory (Safety Stock)	Increase Demand	Inventory Available
Jan.	40[a]	43	3	
Feb.	43	32		11
Mar.	32	73	41	
Apr.	73	178	105	
May	178	61		117
June	61	21		40

[a] Leftover at the end of 1976.

The worksheet in Table 16.7 summarizes the calculations using the modified Land algorithm to schedule Processor assembly. Note that surplus repairman time has been transferred from Table 16.5, with transferred regular time identified by a second source code digit of 1 and overtime by a second source code digit of 2. Regular time and overtime are coded 3 and 4 respectively. The first digit in the source code once again identifies the month.

In Table 16.7 the cost of assembler time was costed at $4.00 per regular time man-hour. Assemblers received no guarantees as to the minimum number of hours of work per week. The regular time in Figure 16.8 available for assemblers has been adjusted to reflect time necessary for Midamatic assembly, as per Table 16.1. The total scheduled man-hours of work for assemblers in each month was allocated in decreasing order of seniority, up to a maximum of 35 hours per week on regular time per assembler. This meant that assemblers with the least seniority could work only part time during some months. A number of housewives, who wished to work only part time, were employed as assemblers by the company.

Table 16.7 Worksheet for Six Month Production Schedule—Processors

Month (1)	Source (2)	Cost (3)	Available at t (4)	Demand at t (5)	Production (6)	Available at t (7)	Remarks (8)
Jan.	1 0	0	0	~~160~~ 163	0	0	Inventory
	1 1	0	0		0	0	R/T Repairmen
	1 2	9	93			0	O/T Repairmen
	1 3	4	1257		163	1000	R/T Assemblers
	1 4	6	377			0	O/T Assemblers
Feb.	2 0	0	11	240	11	0	
	2 1	0	23		23	0	
	2 2	9	200			0	
	2 3	4	397		206	191	
	2 4	6	359			359	
	1 3	6.50	1000			450	
Mar.	3 0	0	0	~~480~~ 521	0	0	
	3 1	0	431		431	0	
	3 2	9	220			0	
	3 3	4	817		90	727	
	3 4	6	395			273	
	2 3	6.50	191			0	
	2 4	8.50	359			0	
	1 3	9	450			0	
Apr.	4 0	0	0	~~960~~ 1065	0	0	
	4 1	0	469		469	0	
	4 2	9	220			0	
	4 3	4	317		317	0	
	4 4	6	395		279	116	
	3 3	6.50	727			727	
	3 4	8.50	273			157	
May	5 0	0	117	1200	117	0	*The inventory control manager chose to use (5, 2) before (3, 3) because it delays production commitment and repairmen are more skilled
	5 1	0	268		268	0	
	5 2	9	220		220	0	
	5 3	4	0		0	0	
	5 4	6	395		395	0	
	4 4	8.50	116		116	0	
	3 3	9	727		84	643	
	2 4	11	157			157	
June	6 0	0	40	400	40	0	
	6 1	0	147		147	0	
	6 2	9	210			210	
	6 3	4	557		213	344	
	6 4	6	377			377	
	3 3	11.50	643			69	
	3 4	13.50	157			0	

It was decided by the Scheduling Committee that, because of space limatations and cash flow considerations, the maximum inventory at the end of any month would be limited to 1000 man-hours of Processors. The cost of carrying one man hour of Processors for one month was estimated at $2.50.

Table 16.8 summarizes the production plan calculated in Table 16.7. In Table 16.9 surplus man-hours of repairman and assembler time that can be transferred to the breaking of bulk chemicals are given. Note that if the plan in Table 16.8 is implemented, then the nine assemblers would be greatly underutilized in January. This was a problem that recurred each year as a result of low demand for Midamatics in January and because MIDAS always tried to reduce their year-end inventories to a minimum to reflect a favorable financial position on their balance sheet.

Table 16.8 Six Month Production Plan—Processors

Month (1)	Starting Inventory (2)	Production (3)	Demand (4)	Closing Inventory (5)	Safety Stock (6)	Anticip. Stock (7)
Jan.	40	163	160	43	43	0
Feb.	43	229	240	32	32	0
Mar.	32	605	480	157	73	84
Apr.	157	1181	960	378	178	200
May	378	883	1200	61	61	0
June	61	360	400	21	21	0

Table 16.9 was derived as follows: The available regular time capacity in column 2 is the same as that given in column 4, Table 16.5 for repairmen and in column 10, Table 16.1 for assemblers. Similarly, the available overtime capacity in column 5 is the same as that given in column 7, Table 16.5 for repairmen and in column 11, Table 16.1 for assemblers. The Processor regular time production schedule in column 3, and the overtime schedule in column 6 in Table 16.9 are from column 6, Table 16.7. For example, in February (all source codes starting with 2) the total processor production consists of 23 repairman-hours and 206 assembler hours on regular time. In April the situation is somewhat more complex. The total demand for April of 1065 (column 5, Table 16.7) was met by working 469 repairman man-hours and 317 assembler man-hours on regular time, supplemented by a further 279 assembler man-hours on overtime. The total of 395 assembler man-hours on overtime reported in column 6, Table 16.9 also includes 116 man-hours of production in April for demand in May (see source (4, 4) under May, column 6, Table 16.7). Finally in Table 16.9, column 4 equals column 2 minus column 3 and column 7 equals column 5 minus column 6.

Table 16.9 Surplus Man Hours Repairmen/Assemblers (After Production Plan For Processors)

Month (1)	Regular Time			Overtime		
	Avail. Capacity (2)	Sched. (3)	Transfer to Bulk (4)	Avail. Capacity (5)	Sched. (6)	Transfer to Bulk (7)
Jan.	0 / 1257	0 / 163	0 / 1094	93 / 377	0 / 0	93 / 377
Feb.	23 / 397	23 / 206	0 / 191	200 / 359	0 / 0	200 / 359
Mar.	431 / 817	431 / 174	0 / 643	200 / 395	0 / 0	220 / 395
Apr.	469 / 317	469 / 317	0 / 0	220 / 395	0 / 395	220 / 0
May	268 / 0	268 / 0	0 / 0	220 / 395	220 / 395	0 / 0
June	147 / 557	147 / 213	0 / 344	210 / 377	0 / 0	210 / 377
Totals	1338 / 3345	1338 / 1073	0 / 2272	1163 / 2298	220 / 790	943 / 1508

16.5 *Scheduling Manpower Requirements for the Breaking of Bulk Chemicals*

The final stage of the new decision system involved the scheduling of surplus assembler and repairman time from Table 16.9, columns 4 and 7, to package processing chemicals which arrived in large bulk containers. The forecasted manpower requirements from Table 2, Case F were first modified by the addition of safety stock as shown in Table 16.10. Once

Table 16.10 Modifications Resulting From Adding Safety Stock—Bulk

Month (1)	Starting Inventory (2)	Closing Inventory Safety Stock (3)	Increase Demand (4)	Inventory Available (5)
Jan.	0	22	22	
Feb.	22	11		11
Mar.	11	10		1
Apr.	10	20	10	
May	20	6		14
June	6	9	3	

again two standard deviations of each month's demand during the past 5 years was added to each month's forecast.

Note from Table 16.9, column 4, that no surplus regular time repairman capacity is left over. The assembly manager decided not to schedule any overtime for the breaking of bulk. As a result, in Table 16.11 only two sources are available to meet demand each month: inventory (source code 0) and regular time assemblers (source code 3). It cost approximately $1.20 per man-hour to carry bulk chemicals in inventory for a month. No maximum inventory limits were imposed on the carrying of bulk. The resulting production plan is given Table 16.12.

16.6 *The Proposed New Master Plan for* 1977

The proposed Master Plan in Table 16.14 represents a potential cost saving of 23.2 percent over the original plan developed by the assembly manager (see Table 16.15 and Table 8 in case F). The saving of 23.2 percent is contingent upon a number of assumptions. It is assumed in Table 16.14 that only 95 percent of each regular time man-hour and each overtime man-hour is available for actual production. The cost savings are overstated in that the cost of training new assemblers who may quit when laid off under the new Master Plan is not included.

As is clear from Table 16.13 the regular time capacity available from the nine assemblers is greatly underutilized in January. Top management considered a number of alternatives. It was decided that all but two of the most senior assemblers should be laid off during January, 1977. This eventually

Table 16.11 Worksheet for Six Month Production Schedule—Bulk

Month	Source	Cost	Available at t	Demand at t	Production	Available at $t+1$	Remarks
Jan.	1 0	0	0	~~45~~ 67	67	0	Inventory
	1 3	4	1094			1027	R/T Assemblers
Feb.	2 0	0	11	136	11	0	
	2 3	4	191		125	66	
	1 3	5.20	1027			1027	
Mar.	3 0	0	1	91	1	0	
	3 3	4	643		90	553	
	2 3	5.20	66			66	
	1 3	6.40	1027			1027	
Apr.	4 0	0	0	~~79~~ 89	0	0	
	4 3	4	0		0	0	
	3 3	5.20	553		89	464	
	2 3	6.40	66			66	
	1 3	7.60	1027			1027	
May	5 0	0	14	102	14	0	
	5 3	4	0		0	0	
	3 3	6.40	464		88	376	
	2 3	7.60	66			66	
	1 3	8.80	1027			1027	
June	6 0	0	0	~~91~~ 94	0	0	
	6 3	4	344		94	250	
	3 3	7.60	376			376	
	2 3	8.80	66			66	
	1 3	10	1027			1027	

Table 16.12 Six Month Production Plan—Bulk

Month (1)	Starting Inventory (2)	Production (3)	Demand (4)	Closing Inventory (5)	Safety Stock (6)	Anticip. Stock (7)
Jan.	0	67	45	22	22	0
Feb.	22	125	136	11	11	0
March	11	267	91	187	10	177
April	187	0	79	108	20	88
May	108	0	102	6	6	0
June	6	94	91	9	9	0

Table 16.13 Surplus of Man Hours of Assemblers (After Breaking of Bulk)

	Regular Time			Overtime		
Month (1)	Available[a] (2)	Sched. (3)	Surplus (4)	Available[a] (5)	Sched. (6)	Surplus (7)
Jan.	1094	67	1027	377	0	377
Feb.	191	125	66	359	0	359
March	643	267	376	395	0	395
April	0	0	0	0	0	0
May	0	0	0	0	0	0
June	344	94	250	377	0	377
Totals	2272	553	1719	1508	0	1508

[a] From Col. 4, and Col. 7 in Table 16-9, respectively.

Table 16.14 Total Cost of Revised Six Month Master Plan for 1977 (Using New Decision System)—see page 644 for detailed explanation of this table.

Month	Repairmen			Assemblers			Inventory (Man hours)			Cost			
	R/T Hrs.	O/T Hrs.	No.	R/T Hrs.	O/T Hrs.	No.	Rep.	Proc.	Bulk	R/T	O/T	Invent.	Total
(1)	(2)	(3)	(4)	(5)	(6)	(7)	(8)	(9)	(10)	(11)	(12)	(13)	(14)
Jan.	737	123	5	295[a]	0	2.00[a]	15	43	22	5,598	1,107	149	6,854
Feb.	700	0	5	1,191	0	8.51	57	32	11	8,964	0	150	9,114
Mar.	768	0	5	991	0	6.45	26	157	187	8,572	0	643	9,215
April	768	0	5	1,386	416	9.00	25	378	108	10,152	2,496	1,100	13,748
May	768	232	5	1,386	416	9.00	42	61	6	10,152	4,584	202	14,938
June	737	0	5	1,060	0	7.19	93	21	9	8,662	0	156	8,818
Totals	4,478	355		6,309	832		258	692	343	52,100	8,187	2,400	62,587

[a] The assembly manager insisted on having a minimum of two assemblers available fulltime during January.

Table 16.15 Total Cost of Six Month Master Plan (Using Existing Decision Procedures as Described in the MIDAS (F) Case)—see page 645 for detailed explanation of this table.

Month	Repairmen			Assemblers			Inventory[a] (Man hours)			Costs			
	R/T Hrs.	O/T Hrs.	No.	R/T Hrs.	O/T Hrs.	No.	Rep.	Proc.	Bulk	R/T	O/T	Invent.	Total
(1)	(2)	(3)	(4)	(5)	(6)	(7)	(8)	(9)	(10)	(11)	(12)	(13)	(14)
Jan.	884	0	6	1,621	0	11	489	164	245	11,788	0	1,193	12,981
Feb.	840	0	6	1,540	0	11	244	528	98	11,200	0	1,682	12,882
Mar.	922	0	6	1,691	0	11	98	1,116	269	12,296	0	3,211	15,507
Apr.	922	0	6	1,691	0	11	98	896	196	12,296	0	2,573	14,869
May	922	0	6	1,691	0	11	0	164	98	12,296	0	528	12,824
June	884	0	6	1,621	0	11	0	332	0	11,788	0	830	12,618
Totals	5,374	0		9,855	0		929	3,200	906	71,664	0	10,017	81,681

[a] See Table 9, Case F.

resulted in two assemblers seeking alternative employment. Subsequently it took about a week to train each of the new assemblers and about another 3 weeks before the new assemblers became proficient. It was also decided that in the future special sales promotions will be held to encourage Midamatic installations in January. The Scheduling Committee also decided to explore in earnest the cost of building Midamatic subassemblies so as to smooth out the Midamatic production schedule over the calendar year.

The new decision system described in this chapter was adopted at MIDAS. A new Master Plan, using a six month decision horizon was subsequently calculated monthly. Over time parts of the new decision system were changed. The number of columns and the headings of the various tables were modified by the assembly manager to suit his own style. The Scheduling Committee found the new decision system particularly useful in their deliberations.

Explanation of Table 16.14

In Table 16.14 calculations for January were derived as follows:

Column 2: 5 repairmen × 140 Hrs./mo. × 1/0.95 = 736.8 Hrs. (See col. 3, Table 16.1)

Column 3: (210 − 93) Hrs. used × 1/0.95 = 123.2 Hrs.
(210: Total capacity, col. 7, Table 16.1; 93: Surplus, col. 5, Table 16.9)

Column 4: 5 repairmen were guaranteed full regular time employment.

Column 5: 2 assemblers × 140 Hrs./mo. × 1/0.95 = 294.7 Hrs.
[For February: (1197 − 66) Hrs. used × 1/0.95 = 1190.5 Hrs.]
(1197: Total capacity, col. 8, Table 16.1; 66: Surplus, col. 4, Table 16.13)

Column 6: (377 − 377) Hrs. used × 1/0.95 = 0 Hrs.
(first 377: Total capacity, col. 11, Table 16.1; second 377: Surplus, col. 7, Table 16.13)

Column 7: Set by managerial intervention. (It could be argued that this is a sunk fixed cost.) (For February: 1191 × 0.95 Hrs. used/133 Hrs./mo. = 8.95 men)

Column 8: See column 5, Table 16.4

Column 9: See column 5, Table 16.8

Column 10: See column 5, Table 16.12

Column 11: (737 Hrs. × \$6 + 295 Hrs. × \$4) = \$5,598.00

Column 12: (123 Hrs. × \$9 + 0 Hrs. × \$6) = \$1,107.00

Column 13: (15 units × \$1 + 43 units × \$2.50 + 22 units × \$1.20) = \$148.90

Column 14: Total = Col. 11 + Col. 12 + Col. 13

In a similar way all the costs for the other months were also computed.

Explanation of Table 16.15

In Table 16.15 the calculations for January were derived as follows:

Columns 2 and 4: It was decided after some discussion that of the 17 employees, at least 6 should be classified as repairmen. MIDAS did not previously stick to strict job classifications. Note that theoretically 6 repairmen cannot handle on regular time the repairs scheduled in Figure 8, column 6 under January. (i.e. (0.053 × 24,453 Hrs.)/140 Hrs./man/mo. = 9.26 repairmen). Nevertheless, since only 6 workers received \$6.00 per hour we calculated regular time repairmen hours to be:

(6 × 140 Hrs.)/0.95 = 884 Hrs.

Columns 5 and 7: Since 6 workers were classified as repairmen above, the remainder were assumed to be assemblers:

(11 × 140 Hrs.)/0.95 = 1,621 Hrs.

Column 8: See Table 9, Case F, row 4.

Column 9: See Table 9, Case F, row 2. 41 units × 4 Hrs./unit = 164 Hrs.

Column 10: See Table 9, Case F, row 5. 7,336 lbs. or gals. × 2 min./lbs. or gal. = 244.5 Hrs.

Column 11: 884 Hrs. × \$6 + 1621 Hrs. × \$4 = \$11,788.00

Column 13: 489 Hrs. × \$1 + 164 Hrs. × \$2.50 + 245 Hrs. × \$1.20 = \$1,193.00

Column 14: Total = Col. 11 + Col. 12 + Col. 13.

16.7 *Some Observations*

Recurrently we have discussed in this book the merits of implementability versus mathematical optimality. In the introduction to this part of the book we advocated "direct extensions of existing managerial decision procedures." The manual decision system presented in this chapter illustrates in detail these basic tenets. The MIDAS decision system is not, mathematically speaking, new. Components of the system have been known to us for some time. The power of this particular decision system derives from the many explicit tradeoffs that were made in an organized, easy-to-understand, even modularly-optimal, way that did not get in the way of management's perception of *their* problems.

A number of technical issues remain. In what order should the various labor skill classes be scheduled? Suppose repairmen were also considered to be a variable cost, how should one allocate the available capacity from the two classes of labor? In what order should products be scheduled for production? Should the products, for example, be scheduled in order of increasing cost per man-hour utilized? How could these and similar refinements be introduced into the new MIDAS decision system successfully?

The authors believe that much research, which flows directly from needs identified by similar implementations in the field, as illustrated in this chapter, needs to be done. A recasting of more aggregate scheduling research into this context holds a great potential. Researchers who are interested in pursuing this tack are referred to an article by Rand[6] and to the original papers by Land,[4] and Beale and Morton.[1]

PROBLEMS FOR CHAPTER 16

Problem 16.1

Compare and contrast the manual-heuristic planning procedure in the MIDAS(F) case to that discussed in Chapter 16. What are the major deficiencies of the existing planning method? Are these adequately dealt with by the method described in Chapter 16? What remains to be improved upon? Comment on the observations in section 16.7.

Problem 16.2

The existing aggregate planning procedure at MIDAS-Canada was designed and implemented by a consulting firm in 1971 for $17,000. Do you think the company got its money's worth? Comment.

Problem 16.3

Do you think that the Master Plan prepared in Chapter 16 is realistic in proposing a reduction in total manpower from 17 to 14? Discuss.

Problem 16.4

How would you modify the decision system described in Chapter 16 to allow for the production of a limited number of subassemblies of MIDAMATICS and/or PROCESSORS? How would you go about deciding which subassemblies should be produced?

Problem 16.5

In Table 16.7 under remarks (column 8) the Inventory Control Manager opted to use source (5, 2) ahead of source (3, 3). Do you agree with his logic? Discuss.

Problem 16.6

An improvement of 23.2 percent in total cost over the previous 1977 Master Plan is claimed for the new decision system in Chapter 16. Do you agree with the methodology used for making the cost comparisons? How much of an improvement do you think will really occur?

Problem 16.7

Suppose it was decided by the Scheduling Committee that the existing safety stocks on bulk chemicals should be tripled. Recalculate Tables 16.10 to 16.14 to reflect the effect of this change in policy. How much extra would this new policy cost?

Problem 16.8

If top management wanted to maintain a constant workforce, how many persons (and with which skills) would you recommend be hired? How much would such a policy cost? Explain how you arrived at your recommendation.

Problem 16.9

Under the proposed 1977 Master Plan, layoffs are predicted for January. Suppose top management insisted that at least 6 assemblers and 5 repairmen be carried through January. How would you utilize these workers and by how much would the total cost change?

Problem 16.10

The vice-president of marketing at MIDAS pointed out that films and chemicals deteriorate over time. He felt that because of production smoothing inventories some bulk would be carried in stock too long under the proposed plan in Chapter 16. Do you agree? What would be the effect on total cost of a policy limiting the carrying of bulk inventories to a maximum of 1 month?

Problem 16.11

The Inventory Control Manager had recently attended a lecture on learning curves (i.e., the productivity of workers increases the longer they work at a task on regular time). How would you modify the decision system described in Chapter 16 to introduce such a concept?

Problem 16.12

The Galt Gadget Company is a manufacturer of automotive parts. For a particular line of products the demand in the next 6 periods (each of 2 months duration) is estimated to be

Period, j	1	2	3	4	5	6
Demand, $D(j)$ (in shifts of output)	30	60	60	60	160	50

The company does not permit deliberate backlogging. However, the requirements shown for a period can be satisfied (if necessary) by production in that period. With a prespecified manpower schedule the production available is as follows:

Period	Type of Production	Cost (hundreds of dollars) per shift of output	Capacity (shifts)
1	Regular	8	46
2	Regular	8	44
	2nd shift	11	22
3	Regular	8	44
	2nd shift	11	44
4	Regular	8	43
	2nd shift	11	43
5	Regular	8	43
	2nd shift	11	43
	3rd shift	17	20
6	Regular	8	42
	2nd shift	11	42

The initial inventory (at the beginning of period 1) is 20 shifts of output. An inventory carrying charge of $200 per shift of output is incurred when material is carried forward from one period to the next (no charge is incurred during a period). Warehouse limitations restrict the inventory at the end of any period to be no larger than 70 shifts of output.

a. Using Land's procedure determine the production plan for Galt Gadget that minimizes the total of production and carrying costs over the 6 month period if an ending inventory of 15 shifts of output is desired. In particular show the actual production by period-shift and the ending inventory of each period.

b. From your solution can you infer the value (in terms of reduced costs) of increasing the warehouse capacity to 72 shifts of output? 75 shifts of output?

REFERENCES FOR CHAPTER 16

1. Beale, E. M. L. and Morton, G. "Solutions of a purchase-Storage Programme: Part I" *Operational Research Quarterly*, Vol. 9, No. 3, 1958.

2. Griffiths, B. "A Production Planning and Stock Control Problem in the Textile Industry." *Operational Research Quarterly*, Vol. 12, 1961.

3. Hurst, E. G. and McNamara, B. A. "Heuristic Scheduling in a Woolen Mill." *Management Science*, Vol. 19, No. 4, December, 1972.

4. Land, A. H. "Solution of A Purchase-Storage Programme: Part II." *Operational Research Quarterly*, Vol. 9, No. 3, 1958.

5. Pengilly, P. "Production Planning in the Seventies." *International Journal of Production Research*, Vol. 9, No. 1, 1971.

6. Rand, Graham K. "A Manual Production Scheduling Algorithm." *O. R. Quarterly*, Volume 25, No. 4, December, 1974.

7. Spurrell, D. J. "A Simple Method of Production Planning in Multi-Item Situations." *Operational Research Quarterly*, Vol. 9, No. 3, 1958.

CHAPTER SEVENTEEN

Mathematical Models for Aggregate Production Planning

In the previous two chapters we examined the aggregate production planning problem in detail and also considered a simple optimization technique (the Land transportation model). Models presented in this chapter allow the optimization of a greater number of decision variables. In particular, all optimization models considered will allow the inclusion of the size of workforce as a decision variable through the introduction of hiring and firing costs directly into the cost tradeoffs. This was not possible with the simpler Land decision procedures considered in Chapters 15 and 16.

We shall present only the three mathematical approaches to aggregate scheduling which we believe to be the most practical. The first set of models which we shall discuss, assume a linear objective function, and are in fact more complex formulations of the simple linear programming model which we have already examined in the Transportation problem format. In addition we shall discuss decision models which allow non-linear objective functions (Search Decision Rules) and which do not explicitly assume any specific form for the objective function (Management Coefficients).

17.1 *Linear Programming Models and the Aggregate Production Planning Problem*

Linear programming (LP) models can be tailored to suit the particular cost and decision structure faced by most any company. This accounts in part for the relatively large number of formulations in existence. Many complex mathematical programming models, including both linear and integer (fixed) cost components, have been proposed. For example see those by Hanssmann and Hess,[15] E. E. Bomberger,[2] and C. H. Von Lanzenauer.[32]

Because of the large variety of possible formulations, we shall start by listing the common assumptions made by most formulations and then present a relatively simple specific model, one which is similar to those that have been implemented in practice.

Most practicable linear programs are structured as follows:

a. Demand is taken as deterministic and known

0_t in period t $\quad (t=1,2,\ldots,T)$

b. The costs of regular time production in period t are usually described by piecewise linear or convex functions as shown in Figure 17.1 (convex merely means that the slopes of the linear segments become larger and larger, i.e., the marginal cost is increasing).

c. The cost of changes in the production rate is usually taken to be piecewise linear as shown in Figure 17.2. Note that the cost function need not be symmetrical about the vertical axis. An alternate approach in some linear programming formulations is not to assign costs for changes in production rates at all, but rather to limit the size of the change or, alternatively, to simply put upper and lower bounds on the allowable production rates in any particular period.

Figure 17.1 The Cost of Regular Time Production in General Linear Programming Models.

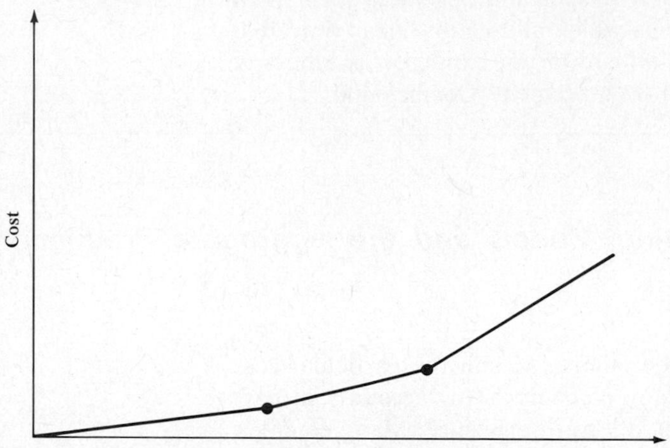

d. Upper and lower bounds on production rates are usually specified. A similar statement holds for the inventory levels.

e. The inventory carrying cost can be different for each period.

f. It is usually assumed that there is a single production facility serving a given market.

g. In most formulations, backorders or lost sales are not permitted.

Figure 17.2 Costs of Changes in the Production Rate in General Linear Programming Models

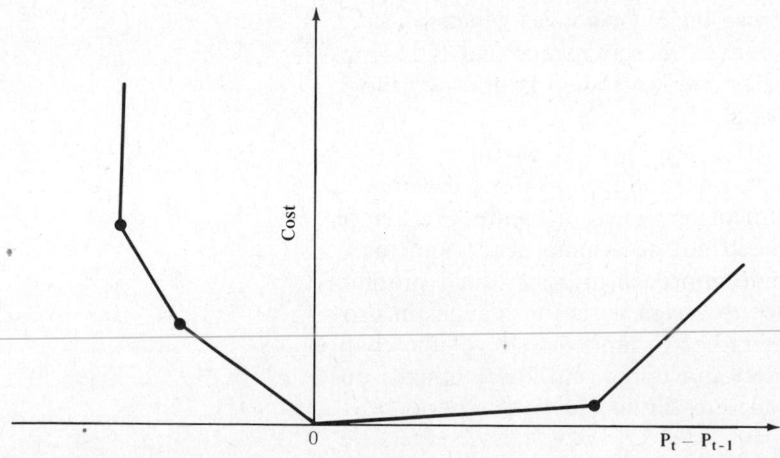

One of the most important characteristics of linear programming models is that many constraints can be directly incorporated in the problem formulation. Also many product categories can be included in the formulation rather than having to define a single, overall surrogate measure of production.

These characteristics are illustrated in the following LP model:

Minimize:

$$C_{\mathrm{TOT}} = \sum_{t=1}^{T} \sum_{i=1}^{n} [c_{i1} I_{it} + c_{i2} W_{it} + c_{i3} W'_{it} + c_{i4} H_{it} + c_{i5} F_{it}]$$

Subject to:

$$\left.\begin{aligned} I_{it} &= I_{i,t-1} + W_{it} + W'_{it} - O_{it} \\ W_{it} &= W_{i,t-1} + H_{it} - F_{it} \end{aligned}\right\} \begin{aligned} i &= 1, \ldots, n \\ t &= 1, \ldots, T \end{aligned} \qquad (17.1)$$

$$W'_{it} \leq a_{it} W_{it}$$

and

$$I_{it}, W_{it}, W'_{it}, H_{it}, F_{it}, O_{it} \geq 0 \quad \text{for all} \quad i, t.$$

where:

n is the number of product groups.

T is the length of the decision horizon.

I_{it} is the inventory of product group i at end of t.

W_{it} is the work force level (expressed as a regular time production rate) of product group i at the end of t.

W'_{it} is the amount of overtime of product group i during t.

a_{it} is the percent maximum overtime allowed for group i in t.

H_{it} is the amount of hires for product group i in t.

F_{it} is the amount of fired W_{it} for product group i in t.

O_{it} is the forecasted requirements (orders) for group i in t.

c's are unit cost coefficients.

While this may look complicated, the basic ideas expressed in the Total Cost objective functions are quite simple. Total Cost is the sum of the costs of carrying inventory, regular work force, overtime, hiring and firing for each product group i during each period t. These decision variables are constrained by three equations. The inventory at the end of t (I_{it}) is equal to the inventory in the previous period, plus the amount of product produced on regular time (W_{it}), plus the amount of product produced on overtime (W'_{it}) less the amount of product shipped to meet requirements (O_{it}). The second constraint specifies that the regular time work force in this period must be equal to that in the previous period plus the amount hired less the amount fired. (H_{it} and F_{it} will never both be greater than zero at the same time.) The third constraint sets available overtime in any period equal to or less than a_{it} percent of the regular time work force capacity. The last line of Eq. 17.1 states that all decision variables must be positive or zero.

Note the similarity of the objective function in Eq. 17.1 to the way we evaluated costs in the graphical-tabular method in Chapter 15. But compared to the graphical-tabular methods the LP model in Eq. 17.1 yields an optimal rather than near-optimal solution. It also determines the size of the workforce $W_{i,t}$ directly by including changeover costs in the objective function rather than requiring a manager to specify it exogenously as was the case in the models we considered in Chapters 15 and 16.

In Eq. 17.1 no constraints are placed on the maximum or minimum levels of inventory, workforce or production, nor are back orders allowed. Note that such limits could be introduced without difficulty by defining additional constraint equations. However, each additional constraint specified, as well as each additional product group chosen for individual attention, increases the computational effort required.

The criteria for selecting products to be aggregated into a product group should be evident from the structure specified in Eq. 17.1. Members of the same product family should share similar seasonal patterns (O_{it}), production costs (C_{i2}, C_{i3}) carrying costs (C_{i1}) and hiring/firing costs (C_{i4}, C_{i5}). Obviously, to reduce the number of equations needed, some severe compromises have to be made in defining product families. Lower bounds on inventory levels, when introduced into the linear programming formulation, provide safety stocks to meet the uncertainty present in all demand forecasts. For a discussion and example of how this can be done see Section 16.3 in the previous chapter. One key difficulty with Eq. 17.1 is the fact that it does not allow the transfer of workforce from one product group to another. This can in practice lead to unreasonable solutions. Recall that the heuristic procedure in Chapter 16 allowed for the transfer of work force exogenously.

17.1.1 *Strengths and Weaknesses*

One of the basic weaknesses of linear programming approaches (and most other aggregate planning techniques) is the assumption of deterministic demand. In most applications there is considerable uncertainty in the forecasts of demand. However, tests have been done by Dzielinski et al[7] using a deterministic model under stochastic conditions which indicated that under many situations the deterministic model can perform favorably, particularly when one recognizes that the solution is adapted as new forecast information becomes available.

Another shortcoming of linear programming models is the requirement of linear cost functions. However, the possibility of piecewise linearity improves the validity (at a cost of additional computational effort). Experiments conducted by Kolenda[21] suggest that linearity may be a reasonable assumption for most practical situations.

An important benefit of a linear programming model is the potential use of the dual solution to obtain the implicit costs of constraints such as on maximum allowable inventory levels. Also parametric methods allow a simple determination of the production plan for conditions somewhat different from those for which the primary solution is obtained. This last property is useful for two purposes; first, for sensitivity analysis on the estimated cost parameters; secondly, as a means of measuring the effects of one or more of the uncertain conditions changing slightly.

17.1.2 *The Inclusion of Integer Variables in Linear Programming Formulation*

One or more integer variables are required to include a setup cost and/or a concave cost in a LP model. The reason for the integer variable in the case of the setup cost is because of the discontinuity in the cost function. When production is zero, the cost is zero; however, a very small production quantity incurs the entire setup cost.

The need for the integer variable in the case of the concave function is not as obvious. To illustrate the need let us consider a simple example:

Consider a product whose concave production costs are as follows:

Rate Range (Pieces/period)	Cost per additional piece produced
0–10	2
11 and higher	1

The basic linear programming model would select production units only from the 11 and higher range because they are less expensive than those in the 0 to 10 range. Of course, this is physically impossible. An integer variable is needed to force the use of all of the 0 to 10 range before any production can be taken from the next higher range. The integer variable takes on only the value 0 or 1. The 11 and higher range can only be used when the integer variable is 1. The logic is arranged such that it is 1 only when the entire 0 to 10 range is used.

The presence of integer variables drastically increases the computational time. While thousands of continuous decision variables can be handled in a regular linear program, only problems with considerably less integer variables can be solved in a reasonable length of time with existing solution algorithms.

17.2 *Simulation Search Procedures*

In 1966 Vergin[31] observed that in many cases the current state of the art does not allow the analytical solution of a mathematical decision model that is representative of the situation faced in practice by a manager. Therefore, he argued, it is better to model the actual cost functions very accurately in mathematical or tabular form so that functions more complex than those allowed in such approaches as linear programming could be solved. For an horizon of T months, in general terms, in the case of the aggregate scheduling decision:

$$C_{\text{TOT}} = f(W_1, P_1, W_2, P_2, \ldots, W_T, P_T) \tag{17.2}$$

As in any simulation, the approach is to systematically vary the variables (e.g., the work force sizes and production rates) until a reasonable (and hopefully near optimal) solution is obtained. Normally a computer is required to make the approach feasible, even under the assumption of no uncertainty in the forecasts of demand.

Vergin and many other researchers have found that simulation search procedures perform extremely well. When the true cost structure closely resembles that assumed by one of the optimizing procedures (e.g., linear programming) the search procedures do essentially as well as the true optimizing procedure. When the true costs structure differs from that assumed by the optimizing procedure, the simulation search approach generally outperforms the LP optimizing procedure.

The solution time required for simulation increases rapidly with the number of variables being *optimized* by trial and error (search) methods. A potential tool for a drastic reduction in the number of iterations required is the branch-and-bound technique. In essence, branch-and-bound allows us to eliminate many potential solutions without having to test each of them. A future combination of branch-and-bound with simulation search should allow us to obtain good solutions to even more realistic (that is, even more complicated) models.*

* *For a discussion of Branch and Bound techniques see Harvey M. Wagner,* Principles of Operations Research. *Prentice-Hall,* 1975, *pp. 484–493.*

17.2.1 *Search Decision Rules*

In 1968, Taubert[30] extended the computer simulation methodology to its ultimate generality by developing techniques called Search Decision Rules (SDR). He defined C_{TOT} as a function of $(W_t, P_t, W_{t-1}, I_{t-1}, O_t; t = 1, 2, \ldots, 12)$ and then identified the values within C_{TOT} by the following vectors:

$$\{D\} = \{\text{Decision Vector} = P_t, W_t; t = 1, 2, \ldots, 12\}$$

$$\{S\} = \{\text{Stage Vector} = W_{t-1}, I_{t-1}; t = 1, 2, \ldots, 12\} \tag{17.3}$$

$$\{P\} = \{\text{Parameter Vector} = \text{Cost coefficients at time } t \text{ and } O_t;\ t = 1, 2, \ldots, 12\}$$

His Decision Vector contains 24 or $(2T)$ independent decision variables, the desired output of SDR methodology. The Stage Vector transmits information about the *state* of the system from time $t-1$ to t. The Parameter Vector contains the forecasts and the cost coefficients that could be different from stage to stage. In many previous aggregate scheduling formulations the cost structure as well as the form of the cost equations from stage to stage were *homogenous.* The SDR methodology makes it possible to construct decision systems that are *heterogeneous* in that changes in cost and model structure overtime are easily handled, an important fact of life in practical aggregate planning problems. A heterogenous decision system capability is important because in most firms' reorganizations, the installation of new machinery, changing composition of work force, pay scales, competitive conditions, etc., occur continually and must be allowed for over the time horizon modelled.

SDR searches directly for Decision Vectors that reduce C_{TOT}. Computer search routines attempt to optimize all stages simultaneously generating 24 trial decisions per iteration. The search procedure terminates when successive iterations result in small reductions in C_{TOT}.

The generation of alternative $\{D\}$ for testing the objective function C_{TOT} is a science in itself. The generation technique chosen determines the total time to arrive at a near-optimal C_{TOT}, or whether a near-optimal C_{TOT} is arrived at, at all. We refer the reader to the references at the end of the paper by Taubert[29] for a complete discussion of computer search techniques.

Taubert, using SDR, was able to achieve results that were very close to those achieved by other mathematically optimal methods. His results have been replicated by a number of other researchers.[23] In their book, Buffa and Taubert[4] summarize the advantages and disadvantages of SDR methodology as follows:

SDR advantages

1. Permits realistic modelling free from many restrictive assumptions, such as closed form mathematical expressions, linear/quadratic cost functions, etc.

2. Permits a variation in mathematical structure from stage to stage (heterogeneous stages) so that anticipated system changes such as the introduction of new products or production equipment, reorganizations, wage increases, etc., can be considered.

3. Provides the operating manager with a set of current and projected decisions.

4. Permits optimized disaggregate decision making.

5. Lends itself to evolutionary cost model development and provides solutions at desired points in the iterative process.

6. Facilitates sensitivity analysis and provides sensitivity data while the search routine is converging on a solution.

7. Easily handles cash flow discounting, nonlinear utility functions, multiple objective functions and complex constraints.

8. Offers the potential of solving many otherwise impossible operations planning problems.

9. The methodology is general and can be applied to single or multi-stage decision problems which are not related to aggregate planning. For example, determining the optimal capital structure of a firm given a forecast of interest rates, stock performance etc., or determining a least cost allocation of manpower to activities defined by a critical path network.

SDR disadvantages

1. Optimization using computer search routines is an art and it is currently impossible to state, a priori, which search routine will give the best performance on a particular objective function.

2. Decisions made by this methodology may not, and in general, will not, represent the absolute global optimum.

3. Response surface dimensionality appears to be a limiting factor.

17.3 Management Coefficients Models

In the previous two sections we examined models which attempted to capture the important tradeoffs required by an aggregate scheduling decision through *explicit* specification of relatively complex mathematical formulations. These modeling strategies confront the analyst-manager with other difficulties that result from his limited ability to measure the more esoteric costs required and the difficulties that result from having to derive solutions to more complex mathematical formulations.

As an alternative, a different philosophy of modeling based on *implicit* cost measurement has evolved. In 1963 Bowman[3] suggested that based on his extensive consulting experiences:

> *Managerial decisions might be improved more by making them more consistent from one time to another than by approaches purporting to give "optimal solutions" to explicit models ... especially for problems where intangibles (run-out costs, delay penalties) must otherwise be estimated or assumed.*

Bowman justified this philosophy by observing that experienced managers are generally quite aware of the criteria and cost factors that influence decisions they must make. Over many repetitive decisions their decision behavior is unbiased, that is, on the average, they make the correct response to the decision environment they face. However, their behavior is probably more erratic than it should be. Spurious influences such as emergency phone calls from superiors, suppliers, and customers can produce deviations from normal (average) behavior when not warranted. Therefore, Bowman argued, why not adopt an approach to modeling that tries to keep a manager closer to his average decision behavior by dampening out most of these erratic reactions. Bowman named his methodology/philosophy the Management Coefficients Model. Kunreuther[22] and Gordon,[13] among others, have reported applications of this approach.

The Management Coefficients approach utilizes standard multiple regression methodology to fit decision rules to historical data on actual managerial decision behavior. By fitting a regression line the analyst attempts to capture the average historical relationship between cues in the environment and management's responses. Erratic behavior (the residuals) is "dampened" by minimizing least squares.

The first step is to select a form of relationship between the decision variable(s) and the historical data on environmental variables. For example, in the production smoothing and work force balancing situation, Bowman chose:

$$P_t = aP_{t-1} + b_1 O_t + b_2 O_{t+1} + c \tag{17.4}$$

That is, the production rate (P_t) in period t is assumed to be *linearly* related to the production rate in the previous period (P_{t-1}) and the estimated orders in periods $t(O_t)$ and $t+1(O_{t+1})$. There should of course be no other reason, except the logic of the relationships involved, to limit such regressions (in general) to linear forms.

Having fit a management coefficients regression equation the analyst can now describe to management how they would have normally (on the average) reacted in the past to any forecasted pattern of future orders, given existing on-hand inventories and prevailing production rates. Presumably this would cause the decision maker to more carefully consider and justify any contemplated deviation from a conventional response to cues in the environment based on his actions in the past.

17.3.1 *Strengths and Weaknesses*

Tests with actual company data have shown that costs can be significantly reduced through the use of the management coefficients approach.* A serious drawback of the procedure is the essentially subjective selection of the form of the rule. It very easily can be selected incorrectly. Implicit in Bowman's approach is the assumption that past decisions are a good basis for future actions. A historical orientation could prevent a manager from quickly adapting to new conditions in a rapidly changing competitive environment.

Kunreuther[22] has proposed general criteria which must be satisfied if a Management Coefficients approach is to have validity in an actual application. The criteria are similar to conditions that must hold for any least squares regression model. Kunreuther makes two recommendations. When a manager has limited information regarding future sales, as when he develops his initial production estimate, then a plan based on average (past) decision behavior is very useful. However, when environmental cues provide reliable information on future sales of specific items (as when subsequent revisions are made in the Master Plan) then actual decisions are

---

* *Strictly speaking one cannot really compare actual company decision behavior with a management coefficients model, or with any of the other explicit models discussed in this chapter. The objective function which management may have tried to minimize with their past decisions may have been far different from any of the ones we have formulated mathematically.*

clearly superior to those suggested by an averaging rule. In such cases, variance in managerial action is beneficial rather than costly to a firm and should not be averaged out.

17.4 *Some Comments on Mathematical Aggregate Production Planning Techniques*

In this chapter we have limited ourselves to three mathematical approaches to the production smoothing and work force balancing problem. Some of the reasons for doing this will now be discussed. Although mathematical development work has been in progress since the early 1950s, until recently, only linear programming has had significant applications in practice. An increasing number of applications of Management Coefficient Models and SDR are being reported by practitioners. The problem of mathematically modeling realistic situations in this area appears to have been solved theoretically. What remains to be done is the training of a new generation of practitioners, management scientists and production planners who can apply these techniques naturally as an integral part of aggregate planning.

Lee and Khumawala[23] in their research concluded that the SDR provides a more efficient and effective approach to the aggregate planning problem than similar techniques like Parametric Production Planning (PPP).[20] SDR is in effect an extension of PPP because it applies a search routine directly to the objective function and thus bypasses the use of a priori postulated decision rules, as in PPP. (For this reason we have not discussed PPP in this chapter.) Lee reports that PPP models take almost as long to develop as SDR:

> *I can visualize some unique situations where I would rather use PPP than LDR or SDR. Specifically, if the objective function is so complex that an efficient search is not feasible on a frequent basis, then it may be desirable to perform the search infrequently and to use the PPP decision rules for decision-making purposes.**

The Management Coefficients Model (MCM) is the simplest and easiest of the three to implement. In a firm where Lee was very familiar with the accounting system and mode of operation it was a matter of a few man-days before an operational model was complete:

> *One needs only to speculate with management about the relevant factors considered in the aggregate planning decisions, to collect the historical data on*

* *Private correspondence, September and August, 1974.*

> *these factors, to hypothesize a set of possible decision rules and to run a series of regression analyses to test the hypotheses. I have since done this with two other firms and have had similar results . . . two of my MBA students did an MCM analysis as a term project. I doubt that they had to spend a great deal more time at it than I!*

Commenting on another commonly discussed technique, Linear Decision Rules,* Lee reported that LDR are much more difficult to implement, requiring between 1 to 3 man-months for model development. The LDR approach contains some complex concepts that are not included in a standard accounting system. In particular, restricted mathematical forms must be "shoe-horned" to fit observed cost structures. "In my one experience with implementing the LDR," reports Lee, "I found that a managerial consensus based on subjective feelings was all I could hope for. I did not find that it required heavy OR-type skill. Rather, the most important type of expertise required seemed to be the ability to translate managerial feelings into a quadratic cost function."

SDR can also be developed, in 3 to 6 man-months. But one is not restricted to selected mathematical forms. Developing the SDR requires considerable knowledge about how a firm operates and skill in building simulation models. Lee believes that the future of aggregate planning models lies with simulation techniques. "It's the old 'what if' game that management likes to play. I get a lot of mileage out of the MCM in discussion with managers, while I spend time developing a more sophisticated simulation model for the SDR approach."

We find these comments by Lee and Khumawala in agreement with our own experience. In most companies, the authors surmise, the *most* important aggregate scheduling decision involves the selection of a management decision making style which includes either no modeling, or simple models such as discussed in Chapters 15 and 16, or more complex models as in Chapter 17, or large comprehensive multi-stage decision systems such as will be discussed in Chapter 18. Once this major policy decision is made the choice between LDR, SDR, LP, PPP, etc., is, by comparison, easy and at least to a degree, a matter of personal taste.

---

* *We have not discussed LDR because we believe it is primarily of theoretical interest. LDR is presented, for example, in the following articles, C. Holt et al.*[17] *and Bergstrom and Smith.*[1]

Problems for Chapter 17

Problem 17.1

A version of the linear programming model of the aggregate scheduling problem that has been used in practice is:

Minimize:

$$C_{\text{TOT}} = \sum_{i=1}^{N} \sum_{t=1}^{T} (v_{it} X_{it} + r_{it} I_{it}) + \sum_{t=1}^{T} (c_w W_t + c_O W'_t)$$

Subject to:

$$X_{it} + I_{i,t-1} - I_{it} = O_{it} \quad \begin{cases} t = 1, \ldots, T \\ i = 1, \ldots, N \end{cases}$$

$$\sum_{i=1}^{N} k_i X_{it} - W_t - W'_t = 0 \quad t = 1, \ldots, T$$

$$0 \le W_t \le W_{t,\max} \quad t = 1, \ldots, T$$

$$0 \le W'_t \le W'_{t,\max} \quad t = 1, \ldots, T$$

$$X_{it}, I_{it} \ge 0 \quad \begin{cases} i = 1, \ldots, N \\ t = 1, \ldots, T \end{cases}$$

a. Define all symbols, giving the units of all variables as well as the point in time when they must be measured.

b. Which data must be collected or estimated?

c. Which variables must be assigned values and which variables are decision variables whose values will be assigned by a LP algorithm?

d. Under which practical circumstances is this LP model appropriate? How does it compare to the model discussed in Chapter 16? Discuss.

Problem 17.2

For the historical data given below, fit by linear regression suitable management coefficients' equations similar to those in Eq. 17.4. Explain your reasons for selecting the number of variables in your model. Is it a good enough fit that you would recommend it for future decisions? Discuss.

Period, t	O_t	S_t	W_t
1	—	—	84
2	445	445	79
3	438	426	75
4	321	356	72
5	396	388	69
6	376	373	68
7	292	331	67
8	455	416	67
9	400	386	67
10	355	363	69
11	289	338	71
12	430	427	74
13	395	475	77
14	513	496	81
15	505	503	85

Period, t	P_t	I_t
1	515	302
2	447	303
3	418	295
4	390	329
5	380	321
6	371	319
7	365	353
8	377	314
9	376	308
10	376	316
11	386	364
12	386	358
13	455	337
14	482	323
15	504	325

*Problem 17.3**

Table 1 shows sales of a washing machine in successive 5 week periods. (The last period in each year is 6 weeks plus a couple of days—assume it is actually 5 weeks.) It is required to develop methods of planning production when the only information on which to base the decisions is current inventory and current production rate. There are four possible production rates which can be used: 7,500, 15,000, 22,500, 30,000 per period. The costs of changing production rates are: increase by a step of 7,500 per period—$70,000, reduction of 7,500 per period—$130,000. The lead time to effect a production rate change is one period.

a. Over the period concerned the rule the company used was to change the production

Table 1 Demand for Washing Machines

Period	1958	1959	1960	1961	1962	1963	1964
1		17,103	15,876	33,059	17,409	13,110	17,877
2		18,494	19,727	18,093	26,633	21,647	15,741
3		15,474	18,571	16,078	19,303	19,349	19,207
4		26,978	34,800	24,542	24,994	23,893	
5		24,021	20,042	24,705	17,251	17,162	
6	13,974	23,488	9,369	24,301	22,672	16,220	
7	14,342	22,984	12,460	19,199	22,014	25,078	
8	17,350	24,931	33,746	20,049	27,144	24,342	
9	21,612	27,837	26,861	21,518	26,579	20,866	
10	22,439	24,416	23,247	16,982	32,407	20,150	
Year	89,717	225,726	214,699	218,526	236,406	201,817	52,825

Table 2 Decision Rule for Setting Production Rate

	Present Production Rate			
Inventory	7,500	15,000	22,500	30,000
<0	30,000	30,000	30,000	30,000
0–10,000	22,500	22,500	30,000	30,000
10–20,000	22,500	22,500	22,500	30,000
20–30,000	15,000	22,500	22,500	22,500
30–40,000	15,000	15,000	22,500	22,500
40–50,000	15,000	15,000	22,500	22,500
50–60,000	15,000	15,000	15,000	15,000
60–70,000	7,500	15,000	15,000	15,000
70–80,000	7,500	7,500	7,500	15,000
>80,000	7,500	7,500	7,500	7,500

* *The solution to problem 17.3 requires the use of simulation. We are indebted to Professor John A. Buzacott of the University of Toronto, for making this problem available to us.*

rate whenever inventory exceeded 70,000 or fell below 20,000. The inventory at the beginning of period 6, 1958, was 33,000 and the production rate in that period was 15,000. Evaluate the number of changes and the cost of changes if the company's policy is used.

b. Suppose shortages can be estimated at $100 per unit demand not met when it occurred (demand is backlogged). The value of a washing machine is $200; thus it is possible to estimate inventory and shortage costs (no great accuracy is required—assume carrying charge 15 percent).

c. Compare the rule in part (a) with a rule described by Table 2. The new production rate is given by the intersection of the present inventory row and the present production rate column.

d. Develop some other reasonable rule which could be used and compare it with (a) and (c).

REFERENCES FOR CHAPTER 17

1. Bergstrom, G. L. and Smith, B. E. "Multi-Item Production Planning—An Extension of the H.M.M.S. Rules." *Management Science*, Vol. 16, No. 10, June, 1970, pp. 614–629.

2. Bomberger, E. E. "A Dynamic Programming Approach to a Lot Size Scheduling Problem." *Management Science*, Vol. 12, No. 11, July, 1966.

3. Bowman, E. H. "Consistency and Optimality in Managerial Decision Making." *Management Science*, Vol. 9, 1963, pp. 310–321.

4. Buffa, E. S. and Taubert, W. H. *Production-Inventory Systems: Planning and Control.* Revised Edition, Richard D. Irwin, Inc., 1972.

5. Buffa, E. S. and Taubert, W. H. "Evaluation of Direct Computer Search Methods for the Aggregate Planning Problem." *Industrial Management Review*, M.I.T. Press, Fall 1967, pp. 19–36.

6. Dutton, John M. and Starbuck, William H. "Finding Charlie's Run-Time Estimator." *Computer Simulation of Human Behavior*, John Wiley and Sons, 1971, pp. 218–242.

7. Dzielinski, B., Baker, C. and Manne, A. "Simulation Tests of Lot Size Programming." *Management Science*, Vol. 9, No. 2, January, 1963.

8. Eilon, Samuel. "Comments on Optimal Smoothing of Shipments in Response to Orders." *Management Science*, Vol. 17, No. 9, May, 1971, pp. 608–609.

9. Eilon, Samuel. "Five Approaches to Aggregate Production Planning." *AIIE Transactions*, Vol. 7, No. 2, June, 1975, pp. 118–131.

10. Eismann, K. and Young, W. M. "Study of a Textile Mill With the Aid of Linear Programming." *Management Technology*, No. 1, January, 1960.

11. Fabian, T. "Blast Furnace Production Planning—A Linear Programming Example." *Management Science*, Vol. 14, No. 2, October, 1967, pp. 1–27.

12. Fairhurst, J. H. and Livingston, D. "A Simulation Model for Production/Inventory Decisions." *Operations Research Quarterly*, Vol. 24, June, 1973.

13. Gordon, J. R. M. "A multi-Model Analysis of an Aggregate Scheduling Decision." unpublished Ph.D. Dissertation, Sloan School of Management, Massachusetts Institute of Technology, 1966.

14. Greene, J. H., Chatto, K., Hicks, C. R. and Cox, C. B. "Linear programming in the packaging Industry." *Journal of Industrial Engineering*, Vol. 10, No. 5, 1959.

15. Hanssmann, F. and Hess, S. W., "A Linear Programming Approach to Production and Employment Scheduling." *Management Technology*, No. 1, January, 1960.

16. Hausman, W. H. and McClain, J. O. "A Note on the Bergstrom–Smith Multi-Item Production Planning Model." *Management Science*, Vol. 17, No. 11, pp. 783–785.

17. Holt, C., Modigliani, F. and

Simon, H. "A Linear Decision Rule for Production and Employment Scheduling." *Management Science*, Vol. 2, 1955, pp. 1–30.

18. Holt, C. C., Modigliani, F., Muth, J. F. and Simon, H. A. *Planning Production Inventories and Work Force.* Prentice-Hall, Englewood Cliffs, N.J., 1960.

19. Holt, C. C. "Dynamic pricing and Economic Instability—A Comment." *Management Science*, Vol. 17, No. 9, May, 1971, pp. 608–609.

20. Jones, Curtis H. "Parametric Production Planning." *Management Science*, Vol. 13, No. 11, July, 1967, pp. 843–866.

21. Kolenda, J. F. "A Comparison of Two Aggregate Planning Models." Unpublished Master's Thesis, Wharton School of Finance and Commerce, 1970.

22. Kunreuther, H. "Extensions of Bowman's Theory on Managerial Decision Making." *Management Science*, Vol. 15, 1969, pp. 415–439.

23. Lee, William B. and Khumawala, Basheer M. "Simulation Testing of Aggregate Production Planning Models in an Implementation Methodology." *Management Science*, Vol. 20, No. 6. February, 1974.

24. Moskowitz, Herbert and Miller, Jeffrey G. "Information and Decision Systems for Production Planning." *Management Science*, Vol. 22, No. 3, November, 1975, pp. 359–370.

25. Moskowitz, Herbert. "The Value of Information in Aggragate Production Planning—A Behavioral Experiment." *AIIE Transactions*, Vol. 4, No. 4, 1972, pp. 290–297.

26. Peterson, R. "Optimal Smoothing of Orders." *Management Science*, Vol. 17, No. 9, May, 1971.

27. Panne, C. Vande and Bosje, P. "Sensitivity Analysis of Cost Coefficient Estimates: The Case of Linear Decision Rules for Employment and Production." *Management Science*, Vol. 9, No. 1, October, 1962, pp. 82–107.

28. Simon, H. A. "Dynamic Programming Under Uncertainty with a Quadratic Criterion Function." *Econometrica*, Vol. 24, 1956, pp. 247–268.

29. Taubert, W. H. "A Search Decision Rule for the Aggregate Scheduling Problem." *Management Science*, Vol. 14, No. 6, February, 1968, pp. 343–359.

30. Taubert, W. H. "A Case Study Problem in Aggregate Manpower Planning." in M. J. C. Martin and R. A. Denison. *Case Exercises in Operations Research.* John Wiley, 1971.

31. Vergin, R. C. "Production Scheduling Under Seasonal Demand." *Journal of Industrial Engineering*, May, 1966, pp. 260–266.

32. Von Lanzenauer, C. H. "Production and Employment Scheduling in Multistage production Systems." *Naval Research Logistics Quarterly*, Vol. 17, No. 2, July, 1970.

CHAPTER EIGHTEEN

A Multi-Echelon Integrated Production Planning and Scheduling System

18.1 *Introduction*

In the area of production planning it is possible to identify a hierarchy of managerial decisions which influence the utilization of a firm's resources. The hierarchy ranges from the planning of basic plant facilities (location, capacity, layout), through the allocation of aggregate resources within a plant (work force, inventories, production rates), to the detailed or item scheduling and planning which must be carried out daily. In terms of Robert Anthony's taxonomy of planning and control systems[1] the hierarchy ranges from strategic planning, through tactical planning to daily operational control. In previous chapters we have emphasized the management of individual item inventories by examining a variety of single-stage decision systems suitable for daily operational control. We touched upon aggregate considerations when we discussed Exchange Curves, the nature of inventories and the corporate policy context of inventory decisions. In this chapter we will examine an integrated four-level production planning decision system in which scheduling becomes increasingly more specific at each level of authority.

18.1.1 *Long-Range (Strategic) Plans*

Strategic Plans usually attempt to look more than two years ahead. They can involve top management's policy decisions regarding a company's physical facilities, for example, the projected number and location of warehouses or the projected size and nature of manufacturing capability at existing and planned production plants. Major changes in competitive policy (for example at a merchandising firm, the decision regarding the timing of how and when a department store chain should revert to discount operations) can also be a part of strategic planning. Most long-range strategic plans deal with highly aggregated financial and operating data that capture only the most important interdependencies between the various levels and plans within an organization. The long-range plans, because they define total available financial, human and material resources over time determine the constraints within which operating management (using medium-range and short-term plans) must function. Overall company strategy, in the context of aggregate production planning, is transmitted to the next level of medium-range plans via the specification of production capacities and shipment requirements per month.

18.1.2 *Medium-Range (Tactical) Plans*

Medium-range plans, with a planning horizon from six to eighteen months into the future, take the basic physical production capacity constraints and projected demand pattern established by a long-range plan and ration available resources to meet demand as effectively and as profitably as possible. Even though basic production capacity is essentially fixed by long-range considerations, production capacity can be increased or decreased within limits in the medium-run. One can decide to vary one or more of: the size of the workforce, the amount of overtime worked, the number of shifts worked, the rate of production, the amount of inventory, and possibly the amount of subcontracting let out by the company. An example of such an approach is given in the MIDAS (F) case. Improvements to the MIDAS tactical planning system were discussed in Chapter 16.

18.1.3 *Short-Term (Operational) Plans*

Short-term schedules provide the day-to-day flexibility needed to meet daily sales within the guidelines established by the more aggregate plans discussed above. In Parts 2 and 3 of the book we described in detail how inventory decision systems for individual items can be designed. Short-range operating schedules are prepared by *producers only* and take the orders generated by the inventory decision system and plan in detail how the products should be processed through a plant. Detailed schedules are drawn up for one week, then onc day and finally one shift in advance. They involve the assignment of products to machines, the sequencing and routing of orders through the plant, the determination of final product quantities for each and every stockkeeping unit.

18.1.4 *Integrated Production Planning*

To achieve some sort of rational and reasonable tradeoff between competing interests and attitudes held by various groups, most companies prepare and continually update three operating plans, each of which, as we have seen, has a planning period of a different duration. Long-range plans must merge into medium-range plans and ultimately appear as short-term individual item schedules. Forecasts for different purposes must be prepared along the way to provide data for these planning processes and to monitor actual progress made. Much of the planning in the corporate planning systems used today is being carried out with the help of only a limited amount of decision making technology. The state of affairs we believe can and should be improved upon in the future. Better decision systems that serve top management purposes can be designed given existing technology. What is needed in practice is a better balance between intuitive reasoning and structured rationalization, keeping in mind the limitations of both processes.

18.2 *The Hax–Meal Integrated Planning and Scheduling System*

In the remainder of this chapter we present one possible solution to the problem of integrating the plans at different levels within an organization. The integrated planning and scheduling system that we will describe was suggested by Hax and Meal,[12] although we have modified some portions of the system that they described and implemented in practice. There is no doubt that hierarchical approaches to the aggregate scheduling decision are important to the effectiveness of a firm. However, the Hax and Meal example is one of the very few implementations reported in the literature.

While the philosophy and approach were developed on the basis of a specific implementation the general structure and conceptual framework are applicable to almost any situation.

Hax and Meal point out that at the present time a hierarchical system constitutes a very natural approach to support the variety of complex decisions encountered in the management of the overall production process because:

1. Existing data processing capabilities and comprehensive analytical decision models are not adequate to develop a single model that "optimizes" an entire production system.

2. If one is to partition the overall production decision process then the hierarchical levels represented in the system should (and do in our example) correspond to the organizational echelons of the firm, which facilitates the interaction between the system outputs and the responsible manager at each level.

3. Hierarchical decision systems permit effective coordination throughout the organizational structure, establishing consistent subgoals at each level that become progressively more specific as they approach the actual day of manufacture.

Before adopting the hierarchical approach to be discussed in this chapter Hax and Meal considered a number of existing models which were designed to provide some integration between decisions made at different levels within an organization.[12] They concluded that these approaches were generally hard to implement, both from a computational and a managerial point of view. In addition, these papers tend to ignore the impact of uncertainties on the planning process. As a result, they set themselves a basic goal of designing a relatively simple conceptual system that would be easy to implement in practice.

The decision system they propose has four levels:

1. Products are assigned to plants using a mixed-integer linear programming model, making long-term capacity provision and utilization decisions.

2. A seasonal stock accumulation plan is prepared based on the decisions made in (1) above. Hax and Meal used linear programming at this stage, whereas we have opted for the Beale-Land Algorithm of Chapters 15 and 16.

3. Detailed schedules are prepared for each product Family using standard inventory decision rules and systems (as discussed in this book) at the third stage. The purpose of decision rules at this level is to allocate the available production capacity among the many Families of items in the system.

4. Finally, individual run quantities are calculated for each s.k.u. in each Family using standard inventory control methods.

We will present the Hax and Meal approach in the context of a very simple example.

Example—In our simple example we will assume that 2 plants exist, manufacturing 2 Types of Families of items. There are a total of 4 Families consisting of 10 s.k.u. The definition of the terms *Type* and *Family* are given schematically in Figure 18.1.

The decision process starts with the forecast of annual Family demand in each of the 2 plant territories. On the basis of these annual forecasts the production of Families will be allocated to plants, resulting in some transshipment between plants. The need for transshipments arises because at each plant is a finished goods warehouse from which demand for all s.k.u. in the plant's territory must be satisfied. For some s.k.u. it is more economical to produce it at a neighboring plant and transship it to the

Figure 18.1 Classification of S.k.u.

2 Types– Families with approximately Common Seasonal Pattern (summer, winter). S.k.u. also have to have approximately the same production rate as measured by inventory investment produced per unit time.*

4 Families – Each Family includes s.k.u. which share tooling and setup cost and are therefore generally produced together.

10 s.k.u. – The Final Product delivered to the customer.

* Note that this definition of "Type" simplifies the real problem. If two items within the same type have markedly different inventory investments per unit production time, then it follows logically that we would want to produce the item with the lower investment in the seasonal buildup period and the one with the higher investment in the peak demand season, thus saving on carrying costs. Moreover, the value of the inventory at any point in time would depend upon the actual mix of s.k.u. and not just on the amount of production time. This would considerably complicate the modelling of the decision process.

warehouse for resale, than to produce the s.k.u. in the plant in the territory where the sale is made.

Next the annual forecasts for each Family are combined at each plant by Type (seasonal pattern, etc.) and broken down into monthly production requirements. Then family Run lengths are determined on the basis of annual demand projections using economic order quantity concepts, although all order quantities are constrained within upper limits on the accumulation of seasonal stock in any one item. Finally the individual item (s.k.u.) quantities are scheduled for production on the basis of annual forecasts and within the constraints of total production allocated for any one Family by the preceding hierarchical decision subsystems. An overall view of the Hierarchical decision system is given in Figure 18.2.

Figure 18.2 Decision Sequence in Planning and Scheduling.

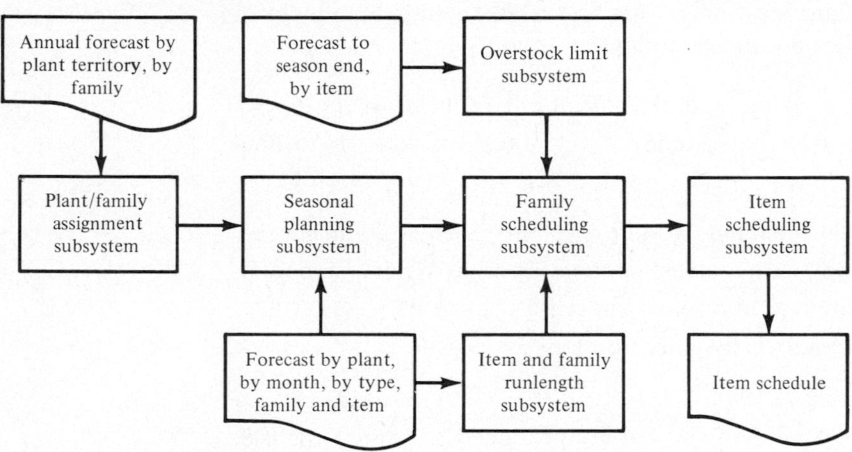

18.2.1 *The Plant/Family Assignment Decision Subsystem*

This decision subsystem balances the cost of interplant freight and handling costs, manufacturing cost differences between plants and the incremental capital investment required to set up proper production facilities. Hax and Meal[12] use the following mixed integer linear program to assign Families to specific plants. Note that Eq. 18.1 must be solved for *each* product Family defined. The cost of producing a Family at any plant i is assumed to be independent of producing any other Family at i. If this were not the case, then Eq. 18.1 would have to include all families in a simultaneous formulation—making it much more difficult, if not impossible, to solve

$$\text{Min. } C_{\text{TOT}} = \sum_{i=1}^{m} c_i x_i + \sum_{i=1}^{m} \sum_{j=1}^{m} g_{ij} x_i y_{ij}$$

Subject to:

$$\sum_{i=1}^{m} x_i y_{ij} = F_j \qquad (j = 1,2, \ldots, m) \qquad (18.1)$$

$$y_{ij} \geq 0 \qquad (i = 1, 2, \ldots, m; j = 1, 2, \ldots, m)$$

$$x_i = 0 \text{ or } 1 \qquad (i = 1, 2, \ldots, m)$$

where:

m = the number of plant-warehouses

c_i = the incremental capital investment required to produce the Family at plant location i. This cost is assumed independent of other Families produced at plant i.

g_{ij} = the cost of making one unit of the Family at plant i *and* transferring it to the warehouse at plant j for delivery to final customer.

F_j = the forecast of demand in units in plant territory j, during the economic life of the investment. (Hax and Meal assumed in their implementation an economic life of 3 years.)

$$x_i = \begin{cases} 1 & \text{if the Family is assigned to plant } i \\ 0 & \text{otherwise} \end{cases}$$

y_{ij} = the number of units of the Family produced at plant i for use in plant territory j.

The first summation in the objective function of Eq. 18.1 calculates the incremental capital investment required to produce the family at plant location(s) i. The second part of the objective function calculates the cost of making y_{ij} units of the Family at plant(s) i and transporting it to the warehouse(s) at plant(s) j. The first constraint sets y_{ij} values equal exactly to the forecast of demand for the particular family at any plant location. Note that when $x_i = 0$ then a plant i is not used to produce the Family. (x_i is an integer variable, constrained to taking on only the values 0 or 1.) This makes Eq. 18.1 a mixed-integer linear programming problem, which must be solved separately for each Family. Note that in Eq. 18.1 *no capacity constraints* are specified.

Example—To illustrate the basic ideas involved in this decision system we will use the following simple contrived example. Results from applying this decision subsystem to this example will be utilized in subsequent decision subsystems in this chapter. We will consider a case of two plants and four Families of products (see Figure 18.3).

Figure 18.3 Possible Interplant Flows.

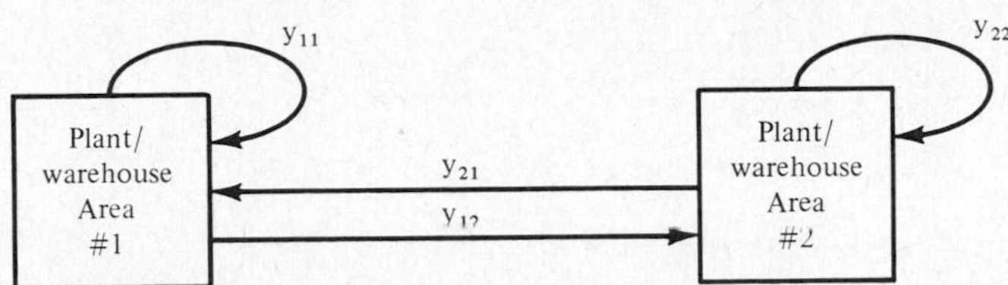

The costs associated with the above flows for each of the families are given in Table 18.1.

Note that in Table 18.1 we have set g_{11} and g_{22} equal to zero. This is equivalent to assuming that the cost of producing any of the Families at Plant 1 or Plant 2 is approximately equal. This is not generally the case, but it does simplify the subsequent illustration of this decision subsystem without doing harm to the generality of the problem solving approach being considered. For the case of two plants three alternatives must be evaluated for each family. We will evaluate each of the alternatives by enumeration. In Table 18.2 are recorded the values of the decision variables that are set by each alternative considered. Decision variables that must be calculated are indicated by a question mark.

In terms of the general model in Eq. 18.1 we can now state the problem described in our simple example as:

$$\text{Min } C_{\text{TOT}} = c_1x_1 + c_2x_2 + g_{12}x_1y_{12} + g_{21}x_2y_{21}$$

Subject to:

$$\begin{aligned} &y_{11} + y_{21} = F_1 \\ &y_{22} + y_{12} = F_2 \\ &y_{11}, y_{22}, y_{21}, y_{12} \geq 0 \\ &x_1, x_2 = 0 \text{ or } 1 \end{aligned} \tag{18.2}$$

Eq. 18.2 must be evaluated for each of the three alternatives and each of the four Families. For each Family we will determine the minimum C_{TOT} by evaluating the relevant costs under each of the three alternatives. Because of our judicious choice of example the evaluation under each alternative becomes quite simple.

Table 18.1 Cost of Interplant Flows and Forecasted Demand per Family

Family	Plant 1, x_1			Plant 2, x_2		
	c_1 (Dollars)	g_{12} (Dollars)	F_1 (Units)	c_2 (Dollars)	g_{21} (Dollars)	F_2 (Units)
1	10,000	1	10,000	0	2	20,000
2	5,000	3	20,000	10,000	1	0
3	0	6	40,000	1,000	2	20,000
4	10,000	2	2,000	5,000	4	30,000

Table 18.2 Possible Alternatives and Decision Variables

Possible Alternative	Decision Variables x_1	x_2	y_{12}	y_{11}	y_{21}	y_{22}
A. Family Produced at Plant 1 only	1	0	?	?	0	0
B. Family Produced at Plant 2 only	0	1	0	0	?	?
C. Family Produced at Both Plants	1	1	?	?	?	?

Under alternative *A* Eq. 18.2 becomes

$$\begin{aligned} &\text{Min } C_{TOT} = c_1 + g_{12}y_{12} \\ &\text{Subject to:} \\ &y_{11} = F_1 \\ &y_{12} = F_2 \end{aligned} \tag{18.3}$$

Note that in Eq. 18.3 no minimization is required because the value of y_{12} is given by the second constraint. Therefore,

$$C_{TOT}(A) = c_1 + g_{12}F_2 \tag{18.4}$$

In general, for a larger number of plant territories than 2, as long as only one plant is assumed to be open (alternative *A*), no minimization will ever be involved. Note that if g_{11} were not assumed to equal zero then an additional term $g_{11}F_{11}$ would appear in Eqs. 18.2 and 18.3. Similarily for alternative *B* the minimization in Eq. 18.3 simplifies to:

$$C_{TOT}(B) = c_2 + g_{21}F_1 \tag{18.5}$$

Once again, a larger number of plant/territories and a non-zero g_{22} would result in an evaluation of an extended form of Eq. 18.5.

Under alternative *C* Eq. 18.2 becomes:

$$\begin{aligned} &\text{Min } C_{TOT} = c_1 + c_2 + g_{12}y_{12} + g_{21}y_{21} \\ &\text{Subject to:} \\ &y_{11} + y_{21} = F_1 \\ &y_{22} + y_{12} = F_2 \\ &y_{11}, y_{21}, y_{22}, y_{12} \geq 0 \end{aligned} \tag{18.6}$$

The minimum value for Eq. 18.6 in general is given by $y_{12} = y_{21} = 0$. That is, because of our contrived example, alternative *C* also reduces to a simple evaluation for each Family, namely:

$$C_{\text{TOT}}(C) = c_1 + c_2 \tag{18.7}$$

In general, for a larger number of plants this is also the case *as long as* g_{ij} *for* $i = j$ *is zero.* That is, as long as the cost of producing a particular Family at any of the m plants is the same. Often in practice the relative production efficiencies vary between plants and one would have to allow for this by assigning a non-zero value to g_{ij} for $i = j$. In such a situation for a case of 2 plants Eq. 18.6 becomes:

$$\text{Min } C_{\text{TOT}} = c_1 + c_2 + g_{11}y_{11} + g_{12}y_{12} + g_{22}y_{22} + g_{21}y_{21}$$

subject to:

$$y_{11}y_{21} = F_1 \tag{18.8}$$

$$y_{22} + y_{12} = F_2$$

$$y_{11}, y_{21}y_{22}, y_{12} \geq 0$$

Now the minimum cost solution to alternative C is no longer as obvious, involving the solution of Eq. 18.8 by a linear programming algorithm. Every computer manufacturer has available for his system a standard solution algorithm for this purpose. The simple two plant case in Eq. 18.8 could also be solved manually by using the steps defined in the Simplex Algorithm.[5] Note that for the cases of more than two plants the number of alternatives that must be evaluated increases rapidly and is given by:

$$\text{Number of Alternatives} = (2^m - 1) \tag{18.9}$$

where m is the number of plants avaliable.

Because of the rapid growth of Eq. 18.9, an analyst may well opt to return to solving Eq. 18.1 directly by a mixed-integer linear programming algorithm.[14] However, for large m the current state of the art in solving integer type problems may make such a solution strategy costly. Luckily, in practice, the largest number of plants that one might consider for inclusion in the Plant/Family Assignment Decision Subsystem is usually in the order of 5 or 6 for most companies. In any case it is *always* feasible to reduce the problem to a series of simple evaluations of C_{TOT} expressions and linear programmes. For example, for 5 plants one would have to compare 5 C_{TOT} evaluation and 26 linear programmes. While this may sound formidable, many of the calculations needed are repetitive in nature (well suited for computer-based operations) and the whole exercise could prove to be well worth the effort in terms of the savings realized in the overall logistics of the distribution system.

Returning to our example (Table 18.1) we will now evaluate for each of the four Families the relevant C_{TOT} for each of three alternatives to identify the minimum cost allocation of Family flows to and from plants in each case. This is carried out in Table 18.3.

Table 18.3 Cost of Producing Families by Each Alternative

Family	Cost of Alternatives	Least Cost Alternative
1	$C_{TOT}(A) = 10{,}000 + 1(20{,}000) = \$30{,}000$ $C_{TOT}(B) = 0 + 2(10{,}000) = \$20{,}000$ $C_{TOT}(C) = 10{,}000 + 0 = \$10{,}000$	Alternative C: $y_{12} = 0 \quad y_{21} = 0$ $y_{11} = 10{,}000 \quad y_{22} = 20{,}000$
2	$C_{TOT}(A) = 5{,}000 + 3(0) = \$5{,}000$ $C_{TOT}(B) = 10{,}000 + 1(20{,}000) = \$30{,}000$ $C_{TOT}(C) = 5{,}000 + 10{,}000 = \$15{,}000$	Alternative A: $y_{12} = 0 \quad y_{21} = 0$ $y_{11} = 20{,}000 \quad y_{22} = 0$
3	$C_{TOT}(A) = 0 + 6(20{,}000) = \$120{,}000$ $C_{TOT}(B) = 1{,}000 + 2(40{,}000) = \$81{,}000$ $C_{TOT}(C) = 0 + 1{,}000 = \$1{,}000$	Alternative C: $y_{12} = 0 \quad y_{21} = 0$ $y_{11} = 40{,}000 \quad y_{22} = 20{,}000$
4	$C_{TOT}(A) = 10{,}000 + 2(30{,}000) = \$70{,}000$ $C_{TOT}(B) = 5{,}000 + 4(2{,}000) = \$13{,}000$ $C_{TOT}(C) = 10{,}000 + 5{,}000 = \$15{,}000$	Alternative B: $y_{12} = 0 \quad y_{21} = 2{,}000$ $y_{11} = 0 \quad y_{22} = 30{,}000$

The net result of Table 18.3 is given in Table 18.4 where we have also converted from units to man-hours, the basis on which the Seasonal Planning Decision Subsystem, discussed in the next section, operates. The solution presented in Table 18.4 was, as the reader will recall, achieved under the assumption that there are no capacity constraints of any sort on the allocation of Families to Plants.

Table 18.4 Total Production Requirements

	Plant 1		Plant 2	
Family	Units	Man-Hours	Units	Man-Hour
1	10,000	32,000	20,000	64,000
2	20,000	25,400	0	0
3	40,000	193,200	20,000	96,600
4	0	0	32,000	114,240
Totals		250,600		274,840

There are a number of constraints that could make the solution infeasible. For example, the line capacity per family at a particular plant may not be sufficient to handle the man-hours of production assigned. Line capacity considerations would require the addition of the following constraints to the general formulation of our 2 plant example given in Eq. 18.2:

$$\begin{aligned} y_{11} + y_{12} &\leq Y_{11} \\ y_{22} + y_{21} &\leq Y_{22} \end{aligned} \tag{18.10}$$

Where Y_{11} and Y_{22} are the maximum amount of a particular family that could be produced at Plants 1 and 2 respectively. Another type of constraint that could be introduced would involve the limitation of total or minimum man-hours assigned to a plant. For example, in Table 18.4 the 274,840 man-hours assigned to Plant 2 may prove to be more than the total work force available or alternatively it may result in seasonal peaks (which would become evident in the decision system we will consider in the next section).

The additional constraints in Eq. 18.2 would make our simple evaluation equations as shown in Table 18.3 invalid. One would now have to evaluate all alternatives using linear programming.

Constraints on total man-hours per plant are in general more difficult to handle analytically because total man-hours at a plant depend upon the assignment of all Families, hence we can no longer analyse each Family separately. Reassignments could be made by trial and error on the basis of cost penalties. That is, reassignment of Families would take place on the basis of moving a Family or Families that would cause the least increase in C_{TOT}. For our expository example we will assume that no constraints are violated by the assignment in Table 18.4 so as not to unnecessarily complicate the basic concept of an hierarchical decision system being presented. A procedure to deal with such capacity constraints appears in Hax.[10]

18.2.2 *The Seasonal Planning Decision Subsystem*

The Plant/Family Assignment Decision, discussed in the previous section, determined for our expository example an allocation of Families to plants. That is, it determined for each plant the workload and product mix to be produced for the coming year. The next step in the hierarchical decision system will involve the planning for work force levels, production rates and inventories so as to meet this allocated demand in an effective manner. This of course involves the aggregate scheduling decision which we have examined in the last three chapters. The only difference being considered here consists of the imbedding of the aggregate scheduling decision within a total hierarchical framework, wherein inputs to the seasonal planning problem are generated from another decision model and where the outputs will become inputs to subsequent systems discussed below. Hax and Meal[12] used a linear programming format to determine a seasonal plan; we will use the Beale-Land Transportation Algorithm first introduced in Chapter 15 and discussed in detail in Chapter 16 to achieve the same ends.

Seasonal planning will be carried out in this section using Types of Families. Recall that we defined a Type as a Family of products which exhibited a similar seasonal pattern and the same production rate, measured in dollars of inventory investment per unit production time. We will prepare an aggregate schedule for Plant 1 only. Exactly the same procedure could be used to plan production for Plant 2. We will assume that Families 1, 2, and 3 are of Type 1, that is they all exhibit a similar seasonal pattern and can be produced at comparable rates per unit time and therefore lead to comparable dollars of inventory investment per man-hour of production. Family 4 will be assumed to be Type 2. Then from Table 18.4 we can see that Plant 1 has been assigned the production of only Type 1 products to a total of 250,600 man-hours for the coming year. Table 18.5 gives the forecasted monthly breakdown of annual demand, as well as the planned work force levels, initial inventories, and maximum and minimum inventory levels specified by management. Minimum inventory levels are based on the degree of uncertainty per monthly forecast using techniques such as discussed in Chapter 8. Production smoothing consideration also play a role in the determination of maximum/minimum levels. Note that in the example we have assumed that the company follows a policy where the regular work force time is kept at a constant level. Table 18.6 shows the details of the calculations on the Beale-Land Algorithm for the four months. This particular aggregate production schedule was computed for a decision horizon of 12 months. Table 18.7 records the results of the application of the Beale-Land Algorithm to Table 18.5. For a detailed discussion of this approach see Chapters 15 and 16.

The Seasonal Planning Decision Subsystem can be used to determine the allocation of the number of hours of production available for each product Type in a Plant. With more than one Type of product the modified Beale-Land Algorithm will produce only a near-optimal solution as was illustrated by the solution to MIDAS (F) in Chapter 16.

18.2.3 *Family Scheduling Decision Subsystem*

To set the Family run quantities correctly and to preserve the aggregate schedule determined in Table 18.7, the decision system in this section must schedule just enough production in each of the Families in the product type to use up the aggregate production time scheduled above. As we shall see the accumulated seasonal stock will be allocated in such a manner as not to incur any additional major setup costs associated with the production of each product Type. At the same time, customer service standard times will be met without violating individual s.k.u. overstock limits. Within these constraints any Family belonging to a Type can be produced. To achieve these ends a four step procedure is recommended by

Table 18.5 Production, Work Force, and Inventory for Plant 1 (All Figures in Man-Hours)

Month t (1)	Allocated Requirements (2)	Inventory at end of t (3)	Minimum Inv. at t (4)	Maximum Inv. at t (5)	Available Regular Time Work Force[a] (6)
0		25,000	10,000	30,000	
1	20,600		10,000	30,000	18,270
2	30,000		10,000	30,000	20,300
3	27,500		10,000	30,000	20,000
4	22,500		10,000	30,000	22,330
5	22,500		10,000	30,000	20,300
6	25,000		10,000	20,000	20,300
7	15,000		5,000	15,000	14,210
8	12,500		5,000	15,000	23,345
9	17,500		5,000	15,000	19,285
10	20,000		10,000	20,000	24,360
11	22,500		15,000	30,000	20,300
12	15,000		20,000	30,000	15,225
Totals	250,600				238,525

[a] The work force levels in column 6 fluctuate because the number of work days per month varies from month to month. For a more detailed discussion see MIDAS (F), Table 3.

*Table 18.6 Beale–Land Algorithm Applied to the Seasonal Planning Problem**

		Type 1						
	Source	Cost	Rank	Avail at t	Prod at t	Avail at $t+l$	Max Inv. at end of t	Min Inv. at end of t
Month 1	00		1	15,000	15,000	0	30,000	10,000
Reg = 20,600	11	0	2	18,270	5,600	12,670		
	12	8	3	5,480	0	5,480		
Month 2	00		1	0	0	0	30,000	10,000
Reg = 30,000	21	0	2	20,300	20,300	0		
	22	8	4	6,090	0	6,090		
	11	2	3	12,670	9,700	2,970		
	12	10	5	5,480	0	5,480		
Month 3	00		1	0	0	0	30,000	10,000
Reg = 27,500	31	0	2	20,300	20,300	0		
	32	8	4	6,090	4,230	1,860		
	22	10	5	6,090	0	6,090		
	11	4	3	2,970	2,970	0		
	12	12	6	5,480	0	5,480		
Month 4	00		1	0	0	0	30,000	10,000
Reg = 22,500	41	0	2	22,330	22,330	0		
	42	8	3	6,700	170	6,530		
	32	10	4	1,860	0	1,860		
	22	12	5	6,090	0	6,090		
	12	14	6	5,480	0	5,480		

* Source 00 refers to the amount of inventory available for use to meet requirements during periods t, or if not required, in subsequent periods. Note that available inventory listed under 00 does not include seasonal (anticipation) inventories previously allocated by the algorithm. Source 00 only lists inventory which has not been committed at any time t. Recall from Chapter 15 that sources 11 and 12 refer to the amount of regular time (second digit equals 1) and overtime (second digit equals 2) available in period 1 respectively, etc. Note that the variable cost of producing on regular time is assumed to be zero and on overtime \$8.00 per man-hour. The cost of carrying one man-hour for one period is given as \$2.00. Overtime is limited to 30 percent of regular time capacity.

Table 18.7 Master Production Plan, Plant 1

Month	Allocated Requirements	P_t Regular Time Production Scheduled	OT_t Overtime Production Scheduled	I_t Inventory at end of t
0				25,000
1	20,600	18,270	0	22,670
2	30,000	20,300	0	12,970
3	27,500	20,300	4,230	10,000
4	22,500	22,330	170	10,000
5	22,500	20,300	2,200	10,000
6	25,000	20,300	4,700	10,000
7	15,000	10,000	0	5,000
8	12,500	20,715	0	13,215
9	17,500	19,285	0	15,000
10	20,000	24,360	0	19,360
11	22,500	20,300	0	17,160
12	15,000	15,225	2,615	20,000

Hax and Meal:

1. Determine the Families in each type which must be run in the scheduling interval to meet s.k.u. service requirements.

2. Initial Family run quantities are determined so as to minimize cycle inventory and changeover costs.

3. Then the initial Family run quantities are adjusted so that all the product time scheduled to a particular Type is used up.

4. At each of the above steps individual s.k.u. overstock limits are checked.

To determine which Families must be scheduled for production this month, Hax and Meal calculate the run out time for each Family using Eq. 18.11. For our example all Families with a run out time less than one will be scheduled. This is equivalent to assuming that Families are scheduled once a month. In general, all Families i whose RT_i is less than the time left until the end of the period being scheduled must be put in the schedule for that period.

$$RT_i = \min_{\substack{\text{items } j \\ \text{belonging to Family } i}} \{(I_{ijt} - SS_{ijt})/d_{ijt}\} \tag{18.11}$$

where:

RT_i = is the earliest expected time at which the available inventory for a member of Family i will reach its safety stock level.

I_{ijt} = inventory of s.k.u. j in Family i at the start of period t.

SS_{ijt} = individual s.k.u. safety stock level at the beginning of period t.

d_{ijt} = forecast demand for the j-th s.k.u. in Family i for month t.

The current status of the ten s.k.u. in our contrived example is given in Table 18.8.

Table 18.8 Inventory Status, at Beginning of Month 1, Plant 1

Type	Family i	s.k.u. j	Available Stock I_{ijt}	Safety Stock SS_{ij}	Forecast Month 1
1	1	1	2,600	730	1,500
		2	2,550	220	450
		3	3,250	480	1,000
		4	3,750	1,150	2,400
		5	2,600	820	1,700
	2	6	3,750	1,520	3,100
		7	1,500	770	1,500
		8	1,250	340	700
	3	9	1,750	2,170	4,500
		10	2,000	1,800	3,750
Totals			25,000	10,000	20,600

From Table 18.8 we can calculate, using Eq. 18.11, the expected run out time for each of the three Families manufactured at Plant 1:

$$RT_1 = \text{Min } [(2600-730)/1500,\ (2550-220)/450,\ (3250-480)/1000,\ (3750-1150)/2400,\ (2600-820)/1700] = 1.05 \text{ (from s.k.u. 5)}$$

$$RT_2 = \text{Min } \{(3750-1520)/3100,\ (1500-770)/1500,\ (1250-340)/700\} = 0.49 \text{ (from s.k.u. 7)}$$

$$RT_3 = \text{Min } \{(1750-2170)/4500,\ (2000-1800)/3750\} = -0.09 \text{ (from s.k.u. 9)}$$

From the above calculations we can see that Families 2 and 3 of Type 1 at Plant 1 must be produced during the period being scheduled.

Hax and Meal define the trial Family run quantity as:

$$RQ_i = \sum_j RQ_{ij} = \sum_j \text{Min}\{Q_{ij}, (L_{ijt} - I_{ijt})\} \qquad (18.12)$$

where:

Q_{ij} is the economic order quantity for s.k.u. j in Family i determined either by the Wilson Economic Order Quantity Formula in Chapter 5 or by the Silver–Meal Heuristic in Chapter 8.

L_{ijt} is the overstock limit for s.k.u. j in Family i at start of t.

I_{ijt} was previously defined as the available stock level at the beginning of month t.

Overstock L_{ijt} could be determined in a number of ways. In our expository example we are at $t = 1$ in Table 18.7, that is the beginning of a seasonal peak in production requirements which abate in approximately six months time. Therefore, as a simple measure one could specify that at $t = 1$, L_{ijt} is equal to six months forecasted demand. Alternatively one could attempt to use one of the single-period techniques described for style items in Chapter 10. The cost of an understock *could* be set equal to the changeover cost associated with having to make an extra run between now and the end of the season, whereas the unit cost of overstock could be set equal to the cost of carrying stock from one season to the next. This was the approach taken by Hax and Meal.* The determination of L_{ijt} will depend on the specifics of the application being carried out. In concept, L_{ijt} attempts to limit individual s.k.u. and Family inventory levels from getting way out of line. Table 18.9 presents the example calculations necessary for Eq. 18.12 in Tabular form.

---

* *Strictly speaking, the overstock cost is not always equal to the cost of carrying stock from one season to the next. Units not sold during a peak season do not always have to be held until the next peak; some could be used up shortly after the current peak. This means, though, that the marginal cost of an overstock increases with the size of the overstock. In the models presented in Chapter 10 we assumed that the marginal cost of an overstock was always constant. Therefore, strictly speaking the models of Chapter 10 would need some minor modifications.*

Table 18.9 Calculation of Trial Family Run Quantities

Type	Family i	s.k.u. j	Available Inventory I_{ijt}	Q_{ij}	L_{ijt}		$(L_{ijt} - I_{ijt})$	Min $(Q_{ij}, L_{ijt} - I_{ijt})$
1	2	6	3,750	1,650	14,500		10,750	1,650
		7	1,500	1,750	7,800		6,300	1,750
		8	1,250	4,000	4,300		3,050	3,050
						Σ	20,100	$RQ_2 =$ 6,450
	3	9	1,750	6,500	21,100		19,350	6,500
		10	2,000	3,400	19,600		17,600	3,400
						Σ	36,950	$RQ_3 =$ 9,900
								Total = 16,350 ($\Sigma_i RQ_i$)

Note: Family 1 is ignored because $R.T. > 1$ and therefore no production is necessary in current month.

Note from Table 18.9 that the trial run quantity total for Type 1, $\sum_i RQ_i$, is equal to 16,350 man hours. For our example the trial quantity is less than the available production scheduled in Table 18.7 for month $t=1$ (18,270 man-hours). The trial Family run quantities must be increased so that this excess capacity is used up and thereby the aggregate production smoothing requirements are met. Hax and Meal recommend the following procedure to determine the final Family run quantity, RQ_i^*:

a. If $\sum_i RQ_i < (P_t + OT_t)$ then set

$$RQ_i^* = \text{Min}\left\{\sum_j (L_{ijt} - I_{ijt}),\ RQ_i + \left[(P_t + OT_t) - \sum_k RQ_k\right] f_i\right\}$$

where:

$$f_i = \sum_j (L_{ijt} - I_{ijt}) / \sum_k \sum_j (L_{kjt} - I_{kjt}) \tag{18.13}$$

P_t = is the regular time production capacity scheduled in month t for the Type under consideration.

OT_t = is the overtime production capacity scheduled in month t for the Type under consideration.

b. If $\sum_i RQ_i > (P_t + OT_t)$ then set

$$RQ_i^* = (P_t + OT_t)\ RQ_i / \sum_k RQ_k \tag{18.14}$$

Note that in Eq. 18.13, the term $RQ_i + (P_t + OT_t)f_i$ sets the *increment* to the run quantity for Family i proportional to the maximum amount that can be run of that quantity (relative to the total maximum amount that can be run of the whole Type). The term $\sum_j (L_{ijt} - I_{ijt})$ is simply the maximum quantity of Family i that may be produced. Similarly, in Eq. 18.14 each Family run quantity is scaled down proportionately.

In our example, Type 1 production in Plant 1 falls into the first case above and requires the use of Eq. 18.13.

For Family i = 2

$$f_2 = \frac{20{,}100}{20{,}100 + 36{,}950} = 0.35$$

$$\begin{aligned} RQ_2^* &= \text{Min}\ \{20{,}100, 6450 + [(18{,}270 + 0) - 16350]0.35\} \\ &= \text{Min}\ \{20{,}100, 7{,}122\} \\ &= 7{,}122 \end{aligned}$$

For Family $i=3$

$$f_3 = \frac{36{,}950}{20{,}100+36{,}950} = 0.65$$

$$\begin{aligned} RQ_3^* &= \text{Min}\ \{36{,}900, 9900+[(18{,}270+0)-16{,}350]0.65\} \\ &= \text{Min}\ \{36{,}900,\ 11{,}148\} \\ &= 11{,}148 \end{aligned}$$

Note that $RQ_2^* + RQ_3^*$ uses up the total production capacity determined in the Seasonal Planning Decision Subsystem (that is, 18,270 man hours as per Table 18.7; see scheduled P_t, OT_t for $t=1$). The $\sum_i RQ_i^*$ derived in the above manner will not always equal the total $(P_t + OT_t)$ available. Consider the contrived example in Table 18.10.

Table 18.10 Contrived Example

Family, i	RQ_i	$(L_{ijt} - I_{ijt})$	f_i	$(RQ_i + 2200 f_i)$	Min (1) or (2)
		(1)		(2)	
1	6,000	9,000	0.56	7,232	7,323
2	3,000	5,000	0.31	3,682	3,682
3	2,000	2,100	0.13	2,286	2,100
	$\sum RQ_i = 11{,}000$	16,100	1.00		$\sum RQ_i^* = 13{,}014$

Table 18.10 assumes that $(P_t + OT_t)$ equals 13,200. Therefore from Eq. 18.13 $RQ_i + [(P_t + OT_t) - \sum_k RQ_k] f_i$ reduces to $RQ_i + 2200 f_1$ as given in column (2) of Table 18.10. Note that $\sum RQ_i^*$ is less than 13,200 the available capacity.

This means that a second iteration is necessary. That is, we must allocate the remaining capacity $(13{,}200 - 13{,}014)$ or 186 man hours. We suggest the following procedure:

$$f_1' = \frac{9{,}000}{9{,}000+5{,}000} = 0.64$$

Therefore,

$$\begin{aligned} f_2' &= 0.36 \\ RQ_1^* &= RQ_1 + 186 \times f_1' \\ &= 7232 + 119 = 7351 \\ RQ_2^* &= 3682 + 67 = 3749 \\ RQ_3^* &= 2100 \text{ (as per Table 18.10)} \end{aligned}$$

Now $\sum RQ_i^*$ equals the available total capacity of 13,200. This method will always work as long as $(P_t + OT_t)$ does not exceed $\sum_i \sum_j (L_{ijt} - I_{ijt})$.

Returning to our main example (as in Table 18.9) what remains to be done now is the scheduling of individual s.k.u. within each Family so that the total run quantities, RQ_i^*, are effectively utilized.

18.2.4 *Individual S.k.u. Scheduling Decision Subsystem*

Hax and Meal recommend the scheduling of individual s.k.u. by calculating quantities which equate the expected run-out times for all s.k.u. in a Family. Effectively, this keeps average inventories as low as possible in that most items will be at reasonably low levels when the family is next scheduled. In doing this overstock limits must be observed. This can be achieved by setting

$$RQ_{ij}^* = [RQ_i^* + \textstyle\sum_k (I_{kt} - SS_{ikt})]\, D_{ijt}/\textstyle\sum_k D_{ikt}) + SS_{ijt} - I_{ijt} \tag{18.15}$$

where:

RQ_{ij}^* is the desired run quantity for the jth s.k.u. in Family i.

D_{ijt} is the forecast demand for the jth s.k.u. in Family i, for period t.

RQ_j^* is the desired Family run quantity determined from the Family Scheduling Decision Subsystem.

Note that in Eq. 18.15 strictly speaking, SS_{ijt} and D_{ijt} are only approximations of the safety stock and demand rates in the future, made at time t. Demand is unlikely to continue at the same rate for all t; neither is a constant safety stock reasonable for all t. Therefore Eq. 18.15 is only an approximation which leads to operationally useful results. From Eq. 18.15 it follows that the *common* expected run-out time for each s.k.u. j in Family i will be given by:

$$RT_i = (RQ_{ij}^* + I_{ijt} - SS_{ijt})/D_{ijt} \tag{18.16}$$

In Table 18.11 we carry out the computation of scheduled quantities for our expository example. The common run-out times of 2.06 and 1.33 months for Families 2 and 3 are given in the last column of Table 18.11. That is, Eq. 18.16 indeed equates run-out times for all s.k.u. in a Family.

Table 18.11 Scheduled Individual S.k.u. Quantities and Run-out Time

Type	Family i	S.K.U. k	Demand D_{ij}	Inventory I_{ijt}	Safety Stock SS_{ijt}	Calculated Order Qty. Q_{ij}	Scheduled RQ^*_{ij}	Run-Out Time RT_{ij}
1	2	6	3,100	3,750	1,520	1,650	4,199	2.06
		7	1,500	1,500	770	1,750	2,361	2.06
		8	700	1,250	340	4,000	533	2.06
	3	9	4,500	1,750	2,170	6,500	6,381	1.33
		10	3,750	2,000	1,800	3,400	4,767	1.33

18.3 *Summary*

We have presented the Hax and Meal approach to integrated aggregate planning in great detail. The two run-out times for Families 2 and 3 in Type 1 were the end result of a four level hierarchical decision system which coordinated the logistics of distribution of s.k.u. to plants and maximized the cost of inter-plant deliveries. The run-out times for individual s.k.u. were set approximately equal for each Family. All this was accomplished in the context of an aggregate seasonal production plan in such a manner that scheduled capacity for month 1 was judiciously allocated across product Families. This is a rather remarkable accomplishment, when you consider the magnitude of the task attempted and the relative simplicity of the approach proposed by Hax and Meal. Note from Table 18.11 that the logic of the hierarchical system is not always obvious intuitively. All the s.k.u. economic order quantities were increased to use up the production capacity available in month 1, except for s.k.u. 8. In this case the Q_{ij} was severely reduced.

All that remains for us to do now is to expedite the production of s.k.u. number 9 through the plant—note that its inventory level is below the safety stock allocation. Hopefully this can be done without causing any major disruptions and let's hope that the recorded inventory figures are correct, or if they are wrong, let's hope there is more of s.k.u. number 9 in inventory. These important details of daily production scheduling have not been covered by the Hax–Meal approach nor are they considered in our book.[4]

Appendix to Chapter 18—Proof

That equation (18.15) equates expected run-out times can be demonstrated as follows:

$$RT_j = \text{the expected time to run-out of s.k.u. } j$$

$$RT_j = \frac{RQ^*_{ij} + I_{ijt} - SS_{ijt}}{D_{ijt}}$$

We want

$$RT_j = RT_k = C, \text{ a constant for all } j,k$$

i.e.,

$$\frac{RQ^*_{ij} + I_{ijt} - SS_{ijt}}{D_{ijt}} = C \qquad (18.17)$$

or

$$RQ^*_{ij} = CD_{ijt} - I_{ijt} + SS_{ijt}$$

We have defined

$$\sum_k RQ^*_{ik} = RQ^*_i$$

$$\sum_k [CD_{ikt} - I_{ikt} + SS_{ikt}] = RQ^*_i$$

$$C\sum_k D_{ikt} - \sum_k I_{ikt} + \sum_k SS_{ikt} = RQ^*_i$$

or

$$C = \frac{RQ^*_i + \sum_k (I_{ikt} - SS_{ikt})}{\sum_k D_{ikt}}$$

Substituting Eq. 18.17 for C gives Eq. 18.15.
Q.E.D.

Problems for Chapter 18

Problem 18.1

In Table 18.1 if you as a manager had the option of reducing one of the g_{ij} by \$1.00, which Family-Plant combination would you choose? Support your decision numerically.

Problem 18.2

Can Eq. 18.2 be solved by the simple algebraic enumeration procedure described in Eqs. 18.3 to 18.7 if one of the constraints were altered:

$$y_{11}+y_{21} \geq F_1$$

Explain your answer in detail.

Problem 18.3

Solve Eq. 18.8 using the cost structure in Figure 18.4 and set $g_{11}=2$ and $g_{22}=3$ for all 4 Families. Is a computer-based algorithm necessary to arrive at a solution? Explain.

Problem 18.4

Using Eq. 18.9 and any other previous equations, write down all linear programs that must be solved for a 3 plant problem. Formulate also the mixed integer linear program that could be solved. Which approach would you use? Discuss.

Problem 18.5

a. If we added to the formulation of the problem described in Eq. 18.2 and Table 18.1 the following constraint for Family 1 only:

$$y_{11}+y_{12} \leq 8{,}000$$

How would the optimal solution given in Table 18.4 be altered? Discuss.

b. How would the optimal solution to the problem described in Eq. 18.2 and Table 18.1 be altered if we limited the total man hours available in plant 2 to 260,000 and in plant 1 to 280,000?

Problem 18.6

Formulate and solve the seasonal planning decision discussed in section 18.2.2 as a linear program. Compare and discuss the results.

Problem 18.7

Using the Beale-Land algorithm as discussed in section 18.2.2, and the example data in Chapter 18, prepare a Master Production Plan for plant 2 in the context of the information given below.

Month	Allocated Requirements		Inventory at t		Min. Inv. at t		Max. Inv. at t		Available R/T	
	Type 1	Type 2	Type 1	Type 2	Type 1	Type 2	Type 1	Type 2	Type 1	Type 2
1	18,600	9,700	18,850	15,250	8,850	3,800	25,000	10,000	11,180	8,600
2	18,000	6,740			8,850	3,000	25,000	10,000	10,660	8,200
3	16,500	6,500			8,850	3,000	25,000	8,000	11,700	9,000
4	13,500	5,000			8,850	3,000	25,000	8,000	11,700	9,000
5	13,500	4,000			8,850	3,000	25,000	8,000	11,700	9,000
6	15,000	6,000			8,850	3,000	20,000	8,000	11,180	8,600
7	9,000	8,500			4,500	3,000	15,000	10,000	6,890	5,300
8	7,500	8,500			4,500	3,000	15,000	15,000	11,180	8,600
9	10,500	10,500			4,500	5,000	20,000	20,000	11,700	9,000
10	12,000	15,000			8,850	8,000	25,000	25,000	11,180	8,600
11	13,000	20,000			10,000	10,000	30,000	20,000	11,180	8,600
12	13,500	13,800			12,000	7,000	30,000	15,000	10,140	7,800
Totals	160,600	114,240							130,390	100,300

Problem 18.8

Using your answer to 18.7 and the procedures described in section 18.2.3, compute the Family run quantities for plant 2, assuming the following inventory status at the beginning of month 1, Plant 2:

Type	Family i	s.k.u. j	Available Stock I_{ijt}	Safety Stock SS_{ij}	Forecast Month 1
1	1	1	2,100	700	2,000
		2	650	200	400
		3	1,400	500	1,200
		4	3,500	1,000	2,000
		5	200	1,200	2,500
	3	9	4,300	2,250	4,500
		10	6,700	3,000	6,000
		Sub Totals	18,850	8,850	18,600
2	4	11	6,100	1,500	4,000
		12	5,700	1,400	3,500
		13	250	500	1,200
		14	3,200	400	1,000
		Sub Totals	15,250	3,800	9,700

The economic order quantities and the overstock limits for Plant 2 are as follows:

Type	Family i	s.k.u. j	Q_{ij}	L_{ijt}
1	1	1	6,450	10,600
		2	460	2,300
		3	9,400	10,000
		4	6,600	11,000
		5	10,600	14,000
	3	9	6,500	21,100
		10	3,400	19,600
2	4	11	8,000	13,300
		12	3,850	11,400
		13	2,250	4,500
		14	3,450	6,000

Problem 18.9

Using your results from problems 18.7 and 18.8, as well as the procedures described in section 18.2.4 prepare an individual item schedule for all s.k.u. to be manufactured at Plant 2 in month 1.

REFERENCES FOR CHAPTER 18

1. Anthony, Robert N. *Planning and Control Systems: A Framework for Analysis.* Harvard University Graduate School of Business Administration, Boston, Mass., 1965.

2. Cohen, J. J. "A Survey of the Warehouse Location Problem." Operations Research Center, M.I.T., Working Paper 022–73, September, 1973.

3. Dzielinski, B. P. and Gomory, R. E. "Optimal Programming of Lot Sizes, Inventory and Labor Allocations." *Management Science,* Vol. 11, No. 9, July, 1965.

4. Garrett, Leonard J. and Silver, Milton. *Production Management Analysis.* Harcourt, Brace, Jovanovich, 2nd Edition, Chapter 20, 1973.

5. Gass, Saul I. *Linear Programming: Methods and Applications.* McGraw-Hill, 3rd Edition, 1969.

6. Green, P. "Heuristic Coupling of Aggregate and Detailed Models in Factory Scheduling." M.I.T., Unpublished Ph. D. Thesis, 1971.

7. Gross, D. "Centralized Inventory Control in Multi-Location Supply Systems," in *Multi-Stage Inventory Models and Techniques,* H. Scarf, D. M. Gilford, M. W. Shelly, Eds. Stanford University Press, Stanford, California.

8. Haber, S. E. "Simulation of Multi-Echelon Macroeconomic Policies." *Naval Research Logistics Quarterly,* Vol. 18, 1971, pp. 119–134.

9. Hadley, G. and Whitin, T. M. "An Inventory-Transportation Model with N Locations." *Multi-Stage Inventory Models and Techniques,* H. Scarf, D. M. Gilford, M. W. Shelly, Eds., Stanford University Press, Stanford, California.

10. Hax, A. C. "Integration of Strategic and Tactical Planning in the Aluminium Industry," M.I.T. Operations Research Center, Working Paper, OR 026–73.

11. Hax, A. C. "Planning a Management Information System for a Distributing and Manufacturing Company." *Sloan Management Review,* Vol. 14, No. 3, Spring, 1973.

12. Hax, A. C. and Meal, H. C. "Hierarchical Integration of Production Planning and Scheduling." *Management Science,* Special Logistics Issue, December, 1974.

13. Lasdon, L. S. and Terjung, R. C. "An Efficient Algorithm for Multi-Item Scheduling." *Operations Research,* Vol. 19, No. 4, July–August, 1971, pp. 946–969.

14. Lemke, C. E. and Spielberg, K. "Direct Search Algorithms for Zero-One and Mixed Integer Programming." *Operations Research,* Vol. 15, 1967, pp. 892–914.

15. Miller, Jeffrey G., Berry, William L., and Lai, Ching-Yi F. "A Comparison of Alternative Forecasting Strategies for Multi-Stage Production-Inventory Systems." Paper No. 441, Institute for Research in the Behavioral, Economic and Management Sciences, Purdue University, 1974.

16. Muckstadt, J. A. "A Model for a Multi-Item, Multi-Echelon,

Multi-Indenture Inventory System." *Management Science*, Vol. 20, 1973, pp. 472–481.

17. Simpson, K. "A Theory of Allocation of Stocks to Warehouse." *Operations Research*, Vol. 7, No. 6, November-December, 1959, pp. 797-805.

18. Wagner, H. M. "The Design of Production and Inventory Systems for Multi-Facility and Multi-Warehouse Companies." *Operations Research*, Vol. 22, No. 2, March–April, 1974, pp. 278–291.

19. Williams, J. F. "Multi-Echelon Production Scheduling when Demand is Stochastic." *Management Science*, Vol. 20, 1974, pp. 1253–1263.

20. Winters, P. R. "Constrained Inventory Rules for Production Smoothing." *Management Science*, Vol. 8, No. 4, July, 1962.

21. Zangwill, W. I. "A Deterministic Multi-Product, Multi-Facility Production and Inventory Model." *Operations Research*, Vol. 14, No. 3, May–June, 1966, pp. 486–507.

PART 6

Synthesis

The two chapters in this, the last part of the book could logically follow the introductory Chapters 1, 2, and 3 in Part 1. An attempt is made to pull together the major themes presented in the book, with the hope of providing the reader with an increased perspective regarding the extensive, complex topics we have examined in much detail. In particular, we shall emphasize the important issues surrounding the implementation of decision systems, and all the other support systems which must also be designed. We shall try to summarize some of the major shortcomings of the operational theory we have expounded. Chapters 19 and 20 are located at the end of our book because "wisdom can't be told." Instead, we hope that the reader, who has read most of the previous chapters, will now take the time to reflect on our musings and theory—and form his own conclusions.

CHAPTER NINETEEN

Planning, Implementation, Evaluation, and Control

Many books on management science modelling have discussed implementation considerations as if they were the last step in a sequential process consisting of: goal specification, problem definition, model construction-solution and testing, and implementation strategy. While implementation of inventory decision systems, *per se*, is discussed in this, one of the last chapters, it is important to recall that throughout the book we have rejected the conventional (sequential) approach. Instead, we have presented the building of decision systems as a process of organizational intervention, whereby a model builder disrupts existing managerial decision processes in attempting to improve on the quality of decisions being made.[20]

By daring to intervene, a management scientist accepts a great responsibility—that of ensuring that the daily routines in his client's organization are carried on, at least as well as before, during the period of transition to the newly designed decision procedures and subsequently during the new steady state that will ensue. Acceptance of such a responsibility implies that implementation considerations have to dominate all phases of the design of an operational inventory decision system. In particular, successfully implemented innovations require careful planning, and once in place must be maintained, and adapted, *ad infinitum*, through an effective monitoring and control system.

Much of the material in this chapter is by necessity experiential and anecdotal. The problems associated with the planning, implementation and control of inventory decision systems have received, relatively speaking, the least attention in the literature.

19.1 *The Psychology of Implementation*

In 1964 Churchman[5] reviewed all the case studies reported in the journal *Operations Research* over its first six years of publication and concluded that there was insufficient evidence to indicate that any of the results or proposed methods had ever been implemented. In addition, most successful implementations apparently did not get reported in the literature. Subsequently, in 1965, Abrams[1] in a study of management science projects in Canada, concluded that probably no more than 75 percent of all studies *which achieve technically competent results* (i.e., not all studies that are ever attempted) get implemented in practice. Turban[32,33], in 1967 and 1970, in two further surveys, put the percentages of such successful implementations at 57 and 67 percent.

A number of persons who read this manuscript before publication questioned these percentages because they felt them to be too high. Issues were raised as to the definition of what constituted an "implemented OR/MS study" and as to what constituted the population of MS/OR studies examined (for example, those achieving "technically competent results"). While exact percentages may be open to debate, it is clear that the development of a new decision technology that is economically superior to existing methods does not in itself guarantee successful implementation in practice.

Churchman[5] hypothesized that the main cause of failure to implement MS/OR results was faulty communication of results from analyst to the manager. However, he was unable to discover any significant correlations between the mode of communication used and successful implementation. Consequently, Churchman and Schainblatt[6] postulated that successful implementation was contingent on whether a management scientist and a manager understood each other's way of thinking about the decision problem under consideration. Their conceptual model suggested that various different implementation strategies be adopted based on whether the management scientist understood the manager and vice versa, or whether the management scientist understood the manager but the manager did not understand him, etc. Dyckman[9] and Duncan [8] tested the Churchman–Schainblatt conceptual model and discovered that both managers and analysts refused to accept any specific implementation strategy as being the most desirable. In particular, mutual understanding between manager and analyst was only one of the variables which affected the success of an implementation.

Huysman,[16, 17] as well as Doktor and Hamilton,[7] examined the different styles of reasoning used by managers and management scientists and how these reasoning modes affected the likelihood of whether a successful implementation resulted. In their work a person's cognitive style was viewed as varying along an analytic-heuristic continuum. Most management scientists are assumed to be analytic. That is, they reduce any decision problem to a key set of causal variables and then attempt to achieve an answer which optimizes some explicit mathematical objective criterion. Most managers, on the other hand, rely on heuristic reasoning, which is characterized by a global, less explicit, approach to any problem where intuition, common sense and unsubstantiated feelings play an important role. This simply means that if a manager has a cognitive style that tends to the heuristic end of the continuum, he is very likely to resist an analytic (non-synthetic) solution which involves mathematics, explicit assumptions and explanations. Note that neither the manager nor the management scientist is using the "wrong" approach to problem solving. It is only a question of previous formal training and conditioning as well as psychological makeup of a person. Clearly, considerable convergence of the two models of reasoning has to occur gradually over time if management science modelling is to impact any managerial decision making situation. At present, when this is achieved, it is usually through involving managers and management scientists in a project right from the beginning.

Wedley and Ferrie [36] have examined the effects of managerial participation on project implementation. The results of their study indicate that there is a statistically significantly higher level of management participation in MS/OR projects in which the findings or methods are implemented than in those which are not. Note that they *did not prove* that management participation is necessarily the *cause* of the greater incidence of implementation. It is possible, for example, that the projects which were implemented had a higher proportion of managers with analytical cognitive styles or alternatively management scientists with a good grasp of synthetic modes of reasoning. Participation does seem to provide on-the-job training to managers in MS/OR techniques and methodology as well as an acid test for the analytical procedures being considered. Involvement also tends to lead to psychological commitment towards problem resolution, on both sides, while lessening the anxiety that unavoidably must result from any change.

While it is generally accepted that many factors affect the success or failure of an implementation, much research remains to be carried out. Rubinstein et al.[30] have suggested that the following factors can have an impact on effective implementation:

1. The degree and level of managerial support
2. The client's receptivity to giving the analyst freedom to select projects, gather data, and implement results
3. The organizational and technical ability of the key analyst and the MS/OR team
4. The organizational location of the MS/OR activity
5. The influence and power of the MS/OR group
6. The reputation of MS/OR activities
7. The adequacy of resources to fulfill the project
8. The relevance of the project
9. The level of opposition to MS/OR
10. The general perception of the level of success of the MS/OR activity

Markland and Newett[23] have devised a method for measuring the importance of various factors over the *life cycle of a project*:

1. Managerial factors:

   Top management interest
   Operating management involvement
   Managerial skills in MS/OR

2. MS/OR team factors:

   Technical ability
   Project management skills
   Orientation towards results
   Ability to communicate

3. Project factors:

   Technical feasibility
   Operational feasibility
   Economic feasibility

The relative importance of these many factors remains to be determined through research. It is clear that technical considerations are of much less importance than they are generally ascribed to be by analysts. The extent to which problems of implementation occur appears to be directly related to the degree to which changes in managerial decision making behavior are being asked for by management scientists. *Finally, and perhaps most importantly, implementation is a long drawn out process rather than a discrete event in time.*

The decision to try an innovation is only the first step in a much longer process. Many (less analytic) managers devote their entire careers to the implementation of a particular set of policies. Economists, because of total devotion to their theories over a protracted period of time, have had a substantial impact on political decision making. Management scientists must have the same degree of commitment to their decision procedures to succeed in implementation.

19.1.1 *The Human Side of Systems*

Wolek* has developed a process model for thinking about implementation in terms of three rising plateaus of commitment: adoption, systematization, and institutionalization. Systematization focuses on the development of formal procedures (instructions, input and output forms, standard methods of data acquistion, software documentation, evaluation of procedures for performance control. etc.). Institutionalization involves the gradual acceptance of the decision system as evidenced by the delegation of routine operating responsibilities by the client organization to the newly designed decision making procedures. Systematization and institutionalization are gradual, sometimes painful, processes that occur over time. The decision to adopt an innovation is an event in time that precedes both processes. According to Wolek the implementation of an innovation is more likely to occur if the adopter is:

> 1. *Predisposed to change.* It is most important that an adopter feel that he has a need for change. In particular he must feel that his problem cannot be solved with methods currently available to him.

---

* *Francis F. Wolek,"Implementation and the Process of Adopting Managerial Technology."* Interfaces, *Vol.* 5, *No.* 3, *May* 1975. *This article includes an excellent set of references and a bibliography on innovation and the psychology of implementation.*

2. *Able to relate to the innovation.* New technology must be logically related to the present thinking of management. The system designer must establish that his new procedures are:

a. definitely relevant to the manager's problem
b. sufficiently different from existing methods,
c. meaningful in terms of the variables and conditions taken into consideration

3. *Able to assess the value of the innovation.* Benefits and costs must be made situationally specific within the adopter's own economic environment. The benefits and costs of new decision procedures are best demonstrated through actual trial use. Alternatively, simulation models and estimation procedures discussed in this chapter can be substituted.

4. *Able to justify a new invention within existing organizational norms.* The recognition by a client organization that a new technology is clearly economically beneficial does not guarantee adoption. A decision to adopt is always followed by the gradual processes of systematization and institutionalization which require, respectively, the expenditure of considerable amount of effort on physical and social adapting of the innovation to the requirements of the particular situation. The cost of these formal and informal disruptions may be judged to be too high. Therefore a prerequisite for the acceptance of an innovation is a determination that the impact of the resulting changes on personalities, careers and social relationships is congruent with the client organization's desired objectives and style.

The manner in which a new technology is introduced is also at least as important as the economic implications of the new technology itself. Lawrence cites a case history where a new technique was successfully defeated not on its merits but because the intended adopters did not want to establish a precedent for change based on an analyst's transparent efforts at "conning" the adopters into thinking they had participated in developing a new technique.[21] Bishop[2] describes a successful implementation where the apparent key factor which led to adoption was a design option within the new decision system which allowed manual overrides of computer decisions by the manager *whenever he disagreed with them.* "Early in the operation of the system, approximately 80 percent of the items were overridden by the use of this feature . . . a year later this proportion had declined to less than 10 percent." According to Bishop the inventory control manager, his staff, and his boss used the new decision system simply because they felt that they were in charge, rather than at the mercy of the innovation.

Before leaving this section, we should point out that in current practice, existing (old) inventory decision systems are resulting in as many challenging difficulties and problems as newly designed ones. The reason for this is relatively simple. Most decision systems cannot be designed (even if all the above steps were followed) to allow for all contingencies. Therefore all extant decision systems depend on a large number of experienced individuals to fill in the gaps that are left in the formal procedures either on purpose or inadvertently. This *invisible* part of inventory decision systems appears to grow increasingly less dependable nowadays because of increased mobility on the part of managers and employees.

The authors were recently approached by the Canadian subsidiary of a major company listed among the Fortune 500. The company was facing the possibility of a total collapse of its highly integrated computer-based inventory decision system—which automatically placed orders for s.k.u. all over the world, and which automatically released shipments to customers from its network of warehouses in Canada, the United States, and abroad. All the original system designers had left the company for other jobs. A relatively fast turnover of personnel meant that experience with the system that had been garnered informally over the several years that the system had worked marvelously, had not been properly passed on. The formal documentation and training manuals (systematization) proved inadequate, especially in that they failed to advise on the simpler tasks that nevertheless were crucial to the routine operation of the physical system.

One day, quite unexpectedly, some errors in the logic of the decision models came to the attention of top management. Upon examining the decision system it became quickly evident that it was nearly impossible for outsiders who had not spent many years tinkering with the computer-based models to untangle all the many interrelationships involved. The company faced a costly and lengthy redesign of its decision system which had evolved without a carefully thought out plan.

The redesign involved the inclusion of many more manual overrides and statistics which will monitor the decision system's performance more closely in the future. A *greater* dependence on inputs from more senior managers was designed into the decision rules. In the past some managers and employees had left the company because they felt that they were stuck in their jobs, unable to progress through the ranks.* An extensive formal

---

* *Needless to say, under the previous decision system the company was reluctant to promote to jobs "on the outside" persons who had garnered very specialized knowledge about the "invisible" decision system.*

training programme and a planned promotion ladder were instituted (institutionalization). A permanent group was created to update and extend all documentation and training manuals on the decision system. When asked as to what he had concluded, based on his recent experiences with computer based inventory decision systems, a top manager at the company replied, "Keep it simple!"

19.2 *Planning an Inventory Study*

As we have seen, no new decision system is completely neutral socially or politically. A systems designer must honestly and realistically face up to the following questions when planning an inventory study:

a. Will there be any change in the personnel who interact with the new decision system?

b. Will there be any change in criteria by which a manager evaluates his or another's skill and performance?

c. Will there be any change in the criteria used to determine the relative status of different persons in the client organization?

d. Will there be any change in the importance of different inputs (thus the power of related persons) to the solution of problems?

If the answer to any of these questions is even a conditional yes, then analysts must allow in the design of their system for the possibility that there will be significant resistance to change.

Urban[34] has developed an approach to systems design which focuses on these questions and in which implementation is dominant throughout. We have modified somewhat the approach originally proposed by Urban, in the diagram that follows as Figure 19.1.

Formulation of Priors—A person who successfully intervenes in an organization's ongoing processes must recognize and deal with his own biases and prior inclinations. Few model builders realize fully the strength of their own priors even though they can clearly see others who are biased towards one particular technique or approach.

Entry—Urban recommends that entry be made at the decision point. A manager's most cherished prerogative is to make a decision and special care must be taken to ensure that the decision models will supplement and not replace the manager in his decision making. A small team,

Figure 19.1 An Approach to Systems Design.

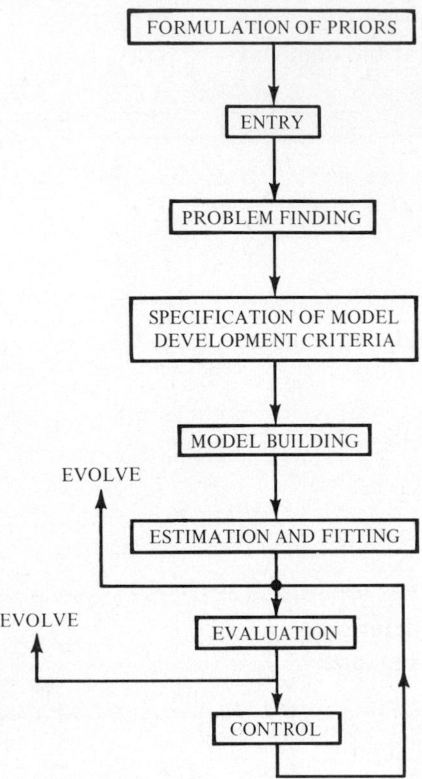

including the decision makers, some staff people, and a change agent who can work effectively from a relatively neutral position within the informal organization to facilitate change and gain acceptance, should be formed. Such a team must have full support from top management.

Problem Finding—It is important to ascertain, at the very beginning, as to why the systems designer has been invited to attempt intervention. More often than not one may wish to admit, an "outside expert" is brought in to help tip the balance in some internal debate. Are you being asked to rubber stamp some imminent decisions or decision procedures? Does the real problem that management is ready to tackle have anything to do with inventory management and production planning? Most managers have some preconceived notions about the problem that a systems-analyst is asked to solve. Unless a manager's preconceptions are proven to be in error, it is very unlikely that he will implement any changes which do not agree with what he had in mind when he hired the analyst.

Given managerial commitment and the resources to pursue model building, effort must be expended on defining the exact boundaries of the decision system to be designed. According to Urban, in his experience, 14 to 21 days is sometimes needed at this stage even for relatively simple situations. Studies must be carried out to identify existing decision models and rules of thumb as well as to determine answers to the four questions about the effects of the proposed changes on the social and political structure of the organization stated at the beginning of this section. Too many systems designers skip over this step or treat it lightly and thereby fail subsequently at implementation.

If a systems designer is new to an organization, it may be wise to identify at the initial stages a trial problem that has a quick and demonstrable payoff and that is currently on management's mind. This is by far the best way to establish credibility. It is possible that at times the trial problem chosen may be one that has nothing or little to do with inventory or production planning decision systems. If top management has had little previous experience with such decision systems, credibility may have to be established in some other arena, where top management can evaluate a system designer's output in a context that is familiar to them.

Specification of Model Development Criteria—Given a good problem definition and a clear understanding of what has to be done, a number of design options must be decided upon. Which parts of the decision system should be descriptive, predictive or normative? The physical, organizational, and external constraints must be ranked in order of priority. In the case of normative decision models, criteria used to define "optimal" and "heuristic" must be agreed upon. Explicit implementation criteria must be identified along with the expected evolutionary steps that will lead to the desired final decision system.

Model Building—It is generally agreed that model building tends to possess many of the characteristics of an art. That is, it is very difficult to prescribe general guidelines or rules that should be followed. However, the most basic factor in model building seems to be the choice of the level of sophistication at which decisions are to be made. Morris,[27] among others, suggests that all decision models should evolve from a version roughly similar to that currently used (perhaps implicitly) by managers. Little[22] suggests that decision models should be (1) understandable, (2) complete, (3) evolutionary, (4) easy to control, (5) easy to communicate with, (6) robust, and (7) adaptive.

It is important to keep in mind that there are practicing managers who have a difficult time in understanding even deterministic mathematical concepts which some model builders take for granted. Therefore, stochastic aspects of models should be introduced gradually and carefully as a decision system evolves. Also, in general, more detailed models: cost more, require more managerial time, take more time to design and maintain, are more subject to problems of personnel turnover, and require more advocation with top management and everyone else in an organization.

Estimating and Fitting—Data for model building and fitting, as we have seen, may come from subjective managerial judgement, the analysis of past numerical data, or experimentation. Generally speaking it is wise to let the decision models (developed through the sequence of steps specified above) specify the data that needs to be henceforth collected routinely in a data base, rather than to try and collect all the data that could be in some way made relevant to inventory decisions.

Evaluation—Monitoring of new decision systems both during a break-in period, and in subsequent use is crucial to successful implementation. Differences from expectations and errors will undoubtedly occur. An implementation must be designed so that discrepancies due to (1) errors in forecasting model inputs, (2) inappropriate cost estimates, (3) incorrect model structuring, (4) changes in the real environment being modeled, or (5) due to random (nonrecurrent) events can be identified quickly and as a matter of routine.

Control—As a decision system is used over time, tracking of how an implementation is progressing (relative to agreed upon model development criteria) is an important process that increases managerial confidence in decision models generally and which usually leads to useful elaboration and evolution. The three components of a decision system: data base, decision models/monitoring statistics, and input/output capability, should be built up and refined gradually. Urban suggests that a five year evolutionary period should not be considered unusual. The controls that continually monitor a decision system should be designed to last the lifetime of the system.

19.2.1 *Preliminary Probings*

Most inventory analysts start the design of inventory decision systems by a series of probing qucstions designed to quickly reveal the major strengths and weaknesses of the extant procedures. By this approach the analysts attempt to locate the tips of the iceberg, so to speak, leaving the more precise identification of the larger body for later on (to be discussed in Section 19.2.2). Surprisingly simple questions usually suffice for this purpose. Such questions also have the advantage of helping to establish an immediate working rapport with top management. Woolsey[38] describes this stage rather picturesquely:

> *. . . When I do work with production and inventory management, I have the funny feeling that I am wandering through machine shops and manufacturing plants like Columbo, the rumpled cop, asking dumb*

> *questions... questions so stupid that nobody that works there would dare to ask... (at the tool room) I go to the bins, select one at random, pull a tool from it and ask the supervisor to produce the card that matches the tool... As a rule he cannot find it... We have learned that the beautiful, computerized ordering system is not kept up to date... the second stop on the required tour is the production line... pick up a gear and ask... How much is this worth?... How many of these are there in the bin?... How long has this bin been here?... What's your cost of money for this company?...*

One usually discovers that management is unable to answer some of the above, apparently simple, questions, thereby revealing possible shortcomings that need to be examined further. For example, if management is unclear about its cost of money it is also very likely that it is unaware how much its inventory investment is costing the company. If management cannot tell how much a s.k.u. costs, for example, because of overhead accounting and transfer costs, then it is unlikely that the total funds tied up in inventories have been effectively rationed between the many purposes for which inventories are held.

In our experience, in response to simple probes, we have encountered situations where management did not believe that it costs money to place an order (see MIDAS Case B). As a result the company placed many small orders to keep "the delivery pipeline full and the total inventory investment low." The decision system proved eventually too expensive to run, especially because of the need for constant expediting of the small orders that inevitably failed to arrive on schedule.

A medium-sized company, run by an entrepreneur–engineer with a Ph.D., replied to one of our simple questions that he placed an order for more transistors whenever the box on the shelf was empty. Furthermore, because of a shortage of funds, he said he was keeping inventory low by ordering only in minimum quantities from his suppliers. The man's problem was immediately obvious, he was not allowing for delivery lead times. Furthermore, by ordering as few as 6 transistors at a time from his suppliers he received poor delivery and service. The suppliers, because it cost them much more to process such small orders than they were worth, routinely held up the small orders for several weeks by grouping five or six orders together before shipment.

A revealing probe, at this stage, can be in the form of an attempt to calculate economic order quantities and reorder points (with the help of management) for a selected few representative *A*, *B*, and *C* items. A comparison with existing decision rules can be dramatic. Similarly it is usually revealing to trace the decision to place an order through all the subsequent procedural and record-keeping steps that must be followed until stock-keeping units (s.k.u.) are on the shelf ready for use.

Every decision system is capable of some improvement at a point in time. Some savings can always be achieved without a loss in effectiveness and often at little cost. The challenge that the analyst faces during these early stages involves the determination of whether the potential savings and the costs (including the attendant social costs) are of a sufficient magnitude to warrant immediate intervention. In our experience we have found that the largest potential savings that can be identified relatively easily occur at the preliminary probing stage. Almost always the allocation of safety stock and record-keeping procedures need improvement.

Because inventory decision sytems evolve over time, an analyst should try through early probings to establish the level of sophistication in existing decision procedures. We have found Table 19.1 useful in fixing in our minds the expectations we should have about improving an existing inventory decision system.

Table 19.1 Stages of Development in the Inventory Decision System

Stage	Inventory Investment is:
1	Residual
2	Recorded
3	Monitored
4	Controlled
5	Managed
6	"Optimized"

Residual inventory decision systems are the most primitive. Inventory investment is viewed as that which is left over at the end of the year when stock is counted because of the requirements of tax law. Daily, implicit decision rules emphasize hand-to-mouth buying with no clearly defined persons responsible for the purchasing function.

A more sophisticated decision system involves the periodic *recording* of inventory transactions, rather than only once at the end of the year. Such systems are often motivated by accounting/cash management requirements. Purchasing decisions often tend to be more centralized in such circumstances.

Monitored inventory decision systems require the periodic reporting of inventory levels to responsible managers. While this feedback is very valuable, usually only a few formal ordering rules exist at this stage. However, it is not uncommon for individual clerks to develop myopic rules of thumb that they follow themselves in order to cope with the workload, especially the paperwork involved.

Controlled inventory decision systems include well-defined weekly, monthly, etc. inventory investment targets. For example, it is common in some department stores to allow buyers to buy up to a monthly limit. If the buyer has spent all of his allotment by the end of the third week, then he must wait until the beginning of the next month to place any further orders. How he spends his monthly allotment is not always controlled. Personalized and sometimes formal rules, such as required turnover ratios, are prevalent.

Managed inventory decision systems involve formal rules which usually attempt limited (heuristic) tradeoffs between competing costs. Most of the decision systems in this book fall into this category. Usually the management of inventories is functionalized by the creation of a formal department at this stage.

Optimized inventory decision systems are comprehensive and automatic, (usually computerized) ordering procedures which attempt to control inventories in several locations and serve many markets simultaneously. The Hax and Meal decision system described in Chapter 18 is of this kind. Recall though that the Hax and Meal decision system was far from being truly *mathematically* optimal.

Surprisingly many inventory decision systems in use today are at stage 1, even in fairly large companies. Only a few organizations have reached stage 6—most notable among these inventory decision systems in the United States and Canada are those in the military establishments and in some of the larger multi-national oil companies. The decision systems discussed in this book are primarily aimed at organizations in stages 3, 4, and 5 and to some extent stage 6. *An analyst should expect considerable resistance to change if he attempts to upgrade an existing inventory decision system several stages at one time!*

19.2.2 *Estimating the Aggregate Characteristics of An Existing Inventory System*

If on the basis of the preliminary probings it is decided to proceed further, then the next thing which an analyst must establish is an agreed upon point of reference. That is, what are the overall performance characteristics of the existing inventory decision system: total average cycle stock, number of replenishments per year and level of customer service provided? Such information is needed to estimate more precisely the potential savings and improvements possible (there may be several alternative strategies) and subsequently to ratify any actual gains garnered when the new decision system has been implemented.

To establish the overall performance characteristics of an existing system, a Distribution by Value curve (DBV) for *all* s.k.u. in inventory must be derived first. This requires the ranking of all s.k.u. according to their Dv values as shown in Figure 19.2. Starting with the highest Dv s.k.u., the percentage contribution to cumulative dollar usage and to cumulative number of s.k.u. in inventory are calculated and plotted.

Figure 19.2 Distribution by Value.

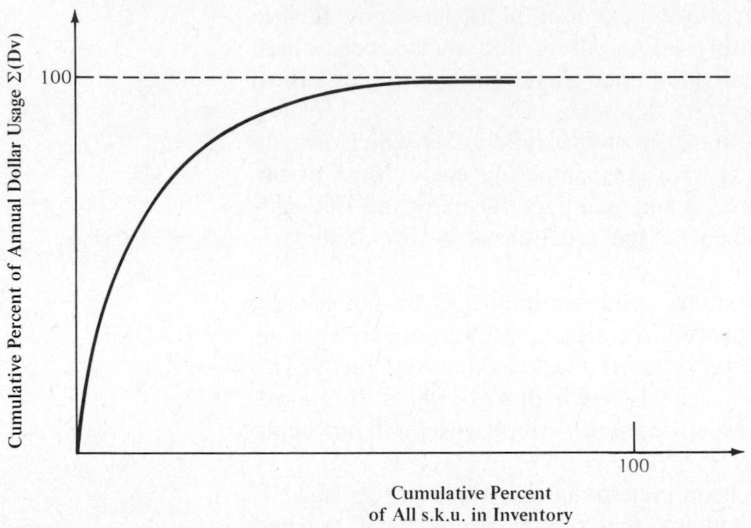

Even if data were in machine-readable form we could face two problems. First there will undoubtedly be some missing data on annual demand, D or variable cost v, etc. Secondly for large data sets the cost of computer time to derive Figure 19.2 for *all* s.k.u. may be deemed prohibitive by management.

When there is some data missing, then there is not much else one can do but ask a knowledgeable clerk or manager who is familiar with the s.k.u., to make a guesstimate. (See also Table 19.3). We believe that the development of a complete DBV is warranted at this stage. A DBV will become mandatory eventually when new order quantities and order points must be derived for *all* s.k.u. Such an expenditure at this stage is also warranted because there is a good chance that a full scale intervention into existing decision procedures is going to take place. Otherwise we should not have proceeded beyond the stage of preliminary probings. Finally, the expenditure of money on a DBV is unavoidable if top management wishes to specify the aggregate operating characteristics that they wish to achieve with a new decision system. Without such a specification an analyst cannot select appropriate values for A, r or the customer service level in the subsequent calculation of economic order quantities and reorder points.

In Chapters 5 and 7 we developed a methodology for deriving exchange curves. We also discussed the estimation of current operating points. Figures 19.3 and 19.4 below were developed for all s.k.u. in the Professional Products Division at MIDAS.*

* *Figures* 19.3 *and* 19.4 *are identical to Figure* 5.4 *and Figure* 7.7*a respectively.*

Note that on both Figures the estimated current operating points are plotted. From Figure 19.3 we see that under the comptrollers' suggested approach the estimated total average cycle stock is approximately $74,000 and the total number of replenishments per year approximately 10,500. From Figure 19.4 we see that the best the current system can do (under the new MIDAS rule) is 800 expected stockout occasions per year with about $185,000 invested in safety stock. The exchange curves plotted on both Figures describe the potential savings available if MIDAS reverted to an EOQ-type decision system described in detail in Part 2 of the book. Any point on an exchange curve that is both to the left and below an

Figure 19.3 Order Quantity Exchange Curve for the Professional Products Division of MIDAS.

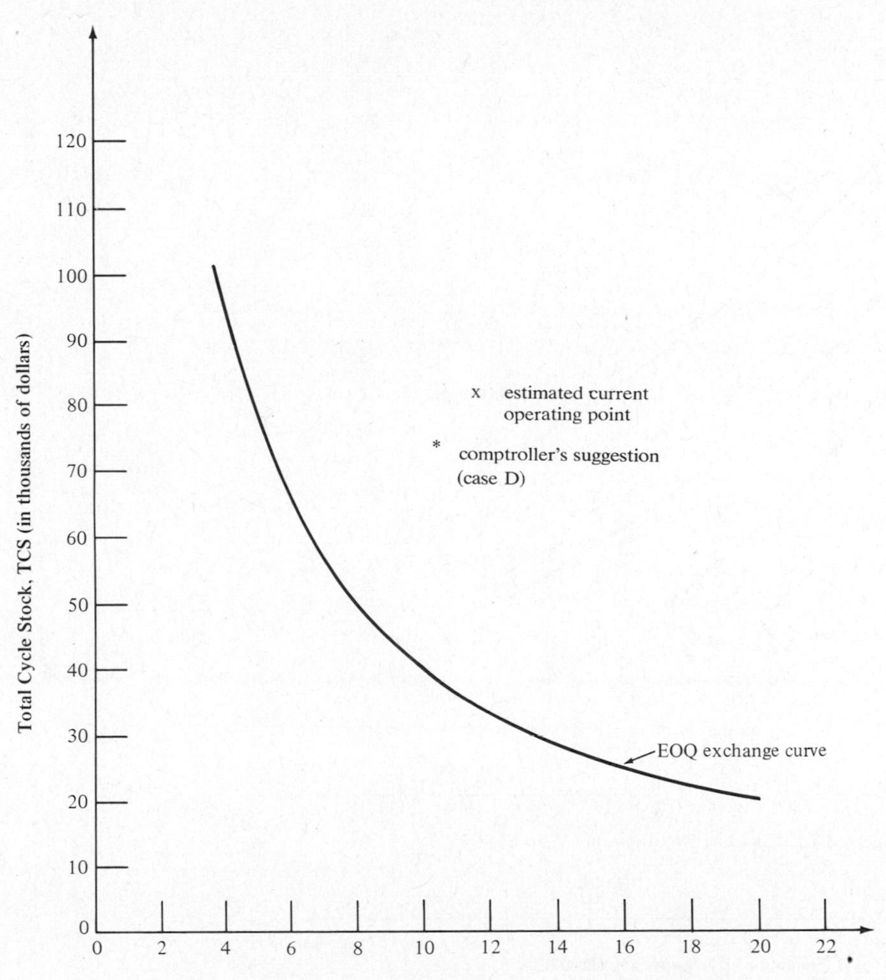

Figure 19.4 Exchange Curves of Safety Stock Versus Expected Stock-out Occasions for Professional Products Division of MIDAS.

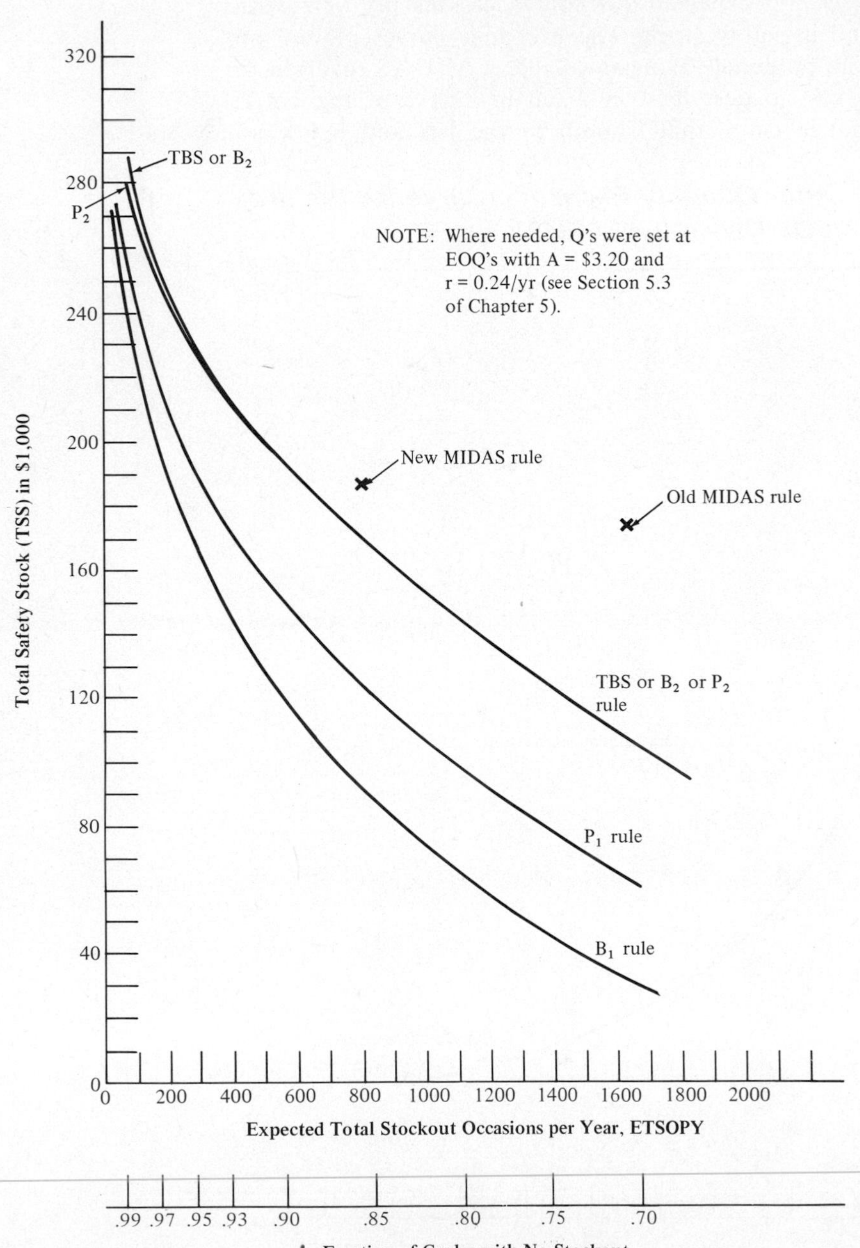

existing operating point describes the savings possible from a new EOQ-type decision system. (For details on this example and on the computation of exchange curves see Section 5.3 of Chapter 5 and Section 7.3.2 of Chapter 7.)

If management is unwilling to spend the money needed to estimate the aggregate characteristics of the existing inventory decision system then we have no other option but to proceed somewhat arbitrarily on the basis of sample data. That is, we must develop a DBV using only a sample of s.k.u. and then *proceed as if the sample DBV was a perfect representation of that for the entire population.* (The data in Figures 19.3 and 19.4 was developed for *all* 849 s.k.u. in the Professional Products Division and took one analyst about a week to compile.)

Little guidance exists in the literature on how to select a representative sample for estimation purposes *given that a complete DBV exists.* Obviously, this is a case for which stratified sampling makes sense in that certain items will contribute disproportionately to measures of effectiveness. However, well defined stratified sampling procedures remain to be derived. Abo El-Ela[10] has derived some preliminary results in this area but considerable work remains to be done. His results do provide an indication that the minimum error variance in an estimated variable (for example, total average stock, total replenishments per year, etc.) is a function of:

1. Total sample size
2. Total population size
3. Number of strata
4. The dispersion of the DBV (which he assumed to be lognormal)

Abo El-Ela also derives results on how to allocate a given total sample size among the strata using as the stratification variable Dv, the annual dollar usage of each s.k.u.

Two crucial problems in this area remain unsolved. How large a sample should one select? Obviously this should involve the balancing of the cost of sampling versus the cost of errors in the estimates, the latter being very difficult to measure. Secondly, if a complete DBV is not available, how should one physically carry out the stratified sampling? Clearly, the more important (the larger Dv) s.k.u. should dominate a sample.

At this stage we face a bit of a quandry as to how to suggest to the reader that he should proceed. Experience, judgment and negotiations with the client determine in practice the size of sample and its stratification. Perhaps all we can do is to give an example. In Table 19.2 we report the composition of an actual judgment sample which we used successfully in a recent consulting study for a large manufacturer of industrial parts.

Table 19.2 Composition of a Recent Judgment Sample

Category	Strata
1	First 100 s.k.u. from DBV
2	50 of the next 300
3	50 of the next 1600
4	100 of the next 4935
5	100 of the next 8065
6	100 of the next 12,600

Within each strata the parts were chosen randomly using a complete DBV. Note that the sample of 500 s.k.u. were selected from a total current inventory of 27,600 items.

For each s.k.u. in the sample we collected the information specified in Table 19.3. By summing, for example, column (7) for each of the 6 categories (see Table 19.2) we estimated the total inventory investment in the population as follows:

$$\begin{aligned}&\text{Estimated Total Inventory Investment}\\&=(100/100)\times\text{Total Column (7) for Category 1 items}+\\&\quad+(300/50)\times\text{Total Column (7) for Category 2 items}+\ldots+\\&\quad+(12{,}600/100)\times\text{Total Column (7) for Category 6 items.}\end{aligned}$$

A similar calculation was carried out to estimate the total number of stockouts in the population, etc. Note that these estimated values should be compared to existing accounting data whenever possible. For example, how close is the estimated inventory investment derived above to that currently reported by the accountants? If the two are within say 5 percent, we probably can conclude that we have selected a reasonably representative sample. If not, then it is usually not obvious what one should do. In particular, one should be careful in concluding that the sample is not representative. Accounting data is probably somewhat out of date, it may not include exactly the same population of s.k.u. for which we are trying to derive estimates and so on. In such circumstances the analyst should consult with a knowledgeable manager in trying to define what is wrong.

Table 19.3 Data to be Collected on Existing Inventory System for Sample of S.k.u.

S.k.u. Identification	Annual Usage, D	Unit Cost, v	Order Cost, A	Reorder Point	Recent Avg. Order Size Q	Current Inventory Level	Estimate of M.A.D.	Assumed Lead Time, L	Number of Stockouts in last 12 months
(1)	(2)	(3)	(4)	(5)	(6)	(7)	(8)	(9)	(10)

Notes:

Col. (2) If demand is seasonal then the demand for each of the last 12 months should be recorded. Most of the estimation procedures described in this chapter do not allow for seasonal fluctuation. But we do eventually need an estimate of seasonal demand to derive ordering decision rules.

Col. (4) It is likely that for many items, A will be unavailable and will have to be assumed.

Col. (5) It is likely that an average of the last few orders will have to be used.

Col. (6) It is likely that an average of the last few orders will have to be used.

Col. (8) Only if a forecasting system such as discussed in Chapter 4 exists, will the value of M.A.D. be available. Otherwise one will have to estimate this value from one of the formulae, given in Chapter 4, that related annual demand and forecast error variance. Sometimes the monthly variation in demand is calculated and used here for each s.k.u.

Col. (9) Actual lead times will usually be different for each order placed in the past. There are basically two ways to develop a value for L. One could use the more precise methodology described at the end of Chapter 6. Alternatively, we suggest that a number of recent lead times be ranked and that the lead time that occurs at about the 80th percentile be assumed to be, L. (This is an aphroximate method that the authors have resorted to when no other data was available. The 80th percentile is used to crop the outliers.

Col. (10) It is likely that this data may not be recorded. One may have to ask knowledgeable persons to make an estimate.

19.2.3 *Estimating the Aggregate Characteristics of a Proposed Economic Order Quantity Decision System*

In earlier chapters we derived the aggregate characteristics of the EOQ decision system proposed for the MIDAS Professional Products Division using computer programmes developed in conjunction with the decision rules of this book. These exchange curves were derived using all 849 s.k.u. in the Division. There is no reason why the calculations could not be done for only a sample of items, whereupon some method of extrapolation to population values would have to be used. For example, one could extrapolate in the manner we did for the sample in Table 19.2 in the previous section. Two other methodologies, which usually give somewhat less accurate results, but require less computational effort, are also available.

Brown's Typical Item Grouping Method—Brown[3] has recommended the grouping of s.k.u. according to annual dollar usage (Dv) from the DBV so that the upper limit for each interval is approximately three times the lower limit (see also Problem 19.14). By selecting interval limits in this manner, Brown takes advantage of the lognormal property of the DBV. For each category the data in Table 19.4 must be collected.

Table 19.4 Example Data for Brown's Typical Item Grouping Method

Category	Lower Limit of Annual Usage	Number of items n	Value of Annual Usage $\sum_i D_i v_i$ in Category	Total Ordering Cost $\sum_i A_i$ in Category	Total Value of Safety Stock $\sum_i SS_i$ in Category	Total Value of Std. Deviation $\sum_i \sigma_{Li} v_i$ in Category	Total Value of Orders $\sum_i Q_i v_i$ in Category
(1)	(2)	(3)	(4)	(5)	(6)	(7)	(8)
.	.	.	.	.	.	.	.
.	.	.	.	.	.	.	.
D	30,000	.	.	.	.	.	.
E	10,000	31	$383,287	$2,523	$19,622.20	$15,337.80	$552,323.90
F	3,000	.	.	.	.	.	.
G	1,000	.	.	.	.	.	.
H	300	.	.	.	.	.	.
I	100	.	.	.	.	.	.
.	.	.	.	.	.	.	.
.	.	.	.	.	.	.	.

Brown defines for each class a hypothetical item that has the average characteristics of that class. For that one typical item in each class all calculations, such as the EOQ, etc., are then carried out. Subsequently, to get the aggregate estimates for the class, all calculations for a typical item are multiplied by the number of items in a category. Then aggregate estimates for each class are summed up to yield overall estimates for the entire system. Note for example, that category E includes all items whose Dv lies between \$300,000 and \$100,000. From Table 19.4 we get for *a typical average item in category* E that:

$$\bar{A} = \frac{\$2{,}523}{31} = \$81.39$$

$$\overline{Dv} = \frac{\$383{,}287}{31} = \$12{,}364.10$$

Therefore using Eqs. 5.8 and 5.9 from Chapter 5 we can calculate that for category E, the total cycle stock (in dollars) and the total cost of replenishments per year, as functions of r, are given by:

$$\text{TCS}(E) \doteqdot \frac{1}{\sqrt{2r}}(\sqrt{\bar{A}\overline{Dv}})(31)$$

$$= \frac{1}{\sqrt{2r}}(\sqrt{81.39 \times 12{,}364.10})(31) = \frac{1}{\sqrt{2r}}(31097.71)$$

$$\text{TCR}(E) \doteqdot \sqrt{\frac{r}{2}}(\sqrt{\bar{A}\overline{Dv}})(31) = \sqrt{\frac{r}{2}}(31097.71)$$

The total orders, per year, from Eq. 5.13 of Chapter 5, are

$$N(E) \doteqdot \sqrt{\frac{r}{\bar{A}}\frac{1}{\sqrt{2}}}\sqrt{\overline{Dv}}\,(31) = \sqrt{\frac{r}{81.39}\frac{1}{\sqrt{2}}}\sqrt{12{,}364.10}\,(31)$$

$$= \sqrt{\frac{r}{2}}(382.08)$$

The total cycle stock for all categories would simply be the sum of the estimates for each of the individual category estimates:

$$\text{TCS} = \text{TCS}(A) + \text{TCS}(B) + \ldots + \frac{1}{\sqrt{2r}}(31097.71) + \text{TCS}(F) + \ldots$$

Similarily we can estimate TCR and N for all the items in inventory. Also, using Eq. 5.14 of Chapter 5, we can estimate the exchange curve given in Figure 19.3:

$$(\text{TCS})(N) = \tfrac{1}{2}\left(\sum_{i=1}^{n} \sqrt{D_i v_i}\right)^2$$

Using column (6) of Table 19.4 and the methodology described for performance measure P_1 in Section 7.2.3 of Chapter 7 we can estimate the expected number of stockout occurrences per year as follows. From columns (6) and (7); for the typical or average item in Category E:

$$k = \$19{,}622.20/15{,}337.80 = 1.28$$

$$\overline{Qv} = \$552{,}323.90/31 = 17{,}816.90$$

Expected number of stockouts per year for Category E

$$\doteqdot p_{u\geq}(k)\left(\frac{\overline{Dv}}{\overline{Qv}}\right)(31) = 0.10\left(\frac{12{,}364.10}{17{,}816.90}\right)(31)$$

$$= 2.15$$

Once again, the total expected number of stockout occasions for the whole inventory system can be estimated by summing the expected numbers obtained for each of the categories.

An Aggregate Lognormal Regression Approach—In Chapter 2 we mentioned that empirically it has been found that annual dollar usage (Dv) across a population of items tends to exhibit a pattern of remarkable regularity that can be described by a lognormal distribution. If for a population of n items (numbered $i = 1, 2, \ldots, n$) a variable x has a lognormal distribution with parameters m and b, where m is the average value of x and b is a measure of the spread of the distribution (the standard deviation of the logarithm of x), then R. G. Brown,[4] among others, has shown that

$$\sum_{i=1}^{n} x_i^j = nm^j \exp\left[b^2 j(j-1)/2\right] \tag{19.1}$$

Suppose a quantity of interest (for example, the cycle stock in dollars) for item i, call it y_i, can be expressed in the form

$$y_i = \sum_{h=1}^{H} c_h (D_i v_i)^{j_h}, \tag{19.2}$$

where the c_h's and j_h's are coefficients
that is, a linear combination of the annual dollar usage raised to various powers. Let

$$Y = \sum_{i=1}^{n} y_i \tag{19.3}$$

be the aggregate across the population of the quantity of interest (for example, the total cycle stock in dollars). Then, because the annual dollar usage is approximately lognormally distributed (with parameters m and b) we have from Eqs. 19.1, 19.2, and 19.3

$$Y = n \sum_{h=1}^{H} c_t m^{j_h} \exp\left[b^2 j_h (j_h - 1)/2\right] \tag{19.4}$$

We now present two illustrative uses:

Illustration 1—EOQ Exchange Curve—The cycle stock of item i in dollars is

$$\frac{Q_i v_i}{2} = \sqrt{\frac{A_i D_i v_i}{2r}}$$

$$= \sqrt{\frac{A}{2r}} (D_i v_i)^{1/2}$$

assuming the same A for all items.

This is a special case of Eq. 19.2 with $H = 1$, $c_1 = \sqrt{A/2r}$ and $j_1 = \frac{1}{2}$. Thus, from Eq. 19.4 we have that the total cycle stock in dollars is given by

$$\text{TCS} = n\sqrt{A/2r}\, m^{1/2} \exp(-b^2/8)$$

For the MIDAS Professional Products Division we have from Chapter 2 that $n = 849$, $m = 2048$, and $b = 1.56$. Thus,

$$\text{TCS} = (849)\sqrt{A/2r}\,(2048)^{1/2} \exp\left[-(1.56)^2/8\right]$$

$$= 20042\sqrt{A/r} \tag{19.5}$$

The number of replenishments per year of item i is

$$D_i/Q_i = D_i v_i / Q_i v_i$$

$$= D_i v_i / \sqrt{2AD_i v_i / r}$$

$$= \sqrt{\frac{r}{2A}}\,(D_i v_i)^{1/2}$$

As above, we have that the total number of replenishments per year, N, is given by

$$N = n\sqrt{r/2A}\, m^{1/2} \exp(-b^2/8)$$

and for the MIDAS division

$$N = 20042\sqrt{r/A} \tag{19.6}$$

Multiplication of Eqs. 19.5 and 19.6 gives

$$(\text{TCS})N \simeq 401{,}700{,}000 \tag{19.7}$$

which is the lognormal approximation of the exchange curve of TCS versus N.

The exact exchange curve is

$$(\text{TCS})N = 406{,}500{,}000.$$

The latter was developed by a complete item-by-item computation (extremely time-consuming without the aid of a computer routine). It is shown on Figure 19.3. The lognormal approximation of Eq. 19.7 falls a negligible amount above the exact curve in Figure 19.3, such a small amount that one would have difficulty in discerning any difference between the curves.

Illustration 2—Safety Stock Considerations—Herron,[15] with some reasonable approximations, has extended the lognormal approach to allow aggregate estimates of safety stocks and service measures. We indicate the nature of his methods with a particular case, namely the B_2 shortage costing case (a charge of $B_2 v_i$ is made for each unit short of item i). The appropriate decision rule for selecting the safety factor k_i under these circumstances is, from Section 7.2.6 of Chapter 7, to select k_i that satisfies

$$p_{u\geq}(k_i) = \frac{Q_i r}{D_i B_2}$$

where $p_{u\geq}(k_i)$ is the probability that a unit normal variable takes on a value of at least k_i. Using an EOQ for Q_i we obtain:

$$p_{u\geq}(k_i) = \frac{\sqrt{2Ar}}{B_2}(D_i v_i)^{1/2} \tag{19.7}$$

Suppose we are interested in the total safety stock in dollars (TSS). The safety stock of item i in dollars is given by

$$SS_i v_i = k_i \sigma_{Li} v_i \tag{19.8}$$

Herron uses an approximation similar to one that we discussed earlier in the book, namely that $\sigma_{Li} v_i$ is given (at least for $L = 1$) *approximately* by (see Chapter 2, Eq. 2.4):

$$\sigma_{Li} v_i \simeq a_2 (D_i v_i)^{b_2} \tag{19.9}$$

Thus Eq. 19.8 can be expressed as

$$SS_i v_i \simeq k_i a_2 (D_i v_i)^{b_2} \tag{19.10}$$

Now, we know that k_i depends on $D_i v_i$ through Eq. 19.7. However, we want Eq. 19.10 to end up as a linear combination of powers of $D_i v_i$ (in order to be able to use Eqs. 19.2 and 19.4). Herron accomplishes this by using the following fitted approximation for k_i in terms of $p_{u\geq}(k_i)$*

$$k \simeq 1.391 p^{-0.123} - 2.325 p^{0.618} \tag{19.11}$$

---

* *For simplicity in notation in Eq.* 19.11 *we drop the subscript on* k_i *and let p represent* $p_{u\geq}(k_i)$.

Substitution of Eqs. 19.7 and 19.11 into Eq. 19.10 gives

$$\begin{aligned} SS_i v_i &\simeq a_2(D_i v_i)^{b_2}[1.391(\sqrt{2Ar}/B_2)^{-0.123}(D_i v_i)^{-0.0615} \\ &\quad -2.325(\sqrt{2Ar}/B_2)^{0.618}(D_i v_i)^{0.309}] \\ &= 1.319 a_2(\sqrt{2Ar}/B_2)^{-0.123}(D_i v_i)^{b_2-0.0615} \\ &\quad -2.325 a_2(\sqrt{2Ar}/B_2)^{0.618}(D_i v_i)^{b_2+0.309} \end{aligned}$$

But, this is in the form of Eq. 19.2. Hence, the lognormal distribution of Dv can be used to find the total safety stock by means of Eq. 19.4.

To permit the derivation of aggregate measures of service (such as the expected total value short per year) and to deal with other safety stock decision rules Herron makes use of other approximations (similar to Eq. 19.11), for example,

i. the $G_u(\cdot)$ function expressed as a linear combination of powers of the $p_{u\geq}(\cdot)$ function

ii. k expressed as a linear combination of powers of the $G_u(\cdot)$ function

---

19.3 *Evaluation and Control*

We have described implementation as a process, consisting of a decision to adopt, followed by systematization and in turn by gradual institutionalization. The last of these three phases tends to get the least attention from analysts because it is seen as being (technically speaking) too complex to generalize about. Yet, many implementation failures occur at this stage. After all, it is at this stage that the integrity of a new decision is finally (if ever) proven. The claims of estimation procedures such as discussed in section 19.2, no matter how well conceived, seldom are a match to proven success in daily use.

In parallel to an actual inventory decision system a number of additional monitoring procedures need to be designed. These procedures should ensure that undesirable and unexpected situations are quickly detected, evaluated, and remedial action initiated. Backorders, erroneous forecasts, manufacturing variances, deviations between physical and book inventories, and the assumptions on which decision rules were based all need to be continually monitored, because they may reveal some design flaws in the new decision system. Some of the most important control functions include:

1. Daily comparison of actual production with that being scheduled

2. Periodic checking of actual sales activity versus forecast

3. Periodic review of the backorder situation and the expediting of requirements

4. Periodic taking of physical inventory

5. Periodic monitoring of the design assumptions of the decision models implemented

If these activities are not carried out routinely, then the institutionalization of an innovative decision system is likely not to follow.

19.3.1 *Physical Stock Counts*

Physical stock counts, taken annually in many organizations, are intended to satisfy the auditors that accounting records represent the value of inventory investment reasonably. But the accuracy of stock records is also an important aspect of production planning and inventory management. Most of the decision systems described in this book would be seriously crippled by inaccurate records unless some form of an evaluation and control system is operated in parallel.[24]

As a check on records some physical counting of s.k.u. actually in stock has always been deemed necessary. But physical counts have proven to be expensive and time-consuming. Taking a physical stock count, has in the past, in many companies involved the shutting down of all operations, and thereby the losing of valuable productive time. Because of this large opportunity cost, many companies are starting to adopt different procedures which achieve the same purpose. Given a limited budget allocation to be spent on corroborating inventory records with physical inventory, a system which more effectively rations the available clerical resources is known as *cycle counting*.

In cycle counting, as the name might suggest, a physical inventory of each particular item is taken once during each of its replenishment cycles. There are several versions of cycle counting;[35] probably the most effective one involves counting the remaining physical stock of an s.k.u. just as a replenishment arrives. This has two key advantages. First, the stock is counted at its lowest level. Second, a clerk is already at the stocking position delivering the replenishment, hence a special trip is not needed for counting purposes. Clearly, one drawback is that if the records are faulty on the high side, we may already have gone into an unexpected stockout position. Note that cycle counting automatically ensures that low usage s.k.u. are counted less often than high usage items because the frequency of ordering increases with Dv (at least under a decision system based on economic order quantities). Most auditors agree with physically counting low-value items less often than the more expensive ones.

Some type of cutoff rules are necessary when using cycle counting because paperwork relating to a s.k.u. being counted, can be outstanding at any point in time. When outstanding paperwork exists, a disagreement between counted and reordered inventory may not necessarily mean that the written records are in error. Cycle counts are for this reason in some companies confined to first thing in the morning or the last thing in the day, or on the off shift, when outstanding paperwork should be at a minimum. In any case, some form of cutoff rule such as the following is required:

> i. If a discrepancy is less than some low percent of the reorder point level, adjust your records to the lower of the two figures and report any loss to accounting.
>
> ii. If the discrepancy is greater than some low percent, one must wait a few days and request a recount. Hopefully by this time outstanding paperwork would have been processed. If the discrepancy is the same on both counts we have probably found an error and should adjust the records accordingly. If the second count results in a different discrepancy, the problem requires investigation.

There are some practical disadvantages and problems with cycle counting.[28] Cutoff rules are not easy to follow while normal everyday activity is going on. Checking up on the paperwork in the system, so that stock levels may be properly corroborated, requires considerable perseverance and diplomacy. Responsibility for cycle counting is often assigned to stockroom employees. As a result, too often cycle counting gets relegated a lower priority and, more often than it should, is discontinued, when business activity picks up and stockroom personnel find it difficult to carry out both activities. One solution in such cases is to assign a permanent team to carry out cycle counting all the year round.

Cycle counting rations effort in proportion to annual dollar usage, Dv. It is important to recognize that not all causes of stock discrepancies are a function of Dv. Recently the authors encountered a situation in one company, where it was not necessarily the higher valued items that were missing. Items that could be resold on the black market tended to be out of stock more often. Although it could not be proven, the distinct possibility existed that some of the stolen parts were being resold back to the company through supposedly legitimate wholesalers. Therefore the physical size and resaleability of items, as well as their Dv, must be considered in establishing procedures for stock counts. However, physical size is apparently not necessarily an undue impediment. A puzzled manufacturer approached us once when he discovered that somehow engine blocks were apparently being smuggled past the guards at the gates around his plant.

19.3.2 *Monitoring the Design Assumptions of Decision Rules and Decision Systems*

In Chapter 3 we explored the difficulties encountered in estimating the various parameters for the decision rules developed in the rest of the book. Resistance to new decision systems results in part from the fact that management science decision models require a greater deal of explicitness and preciseness than most managers can comfortably deliver. The cost of carrying inventories, through a company's cost of capital, is affected almost daily by world events. Therefore, the total dollar investment in inventories and the quality of customer service that is "right" in keeping with these events should ideally also be subject to constant revision by top management. In a dynamic environment, management science models must keep pace with changes in the economic environment to maintain management's confidence in the inventory decision system. Decision systems whose design assumptions become outdated are the most frequent cause of failure over the long implementation period.

Most managers are by necessity results-oriented. When a decision system fails to be supportive of managerial actions, more often than not, a manager under such circumstances, is unwilling to distinguish between problems of data measurement and a failure to appropriately model the decision environment. Therefore a systems designer must accept responsibility for monitoring both whether the model he built is appropriate, as well as whether the model parameters (data) are being properly estimated.

In Chapter 4 we discussed various methods for monitoring of the accuracy of forecasts and of the continuing appropriateness of different forecasting procedures. Such monitoring and control systems are relatively common in practice. Often ignored in practice, though, is the routine monitoring of the appropriateness of the economic order quantity cost parameters, A, v, and r, the shortage costs or service levels and the costs of hiring and firing, regular and overtime production, etc. used in the aggregate scheduling decision. From our experience we have found that the cost parameters for the EOQ's and reorder points (order-up-to-levels) should be updated once or twice a year. For the important A items these parameters should be reviewed every time an order is placed. The maintenance of aggregate scheduling costs should be integrated with regular cost accounting procedures with revised costs reported at least once a year.

The monitoring of individual item cost parameters is necessary to establish control in aggregate over the measures specified by the top management filter that we discussed in Chapter 1. In Figure 1.1 three primary top management measures were identified: aggregate inventory constraints, aggregate stockout performance goals and aggregate budget constraints. Changes in such aggregate measures can only be achieved through the adjustment of individual item decision rule parameters.

19.3.3 *Dynamic Effects—The Transition to a New Steady State*

Each time the parameters of a set of decision models are adjusted a series of transitory effects results which must be carefully monitored and controlled. Consider the recommendation of an analyst who affects the reallocation of inventory tied up in safety stocks in such a manner that *total inventory investment is not changed in the long run.* The reorder points for some s.k.u. are raised, for others the reorder points are lowered, and for the balance there is no change. If management implemented all of the new reorder points at the *same* time, some of the newly calculated reorder points, raised from previous levels, would immediately trigger orders. If there were many changes then a sudden wave of orders could overload a company's manufacturing plant and/or order department and also result, after a lead time, in an increase in on-hand dollar inventory investment as shown in Figure 19.5.*

The obvious solution is, of course, not to make all the changes at the same time. Some form of phased implementation strategy that lengthens the period of transition and thereby dampens the disruptions in the system must be chosen. To determine an acceptable transition strategy the following need to be balanced:

1. The cost of carrying extra inventories during the transition period

2. The expense of a higher than normal ordering rate

---

* *Discussion herein is based on a consulting study by Rein Peterson. "Determination of Feasible Transition Strategy for Changing Decision Rules in an Existing Economic Order Quantity, Reorder Point Inventory Control System." Unpublished Manuscript,* 1966.

Figure 19.5 Schematic Diagram of a Dynamic Effect.

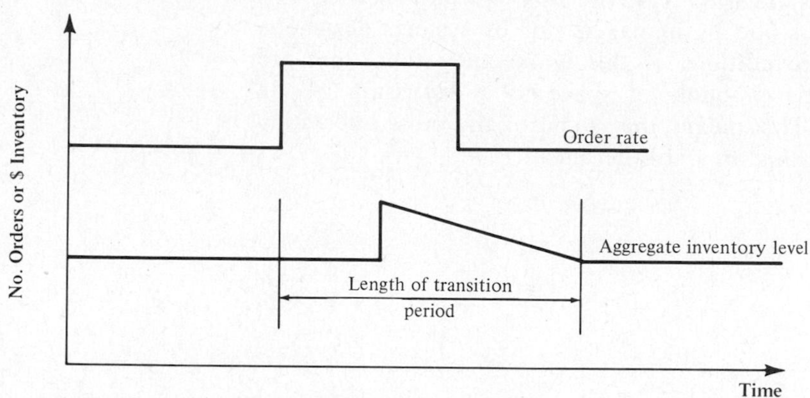

3. The opportunity cost of delaying benefits from a new inventory decision system that is not implemented all at once

4. Any benefits resulting from better than the normal service level resulting from extra inventory on hand during the transition period

In practice, the changeover to new decision rules is often carried out at the time when a s.k.u. is reordered, the assumption being made that a dispersion of transitory effects will result through "random" times when a particular item reaches its reorder point. There is of course no guarantee that large blips such as illustrated in Figure 19.5 would not occur. Alternatively, revised decision rules are implemented in phases, starting with the most important, *A* items first.

In either case, it is best to try and plan a large transition carefully, in particular one should carefully monitor the resulting stockout rate, the net increase in orders placed and the rise in total dollar inventory. It is unlikely that the costs of transition can ever be determined and balanced analytically. Therefore the simulation of transition effects that result from alternative implementation strategies should be undertaken whenever the scope of the problem warrants such an expense.

19.4 *Summary*

While this is the fourth chapter in this book that has been devoted to a discussion of the environment in which new inventory management and production planning decision systems must be implemented, we have but scratched the surface of all the practical issues involved. The process of decision making that utilizes decision systems such as proposed in this book is not completely understood by managers nor by systems designers. We are convinced that future editions of this book, and others that are similar, will devote increasing amounts of space to a discussion of the issues raised in Chapter 19. This means that some of the most interesting and exciting achievements in this area still lie ahead.

Problems for Chapter 19

Problem 19.1

A large wholesaler carried out a preliminary study in which they estimated the effects of introducing an order point, order quantity inventory control system in place of their current system. Because significant potential savings were estimated to be available, the new decision system was installed. Actual savings in carrying costs, replenishment costs and shortage costs during the first year of operation turned out to be much lower than the estimated values. Give some possible reasons for why this might have happened. What action would you take? Elaborate.

Problem 19.2

The following statements were made by a lecturer on the system designer:

1. "His very presence implies that something is wrong—a criticism of some person or group."
2. "He must be totally objective."
3. "He must constantly remind himself that he should not oversell the ideas he is trying to implement."
4. "His final report, very detailed, involving a tremendous amount of analysis and manhours in preparation, will be received by top management as just one of many other items competing for management attention."
5. "He is usually a relatively narrow specialist who understands techniques and computers, but lacks training on the human side of systems."

Comment on and discuss each statement in turn. Do you agree with the sentiments expressed?

Problem 19.3

"It is important that the operating characteristics of an existing inventory management or production planning decision be established before any revisions are started." Do you agree? Give at least 5 reasons for your opinion. Discuss.

Problem 19.4

In Section 19.1 the results of a number of research studies are summarized. Select a recent study that is not reported here, compare and contrast the views expressed. Illustrate your discussion with examples of implementation problems from your own experience and that of your colleagues.

Problems 19.5

Visit a business of your choice and try to establish on the basis of, at most, a one hour interview how sophisticated their existing decision systems are. Write a two page memorandum describing their decision rules and summarize your impressions in terms of the concepts presented in Figure 19.2. What is their highest priority problem? Where would you start to revise their decision systems? How large are the potential savings and improvements likely to be? Does top management appear to be receptive to some changes in the existing procedures?

Problems 19.6

A sample of 30 items has been randomly selected from the inventory files of a company. The company stocks 7000 items in total. Perform the following operations using the information shown in the table.

a. Develop a curve similar to that given in Figure 19.3.

b. What fraction of the items make up 80 percent of the total annual dollar movement?

c. What is your best estimate of the total annual usage of the 7000 items?

Item No.	Annual Usage, Dv($/yr)
1	80
2	120
3	440
4	3
5	17
6	70
7	90
8	0
9	480
10	420
11	320
12	20
13	1330
14	800
15	80
16	2080
17	1400
18	400
19	450
20	410
21	60
22	80
23	440
24	150
25	4100
26	490
27	3400
28	40
29	220
30	120

Problem 19.7

During the preliminary probing of an existing inventory decision system you collect the following data:

Item A	Item B
$A = \$10.00$	$A = \$10.00$
$v = \$4.58$	$v = \$1.82$
$D = 4000$ (last year)	$D = 6100$ (last year)
Current Order Quantity = 1000	Current Order Quantity = 500
Current Reorder Point $\doteq$ 350	Current Reorder Point $\doteq$ 500
$L = 1$ to 3 weeks	$L \doteq 1$ month

Here is your chance to play rumpled cop. Based on this data what would you conclude? What questions would you pose to management? What other data would you seek? Would you request a full scale investigation? Assume that A was estimated by the bookkeeper and v was the value assigned by accountants for purposes of evaluating inventories. The rest of the data was compiled by you from available records.

Problem 19.8

a. What would you conclude about the total inventory decision system described, in part, in Problem 19.7 above, if in addition you were able to compile (using the methodology in Section 5.3 of Chapter 5 and in Section 7.3.2 of Chapter 7) for a total of 50 items the exchange curves given in Figure 19.6?

Figure 19.6

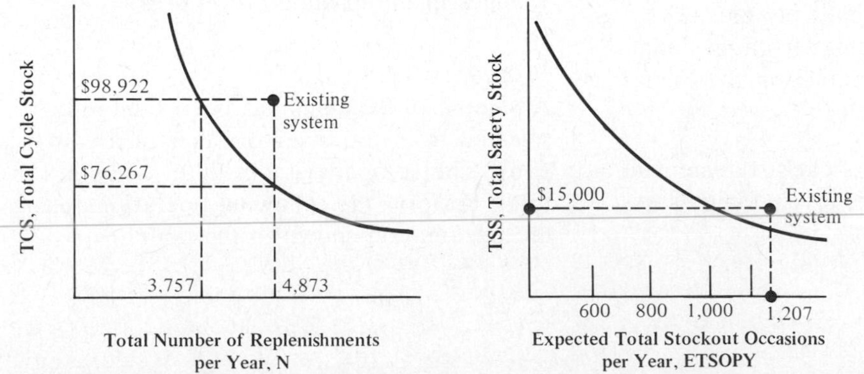

b. Discuss some of the general approaches you would consider in attempting to improve the existing decision making procedures.

Problem 19.9

In the first part of Section 19.2.3 it was suggested that to estimate total orders per year the following equation be used:

$$N = \frac{\bar{D}}{\bar{Q}} = \text{number of items}$$

a. Show that the above equation does not hold true for the data below:

Item, i	D_i	Q_i
1	2,000	400
2	500	400
3	100	200

b. Why then should Brown's method ever be used to make an aggregate estimate?

Problem 19.10

Suppose for category H of Fig. 19.8 the following values were collected:

$$n = 1203$$

$$\sum Dv = \$638{,}720$$

$$\sum A = \$11{,}764.34$$

$$\sum SS = \$100{,}539$$

$$\sum \sigma v = \$70{,}307$$

$$\sum Qv = \$83{,}808$$

Use Brown's typical item grouping method (*Section* 19.2.3) *to estimate for category H*: the EOQ exchange curve and the expected number of stockout occasions per year with the current safety stock (assuming a P_1 service measure).

Problem 19.11

For the data in Problem 19.10, estimate the total safety stock, expected number of shortages per year, and the expected value of backorders per year (see Eq. 7.30 in Chapter 7) for each of the following strategies:

a. A five week safety stock for each item.
b. A value of $k = 1.2$.
c. A 96.3 percent service level (fraction of demand satisfied without backorders).
d. How do the values under part (a) of this question compare to those you derived in Problem 19.10? Discuss.

Problem 19.12

a. Using the methodology described in the second part of Section 19.2.3 estimate the value of total cycle stock (TCS) and the total number of orders per year (N) for a lognormal DBV consisting of 12,387 s.k.u. with the following parameters:

$$m = 1856$$

$$b = 2.03$$

$$\bar{A} \doteq 10.00$$

$$r = 0.20/\text{yr}.$$

b. Draw the exchange curve of TCS vs. N.
c. What are the advantages and disadvantages between this method of estimating total cycle stock, that discussed in problem 19.10, and that described in Section 5.3 of Chapter 5.

Problem 19.13

In Chapter 19 we discussed four methods of estimating the performance of an existing inventory decision system using:

1. All s.k.u. in inventory.
2. A representative random sample.
3. Brown's typical item grouping method.
4. A lognormal regression approach.

Evaluate and contrast each of the above methods, indicating the circumstances under which each would be appropriate to use in practice.

Problem 19.14

Consider the situation where all the items in a population have the same values of A and r. Suppose aggregation into ranges of Dv is to be done as described in Table 19.4 and the *mid-value*, $\overline{Dv}$, of each range is to be used for the EOQ calculations for all items in the range. The ranges are to be selected so as to not make a percent cost error greater than p. Let $(Dv)_B$, $(Dv)_T$, and $\overline{Dv}$ be the bottom, top and average points of a particular range.

a. Verify that:

$$\frac{(Dv)_B}{\overline{Dv}} = \frac{\overline{Dv}}{(Dv)_T} = \text{constant}$$

where the constant is a function of p, but is independent of the particular range.

b. Show that because of the result in part (a), ranges should not be chosen to be of equal width, but should have a constant difference between the logarithms of the upper and lower limits.

Problem 19.15

Discuss the economic considerations, physical constraints and other possible factors that could influence the choice of the method, the frequency and the timing of physical inventory counts. Illustrate your discussions with actual examples from your experience whenever possible.

REFERENCES FOR CHAPTER 19

1. Abrams, John W., "Implementation of Operational Research: A Problem in Sociology." *The Journal of the Canadian Operational Research Society*, Vol. 3, No. 3, November, 1955.

2. Bishop, Jack L. Jr. "Experience with a Successful System for Forecasting and Inventory Control." *Operations Research*, Vol. 22, No. 6.

3. Brown, Robert G. *Decision Rules for Inventory Management.* Holt Rinehart Winston, 1967.

4. Brown, R. G. "Estimating Aggregate Inventory Standards." *Naval Research Logistics Quarterly*, March, 1963.

5. Churchman, C. W. "Managerial Acceptance of Scientific Recommendations." *California Management Review*, Vol. 7, Fall, 1964.

6. Churchman, C. W. and Schainblatt, A. H. "The Researcher and the Manager: A Dialectic of Implementation." *Management Science*, Vol. 11, No. 4, Feb., 1965.

7. Doktor, Robert H. and Hamilton, William F. "Cognitive Style and Acceptance of Management Science Recommendations." *Management Science*, Vol. 19, No. 8, April, 1973.

8. Duncan, W. Jack. "The Researcher and the Manager: A Comparative View of the Need for Mutual Understanding. *Management Science*, Vol. 20, No. 8, April, 1974.

9. Dyckman, Thomas R. "Management Implementation of Scientific Research: An Attitudinal Study." *Management Science*, Vol. 13, No. 10, June, 1967.

10. El-Ela, Maged A. Abo. "Statistical Sampling for Inventory Parameters." Unpublished M.Sc. thesis, University of Waterloo, Waterloo, Ontario. Canada, June, 1975.

11. Emma, C. "Observations on Physical Inventory and Stock Record Error." *Journal of Industrial Engineering*, Vol. XVIII, No. 7, July, 1967.

12. Gross, D., Harris, C. and Roberts, P. "Bridging the Gap Between Mathematical Inventory Theory and the Construction of a Workable Model—A Case Study." *International Journal of Production Research*, Vol. 10, No. 4, 1972.

13. Gross, D. and Schrady, D. "A Survey of Inventory Theory and Practice." Working Paper Serial T-303. Program in Logistics, George Washington University, August 1074.

14. Hayes, R. H. "Statistical Estimation Problems in Inventory Control." *Management Science*, Vol. 15, No. 11, July, 1969.

15. Herron, D. P. "Profit Oriented Techniques for Managing Independent Demand Inventories." *Production and Inventory Management*, Vol. 15, No. 3, 1974.

16. Huysman, Jan H. B. M. *The Implementation of Operations Research.* New York: Wiley Interscience, 1970.

17. Huysman, Jan H. B. M.

"The Effectiveness of the Cognitive-Style Constraint in Implementing Operations Research Proposals." *Management Science,* Vol. 17, No. 1, September, 1970.

18. Iglehart, D. and Morey, R. "Inventory Systems with Imperfect Asset Information." *Management Science,* Vol. 18, No. 8, April, 1972.

19. Jordan, Henry. "How to Start a Cycle Counting Program." *1975 A.P.I.C.S. Conference Proceedings.*

20. Kolb, David, A., and Frohman, Alan L. "An Organization Development Approach to Consulting." *Sloan Management Review,* Vol. 12, Fall, 1970.

21. Lawrence, P. R. "How to Deal with Resistance to Change." *Harvard Business Review,* January–February, 1969.

22. Little, John D. C. "Models and Managers: The Concept of a Decision Calculus." *Management Science,* Vol. 16, No. 8, April, 1970.

23. Markland, Robert E. and Newett, Robert J. "A Subjunctive Taxonomy for Evaluating the Stages of Management Science Research." *Interfaces,* Vo. 2, No. 2, February, 1972.

24. Moore, Michael D. "Stock Record Accuracy and Cycle Inventory Counting." *Production and Inventory Management,* 2nd Quarter, 1973.

25. Morey, R. "Inventory Systems with Imperfect Demand Information." *Naval Research Logistics Quarterly,* Vol. 17, No. 3. September, 1970.

26. Morgan, J. "Questions for Solving the Inventory Problem." *Harvard Business Review,* Vol. 41, No. 1, July, 1963, pp. 95–110.

27. Morris, William T. "On the Art of Modelling." *Management Science,* Vol. 13, August, 1969.

28. Plossl, G. W. and Wight, O. W. *Production and Inventory Control.* Prentice-Hall, Englewood Cliffs, N. J., 1967.

29. Rosenman, B. and Olejarz, G. "Logistic Performance Indicators for Cost-Benefit Analyses of Automatic Data Processing Systems." Philadelphia, Pa., April, 1973.

30. Rubenstein, Albert H., et al. "Some Organizational Factors Related to the Effectiveness of Management Science Groups in Industry." *Management Science,* Vol. 18, No. 8, April, 1972.

31. Schrady, D. "Operational Definitions of Inventory Record Accuracy." *Naval Research Logistics Quarterly,* Vol. 17, No. 1, March, 1970.

32. Turban, Efraim. "The Use of Mathematical Models in Plant Maintenance Decision Making," *Management Science,* Vol. 12, No. 6, February, 1967.

33. Turban, Efraim. "How Companies are Using Operations Research Techniques." *Management Review,* Vol. 59, No. 3, March, 1970.

34. Urban, Glen L. "Building Models for Decision Makers." *Interfaces,* Vol. 4, No. 3, May, 1974.

35. Van De Mark, R. L. *Wholesaler Inventory Control.* Van De Mark Inc., St. Clair, Michigan. 1961.

36. Wedley, William C. and Fer-

rie, Adam E. J. "Some Effects of Managerial Participation on Project Implementation." Simon Fraser University, British Columbia, Canada, Mimeographed.

37. Wharton, F. "On Estimating Aggregate Inventory Characteristics." *Operational Research Quarterly*, Vol. 26, No. 31, September, 1975.

38. Woolsey, R.E.D. "On Doing Good Things and Dumb Things in Production and Inventory Control." *Interfaces*, Vol. 5, No. 3, May, 1975.

CHAPTER TWENTY

In Perspective

(Including "Some Goodies for Our Academic Buddies")

Throughout the book we have advocated a decision systems approach to inventory management and production planning, where decision systems were defined in Chapter 1 as consisting of three basic elements: a data-processing information system, a set of automatic decision rules, and a built-in capability for intervention, at will, by a human decision maker (see Figure 1.3). In this last chapter we first present, in section 20.1, a brief discussion of the data-processing information system. Then in section 20.2, the "software" make or buy decision is discussed. Next in section 20.3, we highlight some applied research problems that we believe should be addressed by our academic friends working in close consultation with practitioners. Finally, section 20.4, provides some concluding remarks.

20.1 *Some Comments on the Data-Processing Information System*

To date, many organizations have been mostly preoccupied with the design and implementation of the data-processing information system. This is really not very surprising if we recall the discussion in Chapters 1, 2, and 3 where the problem of inventory management and production planning was identified as being primarily one of coping with the coordination of a large number of s.k.u. and the balancing of a multitude of cost-benefit variables. Because the motives and goals of different groups (top management, finance, marketing, manufacturing) within an organization are not always the same, good data, as to what is really going on, is vital to the achievement of valid compromises. The design of such a data-processing information system has proven to be no easy task, as should be evident from the demanding requirements listed for a typical manufacturing and distribution firm in Table 20.1:

Table 20.1 Informational Requirements for Materials Management[a]

Inventory Control	Production Planning
Inventory status	Production requirements
Ordering (or setup) cost	Regular production cost
Inventory carrying cost	Hiring and firing cost
Purchasing quantity discounts	Capacity availability
Desired service levels	Production rates
Forecast requirements and feedback	Production smoothing inventory
Procurement lead times	Capacity planning
Imported product procurement plans	Overtime production cost
Traffic	**Purchasing**
Bill of lading	Vendor information
Carrier characteristics	Vendor performance
Rates and routings	Product specification
	Open orders
Warehousing	
Operations expense vs. plan	
Operating performance	
Finished product status	
Custom clearance and packing costs	

[a] Adapted from Arnoldo Hax.[6]

In the future we must become increasingly more careful to not lose sight of the fact that a data handling system is only part of the total challenge. A mere data-processing system:*

> Does not overcome vagueness of organizational responsibilities
>
> Does not replace the painful need for forecasted plans
>
> Does not provide evaluation if there is no definition of policy against which one can evaluate performance
>
> Does not automatically provide sophistication and precision in decision making

At the same time, a mere data-processing system:

> Does tend to foster a "leave it to the experts" attitude
>
> Does make it possible for managers to retreat from direct involvement with daily inventory decisions

Robert Heller[9] has focused the challenge facing the designers of decision systems by concluding that:

> *The (managerial) task isn't to understand what is meant by, say, a system using doubly exponentially smoothed average demand forecasts, etc. It is to know rules of thumb such as this: operational research techniques will enable most companies to cut stocks by* 30 *percent, saving delicious sums, but eight tenths of that saving will come from better recordkeeping.*

The fact that Heller believes 80 percent of the gains are to be found in better recordkeeping is a reflection of how poorly we have managed inventories in the past. It does not imply, as some may conclude, that logical management science decision rules have relatively less to contribute. Measurement, and thereby data-processing, always implies the existence of a theory, a theory about what needs to be measured to feed the requirements of logical deduction. In effect, Heller is (at least to some degree)

---

* *Adapted from a speech by Morton H. Broffman. "Top Management View of Production and Inventory Management." Annual Meeting of A.P.I.C.S., Atlantic City, New Jersey,* 1964.

implying that we may have too often collected and recorded the wrong data in the past. We must therefore be careful that we do not repeat these past mistakes again, only this time doing it faster and in greater bulk than ever before through the use of computers.

20.2 *To Make or Buy*

In considering the problem of how to improve existing inventory management and production planning decision making procedures, top management in effect faces the familiar *make or buy decision.* Management has the choicc of either building an inventory decision system from scratch or, more likely, gradually improving their existing procedures, using some of the ideas we have presented. Alternatively, management could adopt one of the many computerized software (canned) packages or one of the manual systems (as in the MIDAS cases) available on the market. These prepackaged systems contain decision rules and concepts that try to deal with problems similar to the ones we have discussed in our book. But the quality and sophistication of the decision making technology used in *some* of these systems can be open to question. This appears to be a reflection of the fact that prepackaged systems are being sold by a variety of organizations: computer software/hardware companies, consulting firms, data-processing companies, computer service bureaus and by private manufacturing concerns attempting to recoup some of the investment that went into developing a custom-built inventory decision system for themselves. Some of these organizations do not possess the know-how required to properly develop such systems and/or provide appropriate assistance in their implementation. Recall our critical examination in Chapter 5 of the MIDAS ordering decision rules (see case D) and the production planning procedures implemented by the consulting firm discussed in Case F and Chapter 16. Such *ad hoc* procedures are common in the prepackaged systems being sold. Many of these organizations do have one thing in common. They either entered this phase of their business through a desire to sell hardware (including manual card systems) or because they possessed skills in the area of data-processing (as opposed to managerial decision making procedures).

It seems reasonable to assume that the relative effectiveness of different decision systems should be justified on the basis of cost savings. To date, however, most attempts to identify the benefits expected from automation in the logistics area have tended to be qualitative rather than quantitative. Intangible benefits that have been pointed to include: improved customer service, faster response time, greater management flexibility, standardization of operating policies, decreased processing errors, and improved decision making ability. Some of the considerations involved have been spelled out by Hoyt,[10] who spent 4 months as a member of a team of managers from the Sundstrand Corporation looking at alternative prepackaged decision systems. Table 20.2 contains a partial listing of the factors considered by this management team.

Table 20.2 The Software Make-or-Buy Decision[a]

A. Why Buy a Package?

Packages, in theory, are supposed to:

1. Take less time to install since the thinking, coding, and documentation has been done already.
2. Provide quicker benefits so that payback can start sooner.
3. Involve less development cost.
4. Yield better computer utilization since the vendor can afford to fine-tune his coding to use the most efficient programming techniques.
5. Come with superior documentation since the vendor can amortize his efforts across all future buyers.
6. Utilize the vendor's "Project Management Know-how" since he acts as a consultant and presumably has installed many packages before.
7. Provide an avenue for technology exchanges more easily than in-house developed programs. Packages make it easier to talk the same language as other users of the same package.

Other reasons to buy a package:

1. Why re-invent the wheel? Supposedly packages have undergone several generations of logic iterations. They are said to include a more advanced state-of-the-art than your own company people could hope to produce.
2. Projects are often too big for in-house development. The size of many projects often means getting outside help in order to get results in a reasonable period of time. Packages are one form of help.
3. Packages may free up your data-processing resource. In-house projects typically consume a larger percentage of your data-processing (D.P.) staff. A package may leave some analysts and programmers for other worthwhile projects.
4. D.P. personnel who developed and who programmed existing systems are often gone. D.P. has a high turnover rate. The technical understanding of your current systems may be just as foreign to your staff as a package.
5. Packages are tangible and in-house development proposals are not. This means a lot to top management.
6. Packages get more visibility than in-house projects, mainly since a substantial amount of cash had to be justified and paid out. In-house projects are "sunk costs" and don't get the same exposure.
7. Package cost may be capitalized, which can mean a considerable tax advantage.

B. Why Not Buy a Package?

If packages are so great, why aren't there more success stories. It's estimated that U.S. Companies spend 50 times as much on in-house development as they do on packages. In other words, packages are hardly making a dent in their potential market. Some of the reasons include:

1. It's an infant industry—technology is just now developing to make packages a viable alternative. As is the case with all infant industries, there is a high mortality rate. What may be the best buy today may be obsoleted overnight. The vendor may go out of business.
2. All packages must be customized to some degree.

3. Package evaluation is hard—each package has hundreds, even thousands of features. No two packages are alike, or even close. Each has its strengths and weaknesses. It becomes mind-boggling to compare packages in a rational way.
4. Pride of authorship phenomenon—packages are an affront to D.P. As a result, they have a hard time being objective in the evaluation process. They would normally rather do it themselves. It's hard to motivate them to change somebody else's code.
5. Packages use different conventions—naturally whoever wrote the package was familiar with different terminology. Different codes, data names and formats will be a certainty.
6. People resist change—packages mean more change to the users than in-house projects since additional and different codes, input forms and output reports will naturally result.
7. Packages are frequently overly sophisticated—part of the customization process includes de-tuning the package or suppressing features not immediately desired.
8. Maintenance is harder—since your D.P. staff didn't originate the programs it will definitely be harder for them to incorporate changes resulting from bugs or enhancements. Your turnaround time will deteriorate.

---

[a] Adapted from George S. Hoyt.[10]

Perhaps the most striking factor that stands out from the listing in Table 20.2, is the fact that it is highly probable that *all* prepackaged decision systems would have to be customized (to some degree) to be useful in a specific application. Presumably, larger companies, because of their financial and technical capabilities, are more able to develop their own customized compilers, languages, and other specialized features that are needed to increase the operational efficiency of generalized prepackaged decision systems. Smaller companies, on the other hand, if they adopt a prepackaged decision system, usually must resort to the expedient of simply suppressing (rather than eliminating) many of the options and routines available in a software package that was designed for a wider range of market needs. Suppression, rather than elimination, leads to inefficiencies from a computational standpoint. Thus, the repeated use of such a package is relatively quite expensive.

According to Hoyt, often one of the biggest problems in installing a software package is controlling the rate of subsequent customization. Data-processing personnel tend to find many reasons for changing the coding and users are apt to ask for continual changes in the basic logic of the output. Customization of a computer package is usually also accompanied by significant changes in the organizational responsibilities and structures among the decision makers involved.

While in larger companies the eventual computerization of all data-processing activities seems certain, this is not necessarily so in smaller firms. Manual systems are at a disadvantage when it comes to the speed of handling large volumes of transactions, as well as in maintaining accuracy in the posting of these transactions. But computerized systems can result in a loss of personalized attention to, and a lack of experience with, detailed inventory decisions as we saw in an example discussed in Chapter 2. With a manual stock control system experienced clerks and managers can be expected to use their judgment more on a daily basis. In a recent informal poll of consulting firms in the Toronto area we were surprised to find how many of the decision systems implemented were manual. In the smaller companies, the advantages of mechanization, it was felt by several consultants, did not outweigh the personalized attention available through manual systems. It would appear that medium sized firms are the ones who are finding computerized software packages to their advantage. Larger companies because of the complexities of their management information systems either undertake considerable customization of the prepackaged software that they purchase or they simply design their own systems.

20.3 *Some Challenging Research Problems*

In Chapter 1 we pointed out that practice has substantially lagged theory in the area of inventory management/production planning. Moreover, we noted that a primary reason was the unrealistic assumptions made in the development of much of the theory. In this book we have attempted to bridge the gap between theory and practice. However, there still remain a number of challenging problems where we believe that *realistic* applied research efforts can lead to substantial benefits through improved decision making. We shall very briefly outline some of these problem areas. The list of topics is, by no means, meant to be exhaustive. Some research in this vein is already under way, for example, in the area of perishable inventory control (discussed in Chapter 14), Nahmias [16,17] is developing operational rules applicable under a broader range of practical contexts. An excellent starting point for a literature search (covering up to 1965) is the book of abstracts by Eilon and Lampkin.[3] A most welcome research effort would be an appropriate updating of such a book.

20.3.1 *Statistical Issues in Inventory Management*

Most models leading to operational decision systems make certain assumptions, some of them implicit. In particular, in control under probablistic demand we have assumed in each case that there is a known form of the probability distribution of demand (for example, normal or Laplace) with known parameters (the mean and standard deviation). In practice σ is not exactly known, nor is the mean, nor is the distribution itself, particularly when conditions are changing with time. How serious, in terms of possible cost penalties, are these simplifying assumptions? Of course, in answering such a question one must include the system control costs as well. After all, the whole point in making simplifying assumptions is to reduce these latter costs and in so doing, hopefully facilitate implementation of a reasonable decision system. Very little has been done on this difficult research topic. Exceptions include the work of Ehrhardt,[2] Hayes,[8] and MacCormick.[14] In addition, Starr and Miller,[27] have looked at distribution-free analyses in which no assumption is made concerning the form of the underlying probability distribution.

20.3.2 *Non Unit-Sized Transactions—Erratic Demand*

An erratic demand pattern is one where most of the transactions are of small size, but there are occasional (unpredictable) rather large transactions. As already indicated in Section 14.2 large transactions complicate life from the analyst's standpoint in that the inventory position can drop from above to well below the reorder point as the result of a single transaction. Such so-called undershoots must be recognized in predicting the service level or shortage cost implications of a particular reorder point.

The typical operating practice of a company faced with erratic demand is to increase safety stocks by a rather arbitrary amount to protect against the occasional large demands. The erratic demand problem is as yet largely unresolved in that, for a *severe* erratic pattern no *practical* decision rules have been developed for routine use on an item by item basis—practical in the sense of not requiring a computer to give the values of the control variables for an item each time conditions change. Further aspects of the problem, including a computer programme useful for research purposes, are discussed in Reference 24. In addition, Archibald[1], has developed computerized procedures that guarantee the determination of the best settings of the control variables. Also, for a *mildly* erratic demand, he suggests simple adjustments to the standard decision rules, the latter based on a smooth demand pattern (in particular, ignoring undershoots).

20.3.3 *Substitutability of Demand*

There are many situations where, if a specified item is out of stock, a customer may be willing to accept instead a substitutable s.k.u. Examples include:

i. Style goods where several units within a style may be substitutable one for another

ii. Retail sales of hardware items such as different types of paint

When items are substitutable, decisions concerning their inventories should probably not be made independently; in fact, one probably should plan for substitutability. For example, we may be able to carry very little of a particular s.k.u. if we stock a large amount of a substitutable s.k.u. This interdependence considerably complicates the analysis. In fact, in Chapter 9, because of the complexity of mathematical analysis, we considered the substitutable item problem as a logical candidate for study through simulation procedures. However, simple decision guidelines, not requiring simulation, would be of considerable benefit to practitioners. An initial step in this direction has been taken by McGillivray and Silver.[15] A more fundamental problem exists, namely "which selection of the substitutable items should even be stocked?" References on the latter issue include Pentico,[20] Rutenberg,[23] and Townsend.[28]

20.3.4 *Coordinated Control When Demand is Time-Varying*

In Chapter 8 we discussed how to cope with a demand pattern where the average level of the demand varies appreciably in time. Then, in Chapter 13, for *level* demand rates we developed a control system that allows coordination of a group of items so as to reduce total setup costs. In reality, many companies are faced with a combination of these two problem areas.

The combination of the two situations is difficult to analyze. The method, advocated for a single item in Chapter 8, centered on determining a suitable time supply (T) *for only the first replacement.* The coordination method of Chapter 13 was based on a *cycle of the same length repeating over and over again.* Besides the cycle length (T) we determined the integer m_i's for the various items in the group (recall that the idea was that item i would be replenished in a quantity sufficient to last for m_iT). When demand is time-varying we can no longer think in terms of repeating identical cycles. In fact, even under deterministic conditions, it now may actually be desirable to replenish an item even when its inventory is non-zero.

20.3.5 *Coordinated Control Under Probabilistic Demand*

In Sections 13.4 and 13.5 we looked at two control systems for coordinating replenishments of items under probabilistic demand. The conclusion was that, although both approaches represented reasonable solutions, any company using them would have to make use of a computerized solution. To make logical coordinated control more widely applicable, simpler procedures are needed. For example, we need:

i. Guidelines as to when the more complex coordinated control (in contrast with independent, individual item control) makes sense.

ii. Simpler methods for establishing the values of the control variables in (S, c, s) systems or for deciding on how to allocate a group order among the items in the service-point, periodic-review system.

20.3.6 *Safety Stocks in Multi-echelon Systems*

Whether we are using a stock replenishment system (involving reorder points, order-up-to-levels, etc.) or a material requirements planning system, there are uncertainties present in the end item demand forecasts as well as in the supply system. The complexity of the situation has so far defied simple methods of establishing where, and in what quantities, safety stocks should be held. References, describing initial work on this problem area, include New,[18] Roberts and Bramson,[22] Whybark and J. G. Williams,[30] and J. F. Williams.[31]

20.3.7 *Uncertainty of Future Supply*

All of the models presented to this point have assumed that any uncertainty that exists is in the demand process and not in the supply process, except in-so-far as we have permitted the replenishment lead time to be a random variable (see Section 6.9 of Chapter 6). As evidenced by the recent times of inflation and short supply, many firms are faced with serious uncertainty about the availability of raw materials in future periods. Under such circumstances most conventional inventory control systems are in danger of being discarded. Simple decision rules, that can be *routinely* used for *many* items, are sorely needed to ascertain how much to acquire at a moment when substantial material is available at a specified price.

20.3.8 *Operational Aggregate Planning*

As discussed in Chapters 15 to 18, the research problem in aggregate scheduling is simple—not enough practitioners are implementing the systems that have been proposed in the literature. Researchers need to put increased efforts on developing methods that *extend* existing decision systems rather than on mathematically optimal models. That is, there is a need to raise our sights to the level of decision processes and top management strategy. This means that more attention must be given to multi-echelon systems such as described in Chapter 18. As a start, an extensive descriptive documentation of systems similar to that described by Hax[6] and Hax and Meal[7] would be a valuable contribution. We badly need to understand better how aggregate scheduling decisions are in practice being transmitted down to the detail level of individual items.

20.4 *The Need for Gradual Upgrading*

Because of the significant investment and because of the very real implementation issues involved (recall the discussion in Chapter 19) we advocate a gradual upgrading of existing decision systems over time. The management of such a gradual process of change requires commitment and guidance from top management whose natural perspective is the longer term and who are less susceptible to being shifted or promoted from one responsibility to another during the long implementation period. Gradual implementation also implies that the theory and decision rules need to be modular in nature, that is, in identifiable chunks which can be introduced on a project basis when the timing is believed to be ripe from an organization's viewpoint.

We developed this approach in Chapter 5 where we introduced the basic building block for all inventory systems, namely the EOQ. Subsequently in Chapters 6 and 7 we showed how to graft on various ways of calculating safety stocks. Similarly in Chapter 10 we introduced the simple "newsboy" decision rule and then showed how it could be extended to deal with a richer variety of problems. In a different, more aggregate context, in Chapters 15, 16, and 17, we presented ways of extending and improving existing decision making procedures for planning production. Then in Chapter 18 we showed how these decision rules can be blended into a hierarchical structure that ranged from long-term corporate planning to the daily scheduling of individual items.

Much hard work remains to bridge the gap between theory and practice. Perhaps this book will inspire such efforts. In particular, recalling the title of this Chapter, we hope that our "academic buddies" will rise to the challenge of the research problems posed so as to truly help practitioners deal with some of the difficult decision problems that they face on a daily basis.

REFERENCES FOR CHAPTER 20

1. Archibald, B. "Continuous Review (s, S) Policies for Discrete, Compound Poisson, Demand Processes." unpublished Ph.D. dissertation, Department of Management Sciences, University of Waterloo, Waterloo. Ontario, Canada, 1976.

2. Ehrhardt, R. *The Power Approximation: Inventory Policies Based on Limited Demand Information.* Technical Report #7, School of Organization and Management, Yale University, 1976.

3. Eilon, S. and W. Lampkin. *Inventory Control Abstracts* (1953–1965). Oliver & Boyd Ltd., Edinburgh and London, 1968.

4. Galliher, H. P., Morse, P. M. and Simond, M. "Dynamics of Two Classes of Continuous-Review Inventory Systems." *Operations Research*, Vol. 7, No. 3, June, 1959, pp. 362–384.

5. Geisler, M. "Application of the 'Excess Distribution' to an Inventory Study." *Operations Research*, Vol. 12, No. 4, July–August, 1964, pp. 620–623.

6. Hax, A. "Planning and Management Information Systems for a Distributing and Manufacturing Company." *Sloan Management Review*, Spring 1973, pp. 85–98.

7. Hax, A. and Meal, H. C. "Hierarchical Integration of Production Planning and Scheduling." *Management Science*, Special Logistics Issue, December, 1974.

8. Hayes, R. "Statistical Estimation Problems in Inventory Control." *Management Science*, Vol. 15, No. 11, July, 1969, pp. 686–701.

9. Heller, Robert *The Great Executive Dream.* Delacorte Press, New York, 1972.

10. Hoyt, G. S. "The Art of Buying Software: Honest Salesmen, Successful Software Packages . . . and Other Fairy Tales." *Proceedings of the 18th Annual International Conference of the American Production and Inventory Control Society*, 1975, pp. 316–324.

11. Iglehart, D. "The Dynamic Inventory Problem with Unknown Demand Distribution." *Management Science*, Vol. 10, No. 3, April, 1964, pp. 429–440.

12. Iglehart, D. "Recent Results in Inventory Theory." *Journal of Industrial Engineering*, Vol. XVIII, No. 1, January, 1967, pp. 48–51.

13. Jesse, R. R. "Production—Inventory Decisions Under Order-Occurrence Risk: The Deterministic Order Quantity Case." *Management Science*, Vol. 22, No. 6, February, 1976, pp. 664–669.

14. MacCormick, A. *Statistical Problems in Inventory Control.* Technical Report #2, School of Organization and Management, Yale University, 1974.

15. McGillivray, A. R. and Silver, E. A. "Accounting for Substitutable Demand in Inventory Control." Working Paper No. 101, Department of Management Sciences, University of Waterloo, Waterloo, Ontario, Canada, 1976.

16. Nahmias, S. "On Ordering Perishable Inventory When Both the Demand and the Leadtime are Random." Technical Report No.

29, Department of Industrial Engineering, University of Pittsburgh, Pittsburgh Pa. October, 1975.

17. Nahmias, S. "The Fixed Charge Perishable Inventory Problem." Technical Report No. 30, Department of Industrial Engineering, University of Pittsburgh, Pittsburgh, Pa., December, 1975.

18. New C., "Safety Stocks for Requirements Planning." *Production and Inventory Management*, Vol. 16, No. 2, June, 1975, pp. 1–18.

19. Parks, W. H. "The Problem of 'Lumpy' Short-term Demand Variations." *Production and Inventory Management*, Vol. 12, No. 3, 1971, pp. 61–64.

20. Pentico, D. "The Assortment Problem with Probabilistic Demands." *Management Science*, Vol. 21, No. 3, November, 1974, pp. 286–290.

21. Richards, F. "Comments on the Distribution of Inventory Position in a Continous-Review (s, S) Inventory System." *Operations Research*, Vol. 23, No. 2, March–April, 1975, pp. 366–371.

22. Roberts, P. and Bramson, M. "The Commonality Problem in Stock Control for Complex Assemblies." *Operational Research Quarterly*, Vol. 20, Special Issue, 1969, pp. 71–85.

23. Rutenberg, D. "Design Commonality to Reduce Multi-Item Inventory: Optimal Depth of a Product Line." *Operations Research*, Vol. 19, No. 2, March–April, 1971, pp. 491–509.

24. Silver, E. A. "Some Ideas Related to the Inventory Control of Items Having Erratic Demand Patterns." *CORS Journal*, Vol. 8 No. 2, July, 1970, pp. 87–100.

25. Silver, E. A. "Establishing the Order Quantity When the Amount Received is Uncertain." *INFOR*, Vol. 14, No. 1, February, 1976, pp. 32–39.

26. Silver, E. A., Ho. C. M., and Deemer, R. L. "Cost-Minimizing Inventory Control of Items Having a Special Type of Erratic Demand Pattern." *INFOR*, Vol. 9, No. 3, November, 1971, pp. 198–219.

27. Starr, M. K. and Miller, D. W. *Inventory Control*: *Theory and Practice Prentice-Hall*, Englewood Cliffs, N. J. 1962, pp. 58–76.

28. Townsend, W. "A Production-Stocking Problem Analogous to Plant Location." *Operational Research Quarterly*, Vol. 26, No. 2 ii, July 1975, pp. 389–396.

29. Veinott, A. F. The Status of Mathematical Inventory Theory." *Management Science*, Vol. 12, No. 11, July, 1966, pp. 745–777.

30. Whyback, D. C. and Williams, J. G. "Material Requirements Planning Under Uncertainty" Paper No. 545, Institute for Research in the Behavioral, Economic and Management Sciences, Krannert Graduate School of Industrial Administration, Purdue University, West Lafayette, Indiana, February, 1975.

31. Williams, J. F. "Multi-Echelon Production Scheduling When Demand is Stochastic." *Management Science*, Vol. 20, No. 9, May, 1974, pp. 1253–1263.

APPENDIX A

Elements of Lagrangian Optimization

We consider the case where we wish to maximize (or minimize) a function $f(x, y)$ of two variables x and y, but subject to a constraint or side condition which x and y must satisfy, denoted by

$$g(x, y) = 0 \tag{A.1}$$

x and y are not independent; selection of a value of one of them implies a value (or values) of the other through Eq. A.1. Therefore, we cannot find the maximum (or minimum) of $f(x, y)$ by simply equating the partial derivatives of f (with respect to x and y) equal to zero. Instead we could solve Eq. A.1 for y in terms of x, then substitute this expression into $f(x, y)$ to obtain a new function, call it $h(x)$, which depends only upon the single variable x. Then a maximum (or minimum) of $h(x)$ could be found by setting $dh(x)/dx = 0$, etc. The associated value of y would be found from Eq. A.1.

Illustration—Suppose we wish to minimize

$$f(x, y) = \frac{x}{2} + 2y$$

subject to both variables being positive and

$$xy = 4$$

This constraint can be rewritten as

$$xy - 4 = 0$$

which, from Eq. A.1, shows us that

$$g(x, y) = xy - 4$$

The constraint can also be written as

$$y = 4/x \tag{A.2}$$

Substituting into $f(x, y)$ gives us

$$\frac{x}{2} + 2(4/x) = \frac{x}{2} + 8/x, \text{ which we call } h(x)$$

Then,

$$\frac{dh(x)}{dx} = \frac{1}{2} - \frac{8}{x^2}$$

Also

$$\frac{d^2h(x)}{dx^2} = \frac{16}{x^3}$$

At a minimum we require

$$\frac{dh(x)}{dx} = 0$$

in other words,

$$\frac{1}{2} - \frac{8}{x^2} = 0$$

or

$$x^2 = 16$$

Because x must be positive, the only valid solution is

$$x = 4$$

At $x = 4$,

$$\frac{d^2h(x)}{dx^2} = \frac{16}{(4)^3} = \frac{1}{4} > 0$$

Therefore, we have a minimum at $x = 4$. The y value corresponding to $x = 4$ is found from Eq. A.2 to be $y = 1$. Finally, the minimum value of $f(x, y)$ is

$$f(4, 1) = \tfrac{4}{2} + 2(1) = 4$$

We now state, without proof, an alternative method for finding the maximum (or minimum) value of $f(x, y)$ subject to the constraint

$$g(x, y) = 0 \tag{A.3}$$

We set up the new function

$$L(x, y, M) = f(x, y) - Mg(x, y)$$

where M is called a Lagrange multiplier. This new function is now treated as a function of the three *independent* variables x, y, and M. Therefore, we set

$$\frac{\partial L}{\partial x} = 0 \quad \text{that is,} \quad \frac{\partial f}{\partial x} - M\frac{\partial g}{\partial x} = 0 \tag{A.4}$$

$$\frac{\partial L}{\partial y}=0 \quad \text{that is,} \quad \frac{\partial f}{\partial y}-M\frac{\partial g}{\partial y}=0 \tag{A.5}$$

$$\frac{\partial L}{\partial M}=0 \quad \text{that is,} \quad g(x, y)=0$$

The last equation simply regenerates the constraint of Eq. A.3. For any given value of M, Eqs. A.4 and A.5 can be solved for the two unknowns x and y. Of course, this (x, y) pair will likely not satisfy the condition of Eq. A.3. Therefore, we keep trying different M values until this method leads to an (x, y) pair satisfying Eq. A.3.

Illustration—Consider the same problem treated earlier, namely, for positive variables x and y

$$\begin{aligned}&\text{minimize } f(x, y)=\frac{x}{2}+2y\\&\text{subject to } g(x, y)=xy-4=0\end{aligned} \tag{A.6}$$

Our new function is

$$L(x, y, M)=\frac{x}{2}+2y-M(xy-4)$$

Equations A.4 and A.5 give

$$\tfrac{1}{2}-My=0 \quad \text{or} \quad y=\frac{1}{2M}$$

and

$$2-Mx=0 \quad \text{or} \quad x=\frac{2}{M}$$

The following table illustrates values of x, y, and $g(x, y)$ for various values of M.

M	$x=\frac{2}{M}$	$y=\frac{1}{2M}$	$g(x, y)=xy-4$
2	1	$\frac{1}{4}$	−15/4
1	2	$\frac{1}{2}$	−3
$\frac{1}{2}$	4	1	0 ←
$\frac{1}{4}$	8	2	12
$\frac{1}{5}$	10	5/2	21

The behavior of $g(x, y)$ as a function of M is also sketched in Figure A.1. It is clear that there is but a single value of M, namely $\frac{1}{2}$, where $g(x, y)=0$, that is, the constraint of Eq. A.6 is satisfied. From the above table we see that the corresponding (x, y) pair is

$$x=4, y=1$$

precisely the same result we obtained by the earlier more direct method of substitution, etc.

At this stage, the reader may be asking "who needs all this aggravation when the direct substitution method seems so much simpler?" For the example analyzed we certainly do not need the Lagrange multiplier approach. However, the method is directly extendable to the case where there are several, instead of just two, variables involved. Also, in the substitution method we can quickly run into problems if the constraint is of such a form that one variable cannot be easily expressed in terms of the other variables. This would have been the case in the above illustration if the constraint had been instead, for example,

$$x^3y^2-3xy^4=6$$

This type of complexity does not hamper the Lagrange approach.

We now present, without proof,* the general Lagrange approach for maximizing (or minimizing) a function $f(x_1, x_2, \ldots, x_n)$ of n variables $x_1, x_2, \ldots, x_n$ subject to a single equality constraint

$$g(x_1, x_2, \ldots, x_n)=0 \tag{A.7}$$

Step 1 Form the function

$$L(x_1, x_2, \ldots, x_n, M) = f(x_1, x_2, \ldots, x_n)-Mg(x_1, x_2, \ldots, x_n)$$

---

* *A proof is provided on pp. 249–251 of Sokolnikoff and Redheffer.*[1]

Figure A.1 Illustration of g(x, y) as a Function of the Lagrange Multiplier M.

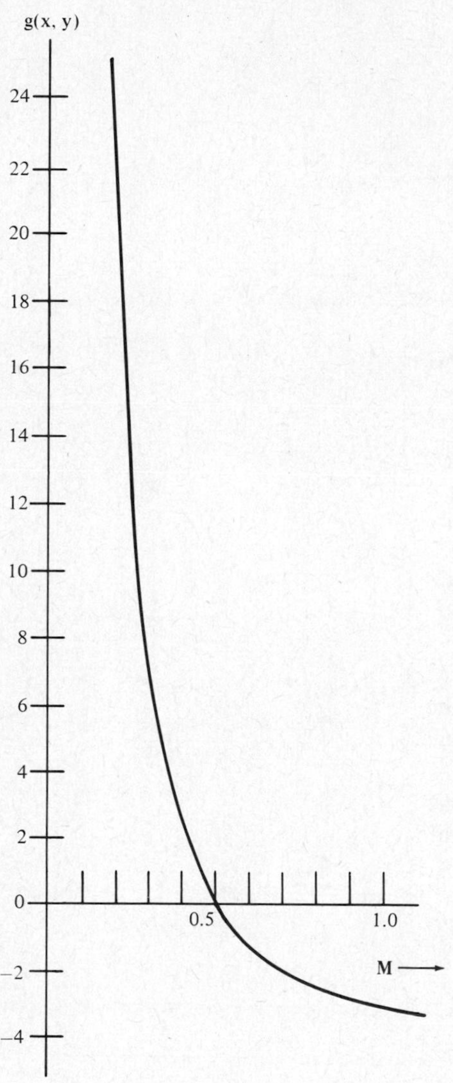

Step 2 Evaluate the n partial derivatives and set each equal to zero.

$$\frac{\partial L}{\partial x_1}=0$$

$$\frac{\partial L}{\partial x_2}=0$$

$$\vdots$$

$$\frac{\partial L}{\partial x_n}=0$$

This gives n equations in the $n+1$ variables $x_1, x_2, \ldots, x_n$, and M.

Step 3 For a particular value of M, solve the set of equations (obtained in Step 2) for the x's. Then evaluate $g(x_1, x_2, \ldots, x_n)$.

Step 4 If $g(x_1, x_2, \ldots, x_n)=0$, we have found a set of x's which are candidates for maximizing (or minimizing) the function f subject to satisfying the condition of Eq. A.7. Otherwise we return to Step 2 with a different value of M. There are different methods available for searching for the M values where the constraint is satisfied. At the very least we can develop graphs, similar to Figure A.1, as we proceed. This certainly would indicate in what directions(s) to explore M values. In some cases one can actually obtain analytic solutions for the required M values.

REFERENCE FOR APPENDIX A

1. Sokolnikoff, I. S. and R. M. Redheffer. *Mathematics of Physics and Modern Engineering*. McGraw-Hill, New York, 1958.

APPENDIX B

Three Useful Probability Distributions

In this appendix we briefly cover some of the important properties of three probability distributions of particular interest in the text. A fourth, and actually the most important, distribution, namely the normal, will be treated separately in Appendix C. Additional information on the subject of probabilistic modelling can be obtained from a number of references (see, for example, Drake,[3] Feller, [4] or Parzen[7]).

B.1 The Lognormal Distribution

B.1.1 Probability Density Function and Cumulative Distribution Function

The density function of a lognormal variable x is given by*

$$f_x(x_0) = \frac{1}{bx_0\sqrt{2\pi}} \exp[-(\ln x_0 - a)^2/2b^2] \qquad 0 < x_0 < \infty \tag{B.1}$$

where a and b are the two parameters of the distribution.

It is seen that the range of the lognormal is from 0 to ∞. It has a single peak in this range. A sketch of a typical lognormal distribution is shown in Figure B.1. The name is derived from the fact that the logarithm of x has a normal distribution (with mean a and standard deviation b).

The cumulative distribution function

$$p_{x\leq}(x_0) = \int_{-\infty}^{x_0} f_x(z)\,dz$$

can be shown to be given by

$$p_{x\leq}(x_0) = 1 - p_{u\geq}\left(\frac{\ln x_0 - a}{b}\right) \tag{B.2}$$

where $p_{u\geq}(u_0)$ is the probability that a unit normal variable takes on a value of u_0 or larger, a function tabulated in Appendix C.

B.1.2 Moments

One can show (see, for example, Aitchison and Brown[1]) that the expected value of the jth power (for any real j) of x is given by†

$$E(x^j) = m^j \exp[b^2 j(j-1)/2] \tag{B.3}$$

---

* $f_x(x_0)dx_0$ *represents the probability that* x *takes on a value between* x_0 *and* $x_0 + dx_0$.

† *In general,*

$$E(x^j) = \int_{-\infty}^{\infty} x_0^j f_x(x_0)\,dx_0 \tag{B.4}$$

Figure B.1 The Lognormal Probability Density Function.

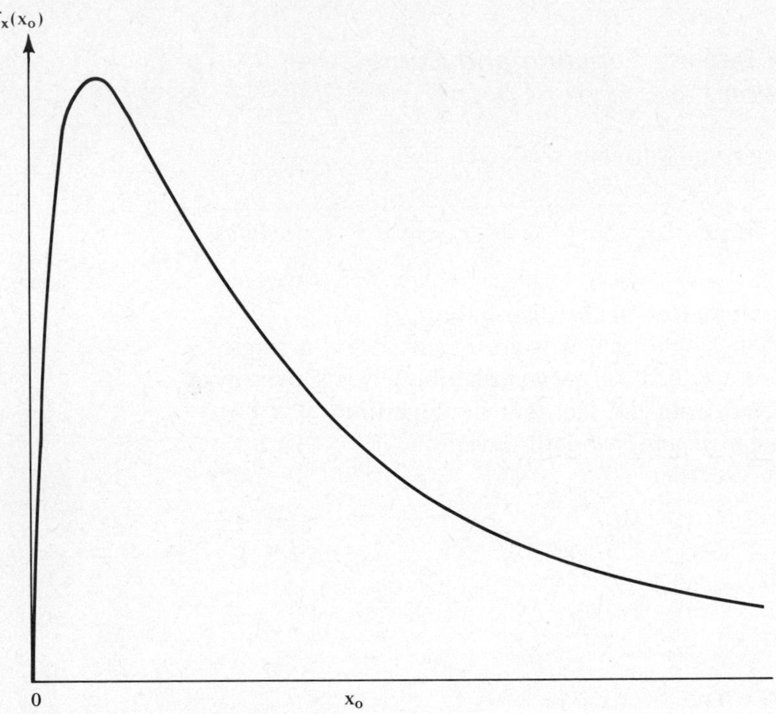

where

$$m = \exp\,[a + b^2/2] \tag{B.5}$$

is the mean or expected value of x itself.

The variance of x, defined by

$$\sigma_x^2 = E(x^2) - [E(x)]^2$$

can be shown, through straightforward use of Eqs. B.3 and B.5, to be

$$\sigma_x^2 = [E(x)]^2[\exp\,(b^2) - 1]$$

Hence, the standard deviation, σ_x is given by

$$\sigma_x = E(x)\sqrt{\exp\,(b^2) - 1}$$

and the coefficient of variation by

$$\sigma_x/E(x) = \sqrt{\exp(b^2) - 1}$$

the latter depending only on the value of b.

B.2 *The Laplace Distribution*

B.2.1 *Probability Density Function and Upper Tail Area*

The Laplace distribution is a two-sided, symmetric exponential function. The density of a Laplace distributed variable x is given by

$$f_x(x_0) = \begin{cases} \dfrac{1}{\sqrt{2}\,\sigma_x} \exp\left[-\dfrac{\sqrt{2}}{\sigma_x}(\bar{x} - x_0)\right] & x_0 \leq \bar{x} \\ \dfrac{1}{\sqrt{2}\,\sigma_x} \exp\left[-\dfrac{\sqrt{2}}{\sigma_x}(x_0 - \bar{x})\right] & x_0 \geq \bar{x} \end{cases} \tag{B.7}$$

where, as can be shown through the use of Eqs. B.4 and B.6, $\bar{x}$ is, indeed, the mean value of x and σ_x its standard deviation. As seen in Figure B.2 the Laplace is symmetric about the mean value, which is also the most likely (or modal) value.

By straightforward integration one can show that

$$p_{x>}(x_0) = \int_{x_0}^{\infty} f_x(z)\,dz = \begin{cases} 1 - \frac{1}{2}\exp\left[-\dfrac{\sqrt{2}}{\sigma_x}(\bar{x} - x_0)\right] & x_0 \leq \bar{x} \\ \frac{1}{2}\exp\left[-\dfrac{\sqrt{2}}{\sigma_x}(x_0 - \bar{x})\right] & x_0 \geq \bar{x} \end{cases} \tag{B.8}$$

Considering the x_0 value of particular interest in inventory theory, namely $\bar{x} + k\sigma_x$, Eq. B.8 gives

$$p_{x>}(\bar{x} + k\sigma_x) = \begin{cases} 1 - \frac{1}{2}\exp(\sqrt{2}k) & k \leq 0 \\ \frac{1}{2}\exp(-\sqrt{2}k) & k \geq 0 \end{cases} \tag{B.9}$$

Figure B.2 The Laplace Probability Density Function.

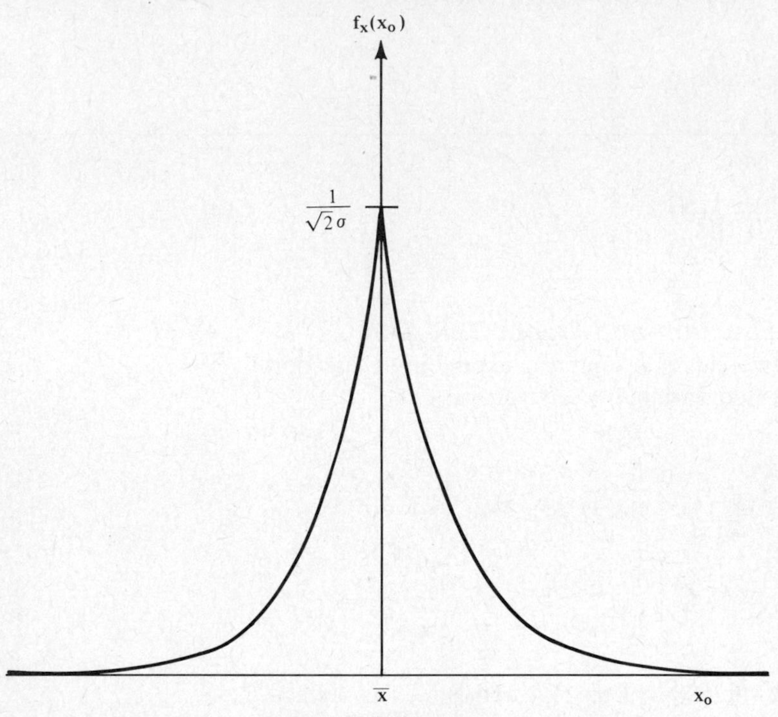

B.2.2 *Another Important Property*

Consider the function w defined by

$$w = \begin{cases} 0 & \text{if} \quad x_0 \leq \bar{x} + k\sigma_x \\ x_0 - (\bar{x} + k\sigma_x) & \text{if} \quad x_0 \geq \bar{x} + k\sigma_x \end{cases}$$

Then

$$E(w) = \int_{-\infty}^{\infty} w_0 f_w(w_0)\,dw_0$$

$$= \int_{x+k\sigma}^{\infty} [x_0 - (\bar{x} + k\sigma_x)] f_x(x_0)\,dx_0 \tag{B.10}$$

Substitution of Eq. B.7 into B.10 gives, after considerable simplification,

$$E(w) = \begin{cases} -k\sigma_x + \dfrac{\sigma_x}{2\sqrt{2}} \exp(\sqrt{2}k) & k \leq 0 \\ \dfrac{\sigma_x}{2\sqrt{2}} \exp(-\sqrt{2}k) & k \geq 0 \end{cases}$$

B.3 The Poisson Distribution

B.3.1 Probability Mass Function

A Poisson variable is an example of a discrete random variable. Its probability mass function (p.m.f.) is given by

$$p_x(x_0) = \text{prob}\,\{x = x_0\} = \frac{a^{x_0} \exp(-a)}{x_0!} \qquad x_0 = 0, 1, 2, \ldots$$

where a is the single parameter of the distribution. A typical Poisson p.m.f. is shown in Figure B.3.

B.3.2 Moments

One can show (see, for example, pages 136–7 of Reference 3) that

i. $E(x) = \sum_{x_0=0}^{\infty} x_0 p_x(x_0) = a$

that is, the parameter a is the mean of the distribution.

ii. $\sigma_x^2 = \sum_{x_0=0}^{\infty} [x_0 - E(x)]^2 p_x(x_0) = a$

Hence, the standard deviation, σ_x, is given by

$$\sigma_x = \sqrt{a}$$

Figure B.3 Typical Poisson Probability Mass Function.

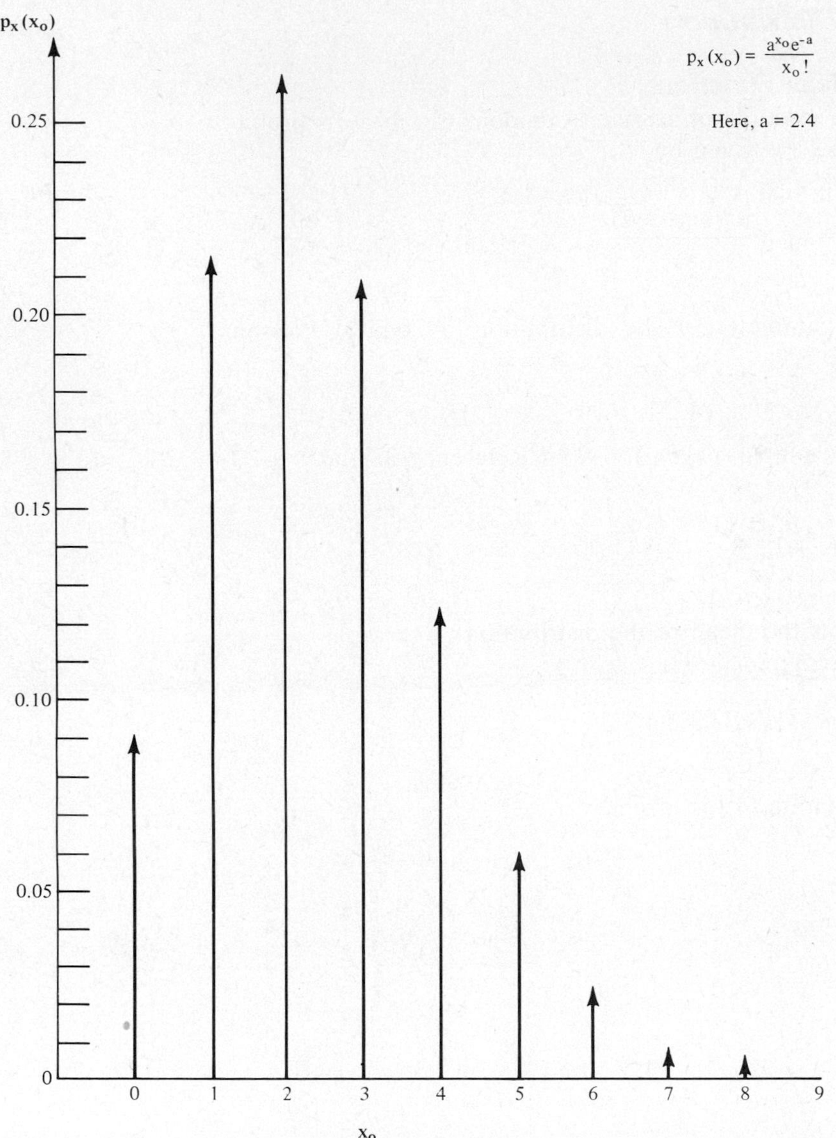

REFERENCES FOR APPENDIX B

1. Aitchison, J. and J. A. C. Brown. *The Lognormal Distribution.* Cambridge University Press, Cambridge, England, 1957.

2. Brown, R. G. *Decision Rules for Inventory Management.* Holt, Rinehart and Winston, New York, N.Y., 1967, pp. 23–27.

3. Drake, A. *Fundamentals of Applied Probability Theory.* McGraw-Hill, New York, 1967.

4. Feller, W. *An Introduction to Probability Theory and Its Applications, Vol. I.* Wiley, New York, 1957.

5. Haight, F. A. *Handbook of the Poisson Distribution.* John Wiley and Sons, New York, N.Y., 1967.

6. Herron, D. P. "Profit Oriented Techniques for Managing Independent Demand Inventories." *Production and Inventory Management,* Vol. 15, No. 3, 1974, pp. 57–74.

7. Parzen, E. *Modern Probability Theory and Its Applications.* Wiley, New York, 1960.

APPENDIX C

The Normal Probability Distribution

The normal is undoubtedly the most important single probability distribution in decision rules of production planning/inventory control, as well as in general usage of probability (particularly in the area of applied statistics). This appendix is devoted to a discussion of the properties of the normal distribution, particularly those needed for the decision rules of the main text.

C.1 The Probability Density Function

The probability density function of a normal variable x, with mean $\bar{x}$ and standard deviation σ_x, is denoted by

$$f_x(x_0) = \frac{1}{\sigma_x\sqrt{2\pi}} \exp\left[-(x_0-\bar{x})^2/2\sigma_x^{\,2}\right] \qquad -\infty < x_0 < \infty \qquad \text{(C.1)}$$

A typical sketch is shown in Figure C.1. This is the familiar bell-shaped curve. As the standard deviation σ_x decreases, the distribution tightens up around the mean value, $\bar{x}$.

Figure C.1 The Normal Probability Density Function.

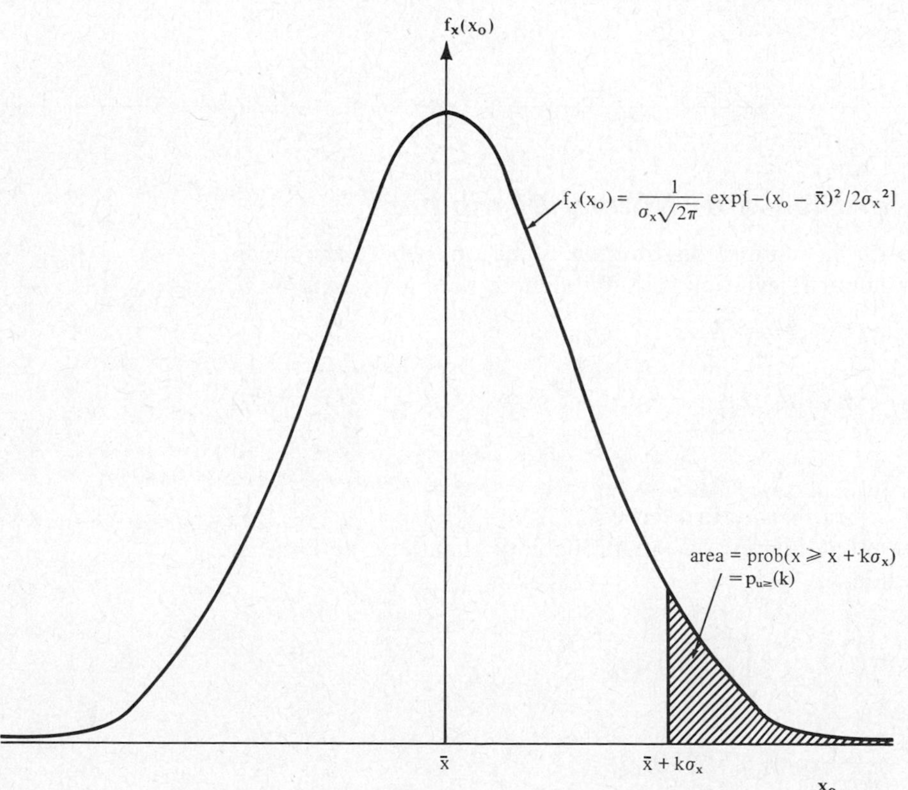

C.2 Moments

The Mean, $E(x)$ or $\bar{x}$, and the Standard Deviation, σ_x—One can verify (for details see page 206 of Reference 2) that the mean and standard deviation are, indeed, the $\bar{x}$ and σ_x in Eq. C.1.

MAD—By definition, the MAD is given by

$$\text{MAD} = \int_{-\infty}^{\infty} |x_0 - \bar{x}| f_x(x_0)\, dx_0$$

Substitution of Eq. C.1 and lengthy algebra and calculus leads to

$$\text{MAD} = \sqrt{\frac{2}{\pi}}\, \sigma_x$$

or

$$\frac{\sigma_x}{\text{MAD}} = \sqrt{\frac{\pi}{2}} \simeq 1.25$$

C.3 The Unit (or Standard) Normal Distribution

A very special case of the normal distribution is the one where the mean value is 0 and the standard deviation is 1. We denote such a variable by u. Thus

$$f_u(u_0) = \frac{1}{\sqrt{2\pi}} \exp\left(-u_0^2/2\right) \qquad -\infty < u_0 < \infty \tag{C.2}$$

with $E(u)$ or $\bar{u} = 0$ and $\sigma_u = 1$.

This p.d.f. is shown graphically in Figure C.2.

A quantity of frequent interest is the probability that u is at least as large as a certain value k,

$$p_{u\geq}(k) = \text{prob}\,(u \geq k) = \int_k^{\infty} f_u(u_0)\, du_0$$

$$= \int_k^{\infty} \frac{1}{\sqrt{2\pi}} \exp\left(-u_0^2/2\right) du_0 \tag{C.3}$$

Figure C.2 The Unit Normal Distribution.

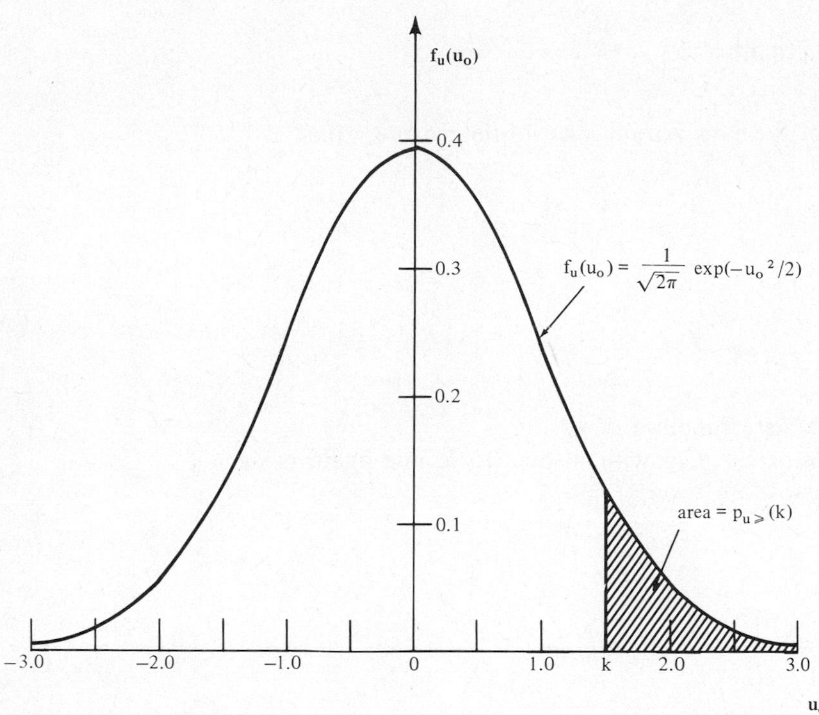

There is no indefinite integral for

$$\exp(-x^2/2)dx$$

Therefore, Eq. C.3 has to be numerically integrated. (The result represents the hatched area in Figure C.2.) This has been done and $p_{u\geq}(k)$ has been tabulated, as in Table C.1, for a range of k values. Only positive values of k are shown in the table. If $p_{u\geq}(k)$ is needed for a negative argument, it is clear from the symmetry of Figure C.2 that

$$p_{u\geq}(-k) = 1 - p_{u\geq}(k) \tag{C.4}$$

It should be noted that, by differentiating both sides of Eq. C.3 with respect to k, and using the theorem in the Appendix of Chapter 10, we obtain

$$\frac{dp_{u\geq}(k)}{dk} = -f_u(k) \tag{C.5}$$

A second quantity of interest relative to production/inventory decision rules, denoted by $G_u(k)$, is given by

$$G_u(k)=\int_k^{\infty}(u_0-k)f_u(u_0)\,du_0 \tag{C.6}$$

Using, a special property of the unit normal distribution, namely tnat

$$\int_k^{\infty}u_0 f_u(u_0)\,du_0=f_u(k)$$

Eq. C.6 can be expressed as

$$G_u(k)=f_u(k)-kp_{u\geq}(k) \tag{C.7}$$

Table C.1 also shows $G_u(k)$ as a function of k.

Differentiating both sides of Eq. C.6 with respect to k, and again using the aforementioned theorem, there results

$$\frac{dG_u(k)}{dk}=-p_{u\geq}(k) \tag{C.8}$$

C.4 Relating any Normal Distribution to the Unit Normal

Consider a normally distributed variable x with mean $\bar{x}$ and standard deviation σ_x. One quantity of direct interest in measuring customer service is the probability of A where A is the event that x takes on a value greater than or equal to $\bar{x}+k\sigma_x$.
Now,

$$\begin{aligned}\text{prob }(A)&=\int_{\bar{x}+k\sigma_x}^{\infty}f_x(x_0)\,dx_0\\ &=\int_{\bar{x}+k\sigma_x}^{\infty}\frac{1}{\sigma_x\sqrt{2\pi}}\exp\left[-(x_0-\bar{x})^2/2\sigma_x{}^2\right]dx_0\end{aligned} \tag{C.9}$$

Consider

$$u_0=(x_0-\bar{x})/\sigma_x$$

We have that $du_0/dx_0=1/\sigma_x$ or $dx_0=\sigma_x du_0$. Also when $x_0=\bar{x}+k\sigma_x$ we have that $u_0=k$, and when $x_0=\infty$, $u_0=\infty$.

Therefore, substituting these expressions into Eq. C.9 results in

$$\text{prob}(A) = \int_k^\infty \frac{1}{\sqrt{2\pi}} \exp(-u_0^2/2)\, du_0$$

Using Eq. C.3 and the definition of event A, we thus have

$$\text{prob}\{x \geq \bar{x} + k\sigma_x\} = p_{u\geq}(k) \tag{C.10}$$

This is represented by the hatched area in Figure C.1.

Another quantity of interest is the expected shortage per replenishment cycle,

$$\begin{aligned} \text{ESPRC} &= \int_{\bar{x}+k\sigma_x}^\infty (x_0 - \bar{x} - k\sigma_x) f_x(x_0)\, dx_0 \\ &= \int_{\bar{x}+k\sigma_x}^\infty (x_0 - \bar{x} - k\sigma_x) \frac{1}{\sigma_x\sqrt{2\pi}} \exp[-(x_0 - \bar{x})^2/2\sigma_x^2]\, dx_0 \end{aligned} \tag{C.11}$$

The key is to again substitute

$$u_0 = (x_0 - \bar{x})/\sigma_x$$

The result, after considerable simplification, is

$$\text{ESPRC} = \sigma_x \int_k^\infty (u_0 - k) \frac{1}{\sqrt{2\pi}} \exp(-u_0^2/2)\, du_0$$

From Eq. C.6 this is seen to be

$$\text{ESPRC} = \sigma_x G_u(k) \tag{C.12}$$

C.5 Further Properties Needed for the Appendix of Chapter 10

In Chapter 10 we have a normally distributed variable x with mean $\bar{x}$ and standard deviation σ_x, and we let

$$Q = \bar{x} + k\sigma_x$$

The first quantity desired is $p_{x<}(Q)$. Clearly

$$\begin{aligned} p_{x<}(Q) &= \text{prob}\,(x < Q) = 1 - \text{prob}\,(x \geq Q) \\ &= 1 - \text{prob}\,(x \geq \bar{x} + k\sigma_x) \end{aligned}$$

Using Eq. C.10 we have

$$p_{x<}(Q) = 1 - p_{u\geq}(k) = p_{u<}(k)$$

The function $p_{u<}(k)$ is sometimes denoted by $\Phi(k)$ in the literature.

The second quantity desired is,

$$\int_Q^\infty x_0 f_x(x_0)\,dx_0$$

We have

$$\int_Q^\infty x_0 f_x(x_0)\,dx_0 = \int_Q^\infty (x_0 - Q) f_x(x_0)\,dx_0 + \int_Q^\infty Q f_x(x_0)\,dx_0$$

$$= \int_{\bar{x}+k\sigma_x}^\infty (x_0 - \bar{x} - k\sigma_x) f_x(x_0)\,dx_0 + Q\int_{\bar{x}+k\sigma_x}^\infty f_x(x_0)\,dx_0$$

Use of Eqs. C.10, C.11, and C.12 gives

$$\int_Q^\infty x_0 f_x(x_0)\,dx_0 = \sigma_x G_u(k) + Q p_{u\geq}(k) \tag{C.13}$$

The third quantity required is

$$\int_0^Q x_0 f_x(x_0)\,dx_0$$

Now, if the chance of a negative value of x is very small, then

$$\int_0^Q x_0 f_x(x_0)\,dx_0 \simeq \int_\infty^Q x_0 f_x(x_0)\,dx_0$$

$$= \int_{-\infty}^\infty x_0 f_x(x_0)\,dx_0 - \int_Q^\infty x_0 f_x(x_0)\,dx_0$$

$$= \bar{x} - \int_Q^\infty x_0 f_x(x_0)\,dx_0$$

Then use of Eq. C.13 leads to

$$\int_0^Q x_o f_x(x_0)\,dx_0 \simeq \bar{x} - \sigma_x G_u(k) - Q p_{u\geq}(k)$$

Table C.1 Some Functions of the Unit Normal Distribution

k	$f_u(k)$	$p_{u\geq}(k)$	$G_u(k)$	$G_u(-k)$	k
0.00	0.3989	0.5000	0.3989	0.3989	0.00
0.01	0.3989	0.4960	0.3940	0.4040	0.01
0.02	0.3989	0.4920	0.3890	0.4090	0.02
0.03	0.3988	0.4880	0.3841	0.4141	0.03
0.04	0.3986	0.4840	0.3793	0.4193	0.04
0.05	0.3984	0.4801	0.3744	0.4244	0.05
0.06	0.3982	0.4761	0.3697	0.4297	0.06
0.07	0.3980	0.4721	0.3649	0.4349	0.07
0.08	0.3977	0.4681	0.3602	0.4402	0.08
0.09	0.3973	0.4641	0.3556	0.4456	0.09
0.10	0.3970	0.4602	0.3509	0.4509	0.10
0.11	0.3965	0.4562	0.3464	0.4564	0.11
0.12	0.3961	0.4522	0.3418	0.4618	0.12
0.13	0.3956	0.4483	0.3373	0.4673	0.13
0.14	0.3951	0.4443	0.3328	0.4728	0.14
0.15	0.3945	0.4404	0.3284	0.4784	0.15
0.16	0.3939	0.4364	0.3240	0.4840	0.16
0.17	0.3932	0.4325	0.3197	0.4897	0.17
0.18	0.3925	0.4286	0.3154	0.4954	0.18
0.19	0.3918	0.4247	0.3111	0.5011	0.19
0.20	0.3910	0.4207	0.3069	0.5069	0.20
0.21	0.3902	0.4168	0.3027	0.5127	0.21
0.22	0.3894	0.4129	0.2986	0.5186	0.22
0.23	0.3885	0.4090	0.2944	0.5244	0.23
0.24	0.3876	0.4052	0.2904	0.5304	0.24
0.25	0.3867	0.4013	0.2863	0.5363	0.25
0.26	0.3857	0.3974	0.2824	0.5424	0.26
0.27	0.3847	0.3936	0.2784	0.5484	0.27
0.28	0.3836	0.3897	0.2745	0.5545	0.28
0.29	0.3825	0.3859	0.2706	0.5606	0.29
0.30	0.3814	0.3821	0.2668	0.5668	0.30
0.31	0.3802	0.3783	0.2630	0.5730	0.31
0.32	0.3790	0.3745	0.2592	0.5792	0.32
0.33	0.3778	0.3707	0.2555	0.5855	0.33
0.34	0.3765	0.3669	0.2518	0.5918	0.34
0.35	0.3752	0.3632	0.2481	0.5981	0.35
0.36	0.3739	0.3594	0.2445	0.6045	0.36
0.37	0.3725	0.3557	0.2409	0.6109	0.37
0.38	0.3712	0.3520	0.2374	0.6174	0.38
0.39	0.3697	0.3483	0.2339	0.6239	0.39
0.40	0.3683	0.3446	0.2304	0.6304	0.40
0.41	0.3668	0.3409	0.2270	0.6370	0.41
0.42	0.3653	0.3372	0.2236	0.6436	0.42
0.43	0.3637	0.3336	0.2203	0.6503	0.43
0.44	0.3621	0.3300	0.2169	0.6569	0.44
0.45	0.3605	0.3264	0.2137	0.6637	0.45
0.46	0.3589	0.3228	0.2104	0.6704	0.46
0.47	0.3572	0.3192	0.2072	0.6772	0.47
0.48	0.3555	0.3156	0.2040	0.6840	0.48
0.49	0.3538	0.3121	0.2009	0.6909	0.49

k	$f_u(k)$	$p_{u\geq}(k)$	$G_u(k)$	$G_u(-k)$	k
0.50	0.3521	0.3085	0.1978	0.6978	0.50
0.51	0.3503	0.3050	0.1947	0.7047	0.51
0.52	0.3485	0.3015	0.1917	0.7117	0.52
0.53	0.3467	0.2981	0.1887	0.7187	0.53
0.54	0.3448	0.2946	0.1857	0.7257	0.54
0.55	0.3429	0.2912	0.1828	0.7328	0.55
0.56	0.3410	0.2877	0.1799	0.7399	0.56
0.57	0.3391	0.2843	0.1771	0.7471	0.57
0.58	0.3372	0.2810	0.1742	0.7542	0.58
0.59	0.3352	0.2776	0.1714	0.7614	0.59
0.60	0.3332	0.2743	0.1687	0.7687	0.60
0.61	0.3312	0.2709	0.1659	0.7759	0.61
0.62	0.3292	0.2676	0.1633	0.7833	0.62
0.63	0.3271	0.2643	0.1606	0.7906	0.63
0.64	0.3251	0.2611	0.1580	0.7980	0.64
0.65	0.3230	0.2578	0.1554	0.8054	0.65
0.66	0.3209	0.2546	0.1528	0.8128	0.66
0.67	0.3187	0.2514	0.1503	0.8203	0.67
0.68	0.3166	0.2483	0.1478	0.8278	0.68
0.69	0.3144	0.2451	0.1453	0.8353	0.69
0.70	0.3123	0.2420	0.1429	0.8429	0.70
0.71	0.3101	0.2389	0.1405	0.8505	0.71
0.72	0.3079	0.2358	0.1381	0.8581	0.72
0.73	0.3056	0.2327	0.1358	0.8658	0.73
0.74	0.3034	0.2297	0.1334	0.8734	0.74
0.75	0.3011	0.2266	0.1312	0.8812	0.75
0.76	0.2989	0.2236	0.1289	0.8889	0.76
0.77	0.2966	0.2206	0.1267	0.8967	0.77
0.78	0.2943	0.2177	0.1245	0.9045	0.78
0.79	0.2920	0.2148	0.1223	0.9123	0.79
0.80	0.2897	0.2119	0.1202	0.9202	0.80
0.81	0.2874	0.2090	0.1181	0.9281	0.81
0.82	0.2850	0.2061	0.1160	0.9360	0.82
0.83	0.2827	0.2033	0.1140	0.9440	0.83
0.84	0.2803	0.2005	0.1120	0.9520	0.84
0.85	0.2780	0.1977	0.1100	0.9600	0.85
0.86	0.2756	0.1949	0.1080	0.9680	0.86
0.87	0.2732	0.1922	0.1061	0.9761	0.87
0.88	0.2709	0.1894	0.1042	0.9842	0.88
0.89	0.2685	0.1867	0.1023	0.9923	0.89
0.90	0.2661	0.1841	0.1004	1.0004	0.90
0.91	0.2637	0.1814	0.09860	1.0086	0.91
0.92	0.2613	0.1788	0.09680	1.0168	0.92
0.93	0.2589	0.1762	0.09503	1.0250	0.93
0.94	0.2565	0.1736	0.09328	1.0333	0.94
0.95	0.2541	0.1711	0.09156	1.0416	0.95
0.96	0.2516	0.1685	0.08986	1.0499	0.96
0.97	0.2492	0.1660	0.08819	1.0582	0.97
0.98	0.2468	0.1635	0.08654	1.0665	0.98
0.99	0.2444	0.1611	0.08491	1.0749	0.99

k	$f_u(k)$	$p_{u\geq}(k)$	$G_u(k)$	$G_u(-k)$	k
1.00	0.2420	0.1587	0.08332	1.0833	1.00
1.01	0.2396	0.1562	0.08174	1.0917	1.01
1.02	0.2371	0.1539	0.08019	1.1002	1.02
1.03	0.2347	0.1515	0.07866	1.1087	1.03
1.04	0.2323	0.1492	0.07716	1.1172	1.04
1.05	0.2299	0.1469	0.07568	1.1257	1.05
1.06	0.2275	0.1446	0.07422	1.1342	1.06
1.07	0.2251	0.1423	0.07279	1.1428	1.07
1.08	0.2227	0.1401	0.07138	1.1514	1.08
1.09	0.2203	0.1379	0.06999	1.1600	1.09
1.10	0.2179	0.1357	0.06862	1.1686	1.10
1.11	0.2155	0.1335	0.06727	1.1773	1.11
1.12	0.2131	0.1314	0.06595	1.1859	1.12
1.13	0.2107	0.1292	0.06465	1.1946	1.13
1.14	0.2083	0.1271	0.06336	1.2034	1.14
1.15	0.2059	0.1251	0.06210	1.2121	1.15
1.16	0.2036	0.1230	0.06086	1.2209	1.16
1.17	0.2012	0.1210	0.05964	1.2296	1.17
1.18	0.1989	0.1190	0.05844	1.2384	1.18
1.19	0.1965	0.1170	0.05726	1.2473	1.19
1.20	0.1942	0.1151	0.05610	1.2561	1.20
1.21	0.1919	0.1131	0.05496	1.2650	1.21
1.22	0.1895	0.1112	0.05384	1.2738	1.22
1.23	0.1872	0.1093	0.05274	1.2827	1.23
1.24	0.1849	0.1075	0.05165	1.2917	1.24
1.25	0.1826	0.1056	0.05059	1.3006	1.25
1.26	0.1804	0.1038	0.04954	1.3095	1.26
1.27	0.1781	0.1020	0.04851	1.3185	1.27
1.28	0.1758	0.1003	0.04750	1.3275	1.28
1.29	0.1736	0.09853	0.04650	1.3365	1.29
1.30	0.1714	0.09680	0.04553	1.3455	1.30
1.31	0.1691	0.09510	0.04457	1.3546	1.31
1.32	0.1669	0.09342	0.04363	1.3636	1.32
1.33	0.1647	0.09176	0.04270	1.3727	1.33
1.34	0.1626	0.09012	0.04179	1.3818	1.34
1.35	0.1604	0.08851	0.04090	1.3909	1.35
1.36	0.1582	0.08692	0.04002	1.4000	1.36
1.37	0.1561	0.08534	0.03916	1.4092	1.37
1.38	0.1539	0.08379	0.03831	1.4183	1.38
1.39	0.1518	0.08226	0.03748	1.4275	1.39
1.40	0.1497	0.08076	0.03667	1.4367	1.40
1.41	0.1476	0.07927	0.03587	1.4459	1.41
1.42	0.1456	0.07780	0.03508	1.4551	1.42
1.43	0.1435	0.07636	0.03431	1.4643	1.43
1.44	0.1415	0.07493	0.03356	1.4736	1.44
1.45	0.1394	0.07353	0.03281	1.4828	1.45
1.46	0.1374	0.07215	0.03208	1.4921	1.46
1.47	0.1354	0.07078	0.03137	1.5014	1.47
1.48	0.1334	0.06944	0.03067	1.5107	1.48
1.49	0.1315	0.06811	0.02998	1.5200	1.49

k	$f_u(k)$	$p_{u\geq}(k)$	$G_u(k)$	$G_u(-k)$	k
1.50	0.1295	0.06681	0.02931	1.5293	1.50
1.51	0.1276	0.06552	0.02865	1.5386	1.51
1.52	0.1257	0.06426	0.02800	1.5480	1.52
1.53	0.1238	0.06301	0.02736	1.5574	1.53
1.54	0.1219	0.06178	0.02674	1.5667	1.54
1.55	0.1200	0.06057	0.02612	1.5761	1.55
1.56	0.1182	0.05938	0.02552	1.5855	1.56
1.57	0.1163	0.05821	0.02494	1.5949	1.57
1.58	0.1145	0.05705	0.02436	1.6044	1.58
1.59	0.1127	0.05592	0.02380	1.6138	1.59
1.60	0.1109	0.05480	0.02324	1.6232	1.60
1.61	0.1092	0.05370	0.02270	1.6327	1.61
1.62	0.1074	0.05262	0.02217	1.6422	1.62
1.63	0.1057	0.05155	0.02165	1.6516	1.63
1.64	0.1040	0.05050	0.02114	1.6611	1.64
1.65	0.1023	0.04947	0.02064	1.6706	1.65
1.66	0.1006	0.04846	0.02015	1.6801	1.66
1.67	0.0989	0.04746	0.01967	1.6897	1.67
1.68	0.0973	0.04648	0.01920	1.6992	1.68
1.69	0.0957	0.04551	0.01874	1.7087	1.69
1.70	0.0940	0.04457	0.01829	1.7183	1.70
1.71	0.0925	0.04363	0.01785	1.7278	1.71
1.72	0.0909	0.04272	0.01742	1.7374	1.72
1.73	0.0893	0.04182	0.01699	1.7470	1.73
1.74	0.0878	0.04093	0.01658	1.7566	1.74
1.75	0.0863	0.04006	0.01617	1.7662	1.75
1.76	0.0848	0.03920	0.01578	1.7758	1.76
1.77	0.0833	0.03836	0.01539	1.7854	1.77
1.78	0.0818	0.03754	0.01501	1.7950	1.78
1.79	0.0804	0.03673	0.01464	1.8046	1.79
1.80	0.0790	0.03593	0.01428	1.8143	1.80
1.81	0.0775	0.03515	0.01392	1.8239	1.81
1.82	0.0761	0.03438	0.01357	1.8336	1.82
1.83	0.0748	0.03362	0.01323	1.8432	1.83
1.84	0.0734	0.03288	0.01290	1.8529	1.84
1.85	0.0721	0.03216	0.01257	1.8626	1.85
1.86	0.0707	0.03144	0.01226	1.8723	1.86
1.87	0.0694	0.03074	0.01195	1.8819	1.87
1.88	0.0681	0.03005	0.01164	1.8916	1.88
1.89	0.0669	0.02938	0.01134	1.9013	1.89
1.90	0.0656	0.02872	0.01105	1.9111	1.90
1.91	0.0644	0.02807	0.01077	1.9208	1.91
1.92	0.0632	0.02743	0.01049	1.9305	1.92
1.93	0.0620	0.02680	0.01022	1.9402	1.93
1.94	0.0608	0.02619	0.009957	1.9500	1.94
1.95	0.0596	0.02559	0.009698	1.9597	1.95
1.96	0.0584	0.02500	0.009445	1.9694	1.96
1.97	0.0573	0.02442	0.009198	1.9792	1.97
1.98	0.0562	0.02385	0.008957	1.9890	1.98
1.99	0.0551	0.02330	0.008721	1.9987	1.99

k	$f_u(k)$	$p_{u\geq}(k)$	$G_u(k)$	$G_u(-k)$	k
2.00	0.0540	0.02275	0.008491	2.0085	2.00
2.01	0.0529	0.02222	0.008266	2.0183	2.01
2.02	0.0519	0.02169	0.008046	2.0280	2.02
2.03	0.0508	0.02118	0.007832	2.0378	2.03
2.04	0.0498	0.02068	0.007623	2.0476	2.04
2.05	0.0488	0.02018	0.007418	2.0574	2.05
2.06	0.0478	0.01970	0.007219	2.0672	2.06
2.07	0.0468	0.01923	0.007024	2.0770	2.07
2.08	0.0459	0.01876	0.006835	2.0868	2.08
2.09	0.0449	0.01831	0.006649	2.0966	2.09
2.10	0.0440	0.01786	0.006468	2.1065	2.10
2.11	0.0431	0.01743	0.006292	2.1163	2.11
2.12	0.0422	0.01700	0.006120	2.1261	2.12
2.13	0.0413	0.01659	0.005952	2.1360	2.13
2.14	0.0404	0.01618	0.005788	2.1458	2.14
2.15	0.0396	0.01578	0.005628	2.1556	2.15
2.16	0.0387	0.01539	0.005472	2.1655	2.16
2.17	0.0379	0.01500	0.005320	2.1753	2.17
2.18	0.0371	0.01463	0.005172	2.1852	2.18
2.19	0.0363	0.01426	0.005028	2.1950	2.19
2.20	0.0355	0.01390	0.004887	2.2049	2.20
2.21	0.0347	0.01355	0.004750	2.2147	2.21
2.22	0.0339	0.01321	0.004616	2.2246	2.22
2.23	0.0332	0.01287	0.004486	2.2345	2.23
2.24	0.0325	0.01255	0.004358	2.2444	2.24
2.25	0.0317	0.01222	0.004235	2.2542	2.25
2.26	0.0310	0.01191	0.004114	2.2641	2.26
2.27	0.0303	0.01160	0.003996	2.2740	2.27
2.28	0.0297	0.01130	0.003882	2.2839	2.28
2.29	0.0290	0.01101	0.003770	2.2938	2.29
2.30	0.0283	0.01072	0.003662	2.3037	2.30
2.31	0.0277	0.01044	0.003556	2.3136	2.31
2.32	0.0270	0.01017	0.003453	2.3235	2.32
2.33	0.0264	0.009903	0.003352	2.3334	2.33
2.34	0.0258	0.009642	0.003255	2.3433	2.34
2.35	0.0252	0.009387	0.003159	2.3532	2.35
2.36	0.0246	0.009137	0.003067	2.3631	2.36
2.37	0.0241	0.008894	0.002977	2.3730	2.37
2.38	0.0235	0.008656	0.002889	2.3829	2.38
2.39	0.0229	0.008424	0.002804	2.3928	2.39
2.40	0.0224	0.008198	0.002720	2.4027	2.40
2.41	0.0219	0.007976	0.002640	2.4126	2.41
2.42	0.0213	0.007760	0.002561	2.4226	2.42
2.43	0.0208	0.007549	0.002484	2.4325	2.43
2.44	0.0203	0.007344	0.002410	2.4424	2.44
2.45	0.0198	0.007143	0.002337	2.4523	2.45
2.46	0.0194	0.006947	0.002267	2.4623	2.46
2.47	0.0189	0.006756	0.002199	2.4722	2.47
2.48	0.0184	0.006569	0.002132	2.4821	2.48
2.49	0.0180	0.006387	0.002067	2.4921	2.49

k	$f_u(k)$	$p_{u\geq}(k)$	$G_u(k)$	$G_u(-k)$	k
2.50	0.0175	0.006210	0.002004	2.5020	2.50
2.51	0.0171	0.006037	0.001943	2.5119	2.51
2.52	0.0167	0.005868	0.001883	2.5219	2.52
2.53	0.0163	0.005703	0.001826	2.5318	2.53
2.54	0.0158	0.005543	0.001769	2.5418	2.54
2.55	0.0154	0.005386	0.001715	2.5517	2.55
2.56	0.0151	0.005234	0.001662	2.5617	2.56
2.57	0.0147	0.005085	0.001610	2.5716	2.57
2.58	0.0143	0.004940	0.001560	2.5816	2.58
2.59	0.0139	0.004799	0.001511	2.5915	2.59
2.60	0.0136	0.004661	0.001464	2.6015	2.60
2.61	0.0132	0.004527	0.001418	2.6114	2.61
2.62	0.0129	0.004396	0.001373	2.6214	2.62
2.63	0.0126	0.004269	0.001330	2.6313	2.63
2.64	0.0122	0.004145	0.001288	2.6413	2.64
2.65	0.0119	0.004025	0.001247	2.6512	2.65
2.66	0.0116	0.003907	0.001207	2.6612	2.66
2.67	0.0113	0.003793	0.001169	2.6712	2.67
2.68	0.0110	0.003681	0.001132	2.6811	2.68
2.69	0.0107	0.003573	0.001095	2.6911	2.69
2.70	0.0104	0.003467	0.001060	2.7011	2.70
2.71	0.0101	0.003364	0.001026	2.7110	2.71
2.72	0.0099	0.003264	0.0009928	2.7210	2.72
2.73	0.0096	0.003167	0.0009607	2.7310	2.73
2.74	0.0093	0.003072	0.0009295	2.7409	2.74
2.75	0.0091	0.002980	0.0008992	2.7509	2.75
2.76	0.0088	0.002890	0.0008699	2.7609	2.76
2.77	0.0086	0.002803	0.0008414	2.7708	2.77
2.78	0.0084	0.002718	0.0008138	2.7808	2.78
2.79	0.0081	0.002635	0.0007870	2.7908	2.79
2.80	0.0079	0.002555	0.0007611	2.8008	2.80
2.81	0.0077	0.002477	0.0007359	2.8107	2.81
2.82	0.0075	0.002401	0.0007115	2.8207	2.82
2.83	0.0073	0.002327	0.0006879	2.8307	2.83
2.84	0.0071	0.002256	0.0006650	2.8407	2.84
2.85	0.0069	0.002186	0.0006428	2.8506	2.85
2.86	0.0067	0.002118	0.0006213	2.8606	2.86
2.87	0.0065	0.002052	0.0006004	2.8706	2.87
2.88	0.0063	0.001988	0.0005802	2.8806	2.88
2.89	0.0061	0.001926	0.0005606	2.8906	2.89
2.90	0.0060	0.001866	0.0005417	2.9005	2.90
2.91	0.0058	0.001807	0.0005233	2.9105	2.91
2.92	0.0056	0.001750	0.0005055	2.9205	2.92
2.93	0.0055	0.001695	0.0004883	2.9305	2.93
2.94	0.0053	0.001641	0.0004716	2.9405	2.94
2.95	0.0051	0.001589	0.0004555	2.9505	2.95
2.96	0.0050	0.001538	0.0004398	2.9604	2.96
2.97	0.0048	0.001489	0.0004247	2.9704	2.97
2.98	0.0047	0.001441	0:0004101	2.9804	2.98
2.99	0.0046	0.001395	0.0003959	2.9904	2.99

k	$f_u(k)$	$p_{u\geq}(k)$	$G_u(k)$	$G_u(-k)$	k
3.00	0.0044	0.001350	0.0003822	3.0004	3.00
3.01	0.0043	0.001306	0.0003689	3.0104	3.01
3.02	0.0042	0.001264	0.0003560	3.0204	3.02
3.03	0.0040	0.001223	0.0003436	3.0303	3.03
3.04	0.0039	0.001183	0.0003316	3.0403	3.04
3.05	0.0038	0.001144	0.0003199	3.0503	3.05
3.06	0.0037	0.001107	0.0003087	3.0603	3.06
3.07	0.0036	0.001070	0.0002978	3.0703	3.07
3.08	0.0035	0.001035	0.0002873	3.0803	3.08
3.09	0.0034	0.001001	0.0002771	3.0903	3.09
3.10	0.0033	0.0009676	0.0002672	3.1003	3.10
3.11	0.0032	0.0009354	0.0002577	3.1103	3.11
3.12	0.0031	0.0009043	0.0002485	3.1202	3.12
3.13	0.0030	0.0008740	0.0002396	3.1302	3.13
3.14	0.0029	0.0008447	0.0002311	3.1402	3.14
3.15	0.0028	0.0008164	0.0002227	3.1502	3.15
3.16	0.0027	0.0007888	0.0002147	3.1602	3.16
3.17	0.0026	0.0007622	0.0002070	3.1702	3.17
3.18	0.0025	0.0007364	0.0001995	3.1802	3.18
3.19	0.0025	0.0007114	0.0001922	3.1902	3.19
3.20	0.0024	0.0006871	0.0001852	3.2002	3.20
3.21	0.0023	0.0006637	0.0001785	3.2102	3.21
3.22	0.0022	0.0006410	0.0001720	3.2202	3.22
3.23	0.0022	0.0006190	0.0001657	3.2302	3.23
3.24	0.0021	0.0005976	0.0001596	3.2402	3.24
3.25	0.0020	0.0005770	0.0001537	3.2502	3.25
3.26	0.0020	0.0005571	0.0001480	3.2601	3.26
3.27	0.0019	0.0005377	0.0001426	3.2701	3.27
3.28	0.0018	0.0005190	0.0001373	3.2801	3.28
3.29	0.0018	0.0005009	0.0001322	3.2901	3.29
3.30	0.0017	0.0004834	0.0001273	3.3001	3.30
3.31	0.0017	0.0004665	0.0001225	3.3101	3.31
3.32	0.0016	0.0004501	0.0001179	3.3201	3.32
3.33	0.0016	0.0004342	0.0001135	3.3301	3.33
3.34	0.0015	0.0004189	0.0001093	3.3401	3.34
3.35	0.0015	0.0004041	0.0001051	3.3501	3.35
3.36	0.0014	0.0003897	0.0001012	3.3601	3.36
3.37	0.0014	0.0003758	0.00009734	3.3701	3.37
3.38	0.0013	0.0003624	0.00009365	3.3801	3.38
3.39	0.0013	0.0003495	0.00009009	3.3901	3.39
3.40	0.0012	0.0003369	0.00008666	3.4001	3.40
3.41	0.0012	0.0003248	0.00008335	3.4101	3.41
3.42	0.0012	0.0003131	0.00008016	3.4201	3.42
3.43	0.0011	0.0003018	0.00007709	3.4301	3.43
3.44	0.0011	0.0002909	0.00007413	3.4401	3.44
3.45	0.0010	0.0002803	0.00007127	3.4501	3.45
3.46	0.0010	0.0002701	0.00006852	3.4601	3.46
3.47	0.0010	0.0002602	0.00006587	3.4701	3.47
3.48	0.0009	0.0002507	0.00006331	3.4801	3.48
3.49	0.0009	0.0002415	0.00006085	3.4901	3.49

k	$f_u(k)$	$p_{u\geq}(k)$	$G_u(k)$	$G_u(-k)$	k
3.50	0.0009	0.0002326	0.00005848	3.5001	3.50
3.51	0.0008	0.0002241	0.00005620	3.5101	3.51
3.52	0.0008	0.0002158	0.00005400	3.5201	3.52
3.53	0.0008	0.0002078	0.00005188	3.5301	3.53
3.54	0.0008	0.0002001	0.00004984	3.5400	3.54
3.55	0.0007	0.0001926	0.00004788	3.5500	3.55
3.56	0.0007	0.0001854	0.00004599	3.5600	3.56
3.57	0.0007	0.0001785	0.00004417	3.5700	3.57
3.58	0.0007	0.0001718	0.00004242	3.5800	3.58
3.59	0.0006	0.0001653	0.00004073	3.5900	3.59
3.60	0.0006	0.0001591	0.00003911	3.6000	3.60
3.61	0.0006	0.0001531	0.00003755	3.6100	3.61
3.62	0.0006	0.0001473	0.00003605	3.6200	3.62
3.63	0.0005	0.0001417	0.00003460	3.6300	3.63
3.64	0.0005	0.0001363	0.00003321	3.6400	3.64
3.65	0.0005	0.0001311	0.00003188	3.6500	3.65
3.66	0.0005	0.0001261	0.00003059	3.6600	3.66
3.67	0.0005	0.0001213	0.00002935	3.6700	3.67
3.68	0.0005	0.0001166	0.00002816	3.6800	3.68
3.69	0.0004	0.0001121	0.00002702	3.6900	3.69
3.70	0.0004	0.0001078	0.00002592	3.7000	3.70
3.71	0.0004	0.0001036	0.00002486	3.7100	3.71
3.72	0.0004	0.0000996	0.00002385	3.7200	3.72
3.73	0.0004	0.00009574	0.00002287	3.7300	3.73
3.74	0.0004	0.00009201	0.00002193	3.7400	3.74
3.75	0.0004	0.00008842	0.00002103	3.7500	3.75
3.76	0.0003	0.00008496	0.00002016	3.7600	3.76
3.77	0.0003	0.00008162	0.00001933	3.7700	3.77
3.78	0.0003	0.00007841	0.00001853	3.7800	3.78
3.79	0.0003	0.00007532	0.00001776	3.7900	3.79
3.80	0.0003	0.00007235	0.00001702	3.8000	3.80
3.81	0.0003	0.00006948	0.00001632	3.8100	3.81
3.82	0.0003	0.00006673	0.00001563	3.8200	3.82
3.83	0.0003	0.00006407	0.00001498	3.8300	3.83
3.84	0.0003	0.00006152	0.00001435	3.8400	3.84
3.85	0.0002	0.00005906	0.00001375	3.8500	3.85
3.86	0.0002	0.00005669	0.00001317	3.8600	3.86
3.87	0.0002	0.00005442	0.00001262	3.8700	3.87
3.88	0.0002	0.00005223	0.00001208	3.8800	3.88
3.89	0.0002	0.00005012	0.00001157	3.8900	3.89
3.90	0.0002	0.00004810	0.00001108	3.9000	3.90
3.91	0.0002	0.00004615	0.00001061	3.9100	3.91
3.92	0.0002	0.00004427	0.00001016	3.9200	3.92
3.93	0.0002	0.00004247	0.00000972	3.9300	3.93
3.94	0.0002	0.00004074	0.000009307	3.9400	3.94
3.95	0.0002	0.00003908	0.000008908	3.9500	3.95
3.96	0.0002	0.00003748	0.000008525	3.9600	3.96
3.97	0.0002	0.00003594	0.000008158	3.9700	3.97
3.98	0.0001	0.00003446	0.000007806	3.9800	3.98
3.99	0.0001	0.00003304	0.000007469	3.9900	3.99
4.00	0.0001	0.00003167	0.000007145	4.000	4.00

REFERENCES FOR APPENDIX C

1. Freund, J. E. *Mathematical Statistics.* Prentice-Hall, Englewood Cliffs, N.J., 1971, pp. 372–374.

2. Parzen, E. *Modern Probability Theory and Its Applications.* Wiley, New York, 1960.

Subject Index

Author Index

Starr, M. K., 14, 85, 626, 749, 754